Encounters Across Borders

Encounters Across Borders

The Changing Visions of Spanish Modernism, 1890–1930

Mary Lee Bretz

Lewisburg
Bucknell University Press
London: Associated University Presses

Associated University Presses
440 Forsgate Drive
Cranbury, NJ 08512

Associated University Presses
16 Barter Street
London WC1A 2AH, England

Associated University Presses
P.O. Box 338, Port Credit
Mississauga, Ontario
Canada L5G 4L8

The paper used in this publication meets the requirements of the American National Standard for Permanence of Paper for Printed Library Materials Z39.48-1984.

Library of Congress Cataloging-in-Publication Data

Bretz, Mary Lee.
Encounters across borders : the changing visions of Spanish modernism, 1890–1930 / Mary Lee Bretz.
p. cm.
Includes bibliographical references and index.
ISBN 0-8387-5484-8 (alk. paper)
1. Spanish literature—20th century—History and criticism. 2. Spanish literature—19th century—History and criticism. 3. Modernism (Literature)—Spain. 4. Difference (Psychology) in literature. I. Title.

PQ6073.M6 B74 2001
860.9′112—dc21

2001025672

PRINTED IN THE UNITED STATES OF AMERICA

To Norton and a lifetime of breaking borders

Contents

Acknowledgments

THIS BOOK REALLY BEGAN WHEN MY GRANDMOTHER FIRST TOLD me stories of studying in Switzerland and traveling in Europe before World War I. Through visits to museums, historical sites, but mostly stories of her life, she gave me a love of travel and history that led me to study in Spain. Many friends and experiences have enriched my encounter with the Spanish culture and have helped me to enjoy as well as study Spanish life and literature. I am especially grateful to Sonsoles Díaz-Berrio, Elvira and Laura Alcalá Zamora, Carmen Portela, Francisco Fernández de Ana Magán, Manolo López López, and the late and much-missed Dolores Sacristán Pérez. Numerous colleagues at Rutgers have helped me to think and rethink my work and have been extremely generous in their support as friends and scholars. Susana Rotker's work on otherness, national memory, and selective amnesia in Latin America inspired me to consider modern Spanish history and culture from new perspectives. Her death leaves an enormous gap in my intellectual and personal world. She and other colleagues, especially Jorge Marcone, Tomás Eloy Martínez, Carlos Narváez, Margo Persin, and Tom Stephens have made it possible for me to finish this book, through intellectual dialogue, support in departmental administration, reading and critiquing my work, and most importantly, being there as friends and colleagues. A Rutgers University FASP leave allowed me to devote myself intensively to writing and my undergraduate and graduate students at Rutgers have been enormously important in helping me to develop my ideas and consider their implications. As always, I am grateful for my extended family—siblings, cousins, in-laws—and for the wonderful patience, humor, and support of my husband, Norton, and my children Lee, Jay, and now Chris.

Encounters Across Borders

1
Modernism and Its Borders

The "Other" in Practice and Theory

Twentieth-Century Heirs to the Black Legend

> There is yet another phenomenon highly characteristic in some cases of degeneracy, in others of hysteria. This is the formation of close groups or schools uncompromisingly exclusive to outsiders, observable today in literature and art. Healthy artists or authors, in possession of minds in a condition of well-regulated equilibrium, will never think of grouping themselves into an association, which may at pleasure be termed a sect or band; of devising a catechism, of binding themselves to definite aesthetic dogmas, and of entering the lists for these with the fanatical intolerance of Spanish inquisitors. (Nordau 1968, 29)

> Ruskin is one of the most turbid and fallacious minds, and one of the most powerful masters of style, of the present century. To the service of the most wildly eccentric thoughts he brings the acerbity of a bigot and the deep sentiment of Morel's "emotionalists." His mental temperament is that of the first Spanish Grand Inquisitors. He is the Torquemada of aesthetics. He would liefest burn alive the critic who disagrees with him, or the dull Philistine who passes by works of art without a feeling of devout awe. (Nordau 1968, 77)

> Esto (Murcia)[1] ya no es España. Es el Oriente. En Argelia misma no he sentido tan intensa la sensación africana. Es el Oriente con sus cipreses, con sus casas bajas, con sus minaretes, con su cielo de incendio. Los moros están ocultos tras aquellas montañas, dispuestos a reconquistar su ciudad. Oíd . . . Es el muezín. (Lorrain 1905?, 125)

> [This (Murcia) is no longer Spain. It is the Orient. Not even in Algeria have I felt so intensely the African feeling. It is the Orient, with its cypress trees, its low houses with their minarets, its flaming sky. The moors are hidden behind those mountains, ready to reconquer the city. Listen . . . It is the muezzin.]

Cameron, a British man who has spent eighteen months in Spain, is about to leave *"the Black Country"* when his sister requests that he guide her and her new husband on a trip through Andalusia, a land populated by *"affable barbarians,"* existing in a *"lawless state."* The trio journeys inland to an ancient town. *"A strong illusion of the Orient, extreme antiquity and dreamlike stillness marked the place."* While exploring the local church, the travelers find themselves locked inside and witness the sacrifice of a woman, who is buried alive in a ceremony attended by a long procession of monks. The victim wears a white linen robe with her face uncovered during the initial ceremony, but veiled for the final burial. After escaping to the nearest Consulate, Cameron and his sister report the crime but are informed that Spanish law works poorly at best. *"And this was not a civil matter, where the wheels might often, certainly be oiled. The wheel ecclesiastic was more intractable."*

"He asked if we were leaving Spain immediately. We said, 'Perhaps in a few days.' 'Take my advice,' said he, 'and make it a few hours.'"

"We did." (Mew 1981, 146–59. Synopsis of "A White Night" with quotations from the original)

Date: September 14, 1994
To: International Atomic Energy Agency Attendees in Seville, Spain
Subject: Travel to Spain Awareness

As a cautionary measure, please note the attached article.

COLOMBIAN MUGGERS USE HYPNOTIC DRUG

White powder causes victims to hallucinate, lose memory

By Chris Torchia, Associated Press

Bogota, Colombia—All Juan Carlos Cuervo was planning to do when he stepped out on a recent night was grab a beer. He was found three days later, wandering about his neighborhood in a zombie-like state and robbed of all his money—a victim in a bizarre crime wave in which thieves use a powerful drug as a weapon.

Thousands of people have been robbed or raped in the past two decades after being slipped the drug scopolamine, known as "burundanga" on the street, prompting a U.S. State Department warning to travelers to Colombia.

"The drug renders the person disoriented and powerless to resist the criminal's orders," the State Department says in a travel advisory.

Although the plant from which burundanga comes is found in many parts of the world, including the Andes Mountains, its use as a weapon is uniquely Colombian.

Attacks have been reported in Spain and Panama, but even in those incidents it's suspected Colombians were involved.

Interoffice memorandum. Princeton Plasma Physics Laboratory.

THE PRECEDING QUOTATIONS ARE DRAWN FROM FOUR DISTINCT text-types and originate in different countries and periods of the twentieth century: literary criticism, travel literature, fiction of the early decade, and an interoffice memorandum from the 1990s. However, all share a vision of Spain as "other," sometimes an exoticized object of desire, but more often, a sinister, alien stimulus of fear and disquiet. Nordau's famous study incorporates several gratuitous allusions to the Spanish Inquisition while describing the decadents that, in his view, threaten European culture. The reference to Torquemada follows a discussion of the Romantic movement in Germany, France, and England, with no mention of Spain. Spain appears only in the negative reference to Ruskin as the Torquemada of aesthetes; she surfaces exclusively as the outsider, the negative of all the text posits as healthy and worthy. Echoes of the "black legend" and the vision of Spain as fanatical, dark, and violent linger subtextually in Nordau's *Degeneration* and surface in many other works of the period. Jean Lorrain conjures up a less threatening image of Spain while reenforcing the traditional view that "Europe begins at the Pyrenees." Centuries of Moorish, Jewish, and Christian mixing in a multicultural Spain produce fear of her racial difference and lingering doubts among continental writers as to her membership in the European community. For Lorrain, remnants of African culture produce excitement and a taste of the exotic without leaving Europe's safety, but in an era of racial typing and Eurocentrism, this image of Spain has significant negative effects.

Charlotte Mew's short story combines attributes present in Nordau and Lorrain. The specter of a fanatical, inquisitorial Catholic Spain combines with evocations of a culture of human sacrifice deep in the heartland of a country that could easily be taken for interior Africa, Aztec Mexico, or Inca Peru. Whereas Nordau evokes memories of a relatively distant past, with echoes in the present, "A White Night," written in 1903, places the action in 1876, thus representing a modern Spain that has barely changed since the days of Torquemada. The narrator's allusions to Spain as "the Black Country" and the covering of the sacrificial victim in a white robe summon images of North Africa and Muslim chador. In every aspect, Spain appears as a dark, savage land, that shares more with a feared Muslim, Aztec, or barbaric other than with British culture. The interoffice memorandum continues negative stereotypes of Spain. The news item contains only a brief mention of Spain, with reports that Colombian criminals may have used scopolamine there, but this tangential reference suffices to prompt a warning to a group of presumably well-traveled, well-educated physicists who are to attend a conference in Seville. It is interesting that the AP writer prefers the term "burundanga," with African roots and connotations, over the scientific "scopolamine" and the leap from reports of criminal activity in Colombia and possible incidents in Spain to a general warning of danger in Seville suggests the conflation of Spain and Latin America into a violent, menacing stranger.

Theories of Alterity

The homogenizing sweep of the opening epigraphs brings Spain, Africa, and South America under a single rubric of feared, dangerous other and represents the traditional xenophobic approach to alterity. Lorrain's rapture in the face of an exoticized Spain reflects a contrasting xenophilic vision, in which dissatisfaction with the hegemonic culture, in this case European rationalism and bourgeois control, expresses itself through the idealized portrait of an Arab-Hispanic culture that embodies values and customs perceived as lacking in the dominant society. Despite apparent differences, as Angelika Bammer argues, "-philic" exaltation and "-phobic" rejection share a refusal to enter into a relation with the other (1995, 50–51), and as Todorov remarks in a slightly different context, both depend for their continued existence on a lack of knowledge of and a blindness to differences within the culture under consideration (1993, 265). Knowledge reveals similarities as well as differences between self and other and disallows the totalizing vision of a dreaded foreigner as well as the idealization of a wondrously different outsider. A consideration of alterity is central to the contemporary disciplines of anthropology, philosophy, history, and literary studies, all of which struggle to sort out the problematic relation between the inquiring subject and the object of investigation. The danger is ever that in describing what lies outside, the viewing subject unintentionally, but inevitably imposes his or her values, ideology, or identity on the other: "How to know alterity—what is beyond the Self or the Same—without reducing it by assimilation," as Mark Millington states the dilemma (1995, 24). This puzzle proves particularly vexing in light of the traditional Western propensity to impose its values on other cultures, a process in which Spain participates but of which she is also a victim, both a member of a colonizing European expansion and also an excluded other of dubious cultural and racial purity.

Zygmunt Bauman studies the transition from pre-modern divisions of "friend" and "enemy" to modern nation states that include within their borders groups previously viewed as the enemy. The drive to unite this new collectivity led nations and empires to impose their religion, language and political and economic systems on others now residing within (1991, 54–69). This assimilation negates the value of the minority culture, actively erasing its difference. Voices opposing the imposition of Eurocentric views surface early in the process of imperial expansion that begins in the early modern period and continues to the present. Todorov traces French dissident opinion in *On Human Diversity* and within the Hispanic world, Bartolomé de las Casas and the Jesuit defenders of the Guaraní peoples of colonial Paraguay challenge hegemonic values. Today's discussions of relations with the other continue to wrestle with the ethical issues arising from cross-cultural communication. Contemporary cultural and post-colonial criticism still struggles with the dangers of phobic rejection, phobic appropriation, or philic assimilation in a world in which encounters between cultures have become the norm. The uneven power relations that often mark cross-cultural meetings has led postcolonial critics like Gayatri Spivak to emphasize the persistent muting of the subaltern in relation to the hegemonic speaker (1998). The philosopher Emanuel Levinas devoted his life to the study of this problem and coincides with Todorov and others in viewing culture as on-going, in-process, and heterogeneous and also in emphasizing engagement with the other, but Levinas frames his discussion in terms of an ethical relationship that recognizes the "otherness of the other." In contrast to approaches that seek to define other cultures or subjects, aspiring to knowledge about the other, Levinas proposes dialogue, an on-going encounter that involves ethical commitment and privileges the act of "saying" over the final product of the stated word. "Saying" involves a fluid relationship that does not stabilize, neither appropriates nor allows appropriation, but persists in a dynamic social relation that transcends knowledge: "The *Saying* is not exhausted in the giving of meaning as it inscribes itself—fable—in the Said. It is communication not reducible to the phenomenon of the *truth-that-unites:* it is a non-indifference to the other person, capable of ethical significance to which the statement itself of the Said is subordinate" (1993, 142).

Bernhard Waldenfels theorizes a similar relation with alterity, suggesting that the other be seen as an entity that evokes a response rather than an object of study to be defined. In the encounter, the subject develops a new answer that arises from the intersubjective/intercultural meeting, a "between" that constitutes neither self nor other but rather creates what neither possessed prior to the dialogue (1995, 43).

Spanish writers of the late nineteenth and early twentieth centuries anticipate current discussions of alterity and cross-cultural communication in their varied responses to the peculiar historical conditions that mark Spanish national development as the first post-imperial European nation. Located in a cultural, geographic, historical, and racial "in-between," Spain stands in an uneasy relationship with a hegemonic, imperialistic Europe. The loss of her last major colonies in 1898, the proximity of Africa, the many centuries of racial/ethnic mixing in the period of Arab-Jewish-Christian co-presence, the residues of Arab culture in the peninsula, among other marks of difference, distance Spain from a Europe intent on constructing a self-image as racially pure and culturally distinct from the African, Asian, and Middle Eastern areas just recently brought under imperial control. On the other hand, Spain has her own long history of conquest and colonization, in which Eurocentric values and views served to justify territorial, economic, and cultural expansion. Both the recipient of a xenophobic European gaze and the agent of xenophobic appropriation in Latin America and to a lesser degree, in Africa, Spain's reconsideration of intercultural relations as she moves from imperial to post-imperial status encompasses all aspects of her external and internal history. The reexamination of intersubjectivity and interculturality and the exploration of new forms of encounter constitutes the central aspiration of Spanish cultural production of the late nineteenth and early twentieth century, with considerable advances in the theorization of cross-cultural communication. The persistent "othering" of Spain has impeded the inclusion of the Spanish modernist exploration within studies of European and global modernism and remnants of an imperial, xenophobic Spanish ideology have similarly obstructed the mapping from within of connections between the Spanish culture of the period and the rest of Europe and the world. *Encounters Across Borders* attempts to break through external and internal forces that have constructed artificial barriers between Spanish and international modernism and to forge productive links between Spanish theorizations of alterity and contemporary concerns regarding the encounter with the other.

Spanish Modernism: Exclusion from Without and Isolation from Within

The traditional European vision of Spain as alien or exotic has impacted many different fields, including the study of contemporary literary history and culture. In recent decades, literary critics and theorists have moved increasingly towards a vision of culture that cuts across traditional national borders and places cultural production within a global context. Postcolonial studies and theories of modernism and postmodernism reflect an interest in exploring commonalities that transcend the local and specific. Both within and in opposition to this trend, scholars have cautioned against the inappropriate imposition of criteria derived from one or several national cultures on others that have followed a slightly or radically different course. In the study of global or international modernism,[2] a recurring tension emerges between the desire to construct an overarching definition that applies to multiple literatures and the recognition of the danger of this impetus. Others reject global definitions out of a reluctance to accept certain literatures as equal in value or importance. Peter Brooker explicitly articulates this view in *Modernism/Postmodernism:* "There is plainly more than one modernism, and not all modernisms are equal" (1992, 1). As a result of this hierarchization of modernisms, in combination with the traditional exclusion of Spain from analyses of European culture, studies of global modernism invariably overlook the development of a rich modernist literature within the Hispanic world. Major works published during the recent explosion of interest in modernism and postmodernism typically deny any relation between Spanish or Spanish American *modernismo* and international modernism, dismissing late nineteenth- and early twentieth-century Spanish/Spanish American culture as either alien or inferior in relation to developments occurring in other parts of the globe. The phobic exclusion of Spain accompanies philic assimilation in persistent references to the writings of the Spanish José Ortega y Gasset, whom many scholars cite as a theorist of modernism, even as they deny the existence of such a movement within his country of origin and residence. Neither approach allows for a dialogic exchange between Spanish modernism and the other national modernisms that develop during the late nineteenth and early twentieth centuries.

Responsibility for the exclusion of Spanish culture from considerations of global modernism also lies within Spain and a significant branch of Spanish tradition that works to isolate the nation from outside contacts and influences. Fear of the other and desire for cultural uniformity have traditionally marked movements of national consolidation and in Spain's case, a strong impulse for religious, racial, and linguistic homogeneity has surfaced at various historical junctures in opposition to a countervailing current that celebrates religious tolerance, racial and cultural diversity, and linguistic pluralism. The early decades of the twentieth century witness the increasing authority of a defense of heterogeneity, which collides with forces favoring centralism and homogeneity in the period of the Spanish Civil War. The Franco victory of 1939 imposes a single voice and perspective and redefines national culture according to an inward-looking, xenophobic vision. During the post Civil War period, Francoist scholars struggle to recuperate the great writers of early twentieth-century Spain as part of an unbroken heritage, and to this end, they divide Spanish culture of the late nineteenth and early twentieth centuries into two discrete movements, the so-called "Generation of 1898" (corresponding to the patriarchal, Castilian tradition that they esteem) and *modernismo* (representing a disparaged reaching out to international currents).

Early resistance to this Manichean division of late nineteenth- and early twentieth-century Spanish literature appeared in studies by Juan Ramón Jiménez, Federico de Onís, and Ricardo Gullón and has received increasing support in recent years. John Butt, Richard Cardwell, and E. Inman Fox, among others, have argued that the traditional classification misrepresents the writers and falsifies the literary history of the period. At a conference held in Valladolid in October 1996, the participants signed a manifesto specifically rejecting the use of the term "Generation of 1898" as fossilized and inaccurate (Mainer and Gracia 1998, 177). Within opponents to traditional critical paradigms, a small number has begun to argue for the need to view Spanish literature of the period within the context of international modernism.[3] Such an enterprise offers exciting opportunities to break through the critical borders that have artificially isolated Spain from cultural developments occurring in the rest of the world during this period, but it also requires both a sensitivity to the specificity of the Spanish context and a clear notion of current definitions of international modernism. In part in response to the proliferation of studies on post-modernism, and in part as a result of significant revisions of the concepts of gender, nation, subjectivity, and textuality, the understanding of modernism has undergone considerable transformation in recent years. Spanish cultural developments of late nineteenth and early twentieth century at times anticipate, at times coincide with, and at times lag behind cultural manifestations occurring in other countries and regions. While some characteristics attributed by recent theorists to international modernism mirror traits that have traditionally or more recently been ascribed to Spanish cultural production of the period, others bear only a tangential relationship or differ considerably. Recognizing the need to respect Spanish cultural specificity, I also feel strongly that the rich body of theory and criticism appearing on global modernism in recent years offers valuable insights that both enhance our understanding of Spanish culture during this period and provide a useful perspective from which to reconsider the traditional division of the period into two opposing cultural camps. The present study aims to explore the relations of Spanish and international modernism, seeking out the "in-between" posited by Waldenfels as the site of intersubjective, intercultural communication.

Building on traditional and recent criticism within Spanish literary studies, I will place it in dialogue with theory and criticism produced in response to non-Spanish literature in areas such as theories of gender, nation, subjectivity, space, time, and textuality. While examining the ways in which Spanish modernism presents a unique response to the changes and challenges of the early twentieth century, I will also seek to show how it shares and in many ways anticipates cultural expressions that have come to define global modernism and post-modernism. As I move from global and European theories of modernism and other subjects to a consideration of Spanish culture, I hope also to open avenues of communication that travel in the other direction. The ignorance of Spanish modernism and contemporary Spanish culture in studies of international modernism produces an incomplete portrait and erases voices that could considerably enrich and expand current views of our shared cultural histories and horizons.

In the present study, I use the term "modernism" in a broader sense than has traditionally occurred in Spanish criticism, recuperating the breadth of meaning it enjoyed at the turn of the century when initially employed to encompass the entire field of

Spanish literature of the day under a single rubric. In keeping with studies published in the 1900s and the decades preceding the Spanish Civil War and in contrast with later analyses by Franco scholars or contemporary critics who consciously or unconsciously continue the Franco legacy, I include writers and texts traditionally designated as "*noventayochista*" under the broader, more global "modernism." Chronological limits to cultural periods elude absolute precision and unanimous acceptance and the dates ascribed to both "modernismo" and the so-called "Generation of 1898" have varied widely. There is some consensus regarding the beginnings of the movements, generally set in the late 1880s or early 1890s. The closing dates have created much more debate, ranging from a death-knell for modernism in 1907, from those who wish to dispense with it quickly to make way for generational theories of Spanish literature, to the 1950s in Juan Ramón Jiménez's epochal definition. In this study, I will focus on the period from 1890 to 1930, including works produced in this period, but excluding writers whose major corpus appears in the 1920s and later. I choose these limits in part to reduce the study to manageable dimensions, but also because the relationship between modernism and the vanguardist literature of the 1920s continues to puzzle critics and is even more problematic in the case of Spain, where vanguardist writers have received less attention and the historical and cultural panorama takes on considerable complexity as the country progresses towards civil war.

Changing Visions of the Other in Spanish Modernism

One of the salient and over-looked characteristics of Spanish cultural production during the period under consideration relates to the relationship between self and other. A confluence of different factors—political, demographic, historical, scientific, psychological—converge in late nineteenth- and early twentieth-century Spain to instigate a reevaluation of intercultural and intersubjective relations. This process takes place in a variety of frameworks, all interrelated with none taking precedence over the others. In the impossibility of presenting them simultaneously, I will introduce them in a sequence that neither reflects their order of appearance on the cultural stage nor their level of importance. Anticipating the inevitable loss of the remaining Spanish colonies, late nineteenth century Spanish writers and intellectuals begin to rethink Spain's role in the current global order and as a consequence, also reassess the historical development of the nation and how it came to the present moment. This involves a consideration of the role of religion, race, empire, tradition, and the nature of history itself. As E. Inman Fox argues in *La invención de España* (1997), Spanish modernism breaks with traditional versions of Spanish history and constructs a different narrative that questions the continuity with the past, explicitly confronting the problem of history as textuality.

Building on the work of Inman Fox, Vicente Cacho Viu, and others who have traced the rejection of traditional Spanish historiography in the writers of the period, I will examine how the review of the past entails a reconsideration of relations between Spain and a variety of others. Previous criticism of the period has failed to emphasize the importance of the rejection of empire in the texts produced during these years and of the concomitant reevaluation of relations with Latin America, Africa, and a Europe that finds its current self-definition in imperial domination. The reexamination of international relations in the (re)definition of nation accompanies a reconsideration of the various groups that played a significant role within the geographic borders of what has come to be modern Spain: Arabs, Jews, and linguistic minorities within the peninsula. European theories of race serve as a backdrop and often a foil as Spanish modernists consider the nation's complex racial history and current and future relations with Europe, Africa, and Latin America in an increasingly complex international arena. New perceptions of time and memory affect both the vision of nation and the individual subject. In the context of Spanish social development, relations among the bourgeoisie, aristocracy, and lower classes, both urban and rural, also require reassessment. The interaction of city and country and of individual subjects and rapidly changing surroundings, in spaces ranging from the subatomic to the galactic, figures prominently in the ongoing examination of shifting interactions of self and other. A growing distrust of reason and an openness to irrational processes and the subconscious produce a different vision of the self, often sundering a previously stable subjectivity into one or more selves that now interact as others. Changing roles of women and views of sexuality require renegotiations of traditional gender relations and disrupt the belief in clearly delineated gender differences. The changing relation of self and other also expresses itself in visions of textuality, language, and the reader. A destabilized world sees an increase in irony and ambiguity that transforms traditional interactions of author, narrator, and reader, as well as inherited visions of art and the artist.

Encounters Across Borders traces the transformation of self and other in these various domains, and the completed analysis provides a definition of Spanish modernism. Writers, artists, and texts covered in the study originate in all areas of Spain, including Catalonia. The term Spanish modernism refers to the country in which it develops, rather than the language in which it originates. I will avoid references to the multiple "-isms" that constitute micro-movements within the period unless they prove useful to clarify a particular point. The late Galdós, Pardo Bazán and at least partially Clarín, Palacio Valdés, and other writers traditionally classified as realist or naturalist will appear here as transitional or fully modernist writers according to characteristics exhibited by their works written after 1890. Baroja, Unamuno, Concha Espina, Dicenta, Ortega y Gasset, Miró and others producing during these years will also be considered within the general rubric of "modernism." This does not deny realist, naturalist, symbolist, decadentist, surrealist, or existentialist elements in the writers or texts studied, but rather seeks to avoid carving the Spanish literature of the period into multiple, discrete subsets. The aim is to demonstrate some of the shared values, strategies, aspirations, and innovations that transcend gender, class, geographic, and linguistic borders, tracing productive encounters between various areas within Spain and between Spain and other Spanish and non-Spanish speaking regions of the world. Before turning to the discussion of these multiple encounters across borders, however, it is necessary to review the development of a critical and theoretical literature that has moved slowly from exclusionary to inclusionary definitions of the period. Both within studies of global modernism and those of Spanish culture from 1890 to 1930, recent redefinitions open the way to a productive dialogue across formerly unsurmountable borders.

Modernism in Theory and Practice

Towards a Truly Global Modernism

The term "modernismo" was used to describe late nineteenth- and early twentieth-century Spanish American and Spanish literature as early as the 1880s, about the same time that it enjoyed a more fleeting currency in France and the term "Die Moderne" arose in Germany and Austria. It predates the first mention of modernism in English literary studies by almost three decades and the generalized use of the term by three-quarters of a century. From the start, the definition of "modernism" was hotly debated, taking on various meanings as it evolved in different regional or national contexts. Students of modernism openly recognize the term's complexity and many recent studies underscore the idiosyncratic rhythms of development that characterize the distinctive modernisms, all of which reveal a contradictory mixture of progressive and traditionalist impulses.[4] Notwithstanding this tolerance of diversity and increasing arguments for an inclusive consideration of the period to incorporate multiple nationalities, races, and linguistic minorities, Hispanic modernism somehow remains outside acceptable limits. Astradur Eysteinsson points out that the majority of studies, although arguing for modernism's international character, limit their selection of texts to one specific national literature. He signals Bradbury and McFarlane's *Modernism: A Guide to European Literature 1890–1930* as an important exception, with its inclusion of diverse literatures (1990, 89) and in his own *The Concept of Modernism,* he cites examples from Britain, France, Germany, Ireland, Italy, North America, and Russia. However, neither Eysteinsson nor Bradbury-McFarlane include Spanish or Spanish American literatures. On the contrary, in Eysteinsson's very first footnote, he explicitly excludes Hispanic "modernismo" as alien to his concept of modernism (1990, 1).[5]

The omission in *Modernism: A Guide to European Literature* is even more startling. The 34 studies in the volume cover artists or writers from Austria, Belgium, Czechoslovakia, Denmark, England, France, Italy, Norway, Germany, Ireland, Poland, Russia, Sweden, Switzerland, and the United States. No Spanish writer warrants attention in the text itself, although three appear in the appended "100 Brief Biographies" (Juan Ramón Jiménez, Federico García Lorca, and Miguel de Unamuno). Pablo Picasso's name appears in several articles, typically inserted between Braque and Matisse and subsumed under the category of French. At least one essay identifies him as a young French painter (Bradbury-McFarlane 1978, 274)![6] The lengthy Chronology of Events incorporates additional information but here and in the Brief Biographies, Spanish entries display glaring errors: Juan Ramón Jiménez appears as Jiminez (598), accents are lacking on numerous titles [*prologo* for *prólogo* (602), *tia* for *tía* (603), *poesia* for *poesía* (624), *pedagogia* for *pedagogía* (638)] and author's names and book titles are comically misspelled. Federico García

Lorca appears as Frederico Garcia Lorca and his famous play acquires the new title of *La casa de Bernada Alba* (627). Unamuno, the Greek and Latin scholar, would probably chuckle to see his *La agonía del cristianismo* remitted to its classical roots as *La agonia del Christianismo* (638), but would likely respond less indulgently to the transformation of his study of surely the greatest narrative of male bonding to a feminized romance in the rebaptized *Vida de don Quijote y Sancha* (587). The ignorance of things Spanish stands out in this extraordinarily rich study of modernism and its manifestations in other literatures.

Monique Chefdor opens *Modernism: Challenges and Perspectives* with a recognition of the "semantic confusion" created by the term, but then goes on to state that "Only the Hispanic and Luso-Brazilian traditions are saved from such ambiguities, since in their case *modernismo* designates clearly delineated movements" (1986, 2). This alleged consensus within Hispanic criticism might come as a surprise to Spanish and Spanish American critics who have engaged in continual debate regarding the origins, nature, and extent of "modernismo." From the very beginning, Hispanic modernism provoked considerable argument, not solely from those who opposed the movement as dangerous and subversive, but also from those who welcomed it with a desire to channel it for their own purposes. The history of the debate follows the same general outline that occurs in studies of international and, in particular, Anglo-European modernism. In broad terms, studies of English modernism initially associate it with decadence and end-of-century crisis, as in the 1908 publication *Modernism and Romance* by R. A. Scott-James. A shift occurs in the next 20 years, exemplified by T. S. Eliot and his definition of art as a means of ordering the chaos of the world and by Laura Riding and Robert Graves's *A Survey of Modernist Poetry* (1927). As Eysteinsson remarks, the formalist/New Critical perspective dominates literary studies through the 1950s and continues to play a significant role even later, privileging a reading of modernist texts as autonomous, formally harmonious, and ahistorical. With the appearance of feminist and post-structuralist theories of the 1970s and 1980s, a new critical paradigm seeks out the silences and contradictions within all texts, modernist or not, and revises inherited interpretations. The theorizing of postmodernism contributes significantly to a reevaluation of modernism, as attempts to define the latter period necessitate reconsideration of the former.

The evolution of the semantics of Spanish modernism follows a culturally specific time-line, at certain points lagging behind, at others anticipating developments that occur in other countries. Peculiar local, regional, economic, political, and cultural phenomena inflect Spanish modernism in unique ways, while other forces bind it indissolubly to the general European and American trajectory. It is not to be expected that specialists in Anglo-European or global modernism control the peculiarities of Hispanic modernism nor even that they familiarize themselves with the overall outline; however, the rush to exclude and the facility with which Spain and Spanish-speaking nations of the Caribbean and Central and South America are both coalesced into a single unit and frozen in time reflects an elimination of ambivalence and internal complexity only possible through a "-phobic" othering of Hispanic culture and identity. In that modernism is defined as the "art of modernization" (Bradbury 1978, 27) and the mode by which artists respond to the changes occurring in late modern society, the exclusion of the Hispanic world implies that it has yet to undergo modernization or that it produced no worthwhile response.[7]

As theorists of the relationship between self and other have articulated, the process of distancing and differentiation facilitates the belief that local values have universal validity. English modernism *is* modernism, perhaps explaining why it normally appears with a capital "M," and European modernism as defined with the exclusion of Spain *is* European modernism, since Europe begins at the Pyrenees. One of the great theorists of international/European modernism, cited consistently in studies devoted to the topic, is the Spanish philosopher José Ortega y Gasset. Through the process of assimilation, Ortega y Gasset becomes the explicator of a European modernist canon that excludes Spanish writers and culture. Assimilation erases difference and subsumes the alien within the world of the self; the realm of the other becomes one with that of the observing subject. Some twelve pages after declaring that Spanish and Spanish American "modernismo" do not warrant inclusion in his study, Eysteinsson cites Ortega's theory of the dehumanization of art as a primary example of formalist interpretations of modernism (1990, 14). References to Ortega as a leading proponent of this vision of modernism appear in at least five essays in the Bradbury-McFarlane collection and three texts in the Chefdor-Quinones-Wachtel study.[8] The persistent recourse to Ortega as an expert on modernism in studies that exclude, deny, or devalue Hispanic modernism raises the question of how a major theorist of the movement arose in a nation with no equivalent cultural development.

While some might argue that Ortega is not considered a *modernista* within traditional Spanish criticism, it bears repeating that the term *modernismo,* like modernism, evolves over time and even synchronically carries multiple, contradictory significations. It is also worth noting that Ortega never uses the term "modernism" in his writings on dehumanization in literature and this lack of lexical concordance has not impeded his recuperation for the cause of a formalist theorization of European modernism. Ortega y Gasset plays a considerable role in the development of early twentieth century Spanish literature, with direct connections to *modernismo,* as traditionally considered, and to the so-called "Generation of 1898." He collaborates in the early *modernista* journal *Helios,* and publishes a reasonably favorable review of Ramón del Valle-Inclán's quintessentially *modernista* text, *Sonata de estío* in *La Lectura* in 1904 (1965, 1: 20–26). On the other hand, he also writes a scathing review of *La corte de los poetas,* a 1907 *modernista* anthology (1965, 1:49–52). Many of his contemporaries figure prominently among those designated *modernistas,* such as Ramón Pérez de Ayala and Gabriel Miró, and his links to the group are multiple and well-known.[9] Ortega's theory of art and literature develops in dialogue with these writers and out of a desire to channel Spanish culture in specific directions. The appropriation of his perspective, to use his own term, while simultaneously ignoring the culture from which it issues, strips his vision of ambiguity and silences the voices of those with whom it enters into exchange. In some cases, the decontextualization of Ortega leads to serious misreadings of his work or produces a rather limited reading of modernism. Cut loose from his moorings in his own national culture and inserted within a discussion of a European modernism that excludes Hispanism, Ortega y Gasset easily becomes the assimilated other, whose difference and ties to difference disappear so completely that no one questions for a moment the invocation of a Spanish authority while simultaneously denying the existence in Spain of the cultural phenomenon on which he holds forth. A similar process occurs with Pablo Picasso, who has come to represent international modernism, but whose identification with Spain typically recedes in favor of his French residency.

Despite the exclusion of Spain and Latin America from virtually all important studies on international modernism, current theoretical and critical trends in the field open the way for a more productive dialogue with traditional and contemporary criticism of the period within Hispanic literary studies. Recent publications by Art Berman, Marianne DeKoven, Astradur Eysteinsson, Rita Felski, and Richard Sheppard distinguish multiple, contradictory currents within modernism and reject formalist attempts to strip it of subversive, transgressive aspects. In consonance with the field of cultural studies, these critics insist on relating formal changes to the broader socio-historical context and repudiate comparisons with postmodernism that fall into facile, reductionist polarizations of a conservative, formalist modernism in contrast with an oppositional, counter-cultural postmodernism. The emphasis on interrelations between artistic form and social context provides an important link to and corrective of current and previous studies of what was traditionally designated in Hispanic criticism as the formalist *modernismo* and the more socially, politically engaged "Generation of 1898." Both formal and ideological shifts co-exist and interact in modernism, in a complex dynamic that critics continue to explore and define. Eysteinsson's vision of modernism as a distinct sociosymbolic system that remains permanently outside of and in opposition to mainstream culture offers a very useful explanation for certain aspects of Spanish modernism as do Berman's definition of modernism as the union of irreconcilable differences and DeKoven's insistence on paradox, collage, irony, and a resistance to resolution and stability. Rita Felski's repeated observation that specific features in modernism are both repressive and liberating, dissident and conformist, helps to comprehend and reconcile many of the opposing views of the Spanish literature of the period. Richard Sheppard's definition of modernism as "a heterogeneous range of responses to a global process of modernization" (1993, 7) aptly describes the multifaceted reactions to the modern condition found in Hispanic texts of the period. Furthermore, his passing reference to the metaphor of two sides of the same spinning coin in his discussion of the modernist vision of the human subject (23) easily applies to all aspects of modernism, in which alternating possibilities coexist within the same author and the same text.

Contributions to the understanding of alterity by Todorov, Levinas, Waldenfels, and postcolonial studies facilitate analysis of the multiple encounters with the other that constitute Spanish modernism. They also provide guidance in avoiding the pitfalls of appropriation or rejection in order to construct a dialogic exchange that fosters acceptance and allows diversity, without precluding judgement or erasing conflict. If a study of a period wishes to claim any validity, it must possess some explanatory power that applies generally to the various cultural expressions produced therein. This clearly represents a departure from Francoist visions of Spanish culture of late nineteenth and early twentieth century and their continuing echoes in what Richard A. Cardwell has labeled "confrontational criticism" (1998b, 173). Many critics trace the origins of this tradition back to the early part of the twentieth century, and specifically to studies published in 1913 by Manuel Machado and José Martínez Ruiz (Azorín).[10] However, Machado and Azorín in large part continue an on-going discussion that dates back to the 1880s and a reading of their studies as fostering a modernist-Generation of 1898 cultural divide misrepresents the complexity of their argument and the inclusive definition of modernism that arises in the earliest discussions and continues for some three decades. In order to trace the early categorization of modernism as a richly nuanced cultural movement and its very early association with tolerance for difference and encounters across established borders, it is imperative to return to early writings on the subject and to strip away as far as possible the imposition of nationalist and isolationist ideologies.

Regional Rivalries and National Tensions: Catalonian and Spanish American Modernism and National Spanish Culture

In Spain, the first use of the term "modernism" apparently dates from 1884 in a manifesto accompanying the publication of the Barcelona magazine *L'Avenç*. During the next two decades and under the rubric of modernism, Catalan writers, artists, and intellectuals develop a mode of thinking and writing that questions inherited values in the areas of religion, politics, and aesthetics. Catalan modernism[11] does not develop harmoniously and monolithically, but rather incorporates several different forms: a socially progressive group associated with *L'Avenç* and the anarchist Jaume Brossa, a more strictly literary group, with aestheticist tendencies under the leadership of Santiago Rusiñol, and in an intermediate position, the poet/journalist Joan Maragall. Maragall accepts Nietzschean exaltation of will, but fears radical social action while also repudiating what he perceives as pessimism and lack of vitality in the Rusiñol camp. For Vicente Cacho Viu and Oriol Bohigas, the architecture of Antoni Gaudi represents yet another expression of modernism. As this synopsis reveals, attempts at classification quickly break down into a multiplication of subgroups and exceptions, representing the heterogeneity of responses to modernity that Richard Sheppard considers the hallmark of international modernism.

Scholars of Catalan modernism trace its development from the 1880s to 1901, when it is succeeded by *noucentisme,* an officially sponsored movement with institutional bases that Terry describes as both "a continuation and a reduction" of antecedent modernism (1995, 57). Traditional criticism of Spanish literature rarely considered Catalan modernism when discussing Spanish culture of the late nineteenth and early twentieth century, while scholars of Catalan modernism insist not only on its precedence with regard to its Castilian counterpart, but also its difference. Although the context of Catalan modernism and *noucentisme* manifests certain peculiarities that provide interesting contrasts with Castilian modernism, the similarities and contacts between the two movements are considerable, as José-Carlos Mainer has indicated (1988, 140). Although Cacho Viu insists on a chronological asymmetry between Barcelona and Madrid, he also sees certain similarities in the appearance of new cultural groups and leaders (1997, 35). In both cases, younger thinkers and artists reject the politics and values of Restoration Spain and attempt to redefine regional and national identity. While this takes place within a drive for regional autonomy and revival in Catalonia, artists and intellectuals in both regions share an overall repudiation of the traditional vision of a Catholic, imperial, and centralized government. Similarly, the coexistence of a socially committed progressive impulse alongside and sometimes within a drive for aesthetic renovation and autonomy provides a significant link. Scholars of Catalan literature often point to a more optimistic trust in possibilities for change in comparison with Castilian pessimism and sense of loss after the defeat during the Spanish-American War, but this divergence is based on a traditional and questionable limitation of Castilian literature of the period to a rather small set of authors and to a restricted reading of a limited number of their works. Furthermore, the existence of numerous interconnections between Catalan and Castilian artists and intellectuals of the period calls into question a substantial difference between the new cultural movements that surface at this time in these two Iberian cultural centers.

From the early work of Guillermo Díaz-Plaja to the more recent studies of Giovanni Allegra, Geoffrey Ribbans, Vicente Cacho Viu, Carlos Salaün, and EduardoValenti Fiol, critics have pointed to the cultural interactions between Catalonia and France and Catalonia and Castile. Catalan geographic and economic contacts with France facilitate the circulation of ideas from abroad. European writers considered key to the introduction of early modernist thought appear frequently in the Barcelona of the 1880s and 1890s. Josep Jordà translates Ibsen's *An Enemy of the People* and Barcelona theater-goers receive the translation with enthusiasm. Cipriano Montoliù introduces Ruskin's social ideas, the Catalan musicologist Joaquim Marsillach publishes the first study of Wagner and first mentions Nietzsche in his 1878 *Ricardo Wagner,* the magazine *Joventut* becomes the official promulgator of Wagner in Spain and also introduces D'Annunzio, while Joan Maragall produces the first full-length study of Nietzsche for *L'Avenç. La Ilustración Ibérica,* published in Barcelona from 1882 to 1900, introduces readers to the Pre-Raphaelites and works by or about Renan, Tolstoy, Ibsen, Maeterlinck, and Barrès appear in *L'Avenç.* The economic strength of Barcelona's bourgeoisie and their openness to innovation further the rich modernist architectural production of Antoni Gaudi, Lluis Domènech I Montaner and others. Santiago Rusiñol, painter, poet, and playwright with lengthy residencies in France, establishes *Cau Ferrat* in Sitges, a modernist center that sponsors numerous *Festes modernistes.* The 1893 festival includes the first representation of a work by Maeterlinck in Spain, and the 1894 festival fosters a revival of interest in El Greco, with a public procession to celebrate the installation in *Cau Ferrat* of two of his paintings that Rusiñol purchased in Paris.

Catalan modernism quickly becomes a focus of attention for Spanish-speaking writers. Emilia Pardo Bazán visits *Cau Ferrat* and writes admiringly of the unconventional atmosphere, the all-night vigil to witness the sunrise, and the commitment to aesthetic renovation (n. d., 263–69). Ganivet stops at Sitges and praises the group's energy, which he finds unparalleled in Spain, and defends the mix of local, national, and international influences for the creation of a new art: "Y la impresión clara que de todo se desprende es que el *Cau* intenta dar un nuevo impulso a nuestro arte, utilizando los procedimientos de las nuevas varias tendencias que por todas partes despuntan, y apoyando los pies para hacer ese esfuerzo en lo más genuinamente español: en el misticismo" [And the clear impression that all this imparts is that the *Cau* hopes to give a new impulse to our art, using techniques of the diverse new tendencies that are surfacing in many places and, in order to undertake this effort, anchoring both feet in what is most authentically Spanish: in mysticism] (1943 II: 737). In his visit to Spain in 1898, Rubén Darío stops both in Madrid and Barcelona and writes in 1899 that only in Catalonia did he encounter any real modernism (1901?, 311).[12]

Exposure to Catalan modernism also takes place through personal friendships, shared residencies in Paris, and multiple collaborations in journals.[13] *La Vida Galante,* a publication that emphasizes the erotic and challenges traditional gender relations, first appears in Barcelona in 1898 and then moves to Madrid in 1900. *El Nuevo Mercurio* has a truly international flavor. Printed in Barcelona with a national distribution, it is directed by the Guatemalan Enrique Gómez Carrillo, who resides in France. Important Catalan modernists contribute to Madrid-based journals that scholars have identified as the voice of Castilian modernism: Rusiñol and Angel Guimerá write for *Germinal* and *Vida Nueva* and *La Vida Literaria* publishes poems by Jacinto Verdaguer and Angel Guimerá as well as a translation of Joan Corominas's *Las prisiones imaginarias,* the prison memoirs of one of numerous anarchists arrested in the wake of an 1896 bombing of a Corpus Christi parade. The scandal created by the arbitrary arrests and torture of suspects in what comes to be known as the Montjuich case, so named for the infamous prison in which the accused are held, brings together Catalan and Castilian intellectuals in common commitment to change and legal fairness. The short-lived modernist journal *Helios* (1903–1904), with contributions from most of the young Castilian writers, including Juan Ramón Jiménez, Gregorio Martínez Sierra, Ramón Pérez de Ayala, and José Ortega y Gasset, pays special attention to Catalan literature and includes contributions by Rusiñol, José Carner, Joan Maragall, and Verdaguer. At least two important journals founded in Madrid during the early years of the twentieth century take as their title a Castilian version of a name previously used in Catalan modernist publications: *Renacimiento* (1907), directed by Gregorio Martínez Sierra, corresponds to the Catalan *La Renaixensa,* where the modernist architect Domènech I Montaner had published the first theoretical text on the search for a new style; and *Juventud*

(1901–1902) echoes its Catalan predecessor *Joventut* and carries forward its sense of novelty and impulse for renewal. Pablo Picasso creates the fleeting *Arte Joven* after a trip to Paris with the writer Pío Baroja and his artist brother Ricardo and brings ideas from *Joventut,* where he had contacts (McDermott 1993, 238). In *Alma Española,* the Catalan Maragall, the Basque Miguel de Unamuno, the Valencian Vicente Blasco Ibáñez and writers from other regions collaborate in 1904 on a series of articles on the regional spirit. *Renacimiento* devotes considerable space to Catalan writers, dedicating an entire issue to Maragall in collaboration with the Catalan critic José Yxart, a second volume to Rusiñol with comments by Maragall, and articles by the Catalan writers Eugenio d'Ors, Victor Català (Catarina Albert I Paradís), and Gabriel Alomar. Maragall and Unamuno develop a close and enduring friendship, with frequent correspondence and exchange of ideas and Gregorio and his wife and co-author María Martínez Sierra collaborate with and translate Santiago Rusiñol. Works by d'Ors, a representative of modernism and then *noucentisme,* appear in Catalan and Castilian and he publishes in *La Lectura, La República de las Letras,* and *Renacimiento.*

The frequent contacts between leading figures of Catalan modernism and *noucentisme* and Castilian modernism/ *noventayochismo* as well as their similarities in origins, influences, and general contours challenge attempts to separate them into two discrete cultural phenomena. Writers and intellectuals working in Madrid see Catalan modernism as a hopeful opening to a new way of thinking and writing and avidly seek to introduce it to the rest of the country, as stated by the editors of the Madrid-based *Vida Nueva* in 1898: "Barcelona tiene iniciativas, energías, entusiasmo, virilidad, y de allí nos vendrá la vida nueva, ya que en Madrid no se piensa sino en hacer política, hablar de la mar y acudir a los toros" [Barcelona has initiative, energy, enthusiasm, virility, and new life will come to us from there, since in Madrid it doesn't occur to anyone to think except about politics, or to talk except about the sea or to go to the bullfights].[14] José María Llanas Aguilaniedo also welcomes Catalan modernism as a sign of progress and presents Catalan writers as models, praising their work ethic, hunger for new ideas, and openness to foreign experiences through travel and reading (1991, 63). While Ribbans (1993, 10) sees decreasing communication between Catalonia and Madrid with the arrival of *noucentisme,* the period from the early 1890s through at least 1907 witnesses continuous dialogue. The borders between Catalan and Castilian culture of early twentieth century prove to be productively porous, with Catalan modernism providing an impetus and a model for a national cultural renovation.

The relations between Spain and Latin America show a similarly enriching encounter, with various stages and nuances. Rubén Darío's 1888 publication of *Azul* represents for many the inauguration of Latin American modernism and it attracted immediate attention from the well-known Spanish novelist-critic Juan Valera. Valera's ambiguous response typifies that of many established Restoration writers and relates to his campaign to discredit naturalism, his anxieties regarding its socially revolutionary elements, and his desire for a less politicized literature. As a result, the review praises the non-didactic thrust of Darío's work and emphasizes its aesthetic purpose. However, the enthusiasm is tempered by discomfort at the loss of religious faith, the accompanying pessimism, and their direct connection to social instability. Valera very directly queries how to control the hungry, ignorant masses without the checks provided by religion (1888, 222) and in a clear expression of his fear, he censures the final, blasphemous verses of "Anagke" that he inserts to give Spanish readers a sense of Darío's poetry. The review also confesses discomfort at the perceptible French influence in *Azul* and suggests that Darío open himself to English, German, Italian, and perhaps even Spanish sources. Fear of a socially and politically transgressive current in modernist literature produces a gallophobic reaction in many conservative and moderate Spaniards. In a previous study on naturalism and its reception in Spain, I traced the complex interplay of fear of social revolution, sexual liberation, and women's emancipation[15] and these same concerns inform the critical reception of modernism by a number of established writers. Leopoldo Alas (Clarín) targets both the sexual license and dependency on French literature, language, and thought. In one text he refers to Darío's "galicismos internos" [internal Gallicisms] (1893a, 222) and in another he plays with the sexual connotation of the color green in Spanish culture to state his opposition to "cosillas afrancesadas, melancólicamente verdes . . . , desnudeces alicaídas" [little Frenchified things, gloomily green . . . , depressed nudities] (Fernández Almagro 1943, 57–58).

Darío's early comments on his relations with Spain and Spanish literature should be read in the context of his interactions with older, established Spanish writers. During his first visit in 1892, he meets Valera, Menéndez y Pelayo, Pardo Bazán as well as the younger Salvador Rueda. In a second trip in 1899, he comes to know Catalan modernists and declares his affinity with them in contrast to the sterile Castilian literary world of the Restoration. He also insists that Latin American modernism predates its Catalan equivalent and represents a rejection of Castilian literature (1901?, 315). By 1904, however, Darío notes a change in Spain and undergoes a shift in his own position. He states now that the energy characteristic of Barcelona has spread to the rest of the peninsula and insists on a common purpose in Spain and Latin America, joined in opposition to the United States (1917, 16). Subsequent critics, citing either Darío's early or later comments, have argued for a commonality of purpose or a cultural separation between Spanish and Latin American modernism. In his 1934 anthology of modernist poetry, Federico de Onís enthusiastically recognizes Darío's contribution to Spanish literary history and advocates an inclusive, epochal definition of modernism (1961, xv). Juan Ramón Jiménez expresses a similar view in 1953, linking Hispanic modernism to theological, scientific, and literary movements and affirming its continued vitality (1962, 50). Even more significantly, Jiménez openly accepts the circuitous route that modernism took from France to Latin America and then Spain and stresses its repudiation of racial, national, and gender borders. His description of Darío as very Indian and very dark, a composite of diverse races (74–77), reflects his validation of the once colonized other.[16]

An opposing critical tradition defends the existence of a clear division between Latin American and peninsular modernism. Its members come from both sides of the Atlantic and although they share a desire to establish the autonomy and superiority of one literary tradition over the other, the implications of their argument vary according to geographical origin. Many Latin Americans and Latin Americanists seize on Darío's initial declaration of independence from Castilian literary tradition and define Spanish American modernism as the moment when the former colonies find their own voice and artistic expression. The performative strength of this position, given the urgency of the creation of a Latin American post-colonial identity, as well as the recognition of the undeniable cultural contributions of such writers as Darío, Martí, and Rodó, to name only a few, prompt a sympathetic response to this line of thought. However, the construction of a Latin American cultural identity sometimes leads to simplistic and misleading descriptions of the Spanish culture in opposition to which it defines itself. The decadent cultural waste land that Darío observes in the aftermath of 1898 becomes for some Latin Americanists a primary trait of Spanish culture for the last quarter of the nineteenth century, or for the entire century, and the absence of major poets in the 1890s leads to blanket statements about the dearth of creative spirit when Galdós, Clarín, and Pardo Bazán are producing extraordinary works.[17] Other studies posit a stolid, homogeneous Spanish public that reacts with shock at Darío's postcolonial language and vision. In contrast to a monochromatic, single-voiced metropolis, Iris Zavala describes a cultural milieu in which the ex-colonies celebrate plurality and openness (1992, 56). While the impulse toward national redefinition manifests itself in different forms in the former colonies than in the former seat of power, neither Spain nor the Latin American nations respond with uniform acceptance or rejection of Darío or modernism. Opposition comes from the older generation, a complaisant bourgeoisie, the church, and other established powers while acceptance is found primarily, on both sides of the Atlantic, in a younger generation that sees the need for new ways of viewing and expressing the self, the nation, and the social and physical landscape.

In Spain, those who insist on a solid border separating Latin American and peninsular modernism fall into similarly simplistic arguments, with imperialist echoes that make their statements even more problematic. Pedro Salinas's now famous "El problema del modernismo en España, o un conflicto entre dos espíritus" (1938) specifically denies the contention that with modernism, America reversed history and conquered Spain. The study rejects the notion that former colonies could provide leadership to the erstwhile colonizers. To head off such arguments, Salinas theorizes the existence of two distinct groups: Latin American modernists with a purely formal, poetic renovation; and Spanish writers, with an analytical, profound, virile, and nationalist preoccupation (1949, 13–25). The impact that Salinas's text has had on subsequent studies cannot be overstated.[18] It represents a significant break with previous Spanish criticism on the nature and development of modernism and in suggesting an impermeable border between Spanish and Latin American modernism and the "Generation of 1898," it erases the ongoing redefinition of Spanish-Latin American relations taking place on both sides of the Atlantic through dialogue and exchange. Latin American modernism is not the primary focus of this study, but it stands in a dialogic relation to peninsular modernism and a deeper understanding of one necessarily clarifies the other. As in the case of Catalan and Castilian modernism, Latin American and peninsular modernism manifest peculiarities unique to each and within Latin America, the pace and extent of modernism varies according to country and region. However, their differences do not negate nor even outweigh their affinities and to ignore their connections to each other and to the global modernism with which they share common origins and general traits repudiates the internationalist, cosmopolitan, and humanitarian goals that stand along side their individual, regional, and national aspirations. While a significant body of recent Spanish criticism has lamented the legacy of the Francoist division of early twentieth-century Spanish culture in two opposing movements and some studies have traced the origins of this tradition to the Salinas essay, the extent to which Salinas and his successors violently reshaped the definition of the goals and nature of Spanish culture of late nineteenth and early twentieth century has not been fully recognized. A review of early studies of Spanish modernism reveals the distorted lens through which later critics viewed the period and which continues all too frequently to condition contemporary critical studies.

Early Definitions of Spanish Modernism: 1894–1913

The term modernism appears in the Madrid press in the early 1890s to designate a new mode of expression and thought that stood in contrast to Restoration values and realist literature. The somewhat earlier appearance of the term in Catalonia and Latin America undoubtedly encouraged its adoption and contributed to its polemical reception. From the outset, the word became a site of conflict between competing sectors of Spanish society, exemplifying not only the Gramscian vision of culture as a struggle for hegemony (Gramsci, 1992), but also the Bakhtinian concept of the word as a primary location of ideological contest (1986, 94). John Butt has accurately pointed out that during the early years of its circulation, modernism has a fluid meaning (1993, 51). Proponents of the movement represent diverse ideological positions, from radical anarchist to moderate Republican. Virtually all envision the intellectual and artist as key figures in the construction of a new culture; their differences consist not so much in the opposition between socially committed and escapist art or between ideas and their elegant expression, as later critics would have it, but rather in different conceptions of how best to transform contemporary society. A review of the literature on modernism published between 1898 and 1913 reveals an on-going dialogue between advocates of various paths to social and cultural renewal and often the same speaker occupies multiple positions depending on personal evolution and, more importantly, on the interlocutor(s) and previous and anticipated responses.[19] The following discussion identifies 10 basic positions that are repeatedly articulated in early studies on modernism. They are neither stable nor discrete and persistently reflect the co-presence of contradictory goals and methods.

1. Modernism Breaks with the National Past Through International Connections

Proponents of this view emphasize both the disavowal of Restoration and pre-Restoration Spain and the link with non-Spanish writers, whether European or American. Journal titles that underscore newness, youth, and discontinuity (*Juventud, Germinal, Vida Nueva,* and *Renacimiento*) reflect this tenet as do declarations by Azorín, Valle-Inclán, and González Blanco that their generation is iconoclastic[20] and statements by Baroja and Valle-Inclán that to destroy is to create.[21]

2. Modernism Retains a Link with the Past, Combining National Traditions and International Sources

This perspective recognizes a certain continuity with the past, but allows for selective identification of key figures and events from the national tradition, infusing them with new meaning in light of concepts introduced by European and Latin American writers and thinkers. Some critics identify the recuperation of the past as a late event in Spanish modernism and chide writers such as Manuel Machado and Azorín for a softening of progressive modernism in their acknowledgment of a connection to tradition. To the contrary, the affirmation of continuity appears early in discussions of modernism and has multiple, sometimes contradictory motives. It responds, on the one hand, to accusations of cultural treason from traditionalists who invoke hypernationalist discourse to discredit their opponents. It also seeks to reclaim or reevaluate figures and events in order to recuperate progressive energies from the past and wrest nationalist discourse from traditional, anti-modernist forces. Writing in response to *Gente Vieja*'s public competition to define modernism in

1902, both Pascual Ruiz Enríquez and Manuel Cidrón argue that it does not really oppose the past, while also insisting on its potential for social regeneration. Ruiz Enríquez sees it as lacking clear form, but possessing educational value and productive energy (3–4). Cidrón initially affirms its ties to tradition and later clarifies that he refers to the glorious legacy of the French Revolution, the quintessential break with the past (5–6).

Around these same dates, Jacinto Benavente produces a one-act play entitled *Modernismo,* which deconstructs the boundaries between tradition and innovation, past and present. Subtitled "Nuevos moldes," it links with Azorín's "Somos iconoclastas" in suggesting a break with literary ancestors. However, the text recasts this idea, arguing that it seeks to widen rather than break molds. It insists on returning to more remote antecedents, such as Greek tragedy, Shakespeare, or classical Spanish drama. The minimization of intrigue and emphasis on character that typifies the new theater espoused by Benavente contrasts with one-dimensional characters, improbable plot development, and violent emotions of more recent introduction—that is, Echegaray—that the speaker argues do not truly belong to the national literary heritage (1945, 1:431–36). The repudiation of recent definitions of tradition and attempt to construct an alternative version of the past lies at the heart of much modernist discourse. As Inman Fox demonstrates, the struggle to define the limits and character of Spanish history and identity commences well before the debates on modernism, coursing through the nineteenth century in polemics between the conservative Marcelino Menéndez y Pelayo and liberal adherents of Krausism and the Institución Libre de Enseñanza (1997). It hardly seems necessary to reiterate that this conflict continues throughout the twentieth century and that history, tradition, and the past are everywhere sites of contention with fluid, shifting contours. In the context of Spanish modernism, this view of culture has not always prevailed, with the unfortunate result that scholars interpret affirmations of links to tradition as wholehearted acceptance of inherited values, failing to see the transgressive underpinnings of a redefined tradition with new purposes.

3. Modernism is Individualistic and Anarchistic

Although related to the repudiation of the past and apparently opposed to the continuation of tradition, this feature of modernism contains contradictory impulses that have been read alternatively as progressive or reactionary. Early advocates of an individualistic, anarchistic modernism include José Deleito y Piñuelo in *Gente Vieja* (1902)[22] and Ramón Pérez de Ayala in *Helios* (1903a). Deleito y Piñuelo notes a disdain for authority and coexistence of multiple literary currents including symbolism, decadentism, and eroticism. His references to Oscar Wilde and symbolist idealism place him in close proximity to definitions of modernism that later critics identify as aestheticist and antagonistic to socially committed art, but the article persistently identifies modernism with social change and argues that art provides the impetus for transformation: ". . . en el mundo de la belleza la piqueta, demoledora de lo construído, puede penetrar más libremente que en la prosaica vida real, cuyos elementos ofrecen solidísima cohesión" [In the world of beauty the pickaxe, destroyer of constructed objects, can penetrate more freely than in prosaic life, where elements present extremely solid cohesion] (1–2).

Pérez de Ayala addresses both the anarchic nature of modernism and its relation to social and political commitment. "La aldea lejana: Con motivo de la aldea perdida," offers a subjective response to Armando Palacio Valdés's novel about their shared Asturian homeland. The speaker defends subjective criticism as a logical consequence of his repudiation of absolute definitions of beauty and his belief that writers may construct their own individual aesthetic. He further states that many artistic tendencies exist in contemporary literature, all marked by a spirit of aesthetic anarchism (1903a, 5–14). "Liras o lanzas" (1903b) continues to emphasize the pursuit of individual definitions of truth and beauty, which for the speaker reside in poetry. The insistence on the value of poetry and the title's polarization of lyrics and lances has led some critics to read the text as an early affirmation of a modernism that privileges art for art's sake over social concern (1973, 75). However, textual ambiguities and a strong repudiation of militarism call such a reading into question. The speaker refutes the thesis of Alvaro de Albornoz's book *No liras, lanzas* that poetry is useless and the solution to national problems lies in direct social combat, symbolized by the lances of the title. In presenting his argument, Pérez de Ayala adopts the posture of a *bon vivant* who has abandoned all concern for the proletariat in favor of champagne and Cuban cigars. He defends poetry as the milk of the great nourishing udder that has nursed the best, most select members of humanity. The odd combination of earthy metaphor and exaltation of artistic elite introduces an initial gap in the declarations of aristocratic posture that widens in subsequent paragraphs. The speaker reacts strongly to the violent connotations of "lances," declaring that the evangelical fervor of Tolstoi constitutes a fundamental feature of his formation, but then in a sudden about-face, he confesses his admiration for Napoleon.

The text speaker then turns to his duty in the context of Spanish national decadence, quoting Miguel de Unamuno's admonishment that to best serve the nation, citizens should search for profound and eternal qualities that are least connected to the present and national culture. He then remits the reader to Krause's second commandment, which prefigures Unamuno's advice in advocating love of humanity and the universal over the individual and local. Within this context of a progressive tradition, the speaker closes with an attack on militarism and nationalist values: "Lanzas ¿para qué? ¿Para que perduren atávicas preocupaciones de raza e inhumanas fronteras políticas? El clásico ha dicho mi patria es el cielo. Yo, un poco romántico con el romanticismo otoñal de las edades que sacudan, digo: 'Mi patria es la tierra. Más que patria, mi madre; mi Dios; madre de todos, Dios de la humanidad'" [Lances, for what purpose? So that atavistic racial concerns and inhuman political frontiers can continue? The classical writer said my country is the heavens. Somewhat romantic, with the autumnal romanticism of declining ages, I say: 'My country is the earth. More than country, my mother; my God; mother of all, God of humanity'] (1903b, 520). On the heels of the recent war with Cuba and the militarist rhetoric it provoked and in the face of traditional associations of Spain and empire, Pérez de Ayala's stakes out a social and political position that remains well outside the ivory tower enclosure in which later critics seek to imprison both this particular text and modernism in general. The allusion to his preference for Cuban cigars acquires a different meaning, beyond the egotistical pleasure seeker, suggesting the abandonment of war-time animosities and the renewal of contacts with the former colony and military enemy.

The insistence on the anarchistic quality of Spanish modernism continues throughout the decade and beyond. Gómez-Lobo reiterates it in 1908 and Manuel Machado in *La guerra literaria* in 1913. Many writers follow the refusal of Baroja and Unamuno to be identified with a particular school or movement, rejecting the imposition of homogeneity and the validity of grand narratives, to use Lyotard's term.[23] Pérez de Ayala's denial of absolute truth or beauty exemplifies another aspect of this attitude. Some modernists focus on moral issues, others emphasize the social, and still others the aesthetic, but each questions inherited values and forcefully expresses a spirit of independence. The refusal to accept a coalescence under a single, univocal rubric persistently reaffirms modernism's originary transgressive, heterogeneous impetus.

4. Modernism Has Practical, Social Objectives

Many writers on Spanish modernism during the late nineteenth and early twentieth centuries emphasize an essential social component, sometimes in combination with and at times in opposition to an individualist current. Ernesto Bark propounds the need for a practical modernism and includes in the modernist agenda a general elevation of the Spanish cultural level through university extension programs, night schools, and a repudiation of militarist, nationalist ambitions (1901, 8, 86). Bark quotes the doctor and medical researcher Santiago Ramón y Cajal to emphasize the conjoining of science and art in this new national project, a combination that reappears even more strikingly in Camilo Bargiela's *Luciérnagas.* This collection of stories challenges traditional visions of honor and love, using decadentist effects, surprise endings, and psychological analysis. The title and many of the stories reveal sensibilities, themes, and characters associated with aestheticist, *arte por el arte* tendencies, but the incorporated essay, "Modernistas y anticuados" insists on a broad, social definition. The text closes with the separation of the contemporary cultural field into two distinct camps, but they do not coincide with a formalist modernism and socially committed "Generation of 1898" later identified by literary historians. Rather, they place modernism in a broadly defined opposition to antiquated tradition, inclusive of all contemporary artistic and scientific currents: ". . . *modernistas,* que significa tanto como espíritus expansivos abiertos a todas las corrientes científicas y artísticas, y otros varones que yo llamo *anticuados,* por no denominar con adjetivo más fuerte y gráfico" [. . . *modernists,* which means the same as expansive spirits open to all scientific and artistic currents, and others who I call *antiquated,* so as not to resort to a stronger and more graphic adjective] (1900, ii). Rafael Altamira echoes similar sentiments in "El patriotismo y la universidad" (1898) as do Gómez-Lobo (1908) and Manuel Ugarte (1908).

5. Modernism Is Anti-Materialist and Anti-determinist

The rejection of Restoration Spain and the influence of contemporary European thought contribute jointly to the modernist renunciation of a positivist, materialist legacy. While many tenets, values, and discursive strands from the previous period, such as racial, biological, and geographic determinism, survive in modernist discourse, they interweave with principles, values, and language drawn from competing systems that question the universal validity and even relative veracity of the positivist vision. Two distinct elements stand out in anti-materialist modernism: the disdain for commodification, industrialism, and a mass culture that vulgarizes art and creativity; and the disavowal of a philosophy incapable of explaining either humanity's spiritual, irrational component, or, equally important, its potential for change. The anti-industrialist thrust may express itself in a distaste for cities, crowds, or a modernization that intrudes between the individual and nature, beauty, and art. Eduardo Chavarri, the winner of *Gente Vieja's* contest for the best essay on modernism, writes that the new movement reacts not so much against naturalism as against utilitarianism and a world dominated by the cult of the stomach. He laments the displacement of traditional popular poetry by the "chulapismo" and "flamenquismo" of the street-smart, cheeky, lower-class men connected to bull-fighting, flamenco dancing, and the underworld. The city threatens popular culture and all forms of poetry: "El canto popular libre, impregnado de naturaleza, va enmudeciendo en las ciudades, las casas de seis pisos impiden ver el centelleo de las estrellas, y los alambres de teléfono no dejan a la mirada perderse en la profundidad azul; el piano callejero mata la musa popular. ¡Estamos en pleno industrialismo!" [Popular music, permeated with nature, is fading in the cities, six-story houses make it impossible to see the twinkling of stars, and the telephone wires don't allow the gaze to lose itself in the blue heavens. The street piano is killing the popular muse. We are in full industrialization!] (1902, 1–2). In the face of this new threat, Chavarri welcomes an incipient art form that resists commodification. Privileging the unique, or Benjamin's "auratic," contains its own risks, as Chavarri himself recognizes. The impulse for the "new" easily leads to a superficial imitation of novel forms, which paradoxically fall back into the mass-produced artifacts against which modernism arose in the first place. Many modernists condemn imitations of their innovations. Antonio Machado's famous verse "mas no amo los afeites de la actual cosmética" [but I've no great love for the latest in cosmetics][24] ("Retrato," 1951, 731) and Rubén Darío's even earlier repudiation of cheap imitations (1901?, 325) reflect this antipathy toward reproduction. Rather than interpret such statements as a rejection of modernism, as many critics have done, they may be viewed as a continuation of the originary impulse towards authentic and individual artistic creation.[25]

Nietzschean emphasis on the will and irrational aspects of humanity, Charcot, Madame Blavatsky, and pre-Freudian and Freudian explorers of the unconscious as well as Oriental philosophies and religions gain currency at the turn of the century and posit realms of human experience that nineteenth century positivism fails to explicate. Proponents of sexual, racial, and class equality further contribute to a reexamination and eventual repudiation of philosophical and scientific determinism. Deleito y Piñuelo (1902) observes a return to idealism in reaction to triumphant matter and an interest in those elements of nature that remain invisible or inaccessible to the ordinary observer. From symbolism, modernism derives the aspiration to discover the soul or essence of things, which it combines with other artistic and cultural movements. Deleito y Piñuelo and Gonzalo Guasp (1902) both refer to a need to recover a sense of wonder before nature, to defamiliarize the automatic responses that modern observers have assimilated. The return to pre-classical periods, medieval spiritualism, the Orient, and primitive worlds answers this need and facilitates the recovery of a sense of mystery:

> Los hombres, con el transcurso de los siglos, se han familiarizado exageradamente con la naturaleza, no causando el espectáculo del Cosmos la impresión que en las primeras generaciones producía. Por esto, el artista simbolista encuentra en la fábula antigua el eterno misterio; solamente entre el artista primitivo, inventor de la fábula, y el actual existe una diferencia: el primero expresaba espontáneamente su visión de las cosas impregnadas del misterio; el segundo tiene que reconstruir en el espíritu moderno una facultad perdida, el sentido del misterio, para lo cual ha de perturbar las costumbres inveteradas del lector. (Guasp, 1902, 2–3)

> [Humanity, with the passage of the centuries, has become overly familiar with nature, so that the spectacle of the Cosmos no longer causes the impression that it produced in the first generations. For

this reason, the symbolist artist finds eternal mystery in the ancient fable; however between the primitive writer, the inventor of the fable, and his contemporary there exists a difference: the former spontaneously expressed his vision of the mystery that permeated all things; the latter has to reconstruct in the modern spirit a lost faculty, the sense of mystery, to which end he has to disturb the inveterate customs of the reader.]

Guasp closes his sensitive study of the challenge to the modernist writer with a discussion of Taine and the determining power of the milieu. In defiance of determinism, he argues that modernists are not the creations of their surroundings, but rather creators of a new world. The arrogation of artistic agency in opposition to a limiting determinism constitutes an important element of antimaterialist modernism, introduces a note of optimism all too often ignored by critics, and has significant implications for theories of language and style.

6. Modernism Requires a New Language to Express a New Vision

Toward the end of Guasp's discussion of the defamiliarizing impetus of modernism, he alludes to the use of daring syntactical innovations and renovated expressions to jolt the bourgeois reader into new habits of seeing and understanding. Chavarri (1902), writing also in *Gente Vieja,* echoes the same opinion, as does Pompeyo Gener in the prologue to *Leyendas de amor,* where he writes of the need to open the reader to new horizons, to free the spirit and expand the heart (1902b, 11). The magazine *Helios* (1903) opens with a declaration of the intimate relationship between the new word and the new spirit in a statement signed by Pedro González Blanco, Juan Ramón Jiménez, Gregorio Martínez Sierra, Carlos Navarro Lamarca, and Ramón Pérez de Ayala. The emphasis on language has received ample attention from critics who seek to cleave these writers into two distinct groups and associate modernism with expression and style at the expense of content. However, the conjunction of word and spirit in *Helios* and the repeated allusions to battle in the introductory section of the magazine suggest a more complex relationship between form and content.

The writers do self-identify as champions of Beauty, but immediately declare that they wage battles not just of word, but also of spirit: "Y henos aquí, paladines de nuestra muy amada Belleza, prontos a reñir cien batallas de verbo y espíritu" [And here we are, paladins of our beloved Beauty, quick to wage a hundred battles of word and of spirit.] ("Génesis", 1903, 3). They also affirm that freedom serves as the publication's standard and the wide-range of articles and contributors confirms an open, inclusive agenda. Often described as the quintessential modernist journal, in the sense of Ivory Tower preoccupation with form and disinclination to social engagement, *Helios,* in fact, includes a repeating feature called "Fémina," devoted to women's issues and partially from a feminist perspective, as well as numerous articles on such contemporary political issues as socialism, racism in the United States, and the construction of the Panama Canal. Contributions range from texts by the Alvarez Quintero brothers, with their interest in popular Andalusian culture, to excerpts from Angel Ganivet's letters, poems by Manuel Machado, Salvador Rueda, and Juan Ramón Jiménez and articles and stories by the iconoclastic Alejandro Sawa and the classical Juan Valera, not to mention Azorín, Unamuno, Pérez de Ayala, and others. *Helios,* alongside other modernist journals and artistic manifestoes, resists limiting definitions of beauty, language, and spirit in favor of an open and tolerant vision.

7. The Modernist Artist Is a Professional, with the Status and Responsibilities of Other Professionals

The importance of art as a force for social transformation and the recognition of language as a reflection and producer of social change accompanies a redefinition of the artist as a professional, with specialized training and duties. Martínez Sierra insists that literature is labor and that for the first time in history, his generation does not subordinate art to political or journalistic ends (1904, 3, 15). Once again, this defense of the artist easily inspires accusations of elitism and escapism and both contemporary and subsequent critics have taken up the charge. Unamuno thundered against those he saw slipping into an unhealthy exaltation of art and warned Antonio Machado and others that artists should love life, hate art, and reject a professionalization that impedes a broad, cross disciplinary approach to the human experience (1903, 46–50). Maeztu also wrote disparagingly of those he feared were retreating from social awareness to the refined world of art (1903). However, before presuming the aestheticist impetus of these statements, it is helpful to view them in the context of other articles that appear during these years. In "Arte y utilidad," Azorín compares writers' work to that of field hands and other laborers and includes all in the common enterprise of the construction of a new nation. Although at times acknowledging the existence of writers who adhere to an aestheticist vision of art, he minimizes the difference between the two groups, comparing their little ivory tower with his own plain, tile-roofed house. Both look outward from a place of observation and the use of the diminutive brings the tower to the same level as the house. More importantly, he joins Chavarri, Deleito y Piñuelo and Guasp in acknowledging that the most seemingly aestheticist art has a marvelous utility in that it brings people together, refining the sensibilities of the masses and preparing a new social consciousness (1904a, 4). Azorín erases differences even as he identifies them, ever resistant to homogenizing, totalizing systems.

Manuel de Guindos reiterates the parallel of the literary and factory worker, insisting that just as writers fight the privileged class in the world of literature, the proletariat struggles against the bourgeoisie in the socio-economic realm (1902, 3–4). In this same context, it is useful to return to Unamuno's admonition to Antonio Machado. A rereading of the text reveals a dialogic quality that underscores the relativity of his position and the acknowledgment and validation of the other.[26] "Vida y arte" (1903) has complex origins in a tripartite communication among Unamuno, Antonio Machado, and his brother Manuel. The text addresses Antonio and responds to his letter regarding a conversation that Unamuno had undertaken with Manuel about Antonio's poetry. Unamuno quotes Antonio's discussion of his two years in Paris and his statement that the French agree with each other even when in disagreement in contrast to Spaniards, who argue even when in agreement. Unamuno suggests that they leave the French to their ways and work at finding themselves, thus validating the Spanish propensity for dissent and tacitly validating Machado's stance, a position he reiterates towards the end of the article, when he advises Machado to create his own aesthetic. The structure of the text, with multiple voices interweaving in on-going dialogue, sanctions the process of verbal and ideological exchange and encourages a dynamic interaction between self and other, whether as fellow writers and intellectuals or as writers looking inward to define their role and purpose. The original, monologic admonition against excessive aestheticism gives way to a defense of plural trajectories based on individual needs and collective discussion.

8. Modernism Threatens the Stability of Contemporary Social Structures

As indicated in the treatment of the modernist relation to tradition and social commitment and of the development of a new language to foster new social visions and values, many of those writing on modernism at the turn of the century welcome and encourage its revolutionary force. Others who espouse modernism respond with trepidation to its more radical elements, but the definitions of which traits represent dangerous extremes vary and at times contradict each other. Writing in *La Lectura,* Eduardo Sanz y Escartín advocates a humanitarian, democratic anarchism that he associates with Tolstoi, while harshly criticizing an antisocial, selfish anarchism that ignores the principle of solidarity (1902, 169). Sanz links this second, abhorrent anarchism with decadentist art forms, *arte por el arte,* and aristocratic snobbery, the same traits that later criticism associates with escapist indifference to social change. In the same journal, Adolfo Posada (1901) expresses his fear of violence and class warfare, but Posada's culprits are Marx and Zola and his preferred models are Tolstoi, coincident with Sanz, and also Ruskin, whom Sanz condemns. Posada sees Ruskin's interiority and mysticism as an antidote to revolution. Here the text speaker espouses modernism as a substitute for naturalism's social violence and revolutionary tendencies and advocates the same inward-looking, individualist aestheticism that Sanz fears for its disruptive qualities. Both writers sympathize with social change while seeking to control its pace and extent and both identify aspects of modernism that foster transformation and others that threaten social stability. However, they disagree fundamentally on which elements of the new cultural landscape best advance their respective agendas and which represent alarming features. The contradictory responses to decadentism and *arte por el arte* serve as a reminder of the complex character of turn-of-the century cultural expression and problematize its facile designation as formalist and socially and politically unimportant by later critics.

9. Decadentism and Pessimism Threaten the Progressive Energies of Modernism

The multi-faceted response to decadentist currents within early modernism includes a fear by many that it will weaken the radical impulse of the movement by fostering pessimism and inaction. The end-of-century mania that swept Europe poses an even greater danger in Spain, where the loss of the last major colonies could easily convey a sense of ending and closure. In the face of persistent references to extinction and degeneration, modernists call for renewal and emphasize vitality and optimism in an effort to combat national and individual abulia.[27] Writing in 1898 on "El patriotismo y la universidad," Rafael Altamira identifies two essential conditions for national regeneration: a renewed sense of confidence in Spain's propensity for progress and in her history; and an avoidance of a resurrection of past values and institutions. The contradictory coalescence of a call for change and a defense of the past, albeit qualified, stems from fear of a national loss of will. A blanket rejection of the national past risks collective paralysis and a self-image as degenerate and incapable of positive, constructive action defeats all efforts for national transformation (258). A similar argument characterizes Pompeyo Gener's *Literaturas malsanas: Estudios de patología literaria contemporánea* (1894). Gener attacks quietist, mystical tendencies of contemporary literature, which he sees as dangerously akin to hegemonic bourgeois, Catholic forces. Undeniably racist, classist, and sexist, Gener also represents a radical Republican point of view, exalting a Western tradition of revolution and its affirmation of life, liberty, and the pursuit of happiness over Eastern nihilism and self-annihilation (323). Altamira never mentions "modernism," but refers positively to modern developments and calls for leadership from the younger generation, both coded allusions to the movement. Gener specifically mentions modernism, but insists it is a misnomer when applied to decadentists, mystics, and symbolists: "El nombre modernistas les está mal aplicado" [The name modernist is incorrectly applied to them] (231). More appropriately, they are traditionalists, Catholics, and atavists.

The emphasis on action, energy, vitality, and other affirmative values appears constantly in proponents of modernism in *Gente Vieja, Alma Española, La Lectura* and Manuel Ugarte's 1908 study. The link between antipessimism and new forms, new themes, and a new interest in aesthetics also surfaces in an author not normally associated with modernism and certainly not with a formalist modernism, but who early critics include as a contributor to modernist journals and name as a member of the group. The lead article of the first issue of *Alma Española,* entitled "Soñemos, alma, soñemos" is authored by Benito Pérez

Galdós, more typically identified with realism and his own brand of naturalism. In this essay, however, a regenerationist spirit combines with a call for national introspection. As in the Altamira essay, the speaker calls for a dual relationship with the past, respect for admirable aspects of tradition and rejection of asceticism, self-flagellation, and religious and social traditions that encourage passivity or abnegation. Of even greater interest, the text urges the creation of a new landscape, through technological irrigation and spiritual/artistic redefinition. The echoes of Joaquín Costa's demands for a new national water policy combine with a modernist insistence on the importance of beauty: "Preciso es desencantar el viejo terruño, dándole con las aguas corrientes, la frescura, amenidad y alegría de la juventud: preciso es vivificar la tierra, dándole sangre y alma y vistiéndole de las naturales galas de la agricultura" [It is necessary to set the old land free, giving it freshness, grace, and youthful joy with running water: it is necessary to revivify the earth, giving it blood and soul and dressing it with the natural fineries of agriculture] (1903, 1–2). The combination of a practical, technical lexicon with a poetic vocabulary reveals the confluence of these two modernist impulses, both placed in the service of an activist agenda and a rejection of pessimism and abulia.[28] Cultivation of an optimistic energy that fosters a desire to live and look forward surfaces repeatedly in Gregorio Martínez Sierra, whose essay "De cómo el arte en esta tierra no acierta a reír" represents a continuation of Galdós's calls for grace and joy. Martínez Sierra criticizes the heavy satires typically published in the journal *Gedeón* and complains that Spaniards, unlike the British and Germans, don't know how to laugh. He argues that laughter expands the heart, duplicating the language of Pompeyo Gener's previously cited prologue to *Leyendas de amor* and further suggests that laughter may well provide the national pedagogy so necessary to transform the country: "Tal vez riendo se nos ensanche el corazón, tal vez pensemos, merced a la risa, que la vida es hermosa, y tal vez caigamos en la cuenta de que para vivirla hay que desperezarse. . . . Acaso el buen humor de que tan necesitados andamos, sea la gran pedagogía nacional." [Perhaps laughing will expand our hearts, perhaps, thanks to laughter, we will think that life is beautiful and perhaps we will realize that in order to live it we have to shake off our laziness . . . Maybe the good humor that we need so terribly is the great national pedagogy] (1903a, 312).

10. Modernism Is Syncretic, Purposely Promoting the Coexistence of Opposites

Early writers on modernism posit a definition that embraces the simultaneous presence of elements traditionally viewed as oppositional and mutually exclusive. Rather than construe this as a confusion as to the "true" nature of modernism, as some subsequent critics have asserted, it constitutes a persistent rejection of the dichotomous thinking that modernists associate with Restoration culture. Deleito y Piñuelo characterizes the movement as the harmonization of opposites, the ideal and real, the trivial and exalted, faith and doubt, hope and despair, dawn and dusk, decadence and vitality, sentimentalism and cruelty, irony and candor (1902, 1–2). Antonio de Monasterio specifically attacks a bipolar vision of art that opposes Christian and pagan or romantic and classical and characterizes modernism as a fusion of different genres (1903, 5–7). The perception of modernism by its original proponents as a syncretic movement explains the tolerance within early modernist journals of writers of many different literary and political orientations. It also accounts for resistance to efforts to homogenize and limit the complexity of the diverse writers, schools, and tendencies. The easy acceptance of hybrid products and the advocacy of concepts that defy traditional hierarchies and dichotomies provoke the ire of early opponents to modernism and continue to unsettle critics who desire a return to clear, definable categories. Early antagonists target such perceived excesses as extravagant language, bizarre characters, outrageous plots, or the lack of support for the military, but some of their most virulent attacks address the breakdown of traditional borders, whether political, geographic, sexual, literary, or linguistic.

The defense of Castilian Spanish from foreign contacts and opposition to Basques and Catalans who seek to authorize the use of their languages informs a good deal of anti-modernist literature. In an attempt to validate Castilian over other national languages, the Jesuit, Juan Mir y Noguera, formulates a curious linguistic history in which Castilian, like Basque and unlike Catalan, predates Latin. He criticizes the Royal Academy and writers of the seventeenth through nineteenth centuries who have contaminated Spanish with lexical and syntactic corruptions of French origin but in his view, the worst "galiparla" of all is modernism (1908, cxv). The satirical journal *Gedeón* contains many examples of linguistic nationalism. One vignette describes a frustrated visit to Andalusia by the Catalan Santiago Rusiñol, who wants to participate in a traditional Andalusian *juerga,* but meets with rejection by the locals, who take him for a foreigner. The narrator approves and embellishes, with a comment that equates Catalonian and modernist with outsider: "Y tenían razón los andaluces: todo esto del modernismo yo no sé lo que será, pero a español no me huele" [And the Andalusians were right: all this modernism stuff, I don't know what it means, but it sure doesn't smell Spanish] ("De Ojeo," 1897). Antonio Balbín de Unquera finds particularly distasteful the image of Spain as mosaic, and attacks attempts to revivify the Basque language (1901, 8). Within the Spanish language, antimodernist voices oppose the incorporation of words and expressions from Latin America. Fray Candil (Emilio Bobadilla) explodes in indignation at the belief that Castilian needs renovating in order to meet the challenges posed by modernity and attacks those from the other side of the ocean who seek to impose "ese guiriguay galo argentino" [that Galo Argentinian gibberish] (1903, 10). The transnational, translinguistic character of Castilian modernism, with influences from France, Latin America, and Catalonia, proves extremely threatening to those who envision a unitary, centrist, xenophobic national identity. The old polarities—Castile versus France, empire versus and over colonies, center versus and over periphery—must be defended against those who seek to establish contacts and communication across these borders. Curiously, the accusations launched by the original opponents of modernism have been assimilated by later critics and used against modernist writers themselves.

Modernism also provokes rebukes for violating gender and genre divisions. The new women's clothing styles, with straight lines and layers that minimize feminine contours, generates derision in Juan García-Goyena (1901, 641–48) and José Jackson-Veyán lampoons the breakdown of traditional gender roles in a long satiric poem:

La moda con sus patrones
nos convierte en mamarrachos,
¡Parecen hembras los machos,
Y las mujeres, varones!
A la esposa, débil ser,
no presta ayuda el marido.
¡Hoy va el esposo cogido
del brazo de su mujer!
Si al mal no ponemos tasa

la ruina será completa,
y pronto haremos calceta
los caballeros en casa.
. . . Bueno que quieran borrar
usos, costumbres y nombres;
Pero dejar de ser hombres ¿. . . ?
¡¡*Hombre,* eso es mucho dejar!!
(Jackson-Veyán, 1900)

[Fashion with her dictates
is making a real mess,
Men now seem like women
And women seem like men!
Husbands no longer help
their no longer fragile mates,
Today the husband walks
protected by his wife!
If we don't stop this soon,
the fall will be complete,
and shortly we men will be
left knitting in the home.
. . . Fine that they want to erase
habits, customs, and names:
But to stop being a man?
Brother, that's a lot to give up !!]

Vicente Colorado's poem introduces accusations of homosexuality, sex changes, and altars to Sodom (1903, 7). Many texts ridicule innovations in literary and artistic taste. Jackson-Veyán mocks the abolition of action and plot complications in narrative and theater and the replacement of the paintbrush by subjective impression. The crossing of music and poetry produces outrage in Francisco Vidal y Careta, who also attacks the presence of prose in contemporary drama. It is worth noting that Vidal y Careta associates such artistic license with an absence of civilization, as could only occur in the heart of Africa, thus connecting opposition to modernism with Eurocentric traditions and empire building. Like Jackson-Veyán, he detests the use of the impressionist short brush stroke and nostalgically invokes the delicate drawing technique and purity of line of earlier movements (1902, 7–8).

The horror of the abolition of the line or border that separates one object from another resurfaces in multiple texts that oppose modernism, in the context of visual arts or with reference to philosophy, language, gender, and other categories. It relates to the strong belief of anti-modernists in one universal truth, a single concept of beauty or virtue. Antonio de Valmala exemplifies this stance and reveals its complicity with an imperialist, racist, and sexist ideology. *Los voceros del modernismo* (1908) is his second attack on the new movement, following his earlier *Ripios colombianos* (1906), a title that exposes his anti-Latin American bias with the multiple denotations of *ripios* as material garbage and empty verbiage. Throughout his study, Valmala identifies the place of origin of each modernist he refutes, emphasizing their non-Castilian roots: Unamuno is Basque, Gómez Carrillo is Guatemalan, resides in Paris, and publishes his *Nuevo Mercurio* in Barcelona, Manuel Ugarte is Argentinean. Valmala dismisses Latin American writers as overly passionate, rhetorical, and sexual ("sicalípticos"), invoking the eroticization of the other that characterizes historical visions of indigenous Africans and Americans. He also echoes many previous writers in his treatment of Emilia Pardo Bazán, claiming to respect her right to speak on modernism, but warning her of the danger a woman of her stature risks in entering into discussions of risqué topics. Valmala surpasses his predecessors with a not-so-subtle reference to the perils of rape facing a woman who consorts with indecent company: ". . . siempre es peligroso para una dama aventurar especies en un asunto tan shocking de suyo, y muy expuesto por ende a que los chicos nuevos las fuerzan a sus antojos y caprichos" [. . . it is always dangerous for a lady to venture opinions in matters that are in and of themselves so shocking, and very exposed, therefore, to the possibility that the new boys force them at their whim and fancy] (1908, 7). The ambiguous use of the object pronoun "las," which can refer to opinions as well as to a pluralized "ladies," indirectly invokes the specter of rape as an instrument of control of women and their bodies. Valmala specifically refutes Pardo Bazán's contention that humanity and its perception of beauty changes over time. He insists it always and everywhere remains the same, in Spain or Peru, and delivers a long panegyric of the classical Spanish language as noble, chivalrous, virile, the language of hymns and odes, warriors and conquerors, and finally, the most appropriate language in which to address God (99). Valmala consistently situates modernism and its proponents outside and in opposition to essentialized, eternal Spanish (i.e., Castilian) qualities and values, which include conquest, masculinity, and religion at the top of the hierarchy.

Anti-modernist shock and horror surfaces often in the face of the proponents' advocacy of multiple, concurrent visions of beauty, truth, and virtue. Emilio Ferrari, in his acceptance speech to the Spanish Royal Academy in 1905, once more denounces the threat of multiple, competing voices to artistic and social harmony. Opposition to a pluralist, syncretic vision of modernism also inserts itself in the critical literature that develops in the twenties and later. The division of the literature of the period into two discrete movements, a brief and escapist modernism in contrast to a more authentically Spanish, profound, masculine "Generation of 1898," bears a much closer relation to the dichotomous thinking of the early opponents of modernism than to those who wrote in its favor during the 1890s and 1900s. The shift from an earlier inclusive, dialogic discussion of modernism to a subsequent closed and limiting definition that strives to wall out contact with the other deviates fundamentally from the original orientation. The same open and fluid definition continues in the studies by Manuel Machado and Azorín that appear in published form in 1913. Critics have read Machado's "La guerra literaria" as the foundational text of the tradition that equates modernism with formalism, ahistoricism, and escapism[29] and have attacked Azorín's articles as the invention of the myth of the "Generation of 1898," a separate inward-looking, Spanish literary movement that stands in opposition to modernism.[30] Scholars have impugned both writers with ignoble, self-serving motivations, accusing them of trying to distance themselves from youthful radicalism and redefine their early writings to conform with current conservative social and political positions and aspirations. However, both texts carry forward the vision presented in earlier definitions of the period, with emphasis on attributes that have considerable importance to the present study.

Manuel Machado and Azorín: The Continuation of a New Tradition

Manuel Machado's "La guerra literaria" opens with an affirmation of discontinuous subjectivity that anticipates contemporary definitions of the self. The speaker compares life to an unstructured, unbound book as contrasted with a well-planned novel and states that the essence of his character lies in its mutability and propensity for contradiction (1981, 93–95). He also boasts of his use of gallicisms and refusal to accept a purist vision of language. The text identifies the appearance of a new group of writers that surfaced on the heels of the Spanish American War and that initially sought to demolish old forms and ideas by means of concepts and literary currents brought from Europe via Latin America. The new poetics attempted to shake the public from their complaisant acceptance of traditional sounds, ideas, and habits. The text speaker refers to Alejandro Sawa, Benavente, Valle-Inclán, Rubén Darío, Baroja, Azorín, Juan Ramón Jiménez, José Ortega y Gasset, Santiago Rusiñol, and Unamuno as the leading modernist writers and emphasizes a generalized transformation of the cultural landscape from poetry to novel, criticism to painting and philosophy. This vision of modernism clearly extends beyond a purely formalist definition and the range of authors included evidently continues earlier definitions rather than preludes later divisions into modernist versus "Generation of 1898" writers. Attention then shifts to modernist poetry, defined in this instance as a purely formal revolution that touches both external and internal art forms. With respect to content, anarchy prevailed. Modernism is not a school but rather, through its insistence on individual freedom, the end of all schools. It introduces new modes of perception and then disappears as a movement as individual poets establish their own personalities and their own voices.

"La guerra literaria" opens with harsh criticism of liberals and Republicans and closes with derisive comments on the ruling parties and political opposition. These statements, in conjunction with the definition of modernist poetry as a purely formal revolution, have led critics to characterize the text, and in particular the section "Los poetas de hoy," as Manuel Machado's repudiation of socio-political transgression in favor of a conservative ideology designed to curry official favor on the eve of his marriage. However, many of the ideas expressed in "La guerra literaria" appear previously in Machado's response to *El Nuevo Mercurio's* 1907 survey on the meaning of modernism (337–40), and consequently bear no relation to aspirations for a job or social acceptance on the occasion of his wedding some three years later. Furthermore, the 1907 study and its reworking in the 1913 "La guerra literaria" reiterate earlier definitions of modernism that merit further attention and commentary. The exaltation of personal mutability may represent, on the one hand, a justification of a shift towards a more conservative position (Celma Valera and Blasco Pascual, 1981, 34), but also continues early modernist emphasis on a syncretic selfhood. The condemnation of liberals and Republicans may confirm a political turn to the right, but simultaneously restates long-standing disgust with Restoration politics, electoral corruption, and the arranged exchange of power between politicians who perpetuate the status quo. Insistence on new artistic forms carries forward the belief that new modes of thinking and being in the world require new habits of perception and new artistic conventions best cultivated by a modern professionalized artist. I would not deny specific instances of elitism and aestheticism in "La guerra literaria," but suggest they coexist with other contrasting elements that reveal a more complex, multilayered textual fabric.

Numerous intertextual references to the poetry of Manuel's younger brother Antonio, invariably seen as a more socially committed and politically leftist writer, suggest a common bond between the two that exemplifies a heterogeneous and complex modernist poetics with origins in the 1890s and continued predominance in the first decade of the twentieth century. In referring to the period from 1885 to 1898, "La guerra literaria" alludes to a general cultural void among Spanish intellectuals: "Irredimibles, porque, ignorándolo todo, lo despreciábamos todo también" [Unredeemable because, ignorant of all, we closed our minds in scorn] (99). The sentence echoes Antonio's well known and twice repeated verse from "A Orillas del Duero": "Castilla miserable, ayer dominadora, envuelta en sus harapos desprecia cuanto ignora" [Wretched Castile, supreme once, now forlorn, wrapped in her rags, closes her mind in scorn] (1951, 733–34).[31] Written between 1907 and 1912 and published initially in *La Lectura* in 1910 and in *Campos de Castilla* in 1912, the poem represents a strongly politicized description of contemporary Spain and its historical causes. Familiar to Manuel Machado and to informed readers of the day, the intertextual reference interjects the social criticism and oppositional stance that permeates Antonio's poetry of this period. The praise of Antonio that concludes "Los poetas de hoy," designating him the deepest and strongest contemporary Spanish poet, reintroduces the note of political dissidence and reminds the reader of the rich and varied texture of modernist poetry. Manuel's description of Antonio's poetry as a simplification of form "hasta lo lapidario y lo popular" [even to lapidary and popular forms] continues the double voicing. "Lapidario" in reference to style denotes laconic, as in the concise inscriptions cut into stone, but it also brings to mind the reference to sculpting a new nation that appears in Antonio's famous verses in "El mañana efímero," also of 1913: "Mas otra España nace, la España del cincel y de la maza" [But another Spain is born, the Spain of the chisel and the war club] (153). The blending of laconic and popular, traditional and antagonistic to the past and its remnants in the present, etched in stone in a written, permanent language and fluid and ephemeral in the orality of popular verse all combine in this characterization of Antonio's poetry.

The suggestion of coexisting opposites relates to yet another instance of intertextuality in "Los poetas de hoy." In the description of Restoration ideology, the text speaker signals a dichotomous pattern of thinking that divided all into black and white, big or small, Sagasta or Cánovas in politics, Lagartijo or Frascuelo in bullfighting, Campoamor or Núñez de Arce in poetry, with no possibility for shadows or a third notion that comes between and destabilizes the symmetry of the pairs. The defense of a third way harks back to earlier definitions of modernism as syncretic and provides a link between Manuel Machado's description of Antonio's poetry, his definition of modernism, and additional segments of "La guerra literaria," where he discusses his own poetry. In "Génesis de un libro," he explicates his ekphrastic combination of painting and poetry and his purposeful play of imitation and invention in verbally recreating a visual painting with deliberate inaccuracies in his verbal copies. As Margaret Persin suggests, through the intentional introduction of misreadings/mispaintings, Manuel Machado problematizes the traditional separation of visual and verbal, static and temporal, simultaneous and chronological, linear and circular, self and other, mimesis and representation (1997, 49–50). The insistent deconstruction of established categories also surfaces in the treatment of popular poetry in "La guerra literaria." Alongside elitist declarations, the text exalts popular poetry and the blending of the poet's voice with that of the people through a recreation of traditional poetry by published poets. Previous references to the individuality and professionalization of the poet, whose work consists solely and exclusively of writing verses, takes on a different significance in this context. The self-proclaimed importance of individual poet diminishes in the face of collective authorship and the line between popular and erudite breaks down when Manuel Machado appreciatively describes hearing one of his *soleares* sung by a flamenco singer in an Andalusian fiesta as if it were just another anonymous, collective creation.

Celma Valero and Blasco Pascual cite Juan Ramón Jiménez's criticism of Manuel Machado's depiction of the gypsy as a true representative of popular Spain and they further deny that Machado has any sincere interest in popular culture (1981, 41ss). As Juan Ramón points out, the commercialization of flamenco and gypsy culture for the benefit of tourism presents a limited and often distorted picture of popular Spanish and Andalusian culture. However, Manuel Machado's insistence on a reworking of popular Andalusian, Flamencan songs, with their close connections to gypsy culture and customs, places this traditionally marginalized group squarely in the presence of middle-class readers in an important and novel manner. Furthermore, his review of this process in a discussion of modernism and his acceptance of the melding of his voice with that of the gypsy woman performer demonstrates once more an openness to the other within modernist practice and theory that should not be dismissed or diminished. Alongside his acceptance and outspoken recognition of the contribution of Rubén Darío and Latin American literature to the development of Spanish modernism, the merging of the popular and the elite and the repudiation of dichotomous thinking links "La guerra literaria" with many of the earlier proponents of modernism, with the later work of Juan Ramón Jiménez and Federico Onís, and with contemporary theorists such as Eysteinsson and Art Berman.

Azorín's "La generación de 1898" (1969) opens with a rejection of the purported antagonism between the younger and older generations. In his view, the presumed generational division represents a simplistic, overly categorical conceptualization of a cultural phenomenon that requires more careful evaluation. As in Machado's text, the speaker of Azorín's essay rejects liberal politics and the administrative corruption and empty rhetoric that his generation associates with the Restoration. The study also insists on linking calls for change to a tradition of progressive thought or to a previously existing progressive spirit. Focusing on three writers of the period from 1870 to 1898, the speaker comments that the new habit of perception produced by Galdosian narrative revealed tragic national flaws and combined with the cry of passion enunciated by Echegaray and the subversive irony circulated by Campoamor to produce a clamor of protest. In this reading, a tradition of regenerationist literature predates 1898, with antecedents in the seventeenth century and a continuous presence throughout the nineteenth. The text then proceeds to inventory the social criticism produced after the loss of the Spanish-American War and to reiterate its links with a long tradition of social and political criticism.

After establishing the social and political characteristics of the "Generation of 1898" and its links to traditional oppositional thought, the text turns to a consideration of the literary traits of the writers under consideration. The speaker insists on the influence of foreign writers and intellectuals (D'Annunzio, Ibsen, Tolstoi, Musset, Poe, Balzac, Ruskin, Nietzsche, Verlaine, among others) and argues that the literary renaissance that occurred in Spain required significant external enrichment, as had occurred in other moments of great national vitality. Azorín's text cites a wide variety of writers as members of the renewal, including figures subsequently excluded by other critics. Valle-Inclán, Unamuno, Benavente, Baroja, Bueno, Maeztu, and Rubén Darío all form part of the movement, which commences before 1898 and already provokes Pereda's opposition in 1897. Both in Pereda's acceptance speech to the Spanish Royal Academy and Azorín's discussion of it, the term used to designate the writers under consideration is not "Generation of 1898" but rather "modernists." At this point in time, the two terms are used interchangeably, and the definition of membership and goals remains extremely fluid. A spirit of protest mixes with attempts to revive primitive poets, Maeztu's calls for destruction of traditional values and the forging of a new, powerful Spain coexist with Valle-Inclán's marble statues and stagnant ponds, and contacts with Latin America and Catalonia rest easily along side traditional calls for change.

Of the 10 positions initially identified with early proponents of modernism, Azorín specifically reiterates seven: a repudiation of as well as link with the past, a combination of national and international sources, an anarchist tendency, the presence of social objectives, the development of a new language to express a new vision, the attack on contemporary social structure, and the opposition to dichotomous structuration. "La generación de 1898," like "La guerra literaria," carries forward modernism's initial self-definition as a multifaceted artistic movement with both social and aesthetic implications and a strong propensity for renewal through contacts with writers and thinkers from traditional European sources, new European centers of thought—such as Russia and the Scandinavian countries, and new national cultural centers—such as Catalonia and the former colonies, which now stand in a relation of equality and often leadership. Azorín reiterates earlier visions of modernism as continuing long-standing traditions, but, like the previous texts, it focuses on specific historical moments and reads them in the light of their pertinence to the construction of a new national culture. The Machado and Azorín texts vary little from theories of modernism elaborated during the preceding decades.

Modernism and "Generation of 1898": The Evolution of a Separation

The term modernism continues to appear in early twentieth century literature, both as a target of attack by those antagonistic to its values and goals and as a positive force for literary and social change. Although the furor over its advent and the scope of the discussion decrease, no other movement or term displaces it. A character in Blasco Ibáñez's *La maja desnuda* (1906) still sees it as a new art form with exotic styles and an obsession with speed and change that requires resisting. Juan Ramón Jiménez continues to dedicate his books of poetry to fellow modernists such as Azorín and Benavente, designating the latter as the prince of this "renaissance" in *Laberinto* (1911). Writing in 1909, Galdós makes reference to the destabilizing, syncretic aspects of the movement when he describes as a modernist joke an episode in which a women bought a mirror in Paris and upon looking into it, saw not her own face but that of her lover (*El caballero encantado* 47). The statesman Sabas Sicilia in Ramón Pérez de Ayala's 1912 novel *Troteras y danzaderas* refers to his young rival Teófilo Pajares as a modernist and explains that those of his generation cannot join the movement, echoing turn-of-the-century divisions of older versus younger writers (1964–66, 1:525). Between 1908 and 1910, Ricardo León sometimes uses the term modernism and sometimes simply alludes to all things modern, equating both with harmful contacts with the outside that destroy the nobility, religious fervor, and spiritual purity of traditional Spain. Valle-Inclán specifically refutes this vision in "Aleluya," of *La pipa de Kif* (1919), exalting the production of grotesque, extravagant verses that the poetic speaker knows will shock conservatives like Ricardo León and Julio Cejador y Frauco. Cejador's *Historia de la lengua y literatura castellana* had appeared a year earlier and his attack on modernist/'98 writers echoes the nationalist views espoused by León. In contrast with their xenophobic stance, Valle-Inclán's "Aleluya" offers a modern muse, one that joins his Celtic bagpipes with the shadow of Rubén Darío and the ambivalent laughter of Pérez de Ayala. The poem describes a literal handshake between the speaker and Darío, acknowledging connections with early exponents of modernism. Although the muse has evolved, its links to the originary transgressive and progressive internationalism of early modernism remain.

The term "Generation of 1898" does not take hold immediately. In response to Azorín's article, Ramiro de Maeztu appropriates the expression with a specifically nationalist agenda in a series of essays that refute Azorín's emphasis on foreign influences and anchor the origins of the movement in Spain's loss of imperial status. Both Unamuno and Baroja deny the existence of a "Generation of 1898." Unamuno's "Nuestra egolatría de los del 98" stresses the individualist, anarchist character of his contemporaries, as does Baroja's 1924 "La supuesta generación de 1898" (1958, 5:496 ff.), which repeats ideas originally expressed in *Juventud, egolatría.* Baroja includes a reference to modernism, which the text speaker describes as the movement to which the majority of the writers of the period belonged, continuing the synonymous use of the two terms already observed in Azorín. As late as 1932, Valle-Inclán refers alternately to membership in the "Generation of 1898" and the modernist movement (Lima 1988, 117).

The decade following World War I witnesses a move away from socially committed art towards a more formalist aesthetic among large sectors of the European intellectual and artistic community. In Spain, critics and artists commenting on the literature of the preceding decades privilege formalist elements and emphasize writers who best reflect these values. Poetry becomes the genre of favor and the mixing of genres witnessed in the previous period as well as the tendency of authors to cultivate multiple genres becomes considerably less pronounced. The poet Jorge Guillén waxes ecstatic when discussing what he perceives as Valle-Inclán's silence on national affairs, praising him as the only pure poet of his generation (Lima 1988, 234–35). While affirming Valle-Inclán's membership in the "Generation of 1898," Guillén cites characteristics that shortly become synonymous with modernism. The battle lines remain fluid, but the campaign to reclaim literary ancestors for one camp or the other has commenced.

Inman Fox points out that a rigid differentiation of the writers of the period into two distinct groups does not appear until the 1930s (1997). By this time, generational theory has become ascendant and critics attempt to determine with greater certainty the members, traits, and goals of the "Generation of 1898." In "El concepto de generación literaria," Pedro Salinas explicitly rejects the use of "Generation of 1898" and modernism as synonymous, placing modernism in a subordinate role as the generational language developed and utilized by the group (1949). He does not exhaustively list the members of the generation, naming Unamuno, Azorín, Baroja, Valle-Inclán, Benavente, the Machado brothers, and then an inclusive "etcetera." Significantly, Darío's name does not appear, nor do the Catalan modernists, and although the text speaker points out a shared autodidacticism in the writers, all of whom read widely outside of normal university channels, the foreign origins of their sources are not stated. Salinas moves further in the construction of barriers that separate modernism and *noventayochismo* into two distinct cultural spheres in "El problema del modernismo en España" (1949). Victor Fuentes attributes Salinas's imposition of generational theory onto the complex reality of early twentieth-century literature to a conservative fear of the masses, which Fuentes identifies as a continuation of Azorín's earlier insistence on the continuity of the Spanish spirit (1995, 24). I previously traced the presence of multiple, contradictory strands in the texts written by Azorín and earlier writers on modernism, in which continuity and revolution coincide and the return to the past often takes the form of a renewal of prior revolutionary or progressive energies. Salinas's text does emphasize a more passive, inward literary movement, reflecting a sadness and sense of defeat that he projects onto Unamuno, the Machados, Azorín, Baroja, and others. This reading of his predecessors may respond to his personal sense of loss as he writes from the United States in 1938,[32] when Madrid had been under siege for some two years and half of Spain had fallen to Franco, or as he edits the essays in 1941 for their publication in Mexico, while he lives in exile. Whatever the causes of Salinas's separation of early twentieth-century Spanish literature into two separate groups, postwar Spanish critics appropriate his outline and develop it to new extremes.

Critics attempting to undo the legacy of Francoist cultural interpretations point to Pedro Laín Entralgo's *La generación del noventa y ocho* (1945) and Guillermo Díaz-Plaja's *Modernismo frente a noventa y ocho* (1951) as key examples of Francoist reappropriation and redefinition of early twentieth-century criticism. Both echo and amplify the nationalist, introspective, and politically muted vision earlier offered in Salinas and despite increasingly successful attempts to counter their division of Spanish culture into two discrete and opposing movements, their reading of the major writers and texts of the period continues in varying degrees in many contemporary studies. In order to establish the origins and political implications of this approach to modernist authors and texts, I will tease out certain aspects of the Laín Entralgo and Díaz Plaja studies and trace their persistence up to the present. In a clear attempt to recuperate a group of extraordinary writers and cultural icons, Laín Entralgo seeks to insert them into a tradition that flows continuously back through the centuries; however, in contrast to early modernist assertions of links to a dynamic, oppositional, unorthodox national past, in *La generación del noventa y ocho* the tradition which these writers purportedly continue is the Catholic, Counter Reformation, exclusionary Spain of the early Menéndez y Pelayo (Inman Fox 1997, 15). In order to promote this vision, the text insists on the preeminence of Castile in their writing and social imaginary, their repudiation of history in favor of an eternal tradition, their apolitical stance, and an only moderately unorthodox religious deviation from Catholic dogma.

Two of seven chapters focus on the links with Castilian landscape or Madrid and the text glosses over international, cosmopolitan elements. The names of Rubén Darío and other Latin American or Catalan writers play no role in the discussion. Although Chapter I offers a relatively inclusive list of Spanish writers, including Unamuno, Azorín, Antonio and Manuel Machado, Baroja, Valle-Inclán, Menéndez Pidal, Ganivet, Maeztu, Benavente, the painters Ignacio Zuloaga and Darío de Regoyos, the Alvarez Quintero brothers, Manuel Bueno, *Silverio Lanza,* and even Gabriel Miró and Juan Ramón Jiménez, the primary emphasis falls on a limited corpus of texts by Unamuno, Azorín, Antonio Machado, Pío Baroja, Ganivet, and Valle-Inclán, with almost no mention of the other artists and writers in the remainder of the study. The reduced range enables the construction of a unified, coherent set of writers that allows for the application of generational theory and a nationalist vision, as defined in terms of a Castilian, centralized tradition.

In keeping with an inward-looking, exclusionary definition of Spain, the text barely acknowledges the opinion repeatedly expressed by the writers studied that the role of Africa in the constitution of Spain needs further examination, preferring to move away from this subject quickly and with evident discomfort (229–30). Modernist calls for a Europeanization of Spain receive little mention and disappear amidst long discussions of the writers' patriotism. The nationalist impulse assumes that exposure to the foreign only leads to a return to the native and local, with increased commitment and loyalty. In Franco Spain, patriotism and orthodox Catholicism go hand in hand and Laín Entralgo's text exemplifies the coalescence of nation and religion. A clear example of this vision occurs in the discussion of Antonio Machado's poem "Al joven meditador José Ortega y Gasset." Machado's poetic speaker calls on the philosopher, recently returned from Germany, to create a new Escorial, in which the quintessential Counter Reformation Spanish Philip II will look out from his grave with a new tolerance and bless Luther's heirs. In Laín's study, the transgressive character of the poem disappears, as does the clear allusion to Protestantism as a viable, welcome alternative to a closed, conservative Catholicism. In its place, the Francoist text speaker constructs a reading in which Ortega y Gasset's philosophical monument continues rather than opposes Philip's legacy and the new philosophy bears no trace of German or Protestant influences. Rather than a "servile" imitation of foreign thought, or a dialogic hybrid creation, Laín presumes it will develop into a unique, original Spanish product, a way for Spain to speak to the world in its own words (253–54).

This rather clumsy reading accompanies a denial of Machado's confessed links to a revolutionary Jacobin tradition in his "Retrato" and a recasting of his and Unamuno's religious beliefs as only mildly opposed to orthodox Catholicism. In a final erasure of difference between Machado and Menéndez y Pelayo, the text drifts almost imperceptibly from analysis of Machado's poem on the construction of a new Spanish philosophy to a consideration of how Menéndez y Pelayo would have construed such a project. The text speaker imagines a Spanish philosophy that returns to the Catholic traditions that nineteenth and twentieth century progressive writers blamed for the lack of a vibrant Spanish philosophical and scientific tradition. Ortega's travels to Germany and exposure to European philosophy become totally unnecessary in the face of an insistent return to tradition and the interpretation of this "Generation of 1898" as a continuation of, rather than break with, orthodox Spanish thought. Laín Entralgo's text expresses a preference for a reduction of contradictory tenets to a single, stable middle ground, which explains the overt rejection of Unamuno's dialectical thinking, his defense of paradox, and the simultaneity of opposites (148–49). *La generación del 98* radically breaks with earlier definitions of modernism, displacing a multifaceted, transgressive vision with a single-voiced, orthodox characterization.

Guillermo Díaz-Plaja (1966) introduces an even greater move toward rigid categories and exclusionary definitions of the literature of the period, positing an uncompromisingly dualistic structuring of human thought that persists throughout time, across cultures, and rests on the belief in a fundamental difference between male and female modes of experience. The "Generation of 1898" and modernism represent the form this eternal, fundamental dualism takes in early twentieth-century Spain, with differences that reveal a clear valorization of the masculine over the feminine and of Europe over other areas. The generation of 1898 is characterized as virile, energetic, socially and politically committed, governed by reason, in search of precise forms and categories, architectural, metaphysical, Castilian, classical, allied with Velázquez, ethical, and obsessed with time and temporality. Modernism, on the other hand, is feminine, passive, governed by sensibility, individualistic, escapist, ivory tower, vegetable, sensual, Andalusian and Mediterranean, primitive, metaphoric, allied with El Greco, amoral, a mixture of disparate elements, and concerned with instantaneity and the moment.

In consonance with Laín Entralgo and Francoist nationalist, isolationist tendencies, *Modernismo frente a noventa y ocho* equates modernism with Catalonia, Andalusia, and Latin America, reserving the authentic, profound, virile "Generation of 1898" for Castile.[33] In Díaz-Plaja's studies, the accusations lodged against modernists by the early antagonists to the movement and applied across the board to all writers of the period now pertain only to a limited sector, while those categorized as members of the "Generation of 1898," in the tradition of Salinas and Laín Entralgo, become the exemplars of patriotic, Castilian, traditional culture. The charges of modernist sexual, linguistic, and artistic deviancy resurface in contrast to the virile, stable categories that characterize the "Generation of 1898." Syncretism, as a trait that critics from early studies through the 1920s attribute to the writers and cultural products of the period, totally disappears in the exaltation of a hierarchical, orderly Castilian masculinity confronting a passive, feminine chaos originating in foreign, unwelcome languages and cultures. Needless to say, this neat packaging into two discrete compartments requires a significant amount of juggling and critical blindness. The association of El Greco with modernism ignores the impassioned depiction of his rediscovery in Baroja's *Camino de perfección,* often cited as a primary example of '98 literature. Similarly, the insistence on a purely aestheticist motivation and lack of social and political inspiration in Valle-Inclán's *esperpentos* proves problematic. The individual contradictions and deficiencies matter less, however, than the overall impulse toward a reductive, exclusionary definition that walls out outsiders and eliminates women, the lower classes, homosexuals, and any form of otherness.

A number of recent studies on Spanish modernism that reject the limiting definitions provided by Salinas and Díaz-Plaja follow this critical tradition in other aspects, in that the authors and texts studied exclude those designated as *noventayochista* by Salinas, Laín Entralgo, and Díaz-Plaja. Otherwise excellent studies and very useful for an understanding of the period, these works focus on themes and writers traditionally labeled *modernista.* Celma Valero (1989) argues against the separation of turn-of-the-century writers into *modernistas* and *noventayochistas,* but she emphasizes themes such as the rejection of reality, irrationalism, occultism, decadentism, primitivism, exoticism, erotism, and aestheticism, which come from the critical tradition that she refutes. The Cardwell and McGuirk anthology (1993) also positions itself against the tyranny of the Salinas, Laín Entralgo, Díaz-Plaja trinity, but continues traditional parameters to a significant degree. Some studies emphasize decadentism, others compare modernists and *noventayochistas,* sometimes so-designated and sometimes under other rubrics, several emphasize elitist and escapist aestheticism after a brief foray into the socio-political arena, and virtually none make reference to the considerable body of literature on global modernism that has appeared recently.

Generational theory continues to prevail in other quarters. In a study condemning the construction of the concept "Generation of 1898," Antonio Ramos-Gascón (1988) substitutes one generational invention for another, arguing that Ortega y Gasset and the generation of 1914 retroactively give substance and meaning to the "Generation of 1898," and that the latter can only be understood in the light of Ortega's writing and guidance. The insistence on a generational model reveals a discomfort with plurality and an insistent homogenization of cultural and intellectual currents of a given moment, playing one generation against another without considering the implications of their cohabitation and dialogue within a shared cultural space. In the specific case of the "Generation of 1898," the focus on the Spanish American War as cause and origin of a major cultural movement inevitably leads to emphasis on a nationalist, backward-looking posture that erases internationalist, cosmopolitan, and anti-traditional impulses that inhere in the origins and development of the cultural expression of the period.

The vision of the *noventayochistas* as pessimistic, disillusioned activists who gave up on any attempt to change the social and political structures of Spain appears in many contemporary studies and echoes elements central to the arguments of Laín Entralgo and Díaz-Plaja. Moreover, several recent studies transfer accusations of fascism to the "Generation of 1898," accepting as valid Francoist readings of the writers. Jo Labanyi considers four texts written by Unamuno, Ganivet, Azorín, and Baroja between 1895 and 1902, which in her reading confirm the nationalist, ahistoricist, mythic character of their art and lead some thirty to forty years later to a fascist takeover that these writers may not have foreseen, but for which they are somehow responsible (1994, 147).[34] This vision of the literary and cultural production of early twentieth-century Spain differs drastically in political orientation from that of Díaz-Plaja and Laín Entralgo, but in both cases, the complex, multifaceted character of the writers and period are sacrificed to other considerations. An overly politicized scholarship often assumes that only texts and writers that explicitly state a radical message contain transgressive or dissident content. Foucault, Derrida, Bakhtin, and other theorists of language, subjectivity, and nation have demonstrated the complexity of cultural artifacts and institutions and the existence of multiple, contradictory currents within a single author, text, or even statement. In the case of late nineteenth- and early twentieth-century Spanish culture, it is time to abandon limiting and reductive barriers that erase the intricate, tangled forces that enter into play and evolve over time. Only in this way can we recover messages that still have value and contribute significantly to issues of contemporary importance, both within Spain and beyond her borders.

2
Changing Empires

THE LATTER PART OF THE NINETEENTH CENTURY WITNESSES drastic changes in the world order. Areas of the globe that previously had experienced only tenuous contact with each other find their destinies intimately intertwined as European powers vastly expand their imperial domain. Edward Said points out that between 1800 and 1914, Europe's domination of the globe grows from 35 percent to approximately 85 percent (1994, 8). Between 1880 and 1900, the scramble for Africa brings the formerly unexplored interior of this continent as well as previously dominated or explored coastal areas under the control of various European nations. During this same period, the last major remnants of the Spanish empire win their independence.[1] A Spain that once boasted that the sun never set on its far-flung possessions finds itself reduced to a mere shadow of its former self. The loss of Cuba, Puerto Rico, the Philippines, and Guam in the Spanish American War requires a redefinition of relations with the former American colonies, both those recently liberated and those that achieved independence in the early nineteenth century.

The present and future identity of the Spanish nation and her role in European and international relations also necessitates reexamination as a post-imperial Spain finds itself out of phase not only with such longstanding competitors as France and England, but also with such newer aspirants to global power as Belgium, Germany, and Italy. The traditional European vision of Spain as other, as well as the now palpable difference between the international prominence of European powers and the military and diplomatic weakness of post-imperial Spain, raise questions about Spanish membership in the European community. Spanish modernist writers examine these issues and press forward with urgent calls for a revision of the relations between Spain and various other nations, anxious to construct a different world order that eschews violence and conquest and allows for difference and pluralism. Traditional and current criticism of the period that emphasizes ivory-tower escapism or a turning inward towards the Castilian core overlooks the significant body of modernist writing that insistently addresses the need to redefine Spanish international relations. The cosmopolitanism that for so long has been considered a hallmark of Hispanic modernism figures prominently in this international vision, but rather than an escapist rejection of the world, it contains a powerful message of transnational cooperation and interaction. The modernist response to the Cuban struggle for autonomy develops in conjunction with changing relations with Latin America, Africa, and Europe. As in the remainder of *Encounters Across Borders,* I do not suggest that every modernist writer shares the same vision of empire, decolonization, and other topics under discussion, but rather that an identifiable, preponderant attitude reveals itself in a significant number of writers who denounce traditional definitions of Spain to establish a different kind of international community.

The Cuban Disconnection and its Impact

Of the colonies remaining under Spanish control at the end of the nineteenth century, Cuba substantially surpasses others in economic, historical, and psychological importance. After the loss of South, Central, and North American lands in the early to mid-1800s, Cuba represents the largest, most commercially valued possession. While significant portions of the Philippines resist Spanish domination until the very end of Spanish rule in 1898, Cuba's assimilation had been swift and complete. In the liberal Spanish Constitution of 1873, Cuba and Puerto Rico figure along with peninsular Spanish provinces as essential components of the nation in contrast to the Philippines and African enclaves, which receive the designation of "territories." Cuban merchants, mostly of Spanish origin, often make the transatlantic trip back to their birthplace, thus enhancing a continuing emotional connection between the two populations. A considerable amount of Catalan wealth originates in the trade monopoly that Catalonia enjoys with Cuba. By 1894, Catalonia exports some 60 percent of its products to Cuba and total Spanish-Cuban trade equals that between either of Spain's two main European trading partners, England and France.[2]

Economic, historic, and psychological connections between Cuba and Spain inhibit support for Cuban autonomy among some sectors on both sides of the Atlantic. Creole slave-owning landowners had looked with interest to a union with the southern United States, but the northern victory in the Civil War put this hope to rest and resulted in a preference for continued Spanish rule as a hedge against a slave uprising, such as had occurred in Haiti. On the Spanish side, certain politicians and writers view continued control of Cuba as a matter of economic necessity and pride, although they camouflage baldly self-serving incentives behind a rhetoric of sacrifice. In a series of articles written in 1896 and 1897, Juan Valera denies economic motives for retaining Cuban colonial status, insisting that a sacred obligation moves Spain to prevent a return to barbarity in a land she has tended for four centuries (1941, 2:1942–43). Another motivation surfaces in "La mediación de los Estados Unidos," in which he argues the importance of Cuba as a relic of past grandeur and a minimal requirement to uphold Spanish prestige in the European community (1941, 2:1970). Numerous articles of the early 1890s in *La Ilustración Española y Americana* express a fear that German, Japanese, and British colonial expansion threatens to take what has rightfully belonged to Spain since the beginnings of history.[3] Defenders of imperialism typically resist any breakdown of hierarchy and centralization, endorsing the exclusive use of the Spanish language, racial purity, the Catholic religion, and other forms of uniformity that postcolonial studies have shown to exemplify colonizing domination (Tiffin 1994, 230).

Later historians and critics assume that the loss of the colonies precipitates a national depression. Hans Jeschke, writing in the Germany of 1934, states that events of 1898 produce wide-spread pessimism and scholars of varied ideological orientation refer to the war and the Treaty of Paris as a "disaster" or "crisis."[4] I would like to resituate the discussion in various respects. Emphasis on the date of 1898 ignores the long process of imperial disintegration that takes place over the nineteenth century, and in the case of Cuba, over at least four decades. Furthermore, the tendency to view the loss of the colonies as the motivating force for national self-examination and a search for national identity ignores the impact of the change in Spain's status on her relations with former colonies, neighboring colonizers, and other colonized peoples. Reevaluation of the self occurs only in tandem with reexamination of relations with the other and this second aspect has not received sufficient attention in studies on Spanish modernism. Finally, the emphasis on pessimism, loss, crisis, and trauma invests imperialism with a worth that not only goes against the value system of many of the scholars who write on this period and these authors, but also against the goals and strategies of the writers studied.

In opposition to groups within Spain and Cuba that fostered the status quo, others on both sides of the Atlantic worked to change the island's colonial status. Liberal Spaniards long opposed slavery and Krausists and Institutionists worked to end it through the establishment of the Abolitionist society. This brought Spanish liberals into alignment with those middle-class Cuban Creoles who opposed the slave-holding elite. Despite international and national opposition to slavery, economic interests in Spain, Cuba, and Puerto Rico delayed its demise until 1886, to the chagrin of liberals who viewed Cuban autonomy as a step toward justice and abhorred the complicity of the Spanish government with the slave-holding Creole elite.[5] Krausist, Institutionist, and other anti-imperialist arguments influence many modernist writers to reject slavery and to examine the history of the slave trade and its capitalist underpinnings.

Benito Pérez Galdós publishes several works in the early 1890s that repudiate Spanish colonialism. His 1890–1891 three-part novel, *Angel Guerra,*[6] introduces a large extended family with several members who have lived in Cuba. Lazy, opportunistic, and unscrupulous, the Babels represent the corrupting influence of colonialism, one accused of embezzlement in Cuba, another a slaver who put his wife to work as a prostitute, and the whole lot living a parasitic lifestyle in Madrid, dependant for survival on the handouts of Dulcenombre, the youngest family member and mistress of the protagonist. The correlation between racial and sexual exploitation surfaces in this novel and throughout the period, and here as elsewhere, suggested remedies to the one imply a change of treatment of the other. In opposition to various forms of enslavement and abuse, the novel seeks to redefine the connection between church and empire and to recuperate for new ends the religious spirit of early modern Spain and, in particular, of Saint Theresa of Avila. The ethic developed in the text presents a stark contrast to the old imperial order as represented by Pito Babel's justification of his slaving career—to save slaves from even worse treatment by African kings and to introduce civilization and rescue Africans from paganism and barbarity (1967, 5:1351). Leré, the leading female character and proponent of a non-exploitative religious spirit, breaks with traditional Spanish models in several ways. Like her predecessor Saint Theresa, she aspires to found a new religious order, but she differs from her mystical antecedent in her connection with the earth and the body, symbolized by her enormous breasts. Furthermore, her commitment to social activism rejects the cloister's enclosure. Leré gradually transforms the erratic Angel Guerra and together they devote themselves to non-violent but radical social reform. Significantly, Angel condemns the Spanish imperial past and the imposition of a "civilization" that creates only unhappiness and misery (1381). The new community envisioned by Leré and Angel calls for a return to early Christianity while embracing Eastern religions. It gives precedence to charity over ritual and persuasion over violence, introducing social revolution through peaceful means (471, 1513). In this modern organization, the sexes have equal rights and labor together in partnership to create a new order. Existing institutions, such as family, Church, government, private property, and police, will give way to new forms that remain only vaguely insinuated.[7]

The novel's visionary impulse comes into brutal confrontation with the weight of the past in the final chapter, where Arístides, embezzler and colonizer of Cuba and Costa Rica, robs and mortally wounds Angel, his former protector. The challenge to a non-violent philosophy emerges in the ironic taunts that Arístides hurls at his bound victim, reminding him that a true saint would forgive his attackers. Angel replies with a projectile of spit to Arístides's face and both his rejoinder and death could suggest a failed agenda. However, the reader's sympathy for Angel and rejection of Arístides, the survival of the admirable Leré, who marries Angel in a deathbed ceremony and remains to continue their work, and Angel's generous final will all carry the new message forward. The tradition of violence and egotism continues in the Spanish culture depicted in the novel, bred by a legacy of colonialism that extends back to the Greek Arístides, founder of the Delian League and Athenian Empire, and passed down to his modern namesake, exploiter of women and slaves. However, a new, antithetical standard confronts and signals the deficiencies of this tradition while imagining a different world with new possibilities for human interaction.

Other Spanish writers of the period condemn continued Spanish control of the colonies. Nicolás Salmerón, president during the First Republic in 1873 and member of the Abolitionist Society, and the younger historian, Rafael Altamira, both argue this position.[8] Ricardo Macías Picavea writes in an early regenerationist study that in his travels through Spain before the war, he found strong opposition to the conflict and popular desire to give Cuba its freedom (1979, 201). Even Joaquín Costa, whose attitude towards Spanish colonialism reveals nostalgia for past glory and desire for new zones of influence in Africa, advocates justice for Cuba and Puerto Rico (1967, 8). In the midst of jingoistic articles and war fervor, the Catalan Juan Maragall publishes articles that interject a note of rationality and anti-war sentiment. "La obsesión" (1898) describes the mood of expectation that grips the country as successive newspaper articles announce the imminent conflict. The text speaker imagines the emotional release that will follow the announcement of military engagement, but even on the eve of war, he frames the national reaction in muted, non-belligerent terms: either a mild "Thank God" for a break in the tension or a more thoughtful, pacific response (n. d. 2:159). After the outbreak of hostilities, Maragall advocates a swift end to the conflict, undermining arguments of national pride and opposing calls for a fight to the finish. "Voto de calidad" (1898) paraphrases an article by the French author Leroy Beaulieu that recommends that Spain cede Cuba and withdraw from the war. In citing Beaulieu's insistence that Spain risks no loss of prestige in following such a course of action, Maragall deflates national concerns regarding adverse European public opinion. He also reiterates Beaulieu's remarks that Spain's wounds are not yet so deep that she cannot heal and move forward, setting up an opposition between war and progress, imperialism and national reconstruction that other writers continue (n. d. 2:193).

Several short stories by women criticize the war and the carnage. Blanca de los Ríos's "La carta del muerto" (1898) describes the tragic life of a female orphan whose father and husband die in different periods of the Cuban struggle for independence. Pardo Bazán alternates between a nationalistic view in "El catecismo" (1896), where the parents of a young boy defend the absence of his soldier-uncle in patriotic explanations of the reasons for the war, and criticism in "La oreja de Juan Soldado" (1899), which narrates the abuse of returning soldiers by Spanish authorities, in a harsh indictment of the military. Azorín refutes jingoistic discourse in *Madrid Cómico,* contrasting the reactions of a patriot, who insists on death with glory and ruin over defeat, and a practical man, who argues that nations achieve distinction through work, industry, and art, not military victory or defeat (Díaz Plaja 1976, 45). Díaz Plaja remarks that Azorín's article is an isolated case of opposition to the war, but the number of dissident voices during the pre-war period and the war itself reflects a considerable current of anti-imperialist, anti-war sentiment.[9]

The pressures that support war and colonialism include the nationalist fervor that accompanies the outbreak of hostilities and centuries of rhetoric and Spanish self-description that equate empire with national identity. Ramiro de Maeztu writes explicitly of the tension between the pull of the past and the aspiration for a different future and his writing during the period attests to the co-presence of these forces in his thinking. His later role as a theorist and martyr for Spanish fascism has fostered a tendency to emphasize the fascist leanings in his early writings. These proclivities exist in the essays collected in *Hacia otra España* (1899), but they interweave with other discursive threads that reveal the anti-colonialist tendencies of even those who later evolve to one-dimensional, highly partisan views. In a series of articles published before and during the war, he laments the collective inertia of the Spanish nation and cavalierly promotes a dismissal of the past in favor of a new Spain: "Dejémosla dormir; dejémosla morir. Cuando apunte otra España nueva, ¡enterremos alegremente a la que hoy agoniza!" [Let her sleep, let her die. When a new and different Spain appears, we will happily bury the one that is presently dying] (1967, 39). His article "27.500" sarcastically signals the callous egotism of the ruling classes, who ship out only workers and members of the lower class to fight in Cuba. The speaker suggests a Malthusian plot to improve the race by eliminating the poor and closes with a call for General Azcárraga to realize that the nation wants peace, not war. "Contra la noción de la justicia" aspires to construct a new national image, arguing for a definition of justice and rights that abjures war and imperialist dreams:

> . . . con la ruina de la España histórica, con el puntapié dado al derecho, con el naufragio de nuestras ilusiones nacionales, han desaparecido muchos de los tropiezos en los que hubiérase encallado nuestro pensamiento. . . . La ocasión es única para que de España surja nuevamente la ley intelectual. Se nos ha puesto fuera de juego. Así podremos observar serenamente cómo se baraja el naipe. . . . Y ahora veamos cómo ha de hacerse otra España, la España de la producción y del trabajo" (237–38).

> [. . . with the destruction of historic Spain, the kick given to rights, and the shipwreck of our national illusions, many of the shoals on which our thoughts might have run aground have disappeared . . . This is a unique opportunity for a new intellectual order to come into

> being in Spain. They have kicked us out of the game. Consequently, we can serenely watch how they deal the deck. . . . And now let us see how we might create the other Spain, a Spain characterized by productivity and work.]

The second part of the essay repudiates violence and in an intertextual allusion to Costa's cry to imprison the Cid, Maeztu states that this national symbol of military prowess is fortunately and definitely dead. The decline of Spain, which occurred over the previous hundred years, cannot be stemmed through the use of military force, but rather by opposition to it. "La herida aun sangra . . . No es con el fusil, sino contra el fusil como ha de restañarse" [The wound continues to bleed . . . It is not with rifles but rather against them that it will be stanched] (241).

In other articles, Maeztu falls back into imperialist rhetoric and visions of the other. He scoffs at accusations of Spanish abuses from citizens of the former colonies and ridicules Latin American claims to have constructed a new order, pointing to corruption and dictatorial abuses in Spanish American governments ("El himno boliviano"). In the heat of the war, Maeztu's writing slips into patriotic declarations of Spanish nobility and gentlemanly demeanor in battle in contrast to uncouth, undisciplined Yankees. On occasion, the texts eerily prefigure the fascist discourse of the 1930s. "La marcha del regimento" coolly dismisses the loss of life during the war, erasing the presence of death through glorification of the healthy bodies of six young Spanish women who join the crowd to send off the troops. "¿Qué importa la guerra? . . . ¿Qué la muerte? . . . En esas caderas arrogantes cabe otra España, si acaso ésta se hundiera" [What does the war matter? . . . Who cares about death? . . . Those bold hips contain another Spain, if this one should go under] (1967, 119). The same image of Spanish women as baby machines for the new Spanish race surfaces in "Sobre el discurso de Lord Salisbury," where Maeztu responds to a speech by the British Lord that was widely interpreted in Spain as a justification of the right of powerful countries to take over the colonial possessions of weaker nations. Juan Maragall had also written on the controversy, going to great lengths not only to show that Salisbury was not alluding to a "weakened" Spain, but also to refute a biologically-based division of the world into strong and weak nations or cultures ("El discurso de Lord Salisbury"). Maeztu takes a more paranoid approach, bashing the English as pale brutes, given to alcohol and, by implication, infertile, in comparison with his healthy store-keeper neighbors, whose two male children give proof of the vitality of the Spanish peoples (123–26).

"El sí a la muerte" presents a clear example of what Walter Benjamin has termed the "aestheticization of political life" within fascism (1968, 219–53). The text speaker responds to the ignominious Spanish naval defeat at Cavite with calls for unanimous national acceptance of the catastrophe that, although painful, can acquire aesthetic value: ". . . si la Historia expansiva y conquistadora de nuestra patria ha de acabarse con la centuria; si los cañones yanquis han de borrar el *plus ultra* de nuestra raza, quiero, al menos, como español y como artista, que nuestra caída sea bella; quiero al menos que si no hemos sabido decir 'sí' a la vida, sepamos decírselo a la muerte, haciéndola gloriosa, digna de España" [. . . . if the expansive and conquering History of our country is to end with the century, if Yankee cannons are to erase the *plus ultra* of our race, I would at least hope, as a Spaniard and an artist, that our fall be beautiful. I would at least hope that if we have not known how to say "yes" to life, we know how to say it to death, making it glorious and worthy of Spain] (1967, 121). The assumption that calls for accountability by the political opposition somehow spoil the aesthetic quality of national pain privileges passive unanimity over free speech and collectivity over the individual, values that Maeztu will later espouse openly and zealously in *La crisis del humanismo* and his fascist writings. In contrast to his later fascist writings, Maeztu's early texts recognize the equal pull of the past and the aspiration for a different future and explicitly call them to the reader's attention. The introductory comments to the second part of *Hacia otra España* state that in preparing the volume of previously published articles, he could have eliminated the contradictions, but retained them to best express the two opposing tendencies that compete in his personal temperament and in the national debate: a bellicose, historical, and heroic drive in contention with a modern, positivist, and conservative impulse (81). "Tradición y crítica" confronts the two positions and expresses a hesitant preference for the modern, critical tendency. The co-presence of conflicting inclinations marks the modernist experience, as Richard Sheppard and Art Berman signal in the context of international modernism and Cathy Jrade suggests when referring to the eclecticism of Hispanic modernism (1988, 189). In later years, Maeztu abandons the modernist modality for a unilateral fascism, but in *Hacia otra España* the two co-exist in uneasy oscillation.

Other writers of the pre-war and war period rest easier in the unstable region of the in-between. Angel Ganivet's *Idearium español* (1897) appears about the same time as *Hacia otra España,* but represents greater openness to non-dichotomous thinking in a complex textualization that has not received the recognition of previous criticism. Herbert Ramsden's much cited study focusses on what he terms its naive determinism (1967) while in a public lecture in 1995, Eduardo Subirats dismisses the text and the entire period as a failed enterprise that never really questions the past and falls into pre-fascist utopianism.[10] These readings reflect two disparate strands in Ganivet's text, which interweaves positivistic arguments of geographical determinism, as observed by Ramsden, with idealistic aspirations to discover the eternal, invariable spirit of Spain, as noted by Subirats. My own reading deals with both aspects and their intricate interplay. Concentrating on those sections of *Idearium español* that deal with imperialism and Cuba, I will trace the multifaceted argumentative text structure to demonstrate how Ganivet exploits essayistic strategies to move his readers towards a repudiation of the colonial past, the threatened colonial wars of the present, and future colonial aspirations.

Published before the outbreak of the Spanish-American War, *Idearium español* consists of three main sections, designated with the capital letters A, B, and C, and subdivided into smaller parts marked either by asterisks or textual spacing. The absence of titles and clear markers of textual structure represents both a repudiation of nineteenth-century treatise writing, with its long titles and clear indication of the content of each section, and a silencing of textual intent in order to prevent early opposition to unorthodox ideas. Part A analyzes Spain's religious, philosophical, political, legal, and artistic development. The text speaker emphasizes Spain's difference from the rest of Europe, citing Seneca's stoicism and the Arab invasion as determining factors. In contrast to a sterile scholasticism that prevails to the North and derives from St. Thomas Aquinas, Spain remains under the sway of more vital African influences, including Saint Augustine and mysticism. The following subsection theorizes a "territorial spirit" for nations, designated as an essential, permanent trait; the geographic disposition of a country as island, peninsula, or continent determines its "spirit." Ganivet argues that imperial Spain behaved as an island rather than a peninsula, which while allowing for invasion, is difficult to conquer and tends to assimilate the invader. Far from a determinist or essentialist argument, this thesis deconstructs both. Spain has disregarded her peninsular configuration, (thus denying geographical determinism) and has been led astray by external forces that have prevented the discovery of her true spirit, (thus, negating claims to eternal qualities, since these have yet to be discovered). The textual energy moves neither toward the confirmation of geographical determinism nor essentialist national definitions, but rather against colonialist, imperialist traditions and their modern manifestations.

Idearium español seeks to undo external and internal images of an aggressive, militaristic Spain by presenting Spaniards as fighters, not soldiers. They excel in the guerrilla warfare that defeated Napoleon and resisted Rome, but fare poorly in organized military operations. As a consequence, Spain should not build a national army but rather smaller, independent units. The focus of *Idearium español* then abandons military, imperial topics to analyze legal and artistic traditions, returning to the colonial issue in Section B. The rhythm of introduction, abandonment, and reintroduction of polemical topics typifies essayistic discourse and responds to a need to avoid confrontation with views strongly held by the average reader. Written after the renewal of hostilities in Cuba, but before the outbreak of war with the United States, *Idearium español* moves cautiously towards the condemnation of Spanish imperialism. Section B describes the historical union of Castile and Aragon and the erroneous development of a continental military strategy under Charles I and Philip II, which led inevitably to failure because it disregarded the "true" Spanish character as defensive fighter but not aggressor.

The remainder of Section B deals with the current status of Spain and its possessions. In a curious yet significant dissymmetry, the speaker structures the discussion according to the cardinal points of the compass, commencing with the North, moving West, and then East, but never mentioning South. Spanish expansion to the North led to defeat in Flanders and no possibility for territorial growth remains on the European front. In the case of Gibraltar, British possession does not impede Spanish national development and with regard to Portugal, the text advocates fraternity over forced unification. The discussion of Spanish relations with the West clearly touches on the sensitive matter of Cuba, but the text only mentions the island in passing, with praise for the cultural contribution of the Cuban dance form, the *habanera*. Other thoughts about Spanish-Cuban relations surface under the general consideration of relations with Spanish America. In this context, Spain should cultivate fraternal relations with the former colonies and reestablish her intellectual prestige without utilitarian or commercial aspirations. The silence with respect to current tensions in Cuba encourages the reader to consider the island colony in conjunction with other former colonies, in a relation of brotherhood rather than possession or domination. The persistent rejection of commercialization and intellectual and personal property rights throughout the text and in this particular section also insinuates a repudiation of the economic exploitation that characterizes colonial rule and Cuba-Spain relations.

Turning to the East, the text speaker comments on the rich potential for expansion in that direction, but declares it totally unrealizable without a navy, and then quickly goes on to argue against hasty navy-building, reiterating his view that institutions should develop naturally and never precipitously for political or economic reasons. The question of relations with Rome occupies a good deal of the section, but in the middle of a discussion clearly aimed at opposing papal influence in national policies, the speaker interjects a brief warning regarding Spanish expansion in Africa, a venture he views as absurd and unjustified. The text reveals a palpable fear of religiously-based imperialism and undermines such a venture with reminders to the reader that Christianity should never resort to force. The specter of renewed Spanish colonial activity in Africa lurks beneath these statements and, in the face of contemporary calls for expansion in the north Sahara, *Idearium español* moves cautiously and indirectly towards an anti-imperialist conclusion. The speaker provides a summary of the discussion thus far, declaring that Spain can expand neither to the north, west, or east and consequently, must turn inward in search of true national identity. In a clear repudiation of past Spanish and current European values, Ganivet insists that a nation's status does not depend on territorial extension. He then reintroduces the subject of Africa and the view of some that expansion to the south represents a continuation of Isabel the Catholic's legacy. In direct rebuttal, he reiterates previously stated assertions of African inferiority and the inevitable failure of attempts to impose civilization at this stage of African development. He argues that Europeans should have founded a few missions and factories as outposts and waited to see whether Africans would gradually adopt their values and cultures. Following these racist, but anti-imperialist statements, the speaker announces after-the-fact that he has completed discussion of the four cardinal points of potential Spanish expansion, revealing again a desire to deal with the South indirectly, without prior enunciation of topic or intent.

The closing sentences on past and potential colonial expansion abandon the hesitancy of the section on Africa. Having gradually brought the reader through the various points of discussion, the speaker clearly and forcefully expresses unequivocal anticolonizing sentiments:

> Una restauración de la vida entera de España no puede tener otro punto de arranque que la concentración de todas nuestras energías dentro de nuestro territorio. Hay que cerrar con cerrojos, llaves y candados todas las puertas por donde el espíritu español se escapó de España para derrarmarse por los cuatro puntos del horizonte, y por donde hoy espera que ha de venir la salvación; y en cada una de esas puertas no pondremos un rótulo dantesco que diga: *Lasciate ogni speranza,* sino otro más consolador, más humano, muy profundamente humano, imitado de San Agustín: *Noli foras ire; in interiore Hispaniae habitat veritas.* (1962, 124)

> [A restoration of complete Spanish life can have no other point of departure than the concentration of all our energies within our territory. We must close with bolts, keys, and padlocks all the doors through which the Spanish spirit escaped from Spain to spill out to the four points of the compass and through which today hopes persist that her salvation will come. On each of these doors we will put, not the Dantean sign that reads "Leave all hope," but rather a more consoling message, more human, profoundly human, taken from Saint Augustine: "Do not exit; the truth resides inside Spain."]

The preference for the African Augustine over the European Dante subtly deconstructs previous affirmations of African inferiority. Nineteenth century authoritative discourse exalts European values and denies African cultural contributions. *Idearium español* puts both these discourses into play in order to exploit their persuasive powers, but inverts them with a final celebration of Africa over Europe, of the colonized over the colonizer. Ganivet clearly recognizes the novelty of his position and of the attempt to construct a post-imperial role for Spain in an era when other European nations define power in terms of territorial conquest. Spain faces uncharted terrain, but just as she preceded other European nations in forming an empire and also in losing her possessions, she now must lead in establishing a novel socio-political order. Without successful models to follow, Spain must find a way to establish new modes of influence (126–27).

The repudiation of a colonizing, military past does not imply a rejection of foreign influences, as Inman Fox argues (1997, 129), or a retreat from international diplomacy. On the contrary, the text advocates different, more productive relations with the former colonies, based not on economic benefit or territorial aspirations, but generosity and dialogue. Ganivet's antipathy for conflict and domination accompanies a rejection of traditional modes of thought and communication. He advocates what he calls "round" rather than "sharp" ideas, clarifying that the former enable community, solidarity, cohabitation, and work, growing steadily but without stridency, while the latter wound and divide individuals in unproductive combat (1962, 141–42).[11] The construction of this new order constitutes a central goal of Spanish modernism and follows a circuitous path that seeks to avoid the pitfalls of the past without totally erasing Spanish tradition and thus falling into unproductive self-hatred. Traditional Spanish isolationism and the Counter Reformation rejection of European thought clearly present a danger, but so does the prevailing European model of territorial conquest and colonization. Modernist writers strive to construct a new space between these sterile options, reconfiguring and transforming traditional models.

Latin America: Trading the Colonial Past for New Futures

Refiguring the "Indiano"

Traditional justifications of Spanish colonization of Latin America emphasize Spain's civilizing contributions and downplay the value of indigenous cultures. Juan Valera minimizes the importance of an indigenous American presence in the past or the present, asserting that Spanish American literature and culture are more Spanish than American ("Sobre la duración del habla castellana," 1941, 2:1026–27). In other essays, he argues that Spain performed a great service in destroying savage indigenous cultures ("Geometría moral" 2:1104) and helped the indigenous peoples by raising their cultural level. An impassioned reply to the black legend includes outrageous claims of Spanish cultural superiority, with suggestions that Aztec and

Mayan hieroglyphics were actually painted after the arrival of the Spanish by educated, colonized indigenous subjects ("Sobre dos tremendas acusaciones contra España del anglo-americano Draper," 2:1924). Valera's comments on Cuba also reflect commonly held nineteenth-century views regarding race and the need for continued European presence. Written in 1896, after the outbreak of the most recent Cuban resistance, "Quejas de los rebeldes de Cuba" asserts that the Spanish presence in Cuba whitens the racial mix and implies that a freed Cuba, without continued Spanish migration, would rapidly become a black enclave. The newspaper *La Voz de Galicia* publishes numerous articles that reiterate this idea while depicting Cuban rebels as savage hordes that burn, rape, and murder their way to victory ("Nuestras impresiones," 1896) or as men of color who rise up with African hatred against the land of their birth ("Un desengaño," 1896). The subversive black woman who rejects her traditional role as concubine and prostitute also threatens the racial balance and whitening process. "La mulata" laments the aberrant behavior of a female rebel leader who chooses military resistance over her "natural" role as purveyor of pleasures to white male clients. In a revealing admission of the paradoxical relation of intimacy and exclusion, need and domination, the speaker finds solace in the fact that as a soldier, the mulatta will never conquer as she would as a prostitute. Nature destined her for other forms of combat; to abandon Venus for Mars ensures her defeat (1896). The conjoining of female, black, and primitive again signals the close association between various racial, class, and sexual others and their frequent conflation in texts that defend empire and textualize it as virile, cultured, and white.

Traditional justifications of colonial domination on the basis of the racial inferiority of the colonized peoples undergo a curious transformation during and immediately following the Spanish American War. Conservative writers who wish to attack the United States find an easy target in its institutionalized segregation of races and extermination or sequestration of indigenous peoples. *La Ilustración Española y Americana,* with a strongly pro-war, pro-empire stance, includes numerous articles that point to the hypocrisy of United States demands for a free Cuba when the United States black population continues to receive unequal treatment. Becerro de Bengoa (1896) contrasts North American extermination of indigenous peoples with the Spanish policy of conversion and mestizaje. Shared Spanish and Latin American hostility to United States ambitions in Latin America produces a rapprochement between Spain and Spanish America, with strong advocates on both sides of the Atlantic. A defense of Hispanic values and Spanish language increases significantly in opposition to expansionist U.S. policies. In Spanish America, Rodó's *Ariel* and Darío's "A Roosevelt" both reject materialist, utilitarian North American culture in favor of more humanistic, spiritual Hispanic qualities. Rodó hopes for Spanish renewal and envisions Darío's trip to Spain as a possible catalyst (n. d., 309). On the Spanish side, nationalist opposition to the United States and a renewal of close ties with Spanish America run the risk of a recolonization, whether economic or cultural, which traditional forces clearly welcome, but progressive, anti-colonialist circles struggle to avoid.[12] In the interplay of these different discourses and forces, modernist writers attempt to construct a new dialogue with the former colonies, opposing slavery and domination for reasons that go beyond purely nationalist opposition to United States expansion. They also reconsider race and gender relations and their role in the construction of empire and seek a pattern of exchange that might displace the old economic and hierarchical order. Modernist texts and writers seek, not always successfully, to free themselves from a colonial legacy. In many cases, the former colonies become a model and place of hope for Spanish modernists, but unlike traditional dreams of fortune and domination, the voyage now takes a more humanitarian form and often includes a specific repudiation of militarism, theocracy, and patriarchy.

As a consequence, the figure of the *indiano* undergoes significant transformation during modernism. In realist narrative, the *indiano* leaves his village to build a fortune in America and then returns older and wealthy to marry the bride of his choosing and live out a comfortable life surrounded by deferential villagers. This image accentuates the victorious colonizer who successfully dominates and exploits colonial possessions for personal and imperial benefit. Remnants of the virile conqueror persist in Vicente Blasco Ibáñez's *Los argonautas* (1914). Despite Blasco Ibáñez's socialist politics and chronological coincidence with the appearance and development of modernism, in language, narrative technique, and vision he remains more a realist than a modernist, with some exceptions around the time of World War I.[13] *Los argonautas* creates a modern space aboard a German ship that transports citizens of some 28 different nations to Buenos Aires, where they hope to build a new life. The mix of nationalities and the sequestered space in which they find themselves reflect both the globalizing tendency and the creation of new communities that Anthony Giddens views as intrinsic to high modernity (1991, 21–34). Furthermore, the intercalated descriptions of past voyages of discovery breaks with the realist separation of history and fiction. However, the mechanical switches from one discourse to the other and a Eurocentric, exaggerated nationalism impose a monologic vision and reflect a traditional poetics and ideology. The novel initially introduces two characters, Fernando de Ojeda and Isidro Maltrana, who debate issues and provide opposing perspectives, but Ojeda rapidly displaces Maltrana as the focalizing presence. His multiple sexual conquests on the ship, while he fondly remembers the woman he left behind, and his self-description as a new fortune-seeking Argonaut mimic the behavior of the Spanish conquistadors that he vigorously defends. He and other characters judge the presence of indigenous populations a hindrance to progress and praise American nations that have maintained a white majority. The text depicts Latin America as a remarkable racial mixture with a predominantly Spanish component, produced by prolific colonizers who successfully whitened the indigenous population: "¡El enorme envío de virilidad que fue necesario para aclarar la sangre india de su cobre nativo!" [The enormous dispatch of virility that was necessary to whiten the Indian blood from its native copper!] (1961, 3:325–26).

Modernist writers represent a less exploitative relation with the former colonies. In their works, the enriched *indiano* of the realist period acquires new dimensions, often displacing material success with accomplishments of a different nature or redefining the methods of acquiring wealth and its use. Elizabelde, the vagabond of Baroja's 1901 story of the same title, cares little for money and happily returns to his Basque village and a simple life style rather than marry a wealthy Creole. Rusiñol's "El indiano" of *Pájaros de barro* describes a complex process of transculturaltion that reveals the power of the colony over the Spanish *indiano.* The emigré of this text, like his historical predecessors, struggles to build his fortune in America, sustained by memories of his homeland and hopes for eventual return. When he finally reaches Spain as a wealthy, old man, he has become a stranger. Friends and family have died and he finds himself surrounded by shirt-tail relatives who await his death in order to inherit the fruits of his labors. Furthermore, he misses his adopted land and yearns to return, after having spent his years there longing for

Spain. The text refers to a dual displacement from and double nostalgia for his fatherland (*patria*) and motherland (*matria*), creating a Spanish feminine form to express this novel attachment to both Spain and Latin America. The *indiano* now belongs nowhere and dies surrounded by gold, without a land to call his own, neither *patria* nor *matria*.

The contrast between a masculine and feminine form for country and the association of the land of origin with the father and land of adoption with the mother suggests a link between patriarchy and emigration that many modernist writers explore. "El viajero" opens Antonio Machado's *Soledades* (1907) and depicts the return of a defeated *indiano* as a metaphor for Spanish imperial history. The beloved brother of the poetic text departed "en el sueño infantil de un claro día" [a young dream on a clear day], but now stands in the dark family parlor with gray hair and a look of anxiety. The clear day of the youthful dream has given way to an autumn afternoon, which coincides with a vision of Spain as in decline, having wasted her prime in futile adventures and unproductive quests. The traveler has returned, empty-handed and empty-spirited: "la fría inquietud de sus miradas / revela un alma casi toda ausente" [the cool anxiety of his gaze / reveals an almost absent soul] (1917, 12–13). The final verses of the poem signal both the causes of this fruitless escapade and the family's discomfort and resistance to recognizing them:

Y este dolor que añora o desconfía
el temblor de una lágrima reprime,
y un resto de viril hipocresía
en el semblante pálido se imprime.
Serio retrato en la pared clarea
todavía. Nosotros divagamos.
En la tristeza del hogar golpea
el tictac del reloj. Todos callamos.

(1917, 12–13)

[And this suffering that grieves or distrusts
represses the shudder of a tear
and a remnant of virile hypocrisy
marks the pale countenance.
The grave portrait on the wall still
glows. We drift aimlessly.
In the sadness of the home resounds
a clock's tick-tock. All stay silent.]

The repressed tear, grave portrait, and clock all suggest patriarchy and link it to empire-building. The traveler's fear of expressing emotion even amongst his family after years of absence recalls traditional admonitions that men do not cry and the grave portrait on the wall suggests a father, grandfather, or other founding patriarch whose presence continues to influence family conduct and in whose name the traveler may well have departed, as the first-born and namesake, to repair a deteriorated family fortune. The ticking clock represents history, Kristevan maletime (1980, 205), and its resounding beat suggests the oppressive nature of this mode of temporality. The traveler and his nation have moved through history, wasting their youth and arriving at old age with nothing to show but an empty spirit.

Antonio Machado's representation of the colonial past as the cause of the present national malaise echoes a theme repeated by liberal writers throughout the nineteenth century and with roots in theories of national reconstruction that date back even further, as Inman Fox has shown (1997). However, modernist rejection of the colonial past differs significantly from traditional views in linking colonialism and patriarchy and underscoring that repudiation of the imperial past also requires rejection of traditional visions of honor, family, virtue, religion, and related concepts. Benito Pérez Galdós explores these topics in a number of plays written between 1892 and 1904 in his endeavor to reform Spanish theater while transmitting a new way of thinking the nation, gender, and class relations to a middle-class audience. *La loca de la casa* (1892) brings together questions of gender, class, religion, nation, and colonialism. In what borders on parody of the traditional *indiano,* the play presents the wealthy, virulently anti-Catholic, and arrogant José María Cruz, who has returned victorious from his adventures in Mexico and California. He boasts of killing a Native American with a machete blow and of the tiger wounds and tattoo that he wears as bodily inscriptions of his exploits. He now seeks to marry one of the Moncada sisters, who as wealthy, upper-class children had ridiculed his lower-class origins. In a comical scene, Victoria Moncada, who had entered the convent and appears in full religious habit, meets with Cruz and induces him to propose marriage after determining that life with him offers greater sacrifice than the convent's seclusion. The relationship between Victoria and Cruz presents the taming of the conqueror and inverts traditional marital roles in her initiative and control of the finances. The strength of their personalities, both in their enthusiasms and differences, also contrasts with conventional gender definitions. When Victoria leaves Cruz after an argument regarding monies she gave to a former suitor's mother, she realizes how much she relishes the life of activity, honesty, and struggle that her marriage provided. She derives tremendous energies from Cruz and their vitality contrasts favorably with the tired solutions of other characters. When Daniel, the former suitor, challenges Cruz to a duel, the latter flatly refuses, rejecting old standards of honor that have no constructive value. He advises Daniel to emigrate to America, where he will learn to build a new life. While Cruz's racist views as well as the American roots of his wealth replay colonialist narratives, *La loca de la casa* veers away from the model in significant details. Victoria tempers his dominance and although he insists that he holds the power, because she needs him to be indomitable, the text suggests parity and even leans towards superior female power. In addition, Cruz's rejection of traditional religion receives textual support in Victoria's abandonment of the convent and her pro-active charity as well as in the repudiation of Daniel's advocacy of the timeworn religious values of resignation and self-sacrifice. Victoria's active, loving religion combines with Cruz's confidence and energy, but eliminates his ruthless exploitation and resituates his activities in Spain to chart a new internal conquest.

La de San Quintín (1894) continues a positive representation of inter-class marriage and again imagines America as key to the creation of new forms of human relations. José Buendía is of humble origins, but has acquired considerable wealth. His son César has assumed the habits and values of traditional upper-class families. César and his illegitimate son Víctor both want to marry Rosario Morenita, an impoverished aristocratic widow. Víctor, a socialist who has served jail time for his political activism, presently lives with his father and grandfather under the assumption that his good behavior will legitimize his status. Rosario has abandoned her aristocratic roots and now prefers more humble pursuits, as she proclaims while making *rosquillas*. Her praise of "la soberana masa" plays with the double meaning of the Spanish word as both dough and masses and suggests the dual value of mixing and uprising. In the end, Víctor and Rosario determine to marry, thus incurring César's wrath. César ironically reveals the arbitrariness of "honor" when he feels dishonored that his illegitimate offspring aspires to marry the same woman he desires. In order to escape this endless cycle of reinvented aristocracies and hierarchies, Víctor and Rosario plan to resettle in America, where they can build a life free of traditional prejudices regarding illegitimacy and class divisions. The final lines specifically refer to Spain and Europe as ruins and America as a promising, new world. The text emphasizes the break with the Spanish imperial past through classical Galdosian name symbolism and historical allusion. César invokes the figures of the imperial Caesars and his defeat by his illegitimate son suggests that the dynasty has ended and a new line commenced. José, the family patriarch, deliberately hands over leadership to his son, declaring that he will retire to Yuste, the monastery to which Charles I retreated after abdicating to Phillip II. The repudiation of the dynasty by its illegitimate offspring breaks with inherited values of honor, patriarchal naming, and domination.[14] The text also avoids a suggestion of continuity with previous Spanish colonizing emigrations by naming several final destinations, at times specifying the United States and at others, alluding to an indeterminate America.

A well-known Galdosian text that deals with the *indiano* but has not been approached from this perspective is *El abuelo,* written as a novel in dialogue form in 1897 and revised for the stage in 1904. The mixing of genres that irritates early opponents of modernism in this case allows readers to experience hybridity, simultaneously putting into play decoding operations for narrative and drama and signaling that in negotiating meaning, borders are continually traversed. In contrast to other Galdosian texts of the period, here the constitution of a new family comes from the noble patriarch himself and his repudiation of the traditions that ensured his aristocratic privilege. The Count of Albrit, unsuccessful in repairing the family fortune with a trip to Peru, has returned to Spain with only one remaining desire—to determine which of two granddaughters is his legitimate heir. Convinced that the common origins of the illegitimate granddaughter will reveal themselves in her conduct, Albrit carefully observes Nell and Dolly. The obsession with consanguinity and honor gradually gives way to a valorization of loyalty and love when Dolly defies her mother and stays with her grandfather while Nell happily accepts the marriage and introduction to society that her mother has arranged. Albrit's belief in racial purity—with echoes of Inquisitorial tribunals, antisemitic/antimestizo prejudices, and inherited privilege—cedes to a new kind of relation, based on commitment over duty, equality over hierarchy. Dolly, the chosen heir and illegitimate granddaughter, creates a new family unit with Albrit and the simple don Pío and together they abandon the family homestead of Jerusa for Rocamor, lands of former tenants.

The play of names points to a transgressive rewriting of traditional narratives on various levels. Jerusa invokes the Jewish temple city and origins of Judeo-Christian religion, with its links to patriarchy, while Rocamor emphasizes love over law and honor. Two additional details deserve emphasis. First, the traditional focus on continuity through the male line is doubly transgressed in the recognition of the illegitimate female heiress.[15] The text also suggests that Dolly, Albrit, and Pío constitute a new Trinity that refigures the traditional masculine triad. Dolly calls Albrit "Abuelo," and Pío states that God is the grandfather of all creatures, explicitly linking Albrit to God the father, whose severity gives way to a grandfatherly benevolence. Dolly, in turn, displaces the sacrificed Christ, abandoning earthly possessions, mother, and sister to join Albrit and Pío in a desolate area called Calvary. Pío, the fount of classical knowledge, represents both a return to a pre-Christian era and a new, more human Holy Spirit. Derided as the cuckold in Jerusa, he achieves dignity in a new world that measures honor by different standards.

A second element in the mutation of values and reconstitution of community relates to the repudiation of the colonial past. Albrit's disavowal of conventional norms of honor and inheritance comes about as a consequence of his failed enterprise in Latin America. He repudiates his own personal past, that of his ancestors, and his nation and refuses to teach his grandchildren history, stating that he will reconstruct the past from the present. Nell and Dolly also abjure history, continually mixing it with mythology. The rejection of the past and of hierarchies of authority and truth relates to the dialogic form of *El abuelo* in several different ways. The absence of a narrator creates an authoritative vacuum that underscores the egalitarian thrust of the text. Although authorial presence never entirely disappears, as Galdós himself recognizes in the prologue (1979, 8), the use of dialogue interspersed with generally brief, emotionally-neutral explanations of scene places the characters in a relation of equality in terms of control of information and obliges the reader to weigh the evidence with no recourse to higher authority.

The hybrid nature of the text, with narrative and dramatic characteristics, requires the reader to move back and forth from one code to the other in order to construct a new interpretive perspective. This active participation in two distinct systems in order to create a third fosters an openness to hybrid forms of expression and thought. The reader cannot remain within a closed system and construct a meaning for the text. *El abuelo,* however, does not arrive at some final and conclusive prescription, either for behavior or textuality. The open nature of the final scene refuses to reimpose hierarchy and eschews stable meaning for a more dynamic, dialogic form. Dolly, Albrit, and Pío embark on a journey with no set destination or length and just as they depart, Dolly's mother—Albrit's hated daughter-in-law—sends a letter granting Dolly permission to accompany them and wishing them good fortune and long-life. Pío closes the text with the unanswered and unanswerable question, "¿El mal . . . es el bien?" [Is evil good?] (1979, 415). Modernism does not construct, but only barely envisages a new way of living in the world, as Eysteinsson has pointed out (1990, 214–22). However, the indeterminacy of the future does not efface a clear repudiation of major aspects of the past. Galdós insistently critiques a colonial legacy in the years preceding and following the Spanish American War and attempts to imagine a society in which the old values of military domination, economic exploitation, patriarchal control, and an inflexible religion no longer reign. In their place, new forms of interaction occur, not devoid of conflict, but certainly better able to cross traditional borders and explore new terrain.

Other Spanish modernists emphasize a flight from economic deprivation and social injustice as motivating forces for the new *indiano.* Enrique de Mesa's "La sangría española," published in 1910 during the height of emigration to Latin America as a result of economic crisis during this period in Spain, focuses on economic issues, but also mentions that these new, impoverished emigrants to Latin America flee such social impediments as inherited prejudices and a narrow public opinion that suffocates noble ideas and dreams of justice (69). The desire to break with the past often confronts extraordinarily strong legacies that do not easily give way. A patriarchal, hierarchical, colonizing vision permeates the Spanish sociosymbolic system and its residue persists in textual construction even when overt statements aspire to its overthrow. Ramón Pérez de Ayala's *Luz de Domingo* reveals this complex intermixing of transgressive and traditional modes of representation. This short novel originally appears in 1916 in *La novela corta,* a publication that disseminates literary texts to a wide public at reasonable costs. It reappears later the same year with two other short novels, now including intercalated poems at the beginning of the eight chapters. The verse introductions and the epigraph from *Poema de mío Cid* set up a relation between the epic past and the present that alternates between contrast and continuity. The 16 syllable verses with a midline break after the eighth syllable continue traditional epic verse form, but the grandeur of the foundational medieval poems and the heroic deeds of the Cid and his cohorts contrast with the corrupt politics of the novel and the honest but ineffectual deeds of the protagonist, Cástor Cagigal. On the other hand, the poetic representation of aristocratic abuses that accompanied the founding of Spanish social order at the time of the Cid suggests the persistence of arbitrary and unjust exercise of power that continues throughout history and into the present battle between the two local political parties and their backers in Madrid. The difficulty but desirability of breaking this chain constitutes the narrative message and leads to textual ambiguities related to narrative stance.

The story describes the idyllic relation of Cástor and his fiancée Balbina that ends with her brutal rape by seven members of the powerful Becerril clan while Cástor stands bound, gagged, and helpless. Cástor unhesitatingly marries Balbina, insisting that the dishonor falls on the perpetrators, not the victim. Balbina's grandfather Joaco and the local population maintain a more traditional view. The taunts commence in the Asturian village where the events occur and follow the couple to the provincial capital and later the Castilian village to which they flee. Determined to leave the past behind, they finally set out for America, only to discover that fellow passengers from their town are also on board and to realize that the story will soon spread to all emigrants. When the ship hits a shoal, Cástor and Balbina willingly accept death at sea, finally able to free themselves from the tyranny of their past. The textual rejection of the past and aspiration for the construction of a different future plays itself out on several different levels. The couple's journey repeats the historical evolution of the Spanish nation, commencing in Asturias where the Reconquest originated, moving to Castile and then on to the "new world." As in other texts of the period, this duplicate narrative departs from the original in that the motivation for the voyage lies not in economic colonization and exploitation, but in the search for a new and better world where traditional views of honor and legitimacy no longer prevail. America represents a future where the Sunday light of the title shines every day and erases the shadows covering the old world (1964–66, 2:669). The break with the past and the possibility of a new future reveal themselves most clearly in Joaco, the grandfather who initially believes that Balbina's dishonor can never be erased. In time, Joaco comes to love the child he once wanted to murder, and it is he who suggests starting anew in America and who saves the baby when Cástor and Balbina drown. The text remains open in typical modernist fashion, but the reader constructs a final narrative in America with Joaco and his great-grandson finally freed from the cycle of rape, violence, and exploitation.

Luz de domingo signals the injustice of a system that blames the victim and also alludes to the horror of a rape trial, where the victim must publicly relive the abuse in order to convict the accused attackers. The combination of prose and poetry suggests the need to break with prior models of textualization in order to construct new ways of thinking and representing. However, the residue of former modes of seeing and writing intrude and intermingle with the impulse for change. Cástor, whose vision clearly breaks with the traditional insistence on the female body as the repository of male honor, is characterized as an effeminate, inept dreamer who walks right into the trap set for him and Balbina, even when forewarned by his protective, astute landlady. The poem that opens chapter 1 suggests a female speaker, who nostalgically reviews the domestic surroundings and expresses no desire to go out, except to be married. Cástor's introduction immediately following this exaltation of home and hearth feminizes his characterization from the outset and the process continues throughout. In the context of early twentieth-century Spanish gender norms, the protagonist's dubious masculinity undermines his advocacy for a new vision of honor. In addition, Castor's representation as concerned for Balbina and accepting of her son, even when unsure of his paternity, cedes to a more traditional vision when Cástor shows Joaco that the birthmark on the child's ribs exactly matches one on the identical location on Cástor's body, thus confirming his biological paternity.

The anti-colonialist impulse of *Luz de domingo* also loses force in that Joaco's monies and his ability to sponsor the trip back to America come from a prior emigration and his financial success as an *indiano.* Finally, Balbina's depiction reveals the persistence of the traditional male gaze, as studied by Laura Mulvey and Peter Brooks, among others.[16] While the description of both Cástor and Balbina follows the conventional realist depiction of the body through the metonymic listing of parts (Brooks 1993, 102), Cástor's representation differs in significant details. The text presents him in his room and describes his eyes actively studying the surroundings. Balbina, on the other hand, appears twice viewed from the outside, framed by a window, which suggests the myriad paintings that have frozen women as objects of desire. The description of her white teeth then drops to focus on her exposed throat ringed by red coral beads, introducing a color that traditionally invokes passion and sexual desire. The mention of a wool shawl covering her chest also summons memories of a male desire to uncover or undress the clothed female body (Brooks, 105). Balbina's eyes have no active power, rather they are shaded by her hands and remain in the shadow, in imitation of traditional paintings and magazine advertisements in which the female model averts the gaze. On the other hand, on at least one important occasion, Balbina acquires a voice and insists on speaking the unspeakable. When Joaco tells her not to bring up the memory of the rape, she argues that naming it proves they have escaped its control. The suggestion of female agency disappears, however, in her final acceptance of death and also in the revelation that Cástor's energetic landlady, who had lived as an independent business woman to the age of 45, has decided she needs a male protector and has married a man she long despised. The rhythm of affirmation and negation of change speaks to the powerful legacy of the past and the difficult construction of new ways of seeing, thinking, and writing in modernist texts. *Luz de domingo* reveals more than many texts of the period the weight of tradition, but it also continues the impulse for change and the examination of the interconnections between patriarchy and colonialism.

Feminist studies have demonstrated the difficulties facing women who wish to speak with a different voice within patriarchy, but whose only model has been the tradition against which they wish to write.[17] Modernist writers face a similar challenge and revert to analogous strategies to disempower the predominant discourse. Parody, irony, and inversion prove useful to question the validity and authority of military, imperial, and patriarchal traditions. Gabriel Miró parodies the theme of the colonial fortune seeker in *El abuelo del rey* (1912). Arcadio, the local patriarch of an inland Levantine village, resents the arrival of coastal peoples who represent a racial mix of Iberians, Phoenicians, Latins, and Berbers in contrast to the pure Iberian strain of local residents, perhaps mixed with a little Jewish washed clean by baptism. Despite Arcadio's pride of place, a stagnant local economy forces his heirs emigrate. His son Agustín marries a Cuban, who the locals—unable to conceive of a site as distant and exotic as Cuba—assume is from Majorca. On her death, Agustín emigrates to the Philippines, where he ends his life without resolving the family's financial decline. The grandson, also named Agustín and also forced to abandon his impoverished family in a continual repetition of the national narrative, departs for Latin America. His aspiration to earn a fortune with engineering inventions quickly fades and he turns to a more traditional path to economic success, working as a clerk for a wealthy landowner. The version propagated in his home village, however, takes a very different turn. Local pride converts Agustín into a legendary hero, living on a remote island as king of the Ona Indians. The isolationist, xenophobic villagers easily invent a version of history that bears no relation to the more sordid reality of the *indiano.* Their ready acceptance of the exalted legend of conquest in modern times, when newspapers, steam ships, and telegraphs bring the far corners of the world into closer proximity and increased mutual knowledge, raises questions about the veracity of the original conquest, when reporting was much less immediate and verifiable. As in the original Conquest, America's riches fail to build an economically viable Spain. The reader is left to ponder whether the invention of a glorious conquest by a people who reject outsiders and consistently wall themselves off from the world does not also duplicate an earlier fabrication of conquest that perhaps shares more with legend than history.

A second Miró story also foregrounds the inseparability of fiction and history and underscores the impact of the teller of the story on the vision of truth. "El beso del esposo" from the 1912 *Del huerto provinciano* contrasts two versions of the perfidy of the kiss. The female narrator first relates the tale of the wife's poisoned kiss, echoing misogynist traditions that portray female sexuality as destructive of male vitality. Her second account opposes the Eve tradition and its connotations of destructive female sexuality, offering a woman's version of the Spanish conquest of America. The narrative suggests an indeterminate temporality, with allusions to New Spain, as in colonial times, and to a photograph, as in the modern period. The parents of the young woman of the second version of the kiss guard their daughter closely and marry her off to a much older family friend who is away in America, trying like so many others of the period to remedy the family slide toward poverty. The couple, married by proxy, remain separated for five years, during which the young wife lives in a fantasy encouraged by impassioned letters from her husband. When he arrives in Spain, his kiss is that of an old man, whose less than dashing appearance crushes the wife's illusions. The text implies that she soon finds herself widowed and childless. This version of colonialism emphasizes its sterile consequences for the Spanish nation and parodies patriarchy and control of the female body in the name of honor as major factors in the initiation and perpetuation of imperial ventures. The female version of history underscores loss and victimization, which haunt the personal and national participants long after the glory of conquest has disappeared.

Colonizers, Colonized, and Inverted Hierarchies

Spanish modernists move beyond a reconsideration of the *indiano* to question the traditional hierarchy of colonizer over colonized. Several texts imagine Spain as a Latin American colony and envision favorable consequences to such a turn around, whether culturally, spiritually, or economically based. In "Al maestro Rubén Darío" (1904), Antonio Machado welcomes the influx of French and Latin American poetic inspiration that arrives with the Nicaraguan: "Y yo le grito: ¡Salve! a la bandera / flamígera que tiene / esta hermosa galera / que de una nueva España a España viene" [And I yell to him: Greetings! To the glowing / flag that waves / over this beautiful galley / that comes to Spain from a New Spain] (1917, 261). The allusion to the galley ship suggests a reverse voyage of discovery and the welcome extended connotes a warm reception to the vitality that can energize and revivify the former colonizer. Unamuno writes countless articles on Latin American literature and Latin American varieties of Spanish over the period of some thirty years. He welcomes dialectal diversity and often undercuts purist criticisms of Latin American lexical peculiarities by pointing out their similarity with Spanish rural dialects, doubly vindicating Latin American and popular speech. Like many of his contemporaries, he envisions a Spanish spiritual and cultural future that develops through Latin America and carries her imprint:

> España se despuebla; sus hijos braceros corren a América, a la España grande y del porvenir, a la tierra de promisión. ¿Y nuestras ideas? Estas no, éstas no emigran, no pueden emigrar; son fósiles y las tenemos encastradas en el espíritu. Parecíamos tener un papel cultural en la América Latina, nosotros, los de España, la primogénita de las naciones de lengua castellana. Hemos vendido la primogenitura por una olla de garbanzos. Hubo un tiempo en que Bolívar el Libertador, el Quijote de América, soñó quijotescamente

con venir a conquistarnos. Acaso sea este nuestro porvenir, que nos conquiste la América española. ¿Quién sabe si un día la vieja madre tendrá que vivir de sus hijas emancipadas?" (Variedades y revista de revistas. 1907, 4:468–69)

[Spain is becoming depopulated; her laborer sons flee to America, to the great and future Spain, the land of promise. And our ideas? No, our ideas don't emigrate, they can't emigrate. They are fossils, deeply embedded in our spirit. We seemed to have a cultural role in Latin America, we Spaniards, the first born of Castilian-speaking nations. We sold our birthright for a pot of chickpeas. There was a time when Bolivar the Liberator, the American Quijote, dreamed quixotically of coming to conquer us. Maybe this is our future, that Spanish America conquer us. Who knows if one day the old mother will have to live off her emancipated daughters?]

In "La otra España" (1920), he writes that if he were younger, he too would emigrate in search of a Spain that might have been and remains so difficult to locate in his homeland.

The fossilization of attitudes not only impedes the development and exportation of Spanish ideas, but also stands in the way of the integration of the other. In productive dialogue with the many texts that imagine a future in which Latin American vitality and innovative socio-cultural structures energize a dormant, introspective Spain, Santiago Rusiñol questions the ability of Spaniards of all political persuasions and social levels to truly act in accordance with their expressed beliefs. He explores the topic in a three-act play and a short story, both entitled "Libertad." The story appears in *Hojas de la vida,* originally published in Catalan and translated to Spanish in 1906, while Jacinto Benavente translated the play for a Madrid staging in 1902. In the dramatic text, a wealthy Cuban expatriate leaves his freed slave Jaumet in a Spanish village when the local inhabitants proclaim their interest in baptizing and educating him. The religious segment of the population insists on a showy baptismal celebration while the liberal sector seeks to inculcate their beliefs in liberty, equality, and fraternity. The leading liberal takes Jaumet into his home and raises him alongside his daughter Florentina. Notwithstanding this apparent acceptance, Jaumet's integration in village life remains tenuous. The school teacher reveals an appalling ignorance of Africans and racial difference, falling easily into stereotypes and racist generalizations. The religious and political rhetoric of acceptance changes to rejection once the outsider seeks to become one with white Spaniards.

When Jaumet asks to marry Florentina, her father angrily rejects him and when the local workers can guarantee their own job security if they accept the expulsion of outside labor, commencing with Jaumet, they quickly exchange cries of international brotherhood and solidarity for proclamations of individual freedom. The liberty of the title undergoes ironic inversion as the union members defend Jaumet's freedom to leave and pursue his fortune wherever he chooses.

Two characters in the play stand out in contrast with the generalized hypocrisy and fear of the other. Florentina accepts Jaumet as a brother, but confesses that his race prevents her from falling in love with him. Her honesty and fear of the prejudice their children would face reveal that she has at least confronted her feelings and will not hide behind religious or political expressions of equality and acceptance. Martín, a skeptic with anarchist leanings, questions all inherited and recently created myths, forever prodding the villagers and Jaumet himself to look beyond accepted presuppositions. When the teacher attacks African culture as primitive and praises Western enlightenment, Martín ironically critiques such modern European advances as military conscription and organized armies. He rejects as tired and empty the trilogy of liberty, equality, and fraternity, suggesting as substitutes love, goodness, and beauty. Martín defends difference, arguing that order consists not in uniformity, but in acceptance of variety. Jaumet brings to the fore a colonial past that persists in post-imperial Spanish society in the fear of the other, a rigid and formalist Catholicism, empty political slogans carried over from another age, and individual and collective resistance to change. Rusiñol's story and play serve as yet another reminder of the impediments to change even within those who advocate social transformation, while they also identify fragile, isolated possibilities in Florentina, Martín, and Jaumet himself. The presence of the other challenges established social and ideological patterns and destabilizes existing norms, provoking resistence, but also opening up possibilities for change.

A considerable body of modernist texts situate the encounter between Spaniards and the former colonies in Spanish America itself, exploiting modernism's cosmopolitan character to offer new reading of the Spanish colonial legacy. Ciro Bayo's 1927 *Por la América desconocida* is based on his travels in Argentina and Bolivia in the 1890s and concentrates on indigenous peoples of the rural or jungle regions. The narrative stance oscillates between a representation of native South Americans as alien and contemptible and a more comprehending attitude. On many occasions, the distinction between self and other breaks down and the reader faces an "alien" that turns out to be very much the "self." The text speaker initially expresses his disillusion with indigenous customs and individuals who seem more akin to European gypsies than to the poetic, noble renderings of Mayne Reid and similar writers (1927, 17). He criticizes the lack of generosity of certain pampas tribes, but then excuses it because of the harshness of range life and the difficulty of gathering food (66). The description of his encounter with a white captive woman continues this rhythm of distanced critique and proximate compassion. The narrator initially takes the wrinkled old woman for a member of a pampas tribe and only realizes she is a white Spaniard when she relates her story of shipwreck and captivity. He assumes she would want to return to white civilization, but she clarifies that she has two children by a native chief and that as his wife, she has much greater status than she would receive in Buenos Aires, where they would surely disparage her as an "Indian-lover" and lock her up in a state home. The narrator's understanding turns to disgust when she replies to his offer to help her with a request for alcohol. With this portrait of an alcoholic European transplant, the text thoroughly inverts the European stereotype of the degenerate drunken native.

In Bolivia, the narrator continues to interlace criticism with praise. He attributes the country's lack of progress to its high percentage of native peoples, but then states that educated natives have great aptitude for literature, law, and politics. He also describes the mestizo population as extremely bright and praises the local custom of legal cohabitation before marriage as a farsighted measure that serves to test the compatibility of the two parties before sanctioning a permanent arrangement (1927, 155). In describing his experiences in the Bolivian rubber-tapping region, he alternates dispassionate descriptions of the abuses of wealthy rubber barons with comments that reveal his moral disgust. In this ungoverned and seemingly ungovernable geography, the line between civilized and primitive, native and European becomes increasingly blurred. The narrator accompanies Paul, the French-speaking overseer of a rubber plantation, to the jungle on a trip to capture natives and impress them as rubber tappers. Their semi-civilized indigenous guide uses the excursion to search for a native chief who had raped and kidnapped his wife. On raiding the camp, they take the naked chief prisoner, and Paul comments sarcastically in French that their captive is wearing quite a uniform. In equally idiomatic French, the chief responds, "De bous a bout" [From head to toe]. Once again, the other proves to be a European who has chosen to live naked and free in the jungle and states clearly that he has no interest in returning to the "civilized" world. In a modernist twist that insists on a final destabilization of terms and endings, the "white" chief dies poisoned by the indigenous guide, who seeks to avenge the loss of reputation he suffered when his wife was kidnapped. It bears noting that this drama of revenge echoes classic Golden Age honor plays and the European obsession with women as the repository of male honor, here played out on American soil with native-American and European participants and proponents. The distance between the alien and the familiar disappears in *Por la América desconocida* with constant inversion and exchange of presumed differences.

Like Ciro Bayo, Ramón del Valle-Inclán spent time in Latin America in the 1890s. His travels to Mexico inspired several stories as well as his novels, *Sonata de estío* (1903) and *Tirano Banderas* (1926). Various texts in the 1895 *Femeninas* depict Creole rejection of traditional Spanish values. The decadentist thrust of the stories adds to the sense that imperial culture has outlived its time. "La condesa de Cela," written in Veracruz, Mexico according to the place and date inscribed in the text, describes the end of an affair between Aquiles Calderón, a young Spanish American studying in Spain, and a wealthy, older countess. The countess combines a "pagan" desire for pleasure with extreme respect for her mother's nobility, purity, and religious fervor. When she breaks with Aquiles, he explodes in hatred of the aristocratic, Catholic mother. This American rejection of Spanish values and the younger, poorer lover's resistance to the power of the countess mimic the process of decolonization. Significantly, it is only after the break, in a post-colonial relationship, that the countess discovers a certain respect for Aquiles as well as a desire to reform her promiscuous life style. "Tula Varona," written in Pontevedra, Spain, describes a frustrated sexual encounter between a Spanish noble and Tula, a Creole living in Paris. The cosmopolitan story, with authorial and textual links to Spain, France, and Spanish America, continues in the description of Tula's house, where native American statues sit on Japanese tables and Tula dresses in a silk robe carrying a parrot on her shoulder while preparing *mate*. The traversing of national boundaries is replicated in the break down of gender barriers, when Tula, a student of fencing and a cigarette-smoking, husky-voiced tease, challenges her suitor to a duel. After awakening his desire by this inversion of sex roles, Tula calls a black servant to evict her noble guest, abruptly putting an end to any possibility of sexual relations. Alone, Tula undresses to admire her naked body in a mirror. The narcissistic stance reflects decadentist interest in unorthodox sexual behaviors, but the rejection of a Spanish noble by a Creole woman and her preference for solitary pleasure over traditional relations also allows for an anti-imperialist reading that represent one more transgression of boundaries in this multiply transgressive text.

A final story in *Femeninas* serves as the basis for the later *Sonata de estío.* "La niña Chole" appears with an explanatory note that identifies its date and place of authorship as Paris, 1893 and describes it as originally appearing in "Impresiones de Tierra Caliente" written by Andrés Hidalgo. The invention of an apocryphal source and author dilutes the power of single authorship and challenges traditional ideas of ownership and authority, as does the insertion of "La niña Chole" with minimal changes in *Sonata de estío.* The intertextual connection of Valle-Inclán's *Sonatas* with Rubén Darío's "Año lírico" and the choice of both writers to use the less common *estío* (Valle-Inclán) or *estival* (Darío) over *verano* as the title of the segment depicting the summer season as well as comparisons of Chole to a tiger (1963b, 103), the central figure of Darío's poem, furthers the deconstruction of borders, both of individual authorship and national origin. This breaking of clear lines of authority, nation, and possession finds an echo in the multinational origins of the text, written in Paris by a Galician about Mexico.

"La niña Chole" and *Sonata de estío* aggressively pursue the melding of cultures and rejection of racial and cultural hierarchies. The ironic, parodic tone continuously destabilizes categories and leads the reader through a succession of conflicting emotions that resist symmetry and consistency. Early in *Sonata de estío,* the Marqués de Bradomín and author of the memoirs expresses his desire to have been born a woman and a courtesan in order to experience love and pleasure from the other side. The desirability of exchange between the other and the self receives continued play throughout the novel. The transatlantic voyage on a British ship makes Bradomín feel a greater affinity with all Latin peoples and the text constantly conflates Europe, Asia, and Spanish American as well as Creole, mestizo, and native peoples and customs. Bradomín admires the Aztec empire and relates it to remote, mysterious Oriental civilizations. He likens the Mayan *huipil* to the traditional Andalusian *fustán*[18] and writes that the ancient and mysterious Mayan race seems to have emigrated from the depths of Assyria, which also constitutes the cradle of European civilization. La niña Chole, the Mayan beauty and love interest of this *Sonata,* constantly reminds him of Lilí, the European woman he left behind.[19] The repeated allusions to the Mayan other as identical to or originating in a shared heritage echoes the breakdown of racial and cultural barriers that occurs in Ciro Bayo's travel narrative.

A second rupture of traditional borders takes place in the representation of the Conquest and its relation to Bradomín's current activities. In an early chapter, he compares himself to an adventurer from another time (1963b, 84), suggesting a rerun of his ancestor's colonizing exploits in the initial phases of new world exploration. However, multiple examples of self-parody deflate the self-aggrandizing likeness. In an encounter with a native Mexican who threatens him with a knife, Bradomín describes how before entering into combat, he first arranges his wire-rim glasses. The text presents the battle as if it occurred in a dream and Bradomín only vaguely recalls the details. Armed with a Mexican staff, he and his opponent never really come into contact and the stand-off ends when each hurls his weapon without hitting the other and the would-be robber disappears in the fog. At that moment a door opens and two men exit a nearby house. Bradomín fears they may also be robbers and retreats to the sea shore (93–94). It is not clear if the robber flees because the men appear or if Bradomín frightens him away. However, the concern with adjusting the wire-rims, the dreamlike quality of the narration, the lack of physical contact, and the final flight to the beach all depict a rather dubious conquistador.

In a later allusion to conquering Spanish ancestors, Bradomín describes them as heirs of Alarik the Barbarian, the Visigothic king who sacked Rome, and Tarik, the Moorish general who first conquered Spain (1963b, 97). The suggestion of a mixed European-African ancestry mocks the Spanish obsession with purity of ancestry that characterizes imperial Spain at the same time that it suggests the barbarous nature of the conquest and its contrast with a decadentist legacy in the figure of Bradomín. In the presence of Chole, he imagines her desire for him and reads in her eyes a longing to be ravished by the great white victor. With exaggerated proclamations of disdain for the Mayan beauty and of attempts to resist her seductive powers, Bradomín admits his defeat and specifically compares his fall to that of the Spanish nation: "En una Historia de España, donde leía siendo niño, aprendí que lo mismo da triunfar que hacer gloriosa la derrota" [In a History of Spain, which I read as a child, I learned that to triumph is the same as to make defeat glorious] (105). The rest of the novel traces his "glorious defeat." In a battle with mercenaries, he kills two opponents but only survives the encounter when Chole intervenes and buys his freedom. In his confrontation with Chole's father and lover, Bradomín again fails as a man of action. With a clear indication of hierarchies of power, Chole falls to her knees to beg her father's forgiveness, calling him her master and king, just as she had earlier addressed Bradomín. When Chole's father strikes her across the face with a whip and then carries her off on his horse, Bradomín makes no move to resist the abduction, explaining away his inaction as evidence of his ethical conversion and newly found virtue (150). A later torrid sexual reencounter with Chole makes a mockery of these protestations of rectitude and reveals his willingness to play the cuckold in a strange ménage-à-trois. After a circuitous series of events delivers Chole to his ancestral lands, she again addresses Bradomín as her master and king, but without falling to her knees in the subservient position adopted with her father. Bradomín writes that he welcomed her with open arms, convinced that in matters of love the divine maxim orders the forgiveness of affronts (160). Indeed, Bradomín has learned well to imitate the national historical model and make defeat glorious. The novel deals not with victory, but with elaborate justifications and poetizations of a failed conquest.

The parody of the Conquest extends to several other aspects of the novel. The visit to a convent with Chole and the consummation of their sexual relations within its walls mock the church's role in the Conquest, as do the revelation that the convent founder had been the Viceroy's mistress and the episode with Chole and the statue of the Baby Christ. Urged on by Bradomín, Chole breaks the papal prohibition that only members of the religious community may taste the waters and also mocks the traditional separation of religion and sexuality by placing her mouth directly over the male sexual organ of the statue from which the water flows (1963, 115). The narrative signals the complicity of religion and imperialism in the description of the bandit Juan de Guzmán, the mother superior's godson who receives asylum and aid from the convent. Bradomín writes that in another age, this brave adventurer would have fought alongside Hernán Cortés and then returned to Spain to found a noble line and receive Christian burial. Bradomín's lament that the spiritual heirs of the conquistador today have no choice but to become bandits could also be read backwards as a statement that yesterday's heroes were simply common thieves. The ease with which Bradomín embellishes and justifies his cowardly behavior and the constant references to literary sources within *Sonata de estío* as well as the time lapse between the adventures and their transcription clearly signals the textualization of empire. As Tiffin and Lawson point out (1994), there can be no domination without a narrative to maintain and reinforce it. *Sonata de estío* duplicates the transcription of the early Conquistadors, who often wrote their memoirs at some temporal and physical distance from the events themselves. The novel reveals the dependency on prior narratives, the interjection of personal motives and values, and the facile conflation of history and personal and national myth-making, suggesting to the reader that narratives of conquest by definition follow this pattern.

The relation with the other, as Angelika Bammer points out, runs the risk of phobic rejection or philic absorption. Bammer observes that blind acceptance of the culture and values of the other results in a misunderstanding that equals that produced by absolute denial. Emanuel Levinas proposes as a possible solution to the problematic encounter with the other an ethical commitment, a non-indifference to the other party that privileges neither subject nor object but rather the ethical responsibility of each for the other (1995, 142, 149). Modernist thinkers who struggle to construct a new relation with the former colonies and move beyond a critique of the past confront the same issues posed by Bammer and Levinas and move towards similar resolutions. Américo Castro's "El verdadero Hispano-americanismo" addresses the need for increased understanding between Spanish America and Spain and advocates the introduction of courses on Spanish American history and culture within Spanish universities. Castro focusses primarily on relations between Spain and Argentina and carefully points to factors that join as well as separate the two cultures. He calls for a mutual exchange of scholars, with Spaniards making the pilgrimage to Buenos Aires and Spanish Americans traveling to Spain. He rejects proposals for the establishment of a Spanish American University in Spain to service the increasing number of Spanish Americans studying there, calling for a more integrated approach to the problem. True Spanish-Spanish American encounter requires movement on both sides and Castro urges Spanish Americans to create centers of study within the Spanish university, alongside traditional fields of study rather than in separate universities. The call for Spanish-Argentinean collaboration and the integration of Spanish American studies within established Spanish university curriculum as well as Castro's own visit to Argentina represent a first step towards understanding and ethical commitment to the other.

A narrative exploration of mutual ethical commitment in Spanish-Spanish American relations appears in Azorín's *Doña Inés* (1925). The novel commences in Madrid, then moves to Segovia, and finally Buenos Aires. The narrative connection between Argentina and Spain occurs on various levels and involves different characters who make the transatlantic trip in both directions. In order to explore and advocate a new relation between former colony and colonizer, *Doña Inés* examines new ways of looking and representing. Early scenes borrow from cinematic techniques, beginning with a long shot of a barely distinguishable figure walking down a Madrid street and then changing to a zoom shot that focusses down on a woman followed by a cut to an external view of the same woman in the window of a third floor apartment. A different image of the female figure, now identified as Inés de Silva, appears in a daguerreotype, faded and difficult to discern. Chapter 3 introduces yet another viewing point through the appropriation of stage directions. The narrator describes the apartment living room as if it were a theatrical set and the reader sees only what a theater public would perceive: a barely discernible roof-scape visible beyond the balcony, the red brick floor, a door to the right, two doors to the left, and a lithograph on the wall (1990, 75). The action unfolds as if on stage; the narrator describes Inés's movements in and out of this limited space and compares her gestures to those of an accomplished actress.

The description of the lithograph on the wall also emphasizes changing perspectives. The picture depicts a city on an estuary and is initially described as if viewed from above, on horseback (*perspectiva caballera*). The title inscribed on the frame appears in French and reads *Buenos Aires. Vue prise a vol d'oiseau,* but when Inés reads it to herself, she decodes the title into Spanish, *Buenos Aires a vista de pájaro.* Each of these three readings, in two languages and with slight variation in the two Spanish versions, introduces a change and each time Inés reads the title, the intervening time produces a barely noticeable but changed perception. The modernist conception of time focusses on its effects on the observer, the object observed, and their interconnections, as apparent in the daguerreotype and in Inés's self-examination in the mirror. As she checks the tautness of her neck skin and the aging of her body, she must revise her self-image, updating it to match a new, changed self. In Segovia, where Inés escapes after her lover don Juan abruptly drops her, the narrator continues to depict a reality that changes even as words attempt to define it. The cathedral tower appears at different hours of the day in a succession of representations that Elena Catena likens to Monet's paintings of the cathedral of Rouen (1990, 93). The description of daybreak slowly records the changing light and gradual displacement of shadows and darkness (1990, 118).

In conjunction with the exploration of new modes of viewing, *Doña Inés* also examines the position of the speaker within time and space and the limitations of vision produced by this location. In the 1840s, when the narrative action takes place, train travel in certain quarters was still a hypothetical possibility with detractors and defenders. The text mentions Marcelino Calero y Portocarrero and his plan for a train line to connect Jerez de la Frontera to Puerto de Santa María, a project that local skeptics ridicule as impossible, with no real advantages over present modes of transportation and with the danger that people would suffocate while traveling through the projected tunnels. The inability to imagine conditions that represent everyday realities at a later date also figures in the mention of the unknown author of a volume of poetry that Diego el de Garcillán, the local poet and Inés's soon-to-be love interest, is currently reading. The poet, identified as Ramón Campeador or maybe Campoamor, represents at the time of the action and in the narrator's estimation just one of many young writers who publish a first book of poetry and then disappear into oblivion. Campoamor, who went on to publish many volumes of poetry, is, of course, widely recognized as the most important poet of the realist period and the narrator's ignorance simple underscores the difficulty of imagining a future as different from the present. This theme receives extensive treatment in chapter 34, where Pablo, Inés's uncle and a writer, relates a dream in which God appears to him and releases a handful of sand into the atmosphere. The clump of sand, as God explains, represents the universe and each grain an entire world. In a novelistic echo of Einstein's theory of relativity, the dream-divinity explains that two or three human seconds represent thousands upon thousands of centuries in a different time frame and further clarifies that the human conception of the world, based on matter, vacuums, movement and inertia, light and darkness, represents only one of many possible systems. Humans assume that all worlds follow the same rules, but there are many ways to structure reality. In contrast with this human vanity and pride, God recommends humility and love of neighbor. He also states that he intends to improve Pablo's health and give him the strength to complete the work he is presently preparing.

The connection between different ways of viewing the world and Pablo's manuscript relates to the shifting narrative perspectives and to the definition of Spanish-Argentinean links in *Doña Inés.* After the early mention of the lithograph of Buenos Aires, no further allusion to Spanish America occurs until chapter 19, where the narrator introduces Diego, who had emigrated to Argentina at the age of 12. There, while his parents worked on a ranch, Diego spent his days reading under the shade of an ombú tree. According to the narrator, the ombú, of African origins, represents the poetic, sentimental tradition of the gauchos and this spirit remains with Diego after he returns to Spain upon the death of his parents. In Segovia, Diego enters into relations with Plácida, a young Segovian woman and friend of Inés. Local opinion assumes they will marry, but Inés's arrival intervenes. In typical Azorinian understatement, the narrator describes a series of chance meetings between Inés and Diego, both of whom feel drawn to solitary, poetic locations. In particular, Inés feels inexplicably attracted to the chapel where her ancestor, Beatriz de Silva, is buried. Pablo's current manuscript relates Beatriz's story, her marriage to Esteban de Silva, her love for a young troubadour, her husband's secret murder of the young lover, and its cruel revelation to his wife by placing the troubadour's hair in a box where she keeps her jewels. After hearing the story and learning that she is the last surviving heir to the de Silva name, Inés becomes increasingly obsessed with a seeming physical and emotional similarity with her ancestor. While visiting the tomb, and meditating on her own loveless life, Inés encounters Diego and succumbs to his passionate kiss. The narration of the ensuing scandal emphasizes the provincial mentality and the intrusion of small-town politics and church power in personal matters. In the end, Inés abandons Segovia and Spain departing for a new life in Argentina after leaving sufficient monies for Diego and Plácida to marry and live comfortably.

Inés's emigration to Latin America signifies an entirely new way of envisioning the world that becomes apparent in the context of a comparison of the two love stories and also the narrative strategies for relating them. The tragic account of Esteban, Beatriz, and the troubadour represents a typical tale of adultery, dishonor, and revenge. Esteban had served as cupbearer to King Enrique IV, Isabel the Catholic's father and a major force in the construction of a united Spain with imperial ambitions. The text describes Esteban as a man of action who would have been a formidable conquistador and founder of empires had he lived just a few years later. Beatriz, aging and ignored by her husband, succumbs to the sensibilities and youth of the troubadour. When she discovers his hair and realizes he has died at her husband's hand, she goes insane, retreating to a country home to live out a short life with an hysterical fear of the sight of hair or anything soft. The male-dominated trio of the Renaissance story gives way to the female dominated triangle of modern times. Inés clearly duplicates the role of Beatriz as the older woman who embarks on one last search for love and Diego bears some resemblance to the troubadour, in terms of age and profession. However, the tragic sixteenth-century tale has a more humane and productive ending in the modernist version. Where her predecessor retreats to the enclosed world of insanity, Inés adopts an active, constructive posture. She recognizes the futility of continued relations with Diego, generously facilitates his marriage to Plácida, and leaves small-minded, provincial Spain to construct a new, more positive legacy in Argentina.[20] The final chapter describes the school she has built on the outskirts of Buenos Aires, where she educates at no cost the children of poor Spanish immigrants. The heir to Esteban de Silva, the would-be conquistador, represents a different kind of traveler to America. It is noteworthy that she does not duplicate the educational methods of earlier missionaries with their connections to colonial ambitions, but rather educates poor Spanish immigrants whose contribution as future Argentineans will come at no cost to Argentine society.

Inés's response to age-old questions of love, social control, and individual destiny represents a new way of looking at the world and at human relations and the narrative contributes to the reader's reeducation through its own exploration of new modes of viewing and narrating. In addition to the collage of techniques borrowed from cinema and theater, *Doña Inés* reworks and disrupts the legacy of the male gaze. The early chapters and the use of the long shot, close-up, and dramatic scene with Inés at center stage do little to break with traditional formats for female representation. The slow description of Inés in bed examining her body for signs of aging that appears in chapter 7 continues a long tradition of male voyeurism. However, later chapters reveal a concerted effort to bring in other, more egalitarian ways of representing female experience. Chapter 25 describes the simultaneous visit of Diego and Inés to the Alcázar, but purposely refuses to name or describe Inés. She literally disappears from the field of vision and the reader's gaze. The reader knows she is present only because the narrator repeats three times in a two-page span that Diego is not alone on the Alcázar terrace. The following chapter narrates the first exchange of meaningful looks between Diego and Inés and although the text postulates a reciprocity of gaze, the language slightly privileges the male over the female gaze. "Diego ha vuelto la cabeza y ha visto a Doña Inés. La mirada del poeta ha quedado clavada en los ojos de la dama; la mirada de la dama se ha posado en los ojos del poeta. . . . Los ojos del poeta no se apartan de la faz de la dama, ni los ojos de la dama del rostro del poeta" [Diego has turned his head and seen Doña Inés. The poet's gaze stayed riveted on the lady's eyes; the lady's gaze settled on the poet's eyes. . . . The poet's eyes do not move from the lady's face nor do the lady's eyes move from the poet's visage"] (1990, 142). The use of the verb *clavar,* with its connections to iron and ability to penetrate strong materials, invests Diego's look with more power than the gentler *posar,* used to describe that of Inés. In addition, the prior placement of the description of Diego's gaze introduces a scant but still evident hierarchy of value.

The parity between the two and the egalitarian mode of envisioning them succeeds more completely in the next two chapters. Chapters 27 and 28 have nearly identical titles, "Obsesión (Ella)" and "Obsesión (El)." On this occasion, Inés's depiction comes first and parallels almost completely that of Diego. Both characters contemplate the advancing dusk from their respective rooms and both view the evening star while imagining a desired kiss. The narration of Inés's dream refers to the star as Hesperus while in the chapter on Diego, it is called Véspero and also Venus. Traces of the traditional gaze remain in that Inés reclines on a couch while viewing the skies whereas Diego sits at a desk, distracted from his reading. In keeping with contemporary sexual morals, in both chapters Diego's lips initiate the kiss. However, the division of the action into two simultaneous scenes in which an outside viewer observes with equal intimacy the female and male characters, who both engage in dreamy meditation, represents a significant equalizing of the object of the gaze and an effort to develop narrative techniques that allow for such parity.

The description of Inés's departure continues to disrupt traditional representations of women. In the narration of the scandal and the hypocritical response of local authorities, Inés's figure is totally absent, with the action focalized through her uncle, aunt, and other characters. The relation of Inés's decision to depart cedes the textual authority entirely to her, structuring the chapter as a letter from Inés to her uncle. The description of the steamer's departure barely mentions her, focussing on the view of the harbor as seen from the neighboring hillside and on the overall picture of the activity in the port. The final chapter moves forward temporally to find Inés in Argentina, an old, fragile woman who watches her young charges from behind closed windows and waves at them through the glass. This placement parodies traditional images of women in two senses. The old woman framed by the window as in a painting is neither the object of desire nor the passive recipient of the gaze.[21] She actively provokes the children's gaze by knocking on the window and blows them kisses in an act of generosity and love that carries forward the philanthropic vigor of her life's work. Secondly, the filial love and appreciation of the children who look up at her inflect the reader's gaze with a sense of admiration that valorizes ethical commitment over physical beauty and sexual desire.

The novel's final lines introduce another figure whose presence speaks to the ethics of heteronomy that Levinas views as key to equal treatment of the other.[22] The narrator suggests the possible presence of a young boy holding a book under the ombú tree in the garden. Critics of this and other Azorinian texts view this kind of circularity as evidence of a temporal paralysis that reflects his disbelief in the possibilities of change.[23] I will deal with this issue more fully when discussing modernist reconceptualizations of time in the next chapter. For the present, I will argue that the discrepancies between the stories of Beatriz and Inés, the emphasis on novel modes of seeing, and the representation of America as a new world, in contrast to a traditional and socially rigid Europe, all communicate a very real faith in human capacity for change. The insinuated presence of the young reader continues non-hierarchical modes of thinking on several levels. The narrator's refusal to confirm the boy's existence abjures authoritative discourse and invites the reader to imagine new ways of seeing and narrating. The open-ended non-conclusion suggests a continuation of the story, with new characters, either in America or with a possible return to Europe. In a new relationship between Spain and her former colony, traffic flows in multiple directions, with reciprocal influences and contributions. In Azorín and in other writers, the new way of envisioning Spanish-Spanish American relations requires the repudiation of a colonial legacy and the patriarchal, theocratic, hierarchical structures that enabled and accompanied the creation and textualization of imperial Spain.

Spain and Europe: Geopolitical and "Racial" Divisions

The desire for dialogic relations with Latin America and the shared resentment of United States territorial and economic expansion to the South as well as the renunciation of a militaristic, imperial past necessarily accompany a renegotiation of Spanish relations with other European nations. Long-standing visions of Spain as other and internal Spanish debate on the merits of increased European contact acquire new complexity as Spanish modernist writers struggle to throw off a self-destructive tradition of insularity while simultaneously rejecting an aggressive, colonizing European model as inappropriate to post-imperial Spain. The construction of a relation of mutual exchange and even Latin American leadership in the Spanish social imaginary provides an important alternative to traditional definitions of Spanish national identity, but the proximity and power of Europe demand a full consideration of the past and future role of Spain within the continent. Not surprisingly, Spanish modernist rejection of militarism and imperialism leads to condemnation of European foreign policy during this period. In the 1890s and early 1900s, Spanish writers focus their criticism primarily on European empire building in Africa and Asia, but in the pre-World War I years and during the war itself, attention shifts to the issue of military aggression within Europe, its relations to imperial expansion, and the question of European identity. The on-going re-evaluation of European culture enters into dynamic interplay with Spanish national identity (re)formation and follows a complex pattern of assimilation, rejection, and dialogic interaction. Spanish anti-imperialists occupy a tenuous position, in that criticism of European expansion could easily be interpreted as the suspect whining of a thoroughly trounced former contender. Changing relations with Europe affect Spanish self-perceptions in terms of racial and cultural composition and profoundly inflect the vision of past and future Spanish participation in international affairs.

Opposition to European Imperial Expansion

Spanish writers of many different political orientations decry European imperialist expansion. Pi y Margall contrasts the liberation of Latin America with the carving up of Africa and laments the passing of the imperial virus from England to the United States (1901, 8). In his published letters, Ganivet denies any noble motives to Belgium's conquest of the Congo, in which he sees crass commercialism, thinly disguised under a rhetoric of philanthropy, and petty ambition among career military officers, who see service in the Congo as a quick road to promotion (1946–48, 2:832). Eugenio d'Ors also pokes fun at Belgian justifications of the appropriation of the Congo in *Glosas* (1920, 114) and Maragall publishes several articles in the late 1890s in which he critiques imperial expansion. Baroja condemns European imperialism and its effects on both colonizer and colonized in a number of novels. *La ciudad de la niebla* (1909) describes the enormous wealth that passes through the port of London and alludes to the avarice that drives the colonial enterprise through the negative comments of Iturrioz and the portrayal of the huge cranes used to unload incoming cargo as having iron claws that enter into the belly of the ships and come out with their prey (1946–1948, 2:363). The language of the hunt and the novel's depiction of exploited foreign and British workers reveal the dark underside of colonial wealth. *Los últimos románticos* (1906) and *Las tragedias grotescas* (1907) portray the corruption of imperial Paris of Napoleon III. In all three novels, the rapacious and unscrupulous exploitation of foreign and domestic subjects is contrasted with the at times ineffectual, but clearly more ethical, non-exploitative stance adopted by the Spanish protagonists, María Aracil and Fausto Bengoa.

The multi-voiced repudiation of European imperialism receives strong expression in *Paradox, rey* (1906), Baroja's parody of the scramble for Africa. The text describes an international expedition to establish a colony in the fictional African region of Cananí. After a series of organizational disasters, remnants of the group arrive in a different area, suffer imprisonment, become allies of a local tribe, establish a settlement, begin to build a new culture, and then see their work destroyed by newly-arrived

French forces. The dialogue format employed in the text replaces the stable narrative perspective of the classic adventure story and the use of exaggerated and jerky gestures, abrupt transitions from one scene to another, contradictory statements, and a melange of grotesque characters all contribute to a sense of absurdity and irreality. The text continuously satirizes the colonial enterprise and reveals the barbarity that resides within "civilizing" cultures. A Spanish doctor and a Latin American general take pleasure in forcing alcohol down a rooster's throat. In contrast to the drunken general, who falls off his horse and expresses a need to vomit, a serene and dignified Moroccan shepherd appears content and in harmony with his surroundings. *Paradox, rey* does not, however, generally idealize nor exoticize native Africans.[24] The mandingo tribe of Uganga that captures Paradox and his colleagues has a tyrannical king who enjoys watching human sacrifice, an ambitious religious ruler who conspires to amass power and money, and a class system that forces the lower classes to work for the benefit of the aristocracy, priests, army, and royal family. The clear connection to traditional European and, in particular, Spanish society introduces a double voicing that eludes the trap of exoticism as well as racial othering.

Paradox, rey rejects the grand narratives of modern European culture and adopts a strong antifoundational stance.[25] In drafting a political structure for the settlement, different expedition members argue for various forms, including monarchy, republic, democracy, and socialist dictatorship. In regard to religion, the differences prove even greater, with advocates of deism, Anglicanism, Presbyterianism, Catholicism, paganism, Mohammedism and even a local Mandingo leader who believes in manure balls, in keeping with ancestral beliefs. The final system adopted in Bu-Tata represents an idiosyncratic synthesis and although the farcical, parodic tenor undermines attempts to interpret a coherent ideology behind the multiple voices, certain values and goals remain constant across the text and contrast with those introduced by the French army in the final chapters. The use of dialogue allows for the expression of difference and introduction of multiple, contradictory ideas. The co-presence of diverse, transmuting positions receives positive value and stands in opposition to overarching systems. Paradox in both name and actions incarnates variability and transformation over rigidity and coherence. He refuses to adopt an immutable stance and in dialogue with his companions and with changing circumstances and peoples with which he interacts, continually reshapes his ideas and values. The members of the expedition represent a multinational group that communicates across linguistic and cultural differences to construct a temporary and highly unusual culture based on a mobile conception of value and good. In addition to British, German, French, Spanish, Latin American, and Italian members, the Moroccan Hachi Omar and the mandingo Ugú participate in discussions of tactics and social organization. Paradox argues against imposing European standards of government on African cultures (1946–48, 2:208) and Sipsom acknowledges the relative standards of beauty when bribing the locals with promises of dark-skinned, snub-nosed, and sagging-breasted women.[26]

The arrival of the French army introduces an opposing vision that imposes a single, imperial language and disallows the continuation of multiple values. When Paradox and the international group of settlers appear as prisoners before the French colonel, the Frenchman treats them well primarily due to the presence of La Môme Fromage, a French expedition member and former dancer at the Moulin Rouge. Bagú, the African shaman, survived under Paradox's reign, but his attempts to speak to the French military leader provoke a dismissive command for his immediate execution. The final three chapters of the text communicate the consolidation of French colonial power and unfold in monologic or very limited dialogic form. Chapter 10 reproduces the speech given to the French Parliament by the Minister of War, in which he reads a communiqué from the leader of the colonizing expedition. Both the speech and the dispatch constitute one-way communications that allow only for an affirmative, congratulatory response. The following chapter transcribes the conversation between a French doctor and his French assistant, who comment indifferently on the deteriorating health of locals they deem primitive and alien. The final chapter incorporates a newspaper report of a French priest's sermon, given in Bu-Tata, in which he praises the French army and thanks God for the arrival of civilization in Uganga (1946–48, 2:226). This monologic imposition of European colonization in Africa and enunciation of grand narratives and foundationalist systems of belief contrasts with the spirit and structure of *Paradox, rey.* Although the text offers little in the way of concrete alternatives, it proposes a transnational, transcultural approach to human interaction and in its harsh rejection of the past, it carries forward the promise of the cyclops, who offers his own monologue in a Chapter entitled "Elogio metafísico de la destrucción":

"Destruir es cambiar; nada más. En la destrucción está la necesidad de la creación. En la destrucción está el pensamiento de lo que anhela llegar a ser" [To destroy is to change, nothing more. In destruction is the necessity of creation. In destruction lies the idea of what desires to be] (1946–48, 2:203). This very clearly does not refer to the destruction of Bu-Tata and African culture as depicted in the final chapters, but rather to the annihilation of the textualization of empire in the classic texts of Robinson Crusoe, Rudyard Kipling, and others. Parody, dialogue, satire, lyrical interludes, and the heteroglot simultaneity of multiple text types, languages, and discourses counterbalance the old fictions and grand narratives with a more modest, multi-voiced, ever-changing text that stakes out a new, developing sociosymbolic system.

Jacinto Benavente also studies European expansion in Africa in his 1904 play, *El dragón de fuego*. The action takes place in the fictionalized African land of Nirván, where fertile soil and gold have attracted various European powers. Nirván's geographic description suggests a South African referent and the various European powers appear to represent Germany (Suavia), France (Franconia) and England (Silandia). The dramatic action develops in a complex play of fraternal rivalries between two African brothers and chiefs, local African differences of opinion regarding possibilities for independence over colonial domination, and European competition for African resources beneath a rhetoric of legal, moral, and religious entitlement. The delicate balance of European power and the use of such trappings of modernity as the telegraph, newspaper, and public relations to maintain the illusion of legality receive major emphasis in the play. Silandia cannot outright expropriate Nirván for fear of alienating other powers and consequently, has to resort to behind-the-scenes maneuvers that mask the capitalist, nationalist, and militarist motives just enough to avoid diplomatic crisis. After grooming Prince Duraní to serve as titular head of Nirván, Silandia allows him to be killed by local insurgents when his enemies blind him and thus make him ineligible to reign according to local custom.[27] His brother, Prince Dani-Sar, who originally supported a Silandian protectorate as a middle ground between occupation and a now impossible independence, ultimately finds himself prisoner in Silandia, whose government works actively to provoke African insurrection in order to justify full colonial occupation of the country and the ensuing "civilizing" of the inhabitants. To this end, Silandian politicians convince an ailing and drugged Dani-Sar to return to his homeland, where he will be killed and Silandian control of the country will receive diplomatic sanction. *El dragón de fuego* reveals the intimate relationship between the scramble for Africa and tensions within Europe. Imperial expansion continually threatened the balance of power and endangered not just colonized peoples, but also citizens of colonizing countries. The crisis hinted at in *El dragón del fuego* explodes a decade later, with the outbreak of World War I. Spanish modernist reaction to the conflict reflects ongoing concerns with militarism, imperialism, and alternative approaches to international relations.

Spanish Modernist Response to World War I

Spanish reaction to the war responds to a complex interplay of factors, including traditional animosities and affinities as well as the role of Spanish-European relations in Spain's national reconstruction. In general, the Spanish left support the Allied cause while the aristocracy, the Church, and the right back Germany and the Central Powers. Critics often divide Spanish writers of the day into the same two groups, listing Baroja, Benavente, and Eugenio d'Ors as proponents of Germany and Austria and Valle-Inclán, Blasco Ibáñez, Ortega and his followers as supporters of the Allied forces.[28] However, texts dealing with the war belie an easy classification into two distinct camps, revealing instead a persistent rejection of militarism and unilateral perspectives. The same turning coin that characterizes other aspects of Spanish modernism continues in the examination of the European conflict.[29] Many Spanish modernists view the war as an extension of imperialist ambitions and, to a large extent, Spanish neutrality during the conflict reflects her minimal participation in the scramble for Africa and neo-colonial enterprises. Several writers interject pacifist messages in works that take place in other historical periods, but have a clear resonance in the atmosphere of European conflict. Galdós's *Sor Simona* (1915) transpires during the nineteenth-century Spanish Carlist war, but the theater-going public of the day would certainly relate the protagonist's anti-war message to contemporary events. In Galdós's play and in the 1914 publication of Eduardo Marquina's *En Flandes se ha puesto el sol,* a strong female character enunciates opposition to war, joining new visions of gender and nation. A well-known exception to a generally conflicted vision of the war is found in Blasco Ibáñez, who once again discloses a predilection for absolutist thinking and realist narration. His *Cuatro jinetes del Apocalipsis,* published in 1916 and made into a movie starring Rudolph Valentino in 1921, declares unwavering support for the Allied cause. The novel falls into simplistic characterizations of blonde, barbaric Germans who exalt war, proclaim Germanic superiority and combine homosexual inclinations, a refined love of music, and callous cruelty (1961, 3:281). The French, in contrast, display no interest in territorial expansion and exemplify democratic equality and noble purpose in battle. The one modernist note in the narrative surfaces in the depiction of Latin America as a place of hope where anachronistic European conflicts are surpassed through cohabitation and intermarriage of peoples who in other times and places had been bitter enemies. However, since the novel opens in Latin America and closes in Europe, with the division of the multinational, multilingual family that had formed in Latin America, bellicose enthusiasm erases the message of cross-cultural understanding.

Other Spanish writers generally considered to support the Allied Forces continue the disgust at diplomatic machinations observed in Benavente's *El dragón de fuego.* Although Unamuno laments Spanish indifference to the conflict and condemns support for German imperialism in his 1917 "La soledad de la España castellana" (1958, vol. 4), in other essays he expresses revulsion at what he calls the games of old European midwives. In 1913, he describes Japan's militarism and the barbarous fighting during the Mexican revolution as the unfortunate creation of a European system of values ("Voces de Europa," 1958, 3:137). Valle-Inclán relates his visit to the front in *La media noche: visión estelar de un momento de guerra* (1917). In complete contrast with Blasco Ibáñez and his attempt to reconstruct a panoramic vision of the war, in keeping with totalizing realist aspirations, Valle-Inclán adopts in the title and throughout the narrative a limited, mediated perspective. The text aims merely to capture a single moment of the war and openly recognizes that every observer and participant enjoys a unique but partial vision: "Todos los relatos están limitados por la posición geométrica del narrador" [All accounts are limited by the geometric position of the narrator] (6). The soldier in the trenches and the general who oversees the battle plan each have a particular view and neither cancels nor invalidates the other. Utilizing a shifting and fragmented focalization, the narration constructs a collage that includes scenes of pathos, gore, wonder, terror, lyricism, and tragedy. *La media noche* interlaces grotesque, parodic strategies of the "esperpento" with classical epic and tragic depictions to present a vision of World War I that frustrates attempts to create a meaningful whole. A poetic description of the sky precedes a horrendous depiction of rat-filled trenches. A destructive but cruelly effective modern technology, with bombs and planes contributing to new, more potent devastation, contrasts with a disrupted modernity, in which cut telephone lines impede communication and dogs must relay messages. The narrator employs at times a notably simplified prose, imitating telegraphic communications in the use of short sentences and brief chapters and seeking effect through the sheer impact of the events. Alternately, poetic metaphors punctuate horrific descriptions, forcing the reader to adopt ever-changing relations with the text.

The war, with the constant proximity of death, also enables a certain liberation from and transcendence of this final moment. When bloated and rotting German cadavers fill the French coastal waters and approach the shore and then recede with the changing tides, local fishermen gain permission to put sails on the corpses so they will head out to sea. After this operation, a young sailor yells in his Celtic language that he no longer fears the dead, conquering superstitions that have long characterized his people. The ability to look beyond war and death, to see the other side of what appear to be absolute limits, typifies the Spanish modernist vision and precludes a stable, unwavering declaration of support for either Allied or Central powers. *La media noche* continually undermines the validity of a single viewpoint with allusions to its contrary. It articulates accusations of German barbarity through French and British spokespersons and then turns the charges back on the speakers. A French doctor, discussing the rape of young French sisters, links the Germans and primitive, presumably non-European peoples and fortifies this claim by insisting on German hatred of classical culture. In a similar vein, a British general and veteran of colonial wars accuses German soldiers of breaking the rules of war by asking for a truce and then attacking. However, Allied claims to greater civility and closer ties with Western tradition break down as the text underscores the Allied use of Indian cavalrymen with their turbaned heads, native swords, and tradition of taking no prisoners. The distinction between East and West, barbaric and civilized, in turn gives way when the British general who accused Germany of breaking the war code declares that the Allied forces will henceforth give no quarter and impose the same punishment on the Germans that the British had so often applied in colonial campaigns in Africa and Oceania (1917, 106).

José Ortega y Gasset also displays divided and contradictory loyalties during World War I. His admiration for German culture, clearly and forcefully argued in *Meditaciones del Quijote,* contrasts with his measured rejection of such German justifications of the war as Max Scheler's *Der Genius des Krieges und der deutsche Krieg.* Pío Baroja expresses identical sentiments, declaring his Germanophilia in terms of culture and philosophy, but condemning the German invasion of Belgium and German conduct in the war. Despite the critical tendency to identify Ortega as a supporter of the Allied Forces and Baroja as a defender of Germany and the Central powers, their expressed views differ little in terms of overall admiration for German culture and criticism of German aggression. Their differences surface more clearly regarding the ethics of imperialism and its relation to the present conflict. Ortega tacitly acknowledges the right of civilized nations to impose their rule on less advanced societies and condemns German expansion not out of philosophical opposition to aggression, but owing to the lack of a clearly developed legal system and philosophy of law (1965, 2:223). By contrast, he argues that British wars and domination have typically brought progress, human rights, and freedoms to the conquered peoples (223). This Eurocentric, imperialist reasoning contrasts with Baroja's more forceful rejection of the right of one country to take over another. Accordingly, the Barojan text states that German occupation of Belgium clearly violates international law and human rights. On the other hand, the Barojan text speaker finds French and English appropriation of India, Egypt, Indochina, Algeria, Morocco, New Zealand and other areas equally unjustified (1946–48, 5:140). Baroja's writings on the war refuse to support either side, despite clear sympathies for German cultural achievements. Baroja insists that he supports German culture for reasons that differ radically from those prompting conservative Spanish advocacy of the Central Powers. Spanish Catholic legitimists and ultraconservatives admire German militarism and discipline and despise France, because of its anticlerical traditions and separation of Church and State. Baroja admires Kant, Fichte, Heine, Beethoven and abhors the militarism, authoritarianism, and imperialist ambition that the right associates with Germany.

The insistence on questioning existing dichotomies and on crossing World War I battle lines also appears in the work of Sofía Casanova, a Spanish writer married to a Pole and residing in Warsaw. *De la guerra: Crónica de Polonia y Rusia* describes her experiences during the war and her opposition to the violence. As a foreign observer, Casanova seeks to find some ray of truth among the muddled versions she reads in the press and hears from the soldiers she attends as a hospital volunteer. Her war chronicle addresses a Spanish audience and appears in the Madrid paper *ABC* over the course of two years. Casanova is considered a conservative Catholic and accordingly, her loyalties would be expected to lie with the Germans. However, once again, established categories break down. She rejects both the Russians and the Germans who have fought to control the Polish peoples and her writing seeks to dissuade Spanish Catholics from supporting Germany. Casanova claims the role of peacemaker for women and underscores opportunities for reconciliation, as when stressing the ease with which prisoners of war forget their hostility and establish friendships with wounded enemy soldiers when both are confined in a common space. In narrating the evacuation of Warsaw and her relocation in Russia, Casanova's attempts to understand the Russians reveal her conservative biases and her preference for a Europeanized Russian aristocracy over what she sees as the fatalistic, passive, unpredictable, Asiatic lower classes. Although her prejudices predispose her to a phobic rejection of the Russian lower classes, Casanova struggles to overcome the hatred that Polish friends and family have inculcated in her. Her opposition to war in general, approval of Spanish neutrality, rejection of imperial expansion, and defense of Polish rights to self-determination contribute to a nonbelligerent stance that strives to maintain an open, dialogic relation with the other.

Racial Theory and the Relationship with Europe

The dilemma facing Baroja, Ortega y Gasset, Valle-Inclán, Casanova, and others writing on World War I relates to the more general issue of Spanish relations with Europe and to the question of which European tradition, if any, Spain should claim as her own. Historical debates regarding the racial composition of Europe, its membership, and future direction take on new stridency and urgency during this period. The growing power of Germany and Russia in the nineteenth and early twentieth centuries requires a revision of perceptions of modern European cultural and military hegemony as concentrated on the Western boundaries of the continent. Theories of racial superiority, of Aryan, Semitic, Slavic, and Latin identity, multiply in the prewar years and culminate in justifications of territorial expansion. The European struggle for self-definition intersects with Spanish endeavors for national reconstruction in a complex and fluid dynamic. Spanish modernists differ considerably in their response to this exchange, but they share a commitment to open Spain to the outside. In contrast with traditionalist desires to close Spain off and protect the remnants of a once glorious past, modernists aspire to change and dialogue through contact with the outside, but they differ considerably regarding which "outside" best facilitates the national transformation they seek. This reading of early twentieth-century Spanish culture departs substantially from traditional interpretations. Definitions of Spanish *modernismo* that emphasize a depoliticized and escapist cosmopolitanism as well as visions of a "Generation of 1898" that retreats to an exaltation of Castilian landscape and protofascist racialisms theorize an isolationism that continues rather than breaks with the past. Generational approaches that seek to stake out a clear difference between Ortega y Gasset and slightly earlier writers such as Unamuno, Baroja, Azorín, and Machado, emphasize Ortega y Gasset's calls for Europeanization and contrast them with a rejection of Europe among his predecessors.[30] Such a reading oversimplifies the cultural landscape of early twentieth-century Spain. The differences between Ortega and Unamuno are no greater than those of Unamuno and his "contemporary" Baroja or of Ortega and his "contemporaries" Pérez de Ayala or Miró. In addition, allegations of rejection of European culture by such writers as Baroja, Machado, and Unamuno fail to recognize the complex nature of their relations with Europe and the persistence of their search for a dialogue across borders, at times European but on other occasions African, Latin American, or other non-Western entities.

Efforts to bring Spain more in line with European standards of living and thought originate in the eighteenth century and follow an uneven development in succeeding years, with alternating periods of openness and insularity. As Inman Fox has argued, Krausists and Institutionists ardently seek greater contact with European thought and culture, which they perceive as key to Spanish modernization. Traditionalists such as Pereda, Coloma, and Balart exalt a pure Spain that eschews contact with the world beyond its borders. Balart's "Salutación" (1893) invokes Asturias as the place of origin of the Reconquest and the essence of the nation precisely because no foreign presence ever adulterated its soil (1929, vol. 2). Leopoldo Alas (Clarín) parodies this vision in *Doña Berta* (1892), where the family of the protagonist has lived in stubborn isolation in Asturian lands on which neither Roman nor Moor set foot. In other texts that deal with European contact, Alas reveals a certain ambivalence that reflects a generalized attitude among some of those who seek to end traditional isolation. Various essays in *Ensayos y revistas* (1892) reflect Alas's wavering and also reveal the causes of his ambivalence. Spanish communication with Europe traditionally passed through France, and French cultural and political hegemony in the eighteenth and nineteenth centuries produced both admiration and animosity among diverse sectors of Spanish society. Spaniards perceived disinterest and ignorance of Spanish culture among French intellectuals and tourists, and although they observed a similar lack of knowledge among other European peoples, for reasons of historical animosity and geographic proximity, they particularly resented French cultural stereotyping of Spain. Since much European culture arrived filtered through French publications and translations, advocates of increased contact with Europe often balanced calls for openness with cautionary remarks regarding French cultural bias. Clarín abhors French naturalism and condemns its Spanish adherents. In his final years, he advocates a literature and philosophy that transcend the purely physical and to this end, his "Ibsen y Daudet" (1892) aims to bring the Spanish reader into contact with newer literary currents that might displace naturalism and philosophical determinism. In the same essay, he remarks that the French confuse Spaniards with Arabs or Italians, expressing a common complaint of Spanish writers and a continuing cause for concern among those who desire European influence, but also perceive its dangers.

Many writers of the period repeat charges of French insularity. In *La feria de los discretos* (1905), Pío Baroja includes a French teacher of Spanish whose professional preparation proves useless in erasing stereotypes of smoking Spanish women, permanently affixed to their balconies, as propagated by the literature of Théophile Gautier. On seeing young Cordoban women behind the iron grates, he assumes they are members of harems (1946–48, 1:659). Many Spanish modernist publications include essays describing fantastic, stereotypical perceptions of Spain in works of French and other foreign writers. Alejandro Sawa refutes the image of a happy Andalusia, as perpetrated by Dumas and Gautier, and supports instead the bleak portraits of Emilio Verhaeren, the Belgian who collaborated with Darío de Regoyos to present a gloomy, tragic Andalusian people (1903, 573).[31] Manuel Machado writes of a Parisian woman whose knowledge of Spain comes from Gautier, Dumas, and Bizet and leads her to insist that Spanish women have no rights and live only to love and die (1904, 32). *El Nuevo Mercurio* includes a running section on European criticism of Spanish art and letters, and individual articles by the French writer Paul Adam on his impressions of Spain, a translation of L. F. Sauvage's short story about Spanish love, in which kisses always accompany blood and dirt, and a survey of various French authors who have written on Spain, querying them on their knowledge of the Spanish language and the time they spent visiting the country about which they have written ("¿Conoce Ud. España?").

As more middle and upper-class Spanish tourists expand their journeys from the traditional pilgrimage to Rome or Paris to include England, Germany, Russia, and other European areas, writers become increasingly aware of the extent to which French propaganda conditions foreign impressions of Spain. Sofía Casanova and Carmen de Burgos both travel extensively in Europe and lament the ignorance about Spanish culture and the perpetration of traditional misconceptions that they confront in their journeys. Casanova relates a dinner party conversation with Sir Henry Stanley in London at which the African explorer remarks that there is more culture in Equatorial Africa than in Spain. His wife continues the attack, insisting that Spanish women carry knives, despite Casanova's attempts to correct her (1910). Carmen de Burgos describes with tolerant good humor how German and American tourists in Naples ask if there are trains in Spain while another presumes a good knowledge of the country based on a visit to Morocco (1909?, 236). *Revista Nueva* publishes a translation of Dr. Hans Parlow's study of Spanish literature that previously appeared in Paris in the *Revue Encyclopedique*. Parlow states that six or eight weeks suffices to read all of Spanish literature because the literacy rate is so low that not much is written. Spanish recognition of European ignorance and bias concerning Spanish history and culture compounds the difficulties facing those who advocate a greater openness to European thinking and contributes to an ambivalent relationship with Europe.

Arguments favoring Aryan superiority and European cultural preeminence serve to justify imperialist expansion by German, British, and other groups who appropriate dubious but politically useful racial classification systems. The geographic shrinkage of the Spanish empire at the same time that the rest of Europe expands its control of the globe complicates the issue of Spanish membership in the European community. Spain's weakness and loss of empire challenges theories of superior European culture and the peninsula's multiethnic history provides an easy explanation for her anomalous development. Some Spanish writers address this issue by negating Jewish-Arabic influence in Spanish cultural formation. Traditional versions of Spanish national composition emphasize racial homogeneity, tracing the national foundations to Pelayo and his band of Visigoths who initiate the long campaign to expel the Moors. Proponents of this view extol Ferdinand and Isabel as representatives of the true origins of Spanish identity and defend the Inquisition and the expulsion of the *moriscos* and Sephardic Jews as a necessary consolidation of Spanish ethnic, religious, and political homogeneity. Restoration thinkers, such as Menéndez y Pelayo and Valera, vigorously defend this version of Spanish history.

Valera's writings on Spain follow the racist pattern previously observed in his reading of Latin American culture. "Con motivo de las novelas rusas" manipulates the ambiguous meaning of the term Aryan to include Spain. The text speaker rejects Pardo Bazán's praise of Russian literature and denies that European culture is on the wane. Russian achievements awaken a deep fear of the growing power of non-European peoples and accordingly, Valera seeks to classify Spain as one with other Christian, Aryan nations in contrast to this new giant with ties to Asia. "A lo que me opongo, lo que no quiero es que este porvenir sea a costa nuestra; implica la muerte o el mutismo de las demás naciones cristianas, arianas, europeas o descendientes de Europe" [What I oppose, what I do not want is that this future occur at our expense; that it imply the death or silence of the remaining Christian, Aryan, European, or heirs of European nations] (1941, 2:798). The emphasis on Spain as Aryan clearly attempts to counteract foreign or domestic claims of Arabic influence in Spanish culture. "Antología de poetas líricos italianos" denies any real Arab role in the construction of Spanish culture, suggesting a pre-Latin, Aryan base that persists through and beyond African occupation. Valera's insistence on a pan-Latin culture also serves to place Spain within a purely European heritage. He praises the Hellenic-Latin Society (1941, 2:1902) and insists that Rome is the greatest city that ever existed, just as Europe perpetuates the greatest civilization of all time. Spain, Italy, and France represent Latin culture, with Spain and Italy more truly Latin than France ("La poesía lírica italiana").

Theories of a pan-Latin cultural community surface in opposition to hypotheses of pan-Germanic identity and seek to refute arrogations of northern European superiority. Rather than debate a European versus non-European differentiation, pan-Latinists and their antagonists focus on different traditions within Europe and seek to establish Spain's connection with the tradition that in their view best confirms Spanish membership in a vital European community. Eugenio d'Ors labors to reconcile admiration for German cultural contributions with opposition to German militarism and at the same time, to establish a link between Latin and Germanic cultures. Like Baroja, he distances his support for German culture from that of the Spanish right and strives to bring the Spanish reader into greater sympathy with what he considers a model for Spanish culture. His *Cartas a Tina* (1914) adopt an epistolary structure that privileges dialogue and transcultural exchange. The interaction between the young female German addressee and older Spanish speaker structures a consideration of World War I and its consequences for a rapprochement between Germanic and Mediterranean cultures.

D'Ors believes strongly in the unity and value of European civilization and the war challenges this belief. His support for Germany is rooted in a desire to break with the French rationalist tradition and to link Spain with a different, richer philosophical and cultural heritage. Although he decries the German destruction of Louvain, he reserves his harshest criticism for the French use of Senegalese troops and for France's alliances with other non-European nations, such as Russia, Japan, and the Senegalese. He even resents French affiliation with England, a land he considers feudal and external to European identity. Notwithstanding his antipathy for France and her traditions, d'Ors works against dichotomous divisions that could easily ensue from the war and divide Germany or Europe into opposing camps. *Cartas a Tina* refuses to accept the view of two Germanies, one bellicose and expansionary and the other philosophical, humanitarian, and pacific. It also spurns arguments that depict classical and Germanic culture or Latin and Germanic traditions as opposed and mutually exclusive. Instead, it advocates a complex definition of culture that links opposites and evolves dynamically towards ever new combinations. Saint Augustine, Giambattista Vico, and especially the painter Raphael represent for d'Ors the transcendence of separate cultural legacies. Augustine's uneasy coalescence of African and Greek thought gives way to Vico's more comfortable amalgamation of the ideal and the real in a pre-Kantian meeting of Mediterranean and Germanic propensities. And finally, Raphael surpasses both to integrate Tuscan, Latin, and Hellenic tradition and bring together such presumed opposites as poetry and practicality, art and law, figure and norm (123–30).

This integration of multiple traditions does not take the form of a harmonious, stable culmination in Orsian analysis. To the contrary, he states that Raphael transcends these oppositions by way of a smile. He then abandons the subject until later in the text, when he clarifies the meaning of this cryptic declaration. D'Ors had an abiding interest in Zeno, having written a doctoral dissertation on the Greek philosopher's observations on motion. In *Cartas a Tina* he returns to the subject of his dissertation and refutes those who believe that Zeno denies movement in his famous paradox of the arrow. Rather, according to d'Ors, he denies the rationality of motion, the possibility of its schematization. Defining life as movement and flux, d'Ors argues that no figure, formula, or rational conceptualization fully comprehends its complexity and dynamism. In constant motion, life escapes all efforts to contain it. The rationalist tradition, culminating in Descartes and Neoclassical French culture but with roots in Rome and its emphasis on law, privileges an abstract, schematic representation of life that fails to capture its chaos and perpetual movement. In contrast, Germanic thought emphasizes change and chaos. The integration of these two traditions in such figures as Raphael and a new European order as conceived by d'Ors in the post-war period occurs not through assimilation or synthesis but irony. Raphael's smile represents an on-going, persistent dialectic rather than the culmination of a process: "¡Al diablo la hegeliana dialéctica! 'Tesis, antítesis, síntesis,' una detrás de otra, como pendonistas de procesión. En la vida (y también el pensamiento es vida), cuando la tesis da el primer paso, ya trae la antítesis enredada entre piernas. Y este enredarse furtivo de la antítesis con la tesis, yo no quiero llamarlo síntesis: lo llamo *ironía* sencillamente" [To hell with Hegelian dialectics! "Thesis, antithesis, synthesis," one after the other, like standard bearers in a procession. In life (and thought is also life), when the thesis takes the first step, it already has the antithesis entangled between its legs. And this furtive entangling of the antithesis with the thesis, I refuse to call synthesis: I call it simply *irony*] (1967, 141). Orsian irony builds on Nietzschean philosophy to prefigure Derridian aporia and its insistence on the dynamic co-presence of oppositions. It also echoes Unamuno's calls for a humor that devours and disturbs in his prologue to *Niebla.* D'Ors calls irony the great digester and sees it as the force that facilitates the coming together of Germanic and Mediterranean cultures. It breaks down difference without abolishing it and enables the incorporation of the other without assimilation or erasure.[32]

José Ortega y Gasset and Eugenio d'Ors share a strong appreciation of Germanic culture, a desire to Germanize Spanish society, and a hope for a united Europe. However, Ortega differs from his Catalan colleague in a much greater emphasis on rationality and science, in a stronger rejection of Latin tradition in favor of Greek heritage, and in a more explicit repudiation of Asian and African cultures as inferior and threatening. In a series of essays written between 1906 and 1911, he decries the absence of science in Spanish culture and inculpates a moribund Latin tradition for the lack. "Alemán, latín y griego" recommends a major infusion of German culture and the study of German in Spanish schools in order to revitalize Spain. "La ciencia romántica" depicts Spain as given to extremes, discontinuous and illogical, with a romantic science in contrast to German classical tradition. "Teoría del clasicismo" defines European history as a tension between classicism and romanticism, Ormuzd and Ahriman, good and evil and makes clear a preference for classicism. "Asamblea para el progreso de la ciencia" again equates science with Europe and signals scientific achievement as that which distinguishes Europe from Asia or Africa. Many essays, such as "Unamuno y Europa: Fábula" vociferously call for the Europeanization of Spain. Although Ortega specifically denies African influence in Spanish culture in *España invertebrada,* the suspicion of such a connection lurks just beneath the surface in many of his texts. In a long discussion of Wilhelm Wörringer's book on artistic expression among different ethnic and national groups, the text speaker negates Wörringer's contention that the recently discovered cave paintings of Altamira are identical to contemporary African artistic production and argues that Altamira represents not an African, but a uniquely Mediterranean art form that differs from Indo-European abstraction, classical rationalism, and oriental mysticism ("Arte de este mundo y del otro," 1965,

1:186–205). Mediterranean, alternately referred to as Latin in other texts, receives positive valorization over African cultures, but is viewed as inferior with respect to Germany ("La pedagogía social como programa político," 1965, 1:521).

Ortega y Gasset's erasure of links between Spain and Africa surfaces in various works in which the speaker posits that Mediterranean culture only prevailed briefly before being subsumed by Germanic invasions. Europe, in this view, did not really exist until it was Germanized, at which time, Italy, France, and Spain ceased as Mediterranean entities and acquired a Germanic, European identity.[33] Occasionally, Ortega presents the debate regarding Spanish links to Africa in dialogic form, with two perspectives opposing each other, as in "Al margen del libro *Los iberos*," where the textual I enters into a discussion with Rubín de Cendaya, a pseudonym used by Ortega in some early writings. However, the negation of African ties and the denial of value of African, Asian, and Arab cultures prevails in all but a handful of essays. In contrast to d'Ors, who retains a dialogic structure and privileges irony and instability,[34] Ortega yearns for "classical" clarity and strives to establish a univocal tradition. The difference stands out starkly in their definitions of Mediterranean and Germanic cultures. Whereas d'Ors perceives Latin clarity and Germanic chaos, preferring the latter as a more accurate depiction of life, Ortega inverts the characterization. *Meditaciones del Quijote* (1914) posits a Germanic commitment to profundity in opposition to a Latin culture of surfaces. Mediterranean formal elegance hides a radical imprecision and chaos behind which lurks the Asiatic or African gesture (1990, 130). Ortega disallows the possibility of synthesis or ironic co-presence posited by d'Ors: "No metáis en mis entrañas guerras civiles; no azucéis al ibero que va en mí con sus ásperas, hirsutas pasiones contra el blondo germano, meditativo y sentimental, que alienta en la zona crepuscular de mi alma. Yo aspiro a poner paz entre mis hombres interiores y los empujo hacia una colaboración. Para esto es necesario una jerarquía. Y entre las dos claridades es menester que hagamos la una eminente" [Do not introduce civil wars into my heart; do not incite the Iberian within me with his harsh, wild passions, against the blonde man of Germanic heritage, meditative and sentimental, who breathes in the twilight zone of my soul. I try to make peace with my inner personalities and I urge them toward collaboration. For this a hierarchy is necessary and one of the two types of clarity must be made preeminent] (159).[35]

Ortega's writings of the 1910s follow nineteenth-century German cultural theory in portraying Germanic culture as a direct descendant of Greek civilization in contrast to Mediterranean links to Rome. In the 1920s, the exaltation of Germany diminishes in Ortega y Gasset's writings and the consideration of Greece grows more problematic. "Etica de los griegos" depicts a mysterious, only dimly understood Greece, but with profound effects on European culture. Various Ortegan essays of the same period deny the right of any culture to claim superiority over others, insisting that each society contributes in its peculiar area of expertise ("Las Atlántidas," 1965, vol. 3). However, the repudiation of African, Asian, and increasingly American cultural contributions persists. In "Viaje de España" (1916), he states that Cervantes may well count more in the realm of culture than the entire African continent (1965, 1:530–31). *La rebelión de las masas* (1930) argues the superiority of European culture based on its scientific and technological dominance, which neither the Chinese, Asians, Persians, Americans, or Africans possess. His theorization of the historical sense in a number of texts written in the 1920s suggests the superiority of a culture that acknowledges the relativity of its own merits and equates such a recognition of a plurality of value with contemporary European ethnographic studies.[36] Ortega's decidedly Eurocentric stance continues to privilege Greek tradition, gradually downplaying its connection with Germanic culture, but still focussing on a non-Latin, non-African heritage.

Ramón Pérez de Ayala, often cited as Ortega's disciple or fellow traveler, views Europe and its relation to Spain from a different perspective. His short novel, *Prometeo* (1916) traces the link between Greek, Latin, and Spanish culture and underscores both the persistent interweaving of these various traditions and their sterility in the construction of a new Spanish society. The text consists of five chapters, each opening with a short poem that outlines the action to follow. The mixture of prose and poetry introduces a double voicing that grows increasingly complex with the interlacing of numerous discourses including classical epic, educated modern, and popular Asturian. The first chapter commences with allusions to Homer and introduces the protagonist as Odysseus. Although it incorporates some references to modern times and a contemporary narrator, it primarily maintains an epic tone, with invocations of classical muses and intertextual allusions to the *Odyssey.* The shift from the exalted world of the Greek epic to a demythified modern Spain occurs with the introduction of Federica Gómez as the contemporary Calypso. The narrator insists on overlaying epic and modern discourse, continuing to refer to the male protagonist as Odysseus while describing Federica as the aging widow of an *indiano.* Chapter 2 transfers the reader from the duality of ancient Greek/modern Spanish spaces to Italy, with the explanation that this new Odysseus was born in Florence of an Italian mother and Spanish father. After completing course work in literature at the University of Florence and convinced that Italian culture lacked vitality, the hero leaves for Spain, which he imagines as a young, energetic land with a promising future.

In Spain, this modern Odysseus experiences bull fights in Seville, consults wise men in Salamanca, lives the high life in Madrid, and finally takes a position as Greek professor in Asturias. In contrast to traditional representations of Asturias as the site of a racially pure national origin, *Prometeo* depicts it as the final link in a voyage that travels from Greece to Italy and up through Southern Spain. Rather than a beginning, it represents the end of classical European heritage. The tripartite nature of this tradition is represented by the protagonist's three names: Odysseus, Marco de Setiñano, and Juan Pérez Setignano. The Hispanization of the Italian Setignano to Setiñano and the Latinization of the vulgar Spanish Juan Pérez to the more heroic Marco symbolize the intertwining of the two cultures, while the link to Greek recurs in Marco/Juan's aspiration to sire a new Prometheus. Having decided it is too late to achieve personal heroic stature, Juan/Marco determines to raise a son who will accomplish all that he has theorized but not put into practice.

The new heir to the combined Greek, Roman, and Spanish traditions turns out to be physically deformed and mentally perverse. Frustrated in attempts to gain the sexual favors of a young milkmaid, he hangs himself from a fig tree. Prometeo represents the end of multiple traditions that have intermixed and still failed to produce new, productive forms. The tale of Odysseus combines with the myth of Prometheus, but neither the narrative of homecoming nor of creation succeeds. These traditions have run their course and their sterility and that of the new Prometheus stands in stark contrast to the fruit of the fig tree from which he hangs "deforme y liviano como fruto serondo" [deformed and swinging in the air like a sterile fruit] (1964–66, 2:635). *Prometeo* does not suggest a clear alternative to the barren European traditions, although it insinuates several possible options. On the trip from Italy to Spain via Gibraltar, Marco/Juan meets

English explorers and North American businessmen, whom he judges to closely approximate the hero he envisions. However, he ultimately rejects them as too avaricious, carrying forward the anti-imperial, anti-materialist message of other modernist writers and suggesting that Northern (Aryan) cultures prove no more useful as models for future development than their Mediterranean counterparts. In the final chapter, Prometeo attacks two different women, a servant and a milkmaid, and both reject him, possibly implying the power of lower-class women over the degenerate educated heir to Western male narratives, a theme that recurs in other works by Pérez de Ayala. *Prometeo* leaves the reader without a clear vision of a future for European culture and in this sense, departs considerably from Ortega's Eurocentrism. The narrative further distances itself from the philosopher's elitism in the emphasis, through a polyphonic discourse, on culture as multivoiced and multifaceted, a coming together of different social classes, ethnic groups, and national traditions. Returning once more to Eysteinsson's concept of modernism as an oppositional movement that seeks to elaborate a new sociosymbolic system, *Prometeo* rejects hierarchical visions of culture and textualizes a rich, multivoiced discourse that stands as a symbolic substitute to a more static, single-voiced classical tradition.

A number of modernist writers look beyond traditional definitions of Europe, whether Greek, Roman, Mediterranean, or Germanic, to examine other cultures and their potential for reinvigorating Spain. Russia's growing importance in late nineteenth and early twentieth centuries brings renewed attention to this previously marginalized nation. Although Sofía Casanova and Juan Valera both repudiate Russia as an integral part of Europe, sharing with Ortega a definition of the continent that is both limited and homogeneous while still promoting the opening of Spain to some form of European influence,[37] other modernists emphasize Russia's youthful energy and revolutionary vision as an antidote to a tired, stagnant Europe. Pardo Bazán reveals an early interest in Russian culture and promotes its divulgation in Spain as a positive step in recent European cultural developments (*La revolución y la novela en Rusia,* 1887). Carmen de Burgos applauds contemporary Russian revolutionaries and their willingness to sacrifice for future generations in *Por Europa* (1906). At one point, she collapses the distinction between Spain and Russia, referring to "nuestra pobre Rusia española" [our poor Spanish Russia] (140).

Pío Baroja's *El mundo es ansí* (1912) traces the biography of the Russian Sacha Velasco and her attempts to understand the various cultures with which she comes into contact. Sacha's early years transpire in pre-Revolutionary Russia, where multiple forces, social classes, and cultural traditions compete for control of the country. The Russian exile community in Geneva reflects the diversity within Russia itself: Russian Jews, revolutionaries, and middle-class students intermingle with each other and with other European nationalities and ethnicities. The vastness and complexity of Russian society defies any easy classification of its peoples or cultures. Sacha's upper-class father and brother display a brutal, savage nature that coincides with stereotypical views of the Russian peasantry. Russian revolutionaries alternately appear naive and hopelessly idealistic, or enthusiastic, active and poised to establish a new order in comparison with a moribund Western culture (1967, 362). Even Sacha, as a Russian, fails to identify her compatriot Vera, taking her for Swiss Italian.

The various opinions of Russian character and of Spanish, Swiss, Italian, and Jewish culture are mediated in *El mundo es ansí* through different characters. The novel rejects any stable point of view, adopting various formats, including diary, epistolary, third person narration with shifting focalizations, and extended dialogues between characters. The cultures depicted are shown to evade easy characterization and the differences between members of a single national or ethnic group equal or surpass those between individuals of differing national, ethnic, or linguistic identities. Sacha's attempts to understand Spain are thwarted by the variability of individual Spaniards. Juan Velasco, her second husband, and his cousin José Ignacio Arcelu share virtually no common values, tastes, or manners. The unnamed narrator of the first part of the novel also differs considerably from Velasco and when Sacha asks if Velasco or the narrator typify Spaniards, the latter suggests the impossibility of accurately answering such a question.

The difficulty of describing the other matches the difficulty of self-knowledge and the two evolve in a dynamic interplay, continually transforming each other and defying stable, definitive demarcations. *El mundo es ansí* traces this complex dynamic in a modern world that facilitates international travel and brings into intimate contact members of different nations and sexes. Sacha twice marries foreigners and her companions in exile and travel continually meet and become intimate with individuals whom they come to know in a cultural vacuum, stripped of their family connections and cultural roots. Contemporary political, economic, and cultural exigencies contribute to frequent emigrations, and individuals find themselves relocating and reshaping their identities as they interact with multiple others. Sacha discovers that as a result of her contact with other nations and cultures, she no longer feels at home in Russia, now alien in her own land. Toward the middle of the novel, she writes that it is a mistake to leave one's homeland: "Hacemos muy mal en salir de nuestro país, en perdernos en lejanas tierras. Ya no tiene remedio." [It is a mistake to leave one's country and lose oneself in faraway lands. But it can't be helped (1967, 388).] This last statement could refer to Sacha's irremediable otherness on the heels of her travels, but it also suggests the inevitability of travel and cross cultural exchange in a modernity characterized by mobility, transnational communities, and the construction of families and intimate relations across linguistic, ethnic, and national borders. In such a world, the already difficult task of categorizing races, ethnicities, and nationalities becomes virtually impossible. Europe appears as a multiethnic, multinational composite that defies traditional attempts at classification as Aryan versus Semite, northern versus southern, Spanish versus Russian, or male versus female.

Critics have frequently described Baroja as a proponent of racial theories and phobias and his narratives are laced with discussions regarding the Iberian, Semitic, Aryan, and Latin type. The presence of these conversations does not signal authorial conviction, but rather reflects a much debated topic of the period. A Bakhtinian definition of the novel, supported by modern narrative theory, cautions against confusing authorial voice with the multiple, heteroglot voices of fictional characters. This admonition applies to any novelist, but in Baroja's case, the constant shifting of terminology and frequently underscored inconsistencies of characters arguing one point or another communicate a skepticism regarding the positions presented that critics have often overlooked. Baroja often presents characters who are taken as foreigners by their compatriots and who feel as outsiders in their home terrain. After several years in England, the protagonist of *La feria de los discretos* (1905) returns to a Spain he only barely recognizes. The French travelers who share his train compartment and briefly speak with him assume he is English. Race and nationality apparently define one less than clothing, mannerisms, and other transient markers. *La ciudad de la niebla* (1909) portrays a multicultural London in which members of different religions, races, and nationalities come together on Christmas Eve and enjoy an ecumenical celebration. María Aracil's wanderings through London bring her into contact with Russian anarchists, Norwegian artists, Jewish merchants, British chamber maids, all of whom befriend and help her in one form or another. Various characters debate the respective merits of Spanish versus British culture while yet another argues that all people are basically the same orangutan with different collars (1946–48, 2:367). Dr. Iturrioz, who reappears in *El árbol de la ciencia* (1911), here praises British culture as superior, but also comments on a visit to the London docks that commerce accompanies enslavement. The novel presents multiple characters who attest to the truth of this statement, from the newly emancipated women workers who labor for hours at the typewriter to the poor dock workers. When María falls ill after a suitor's rejection and in the face of her difficulties at working to support herself, her Russian roommate expresses surprise at her precipitous loss of energy. Iturrioz explains that Spaniards are an old race with weak bones, lacking imagination, and weighted down by history, in contrast with the youthful Russians, who display energy and resilience. Natalia dismisses Iturrioz's theories as nonsense and the narrator inserts several allusions to the perpetual rebirth of hope in the human spirit that conflict with the doctor's bleak vision. The reader is left to choose among several theories that resurface and receive even greater emphasis in subsequent novels.

El árbol de la ciencia (1911) contains long discussions on racial types and systems of classification. Dr. Iturrioz and his nephew Andrés Hurtado, also a medical doctor, meet on several occasions to debate their views on philosophy and national character. In their dialogues, they present differing opinions without ever coming to agreement. Not only do the discussions remain unresolved, but the interlocutors frequently slip from their initial stances and arguments to adopt variant, even opposite views. Early in the novel, the third person narrator refers to Iturrioz's theory that with regard to ethics, Spaniards fall into two racial types: the strong, warlike Iberians and the scheming, mercenary Semites. The fact that he links racial composition and ethics immediately undermines any claim to a scientific, objective stance. Furthermore, the narrator introduces his skepticism regarding Iturrioz's method and ideas by describing the latter's statements as arbitrary (462). And finally, when applying the theory to Hurtado's friend, Julio Aracil, the narrator states that he probably had Semitic blood and if not, then he still manifested Semitic characteristics. The rhythm of affirmation followed by expressions of doubt or subverting qualifiers frustrates attempts to construct a coherent racial theory.

In part 4 of the novel, Iturrioz and Hurtado argue the relative merits of diverse philosophical systems. Iturrioz continues to praise British culture, maintaining consistency with his role in *La ciudad de la niebla,* while Hurtado defends German thought. Andrés tends toward abstraction and Kantian idealism, finding consolation in the idea that the world ends with us and that time and space do not exist outside of individual consciousness. Iturrioz wants a more empirical solution and dismisses his nephew's ideas as pure fantasy. Not surprisingly, Andrés associates German philosophy with the Aryan race and argues that northern, Aryan models will prevail in the future. Iturrioz's correlation of race and philosophical system follows a more circuitous path. He links pragmatism to Semitic thought and believes that traditional Semitic predominance will continue. Iturrioz incorporates Jewish, Christian, and Muslim peoples under the Semitic rubric and, unlike many contemporaries who link Greek to German and Aryan culture, he associates it with the Semites. The famous discussion of the tree of life and knowledge of the novel's title associates Aryans with science and Greeks and Semites with life. The former sought knowledge even if it brought pessimism and despair, whereas the Greco-Semitic tradition consistently chooses life, optimism, opportunism over knowledge.

The shifting terms of the debate, from Iberian versus Semitic to British versus German to Aryan versus Semitic, take another turn when Iturrioz, the defender of British and Semitic pragmatism, suggests as a possible answer to the contemporary malaise a new international organization modeled after Ignatius of Loyola's Jesuit order. This vaguely defined organization would allow only Iberians, with the exclusion of the Semitic-Christian spirit that Iturrioz previously championed. A final crossing of positions occurs in the discussion regarding procreation. Iturrioz, the erstwhile defender of the tree of life and Semitic traditions, adopts an antivitalist position, arguing that the mere possibility of producing an unhealthy child should suffice to dissuade potential parents. Andrés, the normally dispassionate observer and abstract thinker who privileges the tree of knowledge, argues that unhealthy parents often produce normal children. His desire to marry Lulú and enter the rhythm of life leads him to abandon his former stance. Andrés and Iturrioz recognize their inconsistency and comment on their shift of positions: "Me choca en un antiintelectualista como usted esa actitud tan de intelectual—dijo Andrés. —A mí también me choca en un intelectual como tú esa actitud de hombre de mundo" [Such an intellectual attitude in an anti-intellectual like you surprises me—Andrés said. —The man of the world attitude in an intellectual like you also surprises me] (1968?, 562).

The changing positions and terms of the discussion also characterize discussions of race in *El mundo es ansí.* Once again, consideration of the topic unfolds by way of extended dialogue between two characters with different views. In conversation with Sacha Velasco, Arcelu cites articles published by Iturrioz that theorize two ethnic and moral Spanish types, the Iberian and Semitic. Sacha responds to Ignacio's theories with bemused skepticism, pointing out the contradictions in his argument. Ignacio moves arbitrarily from one set of terms to another. From attacks on the Semitic Spanish character he changes to a dismissal of all Mediterranean peoples, introducing yet another theory posited by an unnamed anthropologist who divides European peoples into two castes: the Alpine, descendants from the gorilla, and the Mediterranean, originating in the chimpanzee. The mixing and sliding of terms as well as the comical exaggeration of nineteenth-century anthropological and racial categories in conjunction with Sacha's repeated incredulity confound attempts to construct a consistent theory of race in this or other Barojan texts. Presented through Sacha's mediation as she transcribes her experiences in her diary, Arcelu's theories receive a final ironic classification as amusing pastimes (1967, 448).

Throughout Barojan narratives, the reader encounters opposing views on European ethnic and racial categories that undergo continual transformation and exaggeration, sometimes within a given text and single character. The theories consistently appear in a dialogic structure with characters mutually invalidating the other's point of view. The shifting terms of the debate and the transformation of such culturally accepted classifications as Iberian and Semitic or German and Latin to the more questionable Alpine versus Mediterranean and finally, the absurd gorilla versus chimpanzee, not only suggests inconclusive, unresolvable differences of opinion, but also delegitimizes the entire question as arbitrary and subjective.[38] The repudiation of absolute or relatively stable European racial types denies the uniqueness of Europeans and by implication, rejects claims to European superiority. Baroja's criticism of European imperialism and the imposition of European institutions in Africa and his general skepticism regarding grand narratives and absolute answers lead him to view Europe as both a promise and a threat, a necessary ally in the modernization of Spain and a danger to her future development. In his essays as in his novels, the speaker and authorial presence behind the voice refuse to adopt a stable position. "Europeización" (1917) rejects traditionalist desires to isolate Spain from European currents, but also refuses calls for wholesale adoption of European culture. In science and areas of philosophy that deal with universal truths, Spain should enthusiastically embark on a program of modernization and assimilation, but in art and ethics, she should develop her own directions. Once again, the negative model of French, British, Dutch, Belgian, and North American colonial abuses inspires a desire to stake out a new ethical terrain (1946–48, 5:96–98). This future Spain will link up not with Europe but Africa. "El tipo psicológico español" (1917) posits this future alliance as does *César o nada,* in which César happily accepts the Dumas dictum that Europe begins at the Pyrenees and advocates a new ideological empire by which Spain may spread a vision that contrasts with the European model (1967, 158). Whether the individual reader takes César's aspirations for a Spanish-African transnational entity seriously or not, the identification of Spain with Africa in opposition to Eurocentrism reappears often in Baroja, notwithstanding his ostensibly racist attitudes. Not only does he seek to open Spain to European culture but also to open European culture to various outsiders who offer alternative visions and values. *Juventud, egolatría* (1917) articulates this view:

> Yo, a veces, creo que los Alpes y los Pirineos son lo único europeo que hay en Europa. Por encima de ellos me parece ver el Asia; por abajo, el Africa.
>
> En el navarro ribereño, como en el catalán y como en el genovés, se empieza a notar el africano; en el galo del centro de Francia, como en el austríaco, comienza a aparecer el chino.
>
> Yo, agarrado a los Pirineos y con un injerto de los Alpes, me siento archieuropeo. (*OC* 5:159)

> [At times, I think that the Alps and the Pyrenees are the only European property that exists in Europe.
>
> In the coastal Navarrese as in the Catalan and the Genoese, one begins to see the African; in the Gaul in central France, as in the Austrian, the Chinese begins to appear.

Clinging to the Pyrenees with an Alpine graft, I feel super-European.]

The association of Basque, Navarrese, and Genoese peoples with Africa breaks with traditional efforts to depict northern Spain and Italy as pure and untouched by the Moorish-African contacts that marked the Southern areas of these countries. The linking of Northern Europe with Asia similarly breaks down continental borders and redefines Europe as a heterogeneous culture with integral connections to what traditional Spanish and European writers and Ortega y Gasset aspire to construct as alien and external. The defense of African and Asian civilizations as equal or superior to European culture occurs throughout Spanish modernist writing in connection with the rejection of racial theories and imperialism. Rafael Altamira forcefully rejects claims of European superiority over African and Asian cultures as unscientific rubbish (1976, 53) in 1902, and decries the use of flimsy suppositions regarding race to whip up patriotic fervor during World War I (1917?, 32). Pompeyo Gener at times reveals a strongly Eurocentric, racist attitude that links Catalonia with a superior Aryan, northern European sector. However, in *Historia de la literatura* he persistently signals the confluence of East and West in the development of European literature and argues the superiority of Asian culture over backward, medieval Europe. In contrast with those who begrudgingly recognize past Asian grandeur but deny continued importance in the contemporary period, the text speaker stresses that Asian culture remains strong through the modern period, as evident in the vigor of contemporary Japan. Gener emphasizes the Omayyad and Abbasid dynasties that ruled Baghdad and Córdoba and points to their cultivation of science and art in contrast to religious fanatics within both Muslim and Christian medieval worlds (1902a, 254–55). Although he praises Aryan cultures, in which he includes Germanic, Greek, Celtic, and other northern European peoples, he clearly seeks to validate Semitic civilizations, such as the Egyptian and Arabic. Writing in *Helios,* Angel Guerra imagines the future return of Arab culture as a welcome response to a decadent Spain and his fantasy of rebuilt mosques openly impugns traditional Catholicism as a cause of national decline ("Fuera de España: Retazos").

Probably the most famous proponent of Spanish national regeneration through renewed links with Africa is Miguel de Unamuno. Critics often identify two distinct phases in Unamuno's approach to Spanish relations with the exterior, arguing an early advocacy of Europeanization that gives way to subsequent calls for Africanization. Such a reading greatly simplifies the complexities of Unamunan thought and presumes a monistic vision in a writer who consistently argues for multi-voiced, multi-perspectivist approaches. Unamuno concurs with other modernists in rejecting the concept of pure races[39] and sustains that racial mixing often benefits a culture (*En torno al casticismo,* 1895). He renounces traditional isolationism and offers a variety of avenues through which modern Spain may construct a new identity in relation with the multiple cultures with which it shares historical, geographical, and cultural borders. Throughout his writing, Unamuno upholds the need for contact with the outside and argues that without continual and profound knowledge of other cultures, Spain cannot progress. His vision of the relationship with the other closely parallels contemporary thinking on the subject in the recognition of what Bammer refers to as the dual dangers of phobic rejection or philic assimilation of the self in the other (1995, 48). While Unamuno consistently advocates the need for a people to cultivate what they lack and to come to understand themselves through knowledge of and contact with others, he also emphasizes the desirability of a dual process of integration and differentiation ("Espíritu de la raza vasca," 1958, 6:160). In early writings, he primarily identifies the other through which Spaniards may come to know themselves as Europe, but always places it in conjunction with another, local collectivity that is equally alien to his educated, urban, middle-class reader. Using the arboreal metaphor of branches and roots, he suggests the importance of contact with popular traditions and lower classes in the search for the Spanish self. The process of Europeanization can best evolve in the study of differences within Spain and between Spain and other European nations:

> Hacerse el español, más español cada vez, es tanto como hacerse más europeo; en nuestro fondo, en el lecho de nuestras entrañas, es donde tenemos que buscar al hombre, a la especie, a lo que nos une y asemeja a nuestros semejantes. Por las raíces han de enlazarse los pueblos, no por las copas . . . tenemos que encontrarnos los individuos y los pueblos. Hay que hacer de lo extraño, entraño (1958, 3:97).

> [To become Spanish, more and more Spanish, is the same as to become more European; deep down, in the bedrock of our being, is

where we have to find humanity, the species, all that joins us and makes us similar to our fellow creatures. It is through the roots and not the tree tops that different peoples must join together . . . we individuals and peoples have to find each other. We must make the other our own.]

Other Unamunan texts offer a somewhat more restricted and, in a different sense, expanded definition of the European culture with which Spaniards should come into contact. "España y los españoles" (1902) represents Roman and subsequently Catholic influence in Spain as the imposition of a legalistic, dogmatic, closed mentality that led to the expulsion of Jews and Moors and the extermination of a more productive, open spirit. The text speaker proudly lays claim to possible Berber and Moorish Spanish cultural roots and clarifies that in calling for increased contact with Europe, he seeks not to continue the Latin, Roman tradition but rather to reach out to Anglo-Saxon and Germanic civilizations and through them to multiple and universal traditions. Once more, he insists that Europeanization or universalization implies a concurrent deepening of Spanish character (1958, 4:1086).

The vindication of the popular and African, both of which break with traditional images of Enlightenment Europe, continues in "Sobre la europeización" (1906), where the speaker denounces the imprecision of the terms "Europe" or "modern" and defiantly rejects European logic. He proudly accepts accusations of Spanish rhetoric and links his mode of thinking and expression to Saint Augustine, whom he baptizes "the great African" (1958, 3:1106). The rejection of European rationalism focusses primarily on French culture and thought, with many links to the writing of Eugenio d'Ors. Unamuno disdains the bourgeois pursuit of pleasure and fear of death. He spurns modern technology and science as ends in themselves, welcoming them only if they lead to wisdom and a better understanding not just of life, but also death. Once again, he advocates a recuperation of medieval Spanish traditions and specifically links calls for Europeanization, Africanization, and immersion in the popular in one complex exchange of self and other: "Por mi parte puedo decir que si no hubiese excursionado por los campos de algunas ciencias europeas modernas, no habría tomado el gusto que he tomado a nuestra vieja sabiduría africana, a nuestra sabiduría popular, a lo que escandaliza a todos los fariseos y saduceos del intelectualismo, de ese hórrido intelectualismo que envenena el alma"

[For my part I can say that if I had not explored the disciplines of modern European sciences, I would not have acquired the taste I have for our ancient African wisdom, our popular wisdom, which scandalizes the Pharisees and Sadducees of that horrid intellectualism that poisons the soul] (1958, 3:1111–12).

Unamuno's need for and commitment to dialogue surface in numerous instances in the text. He develops his argument against French logic and the bourgeois pursuit of pleasure in response to "Triste país," an essay by Pío Baroja that appeared two years earlier in *El tablado de Arlequín* (1904). This same collection contains other texts that more closely agree with Unamuno, including several that praise Africa and reject the imposition of European solutions on Spanish culture without regard for local customs and traditions.[40] However, just as Unamuno advocates the encounter with the other in order to find the self, he requires dialogue in order to articulate his thought and avoid a single-voiced, authoritative quality. His word constantly seeks the word of the other and both find voice in the text in a continual statement and response that refuses closure. Even as Unamuno exalts Spanish rhetoric, Gongorism and arbitrarity, the reader doubts the finality of his word, remembering Unamuno's repeated attacks on Góngora and writers who sacrifice content to form. The arbitrary defense of arbitrarity can easily turn to an arbitrary attack and the reader remains ever ready to adopt a new position in relation to a changing textual world. The absence of dialogue and openness in European perceptions of Spain prompt Unamuno's continual redefinition of the project of Europeanization. European, concretely French, stereotypes of Spain foil a healthy, productive exchange. The speaker argues that the French rob the Spanish of their identity by imposing a vision of Spain that squares with their own self-image. Unamuno's solution lies not in the traditional retreat and rejection of the other nor in the acceptance of the French vision, which would represent a cultural conquest, but rather in a continued, more equal dialogue in which the Spanish carry on their interchange with France and Europe while at the same time seek to Hispanize the interlocutor: ". . . tengo la profunda convicción de que la verdadera y honda europeización de España, es decir, nuestra digestión de aquella parte de espíritu europeo que pueda hacerse espíritu nuestro, no empezará hasta que tratemos de imponernos en el orden espiritual de Europa, de hacerles tragar lo nuestro, lo genuinamente nuestro, a cambio de lo suyo, hasta que no tratemos de españolizar a Europa" [I have the deep conviction that the true and profound Europeanization of Spain, that is to say, our digestion of that part of the European spirit that can become our spirit, will not begin until we try to impose ourselves on European spiritual order, to make them swallow what is ours, genuinely ours, in exchange for what is theirs, until we try to Hispanize Europe] (1958, 3:1124).

Behind the language of imposition, it is important to note the continued call for exchange. To break with centuries of French cultural monopoly, European rejection of Spanish culture, and the resulting self-doubts and low self-esteem created in Spaniards, the text speaker adopts a forceful tone, but continues to invite and validate dialogue. In order to fully digest what Europe can offer Spain, Spaniards must achieve some sort of parity. Dialogue too easily reverts to monologue and loses the capacity for exchange and mutual transformation if one party cannot hear its own words and then observe their transmutation in the words of the other. Neither "Sobre la europeización" nor subsequent texts that repudiate French rationalism and xenophobia and exalt African or Semitic modes of thought and culture propose an exclusive rejection of Europe or absolute acceptance of Africa. Unamuno advocates multiple contacts with the outside and in particular with those cultures with which Spain shares common borders. As he states in "La soledad de la España castellana" (1917), borders are sites of contact as well as separation (1958, 4:1141) and the sea represents a fluid border that brings Spain into contact with France, England, Italy, Greece, America, and Africa. The cosmopolitan nature of modernism, often cited in formalist studies of the movement, takes on a very different meaning in the context of this definition of Spain as historically and contemporaneously linked to all segments of the globe.

Unamuno's 1907 statement in "La Civilización es civismo" (1958, vol. 4) that the modern city and industrial society offer a potential remedy to traditional Spanish individualism reflects a wide-spread understanding among Spanish modernist writers. The tradition of isolationism that commenced during national consolidation under Ferdinand and Isabel and continued during the Counter Reformation and with varying degrees in the eighteenth and nineteenth centuries simply could not continue in a rapidly changing world that facilitates travel and transcultural contact. Modernists travel the globe and as a consequence, they come to a new understanding of borders and nationality. Carmen de Burgos writes that she felt no sense of sadness at leaving Madrid and her familiar world: "Confieso que al salir de Madrid no he sentido la tristeza de dejar la patria. Hoy las fronteras se conservan para la vida política de las naciones; pero el espíritu que nos anima es cosmopolita, las facilidades de los viajes, la difusión rápida de las noticias telegráficas por medio de la prensa y lo universal de las obras literarias, forman esta hermosa fraternidad que nos hace encontrarnos en los países extranjeros tan a gusto como en aquel donde nacimos" [I confess that on leaving Madrid I feel no sadness at leaving my country. Today borders are preserved for the political life of nations but the spirit that animates us is cosmopolitan, the facilities for travel, the rapid diffusion of telegraphic news items by the press and universality of literary works form this beautiful fraternity that makes us feel as at home in foreign countries as in the land of our birth] (1909?, 9). Julio Camba and Pío Baroja write extensively on their European travels. Camba comments on the vast numbers of tourists and exiles that move through Europe in the early part of the century and observes that no Swiss reside in Switzerland but rather Russians, Jews, and other travelers (1934, 335). Baroja reflects this same reality in *El mundo es ansí,* while in other works he incorporates knowledge of England, Italy, and Morocco. Enrique Gómez Carrillo's trips to Asia, Valle-Inclán's travels to America, Juan Ramón Jiménez's voyage to marry in the United States, and Felipe Trigo's military experiences in the Philippines represent but a few first-hand experiences of modernist writers in other lands, cultures, and languages that surface directly and indirectly in their work. Concha Espina, Pérez de Ayala, Sofía Casanova, the Machado brothers, Ortega y Gasset, Salvador Rusiñol, Miguel de Unamuno, Alejandro Sawa, Pablo Picasso, Emilia Pardo Bazán, and Azorín all spend prolonged periods living abroad and incorporate this experience in their writing, both in terms of content and vision of the world. Whereas the Romantic exiles had lived in England and France and made contact with European literary and philosophical currents, the representation of these foreign cultures hardly appears in their work. Realist and naturalist writers had contact with other European countries and German influence on Krausist and Institutionist writers plays a significant role in the cultural transformations that occur in Spain during the nineteenth and early twentieth centuries. However, many important writers, such as Pereda, Campoamor, Rosalía de Castro, Bécquer, and Clarín, had little or no first-hand experience of life in another country. Valera, who traveled extensively as a diplomat, barely incorporates the world beyond Spain until his later works, which coincide with the beginnings of modernism. Spanish modernist artists foreground the contact with the other, including many cultures that had never previously received attention.

In this context, Picasso's "Les demoiselles d'Avignon" takes on a different significance than that assigned by many critics. The depiction of the five nude women mixes two white figures with three white bodies topped by black faces. The portraits range from a fairly realistic depiction to a reasonably faithful reproduction of a black African mask and finally to a Cubist rendering of an African mask. Robert Hughes assumes that Picasso's use of the masks reflects no interest in or knowledge of African culture and that his idea of African tribal society likely coincides with that of the average French citizen, "jungle drums, bones in the noses, missionary stew" (1981, 20). Hughes believes that Picasso saw violence and savagery in African culture and turned to it as a source of vitality and renewal. The persistent representation of Africa as a positive component of the Spanish past and an alternative to French rationalist thinking in Spanish modernist writers as well as Spanish proximity to Africa allow for a different response to the painting. The black face to the left of the painting differs from the two white faces in color only while the increasingly abstract mask-like faces to the right clearly introduce a profound difference. This play of similarity and difference depicts Africa as simultaneously at one with and other than Spanish/European society. African prostitutes are familiar figures in Spanish and Mediterranean brothels. Baroja reflects their presence in *Mala hierba* (1904), and in the Paris of *Las tragedias grotescas* (1907), and Pérez de Ayala makes reference to them in *Troteras y danzaderas* (1913). The fact that Picassos's painting is based on a Barcelona brothel further negates the view that these faces represent savagery, violence, or absolute alterity. The blending of European and African figures, the intermixing of the French title and Spanish subject matter, the collage-like composition, and the combining of stylized realistic and cubist representation all reflect a vision of modern culture as the site of multiple and often contradictory forces that come together in a dramatic breakdown of traditional borders.

In post-imperial Spain, questions of national identity necessarily involve a re-evaluation of historical and contemporary relationships with former colonies, present-day colonizers, and peoples who currently find themselves under European rule. Spanish modernist writers undertake this task with full awareness of its significance. The editors of *Renacimiento* speak of their desire to take the reader to new regions through a new art and reject as small and pale the ivory tower in which some of their contemporary and subsequent critics wish to enclose them. Instead, they insist that the world is their tower ("Al lector," 1907, 1:6). Ganivet's sense that a post-imperial Spain must chart a new course with the opportunity to explore new possibilities for international exchange informs much Spanish modernist writing. Virtually all Spanish modernists advocate contact with the outside. Some privilege cultural ties with Europe and many embrace intercultural exchange with Latin America, Asia, and Africa, but with a clear desire to avoid the militarist, imperialist relations of the past. A great deal of modernist writing addresses these subjects and strives to develop new, dialogic modes of communication to best explore them. Critics who exclude or denigrate the rich body of work dedicated to international relations and focus only on texts that examine Castile silence an important modernist contribution that deserves recognition and contributes in important ways to intercultural understanding.

3
Nation, History, and the Past as Other

THE GEOPOLITICAL TRANSFORMATIONS THAT DRASTICALLY ALTER the global map with the rise and fall of empires in the second half of the nineteenth century accompany and intersect with equally remarkable changes in other areas of human experience. Advances in science, technology, history, linguistics, and archeology produce radical changes in the perception of time and the relation of past to present. Newton's description of time as absolute and objective, flowing incessantly along a line everywhere divisible into equal subunits on which events are sequentially ordered, undergoes some modification in Kant's postulation of subjective, *a priori* forms.[1] However, as Stephen Kern points out, Kant as well as Newton continue to perceive time as universal, experienced identically by all human beings (1983, 11). Nineteenth- and twentieth-century developments introduce a fundamental reconceptualization of temporality, its uniformity, unidirectionality, and sequential ordering. Multiple, contradictory definitions and experiences of time coexist, all in opposition to traditional claims of stability, universality, and uniform succession. New geological theories suggest a previously unimaginable temporal extension that stretches time over a dizzying expanse while archeological discoveries allow for reconnection with previously unfamiliar historical periods, bringing the remote past into the present. The reconstruction of splendid civilizations built by ancestors of peoples presently living in modest, sometimes primitive conditions, questions already fragile notions of progress. Henri Bergson and William James challenge assumptions regarding temporal succession with the idea of flux or flow, arguing that ideas develop in complex association with those that precede and succeed them, following an uneven temporal rhythm and breaking with rigorous chronicity. Freud's emphasis on the early stages of life as critical to adult formation also breaks with strict diachronic narratives and further contributes to redefine temporal ordering.

The changing perception of time produced by a confluence of technological, scientific, philosophical, and artistic factors alters the understanding of the interconnections of past, present, and future and of the formation of individual subjects, regions, and nations. Spanish modernists participate in the general reconceptualization of time that sweeps the modern world and explore its implications. Through their writing, they disseminate novel modes of envisioning temporality to their Spanish readers while simultaneously challenging them to examine the consequences of a transformed vision of time for the Spanish nation and individual subject. Studies of time in the Spanish literature of the period typically focus on the use of *intrahistoria*[2] by members of the so-called "Generation of 1898." This approach originates in Laín Entralgo's desire to reconcile the foremost early twentieth-century writers with the eternal Spanish tradition propounded by Francoist scholars. Many recent critics continue to focus on the presence of *intrahistoria* in the small group of writers studied by Laín Entralgo and emphasize what Jo Labanyi designates escape into myth, "a rejection of history for the immobilism of nature" (1994, 147).

Inman Fox looks at *intrahistoria* in the context of recent studies on nation formation, citing Benedict Anderson's notion of imagined communities and Ernest Gellner's characterization of nationalism as the invention of nations where they did not formerly exist (1991, 18). He traces the development of a new vision of Spanish history from a liberal tradition that appears in early nineteenth century and continues through Krausism and Institutionism and the modernist writers of early twentieth century. This liberal historiography refutes traditional visions of Spanish history in order to construct a different version, a Spain that could have been but was stifled under Hapsburg despotism (46–51). In contrast with conservative historians and thinkers such as Jaime Balmes, José Donoso y Cortés, and the later Menéndez y Pelayo, who emphasize an orthodox, Catholic, evangelizing Spain,[3] Inman Fox traces a national history developed by Krausists, regenerationists, and their modernist successors who look back to medieval Spain in order to retrieve a more democratic, progressive national history. In dialogue with the work of Inman Fox and the theorists of nation formation that he cites as well as others such as Homi Bhabha and Michel de Certeau, I will tease out the implications of the construction of a liberal, progressive historiography for a reconsideration of relations with the racial, ethnic, religious, and regional others who play a role in the creation of Spanish national identity. In contrast with Inman Fox's *La invención de España,* which emphasizes a Castile-centered focus on the part of modernist writers and historians, I will trace the recovery of a history that foregrounds a pluralist, multi-cultural Spain, open to the outside and to non-Castilian regions.

It should be noted that intrahistory represents only one of many different visions of temporality current among the writers with whom it is associated and stands in a dialogic relationship with other notions of time that contradict and modulate it. Furthermore, intrahistory appears in a broad range of authors not normally associated with it, who contribute to refine the concept. In contrast with the exclusionary emphasis of nineteenth-century history on elites and leaders, a new vision of history allows for agency among groups previously ignored or demeaned. Both alongside and within lyrical depictions of Spanish nature and rural life, the modernist vision of the interplay of history and intrahistory recuperates a previously silenced past that demands the transformation of the present. Women writers join in the exploration of change derived from a new perception of time and history and their presence enriches the discussion. In contrast to critics who impugn the contributions of modernist/"Generation of 1898" writers as negative and incapable of constructing alternative systems, I suggest that modernist writers engage in an ambitious project to reposition the Spanish public with respect to official historiography, bringing the reader to view the past as presented under Hapsburg and Bourbon versions of national formation as an alien, distant other that bears little relation to modern aspirations for a post-imperial, pluralist society. Modern views of time as discontinuous, in contrast with nineteenth-century beliefs in a linear temporality, facilitate a distancing of present from past. The Spanish modernist reconceptualization of history and nation, of the past and its connection to collective identity contributes significantly to introduce new ways of imagining and experiencing that are fundamental to a modern and postmodern understanding of the world. Women, religious minorities, the lower class, and other previously excluded groups gain entry to Spanish historiography through modernist revisions of the role of the past in the formation of the present and future.

Temporal Discontinuity and a Sundered Past

Geological and Archeological Discoveries and New Visions of the Past

Over the course of the nineteenth century, the fields of geology and archeology experience remarkable change. The development of uniformitarian stratigraphy in the early 1800s enables the dating of fossil remains according to their location in a particular stratum of earth and opens the way for major shifts in estimations of the planet's age. Excavations in many areas, including caves with Paleolithic drawings in France and Spain, contribute to a greater understanding of early human development. The sophisticated cave paintings of Altamira initially caused observers to assume their late execution, but by 1900 their Paleolithic origins had been established. Arguments rage through the century regarding the earth's age, ranging from thousands of years according to Biblical reckoning to millions of years in Kelvin's calculations to hundreds of millions as argued by Pierre Curie and Albert Laborde (Kern, 1983, 38). By the turn of the century, the earth's time line and human history have experienced an enormous stretching out into the past. The decoding of Egyptian hieroglyphics in 1822 brings new appreciation for the complexity of ancient civilizations and the discovery of the remarkable Sumerian civilization in the late 1800s reveals the forgetting/repression of major cultures and the gaps that occur in historical knowledge.

The extension of time in a vertiginous sweep into the past in a paradoxical twist liberates modernist writers and thinkers from the weight of history as once understood. In the nineteenth century, history and the belief in progress take on the status of a grand narrative, a means of explaining all other stories (Readings, 1991, 63). The privileging of diachronic temporality finds support in Darwin's theory of evolution, Comte's positivism, and Hegel and later Marx's vision of social and economic development. The prestige of history and the view of the present as the product of a diachronic evolution encounter increasing resistance toward the end of the nineteenth century. The geological concept of strata, with variable components coexisting within a thick layer, displaces the image of time as a line. Looking back to remote, forgotten, and now rediscovered ancestors suggests that multiple past moments enter into the formation of the present. Like geological strata, different moments in time have variable thicknesses, with varied degrees of importance and durability. Furthermore, the link with the past can be broken and resumed, with possibilities for reconnection at various points along an unevenly distributed succession of ages and temporal units. The immediately preceding interval may represent only a fleeting moment in comparison to other prolonged and influential periods. A dramatically altered vision of time, translated from subjective to collective levels, has significant implications for Spanish modernist considerations of the past and its relation to the present, allowing for (re)connection with remote eras and the rejection of the weight of the immediate past.

Pío Baroja associates geology and archeology with openness to change and a break with restrictive bourgeois customs. Venancio of *La dama errante* (1908) has a knowledge of the geological past and the history of the universe that allows him to disdain recently imposed social restrictions as transient concoctions. He educates his daughters at home, with excursions to the country and a strong scientific emphasis in contrast with official feminine education based on religion, memorization, and physical restraint. Baroja's *Paradox, rey* (1906) pits the forces of modern technology, based on a knowledge of chemistry and geology, against the resistance to change of apparently immovable geographical and geological constraints. In mid-Africa, with a minimum of supplies, Paradox and his cohorts fabricate dynamite to redirect a river over a bluff, filling a valley with water and converting their city into a defensible island. The intercalated "Elogio metafísico de la destrucción" likens this construction through destruction to volcanic action, chemical transformation, and social change. In each case, mutation occurs through the eradication of previously existing entities and in the present transformation, modern knowledge allows human beings to rapidly alter the geological time scale, accelerating the pace of erosion and channeling the river for their benefit. In keeping with modernist commitment to multiple, contradictory perspectives, the text registers varied responses to the shift in balance between man and nature. The enthusiasm of Paradox and his companions contrasts with the local shaman's defense of natural law, the snake's ire, the fish's gratitude, and the bat's indifference. The parodic tone of the text precludes a univocal reading, but the exultation of modern abilities to overcome the weight of geological permanence and time stands out as an important voice.

The Martínez Sierras' play *Madame Pepita* (1912) introduces social change in the person of the archeologist/historian who takes a paternal interest in a young woman of illegitimate birth and directs her unorthodox education. He eventually marries his pupil's mother, Pepita, who has supported herself and her daughter as a single working woman. In a break with traditional class and national borders that reflects the socially fluid modernist culture, the daughter Catalina marries an aspiring artist from a formerly wealthy family and she and her husband move to Rome. For their part, the archeologist/historian and the spirited Pepita leave for a dig in Egypt. *Madame Pepita* asserts several socially progressive stances, including the depiction of working mothers, the importance of education for women, and the constitution of family based on emotional ties rather than biology. The archeologist plays a crucial role as a catalyst in redefining paternity and family, breaking with the strictures of the immediate past, and linking with other cultures. The Martínez Sierras turn to the geological past for new themes and modes of envisioning reality in "Fuerzas latentes," one of the short texts composing *El poema del trabajo* (1899). The text addresses a female public and seeks to educate women readers by strategically combining a science lesson with a lyrical description of the beauty, color, and light condensed in a lump of coal. In the well-known form and language of the legend, combined with a newer scientific discourse, the narrator describes the beginnings of vegetation and the evolution of the first germs of life from turbid waters to early plants and later, towering forests. Subsequently, the forests deteriorate, the wood submerges in water and eventually converts to charcoal. The coals burning in the stove release light and heat formed in another age and attest to the possibility of tapping into primeval energies in the contemporary world. The narrator specifically suggests a moral to the scientific tale, insinuating the need to draw on reserves of untapped energies in other areas of human endeavor. The remote past contains lessons and forces for change that can beautify and liberate modern men and women in contrast with the limited potential of the more recent past, here reduced to a fleeting, inconsequential moment in the history of human development.

Azorín offers a more muted response to the impact of geological/archeological time, but also emphasizes the transformative power embedded in temporality. Like many writers of the period, he applies the concept of geological sedimentation to the human landscape. The first person narrator of *Las confesiones de un pequeño filósofo* describes centuries of sadness in Yecla, the poor Murcian village where the novel takes place, and speaks of layers of suffering that link back to the original Phoenician settlers who he hypothesizes brought their sadness from the banks of the Ganges and incorporated it into the ancient statues of virgins he has admired in museums: "Yo las he mirado y remirado largos ratos en las salas grandes y frías. Y al ver estas mujeres con sus ojos de almendra, con su boca suplicante y llorosa, con sus mantillas, con los pequeños vasos en que ofrecen esencias y ungüentos al Señor, he creído ver las pobres yeclanas del presente y he imaginado que corría por sus venas, a través de los siglos, una gota de sangre de aquellos orientales meditativos y soñadores" [I have studied and restudied them for long periods of time in the great, cold rooms. And seeing these women with their almond-shaped eyes, imploring and sad mouths, mantillas, small glasses in which they offer essences and ointments to God, I thought I saw the poor women of present-day Yecla and I imagined that a drop of the blood of those meditative, dreamy orientals ran through their veins, crossing the centuries] (1976, 91). A sense of the immutable weight of the past saturates this description and, for many critics, represents the Azorinian vision of time. However, the narrative introduces a number of subtleties that underscore the passage of time and present a second vision of temporality that interweaves with the first. Carmen Hernández Valcárcel, Carmen Escudero Martínez, and other critics comment on a dual conception of time in Azorín: the idea that everything passes, inherited from Heraclites; and the notion that all returns, derived from Nietzsche (62). It is important to note that in the interplay of these two temporalities, Azorín consistently signals the presence of change and estrangement from the past. The mention of the museum statues underscores a sense of temporal distance, reminding the reader that the Phoenician culture has long since disappeared and lives only in isolated place names and reconstructed narratives based on the few artifacts that survive in cold, lifeless museum cases.

The novel's closing pages offer even greater instances of the interplay of perpetuity and impermanence, the weight of the past and the evidence of a different, transformed present. The narrator returns to the school where he had passed a tortured youth and experiences an overwhelming sense that nothing has changed; his own fears and desires resurface as he observes the uniformed students. However, the sense of enclosure in a never-ending cycle conflicts with the narrator's language and intertextual references. In describing the feeling of endless repetition, the narrator refers to another philosopher, one he deems much more significant than the *pequeño filósofo* named in the novel's title. The evident allusion to Nietzsche separates the narrator from the small-minded, religiously orthodox world of the boys' school and also forges a link between the narrator and the educated reader, who share a cosmopolitan, modern knowledge that differs considerably from the traditional schooling received at Yecla. The use of the Italian *ritornello*[4] in the same paragraph serves a similar function. Even more striking, the narrator insists several times during the description of his return to the village and school on his use of a red silk umbrella, a prop utilized frequently by Martínez Ruiz during these years and here, by his fictional counterpart Azorín. The red umbrella serves as a sign of individual idiosyncracy that distinguishes the carrier as other, outside the stultifying provincial norms. It stands out in brilliant color against the drab world of Yecla and signals the distance traveled by the narrator in comparison with the young students with whom he identifies, but in relation to whom he simultaneously reveals his difference.

Unamuno often plays with concepts related to geological or archeological advances, at times comforted by the sense of permanence provided by geological time and at times seeking to transcend it. The poem "Paleontología" reflects on new connections with a remote past, the role of the paleontologist in recreating history, and the always tentative nature of this reconstruction:

> Hay rocas que conservan, alegatos
> al diluvio anteriores, las señales
> que dejaron rastreros animales
> de su paso en la tierra. Los estratos
> pedernosos en esos garabatos
> como con grandes letras capitales
> nos dicen las memoras ancestrales
> de sus vidas. El sabio los hïatos
> de esas huellas supone y con tanteos
> logra fijar la alcurnia de una raza
> que pasó, más el cielo a los ondeos
> del volar de las aves no da caza.
> En la historia del hombre los rastreos
> quedan así, no de sus vuelos traza.

(1911:72–73)

[There are rocks that preserve, evidence
prior to the flood, the traces
that passing animals left
of their stay on the earth. The flinty
layers in these scribblings
as if in great capital letters
tell us the ancestral recordings
of their lives. The specialist the gaps
in those marks ponders and through guesses
manages to establish the ancestry of a race
that existed, but the heights of the circles
of the soaring birds he cannot capture.
In the history of man the tracks are
thus, they do not mark his flights.]

The poem's form mimics the perception of time that it presents, disrupting established units and rhythms and breaking with the traditional end of verse and stanza pauses.[5] In this unorthodox sonnet, the initial eleven verses display enjambment that connects across verses as well as stanzas. The first conventional pause appears in line 12, but since it opens the final tercet, the pause creates a crashing ending to what normally serves to introduce a three-line conclusion. Enjambment sometimes produces an uninterrupted stream of words to accelerate the rhythm, but the introduction of mid-verse and mid-stanza pauses in "Paleontología" breaks the flow into irregular chunks that recall the asymmetrical geological strata in which the fossils of the poem's subject matter are embedded. The paleontologist's interpretive role and need to fill in gaps is also embedded as a fossil trace in the poem. The use of dieresis to separate the word *hiato* into three syllables and its placement at the end of a verse and stanza through the employment of hyperbaton as well as the use of enjambment linking it to the first verse of the next stanza all focus attention on this crucial word. Placed strategically before the white blank that separates the second quartet from the first, it obliges the reader to construct a meaning for the gap just as the specialist decodes fossils and fills in the temporal spaces between different specimens. In the experience of reading the poem, the reader adjusts his/her inherited sense of poetic timing to a new mode of division and succession that emphasizes disruption over continuity, chunking over progression.

Spanish modernists produce varied responses to the revision of temporality inspired by contemporary geology and archeology. They view the stretching out of time into a previously unimagined extension as fruitful for a new relation with an(other) past. At times the incredible weight of layers of former ages challenges the desire for change but often, the reconnection with distant periods proves liberating, either through a reconnection with previously unimagined energies or a realization of the relative newness and impermanence of mechanisms for social control. Geological/archeological advances intersect with changing theories of the universe and of the relation between human perception and external reality and together these features of modern thought contribute to a radical redefinition of the role and meaning of history.

Redefining the Past for the Purposes of the Present

Geological and archeological discoveries contribute significantly to a growing disbelief in history as separate from or superior to legend and literature. Heinrich Schlieman's excavations of the ruins at Troy, beginning in 1879, reveal the accuracy of many descriptions embedded in Homer's epic poems. In Spain, Milá y Fontanals in the 1870s and later Menéndez Pidal demonstrate that early epic poems serve as the basis for medieval chronicles/histories and also popular ballads that persist in a collective memory that has long since forgotten the historical record. Numerous Spanish writers of the 1890s and 1900s reveal a skeptical view of historical objectivity. When Pío of Galdós's *El abuelo* chides Nell and Dolly for mixing history and mythology, Nell responds that the one is as much a lie as the other (153). Alejandro Sawa reiterates the same view in his posthumous *Iluminaciones en la sombra:* "Pertenezco a la escuela crítica de los que afirman que la Leyenda vale más y es más verdadera que la Historia" [I belong to the school of criticism that declares that Legend is worth more and is truer than History] (1910, 163). Similarly, Unamuno refers to history as the height of hysteria (1958, 15:339).

The attack on history challenges the traditional focus on political elites and the State over other aspects of national life. It privileges an alternative reading of the past and represents a shift to a broader, more inclusive vision that anticipates modern/postmodern theories of history and fiction and their interrelationship. Richard Cardwell in "Antonio Machado and the Search for the Soul of Spain" and Inman Fox have shown the importance of Krausist/Institutionist thought in the development of a modernist rejection of history. It was in the *Boletín de la Institución Libre de Enseñanza* that the new theory was elaborated and it warrants noting that this broadening of the field of study to include new sectors of society relates to social and political change. Gumersindo Azcárate attacks the emphasis on war and the deaths of kings, calling for a history of civilization that he designates "sociology" ("Carácter científico de la Historia"). Luis de Zulueta equates Spanish national salvation with the death of history as presently understood: "¿Hay remedio para este país, como no sea en la sepultura de la Historia?" [Is there any hope for this country without the burial of History?] (1920). Altamira elaborates a theory of history in an extensive study published over various issues of the *BILE* in 1890.[6] Like Azcárate, he attacks emphasis on military battles and victories and relates the new conception of history to the modern consideration of life as an organism, with each part of equal value and essential to the whole. Consequently, the historian must weigh contributions from all aspects of social activity, not just the political (November 30, 1890). From geological studies of erosion, historians have learned that a small drop of water, slight changes in temperature, or moderate winds have as much effect as hurricanes and earthquakes. Accordingly, the historian now views life in a new light: ". . . producto de suma de esfuerzos que acumulan todos los seres, obra colectiva, de masa y no de ciertas individualidades salientes, a modo de islas, sobre la base oculta en que se apoyan y sin la cual no podrían existir" [. . . product of the sum of efforts that all human beings accumulate, a collective work, of the masses and not of certain outstanding individuals, like islands, on the hidden base which supports them and without which they could not exist] (April 30, 1891).

Galdós fictionalizes this notion of history in *Angel Guerra*. After Angel shoots a military officer in a revolutionary disturbance, he wonders what a future historian might write about the event. His mistress Dulce, a prostitute who would never figure in conventional recordings of the past, voices her lack of confidence in published histories:

> Dulce creía que era más importante para la Humanidad repasar con esmero una pieza de ropa, o freír bien una tortilla, que averiguar las causas determinantes de los éxitos y fracasos en la labor instintiva y fatal de la colectividad por mejorar modificándose. Y, bien mirado el asunto, las ideas de Guerra sobre la supremacía de la Historia no excluían las de Dulce sobre la importancia de las menudencias domésticas, pues todo es necesario; de unas y otras cosas se forma la armonía total, y aún no sabemos si lo que parece pequeño tiene por finalidad lo que parece grande, o al revés. (1967, 5:1209)

> [Dulce believed that it was more important for Humanity that she carefully mend a piece of clothing or fry an omelet well than to discover the determining causes of the successes and failures in the instinctive and fatal efforts of the collectivity to improve through modification. And, in truth, Guerra's ideas on the supremacy of History did not rule out Dulce's ideas on the importance of domestic trifles, since everything is necessary; from one thing and the other total harmony is formed, and we still don't know if what seems small has as its purpose what seems large, or vice versa.]

In evaluating Dulce's ideas, Galdós's vindication of intrahistory delegitimizes causality and hierarchy. The line depicting the clear relationship between cause and effect or the past and present moment gives way to a thicker, more complex layer. Sawa also rejects the straight line, arguing that progress is better represented by the ellipse or the parabola (1910, 38).

In a 1918 essay "Covadonga," Pérez de Ayala draws from current theories on memory, psychology, and archeology to envision history as a mix of culture (erudite memory), tradition (collective memory), and preconscious personality. The preconscious originates in a temperament inherited from one or more races that predate traditional and cultured recollection, but continue to influence the current social body (1964–66 1:1104). Reconstruction of a preconscious past obviously requires interpretive skills and consequently, the definition of history moves increasingly away from notions of objective reporting to creative selection and recombination. The speaker of Azorín's *Alma española* (1900) argues that each period develops its own linguistic modality and that changes in style reflect alterations in living and feeling. As a result, historians must possess literary sensibility in order to capture the nuances of linguistic variation. Moreover, history continually undergoes rewriting and facts are reconsidered in the light of new contexts. In this definition, his own task as cultural historian takes on a new purpose: "redefinir el pasado para el uso del presente" [to redefine the past for present use] (1947–48, 1:680). Altamira's contention that the past stands not as an obstacle, but rather a useful aid to future reforms reveals a common vision and purpose (1898; 261). The literary and the historical meet within Azorín's text and in the agreement of Azorín, the creative writer, and Altamira, the historian.

The redefinition of the historian's role in the *Boletín de la Institución de Enseñanza* and modernist writings builds on lessons provided by geological and archeological discoveries and also relates to theories elaborated by Freud and Nietzsche. The unintentional forgetting of the past attested to by archeological discoveries becomes purposeful in Freudian theories of repression and the retrieval of past memories through psychoanalysis establishes the value of rereading a distant past for the construction of a productive present. Nietzsche also discusses the need to forget the past, with implications for an understanding of time and social construction that critics continue to debate. Eysteinsson points to Paul de Man's work on Nietzsche as representative of those who interpret the philosopher's admonition to forget the past as belief in a dehistoricized present, a paralysis of history and change. In contrast, Eysteinsson observes that Nietzsche's "On the Advantage and Disadvantage of History for Life" in fact maintains that "forgetting (as an act of modernity) is repeatedly counteracted by its necessary opposite (i.e., the critical act, which Nieztsche also calls 'modern'). . . . being able to 'remember at the right time' is as important as forgetting 'at the right time': 'the unhistorical and the historical are equally necessary for the health of an individual, a people, and a culture'"(1990, 55). The purposeful forgetting and remembering of the past advocated by Nietzsche and Freud weakens the authority of history, as does the modernist rejection of overarching systems of thought, the grand narratives of the nineteenth-century episteme. Without an external principle—God, reason, or progress toward a final goal—to validate the observations of individual subjects, the relativity of judgements grows increasingly evident.

Spanish modernists undeniably reject inherited definitions of history and energetically follow Nietzsche's admonition to forget at the right time. Selected elements of national tradition are shown to be other and no longer vital in the constitution of the present. Modernist writers also reconnect with and continue immediate and remote antecedents in a desire to remember a different past that overwrites hegemonic versions of national history in order to produce more fruitful narratives. The earliest theorizations of Spanish modernism incorporate this aspect, as indicated previously. Both in the exercise of forgetting and in the recovery of a different past, issues related to race, religion, class, and gender take precedence. As in the case of empire, traditional rhetoric and values often intrude within texts that explore new modes of expression and living in the world. At times, traditional biases about race come into play in the very act of debunking prejudices regarding religion or gender and the reverse also occurs. It is not just, as Felski has observed, that "A text which may appear subversive and destabilizing from one political perspective becomes a bearer of dominant ideologies when read in the context of another" (1995, 27), but that aspects of the dominant ideology (racism, sexism, nationalism) may serve as a vehicle for the subversion of other inherited values and discourses. As in other aspects of modernist thought, no single rendering captures the rich range of approaches, but certain identifiable patterns are discernible.

Unamuno develops his theory of (intra)history while (re)constructing a vision of Spanish cultural formation in *En torno al casticismo,* the 1902 collection of four essays previously published separately in 1895. He uses two different but related metaphors to communicate his concept of history as surface event and intrahistory as deep substrate: first he refers to the movement of the flowing river that carries with it a rich sediment, and then shifts to the image of the sea, with noisy, foam-crested waves of history that roll over a deep, silent ocean bottom. In the description of the two images, the speaker underscores different elements, referring to the sudden flooding that brings new soil and enriches the countryside by means of the river of progress in the first metaphor and stressing the quiet depth and sunless sea bottom of the second (1971, 109).[7] Alternation of movement and stasis, depth and surface occurs in each but the balance shifts, with emphasis on the moving sediment in the first image and on the quiescent sea bottom in the second. The dual rhythm and perspective also appears in Unamuno's program for national regeneration, in the insistence on a move outward toward Europe and inward toward national self-study. The regeneration and modernization of Spain necessitates that the educated readers addressed by the text seek their roots in the language and traditions of the *pueblo*[8] in combination with a generous, open examination of European traditions: "Quisiera sugerir con toda fuerza al lector la idea de que el despertar de la vida de la muchedumbre difusa y de las regiones tiene que ir de par y enlazado con el abrir de par en par las ventanas al campo europeo para que se oree la patria. Tenemos que europeizarnos y chapuzarnos en pueblo" [I would like to strongly suggest to the reader the idea that revitalizing the scattered masses and regions must go hand in hand and linked with opening wide the windows to European lands in order to air out the nation. We must become Europeanized and immerse ourselves in the people] (241). Through his assimilation of European ideas and also through a return to traditional Spanish writers viewed from a fresh perspective, Unamuno undertakes his examination of *casticismo* and challenges the traditional association of *castizo* with racial purity and religious orthodoxy in order to introduce a transgressive rereading of Spain and her relations with multiple others.

The conjoining of foreign and domestic, traditional and modern, authoritative and innovative discourse occurs in the consideration of various topics in *En torno al casticismo,* including the discussion of history and its function in the formation of nation. In keeping with strategies of essayistic persuasion, this mixture works to move the reader from conventional to novel modes of thought and expression. The speaker draws on conventional Catholic practices to advocate that the study of history, rather than glorify past sins, should open the way to change through a process paralleling the religious confession: "Mientras no sea la historia una confesión de un examen de conciencia, no servirá para despojarnos del pueblo viejo, y no habrá salvación para nosotros" [As long as history is not a confession resulting from an examination of conscience, it will not enable us to shed the old nation and there will be no salvation for us] (1971, 120). On another occasion, the speaker adopts the language of psychoanalysis, referring to intrahistory as *lo inconsciente* (109) and exhorting the nation and individual reader to strive for self-knowledge. In outlining a theory of knowledge, the speaker links the perception of the mind and time to psychoanalysis and contemporary philosophy and science, postulating that ideas appear in the mind linked in an intellectual web, or *nimbo,* which encircles individual ideas and combinations of ideas that join in a random process of coalescence. The speaker avoids comparisons and terms that connote linearity, emphasizing circular, orbital patterns through analogy with Angelo Secchi's theories of stellar spectra (147). The notion of non-linear interconnections of ideas and memories of varying intensity jostling against each other in what is described as an ethereal sea relates to William James's view that "halos" or "fringes" surround mental images and join them to other past and future ideas (53) and also to the Freudian practice of free association. The text speaker alludes to diverse manners of knowing and distinguishes between a knowledge of forms, which he associates with science, and another more qualitative mode of apprehending by which the subject internalizes the object and in an act of love, makes it part of the self (104). Here Unamuno's thought reveals links with Bergson's absolute knowledge through intuition, the experiencing of a thing as from within (1972, 1149–50), as well as with Bakhtin's observations on Bergson and the dualism of cognition and life in *Toward a Philosophy of the Act*.

En torno al casticismo argues that the Castilian culture, designated as the national tradition by previous generations, exemplifies a pattern of mental perception that totally diverges from the modern, non-linear understanding of the accretion of ideas. Calderonian theater lacks *nimbo* or shading and degenerates into a polarized confrontation of opposites, emphasizing exteriority and absolutes. Such thinking produced the brutal conquest of America and the abolition of other civilizations with which it could not learn to cohabit. In relations between classes, genders, and family members, this tradition precludes mediation or compromise and develops an unforgiving honor code. Its remnants appear in occasional outbursts of militarism, a persistent horror of work, admiration for an externally strong personality, adherence to appearances over inner realities, Manichean modes of thought, and disassociative tendencies that lead to the separation of science and art, realism and idealism. In opposition to this *castizo* past, which represents an imposed, falsified version of national character, the speaker suggests a recuperation of an intrahistorical substrate that he designates as the substance of progress (1971, 110), the key to the future. By implication, this Spain allows for dialogue, *nimbo,* encounters across traditional barriers artificially separating classes, genders, regions, religions, and ethnicities. In order to replace conventional definitions of *castizo* with this richer, more productive past, the text speaker turns to a Semitic, pre-Inquisition Spain that was amenable to external influences and characterized by the coexistence of different religions, languages, and ethnicities.[9]

Of the Spaniards mentioned in *En torno al casticismo,* the speaker reserves strong praise for Fray Luis de León, overtly and repeatedly linking him to Hebraic tradition (1971, 213). A long quotation from Fray Luis incorporates his voice as a living remnant of a still vital tradition. Significantly, the passage emphasizes the dialectical relationship between self and other that recurs in Unamuno's texts as a model for current Spanish exchange with other cultures:

> Consiste la perfección de las cosas en que cada uno de nosotros sea un mundo perfecto, para que por esta manera, estando todos en mí y yo en todos los otros, y teniendo yo su ser de todos ellos y todos y cada uno dellos el ser mío, se abrace y eslabone toda aquesta máquina del

> universo, y se reduzca a unidad la muchedumbre de sus diferencias, y quedando no mezcladas, se mezclen, y permaneciendo muchas, no lo sean, y para que extendiéndose y como desplegándose delante los ojos la variedad y diversidad, venza y reine y ponga su silla la unidad sobre todo. (213–14)
>
> [The perfection of things consists in that each one of us is a perfect world, so that in this way, all people reside in me and I reside in all others, and I possess the essence of all of them and each of them possesses mine. All this universal machinery joins and links together; the multiple differences subside to unity and while they remain separate, they fuse with each other and while they continue as many, they are one. Consequently, as the variety and diversity extend themselves and unfold before our eyes, unity triumphs and places its throne over all.]

The predilection for a mystical, paradox-laden approach to reality continues d'Ors's repudiation of Latin-Roman dogmatism and legalism as well as the polarized, fanatical Castilian tradition rejected by other modernist texts. The alternative suggested in *En torno al casticismo* postulates a profound, complex interrelation of individual ideas, entities, and images that join in a web to other ideas, objects, and impressions. Fray Luis de León's Hebraic tradition preserves *nimbo* while classic Spanish literature erases it in the construction of such polarities as Don Quijote and Sancho Panza or the figures of the *gracioso* and lord in Golden Age theater. The performative energy of Unamuno's essay opposes this tradition and aspires to reconnect with a Hebraic vision and mystical tradition that Counter Reformation Spanish culture interrupted.

The dual entry to the Spanish past through European and Spanish sources continues in Unamuno's 1903 "El individualismo español" (1958, vol. 3), which analyzes the relationship between Spanish, Semitic, and African peoples by means of a dialogue with Martin Hume's *The Spanish People: Their Origin, Growth and Influence.* Hume attributes Spanish individualism to the Iberian substrate, which he argues has Semitic, African, non-Aryan roots. He traces a Spanish lack of solidarity to a tribal tradition, exemplified in the resistance to Rome, the long centuries of Christian-Arab rivalry, nineteenth-century cantonalism, and contemporary movements for regional autonomy. Unamuno's response follows a rhythm of agreement and refutation, assimilation and difference that textually reproduces his suggested protocol for approaching the other. The speaker accepts the depiction of Spanish individualism, but establishes a significant distinction between individuality and personality that ultimately deconstructs Hume's arguments. For Unamuno, individuality relates to external limits while personality refers to interiority. The strong individual, like a simple gas whose molecules move chaotically in a single direction, gives the appearance of movement and energy, but in reality remains simple. The text compares the Spaniard to this simple gas, enclosed within a bottle or thick-walled container and allowing the interior gas no contact with the outside, thus precluding interaction and change. The individual of this composition remains isolated from external influences and tends toward rigid, antagonistic positions with little internal complexity. By contrast, personality is likened to a solid, with a complex crystal-like internal structure and a surface that maintains contact with the atmosphere, influencing external forces and receiving their influences. Unamuno judges that Spaniards have an excess of individuality and lack personality. In dialogue with Hume, he introduces this distinction and simultaneously revises the racial origins of this national trait. Interjecting the Biblical tale of Cain and Abel, he traces the excess of Spanish individualism to the sin of envy, originating in the age-old rivalry between the farmer and shepherd, settled grower of crops and mobile herder of flocks. In a significant inversion, the text reformulates Hume's racial identification of Spaniard and Semite and associates Spanish individualism with a shepherd ancestry that stands in stark contrast with Moorish/Semitic agriculture. While the text does not clarify the shepherd's racial origins, it clearly suggests that modern civilization, with industrial and commercial activity based in a stable, urban society, will inevitably curb the nomadic shepherding tendencies and convert a defective excess of individuality into a more productive virtue. In other words, Spain will return to the agriculture and commerce of Moors and Jews, whose expulsion marked the end of a plural, multicultural society that modern Spain must recuperate in order to regenerate and progress.

Re-visions of Medieval and Renaissance Foundations

The aspiration to recuperate a pluralist Spain relates to the widespread modernist interest in the medieval period. Litvak emphasizes modernist admiration for the artistic achievements of this period and relates it to a general regard for primitive cultures and styles in contrast with a disdain for modernity

(1980, 181). Rather than a rejection of modernity, interest in the medieval period represents a link with the modern experience of cultural diversity and the breakdown of traditional centers of power, including the church, nation, and patriarchy. Rejecting Hapsburg Spain's imposition of racial and religious homogeneity and sexual control of women and rejoining with medieval Spain and historical periods that allowed for other forms of social, racial, and cultural interaction, modernist texts forge new links between past and present. The repudiation of conventional versions of Spanish history as alien and incompatible with modern aspirations leads to a different kind of encounter with the other. Condemnation of Charles I and Philip II recurs frequently in writers of the period and the repudiation of Hapsburg monarchy typically combines with calls for religious and racial tolerance, abolition of the patriarchy, and aperture to the outside.

Philip's monument at El Escorial symbolizes all that modernist writers abhor in Spain's past. Its imposing architecture, uniformity of design, and structural imitation of the gridiron on which Saint Lawrence was martyred invoke unpleasant memories of the immense concentration of power and imposition of a single, unitary vision in terms of religion, race, and gender that nineteenth and twentieth-century advocates for change see as the legacy of Hapsburg rule. Carmen de Burgos describes a visceral response when passing the Escorial on her train trip to Europe, experiencing deep chills and the weight of the thick walls on her body as she contemplates the figure of the fanatical king and the omnipresence of death conveyed by his memorial (1909?, 11). She points out the exclusion from the royal pantheon of the one infertile Castilian queen and protests that contrary to the traditional demeaning of infertile royal women, those who refused to perpetuate a degenerate race deserve their own personal monument. Burgos proceeds to attack Isabel the Catholic, her support for the Inquisition, and her destruction of agriculture through persecution of the Moors. She mocks the queen's unhygienic refusal to change her clothes during the campaign to take Granada and in contrast with this image of a dirty, somber queen, Burgos invokes with pleasure memories of Jewish baths and the white veils and frequent ablutions of the Arabs (11–13). Antonio de Zayas's poem "El Escorial," included in the modernist anthology *La Corte de los poetas,* also disdains Philip's tyrannical rule and religious fanaticism (1907, 46). Unamuno plays with the meaning of the word *escorial* as slag heap in his *Cancionero* to depict Philip's imperial glories as meaningless scum. In the poetic text, worms have eaten both scepter and cross in a material erasure of the period that Unamuno and his contemporaries foster (1958, 15: 541).

Ortega y Gasset reveals a more conflicted relationship with the Escorial and Hapsburg legacy in "Azorín: Primores de lo vulgar," written on the eve of a projected trip to Argentina in 1917. Composed in El Escorial, the shadow of the monument hovers in the background of the textual discussion. Commenting on history and temporality, the speaker expresses his conviction that the past persists in the present, and in this he concurs with other modernist writers and contemporary theorists of time: "Recordar es volver la vista al yo pretérito y hallarlo aún vivo y vibrátil como un dardo que sigue en el aire su carrera cuando el brazo que lo lanzó ya descansa" [To remember is to look back at the former self and discover it alive and pulsating like a dart that continues its flight in the air when the arm that threw it already rests] (1965, 2:161). At times, Ortega seems to share the belief he attributes to Azorín that Spain lives locked in an unchangeable past (176), but other passages reveal a love of modernity and desire for a dynamic, heroic art. The speaker betrays a nostalgia for Hapsburg ascendancy and a wish to recuperate an energized past. The references to the San Lorenzo Monastery underscore its colossal size and powerful profile, which the speaker designates "nuestra gran piedra lírica" [our great lyrical stone] (173). Following this incorporation of the reader and speaker in a collective "we" that physically and emotionally finds solace in the monument, the text expresses hopes for the return of the lost national energies symbolized by the building: "[El Escorial] parece recoger los restos de la energía peninsular, como el caudillo espontáneo asume los residuos del ejército vencido que se dispersaban desorientados. Yo espero que un día no lejano los españoles jóvenes harán su peregrinación de El Escorial, y junto al monumento se sentirán solicitados al heroismo" [El Escorial seems to gather up the remains of peninsular energies, like the impromptu chief who collects the residues of the defeated army that were dispersing in confusion. I hope that some day in the not too distant future young Spaniards will make their pilgrimage to the Escorial, and standing next to the monument will feel inspired to heroism] (173). The military allusion reveals the nature of the longed for heroism and the goal of recuperated energy. Later the speaker again exalts the Escorial's massive materiality and rigid profile, which he likens to the inner strength of a nation that prevent its frontiers from becoming laughable lines (183), expressing a yearning for a return to an expanded territory with unchanging borders. Ortega y Gasset craves a hero and although he states that heroes have neither traditions nor inherited habits, living through incessant invention (*OC* 2:178), the Escorial's contours determine the image of the hoped-for leader and the parameters of his ambitions.

Once again, Ortega stands out as the exception among modernist writers. In contrast to his nostalgic reliving of the past in the shadows of El Escorial, modernists typically leap over the traditionally glorified "Golden Age" of Spanish history to reconnect with a heterogeneous, unorthodox Middle Ages. Ganivet returns to Seneca and Semitic roots to describe Spanish character in *Idearium español.* Unamuno insists on contact with other races, religions, and peoples in order to reconstruct a vital nation in *En torno al casticismo.* He details the role of Castile in the unification of the various regions, but also inserts constant reminders of the diversity that persists beneath an apparent homogeneity. The "eternal tradition" he traces pre-dates the Golden Age and runs counter to the values espoused by official Spanish culture of the sixteenth and seventeenth centuries. In the process of reconnecting with pre-imperial Spain, writers frequently overwrite existing versions of national history, utilizing parody or inversion while simultaneously registering their opposition to national myth making. Pardo Bazán ironically presents the illegitimate birth of Pelayo in Toledo, apologizing to Asturian purists who claim him as a local hero. The story further challenges myths of national and racial purity through intertextual references to the legend of Moses—Pelayo's mother hid her disgrace by placing her son in a covered chest and depositing it in the Tagus River—and references to the Arab sources of the legend. The details, some of which occur in medieval chronicles written at considerable distance from the events, suggest the ease with which "history" incorporates legend and relies on sources of dubious authority. The narrator queries the veracity of the Arab accounts, arguing that Pelayo would surely have suffocated if the chest were as airless as they describe. The emphasis on a multicultural Toledo as Pelayo's birthplace, the reliance on Arab sources for the foundational narrative of Spanish national identity, the suggestion of illegitimate birth for the legendary "father" of the nation, the decision to duplicate medieval blending of Hebrew Biblical legend and national history, the tongue-in-cheek tone and title of the story, "Cuento de antaño (La leyenda de Don Pelayo)," all serve to demythify this national narrative and show the impossibility of accurately reconstructing the past (1990, 4:170–72). Pardo Bazán's "El caballo blanco" offers a modern version of Santiago, patron of Spain and symbol of the nation's retreat from contact with the outside with his legendary battle cry of "Cierra España." In this story, Saint Isidore, the patron of Madrid and a common laborer, displaces Santiago and harnesses the famous white steed of battles with the Moors for use in plowing the fields (1990, 2:266–68), a labor historically associated with the Moors that Santiago expelled.

Modernist writers return to the Golden Age and rewrite the narrative of national formation to incorporate the voices of women and racial and religious minorities in contrast with versions of history that privilege class and racial exclusion and a rigid honor code. The Catalan playwright Angel Guimerà explores the seventeenth century to reconsider Christian-Moorish relations in his 1888 *Mar i cel,* translated to Castilian as *Mar y cielo* and staged in 1891. The action describes a group of Moorish pirates who had been born and raised in Spain and now profess a deep hatred for the land and peoples that expelled them. Said, the corsair leader, descends from a *morisco* father, who was killed by Christians, and a Christian mother, who also died after extracting her son's promise to avenge his parents' death. When the pirates capture a group of Christians, Said protests their hypocrisy with angry comments that strongly attack the religion of the theater-going public: "¡Y asesinos nos llaman, y ladrones, / y hienas! . . . ¡Ellos, no; son almas puras, / son palomas sin hiel, son tiernos niños, / todo amor, bondad, fe, virtud . . . ! ¡Cristianos!" [They call us murderers, and thieves, / and hyenas! . . . . Not them, they are pure souls, / doves without gall, tender babes, / all love, goodness, faith, virtue . . . Christians!] (1912, 26). Said's remarks bring tears to Blanca, a young Christian captive, but her father Carlos expresses anger that she would cry for infidels. In a series of abrupt turns in the action, Blanca and Said confront and threaten each other before finally declaring undying mutual love. While Blanca envisions a heaven that includes all peoples and creeds, her father retains his hatred. His statement that he is her king, God, and father make even more evident the connections with his namesake, Carlos V, and underscore the interconnectedness in traditional Spanish ideology of political centrism, religion, and patriarchy. In a sentimental ending geared to sweep the audience into emotional acceptance of the interracial, interfaith romance, Blanca intercepts the bullet that Carlos fires at Said and Said jumps with her body into the sea. Blanca's final words, "al cielo" [to heaven] offer an ecumenical solution to the conflict and overwrite a long nationalist, patriarchal, and religious tradition of exclusion.

Francisco Villaespesa also chooses to remember with a different slant through the figure of the woman in *La leona de Castilla* (1915). Based on the revolt of the Castilian *comuneros* against Carlos V, the play focusses on the leadership of María de Pacheco after the death of her husband, Juan de Padilla. This version supports women's abilities, depicting María as a better shot and leader than her son. It also attacks the Church, ascribing the defeat of the local movement to ecclesiastical perfidy and complicity with the Hapsburg government. Villaespesa's exaltation of Castilian *fueros* invokes one form of nationalist discourse in the act of discrediting another. The transformation of the lion, regional symbol for Leon and later Leon-Castile, into the lioness of the play's title transgresses established national assumptions, but the passionate exaltation of Castile, even when mixed with the defense of the people over king and nobility, reaffirms inherited histories. A similar intermixing of regressive and progressive rhetoric occurs in Villaespesa's *Aben Humeya* (1913). A reworking of the taking of Granada, the play's first act criticizes Christian brutality and defends Moorish culture. In contrast with the Spanish captain who rapes the young Moorish Zahara, Aben Humeya, leader of the Moorish resistance, frees women and children prisoners. On the other hand, the exoticized invocation of Moorish customs, with emphasis on sensuality and barefoot odalisques, reveals a stereotyped vision of the Arab world that dominates in the remaining acts. Zahara displays a vengeful character, intent on killing her rapist and all Christian prisoners in keeping with the ancient Semitic law of an eye for an eye, a tooth for a tooth. Aben Humeya also mutates from the noble, generous leader of the first act to a wilder, more brooding figure. In describing his efforts to resist his attraction to the Christian Isabel, the stage directions note that he shudders, agitated by the "impetuous violence of his race" (1930, 76). Isabel gradually displaces the Moorish characters as the central focus and embodiment of virtue. Notwithstanding the contradictory impulses evident in the work, *Aben Humeya* reexamines conventional histories and introduces an alternative discourse.

Pompeyo Gener undertakes a similar task in studies of Miguel Servet, the Spanish humanist and discoverer of the pulmonary circulation of blood who was burned at the stake by Calvin in Geneva. Both the biography, *Servet: reforma contra renaci-*

miento: Calvino contra humanismo and the short story "Ultimos momentos de Miguel Servet," published in *El cuento semanal* (1907), attempt to recuperate the Spanish humanist tradition and contrast it with a puritanical, rigid Calvinism. In both texts, Gener stresses Servet's belief in a loving, forgiving God as opposed to the punishing Calvinist deity. Gener does not contrast Servet's beliefs with Counter Reformation Spanish doctrines, but his emphasis on Servet's defense of freedom and tolerance and his description of the horrors of inquisitorial cultures insinuate an equation of Spanish Catholic tradition and Calvinism. The biographical study intimates Servet's mixed racial ancestry on two occasions, inserting references to accusations of Jewish and Moorish blood by his contemporaries (1911, 52, 56). Gener anticipates Américo Castro's assumption that Servet is a *converso* (1971, 97) and hints that this accomplished scientist and humanist would have faired no better in Counter Reformation Spain than in Calvinist Geneva. The story version of Servet's last days underscores the support of a number of women. The abbess Isabel and the innkeeper Rosa try to hide Servet and in the end, Rosa avenges his death by fatally stabbing his executioner. The introduction of the two female characters lightens the tone by inserting a love interest and also communicates Servet's charisma. However, suggestions of Isabel's religious unorthodoxy and Rosa's strength and independence when she intervenes after the men exclude her from what they determine is not "women's work" send a subversive message to the popular readership that constituted the public of *El cuento semanal.*[10] The unorthodox female characterizations and Gener's condemnation of the absence of humanity, love, mothers, and children in Golden Age theater (1902a, 326) reflect a critique of the canon and aspiration for change that coexist with misogynistic currents in his work.

In addition to multiple texts that re-examine Golden Age literature, writers of the period look back to other historical periods in the search for alternate national narratives. Blasco Ibáñez's *Sónnica la cortesana* (1901) stands out in his works as an unusual and interesting exploration of the early history of Sagunto in the Valencia region. The novel describes the multiethnic origins of the local people with Carthaginian, Phoenician, Greek, and Iberian antecedents. The depiction of Celtiberian customs emphasizes the inversion of modern sexual roles, portraying strong women who return to the fields immediately after giving birth and leave the fathers in bed with the newborn babies. The narrator differentiates the unfaithful Romans from the more loyal Africans and consistently disparages Roman culture as patriarchal and tyrannical. The anti-Roman impetus utilizes a strong antisemitic discourse, linking Roman and Jewish cultures in contrast with the Greeks. Antisemitism appears in many Blasco Ibáñez novels and represents only one of several instances of traditional discourse that interweaves with and authorizes other unorthodox views.

Manuel Machado's poem "Castilla" and Eduardo Marquina's play *Las hijas del Cid* (1908) both undertake a revision of the legend of the Cid through the introduction of a female figure. As Cardwell notes in "Los Machado y Juan Ramón Jiménez 'en el 98'," Machado's poem softens the image of the warrior by depicting his compassion for the young girl who entreats him not to stop at her home and thus bring the king's fury on her family (1922, 1:38–41). Marquina takes a more radical approach, casting the Cid's daughter Elvira as an emancipated woman who disguises herself as a knight and avenges her honor in combat with her abusive husband. The play also amends the Cid's portrait, painting him as obsessed with marrying his daughters to royalty. In the end, the Cid of this text confesses that he abandoned his popular roots from a desire to gain wealth and power. The vindication of women and the lower classes exploits the exaltation of Castile that typically surfaces in stories of the Cid as well as anti-Moorish/African rhetoric in standard implementation of specific forms of traditional discourse for the purpose of introducing other, thoroughly untraditional modes of thinking and speaking.

The vision of northern Spain, and particularly Asturias, as the birthplace of a racially pure, religiously orthodox, sexually constrained, and geographically circumscribed nation comes under attack in many modernist texts. The eponymous Doña Berta of Clarín's 1892 narrative finds fulfillment infrequently in her life and in each case it occurs because she leaves the confines of the home where "neither Romans nor Moors" have set foot: first, in giving sanctuary to the wounded captain of the Regent María Cristina's army—who falls just outside the gate of her family estate; second, in giving into a whim and leaving the family property for the first time in years for a walk in the forest where she meets the painter who brings her into real or imagined contact with her long-lost illegitimate son; and finally, in leaving for Madrid where she embarks on a mission to save her "son's" honor, which ends tragically but gives meaning to her life.

Baroja also disavows the north-south trajectory of national reconquest in his novel *El mayorazgo de Labraz* (1903). In consonance with his contemporaries, his rewriting of the past heralds an acceptance of difference with respect to religion, ethnicity, and gender while simultaneously communicating the impossibility of objective reporting and the inevitable alterity of the past. The novel's prologue locates the action in Labraz, a walled, medieval Cantabrian village, but later comments place it in Navarre, which in medieval times reached the Cantabrian Sea. The narrative takes place in late nineteenth century, as indicated by references to the economic effects of the disentailment of lands, but the reader feels immersed in a much older world, in which church and aristocracy continue to rule. The temporal and geographic indeterminacy undermines a sense of a stable reality, which is further weakened by the use of shifting narrators and focalizations. The narrator of the prologue visits Labraz where he meets Samuel Bothwell, an eccentric Englishman who has taken up residence in the town and written a novel about Juan de Labraz, the only surviving remnant of local nobility. The narrator claims he has had Bothwell's manuscript in his possession for some time and has decided just now to publish it, with no additions or deletions. Many of the novel's important scenes are reported indirectly, through secondary characters: the dramatic encounter between Juan and his adopted, prodigal brother Ramiro after years of separation; the reports of Ramiro's adventures in Madrid; and Ramiro's robbery of jewels and vestments from the family chapel. The sense of a second-hand reality, mediated through other observers, persists to the end of the narration, when Juan and his companion Marina arrive at the Mediterranean coast after a long journey on foot to escape the weight of national and personal history. The reader now confronts two different accounts of Juan's location, on the Mediterranean coast with the young and beautiful Marina as depicted in the novel's final pages (1946–48, 1:161–62) or in Labraz, old and in the company of a thin, graying, black-robed woman, as described in the prologue (1:56). It is possible that Bothwell invented a fictional account and equally plausible that the unnamed narrator of the prologue misleads the reader when he states he did not alter the manuscript. In either case, the sense of finality, of a completed narrative, and of full possession of the past unravels and the reader must recognize the impact on the story of the various scribes and narrators who intervene in its telling.

The insistence on mediation in the (re)construction of narrative questions the veracity of inherited stories. Each teller rewrites the past, which continually takes new form. Baroja's text reconsiders the traditional exaltation of northern Spanish racial purity through repeated allusions to illegitimacy. The Beamonte family, the second most important representative of nobility in the village, descends from the bastard son of a French Beaumont. Ramiro is of mysterious origins, discovered alone and homeless by Juan's mother, who adopted him and lavished him with maternal affection after her biological son became blind and pockmarked as a result of smallpox. One local resident thinks Ramiro is the son of gypsies who had been expelled from the village years before, and Ramiro himself has vague memories of a dark man who accompanied him in his early childhood (1946–48, 1:103). The disruptions in lineage and intrusion of illegitimate children of uncertain origin mirrors similar breaks in other temporal chronologies. The memory of the past proves elusive in *El mayorazgo de Labraz*. Ramiro's attempts to reconstruct his childhood leave significant gaps and Juan's memories remain clouded and jumbled. The text insistently avoids clarifying details of the history of Juan's relations with Ramiro's wife Cesarea and her sister Micaela. The specifics of Ramiro's treason and reasons for his flight with Cesarea or later return are never fully explained. The difficulty of reconnecting with the past receives emphasis in the early pages of the novel, when Ramiro and Cesarea continually lose their way on their return to Labraz and comment on their inability to remember and orient themselves. The defenders of the past lament the intrusion of the new, which they try to deter by clinging to a past that escapes them and enclosing themselves, physically, socially, and emotionally. Labraz closes its gates at night and has its own Captain of the keys who ritually locks the doors and controls access to the town. The aristocracy lives in guarded isolation from the lower classes and men view women either as sexual prey or economic booty. Diego de Beamonte attempts to freeze the passage of time in his habit of wearing clothing from the 1830s, but his monothematic conversations regarding the decadence of the present reveal the futility of his efforts.

Ramiro also represents resistance to the passage of time, even as it leaves its mark on him. In classic don Juan tradition, he lives in constant movement, but continually repeats his previous actions, whether seducing women, robbing his brother, or fleeing his pursuers. His marriage to Cesarea and then his love for and escape with her sister Micaela reflect a fear of change, dramatically underscored in the incestuous nature of his relationships. Ramiro confesses his inability to move out of himself, comparing his psyche to a locked and shuttered hut. Juan, in contrast, states that he remains open to all and that each new suffering is a window shedding light on his soul (1946–1948, 1:125). His ability to forgive allows him to erase the past rather than obsessively relive it, and his sense of vitality and justice prevent him from falling under the sway of archaic, empty strictures. Although he initially cedes to church demands to restore the Virgin's jewels stolen by Ramiro, he rebels against religious and social control when local church and political authorities reveal their hypocrisy and social biases. After Juan's cherished niece Rosario becomes ill with typhus, other relatives and peers refuse to help him nurse her or pay for her care. Marina, a local innkeeper's daughter who had been in love with Ramiro, offers to move in despite the realization that the local gossip mill will destroy her reputation. When Rosario dies, the priest, moneylender, and notary public all pressure Juan to banish Marina, suggesting that Rosario's death represents divine punishment for Juan and Marina's licentious behavior. In an irate response, Juan abandons the walled city and in Marina's company sets out for a new life on the shores of the Mediterranean.

The final chapters describe the voyage across the mountains, through Aragon and down to the sea. In "Foucault and Bourdieu," Michel de Certeau describes travel as an attempt "to discover in distant lands something whose presence at home has become unrecognizable" (1988, 50). In "Walking in the City," he refers to travel and walking as substitutes for legends that no longer speak to the traveler, an effort to create a new story that has meaning (1988, 107). Juan's journey to the Mediterranean overwrites versions of national origin that privilege a northern, enclosed, Catholic, aristocratic culture in favor of a new narrative that opens outward, across the Mediterranean, class barriers, religious constraints, and conventions of sexual relations. In the light and sun of the coastal region that looks out to various and diverse cultures of the past and present, an older, blind aristocrat and a young, adventurous lower-class woman embark on a new life together. Although the final lines of the novel and the declaration of love invoke traditional images of male possession of women and of a male head of household, the unconventional relationship and Marina's power as the sighted guide carry forward a sense of newness and disconnection from the past. Juan, who had persisted in using his dead niece's name to refer to Marina throughout the voyage, accedes to her insistence that she is no longer a child and wishes to be called by her own name.

Juan's acceptance frees him from the incestuous cycle that entraps Ramiro and reveals his recognition that the past is over and that he and Marina have entered a transformed present.

Azorín's rewriting of Spanish cultural history also privileges previously unheard voices, temporal discontinuity, and a multiply mediated reality. Golden Age Spanish theater rarely merits his attention while the late medieval–early Renaissance works that incorporate dissident discourse, such as *La Celestina* and *Lazarillo de Tormes,* reappear with frequency. In a rare commentary on Lope de Vega, the speaker focusses on his lesser known *El nuevo mundo descubierto por Colón* in order to stress and champion the dramatist's condemnation of Spanish imperial policies (1947–48, 2:651–52). Studies of Cervantes abound in his publications, but he seeks to uncover a Cervantine spirit that traditional Spanish writers and readers have ignored. *Lecturas españolas* (1912) argues that Spaniards don't really know Cervantes and consequently they accuse writers who most clearly reflect Cervantine influence of a foreign, "modernist" style. (1947–48, 2:544–45). "Los moriscos" of *Clásicos y modernos* (1913) plays two antecedent Spanish texts against each other to open a space for a new national response to the expulsion of the Moors. The text speaker invokes Agustín Durán's collection of ballads as a rich source of information regarding the daily life of the Moors in late Medieval-early Renaissance Spain. In a long recreation of *morisco* culture, utilizing the inclusive first-person plural, the text tries to make their daily routine familiar to the contemporary reader. The speaker alludes to the Celestina's *morisca* identity, thus inserting the Moor within the national literary tradition (1947–48, 2:750). After over three pages of poetic depiction, the text shifts to a consideration of Pedro Aznar Cordura's 1612 treatise justifying the Moors' expulsion. Here the speaker changes to the third person plural to describe both the suffering of those expelled and the lack of pity of those who charge exorbitant fees for water or a brief rest in the shade of a tree as the Moors make their way out of the country. In contrast with the inclusive "we" of the first part of the text, the third person distances the reader from the materials and contributes to a sense of a divided national subjectivity; on the one hand, those like Durán reach back to reveal the commonality of Moor and non-Moorish Spaniard of early modern Spain while on the other hand, those like Cordura construct an alien figure and refer to a divinely sanctioned expulsion. The use of a generalized "they" to describe the greed of those who exploited the exiled *moriscos* enhances the sense of two national responses by pitting the contemporary, ostensibly Christian reader against a cruelly mercenary antecedent. The absence of any reference to Spain or Spaniards or to other markers of national identity, facilitated by the consistent utilization of a depersonalized third person plural, purposefully elides the traditional opposition of Spanish Christian versus Moor.

Two Azorinian texts published in 1900, *El alma castellana* and *Los hidalgos,* include slightly different descriptions of an *auto de fe* under the identical title "La inquisición." With chilling effect, the text speaker enumerates in excruciating detail the rituals, the construction and exact dimensions of the "theater" built to house the victims and royal as well as common spectators, the formal proclamation, an area that would in modern times be called a restaurant, the victims' ages (including girls as young as fourteen), and the long reading of sentences and resultant boredom of the crowd. The excess of information communicates to the reader that this national past is so distant and alien that it requires elaborate reconstruction. The dispassionate tone of the description augments the shocked reaction of a reader who finds the absurd preoccupation with ritual and minutiae inhumane and alienating. The version appearing in *El alma castellana* includes a consideration of the final abolition of the Inquisition, initially proposed by the Cortes of Cadiz in 1813 with enthusiastic support from the Bishop of the Canary Islands and other church officials and then finally effected after a brief reinstatement under Ferdinand VII (1947–48, 1:630–31). The final line of the text states in a one-sentence paragraph that the Inquisition has ended, thus forcefully restating the irretrievable alterity of this once glorified past.

Azorín's recreation of segments of prior history for the purpose of demonstrating their disconnection from the present reflects a very modern conception of time that has been theorized by Michel de Certeau, building on the work of Michel Foucault. In "The Black Sun of Language," de Certeau identifies a change from the classic concept of periodicity, with the smooth progression through various periods toward the present moment, to a belief in the radical discontinuity of time. The discovery of dramatic gaps and uneven shifts posits a present that relates to the past as foreign and in the process, undermines the belief in the present moment as the culmination of a process moving from error toward truth. In addition, the confrontation with a truth from the past, for which individuals died and sacrificed, but which seems alien and incomprehensible from the point of view of the present, reveals the relativity of belief systems and raises questions about the validity of the values that prevail in the present moment. As de Certeau expresses it, "The ground of our certainty is shaken when it is revealed that we can no longer think a thought from the past" (1989, 177). Spanish modernist writers rewrite founding national narratives and through parody, inversion, de- or over-emphasis, defamiliarize the inherited stores and reveal them as strange and remote.

Distancing the More Recent Past

The desire to rewrite the nation also requires an examination of the more recent past. The rejection of Restoration Spain has long been considered a fundamental feature of the Spanish writers of late nineteenth and early twentieth centuries and in their revision of nineteenth-century history, modernists continue to undermine the authority of positivist historiography and champion the voices of marginal groups. Baroja returns to the nineteenth-century in *Memorias de un hombre de acción,* a multi-volume narration of the exploits of his ancestor, Eugenio de Aviraneta, written between 1912 and 1934. The choice of a relative who died in 1872, only forty years before the publication of the first volume of the series, might suggest an effort to foreshorten the distance between past and present, due both to the familial link and temporal proximity. However, in both the *Memorias* and the biographical *Aviraneta, o la vida de un conspirador,* Baroja insists on the random, unreliable, and often inconsequential memories that his parents and aunt retained of their uncle (1946–48, 4:1173). The structure of the novels underscores the difficult access to the past and the very partial reconstruction of Aviraneta's life, despite the brief interlude between his death and the fictional rendition. Aviraneta frequently disappears from view, displaced by less significant figures of dubious historical significance. The action is based more on the availability of documentation and the random survival of written and oral testimony than on historical importance. The prologue to the first volume, *El aprendiz del conspirador* (1913), introduces a narrator who receives documentation from his aunt that had been in the possession of another local woman. The source materials include papers compiled by Pedro de Leguía, Aviraneta's secretary and assistant, who subsequently pursued a career in politics and rose to the rank of minister. The prologuist-compiler of the story confesses that he is unable to sort out what Aviraneta dictated, Leguía added, or he himself contributed. The intermixing of diverse personal and political perspectives signals the absence of a stable, objective, historical viewpoint and the later revelation that the prologuist is none other than Shanti Andía, the protagonist of Baroja's 1910 novel *Las inquietudes de Shanti Andía,* further insinuates the melding of fiction and history, invention and fact. Throughout the series, popular songs and stories intermix with purportedly authentic documents to assemble a multivoiced, multi-perspectivist depiction that emphasizes the common over the heroic and presents the past as distant and ultimately unknowable in all its complexity and completeness.

Ramón del Valle-Inclán's incursions into national historiography deal with an even more proximate period, which he and others of his age experienced and remember. Critics generally describe his early historical novels and Carlist trilogy (*Los cruzados de la causa, El resplandor de la hoguera,* and *Gerifaltes de antaño*) as a rejection of bourgeois Restoration society, but while some observe a sincere admiration for the traditionalist cause,[11] others perceive a lack of ideological basis in an aestheticized, idiosyncratic Carlism.[12] Various characters in Valle-Inclán's works express views of the past and history that coincide with those of other modernists. The Marqués de Bradomín states a preference for legend over history in his first-person memoirs in *Sonata de Invierno* (1963a, 97), echoing opinions expressed by Galdós and Sawa. The *Sonatas* create a legendary world continuously placed outside the reader's realm of experience. The distancing effect results from a variety of strategies, including the first-person narration by the now elder Bradomín, who vaguely remembers his earlier adventures and evidently embellishes them. Constant intertextual references to classical literary models and the exquisite, aristocratic ambience also place the narrative at several removes from the reader. Although some argue that the series nostalgically evokes a past that has lamentably disappeared, a number of textual cues prompt a different reading. Bradomín explains the preference for legend over history on several occasions in *Sonata de Invierno,* stating that while truth leads to sadness and death, the "risueña mentira" [smiling lie] allows for hope and life (98). Later in the novel, he writes that nations, like individuals, achieve happiness only when they abandon historical consciousness for a future that lies outside good and evil and triumphs over death. The evident Nietzschean echoes in the statement join with Dionysian laughter in a subsequent remark in which Bradomín clarifies that should he write his memoirs, he would aspire not to teach but to amuse: "Toda mi doctrina está en una sola frase: ¡Viva la bagatela![13] Para mí haber aprendido a sonreir, es la mayor conquista de la Humanidad" [All my teaching is found in one single sentence: Long live triviality! In my opinion, learning to smile is Humanity's greatest conquest.] (172). The Bishop to whom Bradomín addresses this comment links laughter with the devil and this transgressive aspect of the "mentira risueña" traverses the *Sonatas* and the representation of Carlism in *Invierno.* In combination with the persistent distancing of the world of the Carlist pretender and his saintly queen of medieval demeanor, the novel mocks the cause and its adherents. Bradomín is most moved to support the movement when he hears a sermon in Basque, which he cannot understand (91). The Carlist pretender hardly leaves the Court and when he does organize a military excursion, he quickly becomes bored and sneaks back to Estella for a sexual interlude with several of his wife's ladies-in-waiting. The only military action in the novel occurs when Bradomín is sent on a mission to rescue two Russian travelers from a fanatical Carlist priest and is caught in an ambush, losing his arm as a result. The legend that displaces history cedes to an ironic, demythologizing laughter that undermines the "heroes."

The Carlism of *Sonata de invierno* remains locked in a space that achieves neither the grandeur of legend nor the coherence of historical narrative. As a chronicler of the cause, Bradomín persistently displays a faulty, incomplete memory. He fails to recognize or remember his ex-lover, the Countess Volfani, and has forgotten they produced a daughter. Caught in a narcissistic love of self, he is incapable of change and relishes the reliving of a past of his own invention through memoirs and the recycling of lovers. Concha of *Otoño* and Volfani of *Invierno* represent this return to prior loves and Bradomín's deliberate efforts to seduce his and Volfani's daughter reflects the same inability to move forward evident in Ramiro of *El mayorazgo de Labraz.* Only the sly smile that mocks Bradomín's world, sometimes with his complicity and sometimes in subtextual cues that elude his control, escapes imprisonment in a distant, dehistoricized, but not truly legendary world. Both in the laughter and the distance, the Carlism of the *Sonatas* appears as an alien, estranged episteme whose remnants in the present are on occasion noble and aesthetically pleasing, but more often vapid and archaic.

Critics have noted Valle-Inclán's frequent recycling of characters, language, and plots across textual boundaries. While many modernists share this habit, in Valle-Inclán it occurs with notable regularity and has a marked effect on the reception of the texts. Bradomín and his "uncle" Juan Manuel Montenegro appear in the *Sonatas,* the *Comedias bárbaras,* and the Carlist War trilogy, as well as selected earlier and later texts. Montenegro appears white-haired and older than the aging Bradomín in the *Sonata de otoño* and then resurfaces in the early volumes of *Comedias bárbaras* as a seemingly younger whoring father of five young bachelors. Killed by his sons at the end of *Romance de lobos,* which originally appeared in serial form in 1907 in the Madrid paper *El mundo* (Zahareas, 13), he comes back to life the next year in *Los cruzados de la causa* (1908). The constant reintroduction of these and other characters with slight or considerable alteration reminds the reader of their eminently fictive nature and of the arbitrary power of the author to rewrite events and characters. This has particularly strong consequences in the Carlist War trilogy, which deals with a recent historical event. The decision to construct a historical novel around the figures of Bradomín, Montenegro, and the latter's son, Cara de Plata, introduces at the outset a dual rhythm of repetition and innovation, historiography and invention, that accompanies a shift from the legendary-ironic style of the *Sonatas* to the epic-grotesque narrative stance of the trilogy.

The reader's horizon of expectation, as Jauss defines it, changes constantly in Valle-Inclán's work, requiring repeated adjustment in an unstable fictive world. The publication of *Los cruzados de la causa* in 1908, the same year as *Romance de lobos,* further complicates the interpretation of Cara de Plata and Carlism. This youngest son of Juan Manuel originally appears in the 1907 *Aguila de blasón,* alternately singled out as the only worthy offspring or as a robber of cadavers in his brother Farruquiño's company. Cara de Plata does not appear in *Romance de lobos,* but the depiction of his brothers as an undifferentiated band of mercenary egotists who ultimately murder their father contaminates his image, especially in the absence of direct reminders of his difference. His reappearance alongside Bradomín and Montenegro in *Los cruzados de la causa,* against the backdrop of different characterizations in other works with very different narrative perspectives and styles signals the need for a critical stance that abjures simplistic, unequivocal interpretations and requires continual monitoring and recalibration.

The three novels of the Carlist war series continue the archaic ambience of the *Sonatas,* with allusions to the present conflict as part of an ongoing crusade to expel Moorish infidels (1979, *Cruzados,* 5) and to an epic world of patriarchs and ritual sacrifices of goats before battle (1979, *Resplandor,* 58). However, the reasonably harmonious world of the *Sonatas,* disrupted only by the ironic smile that undermines the legendary cast of the narrative, gives way to multiple and textually expressed tensions between and within the trilogy's two warring factions. A declining nobility and ambitious middle class confront each other in *Los cruzados de la causa,* while in *Resplandor de la hoguera* and *Gerifaltes de antaño,* the characters, including Bradomín and Montenegro, openly debate the worthiness of their respective causes and leaders. The assumption by some critics that these texts support Carlism and favor the continued patronizing rule of the traditional gentry over a humble lower class has little persuasive power. Bradomín's categorical verbalization of such a philosophy in *Los cruzados de la causa* (1979, 71) is textually and subtextually undermined as the narrative unfolds in the three volumes. Cara de Plata, the exemplar of aristocratic military prowess, fails in his first adventure—the smuggling of arms from Galicia to the Carlist front—and never really finds a military role when he goes to Navarre to enlist. The unlikely heroes of the action are members of the lower class. Isabel, abbess and defender of the inherited valor of her class (and Bradomín's lover on the eventful night of the death of Concha in *Sonata de otoño*) dreams of martyrdom at the hands of the Alfonsine enemy (*Resplandor* 77), but it is the lowly Roque, ex-sacristan and drunkard, who endures the fire while hiding in the chimney and then discovers that the heat has left him blind (*Resplandor* 132). Even after losing his sight, Roque continues to spy for the Carlists and carry messages across enemy lines.

Ironically, Bradomín had once disparaged Roque as too lowly to command soldiers, and in agreement, Cara de Plata had said that he himself should have been named to head the small Carlist faction that Roque initially directed. Over the course of the trilogy, Roque occupies a much more central role than any of his noble critics and acquires heroic stature despite his grotesque manners and appearances. The perspective changes continually, focusing first on the upper classes and then the lower, shifting from Carlist to Alfonsine side, or tracking debates by characters who articulate a variety of positions regarding the combatants, the war, and its political outcome. The constant changes of vision aspire to capture the multiple facets of the question and to depict a past that had moments of grandeur, but degenerated all too often into petty rivalries. In remembering this period of Spanish history, Valle-Inclán does not posit the desirability of its recuperation but rather, develops a portrait that celebrates a handful of anonymous, popular figures who stand in for the thoroughly forgettable Carlist and Alfonsine military and political leaders. The Carlist uprising has no continuity in the present and cannot provide a model for contemporary culture.

Azorín turns to a different aspect of nineteenth-century Spain, focussing on the daily operations of city and small town life in a number of his texts. In particular, *España* (1909) exemplifies his practice and theory of the interplay of documentation and invention, history and intrahistory. *España* consists of thirty-one short texts that in their entirety attempt to define the nation. For the most part, the texts stand independent from each other, with only rare cases of linking. The prologue clarifies that some were written in Levante, others in Castile and that some are of recent invention and others older. In grouping them under the title *España,* Azorín disdains the methodical elaboration of narratives of national formation and substitutes a series of fragmentary, seemingly disparate vignettes. The work stands in stark contrast to conventional histories of Spain, opposing the seemingly objective reportage of positivist studies. The "I" of the compiler intrudes frequently with clear reminders of the effect of the observer on the telling of the tale. The use of a dual temporality to depict Spain also breaks with inherited historiography. Fourteen texts with dates as subtitles appear in the first half of the work and follow a chronological progression from 1237 to 1892, representing a diachronic approach to the depiction of nation. Another fourteen texts constitute the second half and reflect a synchronic vision of Spain, eliminating dates to focus on an on-going present. Three additional texts, "Horas en León," "Horas en Córdoba," and "Horas en Sevilla" appear interspersed across the volume, as if to disrupt any neat binary division. These three interludes describe in first person the speaker's wanderings in different Spanish cities and reveal several fundamental features of the attempt to recreate the past. In each, the narrator meanders at will through the city and his chance encounters determine his textual representation. "Horas en León" describes how he accidentally finds a card with brief comments written by a nun. On the basis of this minimal documentation and in conjunction with his knowledge of the period and cross-references to a document by Saint Theresa, the speaker constructs a historical context and coherent explanation of the card's message, in the process revealing that history relies on the random survival of documents, their chance discovery by interested parties, and the construction of narratives that though logical, could take many different forms.

"Horas en Córdoba" underscores the power of the observer to skew reality according to his/her perspective, silencing elements that disrupt the overall vision. The speaker insistently remarks on the harmonious melding of different elements of Córdoba—its white walls, cypress trees, occasional motionless donkey and radiant blue sky. He then describes a visit to the Cathedral and the Patio of the Oranges, completely eliding any mention of the Arab temple in which the Christian church was constructed. Although the text does not clarify if the speaker enters the building proper, the visit to the patio itself suffices to invoke the Moorish design of the structure and the city. The use of the term Cathedral to designate what typically is referred to as the Mosque or Mosque-Cathedral erases centuries of Moorish occupation and the prolonged contest for control of Spain in order to facilitate the construction of a harmonious, uniform present. The language and tone of "Horas en Córdoba" contribute to a sense that this ahistorical vision of peace and unity is completely natural and it is only in the enormity of the silence that the text cues the reader to query the presumed harmony. The thorough elision of the Moorish presence in what was once a major Islamic capital and continues to bear the marks of this history communicates a warning regarding the facile erasure of a contentious past for the benefit of a homogenous, conflict-free present.

The insistence in these and other texts of *España* on the random survival of documents, easy forgetting of major historical occurrences, and fundamental impact of the observer on the materials contribute to undermine the veracity of the materials presented and create a wary, dubious attitude in the reader. The opening text immediately raises questions regarding the accuracy of the dates given. "El mal labrador," subtitled "1237," relates the story of the greedy farmer originally appearing in section 11 of Berceo's *Milagros de nuestra senhora.* The chronology of Berceo's life and works remains incomplete, due to the absence of records for the thirteenth century. Del Río refers to mention of his name in documents ranging from 1220 to 1264 and assumes his first work dates from 1230. To propose a specific date for one story within the general collection of the *Milagros* suggests the arbitrariness of dating in general and critiques the obsession with precision in conventional histories. Other dates mentioned in *España* continue to invite challenges regarding their validity and relevance. "Unas sombrereras," subtitled "1520," describes a group of pretty young milliners from Toledo who appear in passing in the third chapter of *La vida de Lazarillo de Tormes.* Three different editions of this famous picaresque novel appeared in 1554 and although it has been conjectured that an earlier edition existed, no text has been found and no specific date for such a text has been determined. The dates for later periods sometime coincide with standard histories but in other cases deviate by five to twenty years. The subtitle "1600" of "Un pobre hombre" anticipates by two decades the publication of the second part of the *Lazarillo de Tormes* that serves as its source. The years given for Velázquez's *Las meninas* and Washington Irving's arrival in Spain exactly match standard histories, but the date of 1860 for Lorenzo Arrazola's ministry anticipates his actual time in power by four years.

The capricious selection of dates in the process of historical or biographical reconstruction also stands out in the obvious chronological gaps that mark *España.* The texts in the first half of the volume jump some three hundred years from the initial date of 1237 to the second of 1520. Five bear subtitles placing them in the 1500s, another two in the 1600s, and then the chronology leaps over the eighteenth century to concentrate on a final six that cover the 1800s. The random choice of years and centuries signals a deliberate silencing of major phases of national development. The decision to start with Berceo, rather than the *Poema de mío Cid,* calls attention to the mediation of the historian in determining what counts and what doesn't in creating a national narrative. Writing for a public with access to the ongoing work by Menéndez Pidal on epic poetry, the decision to commence Spain's cultural history with Berceo's "El mal labrador," emphasizes one set of values over others and carries forward the rejection of the Cid's military and patriarchal representation already observed in Costa, Machado, and Marquina. Although the farmer of the tale had ample lands and lived comfortably, he schemed constantly to enlarge his holdings, duping his neighbors and using legal loopholes to his advantage. Despite his duplicity, he retains popularity among his subjects and also manages to gain the favor of the Virgin Mary, so that at the moment of death she intervenes to wrest his soul from the devil. Azorín's text underscores Berceo's anger at the farmer's machinations, with the effect that the popular acceptance of his malice by his contemporaries and his final salvation seem alien to the modern reader's sense of justice.

The silencing of the fourteenth and fifteenth centuries leaves a huge gap that elides the violent period of national consolidation, the irregular ascension of Isabel the Catholic to the throne in opposition to the legal heir Juana la Beltraneja, the establishment of the Inquisition, the expulsion of the Jews, and the discovery of America. The concentration of texts in the sixteenth and seventeenth centuries mimics traditional histories of Spanish culture, but ignores the great literary and political figures to concentrate on a less glorious, more humane past. "Unas sombrereras" introduces sixteenth-century working women and focusses on a productive, laborious Spain and another vignette chooses the unorthodox figure of Francisco Delicado, priest and author of the often off-color picaresque novel with female protagonist, *Retrato de la lozana andaluza.* Totally overlooking Golden Age theater and the great titles of the Spanish canon, *España* concentrates on the picaresque and on female characters who resist control by a rigid honor system to stake out an independent life style. "Ana," a character from Lope de Rueda's *Eufemia,* comes alive in Azorín's text as a gypsy fortuneteller and cohort of the more famous Celestina. The speaker makes coded allusions to her talent in mending virgins and opening locks with a special herb, identified as *pico.* In his *Diccionario secreto,* Camilo José Cela identifies *pico* as a metonymic substitution for penis (1975, vol. 2, part 2:404) and this double meaning enhances Ana's representation as transgressor of patriarchal and religious control. In keeping with modernist antipathies to emphasis on kings, battles, and politics, "Don José Nieto" totally effaces the figures of king, queen, and princess portrayed in Velázquez's *Las meninas* to focus on a secondary character who appears in the shadows of Velázquez's famous painting and whose biographical details remain obscure.

The continual questioning of history in the first half of the text gives way to an intrahistorical depiction in the second part. However, just as Azorín challenges conventional historiography in the initial studies, he now undermines intrahistorical reconstruction, insinuating a timeless, eternal Spain only to question its existence. For Ortega, Azorín's strength and defect consist in his ability to not only make the reader feel at one with the past but to feel past (1965, 2:189). This view, which recurs with moderate variation in critics such as Vilanova and Glenn, fails to consider the persistent othering in Azorín and his contemporaries of a past that survives to the detriment of the present and future. "Unas sombrereras" depicts an industrious, populous Toledo that conflicts dramatically with the dusty, barren town of the modern period. "Un sabio" illustrates drastic changes in concept and lexicon over time. The text describes a typical day in the life of a Renaissance scholar-writer, who lives in a comfortable home with servants that fetch his cape to warm him while he works, turn the pages of the manuscript he is studying, and take notes when he dictates. The intrusion of the "I" of the modern writer, who expresses his envy and wishes he could write his articles in similar conditions, further distances the reader from the world of the wise man, today known by the less lofty term of author or scholar. "Un pobre hombre" follows a similar strategy to encourage the repudiation of the past. When a servant informs his master that the Inquisitor has a request for him, the master collapses in terror, imagining that various tortures await him. The text speaker incorporates an extensive quotation from *Praxis ecclesiastica et soecularis* to detail different torture methods. The long, elaborate clauses of the Renaissance text, with ample use of polysyndeton and archaic terminology, conflict with the short sentences and simplified syntax of Azorín's modern prose and appear as strange and remote. The sardonic allusion to national competitions for the most effective torture device and the mockingly chagrined confession that the Italians surpassed the Spaniards as well as the final revelation that the Inquisitor only wanted some pears from the now revived and very relieved gentleman reenforce a sense of estrangement from a world that played a considerable role in the formation of the Spanish nation.

In texts that focus on an intrahistorical present, *España* encourages varied responses. "Toscano o la conformidad" introduces a rich man who has lost all, but accepts his fate with dignity and finds a spiritual peace in his poverty. Other texts harshly criticize the lack of movement and vigor associated with intrahistory. "Una ciudad castellana" attacks the paralysis of provincial life in a town with twelve lawyers, four churches, and a multitude of impoverished farmers. A number of sketches historicize the intrahistorical, revealing that, at times for the better, at times for the worse, "eternal" Spain is disappearing. The barely insinuated backdrop to "Juan el de Juan Pedro" includes a multitude of historical and biographical details behind a seemingly static existence. Economic changes that result in his parents' eviction, the cholera epidemic, the massive emigration of unemployed farm workers to America, and a number of hastily alluded events determine Juan's unchanging suffering and solitude amidst the equally unremitting poverty of rural Spain. The anti-idyllic depiction of country life suggests that rural solidarity, if it ever existed outside of fantasized urban narratives, has definitively disappeared.

"Vida de un labrantín" continues the bleak portrayal of rural life and again historicizes the intrahistorical. The description of the philosophy of the unnamed farmer presents an individual who seems to live outside of time, resigned to the disappearance of his children and impending hardships of old age. Dignified and fatalistic, the farmer lives in an eternal present, refusing to concern himself with tomorrow. Azorín's text does not absorb modernity into the past or into a never-ending present, as Ortega suggests. In "Vida de un labrantín," and other similar works, the poetic recreation of figures from the past or a present that harks back to the past accompanies subtle and not so subtle indicators that place the world of the modern reader at a clear distance from the textual time. Twice the text speaker remarks that the reader will probably find certain aspects of the farmer's life incomprehensible and strange, underscoring the separation of the modern urban world from that of the aging rural worker. The use of a very specialized vocabulary in long lists that describe the farmer's tasks, tools, crops, and fields of knowledge introduces a lexicon unfamiliar to city dwellers. The intrusion of modernity in the death of one son in the Spanish American War and another in a train accident historicizes the intrahistorical and strikes a note of pathos designed to evoke sympathy and a sense of injustice at a situation that allows for the conditions depicted. *España* neither closes itself off in an eternally repeating past nor excludes the cosmopolitanism that informs so much modernist literature. While focussing on the definition of Spain, it repudiates such traditional institutions of exclusion as the Inquisition. The epigraph, drawn from a Petrarchan sonnet, appears in Italian and the epilogue reveals the composition of *España* in Gavarnie, France. It describes the speaker's visit to a French village whose buildings, customs, and residents remind him of Spain. The textual borders open to incorporate other literary traditions and languages just as the nation's borders have and must continue to remain receptive to the spirit, ideas, and cultures of multiple others that live inside and outside of Spain.

The conscious forgetting and remembering of history advocated by Azorín and other modernist writers echoes Nietzschean and Freudian versions of history and anticipates concepts later articulated by Hayden White on the role of the literary in history (1978, 81–120) and by Michel de Certeau on culture as a network of words (1989, 178–81). Such a modern and arguably post-modern vision of history can prove progressive or regressive, depending on the criteria employed in the process of erasure and reconstruction. In the forgetting of the imperial and militaristic national past that excludes women, the lower classes, and racial and ethnic minorities, Spanish modernist writers must simultaneously construct a new history and define the Spanish nation according to a different set of principles. The past requires rewriting and the nation must be (re)membered through a different narrative.

The Search for the Present: Reconsiderations of Region, Religion, and Race

The changing perception of time that affects the notion of history and the past also obliges a reconsideration of the present in relation to the past. The new consciousness of temporal discontinuity and of the ease with which history erases and then rewrites the past combines with philosophical developments, such as Bergson's idea of temporality as psychic flow (1911b, 26–30; 54), to suggest different models for the unfolding of the present from some immediate or distant prior time. The effort to recuperate a pluralistic culture that survived the Hapsburg ambition for a centralized, imperialist, patriarchal, and narrowly orthodox religious society continues in the construction of a present in texts that argue for and represent transculturation and acceptance of the other. Much modernist literature deals with questions of gender and class, and I have emphasized the revision of traditional visions of gender, the patriarchy, the don Juan figure, honor, family constitution, and the interrelationship between these topics and a rejection of imperialism in texts whose action takes place in the historical past. I have also underscored how the critique of empire and colonialism often accompanies a call for greater class mobility and the abandonment of bourgeois affectations in favor of a more democratic social structure. I will further explore modernist representations of gender and class in the chapter on subjectivity, although it is important to emphasize that the treatment of these topics in a chapter that focusses on the individual in no way signifies a diminishing of the role of gender and class in the construction of a national identity. A redefinition of nation necessarily influences the conceptualization of the individual subject and a change in the vision of the subject crucially impacts the idea of nation. Similarly, variations in the definition of religious, ethnic, regional, and racial composition simultaneously traverse the categories of nation and subject. In the following analysis of the modernist reconsideration of region, religion, and race and their role in the production of a new Spain, I will focus primarily on issues of national identity, but the implications for subject formation reinsert themselves throughout the discussion.

War Memories, Regionalism, and the Search for New Forms of National Unity

The interest demonstrated by Unamuno, Baroja, Valle-Inclán, Galdós, and others in the Carlist Wars of the 1800s reflects an ongoing concern with regional rivalries. The traditional conflict between a strong central government and a more diffuse federation with greater regional autonomy takes on new urgency in the context of national reconfiguration at the turn-of-the-century.[14] With the loss of Cuba, Puerto Rico, the Philippines, and Guam, and with the exception of troublesome possessions in Africa, Spain reverts to the pre-imperial geographic dimensions that she acquired with the union of Aragon and Castile by way of the marriage of Ferdinand and Isabel in 1469. The growing strength of Catalan, Basque, and Galician linguistic, economic, cultural, and political power on the heels of the loss of the last major colonies raises the specter of further territorial fragmentation within the peninsula. What would prevent a continuing downsizing of the nation, with the Catalan segment of the Old Kingdom of Aragon or the Basque region moving toward the same autonomy that the former colonies had claimed? Traditionalists oppose the regional movements, supporting a strong central government and continued dominance of the Castilian language. The predominant modernist stance rejects inherited centrist and monocultural, monolingual policies. In their continuing efforts to break down old borders and open new avenues of communication that eschew violence and domination, modernists from Catalonia, Castile, and other areas look to regionalism as a new possibility for national reconstruction while at the same time they address fears of and work against further dismemberment.

During the period following the Spanish American War, Juan Valera's essays exhibit a discernible fear of additional national fragmentation. His 1901 review of José Nogales's anti-war novel *El último patriota* also reveals a link between anxiety over national disintegration and the avoidance of criticism of the government's conduct of the war. Although *El último patriota* barely hints at a Catalan location for the novel, Valera clearly reads the text as a critique of the central government's military and political record. The city in which the narrative action takes place is situated on the coast of an unnamed sea and could be any maritime population. The mention of a visiting French investor might suggest a town close to the Pyrenees, whether Catalonia or the Basque Region, but does not preclude other areas of the peninsula. The clearly non-Castilian location of the action, prompts an uneasy response in Valera, who observes that continuing recriminations for the conduct of the war only exacerbate national feelings of inferiority and lead to disunity, regionalism, separatism, and class conflict (1941, 2:1071).

Valera equates empire, Castile, the Castilian language, and strong central government with traditional Spanish grandeur while regionalism, the resurgence of local languages, racial diversity, and demands for social and gender equality threaten an unacceptable partitioning of power and the nation. "El regionalismo filosófico en Galicia" begrudgingly recognizes the vitality of Catalan language and culture, but vigorously seeks to preempt Galician, Majorcan, and Valencian efforts to establish their linguistic identity, arguing that the proliferation of regional languages bears a direct relation to national decadence (1941, 2:902). Several Valera essays dealing with literary matters betray a zealous Castile-centrism and expose its links with imperialist traditions. In a review of Francisco Blanco García's *La literatura española del siglo XIX,* the speaker calls for future volumes on Portugal and Brazil to be added to the existing tomes on Latin American and Catalan literature: "De esta suerte tendríamos el cuadro verdaderamente completo de toda la literatura contemporánea española, dando al nombre o vocablo España la amplitud que tuvo en el siglo XVI" [In this way we would have the truly complete picture of all contemporary Spanish literature, giving the name or term Spain the breadth that it had in the sixteenth century] (1941, 2:883). The subsumption of Portuguese, Brazilian, Catalan, and Spanish American literature under the rubric of contemporary "Spain" represents an egregious colonizing move that disregards the national sensitivities of the countries and regions mentioned as well as their political and cultural differences.

Modernists who seek to break with the past confront this centrist vision and strive to develop an alternate theory of nation that allows for regional and linguistic differences while averting fragmentation and the construction of new internal borders. Furthermore, in turning away from Castilian hegemony towards a greater appreciation of regional expression, they must avoid a retreat to the conservative ethos of traditional regionalism.[15] Nineteenth-century conservative novelists, such as Fernán Caballero, José María de Pereda, or Luis Coloma, also exalt the regional spirit and bitterly attack Castilian hegemony, but they do so with an agenda that differs markedly from modernist calls for a new national and international program. Traditional regionalism rejects Madrid precisely because it views the capital as a liberal, atheist, and corrupt threat to religious orthodoxy and hierarchical class and gender structures. This school of thought looks to the past as a model for the present and future and although it opposes the capital, it continues to envision centrist control in the form of church power. Modernist writing of the 1890s and early 1900s constructs an alternative to traditional regionalism and in contrast to the closed world of Pereda's Santander or Fernán Caballero's Andalusia, it persistently links regional and international concerns and urges openness and religious tolerance.

Ganivet's call in his *Epistolario* for a return to the ancient city-state suggests a tentative step towards independence from national control and his insistence on radical individualism clearly presents a variation to the theological and social conformity espoused by Pereda, Coloma, and Fernán Caballero. The fact that the modernist journal *Helios* chooses to publish the specific segments of Ganivet's letters that deal with regionalism in 1903, some five years after his death, attests to the continuing currency of the issue in national discussions (1903, 257–70). Santiago Rusiñol, often described as a formalist writer with little concern for social issues, wrestles with the relation between nation, region, and the colonial wars in *L'hèroe* (1903). Although the play clearly arrogates responsibility for the war and the national and personal suffering that it caused to the central government, the anti-Castilian, anti-centrist sentiments are expressed much more cautiously than anti-imperialist feelings. Despite its moderation, Rubén Darío writes in *Tierras soleares* that *L'héroe* provoked a scandal at its opening in Barcelona and as a consequence, the run was discontinued and Rusiñol had to leave for France (1917, 16). The play traces the war's impact on the Catalan owners of a small textile factory. The Hero, so named throughout the play, has returned victorious from the Philippines to the adulation of the local government and citizenry. Accustomed to power, to the voluntary or forced favors of Philippine women, and to the satisfaction of his creature comforts by the Army, Philippine subjects, and now the idolizing Catalan citizenry, the Hero refuses to work and embarks on a drinking, gambling spree. His parents, Anton and Ramona, brother Andreuet, and Andreuet's fiancée Carme represent Catalan values of discipline, industriousness, family loyalty, and thrift that the Hero now disdains. Not only does he squander the monies destined to buy his brother's exemption from military service, he also steals his brother's fiancée while simultaneously seducing the wife of an ailing veteran.

Against the backdrop of the Catalan setting and language, references to the Cádiz March and the Hero's new habit of playing the guitar and shouting *olé* introduce a dissonant, foreign note. The "national" symbols of the guitar and the Andalusian *olé,* derived from the Arabic *wa-lla,* pertain to traditions that remain alien in an area that cultivates the more sedate *sardana,* accompanied by the high, piercing *fiscorns,* oboes, drums, and cymbals. The one character who consistently uses Spanish in the play is the sergeant, representative of a distant national government and unable to speak the local language or share local values. The sergeant often extols manly conduct, the virtues of the nation, and military victory, linking patriarchy, militarism, and empire in intimate association. In a drunken stupor, the Hero reveals the extent to which he has internalized these values when he shouts "Visca la guerra! . . . Visca la mort I visca la victòria" [Long live war. . . . Long live death and victory] (1981, 1034), echoing Maeztu's praise of death with glory over life. Joan, a veteran who is dying from a fever contracted in the Philippines, confronts the Hero throughout the play and in the denouement. Joan rejects the use of arms, but when the Hero provokes him with the unremorseful confession that he had seduced Joan's wife, Joan strikes him with a Philippine sword that had been placed in an arrangement of arms and flowers to honor the Hero. Joan insists he has not killed the hero, but rather the local bum; the real heroes and national treasures are the textile workers and loom (1036).

The play's exaltation of regional values functions as a protest against the colonialist, militarist tradition that modernists associate with the central government and its policies. Regionalism here does not signify a return to traditional village life, but rather a link to a new national and international project. The resurgence of Catalan and other regional languages contributes to new modes of thinking and modernist writers exploit the development. The Martínez Sierras, who translate many Rusiñol plays to Spanish, state that the study of a language that is similar to but still different from Spanish provides them with a vocabulary to express the new sentiments and ideas that characterize modernism (1903c, 385–89). Clarín early recognizes Catalonia's cultural dynamism and its close connection to European cultural advances (*Ensayos* 1888) and in 1906 Azorín analyzes Catalonia's difference from the rest of Spain, arguing that it can contribute a new kind of leadership for the nation, in contrast to traditional Castilian hegemony and current apathy (*En Barcelona*). Silverio Lanza's poem "Barcelona," published in *Revista nueva,* compares the city to a new Columbus, with the potential to discover a new world to replace the old and now discredited one (1899, 199–200).

Unamuno, a Basque residing in Salamanca and writing in Castilian, and Joan Maragall, a Catalan living in Barcelona but publishing in both Catalan and Castilian, carry on a public and private correspondence on a number of topics, including the problem of regionalism in the post-war period. Unamuno considers the issue of nation and region in two different essays in 1905 and 1906. "La crisis actual del patriotismo español" (1958, vol. 3) and "Más sobre la crisis del patriotismo" (1958, vol. 3). Unamuno's footnote to the 1905 text clarifies that in 1896 he previously published an article with the same title in the Barcelona publication *Ciencia Social,* but that the publication ceased when government officials confiscated it during the response to the protests against the Montjuich atrocities. This early reference to Barcelona, Montjuich, and government censure in an article on patriotism notifies the reader that the text will adopt an open definition of nation, inclusive of Catalonia and Castile, and hostile to centrist imposition of a uniform vision. The privileging of multiple, sometimes contradictory discourses within the project of post-war national reconstruction continues throughout the article. In response to those who accuse advocates of change and regional autonomy of a lack of patriotism, he responds that even those regionalists who declare themselves anti-Spanish unknowingly aid in constructing a new national spirit. According to the text speaker, nineteenth-century emphasis on the nation as site and source of collective attachment has shifted in the contemporary context to a dual allegiance to the native region and the international community. The new regional pride in Catalonia, the Basque region, and Galicia stems from a repudiation of a Castile-centered national culture and an aversion to such imposed traditions as bullfights, *sainetes,* and the odious "national" music, previously mocked by Rusiñol. The essay welcomes the regional movements and encourages on-going, dynamic interchange between the various value and cultural systems. Catalans should try to catalanize Castile, Galicians should similarly seek to interject their culture in the national mosaic, and Basques should stop fearing the invasion of Castilian workers and culturally invade Castile. In a vociferous rejection of isolationism, the speaker warns against the dangers of traditional regionalist movements and, in particular, of the co-optation of anti-centrist sentiments by centrist powers. According to this reading of Spanish history, Carlist resistance and its potential for a plural, democratic opposition lost all power when it adopted the Castilian unitary vision and the alliance of politics and religion (1958, 3:951). A people cannot preserve their identity in isolation; strength and growth ensue from encounter with the other and regional movements represent the potential for a new, plural, contentious, but rich national culture.

Unamuno exhibits an unwavering conviction of the value of dialogue, not a civil, cordial exchange that easily falls into philic assimilation, but a loud, passionate argument. He specifically differentiates his verbal stridency from physical aggression in the closing paragraphs, in which he advocates discussion over violence and rejects a tradition of imposed truths. He also attests to his belief in the dialogic quality of the word and of discourse when he writes that his truth will no longer be his when and if it enters the thought of his readers.[16] The insistence on a multi-voiced individual and national discourse surfaces again in "Más sobre la crisis del patriotismo," which includes an epigraph in Spanish by José Rizal, the Philippine independence hero, and another in Catalan by Joan Maragall. The opening sentence alludes to the earlier essay, adding to the sense of on-going conversation and encounter with one or more interlocutors. The second part of the discussion of patriotism rejects even more forcefully a definition of nation as homogeneous and single-voiced, specifically linking this unitary vision with the Spanish state as developed under Castile. The establishment of the Inquisition to ensure religious and national unity, the fashioning of the army to uphold values imposed by the Inquisition, and the imperial spread of this monolithic doctrine must give way to a plural, varied national culture. In order to expedite the construction of the new nation, Unamuno again calls on each region to develop its own personality and to this end, to actively impose itself on other regions: "Nadie se hace una personalidad por acción interna, sino por acción hacia fuera" [No one constructs a personality by turning inward, but rather by moving outward] (1958, 3:1011).

Joan Maragall specifically responds to Unamuno in "Catalunya y avant" (1911) and to the question of regionalism in a series of articles written over twenty years. "La vida regional" (1893) aims to legitimize regionalism while differentiating it from its traditional forms. The opening paragraph distinguishes between a progressive regionalism that seeks new horizons and redemptive solutions, and the anachronistic lyricism of previous regional movements, perhaps referring to such national figures as Pereda or to more local Catalan writers of the *Renaixensa*. The text struggles to preempt accusations of separatism, first by rejecting "el espíritu de mezquinos rencores" [the spirit of petty resentment] (n. d. 1:53), then by citing the widespread appearance of new regional movements in Italy and France, and finally by referring to a fellow "patriot" who has written on the Galician regional movement. The reference to Galicia, which had not produced a political movement equivalent to Catalan separatism, serves to deflect attention from the more threatening aspects of regional revival. Writing as a Catalan for a Castilian-speaking public, Maragall often makes use of strategies of indirect speech and textual ambiguity to defray potential accusations of separatism. A review of Azorín's *El alma castellana* (1900) offers him an opportunity to analyze the causes of contemporary Spanish decline through extended quotations from a Madrid-based author. Without directly identifying the sources of the present Spanish condition, the text speaker suggests a disjunction between the Spanish peoples and their leaders that a mere change in governmental structure will not resolve. He then speculates that if writers from other areas of Spain follow Azorín's example and define the spirit of their various regions, the collective effort might produce a new, much needed national "spirit" (n. d., 3:62). In clear agreement with Unamuno, Maragall writes in a softer, less assertive tone than the Salamanca-based professor as he navigates the difficult terrain lying between Catalan ambitions and national fears of dismemberment.

As memories of the war recede and calls for a new national orientation increase, Maragall's texts become more forceful. "El sentimiento catalanista" (1902) openly admits to Catalan resentment of Castile and argues that in an industrial age that rewards analytical talents and cosmopolitan openness, Catalonian qualities will better serve to lead Spain in productive new directions. "La patria nueva" (1902) continues to encourage outreach and political activism among Catalan youth. Consonant with Unamuno's calls to catalanize Spain, Maragall cautions against complaisant regional pride and urges Catalan intervention at the national level to contribute to the creation of a new country. Events of 1905 lead to even greater calls for active cultural and political intervention. The invasion of two Barcelona newspaper offices by Army officers precipitates the passage of the Law of Jurisdictions, which protects the Army by mandating that offenses against the Army, Police, or nation be tried by court martial. "El ideal ibérico" (1906) specifically cites threats of renewed militarism and encourages Catalan participation in national politics as a way to combat centrist, militarist, Castilian policies. The speaker defines Castilian as a political vision that exists in Catalonia as well as Castile and other regions and that rejects diversity and dialogue in favor of rigid, hegemonic control.

The difficult and tenuous nature of a plural, multilingual, and multicultural society receives ample recognition by the two writers. Both Unamuno and Maragall acknowledge the danger of slipping into a univocal world, whether through retreat into the self or colonization of the other. Maragall's "Catalunya y Avant" (1911) addresses this issue in a complex dialogic interchange with Unamuno and his own earlier texts. Here Maragall refutes Unamuno's calls for a catalanization of Spain and for Catalan writers to use Castilian as the means to this end. The essay opens with a two-verse epigraph by Unamuno: "La sangre de mi espíritu es mi lengua / Y mi patria es allí donde resuene" [My language is my spirit's blood / and my country is wherever it resounds] (n. d., 5:268). This textual speaker fully agrees with those sentiments and consequently denies the ability of Catalan writers to express themselves in Castilian. The speaker further refutes as imperialist the admonition to catalanize Castile and argues that for the moment, introspection offers a better route to the construction of a new national identity. He then refers to another Unamunan essay, the 1900 "¡Adentro!," in which Unamuno had also advocated introspection as a vehicle to self-knowledge. In keeping with traditional criticism of the period, one could interpret both "Catalunya y avant" and "¡Adentro!" as proof of a rejection of Catalan-Castilian collaboration and of activism, in reaction to a failure to influence public policy.[17] However, several details preclude such a reading. In both the Maragall and Unamuno essays, the turn inward involves a search for the other through the self. Maragall's text advises readers from Spain's different regions to look within themselves in order to find a common Iberian root. In the process of self-discovery, they will enhance their understanding of each other and create national unity. Unamuno's text reveals an identical play of inward to outward, self to other: "Reconcéntrate para irradiar; deja llenarte para que rebases luego, conservando el manantial. Recójete en ti mismo para mejor darte a los demás todo entero e indiviso. . . . tienes que hacerte universo, buscándolo dentro de ti" [Concentrate on yourself in order to radiate out; let yourself be filled so that you later overflow, conserving the flowing water. Retire into yourself so as to better give yourself to others entire and indivisible. . . . you have to make yourself the universe, looking for it within you] (1958, 3:427). The two faces of the turning coin revolve in a continual movement that rejects stasis, one-sided resolution, and monologic articulations.

The dates of the various texts refute attempts to show a chronological evolution from one position to the other. Maragall reaches back over Unamuno's 1905 and 1906 essays, which advocate catalanization of Spain, to a 1900 text that suggests another route to self-discovery. Furthermore, Maragall's text foregrounds dialogue and heteroglossia in the very act of advocating introspection. The Catalan title, the epigraph from Unamuno, the use of direct address to rebut Unamuno, and the intertextual allusions to "¡Adentro!" privilege communication across language, space, and time. "¡Adentro!" itself is written as an open letter to an unnamed recipient and maintains a dialogic structure and tone. Emmanuel Levinas and his distinction between the Saying and the Said help to illustrate the importance of this ongoing dialogue between and among modernist writers. Levinas rejects the tyranny of meaning, the reduction of the value of what one says to hermeneutics. The process of addressing the other has a meaning that surpasses that of the words themselves; it is an ethical commitment even as the words spoken reveal a lack of coincidence of ideas or value (1993, 142). Maragall and Unamuno disclose a considerable coincidence of ideas but more importantly, they exemplify through their words, their textual construction, and their intertextual exchange that the modernist process of Spanish national reconstruction must take place in the spaces between borders and in the saying of difference.

This same spirit pervades much of Azorín's work and his studies of Spanish landscape and culture. Traditional and recent criticism has focussed with a vengeance on Azorinian representation of Castile,[18] but a good deal of his writing either places Castile within a broader context or subtly perforates the borders that purportedly separate the central region from neighboring and more distant areas. *El paisaje de España, visto por los españoles* (1917) depicts the different regions as they have appeared in the works of antecedent Spanish writers. Doubly mediated through the earlier writers and yet again through Azorín, the landscapes are presented not as objective reality, but rather as the construct of a human observer. Azorín's textualization of Spain incorporates varied linguistic and cultural traditions and insistently traverses the borders that could potentially separate them from each other. The study opens with a consideration of the borderland that joins Galicia and the Bierzo region of León and then moves to a consideration of Galicia. The speaker reproduces a train trip to this northwest province and remarks that Galicia is more distant and alien than France. He points out that the great Galician poet, Rosalía de Castro, was first mentioned in an anthology authored by a foreigner, Fitzmaurice-Kelly (1947–1948, 3:1162) and when quoting her descriptions of the Galician countryside, he leaves them in the original Galician language, interspersing his Spanish commentary between quotations. The entire text reiterates this pattern of cultural mix and dialogue with constant conjoining of insider and outsider to characterize a specific region. To describe the Basque region, it focusses on works by Pío Baroja, a writer of Basque origins who summers there, but resides in Madrid. Azorín emphasizes Baroja's characterization of the region as a borderland, whose identity originates in the co-presence of French language and culture. Other texts underscore the African nature of Granada, cite the Quijote—a quintessentially Castilian text—to describe Seville, and use the Sevillian poet Gustavo Adolfo Bécquer to depict Aragon. To recreate the insular Majorcan landscape, the speaker turns to the Nicaraguan Rubén Darío. Azorín does not directly address the issue of regionalism, but his textual organization minimizes Castile's preeminence and concentrates on the rich diversity of the periphery. The continual commingling of observers with roots in the region and "outsiders" attests to an open, dialogic vision of region and country.

The privileging of dialogue and respect for regional variation come together in many modernist writers. Carmen de Burgos defends Catalan calls for greater autonomy and uses her visit to Switzerland to illustrate the advantages of a multilingual, multicultural nation (1909?, 497). Santiago Rusiñol includes an impassioned description of Granada and the Alhambra in *Desde el molino e Impresiones del arte,* published around 1894. The Andalusian Manuel Machado adds yet another layer of cross cultural dialogue to the Catalan's rendering of the Moorish Alhambra in his poem "Granada, por Rusiñol," in which he responds to Rusiñol's description (1924, 63–64) and reveals once again the modernist belief that dialogue with the outside enriches the understanding of the self. The vindication of regional culture carries with it a repudiation of Castilian hegemony and militarist, imperialist policies. The magnitude of this stance in Spanish modernist writing negates characterizations of the modernist period as the literary correlative of imperialism.[19] In the Spanish context, the modernist break with the past brings together a critique of international and domestic impositions of monolithic systems. Once again, Ortega y Gasset proves the exception. Although his vision of regionalism, national reconstruction, militarism, and colonialism in some ways reiterates arguments presented in Altamira, Ganivet, Unamuno, Maragall, Azorín, and Rusiñol, in other respects, it differs markedly. Ortega y Gasset's study of Spanish character in *España invertebrada* deals primarily with the relationship between regionalism, militarism, colonialism, and nation and also touches upon race, class, and gender as imbricated in questions of region and empire.

First published in the Madrid newspaper *El Sol* in 1920 and later reissued in book form in 1921, *España invertebrada* repudiates pacifism to argue that while force alone will not produce enduring social and political institutions, it is necessary and beneficial when combined with other elements. Ortega rejects the views of Herbert Spencer and others who believe that the modern industrial spirit is superior to the old warring vigor, distancing himself from the anti-imperial discourse of Ganivet, Maragall, the early Maeztu, and Rusiñol in arguing that the force of arms represents spiritual vigor rather than mere brute strength (1967b, 43). Military force goes hand in hand with the "estro divino" [divine inspiration] (45) that characterizes creative and imperial nations. The allusion to imperial power as equivalent to greatness recurs throughout *España invertebrada,* which asserts that only a successful international policy of ambitious ventures produces a great nation with domestic stability and a respectable internal policy. Thus, Castile arose not from a pre-existing unity, but as the result of a national ambition to conquer first Arab lands and later America. Similarly, Rhodesia sprang from Cecil Rhodes's dream of creating an empire in savage Africa (50).

The speaker dismisses the Reconquest of Spain as of little value, since it took eight centuries to complete, but waxes eloquent on the sublime energies evidenced in the Crusades (140–41), the Conquest of America, and the colonization of the "new world" (145). In open disagreement with those who suggest that, in the current historical context, other regions might provide national leadership, *España invertebrada* argues that Castile created Spain and only Castilians have the ability to lead the nation. In this view, regionalism represents not a potential solution but a manifestation of the process of disintegration, which is both the nation's greatest defect and her most pressing challenge. Invertebrate Spain, without a strong center to anchor her component parts, lost first her European possessions, then the American colonies, and now faces the threat of Catalan and Basque particularism. Like Unamuno, Ganivet, Maeztu, Maragall, and his contemporaries, Ortega y Gasset views national unity as the product of a dynamic interaction of constituent parts. His insistence that in fighting, one acknowledges the other's existence and that body combat closely approximates an embrace closely matches statements by Unamuno and the early Maeztu. However, his emphasis on hierarchy and belief that actions of the elite supersedes those of the masses quickly erases the symbol of the embrace for a less symmetrical relation. "Cuando . . . la parte inferior del grupo se resiste anómalamente a ser dirigida, influida por la porción superior . . . cuando en una nación la masa se niega a ser masa—esto es, a seguir a la minoría directora—, la nación se deshace, la sociedad se desmembra y sobreviene el caos social, la invertebración histórica" [When . . . the inferior part of the group anomalously refuses to be led, to be influenced by the superior sector . . . when in a nation the masses refuse to be masses—that is, to follow the leading minority—, the nation comes apart, society fragments and social chaos, historical invertebration, occurs] (100). The dynamic action that constitutes social cohesion now appears as a one-way flow, top down, with no reciprocal response from the majority (99).

Ortega repeats insistently that he does not refer solely to politics, but rather to all areas of social life, including business, the military, labor unions, and art. In these different sectors, the masses have a biological mission to follow their superiors (105). The unidirectional communication espoused as the social model has its counterpart in the lack of dialogic structure in *España invertebrada,* which offers a striking contrast to other texts of the period. Maragall, Unamuno, and others typically establish an interlocutor early in their essayistic writing, sometimes mentioning an immediate antecedent to whom they are responding, or inserting an epigraph to introduce another voice and view even before the text speaker takes the floor. They tend to avoid or minimally use footnotes, even in longer treatises such as Unamuno's *Del sentimiento trágico de la vida.* Footnotes and source identification invest the text speaker with specialized authority that allows her/him to impart information rather than enter into exchange with the reader or antecedent texts. *España invertebrada* refers to authoritative sources with some frequency and makes no mention of a specific contemporary interlocutor other than a generalized "you" that figures as the subject of repeated imperatives: "Consider the intimate life of any contemporary party" (97), "When you hear: 'Today there are no great men', understand: 'Today there are no followers' (98), or "But let's move on" (143). The reader often confronts opinions that are couched as facts or whose veracity could only be challenged by an uninformed interlocutor. "Don't bring up the trivial argument that . . . "(44), "In my opinion there is absolutely no doubt" (61), "It is completely erroneous to suppose that. . . . "(97), "It is a complete waste of time to discuss whether a society should be constituted by the intervention of an elite or not" (114) and similar expressions do not invite response, but rather foster silence and acquiescence. Furthermore, the sources cited have almost exclusively foreign origins or are deceased. As Jan Mukarovsky points out, monologue is addressed to a listener, but discourages response by creating a distant spatio-temporal context (113). The text further dissuades reader response through the use of frequent self-citation. Of 29 footnotes, seven direct the reader to specific authoritative sources and the remaining 22 either introduce additional personal commentary or remit the reader to previous publications by Ortega y Gasset in a sort of closed circuit that precludes the intervention of other voices and contributes to a monologic quality.

Many of these same discursive strategies appear in other essayists, with the aim of shoring up their authority, but typically they are interspersed with techniques that open the text to the reader's input or link it dialogically with other texts or speakers. In *España invertebrada,* the balance between deference to the reader and construction of textual authority, normally carefully maintained in the modern essay, shifts decidedly in the direction of the speaker. In this sense, the essay textualizes the call for docility and operates performatively to exact submission on the reader's part. It stops short of an excess of power, however, and the risk of alienating the targeted public by establishing a homosocial bond between text speaker and reader that becomes ever stronger in the face of a series of others who stand outside the textualized male community. The reader presumably has attained the intellectual ability to decode the text at hand, having chosen to read it in the first place. This immediately separates the reader from the masses, whose disjointed, mistaken and childish opinions (105) preclude an understanding of the materials. The suggestion of extreme childishness (112) and of an other based purely on age subsequently expands to include class, race, and gender. The text speaker characterizes Spain as an agricultural, rural land that even in the cities has not produced a truly urban, cultured elite. The size of the urban population has no real relevance; the key resides in the masses' acquiescence to a ruling minority and where that fails to occur, a society remains forever locked in the cyclical rotation of sowing and harvesting and thus, outside the great historical struggles. The speaker identifies Sudan as a primary example of such a culture, and although he quickly clarifies that Spain is not unredeemably destined to an African destiny, since she participated in the great Western enterprise of colonization, the specter of Arab and African presence among a rural, unrefined Spanish lower class creates a bond between speaker and presumably educated, urban reader that originates in racial and class exclusions.

The gendering of this excluded other develops slowly over the course of the argument to become exceedingly clear in the final pages. In an early passage, Ortega specifically marks women as separate and distinct: "Hace falta, junto a los eminentes sabios y artistas, el militar ejemplar, el industrial perfecto, el obrero modelo y aun el genial hombre de mundo. Y tanto o más que todo esto necesita una nación de mujeres sublimes" [In addition to eminent wise men and artists, one needs the exemplary soldier, the perfect industrialist, the model laborer and even the brilliant man of the world. And as much or more than all this, one needs a nation of sublime women] (122). In 1920, Spain already had eminent women writers and artists, model women workers, wives and widows who ran businesses, and a long tradition of courtesans who had parlayed their talents into social and economic success alongside the "men of the world" cited by Ortega. The erasure of accomplished women betrays a fear and resentment that receives full expression in the last three pages of the text and grows in importance as the speaker struggles to consolidate the homosocial elite that will stave off the incursions of multiple social, racial, and sexual others. After reiterating that the masses' only mission is to accede to their superiors, the speaker again insists that the lack of docility in politics matters less than in other areas, such as everyday social interactions. The masses must learn to submit in the daily practice of small group conversation. In social encounters in France and Germany, the speaker has observed that in the presence of intelligence, other members of the circle concede their inferiority and surrender the floor. In contrast, the exceptional Spanish individual finds himself continually challenged and interrupted by middle-class women and men who spout banalities. The specific mention of women ("damas burguesas") in a text that uses only masculine referents and its placement prior to the masculine term in this specific sentence draw attention to the contrast between intelligent men and ignorant middle-class women, and secondarily, men. The gendering of the masses acquires greater force in the next paragraph, which emphasizes the urgency of elevating every-day conversation to a level that would preclude women's participation: "Urge remontar la tonalidad ambiente de las conversaciones, del trato social y de las costumbres hasta un grado incompatible con el cerebro de las señoras burguesas" [It is imperative to raise the ambient tone of conversations, of social relations and of customs to a level that is incompatible with the intelligence of bourgeois women] (158).

España invertebrada constructs a national elite of white, urban, educated, Castilian males who are destined to govern the rural, Catalan, Basque, female masses. The text conflates geographic, class, and gender differences and in a colonizing sweep, bundles them together with an African, Arab, primitive people that represent all that Spain has lost and still might be regained. Regionalism clearly threatens the recuperation of a Castilian, militaristic, and imperial hegemony. The desire to stave off the voices, languages, and perspectives of the periphery coincides with a centrist nostalgia for uniformity and hierarchy. The fear and resentment of women relates both to the loss of empire and the rise of feminism. Post-colonial studies have shown a close relationship between narratives of colonial conquest and female domination.[21] Empires, islands, continents and other objects of territorial desire are gendered female while women, the lower classes, and other races are textualized as primitive, childish, and in need of control. Freud's designation of female sexuality as the "dark continent of psychology," with echoes of African colonization, exemplifies this conflation of foreign and domestic aliens (Corbey, 1991a). Women, however, destabilize the opposition self-other, colonizer-colonized, outsider-insider because of their presence in the intimacy of the home and family relationship. With increased calls for emancipation, they threaten to alter the structures holding Western, white, male power in place. Ortega's text reveals fear and sublimated anger at this change on the domestic and public, national and international levels. His views and their textualization stand out in contrast to other modernist writers, who welcome a breakdown of traditional dichotomies and explore alterity on many levels in an effort to foster difference. The response to new forms of regionalism as the hopeful beginning of a plural, decentered nation represents an important aspect of modernism's drive towards a post-imperial Spain. The break with the past and rewriting of a present that stands in opposition to established narratives of the nation continues in the consideration of religion, its relation to feminism, and the role of both in modern Spain.

Spanish Women Modernists: A Catholic Exodus

Studies of the nineteenth and twentieth centuries have long recognized the diminished power of the Church over writers of the period. Baroja's harsh criticism of clergy and church in *Camino de perfección* and *César o nada,* Pérez de Ayala's condemnation of Jesuit education in *AMDG,* Clarín's late concern with religious themes, Antonio Machado's alternately agnostic and atheistic declarations, Juan Ramón Jiménez's pantheistic journey to a transcendent force, Unamuno's public angst over the need for a divinity in which he cannot fully believe, and Galdós's attempts to recuperate the religious spirit of the early church all represent the search for alternatives to the Spanish Catholic Church, both as institution and faith. Even in such mainstream publications as *El cuento semanal,* Andrés González-Blanco's "Un amor de provincia" (1908) depicts life in the town of Episcópolis, with clear connotations of ecclesiastical control, as a society in which social and religious authority suffocate a natural youthful desire for freedom and life. It is generally assumed that women writers of the period remain untouched by this questioning of Spanish religious tradition. Critics typically characterize Emilia Pardo Bazán as a conservative Catholic, notwithstanding her radical feminist writings and activism. Concha Espina is also categorized as a Catholic writer with conservative political views (Domingo 1988, 98). In that modernism represents a rejection of grand narratives and nineteenth century foundationalism, the attribution of an unquestioning submission to church authority presumes the exclusion of these and other women writers from the epistemic changes evident in their male counterparts. Lissorgues overtly expresses this view when he writes that Pardo Bazán's Catholic convictions exempt her from the crisis of confidence that characterizes the period (1991, 174). The role of religion in the social construction of gender produces different response in the women writers of the period, but in rethinking the position of women and actively working for their advancement, they necessarily reconsider the church's role in patriarchal control of the female body.

Modernist women writers who examine the role of religion and patriarchy not only face Church opposition, but also that of liberal and radical male writers and thinkers who associate female religious unorthodoxy with a lack of moral and sexual constraint. Church regulation of female sexuality worked in consonance with bourgeois social controls and male liberals, who abandon the church and advocate religious freedom for men, continue to espouse acquiescence in their wives, daughters, sisters, and mothers. Gumersindo de Azcárate's autobiographical depiction of the conflicts facing a non-Catholic in Catholic Spain in his 1876 *Minuta de un testimonio* presumes and admires his wife's continued faith. Similarly, in Galdós's thesis novels *Doña Perfecta* and *La familia de León Roch,* the victim of religious doubts is invariably male while the female subject continues to uphold traditional faith. Clarín attempts to delegitimize and control Pardo Bazán by questioning her religious orthodoxy, with full recognition of the power of his accusation (1887, 62).[21] Pardo Bazán's response to charges of religious, political, literary, or ethical unorthodoxy takes the form of public declarations of Catholicism, in keeping with societal expectations. Other women writers adopt equally cautious public positions, although their fiction examines the deleterious effects of Catholic power on the nation and women. Socialist women writers reveal animosity to Church control much more openly, but a critical stance surfaces even among such purportedly Catholic writers as Blanca de los Ríos, Sofía Casanova, Concha Espina, and Emilia Pardo Bazán. Ironically, Clarín's accusation of religious dissidence in his effort to silence Pardo Bazán proves more accurate than views of later critics, who dismiss her work and that of other women writers as a defense of the status quo.

A number of Pardo Bazán's stories underscore women's role in the foundations of Christianity[22] while others emphasize love over force. Many explore the contradictions between a patriarchal church and feminist aspirations or between traditional Spanish Catholic animosity to other religions and a truly ecumenical understanding of the other. Pardo Bazán often utilizes multiple narrators and frames to bring in several perspectives that dialogue with each other. "La oración de Semana Santa" (1899) employs this structure to join three traditionally alien cultures and religions that mutually illuminate the contradictions inherent in both the Christian and non-Christian worlds. The unnamed, ungendered narrator, presumably Spanish and Catholic, relates a visit to medieval Avila with an English tourist, who in turn narrates her experiences in the court of Nasaredino, the assassinated shah of Persia.[23] The English Ada Sharpton describes her efforts to convert the Muslim tyrant to Christianity, but Nasaredino rejects a hypocritical Christianity that preaches love and humility while carrying out brutal campaigns of imperial expansion (1990, 2:256). He insists that force alone ensures political power, but by his own admission, daily executions of members of the Bãbist sect, whose doctrines he characterizes as resembling Christianity, has not weakened the movement. Miss Ada, so designated by the narrator in constant reminder of her foreign origins, ultimately succeeds in convincing Nasaredino of the value of Christian forgiveness, and in the process saves the life of a Bãbist Persian. The text does not end with an exaltation of Christian values, however, but proceeds to narrate Nasaredino's assassination by the very Bãbist whose sentence he had commuted. Not only did the Bãbist fail to internalize the concept of clemency, despite links between his faith and Christianity, but Miss Ada, who insists that Christ's word is the only truth, confesses her own difficulty in praying for, and hence forgiving, the assassin. The lines demarcating Muslim and Christian belief and conduct become increasingly indeterminate over the course of the story.

Pardo Bazán also questions traditional religious animosities and divisions in her little studied two-part novel, *Una cristiana—La prueba* (1890). Nelly Clemessy, Maurice Hemingway, and Lou Charnon-Deutch coincide in characterizing the novel as a defense of Christian abnegation and the traditional role of women,[24] and there is no doubt that Salustio, the male narrator, and other male characters such as the priest, Silvestre Moreno, encourage such a view. However, this message intersects with others that contradict and expand it in a complex narrative that reevaluates standard versions of Spanish religious history and challenges the viability of past models. The narrative primarily describes the relationship between Carmiña Aldao, the Christian woman designated in the title of the first part of the work, and three male characters—her confessor, her husband Felipe, and this latter's nephew, Salustio. Emphasizing unstable religious and ethnic identities for all three male characters, the text cues the reader to remain alert to fluid borders and changing definitions. The priest bears two unlikely names, Silvestre Moreno and Aben Jusuf. "Silvestre" connotes untamed, outside the norm and the surname "Moreno," with its evocation of dark skin and racial difference, underscores the priest's connections with Africa and the Arab world. He has lived in Morocco and prefers Arab peoples and desert climates. Salustio frequently refers to him as "el moro" or Aben Jusuf, an identity Moreno adopted to avoid persecution by anticlerical forces during the First Spanish Republic (1873–1874). Felipe, in turn, is identified early as a descendant of Spanish Jews. Salustio describes his uncle as closely resembling stereotypical Jewish portraits and Carmiña also identifies her husband's features as Jewish. Salustio distances himself from his own Jewish heritage and also from his Catholic upbringing in his self-description as free-thinking rationalist.

The constant allusions to Jew, Moor, and Christian invoke memories of Spanish religious history and its role in national formation and gender politics. Despite differences of age, ideology, and religion, the three men share similar attitudes with respect to the role and status of women. Felipe assumes a relationship of ownership and control with respect to Carmiña, parsimoniously doling out money for household expenses, leaving his wife at home while he engages in political networking, and forbidding contact with her father and new step-mother. Father Moreno combines a Christian and Moorish view of life as a place of suffering and of wives as bound to obey and serve their husbands (1910?, 146). He dismisses the concept of romantic love as sensuality (283) and finds perfectly natural Carmiña's discovery of love for her husband while she nurses him after he becomes ill with leprosy. Salustio, who falls in love with Carmiña and defends her right to happiness, finds himself increasingly drawn to her precisely because she represents the self-sacrificing, long-suffering ideal of Christian womanhood. His friend Luis Portal comments on the absurdity of this ideal in a rationalist and nonbeliever, arguing that their generation needs the woman of the future, not the feminine ideal of the past. Carmiña's decision to escape her father's lascivious pursuit of his young maid through marriage strikes Portal as a ludicrous, antiquated solution. In his view, a modern woman would have sought work as a seamstress or servant, rather than cede her liberty and her body to a man who repulses her (156).

The presentation of the narrative through Salustio's mediation makes it difficult to assess Carmiña's feelings and beliefs, although her conduct suggests that she has assimilated the values inculcated by patriarchal culture, whether Christian, Jewish, Moorish, or a combination of the three. Salustio reports that when Felipe insults her after she expresses relief that her father has married his maid rather than engage in adultery, Carmiña blames herself for speaking up: "Ningún marido se irrita contra una mujer que no le contesta. Por la lengua vienen todas las disensiones matrimoniales. Nuestro papel es callar" [No husband gets angry with a woman that doesn't answer him back. All marital dissension comes from the tongue. Our role is to keep quiet] (1910?, 186). *Una cristiana—La prueba* textually illustrates the silencing of the female voice in traditional Spanish society as well as its consequences. The modern rationalist, the Catholic priest and Moorish tradition that he evokes, as well as the Jewish-Christian husband impose a vision of the Christian wife that harks back to medieval times and persists in the silent acquiescence of the modern Spanish woman. Although the text consistently portrays Father Moreno as an admirable figure who wins the good will of all who meet him, including the skeptic Salustio, Carmiña's assimilation of his values does not necessarily reflect textual endorsement of nineteenth-century church visions of life as a valley of tears in which one must suffer in order to secure eternal salvation. Multiple and sometimes opposing strands of the narrative introduce alternative readings that question the validity of traditional patterns of thought and conduct. Moreno's transformation from a strapping man and exuberant hiker who thrives in the Moroccan sun and heat to a frail, lame old man in constant pain after being transferred and confined in humid, gray Santiago de Campostela insinuates both the consequences of physical enclosure and the indifference of the Church to individual well-being. In addition, the only other representative of the Church in the novel seriously undermines institutional credibility. The seminarian Serafín manifests his cruelty when he tortures a bat and proves impertinent and inappropriately intimate with both men and women. He gratuitously touches an old female servant's arm in such a way that she tells him to stop getting smart with her. After knowing Salustio for only a few hours, he enters his bedroom, and, when Salustio slips into bed to get rid of him, the seminarian pinches his shoulder and tries to tickle him. Salustio's discomfort at Serafín's physical contact and at his invitation that they swim naked the next day reflects his own prudish character, confirmed in other episodes in the text, but also insinuates homosexual desire in the seminarian. Later episodes further question Serafín's aptitude for the religious ministry; at Carmiña's wedding he gets drunk and attempts to witness the newlyweds' first sexual encounter by spying through cracks in the ceiling. The prospect that an individual of such proclivities could eventually serve as a confessor and counselor to women raises serious questions regarding the wisdom of Church control of the female body and destiny.

Salustio's initial participation in Serafín's voyeuristic activities introduces yet another conflict that challenges a reading of the text as an apology of female abnegation. From the moment of his uncle's announcement of his impending marriage, Salustio demonstrates a keen interest in Carmiña and a rivalry for her affection. After the death of Salustio's father, the unmarried Felipe partially financed his nephew's education and served as a surrogate father. Salustio's obsession with Carmiña, his insistence that she loves him and not Felipe, his initial willingness to join Serafín in spying on the newlyweds and then his abrupt departure from the house and village, his habit of observing Felipe and Carmiña to determine when they are sexually active, and his anger and hurt when he realizes they have resumed a sexual relationship after a period of separation (1910?, 253) all betray an Oedipal competition. Salustio confesses that his passion for Carmiña stems from his hatred of his uncle (257) and Silvestre Moreno accuses him of combining adultery with incest in his pursuit of Carmiña (283). The inability to individuate and free himself from an incestuous, cyclical desire links Salustio with Valle-Inclán's Marqués de Bradomín, Baroja's Ramiro of *El mayorazgo de Labraz,* and other characters who remain locked in a timeless, unchanging past.

Carmiña, the woman of the past, cannot provide access to a different present. She remits Salustio back to an unending rivalry with his male antecedents in a sterile, repetitive process. Notably, Carmiña and Felipe produce no children and even more significantly, Salustio's hatred for Felipe represents a destructive self-loathing. Throughout the narrative, Salustio generates nasty anti-Semitic remarks about Felipe's curved nose and stingy habits. Since Salustio's mother and Felipe are brother and sister, each statement against Felipe applies equally to Salustio. In this respect, the traditional Carmiña represents a break with the past, in her ultimate acceptance and love for Felipe, while the rationalist Salustio confesses his inability to reject atavistic animosities inherited from centuries of Christian hatred of Jews and exacerbated in the context of Spanish nationalist campaigns for racial and religious purity. The text alludes to the Inquisition on several occasions, once to describe Salustio's mother as the Inquisitor, when she burns the dishes and bedding her brother had used, and again when Felipe, now in advanced stages of leprosy and having lost sensation in his extremities, burns his foot in the fire. In both cases, the reference invokes Catholic persecution of Jews and frames it within a context of self-hatred, whether of sister against brother or individual body part against the whole. Salustio's abhorrence of Jews when he himself shares Jewish ancestry echoes sterile and self-destructive national policies of expulsion of Moors and Jews, who constituted a vital part of the nation.

The individual and national propensity for self-mutilation and the role of the patriarchy and Church in this process surfaces in relation to a final puzzling aspect of *Una cristiana—La prueba.* Clemmessy reports that initial criticism of the novel found the discussion of leprosy repulsive and unrealistic (1981, 1:246). The choice of this disease to test Carmiña's mettle has several possible explanations. The reference to an illness of considerable extension during the Middle Ages calls attention to the metaphorical replaying of Spanish national history and Christian, Jewish, Moorish commingling in the medieval period. The presence of lepers in Spain during the period in which the narrative action occurs and the existence of a treatment center at La Toxa, proximate to the setting of the novel, could also explain the use of the illness as a rare, but not thoroughly unbelievable catastrophe (Clemessy 1981, 1:246). Still another explanation arises in considering that leprosy was historically associated with venereal disease and specifically, syphilis.[25] The two afflictions share a number of traits, including skin lesions, a long incubation, slow progression from one phase to another, and a genesis in close physical contact. Both develop idiosyncratically in different individuals and time intervals between the diverse stages vary considerably. In Pardo Bazán's novel, many of the symptoms described match leprosy or syphilis, including reddish marks on the skin, rheumatoid pains, and a general malaise. The loss of sensation that leads to the burning of Felipe's foot relates specifically to leprosy, but since the foot metonymically and euphemistically stands for the penis (Cela 1975, vol. 2, part 2:405), connotations of sexually transmitted illness persist. Descriptions of Felipe's activities before and during his marriage provide ample evidence of possible exposure to venereal disease. Immediately after announcing his plans to marry, he invites Salustio to accompany him on a visit to several young seamstresses, who "moonlight" as prostitutes. The primary target of Felipe's attentions subsequently becomes the mistress of a wealthy older man and Salustio learns that after his marriage, Felipe tries to renew his relations with her and other women. In an ironic sweep of the pen, Pardo Bazán names the young prostitute Belén [Bethlehem], associating the church and the institutionalization of prostitution.

The possibility that Felipe's illness has sexual origins radically changes the significance of Carmiña's sacrifice and the role of the church and the patriarchy in authorizing her subjection. The narrative specifically underscores church complicity in the description of the ecclesiastical marriage ritual: "Oí leer la que todo el mundo llama epístola de San Pablo, aunque no lo sea. Allí el marido era asimilado a Cristo, la mujer a la Iglesia; y en confirmación de esta superioridad viril, la bordada estola cayó sobre la cabeza de la novia a la vez que sobre el cuello del novio. Carmiña Aldao, cruzando las manos sobre el pecho, inclinó la frente sometiéndose al yugo" [I listened to what everyone calls the epistle of Saint Paul, even though it is not. Therein the husband was subject to Christ, the wife to the Church; and in confirmation of this virile superiority, the embroidered stole fell on the head of the bride at the same time as on the neck of the groom. Carmiña Aldao, crossing her hands on her breast, bent her head submitting to the yoke.] (1910?, 127). The ceremony and Father Moreno's constant reminders to Carmiña of her responsibility to remain by her husband under all circumstances reenforce the church's role in the implementation of patriarchy. The consequences of this "yoke" in a culture that condones and even encourages male sexual experience profoundly affect the married couple and society at large. In a reading that interprets Felipe's leprosy as a euphemism for syphilis, Carmiña's discovery of her love for her husband while caring for him during his physical deterioration takes on a very different meaning. Her prior disgust at sexual contact, as intimated by Salustio, connotes not just prudery, but fear of contamination, and her final passionate kiss to her husband on his death bed signifies not merely Christian sacrifice, but a form of abnegation that proves self-destructive to the wife, any children she might bear, and subsequent sexual partners. Once again, Salustio's blindness to the implications of the self-sacrificing female ideal surface in considering his hopes to someday marry Carmiña. The self-hatred that emerges in his antisemitism reappears in his incestuous fascination for a woman whose sexual health has been seriously compromised. In contrast to this sterile, self-destructive conduct, his friend Luis Portal had argued that in order to replace the fruitless remnants of a past age, Spaniards need to cross with other races and marry foreign women (25). In the end, Luis marries the English Maud who, in his view, does not represent the New Woman of his dreams, but clearly comes closer to it than the Carmiña of Salustio's atavistic obsession. Both in the comparison of the two women and the invocation of the historic commingling of multiple religions and ethnicities, *Una cristiana—La prueba* rejects a tradition that privileges a single vision, single voice, single interpretation. In its complex interweaving of multiple plots and counter arguments, the novel reflects a modernist vision of the world as the confluence of contradictory traditions and innovations and in its depiction of the varied effects of Catholic tradition and contemporary practice, it reveals a clear understanding of the need for a more open, truly catholic—in the sense of universal—religion.

Two decades later, in *Dulce Dueño* (1911), Pardo Bazán continues to examine church complicity in patriarchal control of the female body. Once again, a variety of men seek to determine the female protagonist's future, but in this case, the woman rejects all efforts to curb her freedom and forges her own destiny. Modeling her life after Saint Catherine of Alexander, she aspires to discover a fulfilling love that somehow transcends the ordinary.

Her rejection of the convent and marriage perplex or anger her male protectors, including a virulently anti-clerical rationalist and a priest. The priest can understand her refusal to become a nun if she marries, but cannot comprehend virginity outside a religious vocation. Lina distrusts love and is repelled by the prospect of sex, finally seeking happiness in a small town where she serves an old woman and her homely granddaughter. When Lina nurses the young girl through smallpox, her relatives declare her insane and have her institutionalized. In the modern world, a love that is not defined by men or the Church stands outside accepted norms and must be controlled, if not through marriage, or the convent, then the insane asylum. In the end, only the women Lina had served proclaim her saintly; for the others, she is simply and unequivocally mad.

Concha Espina also examines church control of the female body. Her first novel, *La niña de Luzmela* (1909) describes the tension between the religious message of female self-sacrifice and the need to defend oneself from exploitation. Carmen, the young protagonist, has received a copy of Thomas a Kempis's *Imitation of Christ* and as a result, accepts her relatives' physical and mental abuse as a form of penance. The leading male character, symbolically named Salvador, offers a still strongly religious, but more life-affirming view that ultimately helps her to triumph over the tradition of austerity and abnegation. *La esfinge maragata* (1914) also signals the Church's role in socializing women for a life of subservience, but this novel more directly faults the role of the priest. Father Miguel Fidalgo, whose surname harks back to medieval society and values with the early Spanish spelling of *hidalgo,* plays the role of arbiter in determining the female protagonist's fate. Mariflor has come to the barren region of Maragatería in Old Castile to explore the possibility of marrying her cousin Antonio in order to solve the family financial decline. Mariflor finds herself torn between the model of self-sacrifice and a desire to decide her own future, and perhaps marry Rogelio Terán, a young poet from Madrid. Father Miguel advocates that she distrust happiness and choose suffering as the sure road to salvation (1972, 1:297). Well-meaning and sometimes clearly moved by Mariflor's fate, he fails to understand her or the other women whose destinies he controls. He assumes that Mariflor's cousin has a religious vocation, although the text reveals she is in love with Rogelio. Despite the communicative and affective gap between the priest and his female wards, Father Miguel imposes his authority and convinces Mariflor to submit to a marriage she does not desire, thus reenacting the subservient roles of generations of Maragatan women and a tradition that totally discounts female aspirations.

Espina's *Las niñas desaparecidas* (1927) directly relates the religious tradition of cloister and restricted freedom with prostitution, a seemingly opposed but linked form of patriarchal control. Two young women find themselves enclosed in a Catholic orphanage which they rarely leave and where they spend their days praying, reading about saints, and learning no marketable skills. To outsiders, such as the police inspector who comes to investigate charges that the nuns are sequestering young girls, the story's title refers to the young women who disappear behind the convent walls. The mother superior ascribes to a different interpretation with a view of her charges as "niñas a perpetuidad" [children in perpetuity], whom she strives to protect from the evils of the world beyond the convent. When the two protagonists escape, she refuses to consider their possible return because those who leave are irretrievably lost. The text reports the runaways' first encounter with curious passing men, their lack of knowledge of the world and impoverished financial state. The possibility that they will disappear into prostitution looms large in the final paragraphs. In typical modernist fashion, both readings coexist, but the indictment of a church education that in no way prepares young women for life in the modern world and of a nun who cannot conceive of a female identity outside the confines of the convent and virginity joins with a modernist questioning of traditional religion and the church's role in the containment of women.

Blanca de los Ríos, another conservative Catholic writer, indicts the Spanish past and the church in "Madrid goyesco," in which the young male protagonist is unable to find a place for himself in the modern world and the heroine enters a convent. The text closes with sardonic comments regarding the improductivity of inherited habits and solutions, presenting the convent as sterile and useless to national reconstruction. The Martínez Sierras often deal with issues of women and religion. Their "Margarita en la Rueca," published in 1904 in *Sol de la tarde,* relates the story of two sisters, one paralyzed and the other healthy. Engracia gives up her life to care for her ill sister, putting off marriage to a suitor who eventually marries another woman. Engracia finds happiness in art and in the decision to become a nun when her sister dies; but, when this occurs, she discovers that the convent does not accept women over forty. The secular and religious world join in rejecting women whose biological clock has run its course. "La monja maestra," of the same collection, initially appears in the magazine *Helios* in 1903. It anticipates by almost thirty years Unamuno's famous story of the doubting priest in *San Manuel Bueno, Mártir* and outlines a similar dilemma in a young nun. Not only does the text introduce the possibility of female atheism in an older, educated teacher, but it also presents a young female student who confesses her own inability to believe and pray. In the course of Spanish modernism, women writers express their criticism of the church and their personal religious doubts with increasing frankness. Contrary to traditional critical presumptions of conservative religious orthodoxy, they join with male writers in breaking with a restrictive religious past and in exploring new possibilities for female religious expression.

Jews and Arabs in the Spanish Present

The examination of the religious question in Spanish modernism necessarily includes a reconsideration of relations with Jews and Muslims. As in other areas of cultural transformation, the weight of the past often intrudes in efforts to reimagine relations with the Jewish religion and people, and as always in modernist texts, multiple discourses and values coalesce in a complex dialogue. In a number of Pardo Bazán's stories and her play *El becerro de metal,* she probes possibilities for cross-cultural exchange between Christians and Jews, but in almost every case, it is the Jew who converts to Christianity in the face of a Jewish opposition that is portrayed as violent and often odious. Sofía Casanova treats the subject of religious tolerance and condemns antisemitism in her discussion of World War I and in *Triunfo de amor* (1919). In the story, local German authorities attempt to keep Jews out of their area for fear they will contaminate Lutheranism, but a Lutheran leader's daughter falls in love with a wealthy Jewish philanthropist. Both Jewish and Lutheran powers oppose the mixed marriage and the text strongly denounces religious beliefs that result in hatred rather than love. Like other writers of the period who advocate the transgression of traditional borders, Casanova utilizes a hybrid generic form, constructing a short story as if it were a play. However, the aspiration to depict a more ecumenical religious spirit runs up against traditional teachings regarding Catholicism as the only true religion and Christianity as superior to other beliefs when the text discloses the Jewish philanthropist's dissatisfaction with Judaism and his belief in Christ.

Other writers emphasize Christianity's Jewish roots in order to overwrite traditional animosities. Gabriel Miró's reconstruction of Christ's life in *Figuras de la pasión del Señor* (1916–17) incorporates multiple allusions to Jewish rites and clothing and uses Hebrew to recall the initial foreignness of the central figure of European Christianity. The narrative often refers to Christ as *Rábbi,* preferring the Hebrew spelling to a hispanized *rabí.* The scandal that accompanied the publication of the work, which Ian MacDonald attributes to the sensual decadence of the narration (1975, 20), may also reflect shock at the accentuation of the Jewishness of Christ and his disciples. *La España moderna* includes various articles that deal with historical and modern relations of Jews and Spain. A 1912 article by S. Schwarz decries religious fanaticism and charges that the expulsion of the Jews led to Spain's economic decline and benefitted those countries that gave refuge to the expelled Sephardim. Angel Guerra discusses the Jewish situation in "Cuestiones contemporáneas" (1910) and sympathetically portrays the rise of Zionism and the dream of a return to Israel.

Both Angel Pulido and Carmen de Burgos work to reestablish contact between Spain and descendants of expelled Sephardic Jews. Burgos founds the "Alianza hispano-israelita" in 1909 (Martínez Marín, 18) and advocates the establishment of schools funded by the Spanish government in cities of the diaspora with a significant Sephardic population (Burgos, 1909?, 84). Pulido crusaded throughout his life for cross cultural communication between Sephardic communities and Spain and the repatriation of descendants of expelled Spanish Jews. He advocated a reconciliation that would refute the black legend and to that end, surveyed Sephardic Jews in Europe, the Middle East, and Africa and published their histories in *Españoles sin patria y la raza sefardí* (1905). He also established the "Casa universal de los sefardíes" in Madrid in 1920 and worked to establish a professorship on Jewish language and literature at the University of Madrid. In a letter included in Pulido's book, Unamuno praises his attempts to redefine the nation in a more inclusive way and a number of Spanish intellectuals sign a 1916 letter in solidarity with Sephardics who were facing persecution from the Turkish government. The rewriting of the past and the redefinition of modern Spain accompanies a revision of Jewish-Spanish relations and a desire to foster mutual understanding and revive the commingling of cultures that characterized early Spanish society.

A reconsideration of the relationship between modern Spain and the Arab community at times occurs in conjunction with the discussion of Spanish-Jewish relations, but more often receives separate treatment. The continued existence of Spanish enclaves in Africa, persistent military conflicts with guerrilla resistance, and diplomatic rivalry with an expanding French empire in Northern Africa contribute to the ongoing production of a militarist, imperialist discourse that had virtually disappeared in the context of relations with Latin America and had no place in discussions of Jewish-Spanish exchange. The reexamination of Hispano-Arab relations in modern Spanish culture develops along two different but interrelated axes: the consideration of Spanish military and colonial activity in Morocco and a redefinition of contemporary Spanish national identity as a hybrid entity with a marked Arabic influence.

The authorization of Spanish occupation of Morocco by the papal bull of Calixto III and the continuity of some form of Spanish territorial presence in North Africa throughout Hapsburg and Bourbon rule provides the justification for a continued or expanded colonization of North Africa among traditional sectors of Spanish society. Writing for *La ilustración española y americana,* G. Reparaz rues the abandonment of Oran in 1791, which he sees as the surrender of Spanish imperial ambitions in Africa. He argues that above and beyond Spanish grandeur and glory, the resolution of the Moroccan question determines the nation's very existence (1893, 189). In the same publication, Aldolfo Llanos decries Spanish generosity with respect to the Berber tribes of the Rif, describing them as ignorant, barbarous, and incapable of understanding anything but the harshest of treatment (1893, 233). The appearance of these articles in the years immediately preceding the Spanish American War in part explains their bellicose, nationalist rhetoric, but the same discourse continues in the 1904 discussion of the 1860 war in Morocco in "Cosas que fueron" of *Gente vieja* and a 1910 article in *La España Moderna* by Francisco Espinosa y González Pérez. Given the intermittent outbreaks of military conflict—the War of 1859–1860, conflicts over Melilla in 1890 and 1893, Spanish defeat at the Barranco del Lobo in 1909 and then Annual in 1921—the rhetoric of enmity remains constant over time.

Spanish modernist writers of diverse political persuasions

combat this rhetoric directly and indirectly, through attacks on a militarist tradition or persistent deconstruction of the difference between Spain and Morocco, Spaniard and Arab. Oppositional voices often camouflage criticism of a nationalist, militarist tradition and interweave their arguments with conventional authoritative discourse. A clear and early example of this strategy occurs in the one-act play by Rosario de Acuña that was staged in 1893 and published the same year. On the surface, *La voz de la patria* appears to support Spanish military policy in Morocco, although countervailing messages operate within the play and in the dialogue between the dramatic text and the prologue and epilogue that frame it in the published version. Acuña, who created a scandal and occasioned official prohibition after only one performance of the 1891 production of her anticlerical *El padre Juan* (Simón Palmer 1990, 32–34), interweaves anti-war arguments with patriotic and religious declamations in *La voz de la patria.* The first half of the play articulates a feminist, pacifist message that cedes to a patriarchal, militarist discourse in the second part. When the protagonist receives notice to report for military duty in Africa, his mother and pregnant fiancée curse the war and defend the real, immediate family over an illusory concept of nation, anticipating Benedict Anderson's theorization of the nation as imagined community. The women suggest that Pedro escape to France to elude the draft, but his father recoils in horror and invokes patriotic duty to convince his son, his cynical neighbor, and the previously skeptical women. In the end, all fall into step, exalting the Spanish nation and calling for revenge against the barbarous Berbers who stained the Spanish coat of arms.

Allusions to a glorious past and the celebration of war and religion in an openly anticlerical feminist should in and of itself raise questions for an audience that experienced the governmentally ordered shut down of a play by the same author two years earlier. Furthermore, the ardent and very modern denunciation of war and its unsettling contrast with conventional patriotic rhetoric as well as the rather abrupt conversion of the pacificist characters from opposition to wholehearted support for the war manifest a discontinuity that signals a covert communication. The framed structure of the printed text adds a final and very modernist display of dual signification. The prologue-dedication that precedes the play reveals the speaker's sorrow at her father's death and her doubts as to the existence of life after death. In contrast to an overarching faith in religion, the speaker affirms a subjective belief in the value of work and love. At the conclusion of the dramatic text, Acuña resumes the personal commentary, revealing that she has written the dedication while the play was being performed on opening night. Coterminous with the dramatic text, the introductory and concluding remarks depict the writer alone in a room remembering her father and advocating a message that stands in direct contrast with the propositions advanced in the second half of the play. The frame is alien to the text, advocating love and peace in contrast to hatred and war. "¡Sea la paz con el espíritu, que, a pesar de su agotamiento, ni se para, ni es estéril, ¡ni odia!" [Peace be with the spirit, which in spite of its exhaustion, neither stops, nor is sterile, nor hates!] (1893, 33). In the closing words of the personal remarks, the speaker addresses her readers and encourages them to ignore the pages of the play they have just read and join her in a moment of love as she remembers her father.[26] The exaltation of peace and love continues the discourse of the women characters in the play and overlays the militarist, nationalist rhetoric of the second half of the dramatic text.

Emilia Pardo Bazán and Carmen de Burgos also code their opposition to the Moroccan wars in indirect discourse. Pardo Bazán's 1897 novel *El tesoro de Gastón* and Burgos's short story "El tesoro del castillo," originally published in *El cuento semanal* in 1907, bear remarkable similarities in title and symbolic message. The protagonists of both texts search for a buried Moorish treasure as the solution to their economic and personal problems. In the Pardo Bazán novel, the aristocratic but impoverished Gastón is guided by a self-sufficient, highly educated young widow in a process of personal transformation. Gastón's expressed desire for renewal echoes calls for national regeneration that abound during this period and cues the reader to interpret the personal story as a metaphor for the nation. Following the widow Antonia's advice, Gastón abandons the search for the Moorish princesses's jewels that are rumored to be buried in the tower of his family castle and works instead to educate himself in matters of finance and to regain his energies and sense of purpose. In the process, he loses his imperious manners, begins to treat his faithful servant with dignity and call her "grandmother," and comes to love Antonia's son as his own. When he joins the boy in a search for a weasel's nest, he does find a treasure, not at the base of the Tower of the Moorish Princess and not Moorish monies or jewels, but rather coins and jewels from his eighteenth-century ancestors. Gastón succeeds in his quest for regeneration, but it comes from within rather than from ownership of the riches hidden by another, and it accompanies the rejection of aristocratic privilege and the acceptance of family based on emotional commitment rather than consanguineous ties. On the national level, Gastón's lesson translates to a rejection of foreign, colonial enterprises and in particular, to a repudiation of the search for solutions to the national economic malaise in African possessions.

The Burgos story focusses on a rural, Andalusian community with lower-class protagonists, but issues of economic crisis and traditional social barriers recur. Dolores, the calculating daughter of a comfortable farmer, determines to marry a wealthy, older man and ignores the amorous attentions of the family's farm worker. The text includes several intercalated narratives, each dealing with buried Moorish treasure. In the second of the inserted fictions, a poor farmer dreams he will discover a treasure if he goes to the Triana bridge in Seville, but when he arrives there, he finds nothing. While begging to survive, he meets a blind panhandler who tells of his own dream about a treasure buried in the semi-African, arid land of Almería. The laborer-turned-beggar soon realizes that the site described is his own house and the buried treasure lies in the corner of his farmyard. The night that Dolores hears this story, she feels compelled to leave her house and unexpectedly meets Juanillo, her poor suitor, who relates his own dream of locating buried treasure with her help in a nearby abandoned castle. When the couple excavate the site, they find only an empty grave, but in the process fall in love and in the text's words, locate a different treasure when Dolores, with her father's approval, marries Juanillo. In the intercalated and main story, the treasure exists not in temporally distant Arab lands but at home, in the family and local community.

"El tesoro del castillo" includes frequent comments that link southern Spanish and Arab-African culture, history, geography, and ethnic formation. The dissolution of differences between these two historical and contemporary enemies also surfaces in Burgos's story of the 1909 military campaign in Morocco, "En la guerra (Episodios de Melilla)." Burgos had been a war correspondent in Africa and the text's opening statement reveals that she wrote the fiction in camp from a desire to state her impressions without censorship and that she may not have fully expressed the horror that the war inspires in her. These initial disclaimers signal once more a covert message that intertwines with conventional patriotic declarations. From the outset, Burgos announces a determination to incorporate the enemy's vision by dating her narrative according to the Muslim calendar, the year 1287 of the Hegira. The narration continues to deconstruct differences, pointing out that the absence of women in the Spanish outpost of Melilla reflects the continuation of a Moorish tradition in a Spain that combats Moroccan Arabs in the name of Europe and progress. The text refers to the Mediterranean as a lake that joins rather than divides Africa and southern Spain. Paradoxically, the common ancestry produces rivalry and hatred between the soldiers whereas Alina, the lone female character, invokes the Biblical injunction of fraternal love. The narrator vacillates between a vision that conjoins the two populations and the introduction of strategies designed to estrange the reader from the Arab enemy. The text refers collectively to a group of dirty and unkempt Arab boys, then focuses on one attractive, well-groomed youth, and finally relates how the boy inspires Alina's tenderness. The description of the brutality of the Berber fighters and their mutilation of Spanish soldiers in the battle of the Barranco del Lobo aims to create a phobic rejection of the enemy, but the characterization of a member of the feared Kebdana tribe inverts the stereotype with his sweet and innocent appearance (1989a, 194). The double discourse continues to the end of the story, when Lina discovers that her older husband has survived the battle while the young captain she has come to love has died. She not only curses the war, but also defies the traditional honor code, kissing the dead captain publicly although she had previously remained faithful to her husband and rejected any physical contact. War, honor, inherited enmities, patriarchy, and control of the female body once more come together under a scrutiny that challenges and undermines them.

The Moroccan campaign of 1921 serves as the backdrop for *El blocao: Novela de guerra,* published in 1928 by J. Díaz Fernández. The author writes that the several narratives contained in the collection are based on his military experiences in North Africa and deal with a topic he regards as an open wound in the Spanish conscience. A number of the texts focus on divisions within Spanish society and the increasing internal fragmentation caused by the war. "Magdalena roja" relates the adventures of a female anarchist who opposes the war as imperialist and capitalist and comes to Morocco to sell arms to the Arabs. "Reo de muerte" describes the hatred of a commanding officer for a stray dog adopted by the regiment, his indifference to his soldiers' emotional needs, and the cowardly imposition of his authority when he takes the dog to the desert and shoots it. The soldier's enemy resides within Spanish culture or the regiment itself rather than in the Arab antagonist in these texts and similarly in "Convoy de amor," where a coquettish young lieutenant's wife dies at the hand of her fellow countryman when she awakens the desire of the soldiers who accompany her to her husband's outpost. The commanding officer kills her in the crossfire that ensues as he attempts to prevent her rape.

Three remaining stories reveal a complex relation of love, hate, and desire with respect to the Moroccan Arab community. "El blocao" describes the narrator's decision to free a young Arab girl who appears to spy on Spanish troops. Although the soldiers wish to kill her, the narrator begrudgingly admires her valor and loyalty to her people, indirectly validating her right to independence. "Cita en la huerta" ironically mocks European male fantasies of the enigmatic, veiled Muslim woman. Obsessed with a desire to enter the guarded interior of the Arab home, the narrator bribes Mohamed Huddú, the son of the Grand Visir, to introduce him to an Arab woman. The narrator gains access to what turns out to be the Grand Visir's home and meets Aixa, Mohamed Huddú's fifteen year old sister. The beautiful young woman appears unveiled, fresh, dark, and teasingly aloof. She studies the Spanish narrator with her hands on his shoulders, but when he tries to touch her, she jumps back, grabs a red carnation, and throws it at him as if he were a caged lion. She leaves without speaking a word and he does not see her again until he attends a wedding some time later and realizes that the bride is the lovely, inaccessible Aixa. Mary Louse Pratt remarks in *Imperial Eyes* that standard narratives of colonial domination depict a male protagonist who conquers a young and beautiful native woman with whom he shares a passionate love and sometimes sires children and then eventually abandons (1992, 96–97). "Cita en la huerta" inverts the colonial narrative of conquest and depicts a frustrated male suitor who cannot access the object of his desire, a native woman who studies him with curiosity and then abandons him to marry a member of her own community. "Africa a sus pies" also depicts native resistance, but with a more violent twist. The narrator's friend has acquired a Moorish mistress named Africa, after meeting her in a cabaret in Tangier where she was deserted by a French diplomat. When the friend receives orders to transfer, he plans to leave her money but before he departs, Africa kills him and escapes, dressed as an Arab. In some respects, the story confirms stereotypical representations of violent, treacherous Arabs, but in the context of the other stories that display a balanced vision of the Arab other and given the significance of the name Africa, the story invites a reading that recognizes Africa's agency, retaliation for exploitation, and resistance to the injustice of the ongoing conquest.

Ramón del Valle-Inclán's *Los cuernos de don Friolera* (1921) analyzes the Moroccan wars as an extension of traditional Spanish visions of honor. The play's complex structure includes three different units, each with subunits: a prologue in which the characters Manolito and Estrafalario comment on a painting and a puppet show that takes place on stage within the prologue's frame; a twelve-scene play that reenacts the story of marital dishonor and revenge initially presented in the framed puppet show, here developed from a different perspective; and finally, an epilogue that incorporates the ballad version of the same story and commentary on the ballad and the story by Manolito and Estrafalario. The constant shifts in literary genre with accompanying changes in perspective oblige the public to continually adjust its affective relationship with the text and characters. Farce and tragedy intermix to create *trigedia* (119) and no sooner do the characters seem frozen in stiff, jerky dehumanized motions than they transmute to pathetic figures that evoke a sentimental response. In Valle-Inclán's later works, the modernist turning coin spins with increased rapidity, but the two faces never fuse in harmonic unity. *Los cuernos* theorizes the necessity of their co-presence in the prologue, where Manolito and Estrafalario present two visions of art, one advocating love through laughter and tears and the other defending the surpassing of pain and laughter by observation of the world from the other side (1990, 114). The play, with multiple layers and perspectives, continually crosses from one to the other and textually exemplifies the value of traversing borders to incorporate difference and change. For this reason, *Los cuernos* privileges the periphery in contrast to the centrist Castilian tradition, which it equates with militarism, rigid visions of honor, and imperialism.

The prologue introduces Manolito and Estrafalario as Basque transplants who currently live near the Spanish-Portuguese border and the epilogue catches up with them in another coastal city that looks out towards Africa. They praise the puppet version of the honor play precisely because it melds Latin, Portuguese, Cantabrian, and Catalan traditions in contradistinction to Castilian dramatic history. Valle-Inclán associates the Castilian vision of honor with military inflexibility and Moorish cultural practices that still prevail in Spanish culture. Once again, opposition to the war in Morocco expresses itself in the ironic observation that the Arab enemy mirrors the Spanish national psyche. The military cannot see this shared identity because they remain locked in an absurd reliving of the past and in a rigid Manichean division of the world. Friolera states that his wife's innocence must shine like the sun and that in questions of honor there can be no clouds (1990, 108–9). His behavior follows unyielding codes and his absurdly jerky movements as well as his explicit allusions to his public reenforce the sense of histrionic repetition of old scripts. He speaks of an upper theater gallery that would never tolerate mere separation from his wife (79) and his all too familiar discourse connects through Echegaray's nineteenth-century melodramatic honor plays, literally cited in the text (103), to Calderón's earlier dramas, but in a parodic deformation that highlights their inauthenticity in the modern context.[27]

The reliving of the past on the personal level of the family drama mimics military and imperial inability to move away from established patterns of behavior, which in turn relates to a blindness to the realities of past and present. Rovirosa, the lieutenant who leads the discussion to determine the military response to Friolera's failure to avenge his honor, has a glass eye that often falls out of its socket. His literal blindness accompanies the figurative oblivion of his commanding officer, whose wife carries on an affair with his military assistant under his very nose. The inability to see, figuratively and literally, resurfaces in the epilogue in the figure of the blind ballad singer, who recites in popular form a version of the marital drama that fully supports both the traditional marital revenge through the murder of the wife and the national military revenge through the war in Morocco. In the ballad, Friolera kills his wife, thus earning a medal from General Polavieja—an historical figure who served as Captain-General of the Philippines and advocated national salvation through the army (Carr 1970, 478)—and then sets out for Melilla, where he single-handedly kills one hundred Moors to secure royal honor and national fame. Estrafalario condemns the assimilation of this military ideology and of upper class concerns with honor by popular literature and culture, as expressed in the ballad. The exaltation of colonial wars by a lower class that bears the brunt of the economic sacrifice and the military combat reveals an inability to see political realities. In addition, the ballad's support for traditional concepts of honor on the individual and national level speaks to the ironic persistence of values that purportedly originate in the Arab enemy they so enthusiastically combat. The ballad calls Friolera the panther of Arabia, his wife refers to him as a bloodthirsty Turk (1990, 110), and Rovirosa and his military buddies proudly claim to have more Moorish than Latin blood. Unable to move beyond a rigid tradition or see themselves as other than they have always been, the military pursues a course of action that proves as self-destructive as Friolera's accidental murder of his daughter while avenging his wife's supposed infidelity. The text underscores the connection between entrapment in the past, inability to know the self, and rejection of the other when the military tribunal meets to discuss Friolera's fate in scene 8. Chauvinistic sentiments produce a revisionist history that declares Spaniards always victorious over the French and asserts that foreigners living on Spanish soil inevitably become more and more Spanish, as occurs in Gibraltar and Morocco. The absurdity of the conversation, at a moment when French dominance in Africa and in particular, in Morocco, far surpassed a modest Spanish presence[28] has its origins in the officers' ignorance of the colonies in which they have lived and for which they insist on fighting. When a lieutenant states that one only hears Spanish and Arabic in Morocco, another asks if Moroccans speak Tagalog, and the first responds that it is used by some Moors in the interior, comically transposing the languages of the Philippines and Morocco.

The text emphasizes the officers' inability to look beyond and at themselves and consequently to break with the past, alluding constantly to mirrors and glass that distort rather than reflect or reveal. The men talk in a room with large glass windows that look out to the sea and contrast with Rovirosa's unseeing, constantly escaping glass eye. The stage directions cryptically describe a mirror in the scene as being under a tulle netting, possibly signifying that the cloth hangs above the mirror as a sort of decorative ceiling hanging, but also allowing for a staging in which the fine net literally covers the mirror and distorts the image of the self projected in the reflection. In the stage direction that closes the scene, ambiguity disappears. The officers, having debated but not fully determined Friolera's fate, put on their swords and look out of the corner of their eyes into the mirror, at which point one of them cries, "Off to the Thirty Years' War" (1990, 137). The reference to the seventeenth-century conflict in which France definitively displaced Spain as the major European power once more exposes military ignorance of history, while it also highlights the persistent return to an illusory past and the inability to recognize the self and the present. The military blindness to history and the present receives additional emphasis in scene 10, where Friolera laments his inability to escape from the script set in motion by his neighbor, Tadea Calderón—whose name clearly invokes the tradition of the seventeenth-century author of honor plays—and Rovirosa enters with his hand covering his unseeing glass eye while the wind rips the pages off a calender and disperses them in the night.

In contrast with this suspension of time and paralysis in a preexisting script, Manolito, Estrafalario and the multi-leveled, multi-perspectival text of *Los cuernos de don Friolera* welcome the transgression of borders and assimilation of change that comes with contact with the other. The two Basques who travel through Spain to study its different regions typically look out through open windows or occupy a space that straddles the line dividing outside and inside. In the prologue, they stand by the balustrade of a stairway overlooking the inn yard and in the epilogue, although jailed under suspicion of anarchist activities, they look through the bars to observe and comment on the blind man's ballad. The text demolishes traditional genre borders, borrowing from classical drama and puppet theater, cultured and popular traditions, farce and tragedy, to create a work that welcomes diversity and encourages the audience to explore new modes of response. The linguistic richness of the work continues the privileging of transcultural receptivity. It includes gypsy items (*najarse*—to leave), popular Andalusian expressions (*gachó*—man, *gachí*—girl), Latin Americanisms (*flux*—suit) and classical Spanish spellings and pronunciations no longer in use (*haldudo* for *faldudo*—deeply hollowed or heavily skirted). The use of these terms dissolves national and class boundaries and joins with the hybrid textual construction and rejection of a rigid military and honor code to encourage a vision of culture as fluid and porous, open to change and to a multiplicity of voices and values.

With a very different tone and language, the Murcian poet Vicente Medina launches another direct attack on Spanish governmental policy in Africa and its effects on the rural lower classes. Imitating popular lexicon and pronunciation, Medina's *Aires murcianos* (1898) contrasts capitalist interests in African mines with the loss of rural life and labor and links the Moroccan conflict with the Cuban colonial wars ("La guerra"). "Los oasis de Murcia" shifts from a consideration of the war to focus on the Arab-African presence in contemporary Spanish culture, referring to Murcia as "tierra morisca." A text entitled "Mi tierra morisca" overwrites conventional histories to suggest that Moors remained after the Reconquest and culturally fused with their conquerors. The poem alludes to a Moorish Pelayo, equates the fiesta of San Roque with the Arab celebration of Ab-arán, and signals traces of Moorish and Jewish custom in dress and language. Some critics characterize Medina's poetry as belonging to traditional regionalist literature (Niemeyer 1992, 295) and certainly some regionalist features persist in his poetry, but his ambition to transcend regional borders and explore the connections of the Murcian region with the nation and with transnational communities represents a modern and modernist vision.

Many modernists who do not directly engage in considerations of the Moroccan colonial wars echo anti-war texts in emphasizing links between Spain and the Arab world.[29] Some underscore the African-Arab-Spanish connection to communicate their rejection of Eurocentric imperialistic discourse or European rationalism and others to express a desire to break with confining bourgeois social restrictions. Baroja compares the "civilized" world of a Spanish village, equipped with electric lighting and straight streets, in which children threw stones at him and a sexton would not allow him to enter a church, with an "uncivilized" Bedouin camp near Tangier, where he received a warm welcome and serving of couscous (1946–48, 5:75). Jesús of Baroja's *Aurora roja* escapes to Tangier rather than adjust to regularized work schedules and habits, the unorthodox protagonist of Concha Espina's *Agua de nieve* seeks fulfilment in a temporary engagement to a rich Arab from Tangier, and the four socialists of Pardo Bazán's story of the same title approach Tangier in a steamship, each with a distinct vision of how to achieve economic equality as contrasted with European class differences. The representation of exotic, erotic Arab women corresponds in part to the orientalism described by Lily Litvak as a form of rebellion against a vulgar, modern European society (1985, 23–26). Pictures of half-naked Arab odalisques, lying sensually next to an incense burner or possibly an opium pipe and looking straight into the observer's eye (*La Ilustración Española y Americana,* June 8, 1893) exemplify this use of the Arab world. Gypsy women often fall into the same category, as occurs in Camilo Bargielo's portrayal of a sensuous gypsy whose savage beauty and mournful songs intoxicate him and prove impossible to replace when she resumes her nomadic lifestyle (1900, 75–76).[30] However, the portrayal of an odalisque or a fantasized, wandering gypsy represents only one facet within a tendency that emphasizes the representation of

Arab individuals and cultures as existing within and in dialogic interaction with Spanish society.

In this context, it is important to point out that French or British exoticized depictions of a colonized subject, as studied in Edward Said's *Orientalism,* have a very different significance than the Spanish representation of members of a culture that forms an integral part of their past and present. If other European nations escape from themselves through travel in both space and time to another cultural location, Spanish writers invoke images of people who shared their same space and whose representation recuperates an erased history to enrich the present. Salvador Rueda's poem "El turbante" may have its origins in French orientalism and exoticism, as Niemeyer observes (1992,152), but the linguistic process of its composition and its effect are very different. The choice of *romance* form links the poem with early Spanish literary production and a period in which Moorish presence was culturally dominant in the peninsula. The vocabulary utilized includes words of Arab origin that form part of the Spanish linguistic heritage: some like *arabescos, adüares, caravanas* enjoy relatively widespread usage among educated speakers while others, such as *jaique* or *alfanje,* although included in the Royal Academy Dictionary, remain outside the vocabulary of all but a handful of specialists. Even the average speaker, however, would immediately recognize their Arabic origin, owing to the guttural sound of the former and the common conversion of the Arabic definite article into the Spanish prefix *al-* in the latter.

This combination of recognizably foreign, semi-assimilated, and clearly native terms in the lexical composition of the poem continues in the invocation of customs and places. Allusions to musical instruments and songs range from the familiar *pandero,* of Middle Eastern origins, but thoroughly assimilated into Spain and Europe, to the well-known Andalusian *malagueñas, soleares* and *polos,* and finally to the foreign *guzla.* The Muslim turban evokes in the lyric speaker images of distant Constantinople as well as proximate Cordoba, and the criss-crossing of the cloth reminds him of *celosías,* the slatted windows that allowed Spanish women to look out without being seen and date back to the days of Moorish occupation, but continue in use as window coverings in modern Spain. The closing verses introduce the memory of seven centuries of war, bringing the turban home to Spanish soil and reinserting the "fantastic" object of the initial verse into the cultural heritage of the speaker and reader.

Francisco Villaespesa's poetry and his habit of reclining on a sofa Arab-style, dressed with a long green and gold robe, embroidered slippers and decorated Fez (1954, 1:xxx) represent the desire to become other than the bourgeois European by recuperating a silenced but not totally erased past. Like other poets of the period, in his lyrical autobiography, he insists on the syncretic fusion of multiple cultural traditions, including Christian and Moorish, East and West: "Sangre de emires moros y príncipes cristianos circula por mis venas. . . . El Oriente me atrae y Roma me fascina; a Alá rezo mis suras y a Júpiter adoro; por eso, en nobles cláusulas de claridad latina, lloro en ricas imágenes mi fatalismo moro" [The blood of Moorish Emirs and Christian princes circulates in my veins. . . . The Orient attracts me and Rome fascinates me; I pray suras to Allah and I adore Jupiter; hence, in noble clauses of Latin clarity I lament my Moorish fatalism in rich images] (1:621). The connection to Rome and Greece has no greater claim to immediacy and is no less exotic than the reclamation of the Moorish heritage. Once again, it is important to distinguish between orientalism as it develops in empire building nations with no Arabic cultural legacy and a Spanish invocation of a historically shared heritage.

Manuel Machado expands on Villaespesa's Christian-Moorish syncretism to incorporate Greek, Arabic, gypsy, Parisian, popular, and cultured in "Adelfos" (1922, 1:5–7). His poetry typically maintains a dialogic tone and structure that invites ongoing response and rejects a sense of closure or definitive demarcation, whether by nationality, class or language. The poem's speaker identifies himself as of the Moorish race, a mix of Spanish and Arab, and states that his soul has no contours or perimeters. In part this formlessness corresponds to the diffident image he wishes to present, but it also insinuates an openness to the other and an insistence on dialogue, as observed in the dedication of the original version of "Adelfos" (1899) to Unamuno. Unamuno responds to this dedication some eight years later in a review of Machado's poetry and insists that despite their differences, they share a common commitment to combat those who oppose new ways of writing and thinking.[31] Many Machado poems continue this dialogue with voices of the past and the present. "Cantares" catalogues themes of popular Andalusian songs that the text defines as fatal traces of the Moorish race and presents them in schematic, very incomplete form. Wine, suffering, luck, death, black eyes appear in a list that echoes the incompleteness of much traditional popular poetry and the use of ellipses throughout the text suggests the inevitability of future reelaborations by new generations of singers (1923, 17). Machado communicates his image of Andalusian and gypsy women through the mediation of Julio Romero de Torres's paintings in the poem "Las mujeres de Romero de Torres" and self-identifies in "Retrato" as half gypsy, half Parisian, from the bohemian ambience of Montmartre and the popular Sevillian neighborhood of the Macarena. Many poems have a conversational quality that intermixes colloquial expressions with rhymed verses. The final lines of "Yo, poeta decadente" exemplify this trait:

Porque ya
una cosa es la poesía
y otra cosa lo que está
grabado en el alma mía.
   Grabado, lugar común.
Alma, palabra gastada.
Mía . . . No sabemos nada.
Todo es conforme y según.

(1923, 4:18)

[Now since
one thing is poetry
and another thing what is
engraved on my heart.
   Engraved, cliché,
Soul, commonplace word.
Mine . . . We know nothing.
It all depends.]

The informal, conversational tone invites dialogue and in conjunction with the blending of multiple traditions—foreign and domestic, literary and popular, visual and verbal—breaks the borders that conventionally delimit text, poetry, nation, and ethnicity.

Benito Pérez Galdós explores the connections between Spanish and Arab-Jewish culture in ways that differ superficially from the work of Machado, Villaespesa, and Rueda, but that have similar effect. The novelist participates in protests against the Moroccan campaigns in 1909 and 1911 (Bouchard 1988, 350) and in 1905 publishes *Aitta Tettauen,* an indictment of Spanish military intervention in Morocco in 1860. The expression of opposition to official state policy regarding Morocco bears a significant relation to the novelistic representation of Arab-African characters in his novels. *Nazarín* (1895) relates the bizarre story of the eponymous protagonist, a priest who wanders the countryside professing a new form of Christianity with a small band of devotees. In the initial description, the narrative depicts Nazarín as sexually and ethnically indeterminate. Until hearing his voice, the intradiegetic narrator assumes he is a woman and of Arab origin, describing Nazarín as the most perfect Semitic type he has seen outside Arab lands. The reporter-narrator describes him as a "Moorish priest" and a cross between a Buddhist and a follower of the Greek cynic, Diogenes (1967, 5:1687). Just as the characterization repudiates strict national, religious, sexual, and ethnic delimitations, the open, rambling structure of the book rejects the tightly controlled, diachronic order of conventional nineteenth-century realistic narrative. The novel emphasizes Oriental spirituality (5:1723) and rejects European rationalism and individualism and its expression in Western law, private property, and conventional rules for family and community constitution. *Nazarín* anticipates the Barojan open novel, in the random encounters and continually changing cast of characters and Valle-Inclán's esperpento, in the figure of the hideous dwarf—all head atop two little legs that seem to grow from under his beard—who falls in love with Nazarín's disciple (5:1742). Nazarín's Semitic appearances, the invocation of Biblical Nazareth in his name, allusions to his similarity with Christ link up with other texts of the period to imagine a different form of spirituality that reconnects with early Christianity and with oriental, non-European traditions.

Galdós examines the desirability of a Spanish-Arab-African cultural blending in *Misericordia* (1897), where the exploration of new forms of spirituality accompanies a rejection of traditional Spanish and European models. The well-known story of the blind beggar Almudena and Benina, the old servant who befriends and ultimately lives with him in an undefined but loving relationship, takes on a different significance in the context of the present analysis of ongoing reevaluation of Hispano-Arab-Jewish history and contemporary relations. The text purposely refuses to clarify Almudena's religious and ethnic identity.[32] At times it refers to him as an Arab from deep Morocco (1967, 5:1882), but on other occasions connects him with Israel and Sephardic origins. When Benina asks him what religion he professes, he responds that he is "eibrio" (V:1908), establishing a link with Hebrew tradition that the idiosyncratic spelling suggests is indirect and personally defined. His autobiographical narration includes such family names as Saul and Ruben Toledano, which have a distinct

Sephardic ring, and he prays in a language that the text identifies as a blend of Hebrew and fifteenth-century Spanish. However, other characters and the narrator continually refer to him as Moorish, a fellow beggar describes his fasting and ritual observance of what he describes as Muslim Lent, perhaps indicating the feast of Ramadan, and the Hebrew-Arab scholar/priest who enjoys speaking with him does so in Arabic. Almudena makes no distinction between religions, and at one point states that he was baptized and received the appropriately ecumenical name Joseph Marien Almudena.

Almudena's friendship with Benina crosses multiple borders of age, race, sex, and religion and contrasts with the obsession with order and inherited rules that characterize European culture and its textual representatives. The wealthy Carlos Trujillo refuses to aid his impoverished relatives unless they follow his imposed accounting practices. Paca, the mistress for whose benefit Benina has panhandled and sacrificed, cannot forgive her for accompanying a blind African and stooping to the socially unacceptable activity of begging. The aged, aristocratic Ponte is unable to forgive the imagined assault to his honor when Almudena presumes he is a rival for Benina's affections, and the lower-class Juliana as well as church officials encourage Benina to take refuge in the asylum for the poor and elderly rather than remain with Almudena in an unorthodox lifestyle. Benina's rejection of the bourgeois values assimilated by both the former aristocracy, as seen in Ponte, and the former lower class, as observed in Juliana, leads her to imagine new possibilities for social interaction. Her imaginative talents have been observed by many critics, but it is important to note in what manner they differ from those of other characters who also construct fictional worlds. Paca's daughter Obdulia, her friend Ponte, and Almudena all share an ability to escape a sordid reality to an imaginary world. Obdulia and Ponte regress to the grandiose, imperial past of the Paris of Napoleon III while Almudena envisions a fantastic world in which King Samdai promises buried treasures. It is only Benina's invention of the benevolent priest Romualdo that becomes reality. As she herself states, dreams exist to supplement life and bring justice to the world (1967, 5:1937). Benina's relation to her invented Romualdo mimics Galdós's relation to his fictive creation, in which he invents a space that confronts past imperial narratives, as revived by Obdulia and Ponte, and also Almudena's fantastic, otherworldly fictions. In their place, *Misericordia* proposes conditions that are possible and fair. It recuperates pieces of the past, in Benina's recitation to Juliana of the Biblical admonition to return home and sin no more and in the melding of Christian, Jew, and Moor in Almudena, but also looks toward a different kind of future.

Benina's relationship with Almudena defies conventional definition. He has searched throughout his life for the woman promised to him by King Samdai and he loves her as woman, mother, companion, or in his words, as his own soul (1967, 5:1988). The traditional male gaze that proves so difficult to extricate from descriptions of male-female relations disappears in the novel, emphatically erased in the depiction of Almudena's blindness and Benina's age.[33] The convention of the exotic, desired, conquered female of colonized territory also vanishes. Benina displaces the colonizing Spanish male, represented in the novel in the figure of Paca's deceased husband, who fought in the 1860 Moroccan campaign. Benina's relationship with Almudena rewrites the history of expulsion and reverses contemporary political and military imperial ambitions. In the end, Benina forgives but also breaks with a Spanish bourgeois culture that imposes itself on the upper as well as lower classes. She embarks on a different kind of voyage, even considering a journey to Jerusalem. Galdós's 1897 novel appears early in the modernist period, but it shares with later works a desire to imagine a new kind of social order that recuperates a forgotten and now re-remembered period of Spanish culture and refashions it in the construction of a different present. The persistent exploration of cross cultural understanding between Arab and Spaniard during the period when official state policy upholds colonial expansion in Morocco as an essential feature of historical and contemporary national self-definition constitutes a major effort to introduce an alternative discourse that disrupts traditional militarism and imperialism while simultaneously exploring new possibilities for racial, sexual, and religious interaction.

Spanish modernists, informed by modern conceptions of history, abandon long-standing concerns with empire and domination to consider the (re)construction of the Spanish nation in a post-imperial configuration. Rather than turn inward to an idealized evocation of Castilian geography and intrahistorical timelessness or escape into an exotic, fantasized cosmopolitanism, they devote a considerable portion of their energies to the exploration of a pluralist, multicultural Spanish nation that welcomes connection across external and internal borders, with other nations and between its multiple regions, and that includes groups that had contributed indispensably to the formation of Spanish culture, but had suffered expulsion and erasure in a period of regrettable national amnesia. Homi Bhabha's "DissemiNation: Time, Narrative and the Margins of the Modern Nation" describes nation in terms of a dual temporality: on the one hand, a nationalist pedagogy erases difference and fixes national identity through the evocation of a received past and shared traditions; on the other, a performative impulse operates in an intermediate space between identity, received from the past and suggesting immutability, and the other, a new subject capable of the construction of different narratives and new identities. Bhabha, Foucault, and de Certeau offer a definition of nation that allows for plural and multiple forces within a single set of borders and that coincides fundamentally with the delineation of the Spanish nation that Spanish modernism struggled to recuperate and sustain.

4
Modern Times

THE ADVANCES IN SCIENCE, PHILOSOPHY, AND PSYCHOLOGY THAT transform traditional perceptions of history and the relationship of past to present in late nineteenth and early twentieth centuries also contribute to a fundamental reconceptualization of the experience of time and space in the present. The advent of trains, steamships, trolleys, cars, airplanes, the telephone and telegraph all contribute to a sense of accelerated, increasingly rapid temporality. Other technologies allow for different intersections with time that contrast with or exist alongside the experience of speed. Expansion of geological time into an increasingly vast and ponderous past confronts a present that seems ever more minuscule and fleeting. The camera captures and freezes a moment while early film experiments in slow or reverse-motion allow for new ways of imagining temporal sequence. Electric lights defy the solar clock, turning day into night, while better heating systems rob winter of its power and horticultural advances permit the cultivation of spring or summer flowers during other seasons. Einstein's theory of relativity debunks the idea of absolute time, positing instead that two objects moving in relation to each other experience time differently, and Eastern philosophies, as well as Nietzsche's theory of Eternal return, offer alternatives to traditional Western notions of temporality.

SPEED AND CHANGE

Existing criticism on early twentieth century Spanish writers presumes their rejection of modernity and the changes it produces.[1] However, in Spain as in the rest of Europe, the response to modernity includes enthusiasm as well as fear, excitement alongside disgust. Doreen Massey has pointed out that women writers from other European nations welcome changes in social structure brought about by the growth of cities (1994, 171) and the same attitude appears in many Spanish women authors. Moreover, among the male writers that traditional criticism has identified as antagonistic to modern life a countercurrent of acceptance and even advocacy exists. For these authors, the pace of modern life offers an antidote to the weight of the past and an opportunity to interject new rhythms with distinct possibilities for individual and collective development. Early condemnation of the pace and complexity of modern life comes from nineteenth-century conservative realist writers. Pereda's *Pachín González* (1895) depicts the negative effects of modern technologies on the experience of temporality. When Pachín and his mother arrive in Santander to arrange for his emigration to America, they experience the rapid succession of modern time in the bustle of the port city, accelerated by the mention of steamships in the harbor and the suggestion of a brisk ocean crossing to a once remote, alien land. The narrative underscores modern technology's immense powers of destruction when a steamship carrying illegal shipments of dynamite explodes and kills or maims many of the disoriented, defenseless transplanted farmers. It also confronts the traditional experience of time with its modern equivalent. In the explosion, Pachín loses consciousness and as he recovers his senses and begins to search for his mother, sorting through piles of mutilated victims and wandering through the destruction, he experiences a decelerated, nightmarish temporality. In contrast with the alternately rapid and slowed paces, Pachín dreams of a return to the stable cyclicity of village life. In the end, after locating his mother, they decide to return to the country, opting for poverty, nature, and the single temporality of the routine rural life of their ancestors over greed, speed, and the alternating time patterns that characterize modernity and the possibilities for change.

The danger of new forms of travel, particularly the train and automobile, surfaces in various anti-modern texts of the period. "Los enemigos" by José López Pinillos, published in *El cuento semanal* (1908), depicts the train as a horned monster with flames coming from its mouth, thousands of moving feet, and a colossal lung. When it courses through the newly constructed tunnel, women and peasants run in horror. At the story's end, a train derailing kills the son of the protagonist stage-coach driver, thus vindicating his profound hostility to the intrusion of this modern demon in the tranquil countryside. In contrast to the monolithic attitudes of Pereda and López Pinillos, Spanish modernists discover possibilities for positive change through the introduction of modern technologies and explore with pleasure the multiple temporalities that contemporary life introduces. The Catalan painter Darío de Regoyos pictorially captures the juxtaposition of traditional rural and modern life in *Pancorbo: El tren que passa* (1901), in which a smoke blowing engine pulls through a small village in the mountain pass that links the Basque region and Castile. The rocky peaks punctuate sloping green hills that descend to a traditional rural village. As the train steams through the pass and the village, two young boys raise their hands in the foreground in a gesture of excitement and welcome.

Azorín's previously commented "Vida de un labrantín" describes the death of the protagonist's son in a train accident, indirectly contrasting the intrahistorical time of the father with the faster-paced and perilous life of the succeeding generation. Other Azorinian texts directly link trains and train travel with positive social change. *Castilla* (1912) opens with two texts that describe the introduction of train technology in Spain. "Los ferrocarriles" traces early descriptions of rail travel by Spanish writers in the 1840s and 1850s and stresses that the 1840 Cuban stretch antedates the first railroad of a presumably more modern Belgium. In contrast to typical objections regarding an unpoetic modernity, the text perceives beauty in train stations and in the sounds of passengers and the motor itself, and lyrically describes the dimming of lights as the departing train disappears in the distance. The text speaker links support for train travel to progressive attitudes: Modesto Lafuente, an early proponent, rejects the traditional practice of dueling to resolve questions of honor; the introduction of rail travel in Belgium facilitates the movement of single women, who journey unharassed by male travelers; and Robert Ritchie, an English engineer and train enthusiast, emphasizes the railroad's contributions to transnational communication and world peace. In prototypical modernist fashion, a destabilizing note appears in the closing paragraphs, where Ritchie's promises of improved intercultural collaboration fall victim to the modern reality of train use for war purposes. However, "Los ferrocarriles" quickly deconstructs a one-sided rejection of train technology by citing the international workers' argument that trains will bring peace only when no longer used militarily. Although the text does not specify the link between rail travel and the formation of an international worker community, it is clear that the workers' ability to join across national borders and combat train use in war comes about in part through train travel and its contribution to the rapid diffusion of newspapers and printed information. In a final turnabout, the text closes with a statement that confronts without totally erasing the preceding considerations: "Los ferrocarriles serán la paz (1958, 23)." The use of the future allows for a double reading, either a firm declaration that "Trains will bring peace" or the less definitive future of probability, "Trains will probably bring peace," allowing the reader to move between the two positions, both of which uphold the progressive possibilities of modern technology and speed and the possibilities for the realization of a new international order.

Enrique de Mesa compares the modern experience of time with a more traditional modality in two texts included in *Flor pagana* (1905). "En las ciudades viejas" describes stagecoach travel through Castile, with worn axles and grimy windows that correlate well with the barren terrain and ancient villages of the countryside. The two passengers who share the coach with the narrator imitate in appearance and dialect characters from another age. The speaker compares the woman to the highlander from Malagosto who appears in the Arcipreste de Hita's medieval poetry and the man's concern with crops and weather places him in a cyclical, rural temporality. The text describes the appearance in one village of a pale young girl in the balcony of an old noble residence and then describes the coach's arrival at two other similar homes, leaving indeterminate the identity of the villages and the homes as three distinct entities or a cyclical return to the same location. A sad note of temporal change intrudes with the description of a young girl's death, accompanied by a poetic lament for the young women who fade away in the ancient towns of the Castilian wasteland (1905, 35).

"En el camino" describes another trip through Castile, this time by automobile. The narrative rhythm accelerates to match the vehicle's speed and the text speaker explicitly compares earlier voyages, in which the landscape waited for his arrival and the inns were a place of pleasant rest after a slow, tiring approach, with his car trip, in which trees and villages rush towards him and pass just as quickly to recede in the dust. He no longer needs or desires to stop at the inns and his eyes, bored with the monotonous aridity of his surroundings, prefer to rest on the hair and flowing blue scarf of his young female companion. Spirited, with a stylish haircut, the young woman of this text contrasts markedly with the timeless female stagecoach passenger and introduces a contemporary note that connotes change and resistance to tradition. In their seclusion from the outside world, the automobile passengers barely notice the chickens that scurry out of the path of the speeding car or the young boy who throws a stone at them, although the past intrudes when they must stop to repair a flat tire caused by the deplorably deteriorated road. A passing stagecoach leaves them literally in its dust, oxherders stop to stare at them, and a highway worker offers the thirsty young woman water from his earthenware jug. The car travelers are now other to the rural inhabitants and occupy worlds with distinct temporal rhythms that come into contact only under certain circumstances. De Mesa's texts do not privilege the traditional or the modern, evoking the past with lyricism, but also recognizing temporal paralysis in "En las ciudades viejas" and subtly signaling the growing division of urban, upper-class Spaniards from traditional rural classes and values in "En el camino." However, the overall tone of the second story and the clear attraction of the narrator to the stylish young woman present modernity as an appealing alternative and the exploration of new temporal modalities as both artistically, psychologically, and socially productive.

Antonio Machado also offers a mixed response to the speed of modern travel. The poetic speaker of "El tren" describes his pleasure at traveling light in third-class compartments, but combines this declaration of approval for modernity with a sideways critique of urban spaces, stating that he most enjoys departing the city. A negative vision prevails when the speaker describes the train as a wheezing machine afflicted with whooping cough, but a positive evaluation surfaces in the admiring comparison of train speed to a flash of lightning. "Otro viaje" continues the same dual message, contrasting the advancing train with the poetic speaker's inability to escape the pull of memories of lost happiness. The speed of the rushing train that devours olive groves, meadows, and mountains recalls the pleasure of another trip, when he accompanied a loved one who has since died. In this context, the swift forward movement of the train becomes a monotonous click-clacking that reminds the speaker of his unremitting loneliness.

Carmen de Burgos represents the positive response of women writers to a rapidly changing world that offers new possibilities for freedom. She dismisses nostalgic laments for horse-drawn coach travel, preferring modern comfort (1909?, 10) and views the rapid succession of images through train windows as a metaphor for modern life. One moment passengers fixate on a beautiful young woman who lives near the tracks and a second later she disappears from their consciousness (16). Significantly, this observation follows comments on the role of the modern writer in producing a progressive spirit in the reading public. The rapidity of time and quick succession of images relates to a hoped for social transformation. The Martínez Sierras' poem "La linterna mágica," from the collection *La corte de los poetas* (1907), describes early film projection and the succession of images that cascade before a rapt children's audience: Little Red Ridinghood, a clown, battling horsemen, Pierrot and Columbina, a princess who turns into a butterfly to escape a monster, and more. The poem contrasts the construction of multiple imaginary worlds that rapidly supersede each other with the cold, unchanging luminous circle that shines on the white background at the beginning and end of the performance, positively valorizing speed and change in contrast with dull stability and single perspective.

Manuel Machado's *Apolo. Teatro pictórico* (1911) offers an adult variant of the magic lantern, leading the reader through a world tour of art museums. A series of sonnets describes Botticelli's *Allegory of Spring* of the Ufizzi Gallery, Leonardo da Vinci's *Monna Lisa* of the Louvre, Titian's *Carlos V* of the Prado, among many others. The collection reflects a modern experience of travel, with the quick tour through various galleries, and also the new perception of time as discontinuous, memory as fallacious, and history as amenable to revision. The individual poems follow a rough chronology, but arbitrarily break the order in placing Rembrandt (1606–1669) and Zurbarán (1598–1663?) before El Greco (1541–1614). The allusion to Rembrandt's *Anatomy Lesson* does not clarify whether it refers to *The Anatomy Lesson of Dr. Nicolaes Tulp* of 1632 or the 1656 *Anatomical Lesson of Dr. Joan Deyman* and could well be a composite of the two paintings, an intrahistorical reconstruction of the underlying features rather than the specific dates, locations, and surface details. Persin (1997, 36), among others, has pointed out Manuel Machado's tendency to meld details from different paintings or simply invent a detail that appears in no known model in his ekphrastic recreations. The sonnet "La infanta Margarita" also exemplifies this trait (1922, 2:93–94). Velázquez's name appears above the title, clearly situating the reader before his painting of the Hapsburg princess, but not indicating whether it is the 1653 portrait of the two-year-old princess or the 1655–56 painting of a slightly older *infanta,* both of which hang in the Vienna Kunsthistorisches Museum, or the portrait of the same period that hangs in the Louvre. Other contenders include the famous grouping of the princess and her maids of honor of the 1656 *Las meninas* on display in the Prado of Madrid, the 1659 painting of the adolescent princess of the Kunsthistorisches Museum, or the Prado portrait of the princess standing alone and holding a transparent handkerchief, dating from Velázquez's last years and completed by his disciple and son-in-law Martínez del Mazo.

The mention in the first quartet of underskirt staves that seem to imprison the pale princess rule out the early portrait of the two year old and the depiction of the rich handkerchief of the second quartet would seem to point to the Velázquez-del Mazo Prado portrait, but reference to a small pink bow that only barely pins back her blonde hair remits the reader to either the 1655–56 portrait of the Kunsthistorisches Museum or to *Las meninas,* in both of which the *infanta* is painted with a small, pink hair bow. In contrast, the Velázquez-del Mazo portrait of a more mature princess has a large reddish hair ornament that holds her hair more definitively in a stylized coiffure. Machado's sonnet, like the Velázquez-del Mazo portrait, represents a collaborative effort that rejects the tyranny of history, the authority of the master, and the obsession with an unchanging truth and chooses instead to create a synthesis that joins the scattered remnants of the *infanta's* life, her portraits at distinct ages now housed in museums throughout Europe, into a new and not necessarily permanent version.[2] This playful representation of the old masters in the pictorial theater of *Apolo* undermines the auratic quality of art in favor of an irreverent stance that welcomes the trappings of modernity, a more public access to art across geographical and national borders, and the transgressive possibilities that this allows. "La canción del presente" from *El mal poema* (1909) reiterates the exaltation of the present and abjures the search for a lasting, universal truth. This is not the traditional *carpe diem,* but rather a modern version, in which hatred and love succeed each other in a vertiginous and continual swirl: ". . . siempre dura poco / lo que quiero y lo que no . . ." [. . . what I want and what I don't want / never lasts long . . .] (1923, 4:31). The use of ellipsis, a signature device in Manuel Machado's poetry, signals the expectation and acceptance of a change that rewrites, reverses, or erases the present affirmation and allows for a non-causal, non-progressive link between one moment and its successor.

Pío Baroja shares in this exultation of change and impermanence, which marks his first novel and continues throughout his works with changing emphasis and inflection, but invariable presence. *Las aventuras, inventos y mixtificaciones de Silvestre Paradox* (1901) presents the story of the eccentric Silvestre Paradox, whose name invokes modernist attributes of freedom, independence, and contradiction. An eminently modern anti-hero, the middle-aged Silvestre, unmarried and always on the verge of economic disaster, has traveled the world, growing up in northern Spain and then tracing a nomadic trail through Paris, Egypt, Russia, and finally Madrid. The novel includes constant references to modernity: the telegraph, Salvation Army, Zulu war, Livingstone's African exploration, trains, sewing machines, and a concurrent interest in science and occultism. The mix of disparate values and interests in combination with the speed with which they succeed each other and with which Silvestre moves geographically and philosophically through diverse zones lead him to believe that each day is a new life (1946–48, 2:39). The novel echoes Silvestre's peripatetic and rapid movements, interrupting stories to pursue a tangential narrative, introducing characters and then abandoning them without explanation, or decelerating the brisk pace with intervals of stasis. In consonance with Manuel Machado's celebration of the moment and emotional mutability, Silvestre shifts rapidly from anger to benevolence, animosity to acceptance. After his servant Pelayo points out the moral depravity that characterizes bohemian Madrid, Silvestre explodes in fury, but when he reaches home, his anger turns to irony and singing happily, he lies down and falls asleep (111). The same emotional reversal occurs in his relationship with Juan Pérez del Corral, whose antics amuse and also annoy Silvestre, but whose request for assistance when ill awakens a compassion and generosity normally reserved for close friends. With the speed that characterizes modern life and introduces possibilities for rapid personal and social change, Silvestre recovers from indignation at the social disregard for Pérez del Corral's death and also at his servant's robbery of his money and valuables. In the novel's final paragraphs, he and his partner depart to build an electric factory near Valencia and as they leave Madrid, they lean out the train window to shout their enthusiasm for yet another new project (150). The train and electric factory both invoke modernity, which advances hand in hand with a rapid succession of emotions, a continual recovery of the joy of the present, and the possibilities for becoming other than convention and tradition dictate.

The prologue to *La dama errante* (1908) includes an autobiographical statement in which Baroja self-identifies as more Dionysian than Apollonian, a lover of action and drama. Toward the end of the prefatory comments, he links this characterization with a modern preference for the ephemeral: "Somos los hombres del día gentes enamoradas del momento que pasa, de lo fugaz, de lo transitorio, y la perdurabilidad o no de nuestra obra nos preocupa poco, tan poco, que casi no nos preocupa nada" [We individuals of today are enamored of the passing, fleeting, and transitory moment, and the durability or lack of durability of our work concerns us little, so little, that it hardly concerns us at all] (1946–48, 2:232). In a visual metaphor that links with Manuel Machado's rejection of the old masters, the Barojan speaker states that his text does not seek to paint a picture for exhibition in museums, but rather a less authoritative, more transient impressionist cloth. The narrative action of *La dama errante* reflects the valorization of the ephemeral. Based on the anarchist bombing of the wedding procession of Alfonso XIII and Victoria Eugenia of Battenberg, it unfolds with ample use of newspaper reportage to increase the sense of rapid access to and disappearance from the public eye that occurs in contemporary culture. In a subtle enactment of the short-lived public memory, the text never names the king or his bride and the anarchist Morral becomes Nilo Brull. In the prologue, the Barojan speaker states that Brull is a composite of a variety of anarchist figures, further erasing the identity of this momentarily (in)famous figure. The premise that in the modern world the central figures of today's headlines will shortly recede into oblivion structures the narrative plot. Brull's casual contact with Dr. Enrique Aracil casts suspicion on the latter's involvement in the attack and as a result, he and his daughter María must flee Madrid and Spain until the notoriety subsides. The sense of a rapidly receding past and consistent change marks the text. Iturrioz, the ubiquitous commentator of Barojan novels, remarks on recent transformations that separate modern Madrid from the city of his youth and have affected both such superficial aspects as the removal of gambling houses and more substantive features, as the shift toward a generalized skepticism. Iturrioz believes a skeptical rejection of the status quo may well result in significant changes in the constitution of the nation and its future course (263).

As María and her father travel through the countryside, an accelerated modern temporality enters into contact with traditional rhythms. Rural life exhibits several different experiences of time: an unchanging tradition, a slow but perceptible variation of established patterns, and the intrusion of a modern, rapid pace. Horse-drawn carriages carrying villagers to neighboring festivals, gypsy groups on mangy mules, and families consisting only of women left behind when the men emigrate to America reflect a world in which time leaves no apparent trace. The old woman who owns an inn where the Aracils spend a night enunciates a vision of life as unremitting suffering that invokes medieval asceticism (1946–48, 2:292). An aged farmer speaks with a vocabulary and syntax so unfamiliar to the modern ear that María and her father keep asking him questions to try to better understand his language (291). However, evidence of more modern contacts surfaces even in the decrepit country inn, where a lithograph depicts the death in 1813 of the Polish nationalist hero Józaf Antoni Poniatowski. References to the nineteenth-century program of auctioning church and communal lands and its negative effects on rural populations reveal that the poverty of the countryside is not rooted in some temporally distant event, but has more recent causes. As in Azorín, the "intrahistorical" past has its own internal history and changes over time.

María and other characters comment on the intersection of these distinct experiences of temporality. After observing a rustic celebration in a country hermitage and the toothless, hairy, rural participants, María and a more educated farmer remark that they feel they are living in the Bronze Age. María finds it hard to believe that trains, telegraph lines, and electric lights exist nearby (1946–48, 2:306). In this mix of temporal rhythms, many different stories and modes of narrating are possible. No single narrative sequence issues inevitably from the preceding events; rather, a variety of endings prove equally plausible. Iturrioz, the reporter Tom Gray, and María's cousin Venancio try to imagine the various options available to María and her father as they flee the country and they construct different hypothetical narratives according to whether the Aracils left by train, automobile, horse, or on foot. The present moment contains a range of possibilities that contrast with predictable, unchanging narratives of the past. The thrill of modernity and possibilities for change rapidly displace María's memories of her voyage through the Spanish countryside. On the train and then the ocean liner that takes her to London, she senses the power of civilization and looks forward to this new phase of her life. While María's father feels exhausted by the voyage and unable to energetically look to the future, María manifests a youthful optimism and excitement at the possibilities that await her.

La ciudad de la niebla (1909) narrates María's attempts to establish herself as a modern working woman in London. Typically modernist in the rejection of monolithic views of reality, Baroja mutes the optimism of the final pages of the preceding novel with a multi-perspectivist vision. The challenges of life as a single working woman in London overwhelm María and she ultimately determines to return to Madrid and marry Venancio. However, her reconnection with the past does not imply reentry into the unchanging zone of traditional time but rather, a resumption of a more slowly but still evolving temporality in which she retains a relation of similarity and difference with the past. In London, she meets women of many nationalities who succeed in a more complete break with the past and in creating an altered selfhood and modern life for themselves. Her own marriage, which the text describes in a brief final chapter entitled "Epílogo feliz, casi triste" [Happy, almost sad, epilogue], joins her with an unconventional man who provides his daughters with a scientific education free from the constraints of traditional religious, female schooling. In the next to last chapter, the narrator introduces yet one more indication of faith in the inevitability of change in a modern conception of humanity. Intercalated in a chapter entitled "Raza cansada" [Tired race], the section called "Renacimiento de la esperanza" [Renaissance of hope] describes the perpetual turning of the coin from despair to hope, apathy to activity, tradition to change, similarity to alterity (1946–48, 2:441).

The belief in the persistence of change connects with another modern feature of Barojan considerations of temporality and evolution. Both *César o nada* and *El árbol de la ciencia* make reference to theories of evolution that support an organism's capacity for rapid change. César cites experiments by Hugo de Vries that demonstrate rapid, drastic change in certain vegetable species and he refers to the neoDarwinist contention that species do not evolve gradually, but rather suddenly and with permanent, beneficial results (1967, 244–45).[3] This scientific principle confirms César's belief in action and movement as the essence of life and underpins his commitment to social change (42–44). Andrés Hurtado in *El árbol de la ciencia* refers to Haeckel and his theory that each embryo retraces the entire evolutionary history of the species. Haeckel's views presume the rapid change of an organism, which maps evolutionary changes as they occur and reproduces them in the embryonic form of the next generation. César's discussion of this concept unfolds in dialogue with his friend

Alzugaray, just as Andrés's occur in conversation with his uncle Iturrioz. In both cases, affirmation of possibilities for rapid change meets with challenges from the respective interlocutors and faces assertions of the immutability or painfully slow transformation of biological and social organization. The presence of this opposition does not refute the profession of belief in swift social change but rather, alternates with it in the rapid succession of multiple and contradictory tenets that coexist in modernism.

Neither María Aracil's personal retreat from the struggle for individual and collective change nor that of César Moncada or Andrés Hurtado represent a permanent, unchangeable concession to stasis. In each case, the text leaves open the possibility for some future recuperation of the initial energies: the discussion of the perpetual renewal of hope in the final pages of *La ciudad de la niebla,* the indeterminate ending of *César o nada,* with no definitive indication of whether the protagonist has been assassinated, and the doctor's comment in the closing lines of *El árbol de la ciencia* that despite Andrés's suicide, he somehow represents a harbinger of things to come (1968?, 398). The rapidity with which Barojan texts switch from a defense of change to lamentations of stagnation and then back to energetic declarations of a belief in the dynamic essence of life in itself represents a thoroughly modern understanding of the impermanence and profound relativism of truth statements. Change constitutes a fundamental feature of modernity and studies of the period that focus exclusively on stasis or view these writers as retreating into a nostalgic evocation of the past ignore and ultimately silence a significant and productive aspect of their work. The acceptance of rapid change accompanies an increasing emphasis on chance over causality, temporal jumps over succession, alterity over similarity, and a growing sense of liberation from such seemingly inescapable cycles as day and night, the seasons of the year, and the biological clock.

Multiple Clocks: Days, Seasons, Ages, and Light Years

Stephen Kern describes the imposition of standard time and the 1884 establishment of Greenwich Mean Time as a response to the introduction of rail travel and the need for a uniform gauge to create meaningful schedules and facilitate movement across long distances. Prior to that date, Germany had five different time zones and a traveler from Washington to San Francisco had to reset his watch over two hundred times during the course of the trip (1983, 12). Ironically, the move to standardize time called attention to the arbitrary nature of its measure and other technological advances further underscored the subjective nature of traditional methods for designating temporality. Such seemingly objective standards as day and night proved less and less stable as electric lighting supplanted a setting sun and extended working hours well beyond traditional quitting time. The need for clocks grows precisely because human activity no longer depends on solar time and schedules are increasingly variable. Advances in psychology bring a consciousness that chronological and psychological age do not always coincide and the increasing emphasis on childhood in the formation of the adult inspires new interest in the different phases of life. Bergson's theorization of time as becoming and belief that memories of the past must be brought together in a complex network in order to "create" the present and future (1911a, 211) not only highlights a dynamic relationship between past, present, and future, but also posits the remembered past as a unit, a synchronic web that carries forward feelings and thoughts of previous periods of life to link them with the present and future. Connections between past and present no longer take a linear form, but rather that of a tangle of threads that join with other intermeshed bundles of memories without regard to temporal continuity. In a different vein, the 1881 Michelson-Morley experiment establishes a constant velocity for light, irrespective of the medium through which it passes, and other probings into light and its travel across space allow for heady new speculations about the relative time of light's emission in comparison with its reception at a given location. Einstein's theory of relativity adds further fuel to a sense of multiple clocks and to the repudiation of traditional conceptions of time as always and everywhere the same. The common thread that unites these diverse areas consists in the growing recognition that the experience of time varies considerably according to location in space, psychological state, and relations between self and other(s). The acceptance of multiple clocks produces responses ranging from anxiety to excitement, hope to fear, often coexisting within the same writer.

The disjunction between solar and personal, stellar and terrestrial times receives early treatment in Spanish modernism. Many artists find liberation from centuries of dependance on the sun's rotation an exciting contribution to a general sense that time-honored rules no longer hold sway. Benavente marvels in his poem "La tienda de flores" at the presence of tropical plants and exotic vegetation in a Madrid florist and stops to see spring flower in mid-winter, thanks to advances in hot house techniques. Baroja signals both the drawbacks and possibilities of the disjunction between solar and social time in his trilogy *La lucha por la vida.* The opening pages of *La busca* (1903) comically signal the existence of multiple clocks in early twentieth-century Madrid, moving from the description of a clock striking twelve in the first sentence to the mention of a small watch marking eleven strokes in the next paragraph and finally, to a church bell ringing only once (1946–48, 1:257). The narrator laments his inability to verify which time piece gives the correct hour, confessing his lack of control in the new realm of plural temporalities. The second chapter describes the inversion of solar time in the protagonist's boarding house, with absolute darkness prevailing during the day and dimly illuminated surroundings at night. The disorder of urban life connoted by these temporal variants and transpositions carries with it suffering and economic exploitation, but also freedom and social mobility. Manuel, the rural transplant who explores the varied sectors of Madrid, represents a new kind of *flaneur,* not a strolling adult, male observer, but a child who directly suffers the effects of urban misery while simultaneously learning to negotiate its apparent lawlessness. Over the course of the trilogy, he finds openings through which to discover and then realize his aspirations to become other than his rural past might have dictated.[4] At the end of *La busca,* he divides city dwellers into two groups, those that circulate in the night and those that work in the day, equating the former with vice, pleasure, and darkness and the latter with work, fatigue, and sunlight (373). In contrast to Manuel's rigid separation of these two worlds, the trilogy continually deconstructs his polarities in a modernist rejection of dichotomous categorization, including those as seemingly natural as day and night. The road workers who repair the Puerta del Sol and the bakers with whom Manuel labors are active at night while ragmen begin their work before dawn. These laborers intersect with prostitutes, pimps, and middle-class pleasure seekers who also inhabit the streets at night.

The second volume of the series explores an even more heterogeneous society in which rules of social stratification and temporal order no longer prevail. *Mala hierba* (1904) traces Manuel's entry to the underground world of gambling and also the world of typesetting. His social horizons expand to include bohemian artists, upwardly mobile lower and middle-class schemers, downwardly mobile nobility, lesbians, prostitutes, Jewish typesetters, repatriated Cubans, and Spanish American war veterans. Both gambling and printing activities take place at night and this modern exploitation of nocturnal hours is made possible by the gas factory that looms in the background throughout the second part of the novel. Manuel can see it from his boarding house (1946–48, 1:432), he passes it in his meanderings through the city (453), and it serves as a backdrop on several occasions in the final chapter. In *Mala hierba,* the existence of the new temporality and heterogeneous social world that it produces confuses and overwhelms Manuel, who remains torn between the pull of a stable work and home life and the temptations of the street. At the end of the novel, he finds solace in yet another time and space that becomes increasingly attractive and imaginable in the modern world. Contemplating the stars, he entertains the possibility of other infinitely varied and exciting worlds, without hatred, policemen, judges, soldiers, government, and authority (507).

Manuel's momentary anger at society does not represent a final or permanent stance. Like other Barojan creations, he changes with the rapidity that characterizes modern life. In *Aurora roja* (1904), the trilogy's final work, he turns his attention from dreams of other worlds to the creation of a space for himself within the modern Spanish city. His anarchist leanings now shift to a more skeptical detachment and individual ambition that contrast with his brother Juan's radical politics. These two visions join with others, such as Roberto Hasting's exaltation of Darwinian struggle, to form a complex ideological mapping of early twentieth-century urban ideology. The play of light and darkness, day and night, has a less evident role in this novel, but the rich diversity of life styles that modern lighting allows and the social mobility that comes from a more fluid socio-economic situation continue to receive emphasis. In this network of varied cultures, no single language, value, or ideology takes precedence. Well before Ortega y Gasset's famous theorization of perspectivism in *Meditaciones del Quijote* (1914), Baroja advocates the adoption of cascading, revolving viewpoints in order to capture the complexity of modern culture. Juan's sculpture of la Salvadora meta-artistically reflects the novelistic vision; viewed from one side it appears happy, while from the other it communicates sadness (1946–48, 1:535). The Madrid of the trilogy has the same effect. It is sordid, immoral, callous, with appalling slums and corrupt officials, but it also offers freedom, dynamism, and openness to change, to becoming other and joining with others. The series celebrates the city's linguistic diversity as reflecting the speakers' diverse social, regional, and national origins. The cultural wealth of modern Madrid also expresses itself in musical variety, with French anarchist songs, hurdy-gurdy imitations of classical tunes, delicate waltzes of music boxes, tangos, and Cuban melodies praising the island and the independence movement.

Women characters range from the bourgeois, delicate Kate to the self-sufficient, industrious working-class Salvadora to the once proud, now prostituted la Justa. The series eschews grand narratives and instead interweaves many individual stories, none providing a totalizing solution but each offering a partial answer. Juan's anarchism proves idealistic and unworkable, but his commitment and ideals clearly affect his brother and his views of social justice are ultimately internalized by la Salvadora, who joins Manuel and Juan in their political discussions toward the end of *Aurora roja* (1946–48, 1:633) and aggressively acts to prevent an insistent priest from delivering last rights against Juan's will. Juan believes his efforts to educate a group of beggars and prostitutes has produced no effect, yet when he dies, the Philippine prostitute who imperturbably accepted her pimp's abuse breaks down in tears. Manuel's individual narrative takes him from street life to ownership of a small printing business and marriage to la Salvadora. None of the stories offer global solutions, but all signify the possibilities for change that mark modern society, structured according to an inverted temporality in which the solar cycle no longer determines human activity.

In this remapping of human development, discontinuity displaces chronology and alongside the inexorable succession of clock time, asynchronous reconnections with specific past moments or feelings suggest possibilities for rewriting the present and the future. A loosening of the tyranny of chronology proves especially appealing to Spanish modernists, who feel that for cultural and historical reasons, they have been deprived of childhood and youth. Baroja writes of the inability to experience childhood in Spain in *La dama errante* (1946–48, 2:232) and Pérez de Ayala's Alberto Díaz de Guzmán blames Jesuit education for stealing his boyhood in *La pata de la raposa* (1964–66, 1:433). Born in a moment of national decline, in a bourgeois Catholic culture that privileges order over spontaneity, repressed sexuality over a healthy regard for the body, they feel old before their time. Antonio Machado paints an aged poetic persona in *Soledades* (1907), when he has not yet reached his mid-thirties. In order to recuperate the child's voice and resurrect a never-lived childhood, these authors reject the ordered bourgeois life of their day. Baroja's fascination with the "youthful" world of the circus and carnivals is shared by Pérez de Ayala, who introduces the seductive figure of the strongman in *Tinieblas en las cumbres* and has the adult Alberto Díaz de Guzmán join the circus in *La pata de la raposa*. The bohemian life style of Manuel Machado, Alejandro Sawa, Valle-Inclán, and others represents a refusal to follow expected trajectories toward adulthood and social conformity.

Antonio Machado's participation in the bohemian worlds of Madrid and Paris and his late marriage to a young, almost childish, bride reflect his desire to establish an idiosyncratic time line and delay entry into adulthood, but it is his poetry that most fully and profoundly reveals his exploration of multiple temporalities and their liberating effects for individual and collective selves.[5] He expresses his disdain for the artificial manipulation of solar time for economic gain in "A un naranjo y a un limonero vistos en una tienda de plantas y flores," decrying the shriveled fruit and dwarfed trees that result from transplanting Andalusian citrus trees to a Castilian flower shop (1917, 76). However, the poet finds rich human and poetic capital in a changed conceptualization of the relationship between psychological and biological age and of memory as a bundle of images, sensations, and emotions open to ever new configurations. Machado's poetry continually contrasts various temporalities and while recognizing the inexorable march forward toward death as constitutive of human experience, it also explores temporal leaps and reconnections that allow for the creative assimilation of one's own prior experiences into the present and future as well as the integration and recreation of the past experiences of others. His poetic experimentation aims to transcend traditional clocks—solar, seasonal, biological, and mechanical—and allow for the sharing of experience and sensibility across time. A variety of poems explicate the relation between a lost boyhood and its present and future recuperation. "Acaso . . ." presents a poetic speaker lost in dream and discovering spring's arrival for the first time in a symbolic representation of never-experienced youth. The first three quartets describe the fresh splendor and fertility of the season. The remaining verses explore the relationship between multiple clocks and poetic communication:

"Tras de tanto camino es la primera
vez que miro brotar la primavera,"
dije, y después, declamatoriamente:
"¡Cuan tarde ya para la dicha mía!"
Y luego, al caminar, como quien siente
alas de otra ilusión: "Y todavía
¡yo alcanzaré mi juventud un día!"

(1917, 70)

[After so long a road it is the first
time that I see spring sprout,
I said, and then, declamatorily:
—How late now for my happiness!
And then, while walking, as if feeling
the wings of another illusion:—And yet
I will reach my youth some day!]

The tercet that commences the quoted fragment interrupts anteceding and succeeding quartets to call attention to the speaker's claim that he observes the arrival of spring for the first time. The quartet's intercalated statement, described disparagingly as "declamatory," suggests that the assertion that springtime renewal has come too late is more figure of speech than true statement. In this reading, the contradicting rhetorical assertion calls attention to the fact that the speaker has experienced youth and springtime in the past, but for poetic purposes, he chooses to forget in order to re-experience as if for the first time and thus recreate a pristine sense of discovery for himself and the reader. Furthermore, he will continue to forget and rediscover the sensation of youth in a perpetual lyrical rebirth, as suggested in the final three verses, where he projects future reinventions of the same sensation. Neither his own present moment nor some past epiphany remains frozen in time, but continually changes in a fruitful disjunctive temporality that reaches back or projects forward, in denial of rigid and irreversible progressions.

A number of Machado's poems introduce glass, mirrors, and reflections, which further clarify the relationship between "forgotten" moments of the past and present poetic communication. "Me dijo un alba de primavera" opens indeterminately, as Ricardo Senabre has indicated (1992, 119), leaving the reader to choose between the identification of the spring dawn as a speaking subject or adverbial modifier, in which case an unnamed third party enunciates the sentence and the translation would read "He/She said to me one spring dawn." The poem proceeds in dialogue form with the ambiguous interlocutor addressing the poetic speaker:

"Yo florecí en tu corazón sombrío
ha muchos años, caminante viejo
que no cortas las flores del camino.
Tu corazón de sombra, ¿acaso guarda
el viejo aroma de mis viejos lirios?
¿Perfuman aún mis rosas la alba frente
del hada de tu sueño adamantino?"

(1917, 48)

[I blossomed in your gloomy heart
many years ago, you aged traveller
who doesn't gather the roadside flowers.
Does your heart of gloom, perhaps retain
the old aroma of my old lilies?
Do my roses still sweeten the white forehead
of the fairy of your glittering dream?]

The image of the dream as constructed of a translucent material (*adamantino*) continues in the poetic speaker's response, where he states that his dreams are merely of "*cristal,*" denoting either a chemical crystal, glass, or in common figurative use, a mirror. In the final verses, the speaker refers to the crystalline vase of his dreams and ventures that should it break, the indeterminate interlocutor will perhaps recover the flowers, thus reliving in the present an experience or emotion that had been consigned to the speaker at some former time. The two allusions to dawn, in the first and last stanzas, contrast the seemingly unyielding solar periodicity with a more fluid, productive reach back into the past. The speaker or poet, in a metapoetic reading, resurrects past aromas and images that had remained locked inside the glass walls of his consciousness and now spill forth as if alive and present, impervious to the passage of days or seasons. The description of the poet's consciousness varies throughout the poem and throughout Machado's work to capture this sense of fluidity in response to multiple stimuli and to continually interject diverse temporalities as the essence of poetic creation. The first description of diamond-like dreams, suggested by the interlocutor, transmutes to the poet's trio of possibilities—crystal, glass, mirror—and finally, in the last verses, to a crystalline glass. In other texts, the solid glass takes on qualities of crystal, window, or mirror or the less stable forms of water, lagoons, or fountains. The constantly changing form reflects the imprint of time, for as Abel Martín states, A is not A in two successive moments (1951, 942), signifying that the passage of time and alteration of being mutually implicate each other.

Regardless of size or substance, images of poetic consciousness in Machado invariably communicate the ability to both reflect the self and look outward to the other. The material consistently allows for transparency and reflection, for looking through to the outside and reflecting back to the inside, forward to the future, back to the past, and in the mirror of the present. In the metapoetic "Leyendo un claro día," the speaker turns again to the subject of poetic consciousness, the connection with other ages of his and the reader's life, and to a poetics of communicability across time. He describes his dreams as a deep mirror and defines his role as poet as retrieving and reflecting discarded memory back to the reader:

> El alma del poeta
> se orienta hacia el misterio.
> Sólo el poeta puede
> mirar lo que está lejos
> dentro del alma, en turbio
> y mago sol envuelto.
> En esas galerías,
> sin fondo, del recuerdo,
> donde las pobres gentes
> colgaron cual trofeo
> el traje de una fiesta
> apolillado y viejo. . . .
>
> (1917, 83)

> [The poet's soul
> is oriented toward mystery.
> Only the poet is able
> to see what is far away
> inside the soul, enveloped
> in cloudy and magic sun.
> In these galleries,
> without end, of memory,
> where poor humanity
> hangs like a trophy
> the motheaten and old
> party dress. . . .]

The poet not only looks to his own past to recapture memory and link it to the present, in imitation of Bergsonian duration,[6] but defines his role as penetrating the consciousness of the other(s) and recovering their cast off, impoverished memories to construct a vibrant new image capable of dreaming/creating a productive future. The poet creates new honey from old suffering, fabricating white, pure garments as well as strong, iron armor. This mixture of delicate and bellicose images in combination with the exploration of the consciousness of the self and the other links the poet's lyrical and social poetry, the personal and the collective. Both elements of Machado's poetry, which some critics separate into distinct categories of disparate literary value,[7] follow a similar procedure in the conversion of past memories to a living present with possibilities for a transformed future. Furthermore, both demonstrate the relativity of the terms "past, present, and future" and the arbitrary nature of conventional divisions of life into the categories youth, maturity, and old age. The poet guides the reader through a process by which memories become dreams, the past allows for a different present and future, and age reverses to recover lost youth or rewrite a future.

The poet strives to teach the reader to dream because the inability to do so, and thus recast the relationship with the past and the self, produces grotesque deformation:

El alma que no sueña,
el enemigo espejo,
proyecta nuestra imagen
con un perfil grotesco.
   Sentimos una ola
de sangre, en nuestro pecho,
que pasa . . . y sonreímos,
y a laborar volvemos.

(1917, 85)

   [The spirit that does not dream,
the enemy mirror,
projects our image
with a grotesque profile.
   We feel a wave
of blood, in our heart,
that passes . . . and we smile
and return to work.]

These verses clearly state the intimate relationship between self and other in Machado; the other who does not dream reflects back our own image as grotesque and consequently, the poet must revive the other's dream through a dialogic process of assimilation and communication, reconstruction and restatement, recovery and restitution. The mirror/glass/still water/window/gallery of consciousness reflects the self and opens to the other while also intercepting the passage of time, disrupting chronicity, to capture a moment that refuses to remain in the immediacy of a presence that cannot dream, whether of past or future, and, thus, escapes the grotesque distortion of timelessness. “Leyendo un claro día” textually represents the process described, moving from the activity of the poet reading his own verses—connection with the past and the self—to the final verses where he describes a resurgence of vital energy and a desire to return to writing, to communication with the other through a yet to be completed composition. The progression from the initial reading to the final writing proceeds through memory and then back to the present and towards the future while the sun remains high in the sky, first mentioned in the opening verse through the allusion to the clear day and again in the seventh stanza, which describes the creative labor of poets beneath the sun. The immobile, constant midday sun contrasts with the “clouded and magic sun” that illuminates what is distant inside the soul, which constitutes poetic subject matter as defined in the third stanza. The poet freezes the sun in a Castilian or Andalusian sky to emphasize the contrast with the temporal leaps and multiple temporalities of psychological and poetic experience and to reveal the inability of conventional solar time to measure these new temporal relations.

Machado struggles throughout his work to retain the vital rush of blood he feels in the closing verses of “Leyendo un claro día” and like other modernists, he oscillates between despair, anger, apathy and hope, cordiality, and energy. Whether looking back to childhood and the national past, or forward to the individual/national future, his poetry creates a lyrical subject that escapes a particular moment or age while also marking the passage of diachronic time in the very act of leaping over it, contrasting traditional measures with a discontinuous modern(ist) temporality. “¿Mi amor? . . . ¿Recuerdas, dime?” confronts the inexorable passage of solar and seasonal time with the recuperation of the past, in this case of a lover whose connection with the poetic speaker may have terminated or may still continue. The initial interrogation questions whether this love is, or was, and the rest of the poem contains three additional interrogatives that reconstruct the past in the very act of asking if the addressee remembers the events described. Each question invokes an element of nature as a tangible symbol of a shared (?) past and in each quartet, the natural element undergoes a transformation that reveals the passage of time from one season to the next: the tender rushes of the first stanza almost immediately become languid and yellow; the poppy flower, with connotations of bright color and early summer, turns quickly into a black, crêpe-like object; and the morning sun ray, with suggestion of warmth and light, breaks into multiple refractions in a fountain's frozen waters (1917, 47). Against the rhythm of solar or seasonal succession, the poet recaptures a past sharing of sentiments with a lover whose insertion in time remains indeterminate. The use of the interrogative disrupts the more common declarative sequence to introduce a different temporality, a dialogue with an other in a space that the poem creates across time and between subjectivities.

Anguish at the passage of time never disappears from Machado's poetry, but it coexists with different experiences of temporality that create a constructive communication across time. The convergence of the present with other moments of time and the transcendence of solitude through communication with the other is not limited in Machado to the recovery of a past memory of the self or the collectivity. In "Esta luz de Sevilla" the poetic speaker moves from the present to the past and then the future to connect emotionally and experientially across the temporal and spatial gap that separates him from his deceased father. The poetic speaker and son has now reached the age at which he remembers his father, graying and preoccupied with aging and time. The coincidence of these two critical passages allows for an understanding and sharing of experience not previously possible. However, the Machado poem does not simply capture the correspondence of the speaker's present with the father's past but extends forward, to imagine his own future as inscribed in his father's old age, still not realized in the moment depicted in the poem but anticipated as an impending unfolding. The speaker's aging allows him a compassion for his father that erases their separation across time and space and extends beyond the limits set by human mortality. Compassion and connection with the father occur precisely because the father revealed his own struggle with time and his effort to bring the past into the present. Those who remain locked in an eternal present or subject to absolute chronology, who cannot dream and represent the hostile mirror receive only the grotesque depiction predicted in "Leyendo un claro día." A number of poems of *Campos de Castilla* portray individuals or sectors of the nation that live in this sterile time zone and are incapable of dialogue across time. The provincial gambler of "Del pasado efímero" cannot escape the passage of chronological time; his life is determined by the succession of days and seasons that brings a new bull fight, another round of elections, an anxiously awaited rainstorm. The text describes him as "prisionero en la Arcadia del presente" [prisoner in the Arcadia of the present] and the final verses condemn him to the sterility of a present that cannot reach back or project forward, forever isolated from the creative consciousness of reader and speaker:

> Este hombre no es de ayer ni es de mañana,
> sino de nunca; de la cepa hispana
> no es el fruto maduro ni podrido,
> es una fruta vana
> de aquella España que pasó y no ha sido,
> esa que hoy tiene la cabeza cana.
>
> (1917, 208)

> [This man isn't from yesterday or from tomorrow
> but rather from never; of the Hispanic vine
> he is neither the mature nor the rotten fruit,
> he is an empty fruit
> of that Spain that passed and has not been,
> that white-headed one of today.]

The similarity with "Esta luz de Sevilla" in language, temporal play, and the reference to the process of graying hair only enhances the contrast between the compassionate connection across time of the poem about the father and the temporal separation and hostile antagonism in the description of the gambler, who cannot transcend seasons, days, ages, generations, and moves through life with a single clock. Hope for the individual and the nation lies in the coexistence of multiple clocks, in breaking with the tyranny of chronology to establish a dialogue across time.

"A orillas del Duero," the second poem in *Campos de Castilla,* exemplifies the multiplicity of temporalities that Machado views as a positive contribution of modernity. Critics have read the poem as a pessimistic commentary on a Spain that is caught in the past[8], but the presence of diverse temporal perspectives offers other possibilities for a more productive relationship across time. The poem opens with clear temporal indicators—it was a beautiful day in the month of July. The poetic speaker ascends a hill to view the Duero river and valley, alternately tired and seemingly elderly as he stops to rest and wipe his brow or energetic and youthful, as he clambers over the rocks. From his vantage point on the hilltop, the speaker describes the valley in military terms that recall the Castilian imperial, militarist past. The description of natural and man-made defenses invokes historical Castilian hostility to the outside and the mention of the merino sheep and grazing bull recall traditional Castilian preferences for the open range over agriculture, a theme already mentioned in other texts in relation to the expulsion of the Moors in the early days of the nation. Intermixed with historical allusions, the speaker inserts alternative perspectives and temporalities. In contrast to the curving Duero that protects Soria from Aragon, he calls attention to the long bridge that crosses the river's sparkling waters as well as the river's extension across the heart of Iberia. Reference to the river's considerable length reminds the reader of its course across Portugal and eventual flow into the Atlantic ocean.[9] The sense of motion outward is enhanced by the mention of the river's current and of carts, horsemen, and muleteers who cross the bridge and presumably take their wares to external markets. Subsequently, the text refers to emigrant farmers who also follow the Duero to the sea to seek work elsewhere.

As Cobb and Predmore note, the speaker decries the present condition of the meseta, barren and uncultivated, with decrepit cities and roads without inns. However, he does not assume the permanence of this condition. During the description of the valley as observed from above, he calls attention to the importance of perspective by pointing out the diminutive size of the vehicles and individuals on the bridge. A few verses later, he returns to the notion of perspective and links it to modern conceptions of temporality:

> Castilla miserable, ayer dominadora,
> envuelta en sus andrajos desprecia cuanto ignora.
> ¿Espera, duerme o sueña? ¿La sangre derramada
> recuerda, cuando tuvo la fiebre de la espada?
> Todo se mueve, fluye, discurre, corre o gira;
> cambian la mar y el monte y el ojo que los mira.
> ¿Pasó? Sobre sus campos aún el fantasma yerra
> de un pueblo que ponía a Dios sobre la guerra.
>
> (1917, 115–16)

[Miserable Castile, yesterday dominant,
wrapped in her rags disdains all she doesn't know.
Is she hoping, sleeping or dreaming? Does she remember
the spilt blood, when she suffered the fever of the sword?
Everything moves, flows, passes, runs or turns;
the sea and mountain change and the eye that perceives them.
Did it pass? Over her fields still wanders the phantom
of a people that put God above war.]

The initial verses contrast the present and past and the questions raise doubts as to the relationship of present Castile with future or past versions. Is she hoping for a new or repeated adventure, is she asleep with no thought of antecedent and succeeding times, or is she perhaps dreaming? Does she even remember the violence of her previous actions? The suggestion of discontinuity with the past raised in the second question receives additional emphasis in the following verses, which signal the rapid change that characterizes modern life and also introduce a new vision of the relationship between observer and observed object. The mention of a changing mountain and sea introduces geological time, which often connotes a break with tradition and the weight of history in modernism and here accompanies the introduction of the very modern idea that a change in observer impacts the perception of reality. New eyes bring new visions and the past takes on a different configuration. The following question, *¿Pasó?,* allows for several contrasting interpretations that in their difference confirm the preceding statement about the change in the perceiving eye. In one reading, the question communicates doubt as to whether the past is really over or still continues in a Spain that persists in dreams of empire. An alternate reading asks if the past every really happened, if it has any connection to the present or is alien, other, in the sense analyzed in the previous chapter as a constant in modernist writing. In conjunction with the first interpretation, the description of the phantom still roaming the fields suggests the continued presence of religious fanaticism, while the second reading emphasizes the verb *yerra.* In addition to the meaning "to wander," *errar* signifies "to err" and this signification, in association with the notion of ghost or imagined apparition, implies a non-existent connection with this past or at the very least, a mistaken sense of continuity.

The following stanza illustrates the dramatic separation of present, stagnant Castile and the Castile that conventional historiography presents as past glory, depicting the isolation of contemporary Spanish religion and its indifference to commercial activity in Mediterranean ports and the imminence of war. In the context of the poem, the allusion refers to the Moroccan conflict and the ignorance and disinterest of the religious community regarding a new encounter with the traditional "infidel" indicates that the past in which the Spanish people put God above war has indeed ended. Historical enmities give way to new alliances. Traditional isolation cedes to the economic necessities of poor migrants and the commercial ambitions of those involved in shipments in the Mediterranean ports. Everything moves and changes and the poem traces a variety of differences with the past to end with typical modernist indeterminacy that incorporates both hope and caution, community and solitude. The sun has now begun to set, marking the passage of solar time, and the speaker describes the advancing darkness and changing scenery. From the distance, he hears the harmonious ring of bells and comments that old women in black mourning will be on their way to church to say the rosary. The attractive sound of the church bell contrasts with the introduction of theological time in the announcement of the evening prayers and the seemingly innocent description of the old women in black hints at continued religious control in village life. In contrast, the following verses describe the sudden appearance of two curious weasels who observe the speaker, disappear, and then return to examine him once more. This note of natural curiosity for the outsider is followed by the closing verses:

> Los campos se oscurecen,
> Hacia el camino blanco está el mesón abierto
> al campo ensombrecido y al pedregal desierto.
>
> (1951, 734)

> [The countryside grows darker.
> Toward the white road the inn is open
> to the shadowed country and the desolate rock ground.]

David Darst, in his introduction to "A orillas del Duero" in *Sendas literarias: España,* used in many introductory literature courses, sees the poem as a reflection of Machado's anguish at the irreparable decadence of the Spanish nation and interprets the final lines as the description of the "coming of gloomy night to an equally darkened and desolate nation" (1988, 198). This reading coincides with those who privilege a monolithic, mono-voiced vision of early twentieth-century Spanish literature, but disregards the co-presence of competing discourses and visions. In conjunction with solar time, the poem introduces historical time as both chronological and disjunctive, and also alludes to geological, biological, intrahistorical, ecclesiastic, and psychological temporality. At numerous junctures, the speaker injects indeterminacy and invites the reader to imagine several different outcomes to the narrative of Spanish national development. The closing verses carry forward this amenability to multiple resolutions. The open inn contrasts with the earlier verse that refers to roads without inns. A penchant for pessimistic readings of Machado's civic poetry presumes an empty, dark inn, deserted like the countryside and rock fields. However, a reading that builds on the expressed belief in change, on the impact of the observer on the object of perception, on the disjunction between past and present, and on the importance of multiple clocks as a correlative to communication across time in Machado's poetry arrives at a different interpretation. The open inn sheds a welcoming light on the darkened road and beckons those who travel whether physically, towards other parts of the country, or figuratively, to other possibilities for the nation. The inn contrasts with the church, links up with the curious weasels who immediately precede its description in the speaker's experience, and offers a place for community and dialogue. These two reading exist side by side, on the two faces of the turning coin of modernism. Neither takes precedence nor dominates. The existence of multiple and disparate clocks represents a break with the weight of the past and the inexorability of progressive time. The insistence on such a modern and modernist conception of temporality in Machado's work calls for an equally modern reader response, which allows for indeterminacy and multiple, often contradictory, textual significations.

Among the various scientific advances that contribute to the acceptance of multiple clocks, disrupt diachronic visions of historicity, and pave the way for the diffusion of Einstein's theory of relativity, the Michelson-Morley experiment prompts some of the more innovative literary responses. Art Berman points out that with the discovery that light has a velocity, its traditional definition as instantaneous and as a metaphor for stasis and timelessness gives way to a realization that all aspects of reality are dynamic and in motion (1994, 151–52). The 1888 discovery that the speed of light remains constant, irrespective of the medium through which it passes, leads to increasing speculation regarding the transmission of light from distant planets and the time interval between its moment of initiation and arrival on earth. The Martínez Sierras in "Astros muertos" from *El poema del trabajo* (1899) consider the eery thought that even after a star has died, its light continues to travel across space and communicate the illusion of vitality. For these writers, the implied lesson for humanity lies in a more skeptical relation to time-honored ideals, which may similarly transmit the false light of an already dead tradition. Unamuno emphasizes a different aspect in his meditation on dying stars in "Aldebarán" (1958, 13:882). The poetic speaker vacillates between a traditional view of a stable, timeless heavens and a more modern perception of stellar transience. In the early verses, he assumes the permanence of this giant reddish star, whose identification in the constellation Taurus remits to classical Greek astronomy and whose Arabic name connects with medieval times. The speaker addresses the star and queries if it perhaps witnessed the sun's birth or the creation of the planetary system. Later, he declares a link with prehistoric cavemen who, like the modern speaker, observed the ruby-colored object in the sky. However, this testimony to longevity quickly cedes to considerations of possibilities for the star's death. The speaker questions whether the sky he surveys is the same that looked down on today's dust when it formed part of living human beings. He also imagines that dust in outer space previously constituted a celestial body and ponders whether there is an enormous planetary dung heap for dead suns and stars. Unamuno finds both comfort and concern in the star's permanence and in the possibility of a shared destiny that joins them. Modern cosmology opens up new channels for his preoccupation with eternity and for redefining traditional concepts of transience, permanence, and time.

Valle-Inclán and Azorín respond to modern understanding of light's velocity with similar textual creations. Azorín's *Al margen de los clásicos* imagines that at the time of writing in 1915, the image of Fray Luis de León may still be traveling through space or that on a distant planet, someone with the instruments capable of seeing life on earth, might observe Luis de León as he strolled his garden in the 1500s. Valle-Inclán imagines a more bizarre simultaneity of different clocks in *La lámpara maravillosa* when he interjects the modern discovery of the speed of light to speculate on the observation from a distant planet of an arrow just leaving the quiver when the world has completely lost memory of the archer who released it. The speaker further imagines a situation in which Julius Caesar, transported to a distant planet, witnesses the discharge of an arrow he has carried imbedded in his heart for some fifteen centuries. These ruminations on stellar time and multiple clocks add to the ongoing challenge to the weight of history, the concept of unidirectional time, and the inexorability of causality. New ways of imagining temporality challenge the contemporary Spanish reader to throw off traditional modes of thought and enjoy experimentation with novel possibilities for life and community. Change becomes increasingly imaginable and accessible when solar, seasonal, and biological time no longer determine human behavior and when the existence of multiple clocks allows for previously inconceivable choices and connections. Spanish modernists encourage their readers to imagine themselves, individually and collectively, as other than inherited visions of temporality have dictated.

Time as Flow and Cycle

Two final changes in the conceptualization of temporality mark Spanish modernism: the notion of time as flux or flow, to which I referred while discussing the altered vision of history, and the notion of time as cyclical, whether inspired by Eastern philosophies or Nietzsche's speculations on eternal return. The definition of time as flow breaks with the traditional idea of temporality as the sum of discrete units (Kern 1983, 24) and also with Judeo-Christian definitions of the future. William James's insistence on the human experience of temporality as a stream and Bergson's theorization of duration both posit the present as an unfolding that links past with future. The future flows from the past and cannot be separated as a distinct temporal division. The Nietzschean concept of eternal return and the view of time as flow share important similarities with respect to the vision of the future.[10] Both return to a pre-Socratic notion of time as neverending process, without beginning or end. James's metaphor of the river harks back to Heraclites's statements that "you cannot step twice into the same river; for fresh waters are ever flowing in upon you." The perception of time as process and becoming stands in dramatic contrast to the Judeo-Christian vision of two distinct temporal modes: linear time as experienced by human subjects after the fall from grace and the eternity that follows death. This tradition envisions a beginning and end of time, relating linear time and human life to suffering and sin and ascribing it negative value. Nietzsche's eternal return specifically confronts this notion and as Daniel Chapelle observes, directly opposes the depiction of life as transitory and the presumption that only an external power endows life with value (1993?, 60–61).

The difference between the view of life as linear and sinful, with a final release found only in death, and the contrasting vision of life as flow surfaces in two very different Spanish writers who fortuitously coincide in a lexically similar utterance with ideologically opposed meaning. The narrator of *Pequeñeces* (1890), the Jesuit Luis Coloma's indictment of modern Spanish life, poses the following question regarding the relationship of past and present: "¿Hoy es todavía ayer?" [Is today still yesterday?] (1975, 244). Antonio Machado voices his own succinct definition of temporality in his epigram: "Hoy es siempre todavía" [Today is always yet][11] (1951, 885). In the context of the narrative action and message of Coloma's novel, the question equates linear temporality with weakness and temptation in contrast with a sublime, otherworldly future. It describes the inability of Elvira, the Marchioness of Sabadell, to free herself from the seductive powers of her depraved husband. The narrator reveals that Elvira now recognizes her error in allowing a few moments of happiness early in her marriage to displace God with the false object of personal pleasure (1975, 243). This vision of life as a valley of tears, a series of disappointments that the individual must endure in order to earn eternal salvation, marks much nineteenth-century Spanish Catholic discourse. Individual moments stand as discrete entities without a necessary connection between them, as indicated in the church practice of granting absolution at the moment of death, irrespective of preceding sins. Similarly, a life of virtue that ends in unconfessed, unforgiven sin can warrant damnation. Life after death may take the form of damnation or salvation, but either case is a timeless, unchanging state. When a character in *Pequeñeces* dies in a duel without confession, the text describes his plunge into darkness: "Sólo vería en lo alto a Jesucristo, vivo y terrible, que se adelantaba a juzgarle, y detrás la eternidad, oscura, inmensa, implacable" [He would only see Jesus Christ on high, alive and dreadful, advancing to judge him, and behind him the dark, immense, implacable eternity] (163). The novel aspires to describe the evils of a debauched modern society, in which religion provides the only refuge. In the narrative denouement, the female protagonist, Curra Albornoz, renounces worldly life, recognizes her transgressions, and rediscovers her Catholic faith. Similarly, her daughter determines to enter the convent[12] and her son dies after fighting and then reconciling with his mother's lover's son. Although the conservative Menéndez y Pelayo finds the sacrifice of the children excessive,[13] it correlates completely with the vision of life, time, and eternity advocated in the text. Childhood innocence inevitably perishes in this world and survives only by way of premature death and passage into eternity or the protection of the Catholic Church, representing eternity on earth. Rubén Benítez (1975) characterizes Coloma's pessimism as typical of a generation familiar with Nietzsche, but as the analysis of selected modernist texts will demonstrate, Nietzschean speculation on eternal return opposes the bleak portrait of earthly life presented in *Pequeñeces*. Coloma espouses the traditional Judeo-Christian representation of time as discrete moments leading to a timeless eternity, a vision that stands in marked opposition to the conception of time as flow or as cycle, proposed by Nietzsche and his modernist followers. The two modernist alternatives develop hand and hand and both represent an insistent challenge to traditional definitions of death and its implications for the meaning of life.

Antonio Machado's poetry contains constant references to life as river or road and from his earliest collections, his texts refute a sense of definitive ending or strict borders between past, present, and future. "¿Y ha de morir contigo el mundo mago . . . ?" from *Soledades, Galerías y otros poemas* uses the question form throughout the poem to transcend the finality of death. A dialogic structure, addressing an unnamed interlocutor, also breaks the frame surrounding the poetic text and disallows a sense of ending, requiring each new reader to respond to the unanswered questions. The poetic speaker queries whether the magic world of memory dies with the addressee and in the process defines it as a process that continually brings the past to life and renews it: "¿Y ha de morir contigo el mundo tuyo, la vieja vida en orden tuyo y nuevo?" [And is your world to die with you, the old life you reshaped your way?][14] (1917, 96). The poem does not affirm the persistence of individual memory beyond death, but posits as intrinsic to human subjectivity the continuation of the flow of time from past to present to future. Poems that deal with the death of Machado's wife Leonor strive to rewrite the traditional Catholic vision of death as the cessation of temporality and as absolute break with life. The poetic speaker rebels against divine will in "Señor, ya me arrancaste lo que yo más quería" and insists in repeating his cry of foul in a cyclical rhythm that breaks with linearity to proclaim the vividness of memory across time. A number of poems of this period confront memories and dreams of the past with the sense of loss in the present and close with declarations that death cannot efface the renewal and persistence of memory. The past lives on in the present and the present reshapes past memories as it moves toward the future. It is in this sense that there is no established road, but rather that the road is constructed in the process of walking: "Caminante, no hay camino, se hace camino al andar" (1951, 824). It is also in this sense that Machado's epigram "Hoy es siempre todavía" differs from Coloma's lexically similar question. The future, the "*todavía*" of the epigram, whether in this life or another, is inconceivable as separate and distinct from past and present. The essence of the individual consists of the ongoing, unique play of past, present, and future. The past is not a segmented moment of time that represents the fall from grace and from which the human soul either reluctantly or gratefully separates at the moment of death. Rather, it is imbricated in the present and future and takes on value as a constituent element of consciousness. Coloma's rebuke at the character's inability to relinquish memory contrasts with Machado insistence on the flow of past into present and future.

Ricardo Gil explicitly contrasts traditional Judeo-Christian and modernist visions of time in two poems of *La caja de música.* "Tristitia rerum" suggests a religious backdrop in the Latin title with its message of life as sadness and then presents a contrapuntal conception in the text. The poem describes a closed parlor, abandoned since the death of the woman who once used it. The piano music stands open to her favorite piece, the lace on which she was working lies unfinished, and the climbing plant on the balcony appears dried and forsaken. The perception of dying as a complete break with the past and with earthly life as originally suggested in the title resurfaces in the freezing of the living room clock at the moment of death. The lyrical speaker enters the room in what appears a vain attempt to reconnect with the dead lover and in despair, hits his head against the piano. With this motion, the strings vibrate and invoke the image of the dead woman's sorrow at the speaker's loss. Through this sense of a sharing in the present and a communication across time and space, the speaker remembers the woman's favorite melody and successfully reconnects with the deceased. "Memento" establishes an even clearer counterpoint to traditional religious definitions of death and time. The title refers to the parts of the mass dedicated to the memory of the dead, but in the context of the poem also signifies the pressed flowers that the poetic speaker keeps in remembrance of a past love. The book in which the flowers are placed is a religious text, with Latin admonitions about the brevity of life, the evanescence of happiness, and the inevitability of suffering, but the flowers invoke memories of pleasure, a woman's laughter, and love. The speaker explicitly states his preference for this version over sad and bitter Church teachings.

The perception of time as flow receives added impetus from the newly developed art of cinematography. Manuel Machado's "Vagamente" borrows from the language and experience of film to visualize memory as a repository of half-blurred films that blend past and present, reality and dream (1922, 185–86). Unamuno imagines a movie film played in reverse as a metaphor for memory in "Vuelve hacia atrás la vista, caminante" (1958, 14:542) and his concept of *ex-futuro* challenges the traditional vision of time as inexorable and irreversible. "Polémica" speaks of past hopes of memories as future memories of hopes (14:6340) and in many poems and essays, he alludes to a present that might have been different, a future that did not occur because of a choice at a past crossroads, but that could have been and still might be. Like Machado, Unamuno defines human consciousness as inherently linked to temporal flow and rejects with horror the Judeo-Christian notion of death as finality and eternity as timeless. His sonnet "Ex-futuro" depicts this view of death as a terrible buried forgetfulness in which dreams, hopes, and future disappear (13:626). In poems such as "La elegía eterna" (13:357), the poetic speaker rails at the relentless passage of time, at ancient descriptions of life as a river, and at the Christian teaching that all things pass. Catholic depictions of salvation and life after death thoroughly dissatisfy Unamuno. If life is time and individual consciousness is the confluence of a singularly experienced past that flows into an equally unique present and future, an unchanging eternity erases personal identity. As he repeats time and again in *Del sentimiento trágico de la vida,* to be the same at two moments in time is to die, and a promise of immortality that excludes continued change brings only a form of death (1966, 192).

Unamuno's "Sísifo" argues that nothing is eternal, including divinely ordained punishment. After centuries in which Sisyphus repeatedly rolled the immense boulder up the mountain, he transformed the steep slope and large stone through erosion and friction, producing a smooth surface on which to recline while playing with a small ball. In the closing verse, Sisyphus refutes the concept of eternal punishment and of eternity itself: "'Se acaba todo, ¡oh Jove!, hasta la pena!'" ["Everything ends, oh, Jove, even suffering"] (1958, 13:385). For a thinker who views dialogue as the essence of relationship and identity formation,[15] the beatific vision of the absorption of the self in God represents a form of annihilation that differs little from death with no afterlife. As Levinas writes, "The word is the *between par excellence*. Dialogue functions not as a *synthesis* of the Relation, but as its very unfolding" (1993, 25). The Unamunan speaker aspires to an eternal dialogue, not peace but ongoing struggle and perpetual deferral.

In contrast with the Christian notion of eternal life as integration of the self in God, Unamuno and other modernists appropriate Nietzschean speculation on eternal return, not as a certainty, but as a different way of imagining the future. The text speaker of Unamuno's *Del sentimiento trágico de la vida* mocks Nietzschean conjecture that given the finite number of atoms existing in the universe, there is a mathematical possibility that the combination will eventually repeat itself (90). Notwithstanding this ironic treatment, the speaker recognizes the value of Nietzschean desire to escape progressive temporality and returns to the subject in a number of texts. "Nihil Novum sub sole" finds comfort in the notion that others have already led the way and that the speaker and his companion move towards a future already experienced, duplicating their forerunners' past (1958, 13:636). "A un profesional de su mocedad" combines the concepts of time as flux and eternal return in a consideration of the relationship between a young man and an elderly poetic speaker. Whereas the young addressee only enjoys his youth, the older man takes pleasure in both his remembered past and his present maturity. The dialogic exchange between the two creates an intersubjective communication that introduces the consciousness of the one in the other, allowing for a form of eternal return that the Unamunan poetic speaker finds comforting and productive: "Soy lo que fui y eres o ¿serás lo que soy? / allá adonde te vas me voy" [I am what I was and you are or will you be what I am? / wherever you go I go too] (15:432).

Azorín also examines the notion of eternal return as an antidote to traditional Christian representations of time. *La voluntad* (1902) depicts the pervasive effects of religious thought and temporality in the provincial city of Yecla. Like their medieval forebears, the inhabitants believe that earthly life has value only as the passageway to eternal salvation and willingly sacrifice to construct a new cathedral in a town already rich with churches. Village life revolves around the experience of or preparation for death, funerals, and memorial masses (1919, 61–62). The priest Puche epitomizes the traditional ideology in his admonitions to Justina to prevent her marriage to the free-thinking Antonio Azorín, here a character bearing the surname the writer subsequently adopts as his pen name. In Puche's words, life is sadness, suffering eternal, the world stands in the way of love of God, and divine punishment will mercilessly destroy those who do not heed the call to virtue, poverty, and humility (26–28). Justina's assimilation of this vision reveals itself in her repetition of the nineteenth-century adage that life is a valley of tears (28) and as a result, she breaks with Azorín to enter a convent, where she dies saddened by the loss of love and earthly happiness.

In Yecla, even the secular philosophers have incorporated the view of life as contemptible and of eternity as the goal for which all present gratification must be sacrificed. Yuste, Azorín's teacher and mentor, has incorporated certain notions from contemporary philosophy, but they remain subordinated to Judeo-Christian pessimism as it has evolved in the Spanish context. In part 1, chapter 3, Yuste argues that all passes and that time itself will end, since time and eternity stand in direct antitheses. Whereas life is change, eternity is an unchanging present (1919, 31–32). Both in his sorrowful tone and in the message he conveys, Yuste differs little from Puche and the similarity of their names emphasizes the common origins of their thought. Although Yuste proceeds to outline Nietzsche's concept of eternal return, his interpretation merely reenforces the sense of repetition, monotony, and fatigue that characterizes the Judeo-Christian notion of linear time. Yuste's explanation fails totally to capture the vindication of life and rejection of Christian time that characterizes the vitalist philosopher. Given the eventual adoption by the author Martínez Ruiz of the pen name Antonio Azorín, it is tempting to presume that the fictional Azorín represents the writer's *alter ego.*[16] However, neither Yuste nor Azorín serve as authorial spokespersons or stable, definitive representations. The text continually underscores that the essence of their personalities consists in their somewhat capricious shedding of attitudes and outlooks depending on changing personal circumstances. While this does not preclude their role as spokespersons, it complicates the identification of specific values and beliefs as coincident with authorial views.

Post-structuralist and Bakhtinian definitions of narrative and language challenge the legitimacy of efforts to reconstruct authorial intention and *La voluntad* anticipates this view of narrativity in its structure and characterization. The novel signals the distance between Yuste, his disciple Azorín, and the narrator in a process that underscores multiple, divergent perspectives. Whereas Yuste once advocated force in order to effect social change, he responds to Azorín's defense of violence and action with admonitions of non-violence that in turn provoke Azorín's anger and criticism of resignation and passivity. The differences between mentor and mentee negate the existence of a single narrative stance, a denial which becomes even more evident in the shifting positions adopted by the heterodiegetic narrator. After Azorín explodes at Yuste's defense of pacifism, the narrator expresses a certain compassion and affection for the teacher. However, other episodes introduce ironic distance. Yuste's facile adoption of the traditional philosophy of his friend Father Lasalde undermines his credibility and stature as independent thinker. When Lasalde compares two ancient clay statues and expresses his preference for the figure of the disconsolate old man who represents religious faith over the laughing statue of the skeptical philosopher, Yuste humbly agrees that faith is superior to knowledge. A second instance of recognition of inferior human reason occurs several chapters later, when Yuste acknowledges his envy of insects with their multifaceted, compound eyes and ability to enjoy a panoramic view without moving. Since over a million species of arthropods exist, he believes that the world truly belongs to them rather than to human beings, and feels humbled by this recognition (1919, 139).

The parallel episodes, with Yuste's deferential submission first to religious faith and then to insect vision, ironically place historically antagonistic religious and scientific discourse in a dubious harmony that invites further scrutiny. Yuste's exaltation of the lowly insect borders on the ridiculous, especially in the light of traditional anthropocentric visions of biology. However, the enthusiastic description of insect ability to swim, fly, and walk and the fascinating perspective of multiple vision introduces a note of wonder that oscillates in a precarious balance with ironic scorn. The possibilities of multi-perspectival vision subtly introduce a challenge to the definitive proclamation of the superiority of faith in the analogous episode described just a few pages earlier and suggest that from a different perspective, the traditional exaltation of faith over knowledge may well appear as ridiculous as the more modern admiration for complex insect vision. The double voicing continues two chapters later, when Yuste and Azorín again visit Lasalde and once more the priest and Yuste discuss the passage of time and relate it to the ancient statue of the laughing philosopher. Yuste declares that European civilization will decline and at some future date, cultural leadership will pass to Asia. As in the preceding chapter, his insistence on the transience of life conforms with Lasalde's belief in earthly life as mere passage to a superior world. Lasalde's language reflects the theologic diminution of the value of life that has marked Western Christianity: "Esta tierra no es nuestra *casa*. . . . Somos pobres peregrinos que pasamos llorando . . . llorando como estas buenas mujeres (*señala a las estatuas*), que también sentían que el mundo es un lugar de amarguras" [This earth is not our home. . . . We are poor pilgrims that pass through crying . . . crying like these good women (*he points to the statues*), who also felt that the world is a place of distress] (1919, 148). Again, Yuste accepts the priests pronouncement, but in contrast with his acquiescence, he notices the statue of the laughing philosopher: "Y le ha parecido que este hombre antipático, que este hombre odioso que no conoció a Cristo, se burlaba de él, pobre europeo entristecido por diez y nueve siglos de cristianismo" [And it seemed to him that this disagreeable man, the odious man who had never known Christ, was making fun of him, poor European saddened by nineteen centuries of Christianity] (148). In the context of the earlier comment on the inevitable passing of European civilization, the identification of Europe, Christianity, and sadness insinuates the eventual and desirable disappearance of Christianity. The laughing figure of a pre-Christian skeptic invokes the memory of Dionysus, which in turn remits to the Thracian and Phrygian origins of this god of wine, orgy, and vitality. Dionysus's Asian roots coincide with the narrative's description of the statue of the philosopher as a product of an ancient culture that settled in the region of Yecla and consisted of a mix of peoples from India, Phoenicia, and Greece (115). They further link up with Yuste's prediction that at some future date, European (and, thus, Christian) civilization will cede to a superior, more advanced Asian culture. The suggestion of a future preeminence of Asian culture, with the return of the laughing skeptical philosopher who disdains the resigned, sad representatives of religious faith, introduces the notion of eternal return, but this time in a context and exemplified by a figure that proves much more Nietzschean than Yuste's timid and theologically inflected representation of cyclical repetition in part 1, chapter 3.

La voluntad does not foresee the easy return of Dionysian energy and continually emphasizes the difficulty of recovery of will. Antonio Azorín's extensive exposure to a Spanish provincial culture that exalts resignation and passivity in religion, philosophy, education, and daily living precludes facile change. Azorín has been born too late to recover his energy and remains caught between occasional bursts of activity that reject the effects of his education and the self-analytic, reflective individual in whom the development of the intellect has occurred at the expense of the will (1919, 267). It appears at the end that the oscillation of these two modalities gives way to a stable inertia after his return to Yecla and marriage to Iluminada, who reimposes Catholic control almost immediately, casually placing her prayer book in Azorín's pocket on his second day back. Many critics interpret this narrative ending as a definitive closure and as evidence that Azorín equates eternal return with monotonous repetition of previous patterns of thought and behavior (Fiddian 1976, 170). However, the novel's epilogue problematizes the narrative denouement. A series of letters from José Martínez Ruiz to Pío Baroja report on Azorín's sad state, his loss of will, and apathetic accession to his wife's dominance. The fictionalized Martínez Ruiz establishes a clear distance from his character Azorín and openly criticizes petty provincial life and the ubiquitous presence and power of religion. He expresses guarded optimism that Azorín will recover his energy, since his essential contradictoriness requires action, even if lacking real direction. In his own ironic affirmation of eternal return, Martínez Ruiz suggests that should his character recuperate his will, he may possibly write a sequel to the present novel, a possibility he realizes the following year in *Antonio Azorín,* a continued meditation of eternal return and its implications for individual and national change.

It is important to note, as many critics have observed, that *Antonio Azorín* is certainly not a continuation or repetition of *La voluntad.* In a clear break with diachronicity, here the character Azorín appears unmarried with a love interest named Pepita. The difference between the protagonist of the first and the second novel is considerable[17] and relates to the ability to fully enter into the experience of eternal return. Whereas the Azorín of *La voluntad* had rare, rapidly passing bursts of energy and remained largely dependent on his mentor Yuste and immersed in his Catholic background, in *Antonio Azorín* he has established intellectual independence and his thought is presented directly, without the mediation of a teacher. Although Sarrió appears in the novel as a former mentor, the first mention of his existence occurs in the second part of the text and he exercises little influence on the decisions or ideas of his erstwhile student. Furthermore, the distance between narrator and character, although still marked by a tone that hovers between irony and reportage, does not partake of the clear criticism apparent in the preceding narrative. This Azorín discloses a more idiosyncratic manner that he sustains throughout the text and that parallels the narrator's comments on Spanish society. When the protagonist creates a scandal by requesting that a friend play the piano when other residents of the house are still in mourning over a distant relative who died months earlier, the narrator derides the Spanish rural obsession with death. The Azorín of this second narrative moves with greater frequency and further than his predecessor, transferring from Yecla to Petrel to Alicante, planning a trip to Paris, relocating to Madrid, exploring the Castilian countryside, and still residing in the capital in the final pages of the novel. Both he and his elderly uncle Verdú defend change more consistently and without the shadow of traditional religious discourse. Verdú had once created public uproar by criticizing the historic expulsion of the Moors as anti-Christian and economically disastrous and although he feels saddened that his generation has failed, he defends change and the arrival of younger Spaniards with new voices and ideas. He observes that the concept of beauty varies over time, with the appearance of new syntactical forms and modes of thinking (1953a, 223). The text explicitly links Verdú's statements with Spanish modernism when he remarks that in the end, the older generation accepts the innovations of modernism or whatever name is used to designate the brave young Turks. His definition of the new form of thinking privileges multiple perspectives and anticipates theories of modernism as a shifting, dynamic sociosymbolic system, later developed by de Koven, Sheppard, and Eysteinsson:

> . . . en el fondo de esa volubilidad veo yo un instintivo espíritu de justicia. Los viejos, hombres de una sola idea, no pueden comprender que se vivan todas las ideas. ¿Que los jóvenes no tienen ideas fijas? ¡Si precisamente no tener una idea fija es tenerlas todas, es gustarlas todas, es amarlas todas! Y como la vida no es una sola cosa, sino que son varias, y a veces muy contradictorias, sólo éste es el eficaz medio de percibirla en todos sus matices y cambiantes, y sólo ésta es la regla crítica infalible para juzgar y estimar a los hombres . . . (224).

> [. . . at the source of this volubility I see an instinctive spirit of justice. Old people, believing in a single idea, cannot comprehend that one might live all ideas. So young people don't have set ideas? Not having a set idea means precisely having all of them, liking all of them, loving all of them. And since life is not just one single thing, but rather varied and at times contradictory things, this alone is the effective means of perceiving it in all its shading and changes, and this alone is the infallible critical rule to judge and esteem people . . .]

Verdú's death communicates the definitive passing of the older generation and subsequent to this event, Azorín develops his writing career with a series of articles criticizing the lamentable poverty and tragic resistance to change among rural Castilians. This version of Antonio Azorín abjures the view that life is a pilgrimage to another world, as enunciated by Yuste in *La voluntad.* Arguing against the bishop of Orihuela's opposition to change, this Azorín considers that although everything in life merits respect, if one truly respected everything, there would be no movement and life itself would disappear. Consequently, he defends the necessity of destruction (232). Against Catholic resignation, he proposes Nietzschean vitalism: ". . . habría que decirles que la vida no es resignación, no es tristeza, no es dolor, sino que es goce fuerte y fecundo; goce espontáneo de la Naturaleza, del arte, del agua, de los árboles, del cielo azul, de las casas limpias, de los trajes elegantes, de los muebles cómodos. . . . Y para demostrárselo habría que darles estas cosas" [one should tell them that life is not resignation, not sadness, not suffering, but rather strong and fertile pleasure; spontaneous pleasure at nature, art, water, trees, blue sky, clean houses, elegant clothing, comfortable furniture. . . . And to prove it to them, one should give them these things.] (262).

The narrative style developed by Martínez Ruiz relies more on innuendo than direct statement and consequently, the difference between the Azorín of *La voluntad* and *Antonio Azorín,* while evident, requires that the reader actively participate in the (de)construction of character. The Azorín of Nietzschean caste of the second novel that results from such a process contrasts with the apathetic, resigned figure portrayed in *La voluntad* and his will to life enables him to enter joyfully into eternal return. On multiple occasions, the narrative of *Antonio Azorín* doubles back on itself through the introduction of *mise en abîme* and other metafictional strategies that present the dizzying effect of infinite regression.[18] In the present discussion, the most important example occurs in the closing paragraphs, where Azorín, writing in first person, declares his desire to write a book about Sarrió in Madrid and describes how he sits down to begin his text. The closing words of the novel, "Y comienzo . . ." [And I begin . . .] (1953a, 271) allow multiple interpretations. Azorín may well have begun the story of Sarrió in Madrid or he may have begun a narrative that stands in relation to *Antonio Azorín* as this novel relates to *La voluntad,* a third variant on the protagonist's story. He may also have begun to write the narrative we have just finished reading, directing the reader through ellipsis back to the beginning of the text in a never-ending circle. In all possible variants, the Antonio Azorín presented here in his first-person narration achieves agency and his rejection of Spanish Catholic visions of time and life allows him to begin again or anew but in either case, to live a different life, to become other in relation to his past. The affirmation of vitality in *Antonio Azorín* is neither absolute nor free from qualifiers and challenges. In typically modernist fashion, the text abandons categorical definitions for the multifaceted, multi-voiced representation of life earlier advocated by Verdú. The novel repudiates the Catholic notion of life as progression towards death and in its metafictional circularity, it offers an alternative and intellectually exciting transgression of traditional narrative, whether the Catholic story of life on earth as woeful passage toward death or the nineteenth-century realist narrative with its own temporal and sequential limitations.

The similarities between Azorín's *La voluntad* and Pío Baroja's *Camino de perfección,* also of 1902, have been noted by critics since the appearance of the two novels. The connection between this narrative duplication and the relation of these two novels to *Antonio Azorín* and the Nietzschean notion of eternal return has not received critical attention, although it adds considerably to an understanding of the dialogue between the texts and their authors. Fernando Ossorio of *Camino de perfección* represents another version of Antonio Azorín with a life story that both recycles certain episodes of the Azorín of *La voluntad* and previews specific aspects of the Azorín of *Antonio Azorín.* Ossorio's expressed recuperation of will at the end of *Camino de perfección* differs from the defeated Antonio Azorín of the final pages of *La voluntad,* but the surreptitious placement of Biblical texts in the diaper of Fernando's son by his mother-in-law echoes the power of the Church of Azorín's text. Fernando's desire to allow his son to live freely, even violently, concurs with the character Azorín's more energetic declarations in *Antonio Azorín.* The duplication of episodes by the two authors, such as the description of the delivery of the young girl's coffin in Toledo, and the appearance of Baroja as a character in Azorín's novel break down temporal, spatial, and phenomenological barriers. A reader familiar with Baroja's works will have already learned details of Ossorio's life from *Las aventuras de Silvestre Paradox,* where he appears briefly as a relative of Silvestre's student. Readers may also recognize Ossorio as a briefly mentioned character in Clarín's "La imperfecta casada" of *Cuentos morales* (1896). The introduction and reintroduction of characters with the same name, identical or very similar episodes, and characters with different names but shared character traits in novels by the same or different authors defies traditional notions of borders, chronology, ownership, and contrasts with religious versions of time as either unremittingly marching toward death or eternal and timeless. Modernist writers accept neither eternal return nor time as succession as the only forms of temporality, but they play with various and contradictory visions that Verdú theorized as intrinsic to modernism and necessary to understand life.

The assumption by many critics that Azorín's works signal the never-ending repetition of an unchanging reality fails to recognize the multiple temporalities and his own subtle reminders of change within repetition and repetition within change. The much cited "Las nubes" from *Castilla* exemplifies this mix of same and different, self and other. The transformation of the antecedent text has received little emphasis from critics who prefer to focus on repetition and sameness. The lovers from the classical *La Celestina* in Azorín's version have been married for eighteen years and have a young daughter. Calisto and Melibea, who die tragically in the original story, resurface as middle-aged parents and the once arduous Calisto now appears subdued and melancholy. Azorín's text ends with the sudden entry of a young man pursuing a falcon into the garden, duplicating the opening passages of *La Celestina,* except that here the young woman is not named Melibea but Alisa, like Melibea's grandmother in the classical text. The end of "Las nubes" allows the reader to imagine a story that continues as the beginning of *La Celestina,* a repetition of the original with other characters but identical plot, or a divergent story line building on the differences already announced in the successor text. As the narrator states, quoting the poet Campoamor, "vivir es ver pasar" [to live is to see time pass

(1958, 71)], and then in a slight correction/variation, he adds, "vivir es ver volver" [to live is to see return (1958, 71)]. These different visions of time as passing and as return come together in Azorín and other modernists. Eternal return may represent exaltation of life, it may include slight change and the suggestion of a progression towards a different ending the second time around, or it may offer a radical transformation of character, events, or values. In virtually all cases, it stands in opposition to traditional Catholic representations of time.

The desire to rewrite Catholic notions of time also implies revision of the relationship of death and the body. The process of aging in and of itself links the body to the vision of passing time but as Castoriadis points out, "Nothing in me . . . tells me that I was born and that I will die. . . . That I was born and that I will die is essentially social knowledge, transmitted to/imposed upon me" (1991, 46). The form that such socially transmitted knowledge takes can and does vary across cultures. The Catholic vision of the separation of body and soul at death and of the soul as eternal and the body as mortal, at least prior to Final Judgement, provides one such narrative, but in the expanding cultural horizons of the modernist world, the hegemony of this version breaks down as individuals seek other alternatives. Ramón del Valle-Inclán and Gabriel Miró combine the notion of eternal return with a generalized interest in Asian religions to explore an altered conceptualization of time, the body, sexuality, and death. Valle-Inclán's decadentist work of the 1890s and 1900s serves as an important prelude to Miró's later novels and the combined writings of the two authors demonstrate that the experimentation with death, the body, sexuality, and religion in late nineteenth- and early twentieth-century texts represents more than just a superficial escapism or attempt to shock a puritanical bourgeoisie. Behind such early ventures into decadentist subject matter at the turn of the century and continuing over the next decades in Miró and the later Valle-Inclán lies a deeper need to confront inherited visions of death and time. Valle-Inclán's textualization of the desire to surmount the traditionally perceived omnipotence of death persists throughout his literary career, but varies in expression in his different periods. The *Sonatas* (1902–5) and *Flor de santidad* (1904) interweave the sexual, religious, and corporal with scenes of death and desire. *Sonata de primavera* ends with the death of a young girl who falls from a window while Bradomín tries to seduce her older sister, despite the latter's professed intentions to enter the convent the next day. In *Sonata de otoño,* Bradomín's sexual ardor prevents the dying Concha from confessing and precipitates her demise. The reenactment of the Annunciation takes place in *Flor de santidad* in a modern Galicia that hangs indeterminately between innocence and violence, youth and morbidity, leprosy, corporal deterioration, and a more healthy, natural desire. The active melding of these traditionally differentiated emotions, categories, and activities in and of itself transgresses conventional Catholic polarities of life and death, body and soul, sin and virtue, but beyond the negation of a previous tradition, there is also an effort to imagine a new way of thinking about such fundamental features of human existence.[19]

Gabriel Miró further explores possibilities for surpassing traditional dichotomous thinking on the subjects of death and the body, the body and temporality, and sex and purity. His 1910 *Las cerezas en el cementerio* incorporates in the title a blending of life and death, with the brilliant red of cherries connoting life, passion, blood, and sexuality against the backdrop of tombs and grave markers. The narrative deconstructs conventional polarities and demonstrates in poststructuralist fashion that the presumed differences between two concepts or forms of existence collapse and are imbricated within each other. In Miró, nothing remains stable or fixed within definitive categories. In a textualization of Lacanian *glissement,*[20] characters, emotions, and referents slide from one frame of reference to another. The intuitive and creative working out of concepts later theorized by philosophers and linguists such as Derrida, Foucault, and Lacan occurs in many modernist writers and as Eysteinsson suggests, "it is only with the emergence of postructuralist activities that theory 'catches up with' the literary practices of modernism in this performative sense" (1990, 47). The prefiguring of subsequent theorization makes itself particularly evident in *Las cerezas del cementerio.* Félix, the protagonist, is an engineering student of exaggerated sensibilities whose rationalist, scientific formation easily slips into romantic and idealistic responses to his surroundings. In his struggle to break with nineteenth-century order and reason and with religious censure of the body, he reestablishes significant but fleeting connections with the natural world while simultaneously confronting the barbarity and ugliness that exists in nature. After his return from Barcelona, he feels happy to work in the garden and his encounters with the various women with whom he develops relations typically occur in natural settings or infiltrated with natural elements. His first significant amorous encounter with Beatriz occurs through the mediation of water, which purifies and facilitates their desire. Afraid to look at each other, Beatriz and Félix gaze into the cistern and stare into each other's eyes in the reflection. Their first sexual experience takes place bathed in moonlight in a tower open to the fields, distant mountains, and sea. The description confronts religious condemnation of the body and sexuality in two respects: the narrator describes Félix's physical contact with Beatriz as the embrace of a naked soul produced from moonlight and jasmine, thus spiritualizing the body and elevating through aesthetic transfiguration the carnal act of copulation; the text describes initial guilt that prompts the lovers to see in the clouds the figure of the Angel that expelled Adam and Eve from Paradise, but shortly thereafter, the pair kiss chastely and the figure disappears (1947, 56).

Félix represents his sexual desire through metaphors derived from the reproductive processes of bees. He imagines himself tasting honey inside an enormous white flower that smells of woman and then envisions the figures of Beatriz, her daughter Julia, his cousin Isabel, and the wife of his neighbor Koeveld enveloping him (1947, 84). The various women who figure in the novel represent the mobility of Félix's desire and also the ease with which one signifier transmutes to the other. Beatriz and her daughter Julia replace each other in his fantasies, and Isabel at intervals replaces both. Félix and his uncle Guillermo similarly displace each other in Beatriz's desire. Miró's style reenforces the concept of a sliding signifier, frequently omitting the specific referent and delaying or impeding the clear anchoring of meaning: "Félix soñaba a su padrino y a tío Eduardo. Del cual diremos, en tanto que todos sosiegan, que tenía blando y reducido ánimo" [Félix dreamed of his godfather and uncle Edward. Of whom we will say, while all the others rest, that he was of gentle and subdued spirit.] (77). The text never clarifies whether *del cual* refers to Felix, his godfather, or his uncle, and the referent for *todos* remains equally vague. In the novel's understated climax, the narrative describes a physical encounter between Félix and the obese Giner, but the absence of subject pronouns at key points in the cryptic description leaves unclear until later explanation whether it is Félix or Giner who acts or receives the action (230–32).

The novel's constant duplication of characters and events contributes to the sense of floating signifiers while also introducing eternal return, with implications for a revision of traditional perceptions of time. Félix and his uncle Guillermo share physical and emotional traits that cause other characters to comment frequently on their similarities. In his relationship with Beatriz, Félix relives his uncle's earlier amorous history, as he and other characters repeatedly point out. Both uncle and nephew have the ability to see death among the living and to imagine the living as dead (1947, 37). Félix often confuses the Catalan politician Giner with his uncle Guillermo's enemy, the Dutch merchant Koeveld. Félix, like his uncle, dies young and without heirs while involved in a sexual relationship with Beatriz. The novel makes no specific mention of Nietzsche nor of eternal return, although as Ian MacDonald has observed, Miró's library included several volumes by the German philosopher and the two thinkers share a similar outlook in certain respects (64,165). The link to the Orient, on the other hand, appears frequently in the text, although without specific references to a connection with cyclical time. Beatriz's husband is from Ceylon and she had met Guillermo on an ocean voyage to the island, where Guillermo chose to dress Asian style (33). One of Félix's aunts is presently a missionary in India and Félix imagines that he has lived before, indirectly introducing the concept of transmigration of souls. While listening to Beatriz's description of Guillermo's death, the narrator states that Félix feels a cold rush of blood and hears the footsteps of another life moving over his soul (37) and later he feels transported back to a time before he existed when his soul was already marked by a heritage of mysticism, fear, affliction, joy, and passions (111).

The sensation of cyclical repetition combines with the depiction of labile categories to break down traditional polarities, and in particular, Spanish Catholic notions of body in opposition to soul, life in contrast with death, and sexuality as opposed to spirituality. The descriptions of erotic desire and sexual encounter within a natural world that features light and water bring together elements associated with spirituality and carnality, and a transcendent realm that builds on but supersedes nature. As G. G. Brown has noted, the moments of communion with nature quickly dissipate with recognition of a cruel animal world and Darwinian struggle for survival (1072, 46). In Miró's fictional world, one signifier readily transmutes to another, a reading of human experience easily gives way to its traditional opposite. Immediately after the description of Félix's erotic fantasy of nesting like a bee inside a flower that represents the women of his desire, the narrative depicts a turtle calmly devouring a fly with its wings torn off. In a later chapter, Félix witnesses a vicious dog fight, barbaric shepherds who encourage the animals, and one individual herder who stops the melee by biting the snout of a fighting dog and lifting it with his teeth, blood streaming from his mouth. Félix also recognizes his own cruelty when he quickly shifts from compassion to anger at being duped by a false report of a woman dying from a snake bite.

In Miró's texts, the abhorred enemy and vilified other exists within the self. Nature contains both exquisite beauty and horrific violence and humanity, as part of the natural world, partakes of the same co-presence of oppositional forces. Although the text reveals possibilities for both lechery and a glorified, sublime eroticism within human sexuality, it establishes a more fixed boundary between the representatives of these two forms of sexual behavior. Lambeth, Beatriz's detested husband, represents pure lasciviousness with his propensity for deformed young virgins and the shepherd who publicly describes his sexual interlude with his wife takes on the qualities of the savage dogs whose fight immediately follows his lewd commentary. The behavior of both men reflects the traditional vision of sexuality as transgression with which Félix and the narrative aspire to break. Félix refutes Biblical associations of earth and human carnality and inherited prohibitions of physical pleasure: "¡Mi pobre carne, hecha de barro, qué bien rezuma el frescor purísimo y delicioso que va recibiendo el alma! ¡Qué somos de arcilla! . . . ¡Oh, humana alcarraza, qué llena de goces podrías estar si no te rajesen ni te deshiciesen de seca!" [My poor flesh, made of earth, how well seeps out the pure and delicious freshness that it is receiving from the soul. That we are made of clay! . . . Oh, porous human vessel, how full of joy you could be if they didn't split you in two or dry you up!] (1947, 91). The narrative continually links body and soul as equal and interweaves them as paired recipients of physical and non-physical stimuli. When Félix awakens one sunny morning, he feels his soul and his flesh tremble with pleasure as if he were swimming in the clean, luminous sky (113–14) and when he thinks of the various women to whom he feels attracted, he describes his soul's need for another soul that can provide him with the essence of the sentient. In climbing to a mountain summit, he aspires to escape the indefinition of his desire, diffused across four different woman, and also to escape the pure physicality of his feelings. On the mountain, he recovers a more spiritual attraction, and again feels comfortable in the fluid allure that he experiences.

The ambition to transcend conventional borders also finds expression through the melding of religious and secular discourse and human temporality and eternity. Local custom forbids eating the cherries growing in the cemetery and the prohibition reflects the need to maintain the division of life and death, flesh and soul. Félix expresses his indifference to such a ban and his attitude produces a grimace of repugnance in his aunt Lutgarda and dismays his cousin Isabel. Later when Félix, Beatriz, and her daughter Julia eat the cemetery cherries, his aunt Costanza and cousin Isabel react with shock. Isabel, like her aunts, cannot imagine transgressing the line separating life and death, body and spirit. Lutgarda's repulsion of the flesh and its connection to Catholic teaching reveals itself in her description of a visit to the Vatican, where she had kissed the pope's hand. Her statement that she felt born again when the Pope blessed her relates to the belief in physical life as unworthy and biological birth as requiring a religious rebirth to invest it with value. Her exclamation that in kissing the Pope's fingers she kissed God himself and the description of the papal hand as white, cold, and thin as if of marble emphasizes a vision of divinity and holiness as antithetical to carnality, color, and warmth. In a supremely ironic inversion, Miró appropriates the Catholic doctrine of transubstantiation to overturn church-imposed estrangement of body and spirit, life and death. When Félix and Beatriz see each other after a separation, he calls her his prelate and then expands on the use of religious terminology as he explains that he has kept a piece of bread from Beatriz's plate in order to maintain contact with her during their time apart: "Durante el viaje ha sido mi viático de amor, y no lo comulgué del todo para no quedarme sin nada" [During the trip it has been my viaticum of love and I didn't take full communion so as to not end up with nothing] (1947, 163). He adds that he still finds pleasure in biting the dry bread that might have become her flesh. The parody of Catholic belief that in swallowing the host the communicant literally receives the body of Christ both breaks with and builds on religious doctrine. The application of the article of faith to a sexual relationship transgresses church teaching on the separation of body and spirit, but the process of transubstantiation represents the very exultation in and transcendence of the body to which Félix aspires. To make the body and blood of the other part of one's own flesh represents the height of carnal union, although doing so through repeated ritualistic reenactment invests the act with a symbolic value that moves beyond the purely corporal.

These two possibilities for the erotic relationship take form in

Beatriz and Isabel, who seek contact with Félix through memory and visits to the cemetery after his death. Once more the novel underscores the labile nature of desire and of all categories. Beatriz, who in an earlier episode had illustrated the possibilities for the melding of the physical and spiritual, now represents the physical while Isabel, whom Félix had always envisioned as some vague, misty, non-corporal entity here transmutes to the quintessential embodiment of flesh combined with spirituality. In reenactment of the Eucharist and Félix's consumption of the bread that might have become part of Beatriz's body, Beatriz and Isabel eat the cherries that grow in the cemetery. For Beatriz, here the representative of corporal union, the cherries taste just as they did when she ate them in an earlier episode. In contrast, Isabel, who had never eaten from the tree or tasted the fruits of sexual union, now absorbs the essence of the lover as she consumes the cherries growing in the cemetery where he is buried. The text again uses the verb *comulgar* [to take communion] to convey the melding of spiritual and sexual, eternal and earthly, and religious and erotic. The realization of such an unorthodox blending of categories long perceived as antagonistic takes place in the framework of a novel far removed from the conventions of realism. Miró's narrative does not posit the events depicted as real or even as possible, but aspires to imagine a liberated world that surmounts the limitations of Spanish Catholic temporality with a creative exploration of eternal return, cyclical re-enactment, and fluid categories. The exploration of an erotic spirituality or spiritualized eroticism in *Las cerezas del cementerio* challenges the limits of narrative possibility of the period and the reader's willingness to imagine new ways of thinking. When viewed in the context of the conventional modes of depicting sexuality, the body, death, and accepted categories, Miró's purposely imprecise style, his floating signifiers, and his repudiation of chronicity move towards a very different manner of imagining and inscribing reality that today's reader more readily accepts.

Ramón del Valle-Inclán's *La lámpara maravillosa* (1916) is frequently cited as the expression of *modernista* aesthetic doctrine by those who define Spanish modernism as escapist and decadentist. In recent studies, Carol Maier has investigated the possibilities for a double reading of the text that privileges the disharmonies and contradictory impulses contained within it. Building on Maier's observations, I will examine Valle-Inclán's treatment of temporality in *La lámpara maravillosa* and its relation to the representation of time in other Spanish modernists.

Critics often distinguish Valle-Inclán from his contemporaries as more experimental both artistically and ideologically, particularly in his later works.[21] However, his theorization of temporality links him to antecedent and contemporary works and demonstrates the common concern with temporal redefinition that characterizes Spanish modernism. In keeping with a fluid vision of genre and binary categories, the text incorporates Western and Eastern traditions, elements of prose and poetry, mystical and secular concerns as well as multiple, seemingly contradictory conceptualizations of time. Like Miró, Valle-Inclán aspires to transcend traditional polarities. The title and subtitle immediately introduce two distinct traditions: the magic lamp relates to the oriental legacy of enchantment and genies and the legendary world transmitted in *A Thousand and One Nights* while the subtitle *Ejercicios espirituales* invokes the writings of the Jesuit founder, Ignatius of Loyola. The text invokes these two heritages with their disparate visions of subjectivity, spirituality, and temporality and places them in dialogue. Immediately after discussing the three paths to eternal beauty, which directly parody the three paths to mystical union elaborated by such Spanish mystics as Saint Theresa of Avila, the text speaker proceeds to a consideration of the ring of Gyges, interweaving Catholic teachings with the tale of the Persian king whose magic ring made the bearer invisible. The melding of these seemingly unrelated narratives, both of which describe liberation from the body, points to the Asian origins of mysticism and to the Arabic-Jewish roots of Spanish culture and Catholic spiritualism. The link to Eastern practices continues in the speaker's reference to smoking his pipe of Indian hemp. A drug-induced vision provides him with a new sense of space, self, and time.

The following sections of the text detail an experience of temporality that on the surface exalts atemporality, as in the Christian sense of eternal time, but in the details reveals a rejection of progressive and eternal time in favor of temporality as flow or cycle. The text speaker asserts that to the see life as change and perpetual movement is to view it as satanical absurdity. Hell is constant movement whereas quietude characterizes divinity. However, the speaker also insists on the need to incorporate the past in the present and describes a personal experience to illustrate the imbrication of past in the eternal present: "Hasta entonces nunca había descubierto aquella intuición de eternidad que se me mostraba de pronto al evocar la infancia y darle actualidad en otro círculo del Tiempo. Toda la vida pasada era como el verso lejano que revive su evocación musical al encontrar otro verso que le guarda consonancia, y sin perder el primer significado entra a completar un significado más profundo" [Until then I had never discovered that intuition of eternity that appeared to me suddenly upon evoking my infancy and giving it actuality in another circle of Time. All my past life was like a distant verse that relives its musical evocation upon meeting another verse that maintains consonance with it, and without losing the first meaning joins to complete a deeper meaning] (1954, 532–33). Valle-Inclán's analysis echoes Antonio Machado's vision of time. The recovery of the past through memory and of originary significance in conjunction with an enriched meaning in the present suggests a spiraling movement that recurs throughout *La lámpara maravillosa* to depict the combination of time as flow and circularity. In a section entitled "El quietismo estético," the speaker states that one only discovers the enigmatic eternity of an object through the search for its supreme immobility, but in the same section, he writes that since there can be no direct knowledge of a reality that is mediated through the senses and through the mind that orders them, all knowledge is memory, which of necessity implies time and mobility. Like other modernists, Valle-Inclán's speaker recognizes the limitations of individual perspective and calls for a multiperspectival approach. The individual eye breaks the unity of the universe and in order to capture an object outside of space and time in its ideal essence, an individual must contemplate the same image from a variety of locations (572). The speaker designates this operation "cyclical vision" (572). The ambition to capture reality in its essence continually introduces diverse conceptualizations of time. The speaker views his own life as symbolized by a serpent cut in two, invoking the image of past as other. He rejects history as conventionally understood and calls for a return to the essence of tradition with the goal of recuperating what best serves to produce a better future: "Amemos la tradición pero en su esencia, procurando descifrarla como un enigma que guarda el secreto del porvenir" [Let us love tradition but in its essence, attempting to decipher it like an enigma that holds the secret of the future] (542). On various occasions he repudiates the idea of progressive time and in an adaptation of Bergsonian flux, he posits temporality as concentric circles: "Consideramos las horas y las vidas como yuxtaposición de instantes, como eslabones de una cadena, cuando son círculos concéntricos al modo que los engendra la piedra en la laguna" [We consider hours and lives as a juxtaposition of moments, like links in a chain, when they are concentric circles in the manner that a stone engenders when thrown into a lagoon] (580). He defines the goal of art as a cordial palpitation that engenders infinite circles, as a center that encompasses the idea of quietude and of eternal becoming (582–83), linking flux and circle, past and present.

Valle-Inclán conforms with the other modernists in his vision of history and the relationship of past and present. In many ways, *La lámpara maravillosa* synthesizes modernist aesthetics, using modernist in the broad sense that I have employed throughout this study. The emphasis on a plural perspective, on the simultaneity of seemingly contradictory elements, on a hybrid structure, and on the melding of East and West, national and foreign are all traits routinely observable throughout the period. The textualization of the principles expounded in the work itself further links this study with other modernist productions. *La lámpara maravillosa* consists of an introduction followed by five sections whose titles invoke magical, mystical intertexts, such as Gyges's Ring, Musical Miracle, and Aesthetic Quietism. Individual subsections appear within each segment and while numbered, they break with traditional chronology in that the number and accompanying gloss, which synthesizes the prose commentary, follows rather than precedes the text. A "Guión de las glosas" appears at the end of the work, thus circling back to the individual sections of the text and repeating the glosses, but in a new context now that the entire discussion has occurred. In this sense, the text reproduces the image of concentric circles that emanate out from a single core or of a musical theme that repeats with variations over time at different points in the composition.

A final analogy between *La lámpara maravillosa* and other works of the period consists in the presentation of modernism as aspiration rather than reality. Like the *Spiritual Exercises* simultaneously parodied and revered in the text, Valle-Inclán's work offers a guide towards a goal that remains beyond the present. The reader is addressed as a pilgrim, traveling to a still distant destination, and the glosses include ample use of the future tense, the subjunctive, and other markers of incompletion. Azorín, Machado, Baroja, Miró, Valle-Inclán and other modernists who examine the notion of eternal return and other forms of temporality inspired by modern philosophers and intensified contacts with Eastern religions and philosophies communicate through style, textual structure, open-ended conclusions and direct commentary that their break with traditional conceptions of time remains tentative and exploratory. Subject to constant revision and oscillating between professions of hope and ironic skepticism, it stands in opposition to traditional visions of time that inhibit change and preclude pleasure. The possibilities of eternal return in conjunction with the perception of time as discontinuous, fluid, and subject to multiple clocks open up new avenues for imagining life, death, the body, sexuality, and the borders that separate them. In *Crossfire: Philosophy and the Novel in Spain,* Roberta Johnson suggests that the lack of a modern philosophical tradition in Spain led to a stalemate between conflicting philosophies (1993, 5). While Spain undeniably found itself rushing to catch up to its European neighbors as a result of isolation in the Hapsburg and in part the Bourbon period, the presentation of conflicting philosophical positions that Johnson views as symptomatic of the Spain of this period also existed in the rest of Europe. As Art Berman persuasively argues in *Preface to Modernism,* modernism represents a complex and paradoxical response to the legacies of empiricism and idealism that results in a transcendent realism (1994, 23). This melding of two antagonistic philosophical traditions correlates to an equally paradoxical aesthetic posture that Berman defines as "the union of irreconcilables" (23, 94). Throughout the discussion of time, I have pointed to the self-conscious expression by Spanish modernists of their belief in the need to sustain a complex, multi-faceted vision and in their exultation in paradox. Rather than philosophical confusion, their repeated expression of purposeful multiperspectivism represents a conscious declaration of philosophical principle. In this context, the doctrine of eternal return stands with and against notions of time as flux and progression to break with the past and imagine other futures and other selves, individual and collective.[22]

5
From the Subatomic to the Galactic: Modernist Spaces

ADVANCES IN MICROSCOPE QUALITY AND THEORIES OF SUBCELLULAR/subatomic structures radically change the vision of matter in the nineteenth century. The observation of protoplasm movement under improved magnification and lens quality in the 1830s, combined with Maxwell's electromagnetic theory, reveals a world not visible to the naked eye in which particles and subcellular units exist in a dynamic state. The experience of train, car, and later airplane travel further contributes to the experience of space as dynamic by creating the sensation that the landscape rushes by as the observer moves at increasingly accelerated speeds. As Stephen Kern and Richard Sheppard observe, the traditional view of space as at rest and immutable no longer holds.[1] In contrast with the new experience of space as mobile and dynamic, the daguerreotype and later the camera capture and freeze it. Early photography requires absolute stillness and focus on a specific, limited object that is then developed into a framed segment, a permanently recorded temporal moment and spatial fragment that offers a counterweight to perceptions of a dynamic space. However, at the same time and almost to distance themselves from the field of photography, in the world of visual art painters break with the Renaissance tradition of linear perspective. Impressionists experiment with the dissolution of forms in light and the flattening of space through color while Picasso, Braque, and others dismantle bodies and break with the conventional separation of painted subject and background.

The varied depictions and experiences of space exist simultaneously and mutually influence each other in Spanish modernism. In order to capture a complex and varied reality, authors and artists alternately infuse a static description with movement and temporality, or freeze a moment in time and frame it as in a photograph or painting. The oscillation between various modes of spatial representation in itself introduces change and dynamism, characteristics that are enhanced by the modernist vision of reality as everywhere and at all times mediated, whether through an instrument or individual perspective. No single picture or slide exhausts reality and similarly, no single thought system or theory lays claim to absolute truth. Modernism places different perspectives side-by-side or moves fluidly through various points of view to illustrate that the space which an observer occupies and the instruments utilized to access it condition and relativize the resulting vision. Modernist antifoundationalism contributes to and stems from a new conceptualization of space in a dialectic that produces excitement, amazement, and trepidation among Spanish artists, writers, and intellectuals. Once again, the image of the turning coin aptly captures the continual transformation that occurs in the modernist response to ever-changing reality. In the past, criticism of the period has emphasized stasis or a nostalgic desire to return to a more stable world with little or no recognition of the dynamic impulses that reveal themselves in the modernist aspiration for a new individual and collective selfhood that is other to its antecedents. Scholars focussing on the "Generation of 1898" highlight the representation of an unchanging Castilian landscape while studies of *modernismo* feature exotic, rarefied, but also static locations. These spaces exist within the cultural products of late nineteenth and early twentieth-century Spain, but they neither exhaust nor typify spatial representations of the period. Furthermore, within both the depiction of the Castilian countryside and the exquisite *modernista* spaces, writers make use of techniques that introduce movement or call attention to change.

The Subatomic and the Subcellular in Spanish Modernist Writing

Pío Baroja's training as physician and scientist coincides with his interest in areas of reality not normally visible to the naked eye. In an early text published in 1893 in *La Justicia* with the title "Danza de átomos" and later revised as "La vida de los átomos" and included in *Vidas sombrías* (1900), the narrator describes the sudden transformation of a spark from the chimney into many different atoms that move giddily about the room. The narrator of the revised story playfully declares his disbelief in the existence of atoms while addressing them, mocking resistance to contemporary understandings of the nature of matter. Barojan texts typically depict matter as teeming with subatomic, subcellular activity. *Camino de perfección* describes the decay of a buried bishop's body as a purifying, liberating transformation that combines scientific definitions of matter with modernist desires to supersede traditional visions of death:

> ¡Qué hermoso poema el del cadáver del obispo en aquel campo tranquilo! . . . empezaría a pudrirse poco a poco: hoy se le nublaría un ojo, y empezarían a nadar los gusanos por los jugos vítreos; luego el cerebro se le iría reblandeciendo. . . . Un día comenzaría a filtrarse la lluvia y a llevar con ella sustancia orgánica, y al pasar por la tierra aquella sustancia, se limpiaría, se purificaría, nacerían junto a la tumba hierbas verdes, frescas, y el pus de las úlceras brillaría en las blancas corolas de las flores. ¡Qué hermoso poema el del cadáver del obispo en el campo tranquilo! ¡Qué alegría la de los átomos al romper la forma que les aprisionaba, al fundirse con júbilo en la nebulosa del infinito, en la senda del misterio donde todo se pierde! (1969, 61–62)

> [What a beautiful poem, the one about the bishop's cadaver in that peaceful field! . . . it would begin to rot little by little: today an eye would cloud over, and worms would start to swim in the vitreous fluids; then the brain would begin to soften. . . . One day rain would start to filter through and to carry away with it organic substance, and in passing that substance through the earth it would become clean, it would be purified. Fresh, green grasses would sprout next to the tomb and the puss of the ulcers would shine in the white corollas of the flowers. What a beautiful poem, the one about the bishop's cadaver in the peaceful field! How happy the atoms will be to break away from the form that imprisons them, to join happily the nebula of infinity, the mysterious path where everything is lost!]

Fernando Ossorio does not initially share the narrator's exultance at material transformations, expressing fear of invisible forces surging within nature, but as he gradually liberates himself from the Catholic vision of life and death, he comes to appreciate and accept nature's dynamic power. Even before his epiphany in Castellón, Fernando confesses amazement at the immense vitality hidden within the earth and the continual germination of life in both still and rushing waters. Although he recognizes that the creation of new life accompanies tremendous mortality, he accepts death as the storehouse and source of vitality (179–80) and in the end, aspires to raise his child with a philosophy that favors life over death. Fernando envisions his son as an atom within the masses of humanity and now privileges energy and life over stasis and death (208).

Ramiro de Maeztu expresses a similar vision in early essays and directly relates scientific advances in atomic theory to a Nietzschean will to life and change. "Contra la noción de la justicia," which appears in *Hacia otra España* (1899), argues against a static, harmonic vision of life and justice. Structured as an open dialogue in a format that mimics the dynamic nature of reality the text seeks to present, the essay argues that the apparent repose and order of nature observed by humans is deceptive. Beneath a surface stasis, atoms join and separate with a velocity that imperfectly developed human senses cannot perceive. Maeztu's speaker specifically compares human perception to the photographic camera, with its inability to capture movement. In contrast with the reality perceived by the human eye and camera lens, he posits a world in which objects exist in constant conflict, with life the result of struggle and repeated destruction (1967, 232–33). Azorín similarly relates a dynamic atomic reality with a commitment to vitality and a search for new modes of living. Both references to Nietzsche's speculations on eternal return in *La voluntad* build on the concept of perpetual motion and change at the atomic level, which gives rise to the possibilities of cyclical repetition. In a 1905 article published in *España* and later appended to *Los pueblos,* the text speaker links the modern vision of subatomic/subcellular forces and psychological interest in the unconscious with a shift in aesthetic interest:

> Todo tiene su valor estético y psicológico; los conciertos diminutos de las cosas son tan interesantes para el psicólogo y para el artista como las grandes síntesis universales. Hay ya una nueva belleza, un nuevo arte de lo pequeño, en los detalles insignificantes, en lo ordinario, en lo prosaico; los tópicos abstractos y épicos que hasta ahora los poetas han llevado y traído ya no nos dicen nada; ya no se puede hablar con enfáticas generalidades del campo, de la Naturaleza, del amor, de los hombres; necesitamos hechos microscópicos que sean reveladores de la vida y que, ensamblados armónicamente, con simplicidad, con claridad, nos muestren la fuerza misteriosa del Universo, esta fuerza eterna, profunda. . . . (1954, 376)

> [Everything has its aesthetic and psychological value; the diminutive harmonies of things are as interesting for the psychologist and the artist as the great universal syntheses. There is now a new beauty, a new art of the diminutive, in the insignificant details, in the ordinary, in the prosaic. The abstract and epic topics that up to now poets

have returned to again and again no longer say anything to us. One can no long speak with emphatic generalities about the country, nature, love, men; we need microscopic facts that reveal life and that assembled harmoniously, with simplicity and clarity, show us the mysterious force of the Universe, that profound and eternal force. . . .]

Al margen de los clásicos (1915) again links scientific advances with aesthetic change, citing the twentieth century histologist Santiago Ramón y Cajal and the nineteenth century poet Gustavo Adolfo Bécquer as individuals with different specializations who coincide in speculations about aspects of reality that exist beyond the realm of the senses and that require, in Ramón y Cajal's words, optical and acoustical instruments still beyond the range of human experience, but conceivable in the future (Martínez Ruiz 1921, 221). These advances will allow for more complex conceptual combinations in the human mind to better capture the world's mysteries.

The influence of new views of (sub)atomic energy also impacts the perception of nature and space in the novels of Concha Espina.[2] Espina shares with other modernist writers a varied and sometimes contradictory response to modernity as well as a changing conceptualization of space as a result of developments in the geological, chemical, and biological sciences and their relation to social change. *El metal de los muertos* (1920) depicts the deplorable conditions of miners in the Andalusian Riotinto mines and subtextually supports calls for social and economic reform through a depiction of subterranean nature as a violated, suffering landscape that miraculously resists the onslaught of human avarice in its stubborn revelation of beauty and energy. In describing Aurora's visit to the Asturian mine where the action begins, the narrative emphasizes the vital force of nature that obdurately germinates in the rocky entrance to the mine: ". . . una pujanza verde y milagrosa cunde por la sangre de la tierra y sube a la cima, irguiéndose en el aire azul" [. . . a green and miraculous vigor spreads through the earth's blood and climbs to the summit, raising itself in the blue air] (1972, 1:494). In the mine tunnel itself, Aurora hears the sounds of a vibrant, living matter that speaks a language she cannot fully comprehend, but whose powers of creation and force of life she appreciates:

Sudaban las raíces del monte, se oía el estremecimiento incesante de la tierra, el latido profundo de los gérmenes, el trabajo penoso de la roca; una legión de almas decía con balbucientes revelaciones el eterno milagro de la creación.

Avanza la joven escuchando el esfuerzo que hace la naturaleza por hablar, oyendo con asombro que todos los seres mudos levantan allí su repentina voz, y olvidando en un lúcido ensueño, que se confunde perdida en la huraña lobreguez, sólo siente, con raro gozo, el misterio que yace en las costas y se subyuga bajo la fuerte densidad de la vida, atendiendo fascinada a los diálogos incomprensibles, a las visiones alucinantes (1972, 1:495).

[The mountain roots dripped with moisture, the incessant tremble of the earth could be heard, the deep throb of the germs, the painful working of the rock. A legion of spirits expressed with stammering revelations the eternal miracle of creation.

The young woman advances listening to nature's effort to speak, hearing in surprise that all the mute beings there raise an unexpected voice, and lapsing into a lucid dream, which she confuses as one with the unsociable darkness, she only feels with a rare pleasure, the mystery that lies in the banks and she is overcome by the strong density of life, listening fascinated to the incomprehensible dialogues, the mysterious visions.]

The description of the geological strata of the mines underscores the original and residual energy of the rocks' formation rather than a static, inert mass. The narrative invokes prehistoric fires, freezing, molecular changes, sedimentation, and lava flows (1:519). The verbal rendering of a visit to a gallery with stalagmites and stalactites emphasizes the action of water, the changing forms, and the play of light, sound, and water. The depiction of the various minerals stresses diversity in color and a sensation of motion, describing some with a moving nucleus while all reflect light and change in appearance in transformations that belie "classical description of the Silurian age as *tierra sin vida*" (1:578). During this episode, the American chemist who visits the underground grottos comments that there is nothing inert in nature or humanity, in the mineral crystal or the human soul (1:579). The vision of persistent change and dynamic energy at the atomic/cellular level and expressions of admiration for the beauty and energy of these minute transformations provides a suggestive background to the story of the miner's struggle for social and economic reform and vindicates as natural the human impulse for change.

Espina's *La rosa de los vientos* (1916) interweaves a vision of a natural world teeming with life and energy with the narration of the sexual awakening of the young protagonist. In Espina, the expression of the erotic takes place indirectly and through what Rita Felski has designated the popular sublime in her analysis of the work of Marie Corelli (1995, 115 ff). Like Corelli, Espina depicts the feminine aspiration for love as an unrealizable ideal, a transcendent experience that runs counter to male expectations for the romantic relationship and to a vulgar, crass social reality. The failure to fully realize female romantic desire forms the basis of Espina's narratives and is the central theme of *La rosa de los vientos,* where Soledad Fontenebro, the adolescent protagonist, struggles to establish her identity. The sublimation of the young woman's erotic drives takes place through highly poeticized interactions with a pulsating nature. In an early episode, Soledad describes being driven by a stormy restlessness that compels her to a solitary swim in the ocean, from which she emerges transfigured, as if having bathed in liquid gold, in the moving blood of the heavens and stars. The sense of communion with a palpitating natural world surfaces again in a later episode, where the connection with modern visions of subatomic/subcellular reality becomes even clearer. Soledad's desire to understand the mysteries of life, death, time, space, and eternity lead her this time to seek connection through a grassy garden: "Apoyé en el césped la cara, donde hervía mi sangre, y traté de aplicar el oído a los imperceptibles rumores: átomos de vida; gérmenes ocultos; incubaciones misteriosas que pululan en la tierra maternal" [I rested my face in the grass, where my blood boiled, and I tried to attune my ear to the imperceptible noises: atoms of life, hidden germs, mysterious incubations that pulsate in mother earth] (1972, 1:435). The subatomic/subcellular energy reflects the physical and emotional drive of the young protagonist, who struggles to free herself from external social control and to define a life of her own.[3] As in other writers of the period, the representation of space as dynamic and energized accompanies a transgressive break with established patterns of behavior and inherited values and once more, the oppositional discourse does not fully clarify the substance of the new reality to which it aspires. However, in this still vaguely defined future, a dynamic of change receives positive emphasis, as does reconnection with nature and its forces.

Gregorio and María Martínez Sierra also examine the implications of scientific developments for an understanding of space and its relations with human evolution. Two texts from *El poema del trabajo* treat invisible but potent forces in nature. "Orquídeas" describes tiny insects that enter the orchid's calyx and then, covered with golden pollen, fly to other flowers to bring forth new life. The text speaker specifically relates the role of artist and insect, calling for energetic commitment to the elaboration of fertile, regenerative ideas. "Lucha eterna" describes the earth's formation in a dynamic struggle to trap the minute particles that tried to escape her force. In various stages of the planet's evolution, elements engaged in forceful combat and life slowly evolved from microscopic, single-cell aquatic creatures. The connection between a vision of space as charged with energy and a desire for social change informs the collection and the closing paragraphs of individual texts often overtly relate natural forces and material change with artistic innovation or social transformation.[4] Science and social change also combine in the feminist *Cartas a las mujeres de España* (1916), where the speaker encourages women to study botany, physics, chemistry, geography, and to strive to understand the consistency of moonlight and purpose of stars. This radical female education would not destroy dreams but rather, the text argues, change them (1930, 94–95). For the Martínez Sierras, advances in scientific knowledge provide the impetus for a revision of the formation of the individual and society.

Salvador Rueda explores the implications of atomic transformation in several poems. The title "Escalas" of *En Tropel* (1894) refers both to the scales of the musical world and to the term used for different spatial dimensions. Echoing symbolist aspirations for a musicality that liberates poetry from convention, the poetic speaker calls for freedom from confining form. He also expresses a desire to escape the limiting materiality of the body and it is his realization of a constantly changing atomic world that enables a view of death as transformation rather than cessation. Rueda's poetic speaker finds solace and liberation in imagining that his matter will become part of other bodies and of the substance of a "sublime" universe. The linking of artistic and scientific discourse of the title recurs in the use of "sublime," which refers both to the literary sense of exalted and to the chemical term for the conversion of a solid substance into a vapor and then back to solid form though condensation. The scientific description of atomic transformation allows for a new way of imagining the decay of the human body and its reconfiguration in other forms, and the poet joins such a discovery with a search for new modes of poetic expression. Rueda's "Microscopio" similarly links cellular/atomic energies with poetic creation. The poem describes the discernment of previously invisible crystalline forms in minerals viewed under the microscope lens and depicts the creation of crystals and precious stones using such active verbs as "procreate" or "give birth" to capture a sense of their dynamic formation. It further injects animation by depicting the gem's interaction with light and the resulting refraction. The poetic speaker compares poetry and science and expresses an exultant faith in future discoveries through their joint development.

Gabriel Miró's landscape and nature descriptions also reflect the influence of modern science and advances in the understanding of cells and atoms. "La ciudad. Razón y virtudes de muertos," written in 1916 and included in *Libro de Sigüenza* (1917), ponders the question of life and death in the context of the discovery that human beings consist of some thirty trillion cells that continually die and are replaced. Thousands of an individual's cells may die while she/he still lives or conversely, an individual may die and thousands of her/his cells survive. The narrator cites a French physiologist who describes the death certificate as mere prediction, since hair and finger and toe nails continue to grow after official declarations that life has ceased (1949, 643). The text comically questions inherited definitions of mortality and identity in an era when doctors discuss tissue and organ transplants and offers a new definition of death as occurring only when all the elements comprising an individual have died. Like Rueda, Miró finds artistic and intellectual enjoyment in the exploration of new conceptualizations of life, death, and identity and like other modernists, he draws on the scientific revelations of a dynamic, changing atomic and cellular world to create artistic spaces that similarly depict energy and movement.

Landscapes and Other Settings

The vision of the fundamental units of matter and life as dynamic and energized transfers to descriptions of larger spaces. At times, writers focus on forces within seemingly static objects while on other occasions, they reveal how objects interact with and transmute each other. The exploration of the transformative power of background and light on an object contributes both to the sense of a changing spatiality and to the annihilation of the line separating background and object. Through varied techniques and perspectives, modernist writers and artists prod the reader/observer to explore new dimensions of spatiality and alter their own relationship with their surroundings. Critics often point to a modernist predilection for late afternoon or autumn as reflecting a sense of fatigue that characterizes the period.[5] In some cases, afternoon and autumn represent such a state of mind, as in Antonio Machado's "El viajero." Llanas Aguilaniedo writes in *Alma contemporánea* that the contemporary temperament understands sunset better than sunrise because modern individuals are tired, impotent, tormented latecomers (1991, 7) and the narrator of Miró's *Las cerezas del cementerio* describes the resignation and sadness that the afternoon provokes in Félix. However, Miró's narration mentions in the same passage the powers of the morning sun to awaken the observer to the pleasure of pristine gardens, renewed ideals, fresh air, and life itself (1947, 203). The turning of the modernist coin moves from afternoon to morning, never permanent in any single space or time. Furthermore, afternoon does not necessarily connote sadness or fatigue. Modernists strongly favor periods of the day and year that stand on the border of two different time frames. Night giving way to day, day moving into evening, spring bursting forth, autumnal transitions toward winter constitute the preferred backdrops of the period. In moments of transition, light changes constantly and the play of light and shadow allows for a temporalization of spatiality that responds to the modernist view of life as dynamic and mediated.

Santiago Rusiñol relates the predilection for late afternoon to the modernist preference for nuanced, transmuting representations in contrast with the clear silhouette or line that separates one category from another. He writes of his desire to paint nude women in the snow in order to break with inherited practices of clear delineation of background and artistic subject (n. d. a, 24–25). In such a painting, the contours of the body fade into the background and instead of two stable entities, human body in contrast to physical environment, body and setting mutually inform and flow into each other. Juan Ramón Jiménez struggles to erase the line in his poetry, first by means of a verbal representation of color, shadow, and changing materiality and later by omission of detail and understated allusions that often rely on memory, dream, or metapoetic (re)visions. He aspires to simultaneously present stasis and movement, still photograph and moving scene, in a continual crossing of temporal and spatial borders that persists in the various periods of his production. "Mañana nublada y triste," from the 1905 *Pastorales,* utilizes a cloudy early morning as a backdrop to a play of light and darkness, stasis and activity, temporality and spatiality that seeks to capture a multifaceted, unstable physical world. The poetic speaker of this poem still relies on the line and a stable materiality against which he constructs a more fluid, muted area. The dark green of trees, sharp sound of a gunshot, and bright red flame of fire stand out in contrast to a misty drizzle that does not quite efface their silhouette. Other poems of the collection more completely erase the transition from one physical substance to another. "Aún está alumbrando el día" describes the presence of the moon in late afternoon and the ambiguous origins of the gold that colors the stream and the poplars, perhaps generated by a waning sun or perhaps by the moon. The golden poplars lose their firm contours in their reflection in the stream waters and the fluttering of the leaves in the breeze similarly breaks the stability of their outline.

In Jiménez's early poetry, the transmuting of one physical space or object to another and the transition of one temporal period to the next often evokes sadness or a sense of disconnection between past and present. The transformed space and transitional hour of "En estas horas vagas que acercan a la noche" of *Elejías* (1907–8) bring an anxious feeling of irreality regarding both past and present. The text refers to the memory of old histories that no longer make sense and to the movement of a car traveling toward a train, which in turn leads to a world that may no longer exist. In the laborious elaboration of his poetics from the early 1900s to the mature publications of *Diario de un poeta recién casado* (1916), *Eternidades* (1916–17), or *Piedra y cielo,* (1916–18), Jiménez's depiction of a dynamic, changing natural world reveals a gradual acceptance and exultation in the possibilities available in such a universe. While he still expresses occasional anguish, a predominant note of toleration and even rejoicing displaces the earlier anxiety.[6] "Paseo" juxtaposes the day's passing and the physical movement of two lovers who sense their vulnerability in a temporalized world in continual transformation. The glow of the afternoon sky in the water and the islands of dry leaves that float by inject the site of their romantic encounter with reminders of physical decay. However, in this text, the speaker extracts himself from the anguish of the female partner and finds peace in recognizing the infinite possibilities of life, "el alma innumerable de la vida" (1957, 50).

Diario de un poeta recién casado continues the trajectory towards acceptance of temporalized, transmuting matter. The two-line poem of the collection's second page reveals a new desire for hybrid, mutually constitutive forms: "Raíces y alas. Pero que las alas arraiguen / y las raíces vuelen" [Roots and Wings. But let the wings take root / and the roots soar] (1917, 22). The speaker's meditations on the sea also disclose a new-found acceptance of instability. He moves easily from consideration of the ocean's motion to its absolute stillness, of the sea's transformation of his perception of sky and self. Encouraging an agile shifting of perspectives in the reader, the speaker affirms a continually transformed reality. The disappearance of the line that divides subjects and objects, exterior and interior, physical and spiritual, continues in this later period of Jiménez's poetry, but the poetic speaker's comfortable assimilation of these modern spaces differs dramatically from earlier anxiety. "Tarde" of *Piedra y cielo* expresses with incredibly brevity and clarity the attitude of the mature Jiménez:

> ¡Cómo, meciéndose, en las copas de oro,
> al manso viento, mi alma
> me dice, libre, que soy todo!
>
> (1919, 169)

> [And how, swaying, in the golden treetops,
> to the gentle wind, my soul
> tells me, freely, that I am everything!]

The soul, conventionally envisioned as immaterial, becomes even more fluid in the wind's swaying motion. The golden color of the treetops suggests the play of afternoon and perhaps autumnal light, but the speaker welcomes the moment and possibilities for blending self and surroundings. No line delineates any object mentioned in the poem; the treetops fade into the golden light, the soul moves freely in the atmosphere, and the self fuses with the wind and all that it touches. The unorthodox syntax, with ample use of hyperbaton and floating modifiers that easily attach to a variety of referents, furthers the sense of free-flowing movement and effaced borders. Although his response to and interaction with his surroundings evolves over the course of his production, Jiménez remains constant in his vision of a dynamic, changing spatiality.

Antonio Machado diverges considerably from Juan Ramón Jiménez in temperament, personal history, and poetic vision, but he shares with his Andalusian compatriot and other modernists the predilection for temporalized spaces and transitional time frames. Afternoons appear constantly in his poetry and although they sometimes represent tedium or fatigue, they and other periods of the day and year that frame Machado's poetic spaces not infrequently reflect a vision of nature and space as dynamic and moving towards another way and time of being. "Horizonte" describes the dual movement of day into night and of the poetic speaker towards a different temporal-spatial location:

> En una trade clara y amplia como el hastío
> cuando su lanza blande el tórrido verano,
> copiaban el fantasma de un grave sueño mío
> mil sombras en teoría, enhiestas sobre el llano.
> La gloria del ocaso era un purpúreo espejo,
> era un cristal de llamas, que al infinito viejo
> iba arrojando el grave soñar en la llanura . . .
> Y yo sentí la espuela sonora de mi paso
> repercutir lejana en el sangriento ocaso,
> y más allá, la alegre canción de un alba pura.
>
> (1917, 33)

> [On a bright evening, vast as tedium,
> beneath the swinging sword of the summer's heat
> a thousand tall shadows were lined up in the plain,
> copying the phantom of my somber dream.
> The sunset's splendor was a purple mirror,
> flaming glass relaying toward infinity
> the somber dreaming on the plain.
> And I heard my footsteps ring out like a spur
> and ricochet far off on the blood stained west
> and farther off a pure dawn's joyous song.[7]]

The purple of the sunset, the metaphor of the swinging sword and image of a flaming mirror that projects the scene out to infinity construct a dynamic portrait. The modernist tendency to depict the transition from one temporal period to another occurs in tandem with the poetic speaker's movement through space, in a sort of doubling of activity and focal point that further enhances the sense of motion. In this and other Machado poems, the relationship between the two spaces remains indeterminate. On the one hand, the projection of his somber dreams into infinity suggests their duplication over time and a permanent contrast between the colorless phantoms of the poetic speaker's visions and the brilliant, dramatic skies. On the other hand, the mention of footsteps ricocheting first off the evening sky and then off a pure dawn's happy song insinuates a changing relationship between speaker and surroundings, moving from the decline and sense of ending of the afternoon to the joyful promise of the morning. The oscillation between these two possibilities adds to the sensation of instability and change as the reader moves back and forth between two interpretive locations in response to a text that places the moving poet against the backdrop of a changing sky and contrasts a violent setting sun to the calm of a pure dawn.

A number of poems of the *Galerías* section of *Soledades, Galerías y otros poemas* portray spaces in ekphrastic imitation of a painting. "Ante el pálido lienzo de la tarde" depicts the outline of a church in the evening light, with a silver cloud floating beneath a single star in the blue sky. The church's architectural stability and the stillness of the evening sky acquire movement with the mention of the swinging bells of the church tower and the description of the cloud as dispersed sheep fleece (1917, 92). "¡Oh tarde luminosa!" also focusses on the sky, but increases the sense of motion with the criss-crossing of swallows and storks that endow the massive church roof with life and personality. Conversely, the moving stork becomes a still statue in the depiction of his awkward perch on the belfry (1917, 94). The play of opposites and break down of their difference occurs in another descriptive poem that conjoins day and night, life and death, transience and durability in lyrical co-presence. "El sol es un globo de fuego" describes a burning sun that shares the sky with the deep purple of the moon, effacing traditional opposition of day and night. In three remaining two-verse stanzas, the text continues to deconstruct conventional polarities. A white dove, symbol of purity, innocence, and youth alights on the centennial cypress, a tree the text marks as chronologically aged and that Spanish culture associates with cemeteries and death. The patches of myrtle, traditionally associated with love and Venus, here appear covered with dust. In the final verses the poem introduces the sound of water in a marble fountain, placing the image of aquatic movement, associated with Heraclitan passage of time, in opposition to the durability of marble, but simultaneously deconstructing this contrast with the connotation of a monotonously repetitive sound of water hitting against itself in cyclical recurrence and of the gradual erosion of the marble through this very repetition (1917, 41).

It is tempting when reading Machado to emphasize tedium and sadness, heightened by his young wife's tragic death and the many poems in which he struggles to deal with his loss. The dismissal of his social poetry by some critics further contributes to the sense of a monochromatic, unchanging lyrical voice. However, his poetry includes a range of voices that vary from despairing, sad, bored, and diffident to amused, angry, hopeful, and self-deprecating. In his representation of space, Machado favors change and transformation over stasis and infuses even his more static texts with motion through the use of indeterminacy, the erasure of the separation of background and poetic subject, and the simultaneous presentation and demolition of opposites. Even in his poems devoted to Leonor's death, he introduces life in the very act of lamenting death and seeks to move beyond a Catholic vision of death as finality. In his representation of setting in one of his most beautiful poems related to his wife's death, "A José María Palacios," the interpenetration of life and death, distance and proximity, spring and winter, confirms a vision of space as dynamic and ever-changing, as Claudio Guillén clarified in a now classic study. It bears noting in the present context that the commemoration of the loss takes place through the recollection of the arrival of spring in Soria, interweaving thoughts of death with the renewal of life and constructing a space in the poem that is both temporally and spatially distant from the speaker, but which comes alive through memory and lyrical reconstruction. The play of life and death includes the interweaving of references to age and youth, as when the speaker asks Palacio if the old oaks have any new leaves or contrasts the snow-covered mountains with the flowering daisies. The personal note connects with social and community life and the past with the future when the poetic speaker conjectures that the farmers will probably have begun to plant and illegal hunters will already be active with bird lures hidden beneath their long capes. The dialogic structure of the poem, with spatial separation of speaker and addressee, requires the reader to actively move back and forth between the speaker's location in Baeza and Palacio's in Soria, while also projecting the future movement of Palacio from Soria up to the hilltop cemetery. These geographic displacements against the backdrop of spring bursting forth endow the text with movement and a dialectic tension that animate the poetic space.

Although the tone and psychological status of the speaker of "Poema de un día" differs considerably from "A José María Palacios," the spatial displacements recur, along with emphasis on multiple clocks that measure the passage of time for the townspeople and the poetic speaker. Against the backdrop of monotonous village life, the poem presents a day in the life of the autobiographical speaker, who moves from his paper-strewn study to the local pharmacy and then home again and from private meditations to political conversations and philosophical considerations. The rapid movement through time, philosophical schools, and physical spaces communicates the modernist sense of a constantly changing reality and a human response to it that spins through a range of emotions and values. The text alternately blesses the rain that falls as beneficial to the freshly planted wheat and dismisses it as insufficient. It points to the monotony of small town life while underscoring the varied measure of time within a seemingly monotemporal rural culture. The speaker praises Unamuno as the hope of a new Spain that struggles to be (re)born, but also expresses doubt as to the possibilities for such a project. The philosophy shared by Unamuno and the speaker is described as dilettantish, fickle, and extravagant, underscoring the modernist thinker's mobility in the search for answers to a rapidly transforming intellectual landscape. Monotony, repetition, disbelief in change and the correlative spaces appear in the poem, but they interweave with change, new ideas, hope for a different tomorrow, and the various locations that contribute to and reflect this alternate response.

Gabriel Miro's descriptions of nature and setting also underscore movement and change. An element as static as water in a glass undergoes alterations in color and form: "El agua temblaba en los frescos labios de la vasija, agua gozosa y penetrada de claridades; dentro tenía color de panal; y, a veces, se trocaba en azul de la mañana" [The water trembled in the fresh lips of the container, joyful water and pierced with light; inside it was the color of honeycomb, and sometimes, it changed to morning blue] (1949, 244). Gabriel Torres Nebrera refers to Miró's aesthetic of the scene or vignette in his introduction to *Del huerto provinciano* (1988) and there is in Miró, as in other modernists, the influence of painting or photography in the depiction of ambience but typically, the static picture acquires dynamism and sometimes subtly, sometimes more dramatically, transforms to a space permeated with movement. "El final de mi cuento," published in *Heraldo de Madrid* in 1909 and later included in *Del huerto provinciano,* describes a moonlit night and from the start introduces movement by comparing the moon to a restless sleeping maiden that tosses and turns in her white bedding. The representation of the artist-protagonist's parlor and later bedroom centers on the changing lighting effected by the moon, crystal lamp, and mirror that reflects the artist's face and infuses the space with visual instability as the focus of attention moves back and forth from the artist to his reflection (1988, 104). A description of the mountains refers to harsh sierras that rip apart into gorges or daintily withdraw, tucking their skirts and forming a soft lap. The inanimate hills become the agents of such active verbs as "produce," "swell," "break out" (1949, 625).

Baroja's animated landscapes punctuate his novels. The descriptions of the sunrise and sunset viewed from the mountain top in *Camino de perfección* emphasize brilliant, rapidly transmuting colors and wind-blown clouds scudding across the sky with sudden bursts of bird song and trains in the background (1969, 69–72). In later works, Baroja softens his colors and avoids such imposing terrains, but his representations of space continue to privilege motion and dynamism. He often describes living quarters in a series of short sentences and paragraphs that suggest the passing of characters through the spaces, moving from one room to another with a quick survey of the surroundings. Luis Murguía's report on his aunt's house in *La sensualidad pervertida* (1920) moves from the front door through the entryway, up the stairs, past the landing, and then through various wings and individual rooms in quick succession (1967, 501–3). The space is at rest, but the observer follows the motions of a moving camera that pans the rooms and then moves on to the next location.

Azorín prefers smaller, more limited spaces, but he too emphasizes mobility and energy. *La voluntad*'s opening chapter describes the arrival of morning to Yecla as a process in which the city moves out of darkness and the country separates from the town as increasing daylight differentiates the two spaces (1919, 17–18). A later chapter presents the passing of an afternoon, in which the heat first extends across the panorama and then subsides. The individual elements of nature acquire incredible energy and force throughout the representation of the passing day:

> La verdura impetuosa de los pámpanos repta por las blancas pilastras, se enrosca a las carcomidas vigas de los parrales, cubre las alamedas de tupido toldo cimbreante, desborda en tumultuosas oleadas por los panzudos muros de los huertos, baja hasta arañar las aguas sosegadas de la ancha acequia. . . . Las diversas tonalidades de los verdes se funden en una inmensa y uniforme mancha de azul borroso; los términos primeros suéldanse a los lejanos; los claros salientes de las lomas se esfuman misteriosos. Cruza una golondrina rayando el azul pálido. Y a lo lejos, entre las sombras, un bancal inundado refleja, como un enorme espejo, las últimas claridades del crepúsculo. (1919, 89–92)

> [The impetuous green of the vine shoots snakes along the white pilaster, it coils around the rotten beams of the vine arbor, covers the tree-lined walks with thick swaying cover, bursts in tumbling waves through the fat walls of the orchards, descends until it scratches the resting waters of the wide irrigations ditch. . . . The different tones of green fuse in an immense and uniform smudge of indistinct blue; the closest line of objects welds itself to the furthest ones; the clear projections of the hills fade away in mystery. A swallow crosses scoring the pale blue. And in the distance, among the shadows, a flooded patch reflects like an enormous mirror the last lights of dusk.]

In his later works, Azorín continues to depict movement within nature and physical setting, but he adopts with greater frequency techniques borrowed from cinematography, photography, and art to capture the range of possibilities for imagining spatiality and to lead the reader to new modes of perceiving her/his surroundings.[8] The lenses of cameras, telescopes, binoculars, or human eyes now focus on new locations or from different perspectives to present multiple opportunities for reconfiguring traditional spaces.

Lenses, Frames, and Changing Perspectives

The advent of more powerful lenses with better resolution allows access to formerly distant spaces while the photographic and movie cameras permit the examination of familiar spaces from new perspectives. The sense of stillness, of a space immobilized and perpetually recorded in stasis, as produced by photographic cameras, contrasts with cinema, which focusses on motion and infuses space with dynamism. Salaün and Robin report that the first Spanish cinematographic projection occurs in Madrid in 1896, only twenty weeks after the Lumière brothers' projection in Paris. The following year the first Spanish film is produced and theaters and coffee houses begin to provide access to a growing public (1991, 151). Other methods of capturing space also bring together contradictory experiences of stasis and motion. In focussing the lens of the binocular or the camera lens, spaces move forward or backward, grow clearer or more blurred, although ultimately, the scene becomes static and framed. Viewing reality through the microscope, telescope, binocular, or camera intersects with the modernist realization that access to reality is mediated, whether through the ocular lens in one's own eye, the lens of a viewing instrument, or the historical and cultural narratives that condition access to the world. Perspectives change within a single individual over time and according to vantage point, and this realization interacts with the new perception of space as framed and demarcated.

Numerous characters in texts of the period make use of binoculars or telescopes to change their spatial relationship with the object of observation. Clarín introduces the spyglass in the hands of Fermín de Pas in *La Regenta* (1884), but in this naturalist novel, it represents access to power, a type of panopticon utilized to control Vetusta's inhabitants (1980a, 15). Modernism's more powerful lenses do not lead to domination but rather, to a greater sense of perplexity or wonder in the presence of an increasingly complex reality. The contrast between the representation of Fermín de Pas and Baroja's Andrés Hurtado clearly reveals the difference. In comparison with Clarín's depiction of Fermín's power to capture even the most intimate details of the subjects he views from the cathedral tower, Baroja portrays Andrés with achromatic lenses of only limited magnification, through which images remain blurred and clouded with iridescence. Félix of *Las cerezas del cementerio* dislikes looking through binoculars because they cut the panorama into multiple small pieces, as if this refusal could salvage a whole, harmonious world that escapes him throughout the narrative. Quintín of Baroja's *La feria de los discretos* observes without comment the fragmented images that move across the spyglass he trains on the Cordoban skyline, but the narrator mentions Jupiter's presence in the sky and both the segmented panorama viewed through the glasses and Jupiter's proximity insinuate new spatial relationships and a sense of multiple perspectives (1946–48, 1:673–74). The narrator of Azorín's *Las confesiones de un pequeño filósofo* focusses his telescope on the moon and studying the craters and frozen seas of this once distant body, feels a flash of poetic inspiration accompanied by incredible longing (1976, 54).

The possibility of imagining life on other planets and across once immense spaces surfaces in a number of texts during the period. I previously commented on Pablo and Inés's discussion of different worlds (Martínez Ruiz 1990, 165) and I also mentioned the attempts to visualize life without jails and judges, poverty and suffering on a distant planet in *Mala hierba* (Baroja 1946–48, 1:507). Alejandro Sawa offers his version of a different order of reality in "Micromegas," a short story that condenses in the title the simultaneity of opposites inherent in a modernist vision of the universe. In a comical inversion of conventional human accounts of the solar system and the place of earth and humanity within it, the text presents Micromegas, an inhabitant of the star Sirius who measures some 100,000 feet in height, and another inhabitant of the planet Saturn who, although dwarfed by Micromegas, is over 900 times larger than a human being. Able to travel across space on sun rays and comet trails, the two visit the earth where they at first assume no life exists because human beings are so tiny they cannot perceive them without microscopes. In a continual process of defamiliarization, Sawa's text challenges the reader's assumptions of space, size, and value by confronting commonly held human standards with other possibilities. Micromegas and his friend from Saturn learn to their surprise that human beings, to whom they refer repeatedly as "thinking atoms," easily presume their importance over other possible life forms despite a highly developed mental capacity that should prevent such egocentric notions. Utilizing new and now imaginable connections across spaces previously conceived as impassable, "Micromegas" questions the order of things as traditionally envisioned and invites the reader to enter a world in which old borders disappear and the human being becomes an atom under the microscope of a larger, more intelligent being. In a never ending *mise en abîme,* one level of existence places another under microscopic examination while the entity in the slide in turn has his/her own microscope trained on another smaller and presumably inferior object of observation.

The term *mise en abîme* originates in 1893 in André Gide's *Journal,* but has its roots in heraldic depiction of a miniature shield placed within an identical larger one and in medieval paintings of subjects standing before a mirror that reflects their faces and suggests an infinitely repeating chain of images.[9] Sylvia Tomasch analyzes the use of framing in medieval painting and drama and the practice by which "boundaries are violated, attention is shifted, and other worlds are seen to be very much parts of this one . . . framing paradoxically fosters a simultaneous sense of distance and contiguity, separation and union . . ." (1985, 81). The medieval play of frame and inner text, painting and mirror proves extremely attractive to the modernist eye and relates to the development of the camera, microscope, and other lens types. Viewed through camera lenses, spaces become marked off, delimited by borders imposed by the field of vision. However, by moving the camera, the frame shifts and new borders with different interior spaces appear. In conjunction with the changed perception of a dynamic atomic/cellular world, the mobile world projected by the movie camera challenges traditional visions of space as stable and beliefs in the weight of the past and of existing institutions, habits of thought, and modes of living.

Modernist art reflects this complex intersection of differing experiences of spatiality in the simultaneous presentation of scene and movement, the construction of frames to delimit space and the exploration of techniques that break them and connect spaces across borders. With great frequency, interior spaces are viewed through a window or door that frame exterior spaces. However, the frame fails to contain the demarcated subject matter and the border breaks or fades just as Rusiñol had utilized afternoon light to efface the lines separating foreground and background. Mirrors or reflective materials often appear within framed scenes to create a space that eliminates the visual border by either revealing in the reflection an object that lies outside the plane of the depicted space or an object that resides within the depicted space but is now visible from two or more angles. Salvador Dalí explores these possibilities in early paintings. His *Aunt Ana Sewing in Cadaqués* (1916–17) shows a seated woman in a room with a plain blue wall punctured by an open window looking across water to a beach and what appear to be houses and trees. The blue interior wall flows into exterior blue sky and water, interrupted only by the white band of the window frame, which in turn blends with clouds visible in the sky. The use of oil on sackcloth as the painting's medium further links the two spaces, providing a visually evident textural continuity that traverses already weakened borders. Dali's *Girl Seen from Behind Looking Out of the Window* (1925) portrays a young woman leaning out a window that overlooks water and distant beach scape. The woman's muted blue and white striped dress blends with the blue and white curtains framing the window, which in turn fade into the blue and white water lying both outside the window and inside the window frame in the water's reflection in the glass of the open panel. The earth tones of the room's walls match the color of the sand and stone in the distant landscape. The unyielding solidity of the frame further dissolves through the overlaying of the wooden molding by filmy curtains that seem to sway in the wind and the glass panes that reflect houses and beach that would otherwise remain outside the viewing field.

From the earliest years of Spanish modernism, the construction and destruction of frames and framed spaces recurs in writers who anticipate Dalí's visual breaking of borders. "Medium," of Baroja's *Vidas sombrías* (1900), relates the story of a first-person narrator and his friend Román who come to believe that Román's sister Angeles possesses evil powers. When the narrator takes a picture of his friend's family, he snaps two different shots in immediate succession and on developing the plates, he and Román discover a black smudge above Angeles's head. Later, printing the copies, they perceive a woman's shadow in the first picture and in the second, the shadow seems to whisper in Angeles's ear. Not only do the plates reveal a figure that was invisible to the eye that focussed the camera and that transforms from one state to another in the brief instant it took to snap the second picture, but the figure escapes the limits of the photographic plate and prints and appears to the narrator in the mirror of his entryway. Mirrors and photos do not just reflect an identical likeness in mimetic reproduction, but project alternative images that stand alongside and in opposition to the framed object in a shifting relationship of self and other. The interest in forms invisible to the human eye that materialize in film negatives and in a problematized reality prefigures Cortázar's later meditations in "Las babas del diablo" (1959).

The preoccupation with frames and their dissolution also surfaces in *La lucha por la vida. La busca* (1903) describes Manuel's discovery of his cousin Leandro's death through a series of mediated accounts. He first overhears old women relating a crime that just occurred and as he approaches to learn more, discovers from a friend that Leandro killed his girl friend Milagros and then committed suicide. Continuing toward the scene of the tragedy, Manuel hears yet another version—that Leandro had killed Milagros when she left him for another man. When Manuel visits the clinic to view the two corpses, he observes the scene through a window in a final representation of a modern mediated reality that remains simultaneously within and beyond his grasp. The window frames the image of the two bodies and the respective grieving families as in a picture. The reader observes Manuel, who stands outside and studies the scene within, removed but also touched by the sight. His divided subjectivity, as spectator and participant, is mirrored in the complicated relationships of the individuals in the room. The space enclosed by the window frame divides evenly down the middle, with two distinct groups surrounding the corpses of the former lovers. The separation of the two clusters of antagonistic relatives is emphasized by the mutual look of hatred of the two mothers as they leave the room. However, the narrative reveals the fissures in this clear demarcation in the introduction of a painting within the painting that dissolves any sense of stable borders. Manuel learns that the examining doctor had discovered a picture of Leandro in a locket hanging from Milagros's neck. The face in the locket replicates in small scale the body lying on the other side of the room and in a dizzying process of interior duplication, the scene communicates the unfathomable mystery of human relations and the continual unraveling of seemingly stable locations. Manuel fails to comprehend the varied, contradictory vignettes, bewildered by the conflicting, incomplete messages they communicate. His confusion increases as he compares the sorrow of his aunt and uncle with a group of girls singing in the street and tries to reconcile the loss of life with the children's vitality. Manuel's youth and inexperience in part explain his inability to come to terms with the rapidly succeeding images and transgression of borders, but his disorientation also represents a characteristic response to the modern experience and the simultaneity of opposing emotions and values within a single space, here graphically represented by the traversing of interior and exterior boundaries.

A more mature Manuel witnesses the death of his cousin Vidal in *Mala hierba* (1904) and again the narrative underscores the instability of borders and the mediation of reality through others. His mental and visual processing of the event unfolds gradually through a number of filters. Manuel, Vidal, and friends have gathered at an outdoor café. Vidal excuses himself and shortly, Manuel and others hear a scream they do not initially attribute to Vidal. In the distance they see two men fighting and from the silhouetted hat recognize Vidal as one of the combatants. As if viewing a movie, the witnesses watch as the two men pull apart, Vidal falls, and his rival makes a series of movements that seem to be knife thrusts. When Manuel and his friends reach the spot, Manuel again watches as others examine the body, turn it over, and declare Vidal dead. Manuel views the body in horror, but more importantly, he fixes on Vidal's open eyes and on the late afternoon sky reflected in them. The depiction of the eyes as a surface that reflects images lying outside or only peripherally in the field of vision transforms the scene into a series of frames within frames, pictures within pictures. Manuel's experience of his cousin's death occurs through multiple mediations that provide varied viewing positions and continuously refigure the observed events and the viewer's responses.

Antonio Machado also uses reflective surfaces to open enclosed spaces to the outside and contrast the confining sense of enclosure to a more fluid movement across borders. In the previously commented "El viajero," the exterior is doubly visible through the fogged window panes and also in the reflection of the mirror hanging on the wall. These two images of the garden on a fall afternoon bring nature into the dark parlor to contrast with the portrait of the male ancestor and the rigid patriarchal system he represents. The frame of the portrait remains solidly in place and allows for no passage across the border to new or different spaces. In contrast, the mirror and glass open to other realities that they reveal as diverse and changing. "El limonero lánguido suspende" further exploits the reflected image to reimagine reality and provide alternative visions. The poetic speaker blends the present with memory and the material form of a lemon tree with its reflection in the fountain waters, blurring the lines that mark where past and reflection end and present and lemon tree commence. In processing multiple textual levels, the reader envisions an older poetic speaker remembering a younger self in a courtyard surrounded by lemon trees that are reflected in water. It is March and the trees have not yet flowered or borne fruit, but the reflection in the water reveals golden lemons to the young remembered self, who thrusts his hands in the water to grasp the fruit. Although the poem does not explicitly describe the disruption of the reflection caused by the introduction of the hands in the water, for the reader the mental image of the ripples that propagate across the surface of the fountain further multiplies the lemon branches reflected in the water and adds yet another level to the succession of images (1951, 21–22). In contrast to the sense of enclosure and stasis produced by the depiction of a fountain in the silent courtyard, which a reader familiar with Southern Spain envisions as a walled, contained space, the water and reflection open to the sky, the past, and a dreamed future. The technique of *mise en abîme* constructs and then erases boundaries between levels and the use of aquatic reflection enhances the sense of temporal-spatial fluidity and mobility.

Azorín borrows from science, art, photography, and cinema to construct and then deconstruct spaces in *Castilla.* As mentioned earlier, Ortega y Gasset's "Azorín: Los primores de lo vulgar" (1916) has set the pattern for subsequent readings and studies of this particular work and of Azorín's publications.[10] It emphasizes repetition and stasis in Azorín's writings in order to insinuate and occasionally express contrast with an active, combative Ortega, who stands ready to provide a different kind of leadership. The Ortegan text speaker refers to an aesthetic process of petrification, a lack of vitality in Azorín (1965, 2:174) and to the preference for the minuscule and humble in contrast with Ortega's stated preference for heroism and dynamism. Ortega expresses his own divided response to the Spanish national present, alternately envisioning an active, heroic role as inspired by the monastery at El Escorial, where he situates the composition of his study, and a more discouraged and passive attitude that focusses on an irretrievably decayed Spain. However, he presumes a single, fixed stance on Azorín's part, with invariable emphasis on inertia, repetition, and the past, failing to perceive the subtle strategies developed in Azorín's text to prompt the reader to adopt new modes of perceiving and responding to reality. Stephen Kern points to the link between imperial ambition and the notion that small is bad and big is good. He quotes the German geographer Friedrich Ratzel who equates smallness of land mass with inferior stages of culture (1983, 224). Azorín's concentration on detail and miniature rejects such a vision, but it does not fall into immobility. *Castilla* eschews grand narratives of action and political activity to introduce change in myriad small narratives. Through varied techniques, it requires the reader to abandon old habits of perception and move rapidly through a variety of new, sometimes contradictory perspectives to create a dynamic collage that continually changes shape and alters its borders. The volume's title suggests that the text proposes a portrait of Castile, but the prologue immediately clarifies that it aims only to capture a particle of the region's spirit. The work's composition, consisting of fourteen unrelated short texts, adds to the sense of a fragmentary depiction rather than a large, comprehensive canvas. *Castilla's* focalization shifts continually, at times adopting the framed canvas of the painter, at others the moving camera of cinema or the fixed lens of the photographic camera, but invariably calling attention to shifting perspectives and the insufficiency of any single mode of visualization to apprehend reality, normalizing for the reader the experience of simultaneous, multiple viewing positions.

The opening text, "Los ferrocarriles," underscores the presence of new modes of viewing by references to instructions given to early travelers to fix their gaze on distant objects rather than on the track edges, which will disappear in a blur and make the passenger dizzy. The narrator of "Ventas, posadas y fondas" assumes the mobile position of the movie camera, inviting the reader to accompany him on his spatial explorations of different Spanish inns as depicted by the writers Angel Saavedra, Galdós, and Clarín. The doubly mediated reconstruction of the inns, first through antecedent writers and then the present narrative, finds a parallel in the narrator's divided subjectivity, as evidenced by the alternating use of first person plural and first person singular. The plural form joins narrator and reader in a common viewing stance; the text speaker guides the reader through the various inns, prodding him/her along when he states "No nos detengamos aquí; pasemos adelante; caminemos por un ancho, seco y arenoso ramblizo" [Let's not stop here, let's move along; let's walk through the wide, dry and sandy stream bed] (1958, 39) or forcing him/her to go to sleep after arriving late and wait until the next morning to examine the inn (43–44). Using the "we" form, the speaker criticizes the noisy Spanish inns and comments that a nation's sensitivity and thus, degree of civilization, is measured by the level of intolerance to noise. However, on two occasions the first person singular intrudes to introduce a second, nostalgic perspective: "¡Oh fonditas destartaladas, ruidosas, de mi vieja España!" [Oh dilapidated, noisy inns of my old Spain!] (45). In the second incidence, the speaker again alludes with a certain fondness to these traditional sites, but slightly changes the wording: "¡Oh ventas, posadas y fonditas estruendosas y sórdidas, de mi vieja España!" [Oh, noisy and sordid country inns and lodging houses of my old Spain!] (46). The combination of the negatively charged "noisy" and "sordid" with the first person possessive and clearly stated affection combines two different perspectives, bringing together the desire for modernization and the regret at the loss of this colorful past. The two positions exist side by side, in a relationship of covalence.

"La catedral" combines varied modes of perception to invert conventional definitions of change and permanence. In this text, Virgil's verses and their translation by Fray Luis de León persist unaltered across the centuries while the stone cathedral acquires dynamic character, undergoing constant alteration through redesigns and additions, but also changing according to the time of day, season of the year, and eroding forces of the wind and weather. The photograph of the church taken by Laurent in 1870 now appears yellowed and faded, adding yet another facet to the varied images of the structure. "El mar" introduces complex visual and narrative techniques to explore diverse perspectives and multiple visions of Castile. In this text, access to the Castilian landscape takes place through a magic mirror or photographic negative that projects the opposite of the original, not just a reverse image in the sense of directionality but a completely different portrayal that stands in opposition to the original. Castile here is defined by what it is not, by the sea that surrounds Spain, but from which the nation's landlocked center remains distant. In a continual construction and destruction of borders and frames, "El mar" places the sea in the very center of a book entitled *Castilla.* The speaker reiterates frequently that Castile cannot see the ocean and then proceeds to list the beaches, blue waters, tidal changes and sea gulls that the region cannot enjoy. The focalization shifts in several different senses, moving from daylight to nocturnal representation and then from the Mediterranean to the Atlantic. The waters forming the geographic borders of the Spanish nation here appear enclosed in the very center of a text that proposes to define landlocked Castile. In an inversion of borders and centers, the reader is led across the different land masses to the diverse bodies of water that lie beyond Castile's field of vision and outside the terrestrial national borders. "El mar" represents a conceptual *mise en abîme,* with the visual invocation of the seas that both surround the nation of which Castile is the center and inhere within Castile as the void that defines her. A final duplication of the play of frame and interior, sea and land, appears in the closing paragraph, where the speaker guides the reader back from the distant coasts to the old Castilian city from which the journey began at the start of the text. There, from an upper floor of a Castilian home, framed by a window, the speaker presents the arid, dusty meseta and reminds the reader once again that Castile cannot see the sea. The play of presence and absence continues in this closing mention of the absent sea and the framing of the landscape through the window communicates to the reader that frames and borders are constructed and can easily be traversed and redefined through the adoption of new and changing visual stances.

"Lo fatal" and "La fragancia del vaso" overwrite classical Spanish texts to celebrate a redefined literary canon. "Lo fatal" recreates the episode of *El Lazarillo de Tormes* in which Lazarillo shares a few crumbs of dried bread with his impoverished but noble master. In the second segment of the text, a fictional reinvention now finds the noble master comfortably ensconced in a restored house, saved by inherited fortune but plagued by digestive problems. The text further amends the classical version with allusions to a sonnet by Góngora and a portrait by El Greco that purportedly depict the same gentleman, thus offering additional vantage points from which to reconstruct his likeness. The reader's perspective moves through time and space, poetry, prose, and visual art, to build a composite that is neither complete nor definitive. "La fragancia del vaso" retells Cervantes's *La ilustre fregona,* but this version continues into Costanza's adult life, once again exemplifying the principles of repetition and change that govern *Castilla.* In describing Costanza's failed attempt to recapture the excitement of life as a young servant in a busy inn, in contrast to her present comfortable but monotonous upper-class provincial life, "La fragancia del vaso" communicates the irretrievability of the past, the fragility of memory, and the inevitable revision of what appeared to be a fixed narrative. Costanza cannot go back to once familiar spaces; no one she remembers remains at the inn except for an old woman who is now deaf and blind and has no means to indicate whether she retains a memory of the young servant. In contrast with Ortega's view that *Castilla* and Azorín in general induce the reader to feel the present as if past (1965, 2:189), "La fragancia del vaso" presents the past as definitively other.

"Flauta en la noche" combines cinematographic and theatrical techniques to construct different modes of viewing and capturing space. The text contains three scenes dated 1820, 1870, and 1900, in each of which several characters appear as if on stage or in a series of paintings placed in a continuum. The epigraph from Guillén de Castro's play *Las mocedades del Cid* reenforces the sense of dramatic set, but the incorporation of the cinematographic traveling shot introduces a different focalization. The speaker uses the first person plural to create a sense that the reader accompanies him as he moves with the camera up the hill in a horse-drawn coach, enters the town, and proceeds to a particular house and room. The importance and limitations of viewing stances receive great emphasis in two final texts. "Una lucecita roja" describes a house high on a mountain top and a train in the valley from a variety of temporal-spatial perspectives. In the first and third vignettes, the house appears empty and abandoned, while in the second it is inhabited and full of life. Viewed from above, the activity in the valley seems to stand still and the train whistle sounds like a muffled murmur. The landscapes and noises change according to the observer's distance and no single viewpoint captures a complete picture. Omissions and distortions exist in each spatial depiction, just as the barely delineated story of the individuals described unfolds with gaps and impenetrable silences. The reader can no more reconstruct the "true" story of the man, woman, and child who occupy the mountain house in the middle segment than she/he can capture the totality of the spatial surroundings. To rest in a single viewing position and use a single ocular instrument produces a limited, partial vision of reality.

Castilla relies on varied visual and discursive modes to capture a changing, multifaceted reality. Still camera, painting, movie camera, binocular, bird's eye view, closeup, traveling shot, theatrical scene, combine to offer restricted access to a complex temporal and spatial reality and urge the reader to adopt multiple lenses in the effort to apprehend the surrounding world. The final text reveals that visual approximations in and of themselves remain incomplete and must join with other senses. "La casa cerrada" describes the return of a blind man to his childhood home and his attempts to reconstruct through memory, smell, sound, and touch the sites of his previous life. His verbal descriptions of the town and of the various rooms of his home communicate to the reader visual images of the surroundings. The reader, like the blind character, must rely on recollection, imagination, multiple senses and perspectives, and in both cases reality is mediated through words, memories, previously viewed spaces, and current perspective. *Castilla* induces the reader to explore a variety of traditional and modern viewing and reading modes and to cycle through them in a rapid exchange of perspectives that strives to capture a changing, multifaceted reality. The world depicted by Azorín is neither petrified nor uniformly locked in the past. Rather, it resides alternately in different temporal and spatial zones and the method of accessing it similarly traverses a wide range of historical and modern techniques for apprehending an unstable and invariably mediated reality.

Francisco Villaespesa shares with other modernists an interest in exploring new spaces and reconfiguring traditional ones. "En la alcoba" from *Baladas de cetrería* (1916) provides an interesting adaptation of the cinematographic "cut," combined with ekphrastic intertextuality. The sonnet's opening stanza describes a bedroom, bed, wash basin, four chairs, petroleum light and the smell of soaps, perfume, and cigarettes. The following quartet depicts a woman undressing, indirectly revealing that she makes her living as a prostitute. The two stanzas evoke many contemporary paintings of naked prostitutes, such as Manet's *Olympia.* The closing tercets shift focus to the poetic speaker-observer who describes himself as pensive, with head resting on hand, and imagining a very different scene of an anatomy student dissecting a cadaver. This second representation calls to mind Rembrandt's famous paintings of the anatomy lesson or perhaps a more recent realist canvas. The verbal replication of the movie cut in the rapid shift from the bedroom scene to the laboratory reflects the instability of the modernist perspective and the rapid crossing of frames and borders. "Espirales de Kif" in *Torre de marfil* (1910) ventures into new spaces through the influence of drugs, describing a shadowy world behind a sort of curtain that once again dissolves the defining lines that separate objects and background, silhouette and inner or outer spaces. Villaespesa writes that he abhors the straight line and the always invariable desert horizon (1954, 1:902) and in his drug-inspired poems, he discovers a world in which this traditional geometry disappears.

Valle-Inclán's *La pipa de Kif* (1919) echoes Villaespesa's "Espirales de Kif," but anticipates more boldly the surrealistic spaces of Federico García Lorca. The depiction of gypsies, violent crime, the Civil Guard, and a moonlit tavern with a cat lying in wait as well as the mix of odd colors and unusual images create a strange new space in "Marina norteña": "Con la tristeza de la tarde muerde / una lima de acero. De la fragua / brotan las chispas. Tiene una luz verde / Ante la puerta, la cortina de agua" [With the sadness of the afternoon dies / A steel file. From the forge / the sparks gush forth. The curtain of water / Has a green light in front of the door] (1919, 34). "Rosa de sanatorio" depicts the effects of chloroform on the poetic speaker, who describes himself floating in an unfamiliar space that he likens to the in-between zone of a river dividing two borders. The influence of hashish contributes to mystical experiences in *La lámpara maravillosa* (1916) and to a new communion with nature (1974, 526). In Valle-Inclán's later works, nature and space transmute to new forms before the eyes of the beholder, either under the influence of drugs or the rapidly changing social and physical world of the *esperpento.*

Valle-Inclán's earlier *modernista* works at first blush might seem to present a more uniform and static space but, as in Azorín, multiple temporalities and spaces coexist and the presence of *ekphrasis* and *mise en abîme* alongside the ironic / parodic smile of Bradomín introduce a complex play of stasis and movement. Many scenes in the *Sonatas* are explicitly linked with famous paintings, while others appear as if frozen in a sort of verbal canvas. *Sonata de primavera* compares the profile of the dying Monsignor Gaetani to a reclined statue and likens the Princess Gaetani to Rubens's portrait of María de Medici. On repeated occasions, the first-person narrator invokes classical paintings and religious statuary to describe the princesses and the aristocratic ambience of the palace. The textual world seems frozen in a remote past, a remnant of the Renaissance with no real connection to the modern world. In this regard, the entire novel and the other *Sonatas* assume the form of a painting with an ornate frame that closes if off from the outside, from change and modernity. However, Bradomín's ironic posture continually punctures the otherwise uniform textual world and inserts a second, contrasting discourse that requires the reader to constantly readjust her/his response. Bradomín's cynical opinions regarding the purity of women in *Sonata de primavera* (14) stand in opposition to his portrait of the five virginal princesses and his anticlerical statements and religious indifference introduce a note of disharmony in the monochrome depiction of the church, its dignitaries, and adherents. His assertion that the oldest princess was the only love of his life conflicts with his statements at other points in the text regarding previous and subsequent loves and further contradicts the narratives related in *Sonata de estío* and *Sonata de otoño,* which appeared during the two previous years, 1902 and 1903. Such assertions, in combination with Bradomín's evident propensity for self-invention, clearly signal that events, characters, and locations depicted in the novel and filtered through Bradomín's first-person narration occupy a constantly changing middle range, oscillating between the stylized world depicted through the ekphrastic, static representation and a more modern, ironic stance that questions the permanence of traditional values and the classical world. Mediated through Bradomín's ironic lens, the classical model persists, but alongside a deformed image that transforms it. The presumed stasis of the framed canvas acquires dynamism as it transmutes in parodic duplication. Like medieval paintings that reveal a slightly distorted image of subjects as reflected in the curved mirror, both through the normal directional inversion and the curvature of the reflecting surface, the characters and scenes constructed in the *Sonatas* through comparisons to visual and statuary art undergo perceptible deformation.

In the utilization of multiple viewing techniques for the reconstruction of space, modernist writers and painters propel readers and viewers to explore new modes of access to reality and to construct a multi-perspectivist vision that takes into account the varied, changing faces of the world in which they live. Borrowing from photographic, cinematographic, traditional and modern painting techniques, and scientific advances in microscopes and other lens technology, Spanish modernists portray landscape and physical spaces as simultaneously dynamic and static, familiar and alien, and place the viewing subject in a mobile stance that enters into a continually changing relationship with the object of perception according to the angle of view, the instrument of vision, and a range of other factors that mediate access. New spaces facilitate and encourage a reconceptualization of individual and collective interaction with the surrounding world.

Trains, Planes, Theaters, and Cabarets: Sites for Cross-Cultural Communication

Modernity not only institutes new instruments for viewing physical reality and spatiality, but also creates new spaces for living. Previously non-existent public areas, accessible to individuals of different social classes and genders, allow for more prolonged and intimate contact between groups that had formerly existed in relative isolation. Cars, trains, steamships, and planes accelerate contact with distant parts of the globe or country and enable communication between nations and racial and ethnic groups inconceivable in previous historical periods. The train, ocean liner, and trolley produce contact between passengers who suddenly find themselves enclosed with strangers in a shared, semi-private space over prolonged periods of time. The train also facilitates greater mobility for theatrical troupes and other entertainers and improved roads enable increased touring on the part of circuses and portable performances. In cities and larger towns, the cinema joins conventional theater as a popular pastime and the theater itself undergoes transformation with the rise of the cabaret singer and the *género chico,* ranging from one act plays to short or full length operettas with popular themes in the *zarzuela.* Salaün and Robin write that, between 1887 and 1920, twenty of Madrid's theaters devote themselves fully or partially to this kind of theater (1991, 134). Accessible to all classes, theaters specializing in *género chico,* cabarets, and dance halls bring together members of diverse social groups to hear a more popular music and discourse that breaks with the language and values of bourgeois nineteenth-century drama.

Train travel provides a new mobility for women and facilitates interactions between strangers who share the same space for extended periods of time. Azorín registers the general concern for solitary women travelers in his opening essay in *Castilla* and quotes Modesto Lafuente's observations that the lone female passenger who travels unmolested amidst men on a Belgian train could not expect the same respect in Spain (1958, 17). In the early days, Spanish train cars had special sections for women traveling alone but, as Leopoldo Alas discloses in "Supercheria," the possibilities for error were great. Nicolás Serrano, the story's protagonist, enters what he assumes to be a non-smoking car, but at a later stop in the dark of night a nun enters the same compartment, thinking it reserved for women travelers. In a process that reveals the increased proximity of individuals who in previous spatial configurations would never come into close contact, the nun grows increasingly uncomfortable with sharing space with what she comes to realize is a man. The intimacy of the train compartment and rapidity of new encounters receives further emphasis through the description of the quick succession of events occurring while Serrano repeatedly cat naps: the nun's exit, the arrival of Catalina—a member of a traveling hypnosis and mind-reading show, Catalina's study of Serrano's open journal while he dozes, and her departure. Serrano's subsequent reencounter with Catalina and her use of the knowledge acquired from the journal to demonstrate her mind-reading powers constitute an unlikely chain of events that occurs precisely because of the new space for human interaction provided by train car design and the opportunities it presents for entering the private sphere of another's life.

Antonio Machado also registers the coincidence of a nun traveling alone in the company of strange men in "En tren" (1917, 138–40) and many writers comment on the new community created within the train compartment. The narrator of Azorín's *Los pueblos* (1905) finds himself surrounded by the children of a fellow passenger in a train compartment and, listening to them sing and observing their charm, feels contented with life. Antonio Azorín's train departure from Madrid in *La voluntad* (1902) depicts the scene as a mix of disparate sensorial impressions and rapid motion. The narrative describes fragments of intimate farewells that interweave with train whistles and reports on the varied occupants of a third-class car: two farmers, a woman and her children, a blind singing beggar, and the cultured but impoverished protagonist. Pérez de Ayala creates a very different kind of community in *Tinieblas en las cumbres* when he describes the train excursion of a group of prostitutes and bourgeois men to view an eclipse from a mountaintop. The train cars become the scene for sexual interludes that unsuspecting fellow travelers interrupt to their horror. Emilia Pardo Bazán reveals the new intimacy, the fragmentary nature of this modern contact, and the growing mobility of women in "Sud-Exprés," originally published in *El Imparcial* in 1902 and later in the 1909 collection of the story's title. The action takes place aboard a luxury train en route to Paris. Although Pardo Bazán often makes use of ungendered or male narrators, in this text the narrator's facial veil suggests a feminine focalization. The introduction of a solitary female traveler who observes the actions of her fellow passengers reflects the freedom of movement facilitated by train travel, which is in turn duplicated on the level of plot. From behind her veil, the narrator studies what she assumes are newlyweds enjoying an elegant packed luncheon, intimate conversation, and physical caresses. She notices that at various points the young woman leaves to visit the adjoining compartment and exchange looks with a second young man who feigns sleep. At one point, after sending the presumed husband to look for a bag that the narrator saw the woman hide under the seat, the supposed wife runs to the next compartment and exchanges a passionate embrace with the second man. She then returns to her seat, awaits the arrival of her "husband," and continues the romantic luncheon and affectionate conversation until arriving in Paris, where the duo disembark arm in arm. The narrator offers no explanation, simply presenting the reader with a first-hand account of an intimate interlude that remains unfinished and enigmatic, in typical modernist fashion.

Concha Espina compares the new relationship facilitated by modern train travel with traditional spaces in *La esfinge maragata* (1914). The female protagonist and her paternal grandmother travel by rail from northern Spain, where Mariflor was born and raised on the coast, to the Maragatan village of her father's family. The two women have fallen asleep and the narrative describes them as reclining, in a position they would assume in the privacy of their bedroom. When Rogelio Terán enters the compartment, his examination of Mariflor follows the pattern of the male gaze, fixing his eyes first on her face, which he breaks into individual features, and then moving down to her neck, where his fascination with a red coral necklace insinuates his erotic desire. As she awakens, Mariflor senses the unusual intimacy of the encounter and quickly sits up, adopting a more controlled composure, blushing from embarrassment and avoiding Rogelio's eyes (1972, 1:242–43). The initial discomfort fades quickly and the two young passengers proceed to relate their respective life histories, prompted by the sense of community that the train encourages. The grandmother remains aloof and suspicious and Rogelio and Mariflor regress to a traditional restraint each time the train arrives at a station, where the magic of new communities breaks down: “Cuando éste se detuvo en la estación de Torre, quedó rota de nuevo aquella intimidad, imperativa y fuerte, que a sus mismos mantenedores causaba confusión y asombro” [When it (the train) stopped in the station at Torre, that new intimacy was again broken. Imposing and strong, it caused confusion and surprise in those who experienced it] (1:248).

The delicate nature of this modern space and the difference between male and female experiences of modernity and spatiality constitute a major theme of the novel. Rogelio’s literary ambitions, his references to Valle-Inclán’s *Sonatas* and *Flor de santidad,* and his mention of earlier travels through Maragatería on horseback in the company of other men link him to masculine activities and values. Rogelio had previously visited the mountains, avoiding the Maragatan plains and the sad, poor villages where women remain to work the fields while their men emigrate to Madrid or Argentina. Rogelio and those who share his experiences remain ignorant of the reality of these inner female spaces and enclosures. When Mariflor leaves the train, she enters a different world, in which time has stopped and women live imprisoned, without men but still controlled by their rules. Like Azorín in *Castilla,* Espina defines Maragatería by the absence of water and often compares the vast plains to the sea in a reminder of the void that constitutes its essence. She also replicates the Azorinian observation that the intrahistorical present does not represent an eternal spirit; rather, it results from mismanagement and modern economic failures. The text alludes to the region’s thriving economy under the Moors, when water was plentiful and boats, trees, and flowers filled the landscape (1972, 1:252). The home of Mariflor’s grandmother and aunt speaks to even more recent wealth, which has disappeared only in the past generation, forcing Mariflor’s uncle and father to emigrate. Despite the women’s absolute control of their home and fields, except for a brief period in August when the men return, the female population has internalized patriarchal laws and imposes them without question.

The description of the August celebration of the Feast of the Assumption underscores male authority. The women have tilled the fields, planted, weeded, and harvested, and now they welcome the returning men with a festive meal and subservient inquiries as to their desires and needs. They address their husbands by the formal, respectful *vos* and during the night, when married and engaged couples and families sleep in the open air, the women continue to concern themselves with their men's wellbeing, as exemplified by the timid query of one Maragatan woman who addresses her husband as sir and asks if he is comfortable: "—¿Estades bien, señor?" (1972, 1:348). At this same moment, Mariflor remembers her train journey with Rogelio and the contrast between the two spaces illustrates the difference between a modern world in which equality and openness show promise for future development and a traditional world in which women, even in open fields under expansive skies, remain imprisoned within patriarchy. Espina does not entirely preclude the possibilities that Mariflor's independence and strength of character, derived from her previous education and experience, may leave a mark on the Maragatan landscape. The ambivalent ending allows for some hope of change, albeit modest, and throughout the novel, the construction of alternative spaces that stand in opposition to traditional control and enclosure offer evidence of a different, more promising vision. Feminist criticism early took note of the motifs of flight and enclosed spaces to contrast freedom and confinement in writing by women. Espina utilizes the flight theme, but rather than compare enclosed and open space, she contrasts proximity with nature with culturally constructed locations. She particularly focusses on two groups of birds that play a significant role in village life and underscores the imbalance between a hierarchical human society and an egalitarian animal world. From the attic of the deteriorating family home, Mariflor delights in views of the village roof scape, especially noting the stork nest on the church tower. In the pigeon loft, she enjoys the play of light and shadow and the noise and closeness of the birds. Mariflor senses the freedom and natural rhythms of the doves and observes that her cousin Olalla, normally plain with scarf-covered braids, looks beautiful and uninhibited with a dove feather in her exposed hair. When Mariflor urges her cousin to leave her hair down and uncovered, Olalla refuses because it is not local custom (1:260–61).

The doves and storks represent a balance between freedom and commitment that is absent in the regional and national social structures. The doves leave the coop but return at the end of the day and the storks, who mate for life, share the responsibilities of annually rebuilding the nest and raising the young. By contrast, the women of *La esfinge maragata* have no freedom and the men share none of the responsibility. Husbands and fathers emigrate, the priest awaits a new and better assignment, and Rogelio, described as a modernist Quijote (1972, 1:282), courts Mariflor, promises to marry her, and then breaks off their engagement when the responsibility appears too onerous. Like his own father, who abandoned his family, Rogelio fears and avoids commitment. As he leaves the village, the doves from Mariflor's family coop fly over his head, placing his own inconstancy in contrast with their fidelity. The isolated world of Maragatería can expect little from external sources but change, albeit slowly, comes to the region through female agents. Mariflor herself, with her strength and sensitivity, introduces an exotic note that becomes more subdued, but does not disappear. Her forthright character astonishes and attracts the rich Maragatan cousin whom she eventually agrees to marry in order to save her family from poverty. The train that brought her from the coast and that carries the emigrating men to the port cities from which they leave for America also brings contacts with the outside that slowly leave their mark on local society. A traveling circus visits and exposes the naive villagers to a magician and to a reading of a poem that deeply affects Mariflor and her sensitive cousin Marinela. Throughout the text, various characters confuse Marinela and Mariflor and the similarity of their names and demeanor encourages the conflation of the two young women. Both fall in love with Rogelio and both dream of a life outside the confined Maragatan social structure. Mariflor brings her aspirations for change with her from another place and culture, while Marinela comes to them from within and together, they move toward the creation of new spaces, made for and by women, which aspire to a balance of flight and commitment.

Trains, boats, trolleys and other forms of modern transport also create new links and separations between the passengers traveling inside and the places and peoples they pass in their rapid transit. A number of Barojan texts illustrate the varied possibilities of distance and proximity made possible in modernity. The text speaker of "La venta" from *Tablado de Arlequín* (1904) compares train travelers with those who voyage by foot or in horse-drawn coach and imagines them as two distinct populations that meet only in a passing gesture of greeting through a train window or from a distant building or road. "Lo desconocido" from *Vidas sombrías* (1900) describes a woman who travels through a changing landscape, arrives at a town, and considers leaving the train to start her life anew in a different place. Although she lacks the courage to follow her impulse, the possibility for such a radical personal and geographical relocation provides a comfortable escape valve from the pressures of modern life. Ciro Bayo responds affirmatively to the call to adventure in *El lazarillo español* (1911), in which he hops trains and follows the railroad tracks in his exploration of different Spanish regions. Trains and steamships facilitate a new form of tourism that makes it possible to cover lengthy distances in a short period of time. Women writers are especially gratified at the freedom of movement and cultivate travel literature with pleasure. Sofía Casanova, Emilia Pardo Bazán, Carmen de Burgos, and Concha Espina produce books about their travels through Europe or America. The rise of the tourist industry creates a new demand for hotels and these in turn create new spaces for the production of community across national and linguistic barriers. Baroja writes about life in hotels and the casual and more intimate relationships that occur in these modern, international spaces in *César o nada, El mundo es ansí, La ciudad de la niebla,* and *Los últimos románticos.*

Concert halls and theaters also allow for new communication across class, national, and gender barriers. Jacinto Benavente explores the liberating spaces of the circus, music hall, and tourist attraction in various plays. *La noche del sábado* (1903) takes place in a resort town located between France and Italy where individuals of diverse social classes, national origins, and political and economic ambitions come together in an intimacy not possible in their respective home territories. The connotations of midnight and bewitching hour contained in the title introduce a transgressive note that the drama exploits in cross-class, cross-cultural encounters. Nobles, circus performers, artists, models, poor and ambitious social climbers, degenerates, and drunken and defeated has-beens all come together in a world where origin matters less than talent and new fortunes and social reputations rise and fall with incredible rapidity. The Countess Rinaldi enters into business dealings and a sexual liaison with an elephant trainer, Prince Florencio surrounds himself with ambitious and poor individuals whom he enjoys corrupting and sadistically manipulating, and Imperia, the street urchin from Rome, rises to become the mistress and power behind the throne of the King of Suabia. Benavente's *La fuerza bruta* (1908) revolves around a group of circus performers of different nationalities and again creates a space where rapid change is the norm.

Few texts of the period deal with the airplane, which remains largely outside the experience of all but a few individuals until after World War I. Unamuno compares the plane to Clavileño, the flying horse of the *Quijote,* and also to a wooden horse that has miraculously escaped the confinement of the merry-go-round in "Al aeroplano" (1958, 15:382). Both images link this new mode of transportation to fantasy and freedom. Concha Espina similarly equates the airplane with liberation in "Talín," a story from *Ruecas de marfil* (1917) about a young woman whose search for independence finally eludes social controls in a suicidal airplane flight. The young protagonist, nicknamed Talín after a wild mountain canary, enjoyed freedom as a child in part because her mother has died and her father spoils her, but also because social control and appearances have less import in a small village of poor farmers and herders. Espina's text symbolically introduces the omnipresence of patriarchy in the narration of the encounter between the young girl, dressed in red, and a bull. In her effort to escape, Talín climbs a wall and falls, breaking her foot. The color of the dress connotes a transgressive energy that soon submits to social regulation. A female folk healer recommends faith and ointments, while a male doctor insists on absolute quiet. His advice prevails and in response to his treatment, Talín eventually becomes lame and housebound. In an effort to find a cure, the family moves to Santander where Talín, now able to walk with crutches, works at home as a seamstress. Always looking through the window to the sea and the sky, she hungers for the mobility and freedom (that she associates with these two spaces and that she strives to recover) when she convinces a young pilot to take her flying. Again wearing a red dress, she seeks liberation from her physical and gendered confinement. Shouting her love for the pilot, fully aware that her social class and physical deformity preclude their relationship, she jumps from the plane in a gesture of agency and arrogation of freedom. The text strongly suggests suicide, but leaves the ending open to the reader's interpretation. However, the final paragraph describes an opening in the clouds and the appearance of the sun as if blessing a sacrificial altar, valorizing Talín's choice.

The feminist motif of flight acquires new meaning in the context of aviation and combines with the theme of liberation through suicide, which appears in such modernist women writers as Virginia Woolf, to imagine a different response to spatial and social limitations. Espina joins other Spanish modernists such as Unamuno, Baroja, Miró, Ciro Bayo, and Benavente, who perceive the restrictions, but also highlight the emancipatory potency of new spaces and spatial organization. During modernism, innovative technologies change the individual's relationship with her / his surroundings and also create new locations in which the individual relates to nature and other human beings in a changing relationship. The train, boat, trolley, automobile, and airplane enable a different interaction between individuals who travel within them and a changed relationship with the world outside. Improved modes of transportation allow for greater mobility and communication between city and country and small town and large urban areas increases considerably. Expanding internal markets and a changing demand for labor also lead to greater contact between the urban and rural areas of the nation and contribute to increased commerce between these two zones. The city provides novel ways of experiencing modernity and contributes new locations for human interaction. Spanish modernist texts reflect this transformed spatiality and help to expose the urban, provincial, and rural reader to new forms of living in the world and new ways of being.

Cities, Towns, and Urban Places

Critics often characterize writers of late nineteenth and early twentieth century Spanish literature as antagonistic to modern technology and urban life. Graham and Labanyi assert that the "response of most modernists to modernization . . . was one of trauma and loss" (1995, 14) and Macklin traces the beginnings of modernist narrative to a rejection of urban culture in Unamuno's *Paz en la guerra* and Galdós's *Misericordia* (1993, 202). Comparing the reaction of Spanish American and Spanish writers to Paris at the turn of the century, Luis Fernández Cifuentes posits a Spanish rejection of the French capital and cites their experience of the city as the cause of their affection for rural landscapes (1997, 107–8). The rise of the city and the problems it created on social and individual levels preoccupy modernist writers and constitute a major focus of attention in their works. Their response to urbanization is characteristically multi-faceted with both a recognition of the possibilities for national and individual development inherent in urban life and of the hazards for collective and personal evolution.

Men and women writers alike reflect on the advantages and dangers of the urban experience, but women generally downplay the disadvantages to highlight enhanced possibilities for liberation and personal development. Carmen de Burgos expresses her preference for the modern city even in the case of Rome, where the modern Italian capital appeals to her more than the Rome of the past. Her story "Los negociantes de la Puerta del Sol," published in 1919 in *La novela corta,* describes the attraction exerted by a bustling, noisy downtown Madrid on don Justo, a recent arrival who has fled the boredom of provincial life. His family, particularly his daughter Anita, enjoys walking the city streets and the attention of young men of different classes. The narrative underscores the social mobility, excitement, and freedom available to men and women in the city, describing Justo's attempts to establish himself as a businessman and his final success as a street vendor. Traditional class prejudices give way as he happily takes on a new identity in the fluid society of the urban world. Burgos's *El hombre negro* (1915) offers a less optimistic account, but it too portrays the city as a place of opportunity for women, as Michael Ugarte has previously shown (1996, 102). The narrative blames provincial social formation for the female protagonist's lack of education and exposure, which prevents her from discerning the duplicity behind the pleasant mask of her suitor and then husband Bernardo. In Madrid, Bernardo spends her modest inheritance, pawns her jewelry, and uses her physical beauty to attract other men for his shady enterprises. Through her exposure to city life, Elvira comes to understand her husband's business ventures and acquires the courage to denounce him in court. Urban society facilitates female agency in contrast to provincial passivity and although Elvira must remain legally married to her husband in a Spain without divorce, her public and legally sanctioned separation stands as a demonstration of the growing power of women in an urban society that opens new spaces for female experience and growth.

While male writers betray a less uniform response to urban life, in all cases the traditional dichotomy of city versus country cedes to a more nuanced relationship between city, large and small towns, and country. Commutation between city and country becomes increasingly possible with a resultant reciprocal influence between the two spaces. Modernist writers are city dwellers and this experience permanently marks their perspective, making it impossible for them to see the country without comparing it to the city and vice versa. In the general pattern of encounters across borders, Spanish modernism breaks down divisions between rural and urban Spain both by exposing the urban reader to rural values and spaces through the literary recreation of the rural world and by discovering rural spaces within the city. Whereas the realist / naturalist paradigm portrayed the city and country as antagonists in the struggle for the national soul, modernist representations underscore the interconnections of city and country.

Realism commences with Fernán Caballero's 1849 indictment of urban corruption in *La Gaviota* and condemnation of the city continues through Pereda's depiction of moral dissolution in the Madrid of *Pedro Sánchez* (1883) and Coloma's similar portrayal of the capital in *Pequeñeces* (1890). Galdós and Pardo Bazán invert the terms to paint a regressive rural society in *Doña Perfecta* and *Los Pazos de Ulloa,* but they continue to represent urban and rural locations as oppositional and impervious to reciprocal impact in their realist and naturalist writing. In later works, both Galdós and Pardo Bazán adopt a more complex vision, with frequent displacement from city to country and back to city in a movement of mutual contact and influence. Pardo Bazán's novels and short stories of the 1890s through the end of her writing career in 1920 alternately study urban and rural spaces as sites where the struggle for female and human development plays itself out with similarities and differences that defy facile geographic associations. Galdós's realist and naturalist works of the 1880s reflect his belief that the nation's hope lies in the Spanish middle classes and as a consequence, he abandons the countryside to concentrate on life in Madrid in novels such as *La de Bringas* and *Fortunata y Jacinta.* In the modernist works of the 1890s and 1900s, he returns to a consideration of the countryside in *Halma* and *Nazarín* and to Catalan cities and villages in a number of his plays. His attentions and hopes shift to the lower classes and his depiction of urban and rural spaces turns increasingly to the more heterogeneous zones of contact between city and country and varied social groups. The difference between realist and modernist visions of the world and the city receive clear expression in Pereda's speech at his 1897 induction to the Spanish Royal Academy and Galdós's response. Pereda asserts that the regional narrative, which he defines as excluding the city, represents the only true Spanish novel (1897, 19). He equates modernism with the urban world (13) and attacks cities as sites of foreign influence. In contrast to Pereda's firm beliefs, Galdós specifies that he possesses growing doubts and finds himself increasingly bewildered and restless (32–33). He identifies the city as the place that best reflects his current views and also as the exciting place of encounters between the foreign and the domestic, where free and open dealings between human beings represent the norm (33).

The negative portrayal of the city as a corrupting, dehumanizing force continues in the early 1900s in texts by conservative writers such as Ricardo León in *Casta de hidalgos* (1908) and Wenceslao Fernández Flórez in *Volvoreta* (1917). On the radical left, Blasco Ibáñez also attacks the city, although his portrayal of the countryside and small village share equally in his rejection of modernity and the capitalism that undergirds it. The artist protagonist of *La maja desnuda* (1906) expresses contempt for cars and a younger generation that prefers speed to the tranquil contemplation of landscape. Other novels emphasize insurmountable distances separating classes, genders, and rural or urban cultures. *El intruso* depicts a permanent divide between lower-class miners and wealthy capitalists, inhabitants of the city and denizens of the mountain, and women who enforce church dogma against free thinking men who challenge it. The protagonist provides the only link between these two groups, a connection necessary to facilitate the story that disappears at the end of the narrative when he joins the socialists and lower classes.

Modernists perceive a more fluid dynamic in urban society and explore the space between classes, genders, and geographic zones as the site of promising interactions and fruitful exchanges. Leopoldo Alas retains a certain suspicion of city life, which he shares with regionalist realist literature, but also explores the possibilities for change and personal development in urban society. "¡Adios, Cordera!" pits the simple rural world of the twin orphans raised along with and partially by the family cow against a distant, insensitive urban society that has just recently begun to invade the countryside through the construction of train tracks and telegraph wires. The timeless world of the idyll breaks down through repeated intrusions of a modern time and space, and in particular in the sale of the family cow for slaughter in Madrid in order to pay rent owed an absentee, urban-dwelling landlord. A cruel modernity takes form in the train that carries Cordera away to the city to feed wealthy city dwellers and then takes the drafted male twin off to war. The criticism of the church as part and parcel of Madrid capitalism distinguishes this text from a more conservative Pereda, but in other respects it replicates his theme of the exploitation of the *patria chica* by the capital city. In *Doña Berta* (1892), the stereotype of a dehumanized, dehumanizing urban center exists in the minds of the rural characters and continues to a certain extent in doña Berta, who moves to Madrid and negotiates the urban space with constant fear of crowds and trolleys. However, Berta finds allies in the city and she herself becomes a source of kindness and generosity to other urban dwellers. This Clarín text demonstrates the formation of new communities and new subjectivities in a space where traditional class, gender, and ideological barriers no longer hold and individuals have both the challenge and pleasure of creating value for their lives. Considerably younger than Clarín and with a more enthusiastic acceptance of modernism's aesthetic and ideological tenets, Llanas Aguilaniedo acknowledges the horrors of urban life while simultaneously recognizing it as a force for change. He publishes an early sociological study of the Madrid under classes in his 1901 *La mala vida en Madrid,* with intertextual links to Pío Baroja's earlier essay, "La patología del golfo," and subsequent trilogy, *La lucha por la vida.* Llanas Aguilaniedo analyzes the customs and living conditions of petty thieves, the under- and unemployed, and other marginalized urban groups. Despite a generally bleak portrait, the text speaker insists that inhabitants of the countryside are no more or less moral than city dwellers and sees a tremendous fount of energy and source of future social evolution in lower-class urban residents.

Many modernist writers emphasize the energy and positive benefits of urban social fluidity. The early Maeztu praises the vigor of industrial Bilbao and calls for the industrialization of the Castilian center by the economically, technologically more developed coastal areas (1967, 74, 175–78). Gabriel Alomar praises the futurist movement in the modernist magazine *Renacimiento* (1907) and clamors for the triumph of city over country. The Barojan text speaker of "El vago" profits from new communities available in a socially mobile urban society and finds solace in the figure of a vagabond who leans against the street light and refuses to defer to the structures and strictures of society. The vagrant communicates a sense of independence and individualism to the text speaker, who writes that he feels protected by the presence of this cultural and social other (1946–48, 5:63). Many Barojan texts include the figure of the *flaneur,* who delights in prolonged observation of urban crowds. Fausto Bengoa of *Los últimos románticos* plays this role in the Parisian setting of Napoleon III and María Aracil offers a feminine variant in the London of *La ciudad de la niebla.* Silvestre Paradox of *Aventuras, inventos y mixtificaciones de Silvestre Paradox* moves through various social classes as he acquires new friends and takes new jobs in Madrid and as mentioned earlier, Manuel of *La lucha por la vida* experiences an enormous range of the Madrid social scene and benefits tremendously from the possibilities provided by a mobile urban society. Manuel Machado expresses the incredible pull of the city for writers and the general public of his day in "Regreso" of *Ars moriendi* (1921). The poem includes a slow rhythm and a vocabulary rich in color and pleasant sounds to create a country landscape that the poetic speaker then abruptly contrasts with a rapid, almost hectic invocation of urban life. At the end of each of the first three stanzas, the long description of rural landscape is punctuated by a one-line exclamation: "¡Adiós, adiós! ¡Que la ciudad me llama!" [Good bye, good bye! The City calls me!]. The final stanza depicts an urban landscape devoid of sky, sun, and stars and filled with unpleasant smells and noises (1951, 183). Despite this unattractive representation, the text speaker communicates the excitement and inevitability of the departure through the repeated exclamation. The often repeated negative characterization of city life cannot displace the attraction it holds for the modern poetic speaker.

Azorín reflects on the city's impact on individual subjectivity and on the emancipatory value of modern urban spaces in contrast to small town confinement. *Diario de un enfermo* (1901) intermixes negative comments on urban life with more positive remarks. The narrative's mediation through the neurotic first-person narrator brackets the judgements, leaving the reader with a sense of the imbalanced psychology of the character, but no clear explanation as to its causes. The narrator / diary writer decries the city's depersonalizing effects and the violence visited on the individual through economic exploitation and industrial accidents. He complains of a vertiginous succession of emotions and sensations that the individual cannot assimilate: "Nos falta el tiempo . . . Me ahogo, me ahogo en este ambiente inhumano de civilización humanitaria. Estoy fuera de mí; no soy yo. Mi voluntad se evapora. No siento las cosas, las presiento; trago, sin paladear, las sensaciones . . ." [We don't have any time . . . I am suffocating, I am suffocating in this inhuman atmosphere of humanitarian civilization. I am outside of myself; I am not me. My will is evaporated. I cannot feel things, I sense them; I swallow, without tasting, sensations . . .] (1947–48, 702). To ward off sensorial overload, the narrator goes to Toledo, but change of place does not fundamentally alter his neurotic behavior. Furthermore, it is the city that facilitates his love and marriage, providing a space for the fortuitous encounters with the young woman he eventually marries. Unnamed throughout the text, this central female figure in the diary writer's life appears first as a face in the crowds and through repeated re-encounters comes to occupy a key role in his life. Although this positive event quickly unravels when the bride dies of tuberculosis, the tragic denouement is not directly or exclusively related to an urban environment.[11]

Alejandro Sawa and Santiago Rusiñol both focus on Parisian city life. Sawa spent a great deal of time in the French capital and much of his autobiography recalls his time in France.[12] Darío wrote that Sawa felt like a stranger in his own country and missed Paris when away from it (Sawa, 1910, 13). Rusiñol expresses his disdain for technological progress on numerous occasions, including his prologues to *Hojas de la vida* (8) and *Oracions* (9). Several texts within *Hojas de la vida* continue the anti-modern, anti-urban tone. "Una fábrica de santos" laments the industrialization of the art of religious statuary and the assembly line production in which one person specializes in painting knees and another the staff. "Un entierro" describes the trajectory of a cadaver that travels the length of the Seine River from Paris to the sea, passing under various bridges where it mixes with discarded letters and other urban detritus, moving by Notre Dame and the Morgue to the open ocean. The text allows the reader to imagine a possible suicide, accidental fall, or other cause in order to focus on depersonalized abandonment in the midst of urban activity. *Desde el molino* offers a different version of urban life, noting the poverty and suffering but also the mixes of peoples, pleasant solitude of small plazas with background city noises, varied colors and information on posters and wall advertisements, the picturesque, anarchic spaces carved out by immigrants who build impromptu shelters, and the night life of Montmartre with nationally specialized music halls of Japanese, Spanish, and French theme and music. Rusiñol's play *La alegría que pasa,* translated to Spanish and performed in Madrid in 1906, confronts two groups of characters, one that praises the advantages of city life with its promise for a better future and the other that exalts village life. The protagonist ultimately and somewhat sadly accepts the inevitability of his residence in the village and in his final monologue, the monotony and limitations of rural life receive clear emphasis.

Unamuno, generally depicted as a lover of country and hater of modern city, shares with other modernists the ability and need to view the question from various, changing angles. Like his contemporaries, he prefers to occupy both spaces, moving back and forth from country to small city. His view of the urban and rural landscape no longer maintains them as separate entities, but as spaces that mutually constitute and continually invade each other in his memories and perceptions. The speaker of "¡Adentro!" counsels the young interlocutor to leave the city and find himself in the country but, as previously mentioned, he simultaneously commands his addressee to seek society and reach the other through the self (1958, 3:426). The same concept informs "Soledad," where the text speaker states that his love for the masses prompts him to seek solitude because, alone in the country, he is able to break down the layer of shyness that separates him from himself and others: "Sólo la soledad nos derrite esa espesa capa de pudor que nos aísla a los unos de los otros; sólo en la soledad nos encontramos; y al encontrarnos, encontramos en nosotros a todos nuestros hermanos en soledad" [Only solitude melts away that thick layer of shyness that separates the one from the other; only in solitude can we find ourselves and by finding ourselves, we find within us all our brothers and sisters in solitude] (3:882). The double rhythm of inward self-examination in the country's solitude and outward communication in the social network of larger population centers characterizes Unamuno's writing. No single location offers a respite from the obligation to create a space for the self and the self can only develop in dialogue with the other. The tenuous balance between these forces consistently surfaces in Unamuno's texts and whether in city, town, or country, the individual must struggle to resist the imposition of one or the other.

I have commented throughout the study on Unamuno's commitment to non-dichotomous thinking and his view of urban and rural spaces develops along these same lines. The city, village, and country offer opportunities for personal development and space for aesthetic renewal. "En Alcalá de Henares, Castilla y Vizcaya" presents a dialogue between the text speaker and a Basque friend, in which the former insists that even the Basque factories, steam boilers, iron roofs, and coal deposits have their own poetry (1958, 1:224). "La civilización es civismo" equates rural society with conservativism and civilization and progress with the city. In the earlier *Paisajes* (1902), Unamuno argued for a different point of view, when he wrote that cities exploit the countryside and cause civil war. The solution to this division lies in a strengthening of the country and the reduction of cities to islands within a green ocean. Although Unamuno, like all writers, undergoes a certain evolution in his thought, in this case the shifts in position represent a continuous change in emphasis, which in all cases calls for dialogue and communication between locations. The country, without an infusion of new ideas and rhythms, falls into stagnation and regressive tendencies and the urban population center, without the assimilation of spaces conducive to self-analysis and self-healing, leads to the suffocation of the self by multiple others. While Unamuno expresses a personal preference for life in the smaller city, such as the Salamanca where he spent most of his adult years, he praises Barcelona in "La civilización es civismo" as a model of progressive public spirit and many of his novels and stories take place in a city environment and explore possibilities for change in such spaces.

Niebla leaves the specifics of the novel's spatial location to the reader's imagination, but it clearly takes place in a city and Augusto and Eugenia's fortuitous encounters could only occur in an urban environment. Although the excess of stimuli and hurried pace of urban life contribute to Augusto's loss of identity, the city also provides him the diversity of contacts and range of opinions and discourses that allow him to complete his voyage of self-discovery. In one of Augusto's random comments that captures the essence of Unamunan and modernist thought, he compares the world to a kaleidoscope and states that human observers must provide the logic that makes sense of the observed reality (1958, 2:711). As I detailed in a previous study, Augusto's process involves the gradual overthrow of traditional authoritative discourses and the evolution of his own personal but still polyphonic mode of speaking and thinking.[13] Such a trajectory occurs only in an atmosphere of competing value systems and multiple discourses, as characterized by modern urban society. "Un pobre hombre rico o el sentimiento cómico de la vida" (1930) also outlines the development of the self in the urban environment, but with much less tragic tone and vision. The protagonist Emeterio represents the modern anti-hero, a modest bank employee whose fear of exposing his feelings and habit of economizing both financially and emotionally cause him to lose the opportunity to marry his landlady's daughter. Rosita marries another man and throughout a long, uneventful bachelorhood, Emeterio regrets his failure to act. When as an older man he fortuitously meets Rosita's daughter, he abandons all worries about economy, rejection, and ridicule. Emeterio marries Rosita, pays for her daughter's dowry, moves in with his step-daughter and step-son-in-law, and prepares to will his lifetime savings to a grandchild that is not his. He becomes the cuckold, as he himself admits, laughingly welcoming this socially derided role in exchange for the sense of fulfilment that his late marriage and step-family have brought him (1958, 2:1299). Unamuno totally inverts his own philosophy of the tragic meaning of life and here advocates the comic meaning of life, the ability to laugh at oneself and accept the laughter of others in exchange for the creation of community. The text rejects patriarchal notions of male ownership of female bodies and of their offspring and bourgeois social prohibitions of cross-class marriage. Emeterio constructs a new kind of family made possible by a heterogeneous urban society that fosters social and psychological fluidity.

"El Marqués de Lumbría" also defies traditional patriarchal and bourgeois expectations about family and human behavior. In yet another shift of location and angle of vision, Unamuno analyzes the expression of raw will by a female character in a story that transpires in a traditional Castilian town. In contrast with the idyllic depiction of provincial cities and rural world that occurs in some realist literature, this text portrays a noble family completely cut off from the land, living in the somber enclosure of the family manor from the rent they receive from tenants, but lacking all other connection to the lower classes or nature. The family horror of the sun and lower classes, the internal tensions between the various family members, and in particular the two sisters, breaks with the idyllic representation of community.[14] The text also rejects antecedent naturalist studies of small town life. Although Carolina steals Tristán, her younger sister's fiancé, and bears an illegitimate child, her motivations transcend mere physical instinct as she reveals when she speaks of her desire to be the mother of the future marquis and maintain her place as the first-born. The sexual details are totally silenced in this narrative, in part from a desire to distance Carolina's ambitions from pure carnal lust and in part to reflect a society in which euphemism and silence characterize discussions of the most basic elements of human existence.

"El marqués de Lumbría" also differs markedly from the standard critical descriptions of Unamunan intrahistory as escape into an unchanging, essentialized Castilian tradition.[15] Here intrahistory represents the stagnant world of a nobility that has lost all reason for living and in a conscious recognition of its anachronistic survival, retires to the back of the family home. The text links the worthless nobility with patriarchy and local church and civil authority. The family counselor is the local priest and the other two regular visitors to the family *tertulia* are another church official and the registrar of deeds. It is the ecclesiastic advisor who determines to send Carolina and her illegitimate son to the country and marry Tristán to the youngest daughter, Luisa. The aging marquis, imbued with patriarchal norms, clings to life until his younger daughter gives birth to a son, but Luisa soon dies and Tristán brings Carolina back as his second wife. Against traditional values and customs, Carolina rebels violently and stridently, confronting public opinion and private sensibilities to demand her son's recognition as the rightful heir and her title as *mayorazga* (1958, 2:1026). The creation of a previously non-existent feminine form of *mayorazgo* and Carolina's arrogation of the term place her in direct rebellion against patriarchal strictures. Her refusal to accept the notion of illegitimacy for her son and the judgement of "sin" for her act of self-definition also defies church and conventional social values. Carolina negates history and intrahistory to strike out in a new direction, opening the windows, letting the sun stream into the house, and repudiating the noble heritage and blue blood of her ancestry for the red blood of life, as she herself emphasizes in her choice of a new shield for the manor entryway. The novelty of her position, which anticipates the unorthodoxy of Tula of Unamuno's *La tía Tula,*[16] continues to appear outrageous even to the modern reader, but represents a clear effort to break with traditional depictions of female subjectivity and opens conventional society to new modes of thinking and acting.

Juan Ramón Jiménez examines North American urban life in his *Diario de un poeta recién casado.* The prose and poetic entries of the journal of his trip to the United States on the occasion of his wedding to Zenobia Camprubí detail a vision of Boston, New York, and Philadelphia that includes apprehension in the face of the unknown, admiration for the new, and appreciation of heterogeneous mixes. The varied emotions reflect the urban experience and the rapidity of the images and sensations that succeed each other textually reproduce it for a Spanish readership. Descriptions of white Boston snow lead to bleak portrayals of dirt and darkness and then to a lyrical evocation of a small brook that struggles to free itself from the ice and snow that cover it. Selections written in New York capture the speed of city life, the picturesque presence of an old house in the midst of the tall buildings on Riverside Drive, and culture shock at the American obsession with fire that produces ugly fire escapes and hatchets encased in hotel and apartment halls. Other entries communicate a sort of aesthetic map to the reader with guides for the discovery of beauty in details that easily disappear in the larger panorama. "Primavera," composed according to the epigraph while waiting for the bus on the corner of 5th Avenue and 10th Street, contrasts the winter winds that dominate New York streets with small white flowers of magnolia trees that seem to dance in the breeze and aspire to flight. "La negra y la rosa" describes a sleeping black woman holding a white rose in a subway car. The rose, moving gently with the train motion to rest in different positions on the young woman's shoulders, gradually attracts the attention of the other passengers and transforms the atmosphere, sending an aroma of springtime through the car.

"Alta noche" recounts a contrasting response to African Americans, revealing the speaker's fear of the other. Walking alone at night on 5th Avenue, the speaker admires the store windows and complicated bank grates, but the pleasure of this unusual solitude in the midst of the city quickly gives way to anxiety as echoes of footsteps fill the silence. Turning around, the speaker looks directly into an enormous pair of eyes that he describes as black, red, and yellow, synecdochically evoking the various racial identities that his fright assumes for this nocturnal visitor. An older, lame, black man smiles and greets him, leaving the speaker to continue his solitary walk. The grip of panic and evident relief reveal a racist undercurrent, but also capture the individual's sense of vulnerability in the desired but fearful solitude of the city. "La luna" introduces a comical note that reflects the speaker's changing responses to his urban surroundings and also explicates the altered experience of reality in late modernity. The text portrays a contemporary version of the sky, where the changing lights of Broadway advertisements are new constellations and a succession of images appears, from a pig that dances to a bottle that spills its liquid when its cork pops off to a ship that continually commences and recommences its voyage. The speaker then points out the moon over the river between two tall buildings but suddenly has doubts, and wonders if it is the moon or its reproduction in an illuminated advertisement.

In *Los contemporáneos* (1907), Andrés González Blanco states that the perception and appreciation of landscape is an acquired taste transmitted through literature (1907a, 3) and that modernist writers look for the transcendental in the accidental, the inner world in external reality (22). Although he speaks mainly of natural landscapes, his comments also apply to urban scenes. Modernist authors and painters seek to develop a new sensibility in the urban reader with respect to the rural landscape and they similarly aspire to train him/her to locate sites of aesthetic enjoyment in the urban landscape. Jiménez focusses on a large, solitary city tree in "El árbol tranquilo" and on the fountain that reflects the starlit night while distant illuminated signs form a backdrop. The city lights outline the tree branches, which the speaker describes as kissed by spring and inflamed on each point like a golden blossom. The tree remains bound to the city, by the lights and busses that pass, but also provides a site for aesthetic contemplation outside the whirlwind speed of urban life (1957, 366–67). Jiménez feels drawn to the urban cemetery because it also allows for a space of aesthetic enjoyment within the modern city. The borders between life and death and city and country disappear in the American city cemetery, which appears as the focal point of four entries of the one hundred that constitute the section of the *Diario* devoted to the eastern United States. American beautification of cemeteries with trees, flowers, and grass prompts the text speaker of "Cementerio alegre" to wish to rent a tomb and spend the rest of the spring there. "Cementerios" details the encounter across borders that so attracts the modernist eye and links the representation of modern spaces with a desire to reconceptualize traditional visions of death. The text describes a cemetery without fences or walls, connected to the surrounding city. A young girl wends her way through the gravestones and birds fly from tombstone crosses to the windows of nearby houses. In yet another instance of reflected images that break borders, the text describes the image of cemetery crosses in the windows of the neighboring homes: "En los cristales colgados de yedras de las casas próximas se copian las cruces, a la fresca paz cobijada por la espesura que hermana, en una misma sombra, casa y tumba" [In the ivy hung windows of the nearby houses the crosses are reflected, sheltered in the calm peace by the thicket that harmonizes, in one same shadow, house and tomb] (1957, 418–19). The speaker remarks with admiration that beauty and life defeat death and imagines the dead resting easily in this space.

Santiago Rusiñol feels similarly drawn to the Montmartre cemetery, which provides a respite from Parisian city noises and rhythms while remaining thoroughly connected to the urban world. "El cementerio de Montmartre" of *Desde el molino* describes a common skyscape in which trees in the cemetery blend with chimneys of surrounding houses and factories. The text speaker visits at different times of the day, relating the passage of time over the eternal sleep of the dead and the fusion of the mausoleums with the surrounding houses in the dark of the night. He further insists on reviewing the lives of those buried there, transgressing through memory the traditional notion of death's finality. Unamuno focusses on Spanish cemeteries in a number of poems and he too underscores the dissolution of barriers between the world outside and the space within. Starker and more distant from population centers than American or French urban burial places, the Spanish cemetery of Unamuno's texts nevertheless connects with the world around it and with a sense of life over death. "Camposanto junto al río" breaks down the barriers separating life and death, passage of time and eternity, nature and human existence in the description of the river that brings the melted snow of the mountain tops to irrigate the dried bones in the tombs and revitalize the thick brush that covers the crosses, sending its roots in search of those who once lived and are now buried below. Unamuno describes the cemetery's reflection in the river, in another example of *mise en abîme* that erases frames and dividing borders (1958, 14:740–41). "Llueve" joins city and country, past, present, and future, Castile and the Basque region, life and death, in one continuous elimination of partitions. On a rainy day, the Salamancan poetic speaker is transported back to the misty days of his childhood in Bilbao and to the safety of a time in which religious doubts and other worries had no place. The rain joins heaven and earth, bringing the skies down and carrying the dust away. They reach the city and the cemetery and the speaker imagines that this may well be the only message to arrive from the world and console the dead. He projects his own death and burial and finds comfort in the thought that the sounds of the rains will purify his memories and have the reassuring effect of a lullaby (14:764).

The melding of city and country and the desire to present the simultaneity of urban and rural experiences that characterize modernist culture inform many Unamunan poems. He describes Salamanca as a forest of stones and its towers as high thickets in "Salamanca" (1958, 13:216). His depiction of Bilbao through the image of the river that runs through it and connects to the mountains and sea in "Al Nervión" (13:822–25) as well as allusions to the wheat colored walls of Salamanca and the comparison of her towers to giant columns of corn in "Atardecer de estío en Salamanca" exemplify the same practice (13:837–38). Joan Maragall depicts the modernist vision of the interpenetration and mutual constitution of city and country in two essays published in 1901 and appearing in succession in *Artículos.* "La ciudad" presents the city as the synthesis of the nation, the hope for the future and site of productivity and wealth. The speaker describes nature's intrusion in the urban landscape during the quintessentially modernist moment of the sunset, when the city appears like a virgin forest and its noises mimic the sound of wind or ocean. He also depicts other more sinister zones of urban life, including the squalor and egotism, but in the end sees the urban world as a compendium of national life that retains contact with the various rural spaces: "No es una cosa distinta de la montaña solitaria, ni del llano risueño y cultivado, ni de la pequeña población activa, ni del yermo miserable: sino que recibe la vida de todo ello y le da alma y sentido" [It is not something distinct from the solitary mountain or the cultivated, sunny plains, or the small, active village or the miserable waste land. Rather, it receives life from all of those areas and gives them soul and meaning.] (n. d., 3:191).

"La montaña" shifts the viewing angle to consider the advantages of a city constructed at the foot of a mountain, against which it can define and purify itself. The open space of the country provides a release from crowded city conditions and tempts the city with the possibilities of spreading out and reconfiguring its spatial dimensions, but while refreshed and allayed by such hopes, the city resists the impulse in recognition of her reason for being and her essential nature. The nearby mountain calls to the city dweller who ascends the summit, views the horizon, and then returns to the urban world knowing his own strengths and those of the society in which he must continue his labors. A mutual permeation of rural and urban spaces defines Darío de Regoyos's painting *Fum de Fàbrica. Lluna* (1908). A group of buildings representing an industrial center lies exactly midway in the painting between a foreground of plants and a flowing river and a background of hills and moonlit, clouded nocturnal sky. The smoke from the factories rises to cover the moon and link the urban center with the natural backdrop and the industrially permeated sky connects with the rural zone of the river through the reflection of the moon on the water as filtered through the factory smoke. The industrial smoke fades into the night and melds with the clouds in another bond of nature and humanly produced spatiality. The painting joins sky, city, and countryside and also industrial center with nature.

Many authors replicate the sense of concurrent experience of city and county and back and forth traffic connecting the two zones. Maragall describes his train trip to Madrid in "La capital" (1900), in which he interweaves an aesthetic and political response to the Castilian city and national capital. The text speaker emphasizes the blinding light and absence of shading as he crosses the Castilian landscape and links this absolutism of line to the tradition of centrist political power against which his love for his native Catalonia rebels. He finds no connection between Madrid and the countryside and decides to quickly leave the capital to flee this alien space. However, as he departs in the late afternoon in the light of the setting sun, he begins to sense a change and the start of an attachment and forgiveness as he observes varied hues and shadings. Once more, a modernist writer demonstrates the importance of the afternoon as a transitional moment capable of breaking down the rigidity of the line, literally and symbolically.

The transitional zone between urban and rural life also attracts the attention of modernist writers, who recognize the poverty of the marginal groups that reside in the outlying districts, but also see the potential of this hybrid space. Baroja describes this zone in *La busca,* where the ragman who offers Manuel a home and job has built a comfortable, picturesque home constructed of throwaway urban materials, complete with a merry-go-round, fenced area for pigs and chickens, and mounds of used materials classified and ready for resale. The characters of Galdós's novel *Nazarín* and its sequel *Halma* move from city to country and back again throughout the narrative and the two populations learn from and influence each other. When the city dwelling José Antonio de Urrea moves to the country in disgust at urban corruption, he finds a backward, uncultured rural society that initially wounds his highly developed sensibilities, but in time he becomes inured to and appreciative of the frankness of his fellow farmers and they acquire some of his refinement (1967, 5:1852). These Galdosian novels put into play Unamuno's call for the city to free itself from a regressive country and for the country to liberate itself from an exploitative urban culture. The narrative action of *Misericordia* takes place largely in Madrid and the intersection of the diverse individuals, races, religions, and classes described in the novel could only occur in an urban setting. The grinding poverty of the beggars, the dismal privation of a downwardly spiraling bourgeoisie, and the cold ingratitude and quick loss of memory emanate primarily from city life. It is significant that Almudena and Benina move to the outskirts at the end of the novel. In this transitional zone between country and city, the unorthodox couple can survive. They could not find acceptance in a rural or small town world and urban society has already cruelly spurned them. I do not see their move to the city limits as a rejection of urban life as suggested by Macklin (1993, 202), but rather as the statement of a need for a hybrid space that straddles borders, creating new zones of human contact and living.

Many texts create this transitional zone through emphasis on the process of arrival to or departure from the city. Ciro Bayo feels the call of the country in *El peregrino entretenido,* but on leaving the capital, looks back and observes Madrid's profile from the vantage of the country, bringing city and country together in a single perspective. Baroja's *Camino de perfección* relates the odd juxtaposition of trolleys and the bells of a goat herd (1969, 12). Fernando easily reaches the city outskirts and the country in his walks, moving on foot from one realm to the other. When he travels by mule cart from Segovia to Illescas, he passes Madrid and views it from outside, through the vision and temporal perspective of those who like his companion Polentinos continue to live in another world. However, Fernando cannot erase his urban experience and the narration inserts city metaphors in descriptions of nature to emphasize the simultaneity of a dual vision. Describing the trees of the countryside surrounding Madrid, the narrator compares the masses of foliage to the sculptured filigree work of cathedral stones (84). Conversely, in describing the Cathedral pinnacles, he compares them to the cypress trees normally found in a cemetery (77). Manuel and his brother Juan come from the country to the city and their vision of the urban landscape carries within it the experience of the country. Manuel loves his time in the small town outside Madrid in the company of Kate and her mother, but he has become citified and fails miserably in his attempts to raise vegetables. He finally finds success in *Aurora roja* in a neighborhood at the city's edge, where hunters mix with urban dwellers and the cemetery gives the impression of nature within urban congestion. Much of the novel's action describes the transit from the city to the outskirts on Sunday excursions and visits to the tavern Aurora roja, from which the novel takes its title. The meeting site of utopian anarchists lies in the fruitful transitional zone between city and country.

Manuel and other modernist characters learn to appreciate the urban landscape and to create a space for themselves in the city. As Manuel evolves toward a personal solution to modern life, he discovers sites of aesthetic repose in the urban center. He notices the different forms that the smoke takes as it spirals from the factory chimneys (1946–48, 1:522). Lying sick in the home he shares with his sister and la Salvadora, he comes to enjoy the view through the window of the swallows circling overhead and the changing lights of the early evening sky in combination with the glow of city street lights and noise of goat bells. Interspersed between descriptions of Juan's anarchist activities, *Aurora roja* contains many brief delineations of the invasion of the city by the night sky and evening breeze (1:622) or of the sky as viewed through a window (1:643). Pío Baroja, like his brother the painter Ricardo, focusses on roofscapes as a new perspective on nature and spatiality that becomes available in the city. Ricardo's 1928 *Humo* depicts a view from the top of a building or a window on an upper floor from which adjoining tile roofs, chimneys, church belfries, women hanging laundry on clotheslines on rooftop balconies, and windows with varied curtains are viewed.

Pío depicts similar scenes in *Las aventuras, inventos y mixtificaciones de Silvestre Paradox* and *Las tragedias grotescas,* among others, but especially develops this perspective in *El árbol de la ciencia.* When Andrés Hurtado spies through his looking glasses from an attic window, he perceives various patios and tile roofs as well as young girls combing their hair on their balconies and an old woman putting on makeup inside her house. Andrés's cats explore the new terrain, hunting on the rooftops and stealing from the neighbor's kitchens. Andrés's conversations with his uncle Iturrioz all take place on the latter's fifth floor terrace, which is covered with plants and has a view of the Guadarrama mountain range, the rooftop of a military barracks, various church towers, a cemetery, and distant windmills. The philosophical discussions about life's meaning, the advantage of action over contemplation or contemplation over action, abstention or involvement, take place framed by a roofscape that combines rural and urban spaces and symbolizes the modernist melding of opposites in which such a conversation becomes not only possible, but inevitable. The long second dialogue between uncle and nephew closes with a juxtaposition of the lights from Venus and Jupiter with those from the house and street lamps in yet another example of the intermingling of natural and technological worlds that constitutes the modern experience of space. Andrés, like Manuel, seeks to create a space for himself in urban structures and Lulú, his unconventional friend and later wife also actively works to carve out her own locations for self expression and development. At her home, Lulú likes to box herself in, surrounded by chairs and a table behind which she launches her cynical comments, spatially and morally demarcating a zone that separates her from her mother and sister. Later, she insists on setting up her own store, from which she sells linens and children's clothing. Andrés attempts to construct his space when he moves to the attic room of his father's home, and, after marrying Lulú, he has the landlord tear down the walls separating the different rooms to make one large common area that serves as bedroom, study, living and dining room. In this open, airy location, he feels unencumbered by neighbors and walls, as if living in the country.

Modernist writers and painters explore new spaces and modes of living in and representing traditional and modern spaces. They conceive of space as dynamic, whether in the movement that occurs within it or in the requisite mobility of the observer's eye as it shifts from one perspective to another, at times successively but more often in a rapid oscillation that approaches simultaneity. Although modernist texts honestly and at times ruthlessly scrutinize the dangers and evils of modern technology and urban society, they also acknowledge, often with enthusiasm and hope, the considerable benefits of new forms of living in community. In all cases, they recognize the inalterably transformed experience of spatiality that accompanies life in the modern world and in their writing and visual representations, they aspire to educate the Spanish reader of the period in new ways of perceiving and interacting with their surroundings. Spanish modernism takes a dramatic and energetic leap forward in the understanding of time and space and moves the reader to new and exciting discoveries regarding the dynamic interaction of temporal-spatial location and individual and community.

6
Class and Gender in the Construction of Modernist Subjectivity

LATE NINETEENTH AND EARLY TWENTIETH-CENTURY CULTURE witnessed increased contact between different social classes and male and female sectors of the population. Urban living brings about greater intermixing of social classes and city living and modern forms of transportation contribute to increased mobility and public visibility of women of all classes. Greater social movement, with the rapid creation and loss of wealth and status, suggests the intrinsic historicity of class identity, which alters over time in relation to cultural conditions. Similarly, traditional views of gender undergo radical transformation as women enter areas formally considered exclusively masculine and the dandy, the "New Woman," and other turn-of-the-century figures challenge accepted norms of masculine and feminine behavior. In many cases, changing visions of class are expressed in conjunction with altered views of gender, and it is often through the lower-class woman that the middle class begins to reconfigure its identity. In the construction of the modernist subject, the growing presence and power of the lower classes and women challenge traditional views of collective and individual identity and contribute to a comprehensive redefinition of the possibilities and consequences of intersubjective and intercultural relations.

SOCIAL CLASS AND IDENTITY FORMATION

Xenophobic and Xenophilic Representations of the Spanish Lower Classes

New Critical and formalist approaches to literature and their continuing legacy identify European modernism with fear of the masses and a resultant elitism. Andreas Huyssen argues this position in *After the Great Divide* and Scott Lash defines modernism as addressing an elite audience in contrast with realist forms designed for the working class (1991, 25). The association of realism with the lower classes and modernism with a cultured elite elides the complexity of both movements and underestimates the fluidity of early twentieth-century social structures. Perry Anderson's conjunctural model offers a more useful guide to class relations and their impact on artistic expression during this period: the presence of a declining but still powerful landowning class, the appearance of labor movements that challenge a bourgeoisie with a tenuous hold on newly acquired authority, and the proximity of a hoped for or feared revolution (1984, 104).

The fear of the masses and social revolution mentioned by Anderson, Huyssen and others as characteristic of modernism peaks much earlier in Spain, prompted by popular uprisings during the First Republic and the cantonalist movements of 1873. In the artistic world, fear of revolution informs a good deal of realist and naturalist literature and plays an important role in the debate regarding the reception of naturalism in Spain.[1] Although fear of the lower classes and social disorder continues in the modernist period, other elements offset and redirect it. The perception that the Restoration had failed to address the nation's longstanding social and political problems compels intellectuals and artists to seek new solutions. The identification of the Restoration with the bourgeoisie provokes a rejection of middle-class values and a reconsideration of the role of both the lower and upper classes in national formation. The tendency of the Spanish bourgeoisie to identify with the aristocracy, buying titles and marrying into an economically needy nobility, as well as past failures of the aristocracy to provide effective leadership, preclude any serious turn to the aristocracy for direction, although attempts to link the upper and lower classes surface in some writers. More typically, the lower classes attract the attention of those interested in reimagining Spanish collective and individual identity. Both the rural peasantry and urban working class occupy a central role in the search for new identities, in dynamic interaction with each other and with the middle-class men and women who participate in the discussion.

Literary scholars often point to the absence of the urban working class in Spanish modernist texts[2] and although rural figures predominate, the urban lower classes appear with greater frequency than normally acknowledged if a wider corpus of writers and texts is considered and if female lower-class characters are included. The rural lower classes represent by far the largest sector of the Spanish population during the modernist period and up to the 1950s, and artistic production naturally reflects this predominance.[3] Furthermore, the assumption that problems facing the rural and urban working classes are fundamentally different or that textual representations of individuals from one of these two populations has greater power for social transformation does not necessarily hold. Miners and agricultural laborers work in rural environments but share many of the economic, social, and psychological difficulties facing their urban counterparts. Miners often move back and forth from farming to mining depending on the economy and many urban workers are recent arrivals to the city, retaining an attachment to rural life. In terms of impact on the reading public, the focus on a rural as opposed to urban working class matters less than a constructive, compelling portrayal of the marginalized lower-class other and explorations of possibilities for new relations with the dominant classes.

Realist and naturalist visions and techniques continue throughout the twentieth century[4] and strongly impact depictions of lower-class subjectivity. At times in combination, at times in opposition, realism, naturalism, and modernism adopt three different attitudes towards the lower-class subject. The fear of revolution that typifies the 1870s continues in conservative and some liberal sectors and leads to a phobic representation.[5] Although motivated by different political goals, certain radical writers similarly depict lower-class subjects as other and class conflict as inevitable. At the other extreme, a subset of artists erases difference in a xenophilic idealization of lower-class identity, presenting it as a mirror for middle-class subjectivity. Popular discourse and setting provide an escape from modern tensions rather than a site for their examination, although even the most conservative renderings open a space for lower-class agency. In between these two stances, the predominant modernist depiction of rural and urban lower classes moves back and forth from identification to difference, understanding to questioning, in a process that neither effaces the other nor the self, but aspires to reciprocity and intersubjective formation. Popular and mass motifs and discourses interweave with modernist emphasis on individuality and artistic innovation and the two form a polyphonic expression that combines the collective and individual, the spontaneous and mediated. Traditional fears and animosities easily intrude, but a persistent search for new modes of interrelations between classes characterizes the period.

Luis Coloma and Juan Valera exemplify conservative fears of changing social structures and class relations. Coloma's attack on the aristocracy arises largely from a concern that the power vacuum created by their decadence will open the door to lower-class revolution. Early in *Pequeñeces* (1890), a character alludes to a repeat of '93, invoking images of the French revolution and mob violence (1975, 74). The narrative action begins in 1872 during the first Republic and continues through the phase of cantonalist unrest to end with Curra's reconversion, which coincides with the Restoration of Alfonso XII and more conservative social and political conditions. Valera's tone differs from his conservative allies, but his vision of the lower classes coincides entirely. He opposes modernism, as he had previously opposed naturalism, out of a fear that explicit eroticism will attract lower-class readers who might assimilate the pessimistic message and abandon Christian resignation for political activism. Liberal fears of revolution in Krausist and Institutionist writing have been observed by numerous scholars of nineteenth-century Spanish culture.[6] Although Clarín attacks the bourgeoisie in *Su único hijo* (1891), the repudiation of the frivolous world of Emma Valcárcel and Bonifacio Reyes unfolds without any suggestion for an alternative and the lower classes remain strikingly absent in the narrative. Bonifacio's visits to a chemical plant and gunpowder factory include brief mention of the machines, noise, and heat, but the text only mentions in passing the presence of a few *operarios,* using the more cultured term in preference to worker or laborer (1966, 228). Alas's short story "Un jornalero" from *El señor y los demás son cuentos* (1893) moves from omission to commission in the phobic representation of urban workers, referred to pejoratively as *plebe.* The protagonist, designated in the title as a worker, is in fact an intellectual who unwittingly becomes involved in a conflict between the police and a group of anarchists or socialists, terms used indiscriminately in the text, with a casual "o lo que sean" [whatever they might be] to generically disparage labor movements (1893b, 253). The main character describes himself as a spiritual worker and refuses to condemn capitalism, deferring judgement on what he describes as a complex question. In the end, the police arrest him, thinking he is part of a street disturbance and the workers testify against him because they believe he is a police informer. The intellectual here occupies a lonely position, alienated from the establishment and also from an insolent, repugnant lower class.

Armando Palacio Valdés, a co-author of Clarín and fellow liberal, begins his literary career in 1881 during the realist/naturalist period and continues writing into the 1930s. Spiritualist and decadentist traits appear in some later works, but remain largely external and superficial. His "modernist" texts refute the anti-foundationalist impulse and radical doubt of modernist thought by reinserting traditional Catholic values. *La espuma* (1891) follows the pattern set by *Pequeñeces* in the critique of a decadent aristocracy and greedy bourgeoisie. Lower-class subjects have a larger presence in Palacio Valdés's novel, where they echo the crass materialism of the bourgeoisie without their veneer of social graces or function as signs of upper-class abuse, appearing as vaguely characterized victims. The focus of the novel's criticism is Clementina, the illegitimate daughter of the newly-titled Duke of Requena and an English woman of unidentified class. Clementina represents the other in terms of nationality, legal status, gender, and dubious class affiliation. Her sexual appetite and immorality are specifically linked to the lower class in the explanation of her love of the bull fight and her violent nature (1917, 82–83). The primary narrative conflict traces Clementina's rivalry with her father's lower-class mistress in a displacement of criticism of the upper classes onto two lower-class women.

A secondary focus of the novel concerns the unscrupulous accumulation of wealth through bribery and exploitation of the lower classes. The Duke of Requena gains control of a Spanish mining operation and invites his aristocratic friends to visit the site. The guests travel by train in luxurious surroundings and descend by elevator to a beautifully lit cavern, where they eat an elegant meal on a carpeted floor surrounded by candelabras and orchestral music. The narrative describes the miners' poverty, but primarily emphasizes the hostility separating the two groups, filtering the depiction of the miners' conditions through comments by upper-class visitors that serve more to characterize their insensitivity than to portray the lower class. *La espuma* recognizes the miners' hatred but swerves away from the social conflict, reducing the mines to a tangential subplot and moving the action quickly back to Madrid, where the novel ends with a sense that a newly-constituted aristocracy remains firmly entrenched. Evasion of social conflict reveals itself even more clearly in *La aldea perdida* (1903), which describes the rural Asturias of Palacio Valdés's youth that the arrival of mining has largely destroyed. The narrative longs for a return to what is described as a lost Arcadia and depicts the "invading" miners as barbarous and alien.

"Intermedio del editor," one of several short stories in *Papeles del doctor Angélico* (1910), narrates the intervention of the narrator and his friend Jiménez to save a child from a beating by her stepfather, who as a rag collector represents one of the lowliest of workers. The text alternates between a xenophilic representation of the victim, who clasps the narrator's legs in a physical symbolization of their spiritual and moral affinity, and a xenophobic depiction of the stepfather, whose brutality toward the step-daughter recurs in his savage, perhaps fatal beating of a young neighbor who had testified on the girl's behalf. Mediation of the events through a middle-class focalization distances the depiction of lower-class experience, which further recedes when Jiménez and the narrator enter into a long philosophical discussion on the nature of good and evil. The beatings serve as a pretext for an abstract meditation that refutes Schopenhauer, Leibnitz, Buddhism, and Darwinism in order to return to the Christian values of faith and love. Although the final paragraphs, describing the ragman's arrest for the beating of the neighbor and the cries of the distraught boy's mother, challenge the facile acceptance of Christian doctrine, the narrator struggles to impose an overriding message of faith and resignation.

Vicente Blasco Ibáñez's radical political position distances him from Clarín and Palacio Valdés, but his depiction of the rural and urban lower classes similarly emphasizes their difference from the middle-class subject. In keeping with his largely naturalist outlook and literary technique, Blasco Ibáñez portrays an instinctive lower-class behavior. In comparison, the better educated middle-class characters have a more complex motivation. His novels typically segregate these worlds, with only occasional encounters between the classes. *La barraca* (1898) presents conflict between the farmers of the Valencian countryside and the poor family from outside the area that tries to eke out a living in the abandoned lands of an imprisoned local dissident. Animosity to the outsider characterizes this world, which lives isolated from external influences and contacts, governed by tradition and instinctive love of the land. This culture remains locked in the past, hostile to change and intolerant of the other, who may suffer the same class and economic exploitation but is hated and ultimately driven out as an alien invader.[7] *Cañas y barro* (1902) introduces some evidence of change in the Valencian wetlands, owing to the commercial ambitions of the tavern owner and several characters' desires for material wealth over subsistence farming. However, sexual instinct and egotism retain equal if not greater motivating force in determining behavior and the novel closes with no possibility for change, in a total repudiation of capitalism and modernity as well as a bleak portrayal of traditional rural life and the lower class.

Blasco Ibáñez's narratives of urban life similarly render the lower classes as distinct and separated from middle-class experience and subjectivity. *La horda* (1905) bears considerable similarities with Baroja's *La busca,* but differs specifically in the absence of the cultural and class diversity that characterizes Baroja's modernist vision of Madrid. *La horda*'s focus falls exclusively on the working class or unemployed and the title underscores the homogeneity of underclass representatives. The women share an inherited anemia that erases physical differences except for a brief moment of youthful vitality. The two most memorable characters are Isidoro Maltrana, whose university education endows him with middle-class culture, and the anarchistic El Mosco, whose defiance distinguishes him from his anonymous, resigned neighbors. The urban lower class of Blasco Ibáñez's novels remains largely locked in the passive stance of victims who lack the knowledge or energy to act and whose separation from the rest of the population dooms them to submission. The texts display no faith in the lower-class ability to change its destiny. When characters express a will to change, as when Isidoro promises to access a better life for his son in the final pages, it comes late and with little evidence of potential realization.

The phobic representation of the lower classes also characterizes the theory of elites developed in conjunction with that of modern subjectivity by José Ortega y Gasset in *La rebelión de las masas* (1930). Ortega's definition of modernity coincides in certain aspects with studies such as Anthony Giddens's late twentieth century analysis of the modern condition. Both refer to the process of globalization by which individuals from various parts of the world come into increased contact[8] and also observe a break with the past in a modern world in which individuals create a personal trajectory on the basis of choices.[9] However, while theorists like Giddens or Paul Smith assume that the construction of self allows for multiple trajectories and offers emancipatory possibilities,[10] Ortega divides modern subjectivity into two basic types, the masses and the elites, and fears the liberating potential of modern social reorganization. Although the text speaker insists that he does not equate the masses with the lower classes, the examples illustrating mass behavior invoke images of the lower class. The discussion of rights distinguishes an upper class that discovered certain inalienable rights from *el pueblo,* which later arrogated the rights for themselves without fully understanding or even believing in them. On another occasion, the text compares the masses to groups that ransack bakeries in search of bread, invoking the spectre of lower-class violence. Citing mob tendencies to destroy the foundations necessary for self-preservation, the speaker refers both to plebeian and "aristocratic" masses (1993, 87), placing quotation marks around the term *aristocratic* to suggest a natural connection between plebeian and masses that does not pertain to aristocratic and masses. Fear of the masses and the disorder they connote permeates the text, which emphasizes the need for civility and respectful acquiescence to minority leadership. The speaker values regulating norms, democratic tolerance, civil debate, and opposes the forceful imposition in fascism and syndicalism of the will of the many. He refers to courtesy, reason, and justice, but in the prologue to the 1937 French edition, justice takes a back seat to reason, order, and individualism: "Ante el feroz patetismo de esta cuestión [the survival of European individualism] que, queramos o no, está ya a la vista, el tema de la 'justicia social', con ser tan respetable, empalidece y se degrada hasta parecer retórico e insincero suspiro romántico" [In the face of the fierce poignancy of this question [the survival of European individualism] that, like it or not, is clearly before us, the subject of 'social justice', while respectable in itself, pales and diminishes until it seems a rhetorical and insincere romantic sigh] (1993, 35).

An evident distaste for irrationality marks Ortega's work and, in particular, *La rebelión de las masas.* The speaker of the 1937 prologue describes Descartes as the man to whom Europe owes the single greatest debt and based on his discovery of reason denies the value of revolution and rapid social transformation (1993, 38–39). Ortega's vision departs from Cartesian rationality in several significant aspects, however, revealing the influence of modern(ist) thought in his conceptualization of the subject. He acknowledges the insufficiency of language for the expression of thought (12–13) and the impossibility of direct access to reality (148). This view anticipates in a general sense poststructuralist definitions of language and the relationship between subject, language, and reality; however, Ortega pulls back from further exploration of the fluid subjectivity that many of his modernist contemporaries and later poststructuralist thinkers, such as Jacques Lacan, pursue. Despite declarations that statements about reality are always ironic and aware of their inadequacy, Ortega insists that this gap is resolved through the arbitrary construction of an illusory reality, in supposing that things are a certain way (148). Lacan speaks of two moments or operations in the relation of the subject and the unconscious. In alienation, the first operation, the subject finds itself in an unstable dialectic, never fully possessing meaning and recognizing its provisional character. The inevitable separation of subject and meaning leads to a conceptualization of the self as a series of "subject-positions among whose arrangement there is no conceivable equipollence of elements" (Smith 1988, 75). Ortega accepts the provisional character of meaning, but resists defining the subject as constituted by a variety of subject positions, preferring to invent a stable position that anchors the self to a fixed, if illusory, location. He glides over alienation in preference for suture, Lacan's second operation. Suture effaces the separation of subject and meaning to construct a sense of wholeness and a coherent subject.

Whereas Lacan and other modern theorists of the subject envision a continual slide from one position to the other, Ortega recoils from the recognition of the unconscious, the impossibility of access to reality, and the instability that it implies. *La rebelión de las masas* equates the arbitrary construction of reality with the scientific method and strives to erase remnants of doubt and insecurity through repeated allusions to empiricism. Ignoring his own recognition of the subjective construction of reality, the text speaker insists that his belief in the necessity of elites for humanity's survival is not subjective opinion but a "law of social physics," as incontrovertible as Newton's laws (1993, 134). The mention of Newton and exclusion of Einstein, whose theories he had analyzed previously, reveals once more a nostalgia for times in which the human subject believed in a stable, unchanging self rooted in a stable, unchanging reality. Ortega's text reflects the widely recognized view in modernist and postmodernist thought that the individual constructs his/her own selfhood, but it evades the consequences of such a vision by creating an elite subject that recognizes disorder and then dispenses with it through an arbitrary imposition of order (171–72). The homogeneity of this elite—white, male, European, and despite protestations to the contrary, middle class—aims to shore up the construction of a secure subjectivity in control of its surroundings. The tenuous nature of this dominion reveals itself in explicit and implicit admissions of fear of the others who threaten traditional power structures and theories of subjectivity. Graham and Labanyi point out that critics inside and outside of Spain too often accept Ortega's elitist view of culture as the prevailing current of thought in Spanish modernism (1995, 3). With respect to subjectivity as well as to topics treated earlier, Ortega y Gasset differs markedly from other modernists, who develop different and at times contradictory visions of the subject, but who more clearly anticipate postructuralist theories of subjectivity and more fully explore the range of subject positions available to the modern individual.

In contrast to the phobic othering of the lower classes observed in the preceding analyses, Spanish popular theater often displays a philic assimilation of popular culture. The Spanish *zarzuela* and *sainete* present a stereotyped vision of urban and rural lower-class culture that typically reflects a middle-class ethos in defense of work, honor, and family. Carlos Arniches's *Las estrellas* combines a depiction of the lower class as other with a dramatic resolution that assimilates the characters into middle-class life style and beliefs. The father aspires to a career as tango singer for his daughter and bullfighter for his son, while the mother pushes the son to become a typesetter and the daughter a dressmaker. The slapstick humor that characterizes the *género chico* mocks both the lower-class aspiration for tango-bullfighting renown and the would-be middle-class mother, who beats husband, son, and daughter to realize her dream, but in the end, the mother's imposition of middle-class norms receives acclaim as she salvages the family business and saves husband and children from social and economic disaster.

Ricardo de la Vega's *Amor engendra desdichas o El guapo y el feo y verduleras honradas* epitomizes the *sainete* in the extensive title, mix of verse, prose, and music, slapstick plot, and idealization of urban lower-class life, although it also contains small seeds of social protest that counter the genre's predominant elision of conflict. The lead characters are two motherless but happy sisters who live in a poor, clean garret and sell vegetables in the local market. One sister has fallen in love with a bullfighter and father of a child by another woman, but in the course of the drama she learns to love her ugly but honest neighbor, who unmasks the bullfighter's duplicity. The text includes passing references to conflicts between the vegetable sellers and middle men who want to raise their prices, although the play only presents lower-class characters from the immediate neighborhood. Accordingly, the tensions play out within the confines of this space and quickly dissipate in comical exchanges between the women and the local policeman. José Alvarez Junco points to the idealized urban lower-class stereotypes that appear in *zarzuelas* and *sainetes* and suggests that this image may have influenced lower-class audiences to imitate the distortion of their culture that they observed in the theater (Graham, 1995, 86). This very plausible hypothesis suggests a strictly unidirectional influence and precludes the possibility that the depiction of lower-class urban life, albeit idealized and often filtered through middle-class expectations, might impact the middle class. The use of music in the *sainete* and *zarzuela* encourages the repetition of memorized songs that often include declarations of social injustice and vindications of workers' rights. The musical segments of *Amor engendra desdichas* include the announcement of an impending vegetable sellers' protest and a chorus that repeats the characters' call to prepare to fight (1899, 27), as well as a final song in which an older woman wrests a billy club from the policeman and turns it against him. The easily memorized songs from *sainetes* and *zarzuelas* allow for continual repetition of expressions of romantic desire as well as socially transgressive messages that over time become internalized by the theater-going population.

Speaking for the Other: Mobile Subjectivity Across the Class Divide

The growing field of sociology attracts the attention of modernist writers who aspire to speak for and about the urban and rural working class and to incorporate them in the project of national reconstruction. Joaquín Costa critiques the unjust and dangerous exploitation of the rural lower classes in analyzing the Spanish variant of residual oligarchical power that Perry Anderson identifies as one of modernism's coordinates. Costa interweaves political, linguistic, and artistic considerations and expresses admiration for popular culture and dialects. Ganivet's *Granada la bella* (1896) argues against certain elements of modern urban planning in favor of traditional, popular forms. The text speaker cites the need to listen to the opinion of the *pueblo,* which he defends as artistic and philosophical and strongly opposes the separation of classes in different neighborhoods (1943,

1:35), in part from a fear that a concentration of lower-class individuals might lead to revolution, but also in preference for dissymetries and mixtures.

José María Llanas Aguilaniedo applies new sociological methods to study Madrid's lower classes in *La mala vida en Madrid* (1901). He defines the *golfo* as a novel social phenomenon, but insists that members of the low life that form the subject of his study do not differ substantially from the general public. In the continual erasure of otherness that characterizes modernism, he speculates that tattoos came into vogue when soldiers saw them on indigenous American peoples and then revived a custom that had been formerly practiced but lost in Europe. Ernesto Bark, a socialist who participates in the modernist publication *Germinal* and publishes his study *Modernismo* in 1901, follows with *Estadística social* (1904). A sociological analysis of urban and rural labor conditions, the work inveighs against capitalism and advocates increased rights for working men and women. Bark alternately treats urban and rural worker conditions, including peasants, newspaper reporters, and sailors as well as working women within his purview and breaking with conventional class, gender, and geographic divisions to address the shared concerns of all modern workers. Both Bark and Llanas Aguilaniedo produce sociological study and literary criticism, exemplifying modernism's combined interest in artistic innovation and social reform. Darío encourages such a mix in *Tierras solares* when he praises Catalan modernism and Santiago Rusiñol for reaching out to workers. Rural and urban workers, men and women, literary and social subjects intermix in modernist writing to depict a culture in which classes intermingle and relocate geographically with continual redefinition of differences and encounters across borders.

Azorín further illustrates this trend in his 1905 *Los pueblos,* which combines fiction, literary criticism, and travel literature, closing with a sociological analysis of Andalusian rural workers that includes statistics on unemployment, tuberculosis, and malnutrition. The text speaker travels through worker neighborhoods of Lebrija and in a strong expression of protest, joins with workers, businessmen, and other writers to demand change and better government (1953b, 367). The same alliance of different classes and professions occurs in "Notas sociales" (1895), where Azorín discusses the connection between increased levels of literacy, growing numbers of labor publications, and artistic production (1947–48, 1:199). The text acknowledges workers as agents of their own cause and recognizes their voice among a chorus that clamors for change. The lower classes are presented with compassion, respect, and understated despair in a series of Azorinian texts that offer a collage of images. In typical modernist rejection of grand narratives, Azorin interweaves anarchist discourse with other political, rhetorical stances. The fragmentary nature of his writing reflects a modern vision of subjectivity, obligating the reader to abandon a fixed positionality and adopt changing responses to the textual reproduction of the modern experience.

Even within the brevity of a two-page, two-paragraph text, Azorín exploits the powers of understatement and textual gaps to encourage a conceptualization of the modern subject as moving through different positions and in relation to the lower-class subject, this mobility necessitates the surrender of inherited attitudes toward the other. "Vaso" of *Pueblo* (1930) presents a minimalist scene that commences with the description of a soft light, moves to the impeccable whiteness of a bed, and gradually introduces footsteps, bottles of varied sizes, medicine droppers, until the reader assembles a picture of a well-equipped hospital room. The absence of verbs requires the linking of different elements in an active process of creating meaning. The method of discovery underscores the active role of the subject in the construction of reality and the interactive nature of knowledge. Additional details complete the picture, with the mention of urine analysis, blood tests, x-rays, but just as the image appears to stabilize and the reader feels secure in the identification of a middle or upper-class sick room, the narrator speaks of a "poor," "miserable" bed. The lack of light, air, and medicines in this second room suggests a new location and different class. The absence of medical care distinguishes the unnamed, never described poor subject from the privileged patient of the preceding paragraph. The clear difference between the two, made more obvious by the interpretive need to return to the initial paragraph in order to verify the accuracy of the reading, subtly obliges the reader to recognize injustices based on class and wealth. The order of the two paragraphs, the antiseptic tone of the treatment of the wealthy patient, and the more emotive depiction of the poor resident encourage a middle-class reader to suspend identification with a fellow class member and empathize with the lower-class patient. The choice of *vaso* [glass] as title and object through which the reader accesses the barely delineated characters suggests a model for the ever-changing relation of self and other, here developed in the context of cross-class relations. Solid yet transparent, open but containing, the glass symbolizes the modernist vision of subjectivity as amenable to exchange with the other but also resistant to assimilation, fluid without absorbing or being absorbed.

Baroja's depiction of the lower classes places them within a mobile society that directly relates to his view of subjectivity as marked by change and instability. He shares Ortega y Gasset's scorn for the masses, but manifests a more complex attitude toward and dialogical relation with the other. Baroja purposely provokes reaction and anger in his reading public with the goal of fostering shifts in the reader's subject positions. He equates social and individual change with the dissolution of traditional ideas and aspires to push his audience toward modern thought by forcing it to break with accepted norms: "Hay que producir en cada español una intranquilidad, un instinto de examen, un anhelo, aunque sea inconcreto de algo mejor. Hay que disociar todas las ideas del ambiente; las ideas nuevas se nutren con los restos de las ideas tradicionales. Algunas gentes temen lo que llaman ideas disolventes. ¿Por qué? Gracias a las ideas disolventes, la Humanidad marcha. Gracias a las ideas disolventes, el hombre vive hoy mejor que ayer" [It is necessary to foster in every Spaniard a sense of anxiety, an instinct for examination, a desire, even if vaguely defined for something better. It is necessary to disassociate all ideas from their surroundings. New ideas feed on the remains of traditional ideas. Some people fear what they call corrosive ideas. Why? Thanks to corrosive ideas, Humanity marches on. Thanks to corrosive ideas, people live better today than yesterday] (1946–48, 5:107). With respect to the lower classes, Baroja resists totalizing visions. He recognizes the dehumanizing effects of modern urban society and like Sawa, remarks on how few human faces can be found in a crowd,[11] but he also exults in the creation of urban and rural lower-class types that embody the complexities of human subjectivity. At the same time that he decries the brutality and ingratitude of the Russian lower classes in *El mundo es ansí,* José Ignacio Arcelu states that the birth of the collective conscience represents the single greatest contribution of modern history (1967, 427). Unlike Blasco Ibáñez and xenophilic *sainetes* and *zarzuelas,* Baroja depicts urban and rural societies in which classes come into contact and intermingle. *César o nada, La dama errante, Las tragedias grotescas,* and *Camino de perfección* present narrative worlds in which individuals from different classes interact in a process that transforms individual subjects. Possibilities for happiness often arise by way of cross-class marriages. Fernando Ossorio chooses

Dolores, the dark-skinned daughter of a lower-class woman and Andrés Hurtado marries Lulú, of marginally middle-class origins but of lower-class values and habits learned from her lower-class community.

Ciro Bayo also trains his eye on a heterogeneous society. In both *El peregrino entretenido* (1910) and *El lazarillo español* (1911), he describes his travels through Spain and his contacts with farmers, traveling puppeteers, a Swiss entomologist, owners and maids of small inns, beggars, and criminals. The text speaker often adopts a dual perspective, as when he forgives the gypsies who trick him, admiring their carefree lifestyle and then a page later impugns them as masters of theft (64). Galdós brings the issue of class mingling to his novels and plays of the 1890s and 1900s. The *Torquemada* series (1889–95) describes the upward trajectory of the money lending Francisco Torquemada and his marriage into an aristocratic family that he saves from financial ruin. The narrative signals the futility of traditional class segregation through the figure of the blind Rafael, who decries interclass mixing. Rafael's sightlessness symbolizes his inability to accept change, a refusal of new forms of interculturality that leads him to choose suicide over life in the new order.

Realidad (1889) also examines a shifting social order, in which aristocratic men borrow money from prostitutes and a ruined noble woman marries a shopkeeper. In this mobile society, individuals lack full understanding of each other and of themselves. Augusta remains a mystery both to her husband, Tomás Orozco, and her lover, Federico Viera. Federico feels mystified by his friendship with the prostitute Leonor, and her feelings for him remain unclarified. The stability of the self and control of one's surroundings disappear in this text, which unfolds in dialogue form in yet another indication of the absence of authority and fixed perspective. Although Orozco and Viera had been close friends, their friendship did not prevent Viera from having an affair with Orozco's wife. Viera at one point blames a hypocritical society for his and Augusta's infidelity, suggesting they put on clown makeup to publicly confess their duplicity, but the masking of identity in the novel goes beyond conventional criticism of bourgeois hypocrisy to examine the difficulty of intersubjective knowledge in the modern world. Orozco, Augusta, and Viera live in solitude, unable to communicate. It is only after Viera kills himself out of remorse that Orozco feels he understands his friend. However, when he tries to embrace the ghost of Viera that appears to him, the image fades, leaving Orozco alone once more.

In subsequent works, Galdós explores new modes of intersubjective, interclass communication, increasingly vindicating the lower classes as the site for the development of relationships based on ethical commitment in *Mariucha, El abuelo, Celia en los infiernos, El tacaño Salomon, Nazarín, Halma,* and *Misericordia.*

The modernist vision of Spanish culture as socially heterogeneous, with frequent encounters between classes, genders, regions, and ethnicities recognizes lower-class agency. In realism and naturalism, interaction between individuals of diverse social strata often developed by way of the amorous desire of a middle or upper-class man for a lower-class woman and the resolution of the conflict typically involved either the death of the lower-class woman or her return to lower-class status. Pardo Bazán's *La Tribuna,* Pereda's *Sotileza,* Galdós's *Marianela,* and even his *Fortunata y Jacinta* exemplify this tendency. Modernist texts allow for more varied encounters between classes and more divergent endings. Relations between the sexes do not develop solely through romantic or sexual desire and the modernist preference for inconclusive endings avoids the definitive closure characteristic of realist and naturalist texts. On the other hand, the rejection of grand narratives also precludes the depiction of absolute lower-class victory.

Joaquín Dicenta's *Daniel* (1906) explores possibilities for lower-class agency. The action takes place in a miners' village during a labor strike and unfolds around the figure of the eponymous protagonist and his three children: Pablo, a miner and labor organizer; Pedro, a soldier; and Anita. The owner's son seduces and then abandons Anita and also orders the soldiers to fire on the strikers, leading to the deaths of Pablo and Pedro. The commanding officer's strong opposition to the shooting avoids a sense of intractable class conflict, as does the depiction of the mine owner and the chief engineer as caring individuals who have been forced to lower wages by competitors and stock holders. By contrast, the mine owner's son and the stock holders who tour the mine remain blind to the miners' condition. Echoes of Palacio Valdés's *La espuma* surface in the depiction of an elevator trip to the caverns, but Dicenta's text ends on a very different note. Daniel determines to avenge his sons' deaths and daughter's dishonor and disables the elevator to send a group of wealthy visitors crashing to death. Although his personal motivations displace a politicized conflict, the political resurfaces in the figure of Cesarea, a female strike leader whose husband had died in a previous protest and who had rejected Pablo's love out of commitment to her children and the workers' cause. Cesarea watches as Daniel realizes his plan, in an attitude that remains open for audience interpretation. The stage directions specifically state that the actress playing the role shall determine the appropriate facial expression (1931, 73) and as Daniel reveals his plan, Cesarea seems to move from surprise to shock, opposition, and finally paralysis. The aspiration of middle-class writers to represent lower-class subjectivity is fraught with the dangers that accompany all attempts to speak for the other; as Millington poses the dilemma: "how to know alterity—what is beyond the Self or the Same—without reducing it by assimilation . . . how to establish a dialogue with a text, while preserving its difference" (1994, 24). Dicenta risks presenting a class hatred so violent and vengeful that it becomes excessively alien. Cesarea's ambivalence provides an opening for connection, both in her role as mother and in the undecidability of her response to Daniel's action.

Several modernist works textually examine the problem of speaking for the lower-class other. Emilia Pardo Bazán explores class conflict in her early *La Tribuna* (1882), which closes with the reimposition of social order, in keeping with the Spanish realist paradigm. The 1894 *Memorias de un solterón* offers a modernist rewriting of *La Tribuna,* with the reappearance of the working-class Amparo and the middle-class Baltasar Sobrado, who had seduced and abandoned her. In contrast to the 1882 novel, where the revolutionary Amparo fails in both political and personal aspirations, leaving the impression of a world in which different classes come into contact but the social order does not change, *Memorias* depicts a society in rapid transformation. An unreliable first-person narrator presents the story, a frequent technique in the later Pardo Bazán that facilitates the introduction of double voicing and destabilized focalization. Mauro Parejo relates the story first as a semi-detached observer and then an increasingly interested party as he becomes more and more enamored of Feíta Neira, the protagonist. Mauro's shift in stance as well as the overlaying of a masculine narrator to present the feminist argument of a woman writer creates a complex set of voices that interact with and inflect each other.

Feíta rejects bourgeois class prejudices and advocates a complete break with the family's aristocratic credentials and now barely middle-class life style. Without the financial means to maintain middle-class status, she suggests her sisters earn money by sewing or singing in the theater, and she personally considers working as a servant. Her ideal consists of becoming *pueblo* in body and economic life style and aristocrat in knowledge and culture (1964, 2:506). Mauro comes to accept Feíta's views and assists in placing her sisters and brother respectively as seamstress, singer, and salesman of female clothing in a department store. However, the multiply inflected narrative reveals reticence in Mauro's acceptance of the working class, especially with regard to lower-class men. Feíta's relationship with Amparo's son, designated throughout the novel as *el compañero Sobrado,* provokes Mauro's sexual insecurities and elitism. During a meeting with his rival, Mauro discloses snobbish disdain for Sobrado's ill-fitting work shirt and envy of his dark, handsome demeanor. He fears that Sobrado epitomizes the dashing lower-class figure that would appeal to the unorthodox Feíta. Sobrado openly refers to the abyss that separates them and although Mauro protests that class distinctions play no role in their relations, he later admits the contradiction between his denial and his initial thoughts on seeing the handsome worker (500).

An advocate of liberal political positions, Mauro avoids admitting his elitism and resists even more the recognition of fears of sexual inadequacy in the face of the younger, stronger, and more attractive Sobrado. Early in the novel, Mauro confesses his anxieties with respect to women and marriage, explaining his fear that after the wedding ceremony, there will follow only a few brief hours of not always mutual physical pleasure (1964, 2:455). Concerns regarding his ability to sexually satisfy a wife remain only barely insinuated, but take on greater force when Mauro studies *el compañero Sobrado*'s physical appearances as he imagines they would appear to Feíta. Mauro's feelings of envy, jealousy, and barely disguised scorn reveal a sublimated fear of lower-class sexuality.[12] His concerns prove groundless when Feíta discloses her disdain for Sobrado after he abandons the workers' cause for the trappings of bourgeois life. Feíta's clear expression of her feelings and rejection of middle-class values contrast with Mauro's more conflicted emotional and ideological response. *Memorias de un solterón* puts these different discourses into play to underscore the difficulty of representing the lower-class subject. Middle-class sensibilities and anxieties occlude access to this other and at the same time that the text advocates the desirability of cross-class encounters, it points out the difficulties of such a rapprochement.

Pardo Bazán's *La piedra angular* (1891) more fully explores the difficulty of representing the lower-class other. Clemessy (1981, 248–49) and others characterize the novel as an apology for the abolition of the death penalty, but it also probes liberal ideological inconsistencies and underlying bourgeois masculine disdain for women and the lower classes. The novel relates the story of the liberal doctor Moragas, his condemnation of the death penalty, and strained relationship with Juan Rojo, the local executioner. Moragas determines to redeem Rojo, save his son Telmo from social ostracism, and prevent the execution of a lower-class woman accused of murdering her husband. The extradiegetic narrator stands at a palpable distance from Moragas and other middle-class characters who treat lower-class subjects with patronizing arrogance. Moragas disdains the executioner and only condescends to treat his wounded son after the intercession of a pleading woman neighbor. The doctor finds it normal that boys from the local private school stoned Telmo and tells Rojo that executioners' children are better left to die than saved to live as outcasts.

The lawyer Lucio Febrero privately expresses liberal attitudes toward crime and opposes the death penalty, but he publicly moderates his position due to political aspirations. His uninspired defense results in prosecutorial victory and the woman receives the death penalty despite the mitigating circumstances of a lifetime of sexual abuse. The full story of the crime never unfolds in the novel, insinuated in fragments intercalated in conversations between middle-class men. When Febrero and Moragas visit the nameless and largely voiceless woman, they paternalistically deceive her with false promises that she will never face execution. Febrero openly voices his belief that the lower class responds better to deception than reason and coolly remarks that the woman's loss of life matters less than the struggle for the noble ideal of abolishing the death penalty (1964, 2:336).

Moragas's desire to prevent the execution coincides with his dream of reforming Telmo and he determines to effect both at Rojo's expense. The doctor promises to pay for Telmo's education and in return, requires that Rojo refuse to carry out the execution and also deliver Telmo to Moragas's keeping. Rojo explodes in anger at the thought and Telmo, despite Moragas's assumption that he could not love his father, reveals his deep filial attachment. Moragas's inflexible, inhuman demand finally prevails. The description of his victory reveals the overwriting of lower-class aspirations and discourse by a smugly righteous, liberal middle class:

> Telmo quiso decir algo, apretósele el corazón, mitad de alegría, mitad de otra cosa . . . , y sin acción ni resistencia se dejó conducir por Moragas. . . . El filántropo sonreía: orgullo inefable dilataba su corazón; sus pulmones bebían la brisa salitrosa; sus pasos eran elásticos, iguales; no tropezaba en las piedras; creía volar. Más poderoso que el jefe del Estado, acababa de indultar a dos seres humanos y de regenerar a otros dos. Y como Telmo no le siguiese todo lo aprisa posible, aun volviese de cuando en cuando el rostro atrás, mirando hacia la barraca maldita, el doctor se inclinó, echó un brazo al cuello del muchacho y murmuró con ternura: —Anda, hijo mío. (1964, 2:346)
>
> [Telmo wanted to say something, his heart ached, half from happiness, half from something else . . . and without action or resistance, he let Moragas lead him. . . . The philanthropist smiled. Ineffable pride filled his heart, his lungs drank in the salty air, his steps were elastic and even, with no stumbling on the rocks. He felt like he was flying. More powerful than the head of government, he had just pardoned two human beings and regenerated two more. And since Telmo wasn't following him as rapidly as he should, and even turned his head back from time to time, looking at the cursed hut, the doctor bent down, placed his arm around the boy's neck and whispered tenderly: —Come along, my son.]

The narrative underscores Moragas's self-serving actions by focussing on his feelings of pride and satisfaction and signaling his blindness to Telmo's emotional distress. Moragas's words preclude a response and Telmo's silence links with the anonymous, voiceless female prisoner who never has the opportunity to tell her story. The lack of forum and voice for the lower classes in a middle-class world receives striking emphasis in the text's closing lines. Rojo, afraid to defy the authorities by refusing to carry out the execution and equally bound by his promise to Moragas, throws himself and his instruments into the sea, where the water gradually fills his lungs and as the narrative explains, suffocates his final scream (1964, 2:349). *La piedra angular* dramatically enacts the difficulty of giving voice to the lower classes and signals liberal middle-class male blindness to issues of lower-class male and female agency and subjectivity.

Gabriel Miró often explores the difficulty of knowing the other and specifically addresses cross-class communication in "La niña del Cuévano," of *Corpus y otros cuentos* (1908). The text uses a first-person plural narration to describe the collective attitude of a numerically indeterminate group of middle-class visitors to the country. Their description of nature unfolds with delicate sensitivity, including minutely detailed portraits of ants and other insects that appear endowed with human traits. In the midst of an idyllic scene, a young girl appears and asks them to buy her homemade basket. The narrators note her ragged clothing, bare feet, almost shaved head and offer small change, but do not purchase her product. With idealistic visions of her life as poor but filled with love, they observe with shocked disbelief when she crushes an insect with a stone. Gradually the narrators see each of their illusions crumble in the face of her brusque replies. They imagine her to come from a distant village, but she is a local resident; they assume she lives with a family that loves her as the youngest member, but her father is dead, her mother mistreats her, and her sister is the single mother of a constantly crying baby.

An ironic undercurrent mocks these idealistic declarations and the girl introduces the final blow to middle-class illusions when she answers their exhortations of generosity and kindness bluntly asking if they are going to buy her basket. The child's commercial ambitions remain completely outside the narrators' realm of imagination. They envision a subjectivity for her that clashes with the self-sufficient identity she has constructed for herself and cannot comprehend or value this other that defies their projections. The text suggests that the young entrepreneur has a more developed ability for intersubjective communication: when the narrators command her to look at the insect she has killed, she refuses, revealing that their disapproval affects her. She has learned enough middle-class discursive protocol to remain attentive to their disquisitions while they endlessly lecture her, breaking her silence only when questioned or actively marketing her basket. The narrators cannot hear her voice. Even when they recognize her dialect as typical of the area, they imagine that she is from some distant place.

Emilia Pardo Bazán and Gabriel Miró seek to open a space for the lower-class speaker by critiquing middle-class discursive hegemony. Their awareness of the dangers of attempting to speak for the other does not entirely erase the pitfalls confronting those who aspire to cross-class communication, but it allows for the exploration of new modes of narrativity and discursivity that foster polyphonic expression. The reader of these modernist texts faces a plural, contradictory presentation that results from Pardo Bazán's use of unreliable narrators and shifting subject positions and Miró's ironic juxtapositions and use of an innovative first person plural that calls attention to the conventions of narrative focalization even as it breaks with them. The plural "we" destroys the fiction of a single, stable speaking position—the narrative I—and inserts the suggestion of multiple viewpoints within an illusory unity.

Other modernist writers incorporate the voice and values of the lower class through the interjection of popular oral or written texts. Victor Catalá's use of legends and folklore in *Solitut* introduces the voices of an anonymous collectivity, largely transmitted by women story tellers, in a dual affirmation of lower-class and feminine subjectivity. Pío Baroja introduces popular songs, poems, and legends in his multi-volume series on the adventures of Eugenio Aviraneta and also in his novels of the Basque region, *Zalacaín el aventurero* and *Las inquietudes de Shanti Andía.* As mentioned previously, Manuel Machado's incorporation of popular verse forms and songs represents an important melding of cultured and traditional, individual and collective authorship that becomes so entirely seamless that popular singers appropriate Machado's creations as if they belonged to the collective repertoire. Enrique de Mesa and Vicente Medina similarly fuse traditional poetic forms and rural dialect in their poetry and alongside Francisco Villaespesa's exotic or drug-induced compositions, he imitates the collective popular voice in "Coplas de mi Andalucía" or the *soleares, seguidillas* of other collections.

Antonio Machado inserts popular verse forms and songs in his highly abstract and cultured philosophical writings, bringing together two traditionally disparate worlds. *De un cancionero apócrifo* and *Juan de Mairena* contain epigrams, aphorisms, *coplas,* original creations in both cultured and popular form as well as quotations from classical poems and poets in Spanish and other languages. In combination with the complex play of levels and speakers present in these texts through the invention of the multiply fictionalized identities of Abel Martín and Juan de Mairena, the rich range of poems of diverse origin introduces a hybridity that blends different traditions, social classes, and nationalities. Francisco Martínez Martínez refers to the rejection of modernity in Machado and to the poet's bucolic ruralism (1989, 83). The attribution of "bucolic" hardly captures the anguish described in the faces of the poor dwellers of the public hospital in "El hospicio" or in the hands of the beggars who stand in the marble atrium of the church (1951, 672). "Un criminal" and "La tierra de Alvargonzález" explore the effects of greed, sexual repression, and envy on rural families. Machado presents "La tierra de Alvargonzález" in two versions, the prose legend and the long ballad, that dialogue with each other and intermix their popular form and voice with his own personal touches. In this recuperation of a double-voiced popular tradition as well as in the varied portraits of popular figures and the utilization of different popular poetic forms, Machado textually reproduces a diverse, polyphonic lower class with which he interacts dialogically, joining popular tradition and the lower-class voice with his literary production.

Unamuno approaches the question of lower-class subjectivity with a different voice and emphasis but like Machado, Baroja, Miró, Pardo Bazán, and others, he prefers a variable, mutable stance. "Razón y vida," published in *Renacimiento* in 1907, appropriates a tone and attitude akin to Ortega y Gasset when castigating the Spanish *pueblo's* failure to recognize natural hierarchies. In this context, *pueblo* appears to refer to the lower classes, although it could also designate the nation in general. In other texts, and culminating for some in his final novel, *San Manuel Bueno, Mártir* (1930), Unamuno discloses a paternalistic attitude towards less educated classes when suggesting that his own doubts regarding life after death and the existence of God would prove too burdensome for them. On the other hand, Unamuno actively seeks to disseminate his doubts through novels, essays, plays, speeches, magazine publications, and poetry, and although he does not specifically address the lower classes, his choice of language and genre and his constant interventions in public affairs with the resulting national fame that they produce encourage a very wide distribution of his ideas. Furthermore, even within *San Manuel Bueno,* the tension between a silencing and proclamation of doubt remains unresolved. The protagonist reveals his qualms to the female narrator and her brother and publicly expresses them in his moving enunciation of Christ's words, "My God, My God, why hast Thou forsaken me?," with the effect that his mother openly breaks into tears and the village idiot internalizes the words and repeats them at intervals as he wanders the streets, profoundly moving all who hear the repeated confession of disbelief.

The presence of two responses to the lower-class subject persists throughout Unamuno's work. The impulse to cocoon the public from religious doubt carries forward to some extent nineteenth century anxiety regarding the proximity of social revolution, but also seeks to resolve or dissolve the tension between risk and security that Anthony Giddens signals as intrinsic to the modern experience. In a world where the grand narrative of religious faith has disappeared, individuals must construct their own meaningful accounts and create their own subjectivity, and Unamuno at times shrinks from this responsibility both for himself and for others of all classes. More typically, he insists on facing the task squarely and on prodding his public to follow his example. His drive to educate the public through every means available in modern society on such varied topics as responsibility, national reconstruction, religious doubt, and identity formation produces an ongoing dialogue with his Spanish audience.

"Los naturales y los espirituales" (1905) superbly reflects the simultaneity of polarities in Unamunan thought and the methods that he employs in communicating with his readers, amongst whom he includes a lower-class public. The text opens in the middle of an on-going discussion between two individuals who debate the merits of tradition and innovation and the tendency of *el pueblo* to favor one or the other. The speakers leave no doubt that in this context they refer to the lower classes. One argues that the Spanish *pueblo* is essentially conservative and resistant to change while the other insists on popular openness to new ideas. Lacking names and physical markers of divergence, differentiation of the speakers relies entirely on their expressed opinions and as they refine their positions in the process of the debate, their separate identities often disappear. One speaker insists that real popular traditions differ radically from institutionalized visions of national tradition, which schools and churches must continually reteach because they have in fact no roots among the people. The same speaker rails against the Spanish expression *fe de carbonero,* with its connotations of blind acceptance of religious or other ideas. He insists that all people must understand their beliefs, emphasizing the need for lower-class faith in the validity of their knowledge and in themselves. In this essay, the speaker who advocates intelligence and doubt predominates over the representative of faith and security, in contrast with *San Manuel Bueno, Mártir,* where the reverse occurs. However, "Los naturales y los espirituales" eschews hierarchical ranking and presents the speakers as twins who accept as necessary and beneficial that they will never come to agreement, fusing into a single figure in the closing sentence (1958, 3:841). The revolving coin stops momentarily, but the two faces that continually succeed each other will resurface over the next decades in Unamuno's writing.

Ramón del Valle-Inclán brings the lower classes into his works through varied strategies. The stylized, rural figures of his earlier publications often include older women servants, who have become members of the household and stay on after they can no longer work, frequently serving as transmitters of family and folk lore from one generation to the other. With the *esperpento,* the presence of lower-class characters accompanies a concentrated effort to incorporate their discourse. Rural and urban lower classes appear in *Divinas palabras,*[13] *La hija del capitán, Los cuernos de don Friolera,* and *Luces de bohemia,* with its famous definition of the *esperpento* as the reflection of classical heroes in the deforming curvature of a carnival mirror, a reference that in itself brings together cultured and popular traditions. *Luces de bohemia* has long been recognized as a radically transgressive text. For the purposes of the present study, I would like to point to its links with the origins and theorization of the modernist movement at the turn of the century and ongoing concerns within modernism for the lower classes and cross-class intermingling of values and discourse. Like many of his contemporaries, albeit in more extreme form, Valle-Inclán introduces Bakhtinian *heteroglossia* through the intermixing of popular speech with classical discourse as well as through constant parody. The mix of gypsy and other lower-class slang, Latin Americanisms, comically translated French terms (e.g., Jefe de Obra for the French chef d'oevre to indicate masterpiece [1968, 41]) and an ironized cultured discourse reflect the intense social melding that occurs in the play and in the society that contributes to its form, content, and ideological perspective. The down and out writer Máximo Estrella and his sidekick don Latino de Hispalis wander through Madrid in the course of a night, encountering prostitutes, book dealers, street venders, policemen, newspaper writers, and on the occasion of Máximo's run in with the police, judges, the Minister of Interior, and other representatives of official Spain. In jail, Máximo shares a cell with an Anarchist prisoner who had refused to serve in the army and had worked as a union organizer. The poet and the political prisoner embrace at the end of the scene in an important symbolization of modernism's blending of artistic and ideological missions.

The intellectual's assimilation of the language and ideology of the lower class recurs throughout the text, in the episodes with the Anarchist and in scene 11, where the voice of a mother whose child has been killed by police bullets moves Máximo to tears of frustration and solidarity. Immediately after this scene, he spells out his theory of the esperpento and the new literary form, the radical political stance, as well as the lexical and discursive hybridity all come together in the production of a novel experiment in artistic genre. Máximo represents the intellectual as worker who shares the sufferings of other laborers and in this sense, his self-identification harks back to early modernist writings that link writer and worker, as mentioned in chapter 1. The reference to Alejandro Sawa, the model for Máximo Estrella, also provides a connection between the *esperpento* and early modernism. Along with Sawa, an active participant in turn of the century anti-establishment modernist journals, the poet Rubén Darío and the fictional Bradomín of Valle-Inclán's earlier narratives make their appearance in the play, accompanying Max's body to the cemetery. While many critics have interpreted the presence of Bradomín and Darío at this funeral as a declaration of a break with his previous works and aesthetic, it can also be read as a refiguring that both continues and revises, simultaneously presenting the original and the deformed version as seen through the curved mirror. In the representation of the Nicaraguan poet and the fictional protagonist of the *Sonatas,* the text minimizes deformation to emphasize continuity. Darío still writes poetry, even as he leaves the cemetery, and he and Bradomín concur that the latter will probably live on forever. The conjoining of a historical person with a fictional character adds one more element of hybridity to an already multifaceted text. The dialogue between the aristocratic Spanish marquis and the Nicaraguan poet, whose indigenous features are textually emphasized (1968, 127), also traverses national, ethnic, and class borders. The rapid succession of distinct literary traditions, emotional perspectives, and lexical and discursive modalities contributes to the richness as well as the interpretive difficulty of Valle-Inclán's *esperpentos.* Critics often assume that these creations represent an elitist art form, available only to a minority audience (López Martínez 1988, 257). To the contrary, in another democratizing move, Valle-Inclán places all readers in a position of otherness with respect to the text. Lower-class readers would find certain scenes and vocabulary thoroughly familiar, although they might have difficulty with the work's non-representational aspects and classical allusions. Cultured readers presumably comprehend these latter features, but face significant challenges in penetrating the fast-paced dialogue with its popular, slang expressions. Like other modernists, Valle-Inclán fosters the creation of a new subjectivity in the Spanish audience, which must incorporate elements of lower and upper classes, Spanish and

Latin American and gypsy languages, and classical literary tradition as well as its parodic deformation.

The lower classes play multiple roles in Spanish modernist texts, confronting in language, life style, and ideology the middle and upper classes with new modes of speaking and experiencing reality. Their growing presence and power in society challenge traditional attempts to confine them to certain regions or freeze them in nostalgic *costumbrista* portraits. In modernism, lower-class subjectivities compete actively with bourgeois and upper-class visions of identity and Spanish modernist texts reflect this process in an ongoing examination of the mutual influence that occurs between classes and contributes to a redefinition of both nation and subject.

The Intersection of Women and the Lower Class in Redefining the Modernist Subject

The changing vision of social class takes place in conjunction with a transformed perception of gender and in the context of a struggle on the part of both women and the lower class for increased power and agency. The intersection of gender and class in modernism, as in the present, leads to a constant shifting of alliances and oppositions, shared concerns and mutual suspicions. Despite obvious and subtle dissimilarities between class and gender, hegemonic male culture traditionally subsumes both under the homogenizing designation of irrational and disordered. Felski identifies the attribution of female irrationality at the turn of the century to fear of growing feminism (1995, 3) and Showalter relates fear of female emancipation to anxiety regarding the breakdown of racial and class divisions (1990, 4–5). The link between women, the lower class, and primitive peoples has a long history in Western thought and continues in Freud's description of female sexuality as the "dark continent" of psychology (Corbey, 1991b, 50) and in Ortega y Gasset's association of women, non-Europeans, and the lower classes.

Sexual desire and patriarchal concerns regarding the legitimacy of offspring complicates the relationship between the male bourgeois subject and the feminine other. The conflict between the drives for sexual gratification and control of succession leads to the paradoxical co-presence in Spain and other Western cultures of the masculine ideal of the don Juan and the feminine ideal of the virgin. Obviously, the successful implementation of the male model seriously undermines possibilities for the effective realization of the female paradigm, and a partial resolution of this contradiction appears in the division of women into the opposing categories of virgin and prostitute, wife and mistress, Eve and Mary, that characterizes much Western cultural production. In a continuation of this dichotomous thinking, women associated with sexual activity are generally assigned lower social status. Domestic maids often functioned as sexual partners for male employers or their sons, at times initiating young men into sexuality with their parents' tacit approval. Prostitutes either originated in the lower classes or descended in social category once sexually active. The separation of sexual lower-class women from middle and upper-class wives, sisters, and daughters always evidenced a certain fragility in that men of power could legitimize their erotic relationships through marriage or legal recognition of illegitimate offspring. The tenuous nature of the divide between the two classes of women and attempts to maintain it constitute a major focus of literary production throughout history and into modernism. Attempts to separate women into two social and sexual classes also run counter to the intimate bonds formed between female servants and the families they serve. Lower-class wet nurses and nannies share maternal duties with upper-class biological mothers, bringing the two classes of women into intimate contact and exposing each to different ways of experiencing female subjectivity.

The hostility expressed toward urban culture and the nostalgia of certain realist writers for a return to rural cultures stem from a fear of the masses and of the breakdown of social and sexual barriers. Middle and upper-class female mobility in the city inevitably entails contact with the "instinctive, sexually licentious" lower classes and with men from all classes in a world in which surveillance becomes increasingly difficult. During realism and naturalism, the response to the new freedoms varied from panic and condemnation in Pereda, Fernán Caballero, and Coloma, to moderate to strong enthusiasm for new artistic and social possibilities in the early Galdós, Clarín, and Pardo Bazán. Elizabeth Wilson and Doreen Massey point out that women writers generally express greater enthusiasm for the city than their male counterparts and as indicated previously, Pardo Bazán and Carmen de Burgos celebrate the increased freedom available to urban women. Male modernists vary in their response to changing gender and social roles, but they too explore the intersection of gender and class in the search for new individual and social models.

The weight of traditional visions of female and lower-class subjectivity often overwhelms aspirations for change and rarely do writers and texts succeed in constructing both a modernist female and lower-class selfhood. Whether out of personal anxiety, pressures from the reading and viewing public, or the inability to overwrite tradition simultaneously on both fronts, modernist writers and texts often interweave conventional visions of female subjectivity with a rhetoric of social revolution or inversely, explore new possibilities for lower-class female identity within a more conservative political discourse. As Felski points out with respect to modernism and gender, the old dichotomies of tradition and modernity fail to capture the complexities of the period (1995, 211). In the context of Spanish culture, Graham and Labanyi remark that in the consumption of culture, the same segment of society "can respond in ways that are simultaneously conformist and contestatory; indeed the same response can be both at the same time" (1995, 5). An identical duality holds for the producers of culture, who work within inherited definitions and discourses in dialogue with their ancestors and contemporary interlocutors. The traditional othering of women and the lower class in one homogenized categorization and the coincident arrival of feminism and syndicalism that further encourages such a link in some instances provoke the displacement of fears of class rebellion onto women and of anxieties regarding feminist demands onto the lower classes. However, the conflation of women and the lower class also enables a new representation of both in that alteration in the identity of one translates to the other. Emphasis on male subjectivity in modernist works has led critics to overlook the significant presence of lower-class female subjectivity and the mutual implications of revised visions of gender and social class.

Persistent Echoes of Tradition in Visions of Class and Gender

Resistance to female and lower-class emancipation characterizes much realist and naturalist literature and continues into the modernist period in writers who remain largely within nineteenth-century sociosymbolic patterns. Wenceslau Fernández Florez depicts a totally othered lower-class female subjectivity in *Volvoreta* (1917). Despite a sexual interest in the eponymous female servant, the protagonist Sergio has internalized his mother's middle-class values. Although he runs away with Volvoreta, his rebellion relates more to a desire to free himself from his mother's control and establish masculine credentials than to an emotional attachment. He acts out his need for individuation and sexual coming of age through Volvoreta's body, but retains a deep suspicion and revulsion of her as subject, responding with disgust when she arrives unsuitably groomed for their first meeting in La Coruña. The depiction of his sexual maturation within a conservative, patriarchal ideology unfolds in a dual rejection of women and the lower class that increases in proportion to his perceived loss of masculinity. When Sergio attempts to confront the older rival who has taken Volvoreta as his mistress, he is unceremoniously and literally thrown out and determines to avenge his disgrace by reporting the affair to the man's wife and daughter. The upper-class daughter, with some access to power, has Sergio escorted to the door, but the lower-class Volvoreta remains a silenced, alien shadow who functions merely as a physical outlet for the various upper-class men who make use of her. Depicted as amoral and coarse, Volvoreta reflects a general repudiation of the lower class by the middle-class narrator and protagonist.

Other realist writers who continue to write during the modernist years incorporate the lower-class female through a process of assimilation, ultimately erasing any remnants of lower-class subjectivity. Juan Valera's personal sophistication precludes his wholehearted adoption of intransigent conservative values, but he clearly feels uncomfortable with feminist and working-class demands for greater social and political power. His novels of the 1890s incorporate certain aspects of the modernist aesthetic, as in the cosmopolitan and marginally decadentist ambience of *Genio y figura* (1897), but behind a veneer of stylistic innovation and an ironic stance that appears to brook no quarrel with modernity lies a traditionalist vision of gender and class. Several Valera novels relate the story of a lower-class woman who rises socially and economically, but the narratives only legitimize such a breaking of traditional borders if the woman's behavior reveals a clear, sustained repudiation of lower-class mores. *Pepita Jiménez* (1874) represents an early version of the story of a socially mobile young woman, although Pepita's lower-class origins remain somewhat unclear. Her father was an army captain and the class of her coarse and uncultured mother remains unclarified. The suggestion of her sexual impropriety receives more direct treatment, first in the questionable motives for her marriage to her geriatric husband and then on the occasion of her premarital relations with Luis Vargas. Although the narrative goes to great lengths to depict the sexual interlude as a one-time lapse in Pepita's otherwise exemplary life, the novel at least in part breaks down the binarism of virgin versus whore, Eve versus Mary.

Some two decades later Valera publishes *Juanita la Larga* (1895), returning to a cross-class love story in rural Andalusia. However, in response to growing pressures from the lower class and women, this novel reverts to more traditional binarisms and demands total assimilation of middle/upper-class conduct in the illegitimate, lower-class female protagonist. Despite the narrator's protestations that the novel contains no thesis and aims only to entertain, the subtext communicates that self-control and playing by the rules offer a surer path to social improvement than even moderately unconventional behavior. Juanita has grown up with considerable freedoms and participated in what the narrator designates as boyish activities. She continues to enjoy unusual independence as a young woman, visiting the public fountain where her beauty attracts the attention of the local men. Virtuous and innocent, Juanita also possesses a sensuality that the text relates to her lower-class origins. The tension between these various attributes—purity and sexuality, candor and cunning, lower-class spontaneity and upper-class restraint—play themselves out over the course of the novel. Juanita learns to curb her aspiration to "masculine" freedom of movement and to mask her pleasure at the exhibition of her physical beauty. Before she assimilates this lesson, she cedes to the temptation to flaunt her beauty and her body in the dress she makes from the Philippine silk given to her by don Paco, her fifty-three-year-old upper-class suitor.

The association in the social imaginary of lower-class and feminist demands for change finds expression in the priest's sermon, when he publicly castigates Juanita and interweaves censure of female depravity and materialist aspirations with warnings against socialism and challenges to existing social structures. He insists on the inevitable continuity of social and economical hierarchies and admonishes his listeners to respect the established system in order to enter paradise (1982, 93–94). Juanita realizes her mistake in defying social dictates regarding acceptable conduct for lower-class women and adopts a different behavior to regain public approval. She subsequently avoids public outings, dedicating her time to the feminine activities of sewing, embroidering, and regular church attendance. She gradually gains the acceptance of Paco's daughter Inés through proof of her virtue, her skills as seamstress, and successful deflection without public scandal of the amorous attentions of both the local *cacique,* Andrés Rubio, and Inés's husband. Juanita's transformation is sanctioned by her marriage to Paco in a narrative legitimization of cross-class relations on the condition of lower-class obedience of social norms.

Juanita la Larga reveals with surprising candor the conservative ideology underpinning the narrative. The narrator introduces initial doubts regarding women's virtue in a comment by Andrés Rubio, whose personal experiences have made him skeptical of women's purity. The epilogue further clarifies this view when the narrator indirectly but unmistakably reveals that Andrés has had a longstanding affair with Inés, the model of religious and social decorum, and is apparently the father of all or most of her twelve children, the last two arriving since Inés's husband became paralyzed (1982, 288). Inés heeds the demands for external adherence to hierarchies and norms and consequently, her sexuality represents no threat to the existing order. The narrator at times reveals discomfort with the blatant expression of such hypocrisy and attempts to explain the disjunction between Inés's private and public personae by outlining her belief in the Platonic doctrine of three souls—the sensual, sentimental, and pure or ideal—but the ironic tone and overall depiction of Inés as shallow and superficial undercut any serious consideration of belief in tripartite selfhood. The novel fundamentally upholds a traditional vision of subjectivity, where a consciously motivated separation of public and private identities allows for the reconciliation of the conflicting pulls of personal desire and public order.

Clarín's participation in Krausist and Institutionist activities and his involvement in the University of Oviedo's outreach programs speak to a liberal social and political commitment that differs radically from Valera's skeptical cynicism. However, Clarín's anxiety in the face of changing gender and social relations proves equally profound. His later works reveal increasing discomfort with social and literary changes and he openly declares that he feels old-fashioned and out of touch (1893a, 53). The same essay attacks a perceived democratization of literature and the growing insolence of readers who invade the terrain of the literary critics (54). Most of his writings on women deal with middle and upper-class subjects, but his one-act play about Asturian miners intermixes considerations of class and gender. *Teresa* (1895) depicts a mixed agrarian, industrial economy and although it incorporates politically charged terms such as *los miserables* and *los compañeros,* which apparently disturbed critics of the day,[14] the vindication of lower-class rights pales in the face of the very critical portrayal of the miner Roque and the displacement of a political focus to the question of women's role in the confluence of gender and social change. Roque's hatred of the upper classes relates less to social injustice than to personal resentment and jealousy of an upper-class rival. The dramatic attention shifts from the social to the sentimental in the latter part of the play, where Teresa comes to embody a feminine abnegation that repudiates women's rights to personal fulfillment and lower-class demands for social justice. Roque's hatred for the ruling classes plays itself out in his abuse of Teresa, beating her until he draws blood, and Teresa accepts her part unquestioningly: "Es mi hombre, soy suya" [He is my man, I belong to him] (1975b, 106). In addition, Teresa suffers on behalf of her upper-class admirer Fernando, steadfast in her loyalty to her husband but understanding of Fernando's love for her. The final scene utilizes the symbol of the cross to equate Teresa with the Christ figure and define her role as perpetual suffering for the redemption of the men who love her and for the circumvention of class conflict.[15]

The dramatic and narrative works of Joaquín Dicenta demonstrate the contradictory stances that ensue in the modernist examination of gender and class conflicts. His most famous play dealing with the urban working class, *Juan José* (1895), offers an interesting counterpart to Clarín's *Teresa,* with a shift of emphasis from resignation to agency and from the restricted world of the home to the public arena of streets and tavern. The first act unfolds in this public ambience, with discussions of salary injustices, past strikes, and future revolutions, but in acts 2 and 3, the focus moves from political issues to the amorous triangle formed by Juan José, his lover Rosa, and his foreman Paco. In a melodramatic ending, Juan José kills Paco and Rosa and then hands himself over to whatever sentence awaits him. The text manifests the change of emphasis from a modern social drama to traditional themes and tensions with the introduction of intertextual allusions to classical texts, in particular the *Celestina.* The presence of a go-between to unite Paco and Rosa totally breaks with Rosa's character as initially depicted and the audience's knowledge that she has been previously sexually active. The revised portrayal of Rosa as coy and indecisive, requiring the enticement of an experienced older woman to enter into another sexual relationship, reflects the weight of traditional visions of female dramatic heroines and the inability to imagine or fear of depicting a different female subjectivity. Despite this hesitancy, the dramatic dialogue places several different discourses in conflict and in so doing, gives voice to some of the contradictions that stand in the way of a transformation of traditional visions of class and gender. Juan José refutes the notion that Paco's power as supervisor justifies his control over other aspects of his life in a vindication of the right to self-sufficiency that he contradicts with his statements that Rosa belongs to him in a sense of material ownership. One lower-class woman character and many of the men defend a male right to control women by physical abuse, but Isidra, the go-between, disparages this view as the offshoot of cheap literature and also opposes the notion that women must sacrifice themselves for the happiness of others. Juan José's final acceptance of his fate conflicts with his earlier determination to act and with his agency in the double murder of Rosa and Paco. And finally, the melodramatic, Echegarayan ending and the projection of concerns with honor onto and in substitution for lower-class calls for social justice, represent a clear case of assimilation of the lower class other into a middle-class subjectivity and an elision of the threat of social revolution. Notwithstanding these concessions, the introduction of a range of lower-class characters allows for the articulation of oppositional values that stand in contradiction with each other and with conventional middle-class attempts to silence new discourses.

Los bárbaros (1912) follows the same pattern of initial political and social class conflict gradually ceding to a personal confrontation, but in this case the separation between the two spheres diminishes considerably. Furthermore, the representation of lower-class female agency directly addresses the issue of male power and its imbrication in the intersection of gender and class. The narrative action takes place in a rural environment and revolves around the love story of the forty-year old Manuel and María, a farm girl of 20 years. The symbolic names, invoking the figures of Christ and the virgin mother, point to a new order that the text defines as a blend of a revived, invigorated aristocracy and an energetic lower class. This social transformation requires the abolition of the current ruling class, a decadent nobility intermingling with a greedy bourgeoisie. The explication of this political program remains nebulous, but the delineation of women's role in the conflict receives greater definition. In the early chapters, the novel emphasizes the overarching power of patriarchy over lower and upper-class women. Male control of María's body surfaces repeatedly in the voyeuristic representation of her bathing by an evidently masculine narrator and in her own insistence on proving her feelings for the older Manuel by inviting him to make love to her. When she becomes pregnant and determines to marry Manuel, her father's violent opposition continues the theme of masculine control of the female body and its progeny. María's statement that an honorable woman only gives herself to the man she truly loves reveals the extent to which she has assimilated the view that a woman's body belongs more to others than to the female subject. It also reveals a conscious, noninstinctive decision on María's part and distances her from the purely instinctive characters of the naturalist novels of Blasco Ibáñez.

The upper-class women of the text similarly reveal the definition of their value through the exchange of their bodies. Julia, a duke's illegitimate daughter, enters into marriage with a financially ruined count in order to access upper-class Madrid society. However, in the latter part of *Los bárbaros,* Julia and María both evolve towards a different understanding of their power and relation with male authority. In Madrid, Julia becomes the king's mistress and her physical strength, reflecting her rural and lower-class origins, expresses itself in a sexuality that rapidly debilitates her lover, a degenerate heir to a deteriorating noble line. Julia's body and passion, however, remain entirely under her own control. She derives no pleasure from her sexual liaisons, preferring moments of solitude in which she treats herself to long baths and admires her naked body in the mirror. The narrator displays a complex relationship with the figure he voyeuristically describes, depicting with admiration and sensuous detail her magnificent naked body and alluding to her masturbatory pleasures with a combination of erotic curiosity and moralistic censure. He also insinuates her desire to rid herself of the odors and stains left by her male visitor, revealing a female loathing of male possession and a passive but evident rejection of control of her body.

María's repudiation of patriarchy takes a more aggressive form. She resists the village priest, local political powers, and her father's control by escaping to the mountains with Manuel. After a series of natural disasters compounded by political corruption and graft, María and Manuel return to the village, where the lower class finally rises up against the wealthy. The novel describes an incredibly violent confrontation, with wholesale destruction and killing of those who had exploited the poor. Fernando, a noble who has lived in retirement in protest against the present government, sees the rebels and their actions as the return of his grandfathers, thus justifying the current revolutionary activity through links with Spanish tradition (1912, 218). Julia, who is visiting the village, attempts to avoid her fate by once again using her body, this time to seduce Manuel. However, when Maria sees her husband's desire, she intercedes and kills her rival with an axe blow. In María's actions, lower-class and female resistance combine in a gesture of fury that radically breaks with the tradition of female abnegation and passivity. It might be argued that María's conduct confirms representations of female and lower-class subjectivity as irrational and primitive, and the text invokes this tradition by comparing her intervention to the fury of a female animal fighting over her mate (222). However, this represents only one of many different subject positions that interweave in María's psychological makeup. The legitimizing comments made by the aristocratic Fernando, the text's overt call for the equality of sexes and classes in the words of a middle-class doctor (175), and María's long history of loyalty, integrity, and self-sacrifice introduce alternative discourses that counter the stereotype of the irrational, possessive woman as the single, all-encompassing account of lower-class female subjectivity. María combines diverse behaviors and her final act of personal agency stands as one among many possible responses to the conditions of her existence. Perhaps evading the more fundamental conflict by turning woman against woman, María's action stands out, along with the vigorous self-assertion of Carolina of Unamuno's *El marqués de Lumbría* and a handful of other modernist texts in which female agency acquires a force and complexity traditionally reserved for middle and upper-class men.

Explorations of Female Sexuality and Changing Visions of Honor

Writers and publications that aspire to transform Spanish visions of human sexuality continue the ambivalent vision of lower-class and female sexual activity observed in Joaquín Dicenta. The magazine *La vida galante* (1898–1905) proposes to modernize Spanish attitudes toward love, honor, and the body through brief narratives, photographs, jokes, and poems. Celma Valero describes it as devoted exclusively to the erotic and exotic (1991,

47–49) and while this is largely true, the magazine also continues the linking of gender and social class that occurs in other publications of the period. Photographs of semi-nude actresses and teasing narratives offer continuous examples of a male gaze that invades female intimacy and enjoys unveiling the female body in a tradition extending back to the earliest narratives (Brooks 1993, 28–38). Pictures of the scantily clothed Belgian dancer Cleo de Merode (March 19, 1899:252) and of the fully dressed Spanish actress María Guerrero speak to the growing stature of women entertainers and the access to power and money that acting, singing, and dancing afforded women of the lower classes in the early twentieth century. Many stories and jokes contain strong anti-marriage sentiments and the magazine advocates sensual and sexual experiences as natural for the modern subject. In conjunction with this message, the publication reproaches male brutality toward women in texts such as Eduardo Zamacois's "Lo inconfesable," where a previously faithful middle-class wife finds herself in a compromising situation because of a less than forthright friend. After enduring what today would be considered date rape, the increasingly embittered woman withdraws to spend the rest of her life regretting her conduct. Significantly, the participants in this text are middle-class men and women, while in those that depict pleasurable sexual encounters, the characters are middle-class men, but lower-class women. A positive experience of sexuality for women remains largely confined to the lower class.

Felipe Trigo and Jacinto Octavio Picón devote most of their literary production to a revision of traditional attitudes toward sexuality and honor. Trigo's works include a generous dose of male voyeurism, often teasingly deferring descriptions of sexual gratification. In two of his better known novels, he constructs a dual narrative, in which the discussion of social problems forms a backdrop to the sexual exploits of the main characters. *El médico rural* (1912) describes an impoverished, backward rural village where the doctor protagonist practices before moving to a more prosperous town and embarking on numerous sexual exploits. *Jarrapellejos* (1914) similarly interweaves the social and the sexual. While neither text explicates the relationship between these two realms of experience, their co-presence continues the melding of gender and class considerations that characterize modernist literary production. Picón's narratives more fully intertwine the changing vision of sexuality and social issues affecting women of all classes, such as divorce, education, and career opportunities. In the short story collections *Cuentos de mi tiempo* (1895) and *Mujeres* (1911), gender and class receive equal treatment and the vindication of lower-class rights often takes on a radical tone. "El hijo del camino" presents the progeny of a prisoner and the poor, ugly woman with whom he was allowed to have sexual relations during a prison transfer. The son grows up uneducated and impoverished until he starts working for the electric company and sees the inside of a wealthy home. In frustration that he will never achieve access to this world, he bombs the house, killing its inhabitants. Picón depicts increased class separation as a result of modern urbanization in "La buhardilla," which describes the friendship of a duchess and the maid who had lived in the same building and given birth at the same time. In a reversal of standard narratives of the lower-class wet nurse, in this case the duchess nursed the maid's child to help her sickly neighbor. When the duchess moves to a newly-built home on the Castellana, the two women lose contact until a violent labor strike, in which the maid saves her noble friend and expresses her sorrow that new patterns of urban residence impede the formation of cross-class female solidarity. Another example of women bonding across classes appears in "Decadentes," in which two middle-class men make fun of a country woman who fails to load a heavy bundle of branches on a mule. The middle-class woman they are courting challenges them to complete the task and when they too fail, she takes off her gloves and easily completes the job.

Despite the feminist message of numerous Picón texts, his campaign to liberate the body and sexuality from traditional prohibitions continues to distinguish between male and female freedom and lower and upper-class female behavior. Juan de Todellas of *Dulce y sabrosa* (1891) exhibits traits typical of the don Juan model in his distaste for emotional commitment and avid pursuit of sexual pleasures. Cristeta, in turn, incarnates the requisite female behaviors. Innocent until her relations with Juan, inspired by passion and devoid of material interest, of lower-class origins without lower-class coarseness, she remains faithful to her first love despite his unexplained desertion. When Juan sees her with a young child after a two-year absence, he reveals the depths of the double standard in his resentment of the speed with which she has apparently replaced him and his horror at the possibility that she could have had the "criminal impudence" to marry another man without revealing her past (1915, 237). As the first man to engage in sexual relations with her, he invokes a prior and permanent ownership. Cristeta's clever enactment of a fictitious marriage and motherhood successfully reawakens Juan's desire and the couple reunite in the best of all possible (masculine) worlds. Juan professes his love and proposes, but Cristeta refuses on the grounds that marriage will destroy their affection. *Juanita Tenorio* (1910), written almost twenty years later, moves away from emphasis on virginity towards greater tolerance for multiple sexual partners for women. However, despite repeated critiques of a society that does not prepare women for financial independence, the narrative presents Juanita's sale of her body as an inexcusable transgression from which she redeems herself only through extended care of an ex-lover who is dying of tuberculosis. The return to female self-sacrifice and lower-class servitude contradicts the message of sexual liberation and female agency communicated in other Picón texts and in *Juanita Tenorio* itself. In a surprising regression to Clarín's *Teresa,* Picón here advocates the same lower-class female abnegation, but without the safety net of marriage or class solidarity.

In the context of the array of texts that hesitantly attempt to negotiate the difficult terrain connecting social class, gender, and the modernist subject, Benito Pérez Galdós and Ramón Pérez de Ayala offer innovative explorations of lower-class female subjectivity. Galdós's *Tristana* (1892) presents a multifaceted vision of gender and class that reflects the varied forces working for and against new opportunities for lower-class women. Tristana, the orphan who has been adopted and seduced by her guardian don Lope, incarnates a spontaneous aspiration for freedom and self-expression that confronts the formidable controls put in place by patriarchal society. She and her elderly maid Saturna escape the house to enjoy the independence of movement allowed a lower-class older woman in the urban streets. This relatively autonomous female society and cross-class bond is broken by Lope's control and the appearance of a young lover. The aspiring artist Horacio and Lope see themselves as rivals for Tristana's affections, but each represents in his own way an obstacle to her liberation. Horacio introduces Tristana to art and self-expression through painting. She discovers a natural talent that with education and more tolerant social conditions might have led to substantial achievements. However, Horacio's encouragement of her autonomy remains subordinate to inherited prejudices. He finds himself moderately annoyed by the intellectual growth of a woman he envisioned as an admiring subordinate. When they discuss the possibility that Tristana might become pregnant, Horacio responds with irritation at her insistence that the child would be more hers than his and that she would raise it as a single mother.

In the framework of the social conventions of the period, Tristana's desire for both independence and honor introduces an oxymoron that signals an unjust world in which she can achieve neither. Her many-sided personality reveals an incredible potential that just begins to develop in the novel. The narrative endows her with a complex subjectivity, sensitive to the needs of others, insistent on independence, and intuitively alert to the complexity of human personality. Describing Lope to Horacio, she struggles to capture his contradictory qualities, asserting that he has two consciences, one pure and noble, the other murky and reprehensible. In contrast to Valera's superficial enunciation of a theory of unstable, multiple subjectivity, Galdós explores such a possibility and demonstrates its social construction. Lope's morally objectionable side derives from the culturally sanctioned masculine model of the don Juan, while his noble aspect originates in a generous spirit that led him to support Tristana's dying mother even to his own economic detriment and proves likable despite the clear evidence of his sexual abuse of his charge. Lope's control of Tristana interweaves with his declarations of support for her newly discovered independence and artistic talents and reflects the conflicting messages directed to women in Western cultures in the late nineteenth and early twentieth centuries.

Tristana's search for a place in this contradictory cultural landscape requires the invention of an entirely new language. Like Feíta of Pardo Bazán's *Memorias de un solterón,*[16] Tristana interjects popular expressions in her speech in an effort to break with bourgeois social control. She and Horacio create an idiosyncratic Spanish, intermixing Italian, gypsy, and popular speech. Tristana introduces new verb endings to reflect a previously unexperienced subjectivity. When arguing against traditional visions of female assimilation to male identity in the process of love, she invents the first person singular verb *ero,* substituting it for the linguistically correct *era* and borrowing the "-o" ending exclusive to the first person in other verbal tenses to underscore the separation between herself as the speaker and Horacio as the third-person party to whom or about whom she might speak: "Tú como eres, yo como *ero.* Eso de que dos que se aman han de volverse iguales y han de pensar lo mismo, no me cabe en la cabeza" [You as you are, me as I was. This idea that two who love each other become the same and think the same thoughts doesn't make any sense to me] (1967, 5:1583). The narrative develops this new voice and discourse with incredible vigor and imagination, offering a fresh perspective on life, love, and personal identity that dominates over half of the text.

The second part of the novel introduces a fictional version of male backlash, elucidating the powerful array of forces that silence Tristana's newly found voice. Tristana develops a tumor that requires the amputation of her leg and although this reflects the unpredictable nature of illness, it also evokes with perverse cruelty the Spanish expression *La mujer en casa con la pata quebrada* [Keep women at home, house bound, and broken-legged]. In Tristana's case, the biological accident colludes with traditional equations of female identity and physical beauty and neither Tristana nor Horacio overcome this legacy. Tristana senses that Horacio will stop loving her if he sees her mutilated body and when Horacio finally visits, the narrative confirms the accuracy of her intuition. Lope's reaction proves more complex. The enforcer of a contradictory patriarchy, he physically attends the amputation performed by a male doctor and his realization that Tristana will never be able to leave him brings both sadness and relief. His paternal need to protect and sexual desire to possess now cede to a docile companionship that might allow a belated freedom, but Tristana turns inward, abandoning interest in her appearance, in painting, and in the development of a new discourse. With a mutilated body and self, she can turn only to the traditional feminine solution of religious faith. The narrative closes with a subtle acknowledgment of church complicity with patriarchy in describing the pressure Lope's religious aunts put on him to marry Tristana in exchange for financial aid. The ironic emergence of a concern for appearances when Tristana and Lope have long since converted their illicit sexual relationship into a platonic association and the absence of any desire to protect Tristana when she was young, vulnerable, and still capable of developing an independent identity signal the gaps and contradictions that mark the treatment of women and the lower classes.

The final portrait of a silenced Tristana, whose happiness or unhappiness the narrator confesses he cannot ascertain, and the announcement of her marriage to an increasingly senile Lope raise serious questions regarding the conventional depiction of matrimony as the desirable denouement to fictional or biographical accounts of women.[17] It is important to note that this Galdosian ending also departs from traditional narratives of female experience in the treatment of honor. Although Tristana initially feels disgraced when she realizes the nature and implications of her relationship with Lope, once she enters into a relationship with Horacio, she erases terms such as "honor," "guilt," "shame" from her vocabulary. Her retreat into herself has its origins in other factors, such as the loss of mobility and corporal desirability that allowed her to explore new features of female subjectivity. Tristana's development, like that of Cristeta and Juanita of Picón's novels, could only occur in urban spaces, where casual encounters, a certain anonymity, and abundant mobility enable the repudiation of inherited accounts of female development and the creation of new personal histories. Galdós also departs from convention in the representation of a healthy sexuality in the figure of a middle-class woman, although the text retreats from this innovative association by presenting Tristana's middle-class upbringing only briefly and indirectly through a retrospective narration of her life prior to moving in with Lope and after the reader has already learned of her current situation, in which her economic and sexual status distance her considerably from a traditional middle-class environment.

Pérez de Ayala explores cross-class relations and their impact on modern subjectivity in a number of works but most intensely in his four-part narrative series on the aspiring writer, Alberto Díaz de Guzmán. Published from 1907 to 1913, the first and last two novels in the series trace Alberto's search for personal and artistic direction and his alternating interactions with a bohemian world of prostitutes and artists and the middle-class society of his origins. *A.M.D.G,* the second volume in the set, describes Alberto's youth in a Jesuit boarding school and appears to have little relation with the rest of the series. However, the physical, emotional, and sexual abuse perpetrated by the Jesuits within the context of an education that portrays the body as evil contributes substantially to the unhealthy vision of sexuality and self that marks the adult Alberto. *Tinieblas en las cumbres* contrasts a healthy lower-class response to sexuality with a repressed middle-class attitude that expresses itself in abusive behaviors and uncontrolled promiscuity. The account of the love story of Rosina, a young country girl, and Fernando, the circus performer, depicts a mutually consensual sexual relation that unfolds without a shadow of guilt or shame. The text emphasizes the lovers' pleasure and innocence and breaks with the traditional opposition of body and soul, sexuality and innocence, through intertextual references to mystical writing in the description of their physical desire and the representation of passionate sexual activity intermixed with Rosina's gentle singing to quiet her young brothers, who sleep in adjoining beds and wake up at one point during Rosina and Fernando's sexual encounter. The lyrical interlude differs markedly from the rest of the novel, in which sexuality almost invariably involves sadistic behavior. Rosina's presence in both worlds, as the lover and later the prostitute who services middle-class men, highlights the difference between the two attitudes as does the double framing of the episode describing her reciprocally desired and enjoyed encounter with Fernando. It is immediately preceded by descriptions of the middle-class canning factory owner, who lasciviously pursues Rosina despite her manifest repulsion, and it is framed by the novel's description of an excursion of middle-class men and prostitutes to observe a solar eclipse.

The male obsession with virginity and desire for control and ownership of the female body through prior and preferably initial sexual contact surfaces continually in the series. In their excursion to view the eclipse, the men compete with each other for ascendance over the prostitutes, engaging in crude tricks, as when Paco Alvarez throws brandy on the exposed sexual organs of one woman (1964–66, 1:124). All accept the absolute separation of women into opposing categories of sexually active lower-class subjects and pure middle/upper-class individuals. It is precisely the strong belief in such a division that produces their infantile pleasure at defying it. The revelers find it amusing that the train engineer treats Rosina like a young lady, not realizing she is a prostitute. Rosina has come to terms with her condition and calmly accepts the disjunction between her personal ethics and work as a prostitute. In her view, the night of love with Fernando has no relation to the professional sexual activity that she practices to support her daughter, and she easily reconciles the apparent contradictions between her acceptance of self and conventional social visions of her conduct. Alberto's conflicted feelings with respect to Rosina reflect his own inability to deal with the breakdown of the traditional antinomies of virgin and whore, purity and sexuality, that structure Spanish culture. He vacillates between intellectual rejection and emotional attachment to a range of religious and aesthetic beliefs and his inability to resolve the tension precipitates the psychological crisis he suffers in the closing pages of the novel.

La pata de la raposa traces Alberto's uneven trajectory and reveals even more dramatically his painful attempts to harmonize the various forces that play against each other in his construction of identity. He realizes that his education has severed his access to himself and that his artistic formation conditions his vision of reality, causing him to perceive all through the lens of antecedent artists and writers. In open expression of Harold Bloom's later theorization of the anxiety of influence, he states a desire to experience life through a child's soul. His inability to reconcile the divergent facets of his personality reveals itself in his oscillating relationship with his middle-class fiancée. Fina represents in many ways another version of Rosina, but her background and social status protect her from male predatory behavior in a security Rosina never enjoyed. Virginal and delicate but also spontaneous, tolerant, and sensitive, Fina differs radically from her superficial sister and parents and gives every indication that she is capable of developing into a richly multifaceted woman. Alberto's view of her does not allow for the unfolding of multiple subject positions. Fina remains a refuge from his doubts, from other kinds of desire, and other facets of his life. He tells her that he is one person when he is with her and another when they are apart (1964–66, 1:299) and he so fears revealing that other person that he often abandons her.

Alberto's inability to reconcile instinct and sensibility, sexuality and desire for emotional communication lead to an exaggerated internal disjunction. After an idyllic day with Fina, he embarks on a night of middle-class male pleasure, ending the evening in a prostitute's arms. Alberto's divided subjectivity reveals itself in the poems he writes about this experience. In one, a first-person speaker relates his seduction by the prostitute while in a second, a male speaker consoles a friend who believes he has betrayed his fiancée by indulging in sex with a prostitute. The change in speaking voices and tone in the two texts graphically illustrates the split in Alberto's identity, which receives even greater emphasis in the narrator's intervention and explicit questioning of why Alberto adopts the dual subject position manifested in his poetry. The narrator's intrusion interjects yet another focalization, adding to the complex and changing viewing stance that shifts from Alberto's first-person revelations to his projection of himself into the figure of a fictive friend commenting on his behavior, and finally to the third-person narrator. The change from poetry to prose, lyricism to ironic distance and raucous laughter, further entangles the representation of Alberto and contributes to the alternating focalization that mimics Alberto's shifting relationship with the worlds and individuals with whom he interacts.

In early experiments with techniques that better reflect the modern experience of the simultaneity of multiple subject positions, Pérez de Ayala introduces marginal comments instructing the reader to skip a specific section and return to it later (1964–66, 1:265), intercalates poems, diary entries and letters, and moves without warning from Spain to London to Italy in imitation of cinematographic cuts. In a modern world where experiences succeed each other with stunning rapidity and within the confines of the Spanish culture of the period and its rigid class and gender categorization, Alberto repeatedly resolves personal and social conflicts through escape. Unable to imagine a sexual Fina, he cannot bring himself to renew contact with her after his experience with the prostitute. In a letter to a friend, Alberto classifies Fina within the conventional boundaries of virgin and mother. He compares her to a Gothic statue of the Christian mother, in contrast with Greek statues of nude women, which are neither innocent nor maternal (339). Alberto's flight this time takes him to the circus, where he assumes multiple roles as clown, financial backer, and publicizer in a futile effort to return to childhood and evade the conflicting selves that his socialization in the Jesuit school and Spanish culture have created within him. Alberto never comes to terms with his fluid subjectivity. Twice more he returns to Fina, only to abandon her again and ultimately to cause her death with his inconstancy.

The final novel in the series, *Troteras y danzaderas,* shifts the focus from Alberto back to Rosina and a group of women who respond to the experience of modern subjectivity in various ways, all of which prove much more accepting of the decentered self. Rita Felski observes that women best exemplify the modern individual because as objects of the male gaze who have traditionally watched themselves being watched, they achieve a level of self-awareness that eludes men. ". . . it is now the male subject who clings nostalgically to an illusory sense of unitary and non-contradictory identity, whereas woman epitomizes the double, divided, and contradictory self fully conscious of her own exterior determination" (1995, 194–95). I would add that as women achieve greater degrees of agency in modernity, the splits in their identity grow increasingly complex and the legacy of a divided subjectivity allows easier assimilation of new, often contradictory roles.

Troteras y danzaderas fully confirms Felski's analysis, carrying forward the presentation of Alberto's failure to come to terms with his divided selfhood and combining it with a similarly frustrated trajectory in the young poet, Teófilo Pajares. By contrast, Rosina, Verónica, and other lower-class women easily slide from one subject position to another. Rosina assimilates her multiple roles as mother, daughter, professional singer, mistress of a man she does not love, lover of the aspiring poet Teófilo Pajares and also of Fernando, with whom she reunites in this last volume of the series. The narrative describes her recognition of her sexuality in a life-long passion for Fernando and also a more poetic ethereal need in her relationship with Teófilo. Verónica does not share Rosina's easy acceptance of multiple, simultaneous sexual and romantic relationships, but she moves with ease from life as a prostitute to a dancer and without guilt or hypocrisy, redefines herself as an honorable professional woman. Both Rosina and Verónica defy virgin-whore, purity-sexuality dichotomies, retaining an observable innocence despite their sexual histories and creating a personalized vision of honor and respectability that accurately corresponds to their self-image and that others come to accept as well.[18] Unlike Alberto and Teófilo, who remain entrapped in traditional visions of women, sexuality, and morality, these female characters prove extremely susceptible to new modes of thinking the self and new forms of being in the world. Both have an instinctive, highly developed aesthetic sense that mirrors their fluid subjectivity. When Teófilo and Rosina visit the Prado Museum, he observes Velázquez's paintings with indifference while she marvels at the painter's ability to create perspective and states that the experience of art has changed her way of viewing reality. Rosina has the ability to be herself and to get outside of herself at the same time, as when she feels moved by Teófilo's declaration of love but simultaneously experiences herself as a spectator of the scene (1964–66, 1:509).

Verónica's response to *Othello* similarly demonstrates lower-class female sensibility and ease of movement from one subject position to another. As Alberto reads, Verónica lives the experiences of Othello, Iago, Desdemona, and other characters, revealing a facility to internalize the experience and feelings of the other without freezing in a single position. Alberto subsequently models his aesthetic theory on Verónica's response to the literary work: ". . . el hecho primario en la actividad estética, el hecho estético esencial es, yo diría, la confusión (fundirse con) o transfusión (fundirse en) de uno mismo en los demás, y aun en los seres inanimados, y aun en los fenómenos físicos, y aun en los más simples esquemas o figuras geométricas: vivir por entero en la medida de lo posible las emociones ajenas, y a los seres inanimados henchirlos y saturarlos de emoción, *personificarlos*" [. . . the primary reality in the aesthetic activity, the essential aesthetic reality is, I would say, the confusion (fusing with) or transfusion (fusing in) of the self with the others, and even with inanimate beings and physical phenomena and the simplest diagrams or geometric figures: to live entirely to the extent possible the feelings of others, and to *personify,* enhance, and saturate with feeling inanimate beings] (1964–66, 1:600). When a friend clings to inherited norms and says one must become centered, Alberto responds that all Spaniards need to learn to become decentered (601). The famous perspectivism elaborated by Pérez de Ayala and associated with tolerance and justice has its basis in a theory of the other and in a vision of subjectivity that finds its most apt embodiment in the lower-class woman. Although Alberto develops the theory, he personally fails to internalize it. It is Verónica, Rosina, and Juana, Teófilo's mother, who best exemplify the aesthetic that Alberto specifically links to the project of national reconstruction. Juana initially incarnates the rigidity of traditional Spain but in the end, she and Verónica together nurse the dying Teófilo and Juana both forgives and asks forgiveness in confessing to her son that his real father was a priest who abused her. The revelation reconnects with earlier depictions of church teachings on sexuality and female subjectivity. The national and church construction of the virgin-whore dichotomy breaks down in the face of Verónica and Juana's bond and in the refusal of each in her own way to accept such an externally imposed definition of self.

In a characteristically ambivalent ending, Pérez de Ayala interweaves the sad description of Teófilo's death with comical depictions of a young actor's attempt to mimic Teófilo's gestures and expressions in the event that he ever play a character dying of tuberculosis. The fact that Teófilo, whose initial characterization reveals an immature, superficial, and thoroughly untragic figure, changes in the final chapters to a dignified, admirable personality reflects a multi-perspectivist vision. The novel's final lines continue this mutating stance. When a pedantic acquaintance approaches Alberto and repeats the question raised by Masson de Morvilliers in 1782 asking what Spain has contributed to European culture, Alberto responds "Troteras y danzaderas, amigo mío; Troteras y danzaderas." This closing statement remits to the title of the novel, which has been translated as *Mummers and Dancers* by Marguerite Rand, but might more appropriately be expressed as *Trollops and Dancers.* Taken from Juan Ruiz's *Libro de buen amor,* it invokes the tradition of textual hybridity characteristic of medieval literature, with popular and cultured poetry, sexuality and spirituality, laughter and tears. The term *troteras* in traditional Spanish refers to prostitutes or sexually active women and relates to both Rosina and Verónica while *danzaderas* specifically points to Verónica. Alberto's somewhat flippant answer to his pretentious acquaintance and to Masson de Morvilliers includes a serious element that valorizes popular culture and lower-class women in the construction of an alternative Spanish culture. It opposes both the French rationalist tradition to which Masson de Morvilliers belonged and the misogynistic, theocratic tradition that characterizes orthodox Spanish culture and contributes to a rigid, unyielding morality that impedes the development of a subject capable of change and of entering modern culture.

Pérez de Ayala's study of gender and class continues traditional and modern tendencies to associate sexuality and lower-class women,[19] but it progresses considerably towards the construction of a female subjectivity independent of the legacy of guilt, rigid standards of honor, and passivity that characterize inherited visions of women. The importance of the lower-class woman to a reconceptualization of female subjectivity and male-female relations receives emphasis in the works of other modernist writers who stress their spontaneity and freedom from the mind-body split. Baroja introduces a number of women from or with strong ties to the lower classes who incarnate a vitality and spontaneity lacking in middle-class culture: Marina of *El mayorzazgo de Labraz,* Dolores of *Camino de perfección,* and to some extent Lulú of *El árbol de la ciencia,* who has middle-class origins, despite a precarious financial status, but has internalized lower-class values and disdains middle-class taboos. Her easy assimilation of tangos and popular music that she hears on the street demonstrates her temperamental affinity for the spontaneous, freer lower classes and her interest in women's emancipation inspires her choice of songs about women in the military or riding bicycles (1968?, 120).

Unamuno publishes a number of stories that depict cross-class relationships and seek to redefine traditional views of sexuality, combining ethical commitment and sexual attraction. "En manos de la cocinera," published in *Los Lunes de El imparcial* in 1912, relates the story of a middle-class man who is about to marry when he falls and breaks a leg. His very proper fiancée will not visit him, much less care for him, so his maid nurses and bathes him, knowing she will be fired after the wedding because she broke bourgeois taboos regarding intimacy and bodily contact. In the end, the now healed young man decides to marry his servant. "El sencillo don Rafael, cazador y tresillista," also appearing in *Los lunes de El Imparcial* in 1912, breaks with middle-class strictures regarding legitimacy, honor, love, racial and class divisions. A bachelor adopts a foundling and hires a sensuous gypsy-looking wet-nurse who had recently lost an illegitimate child. The bachelor never thinks about social norms, brings the wet-nurse Emilia to live with him, and when the baby is sick, has her stay in his bedroom to nurse on demand. The text presents a different kind of male gaze, in which the adoptive father watches Emilia breast feed the baby and experiences a desire for paternity more than sexual possession (1958, 2:528). That very night they set the process in motion, and subsequently marry, have ten children, and live happily in a "blended" family that joins adoptive and biological children as well as different classes and possibly different ethnicities.

Cross-Class Representations of Female Subjectivity by Spanish Women Writers

Spanish women writers of the period similarly explore the possibilities for cross-class relationships between men and women and among women. The more conservative women writers uphold traditional injunctions against class mixing, but many women authors seek to forge new connections or redefine old ones. A traditional vision governs Blanca de los Ríos's "La caridad de Malvina" (1902), which depicts the disastrous effects of a well-meaning countess who takes in a lower-class girl. When the child grows up, she refuses to marry within her class, runs away with a playboy, and eventually becomes a prostitute. The narrative presents the tale as a warning against meddling with established boundaries. The jointly authored play *Buena gente,* by the Martínez Sierras and Santiago Rusiñol, responds to such a stance, presenting a young adoptee who rejects the family fortune and requests that her adoptive father donate his monies to the poor.

Concha Espina moves toward a more positive vision of cross-class relations, but recoils from a full exploration of such a possibility. *La niña de Luzmela* (1909) pairs the aristocratic female protagonist with her lower-class savior, but his middle/upper-class formation and the late revelation of his origins considerably lessen the unorthodox class mixing. *La rosa de los vientos* (1916) introduces a potential love match between a man of lower-class life style and an upper-class woman, but again shies away from such an alliance. Soledad Fontenebro's rejection of middle-class rituals and her love of nature and village culture suggest a natural affinity for the life style and values of Agustín, her lower-class childhood friend. When he declares his love, Soledad almost immediately realizes that their class difference matters little in comparison with the value of their feelings. However, the text never allows her to test such a conviction, since Agustín falls to his death in a melodramatic ending to what might have been a radical departure from conventional narratives of cross-class romantic relations.

María (and Gregorio) Martínez Sierra, Margarita Nelken, and Emilia Pardo Bazán explore the possibilities for a female solidarity that transcends class and joins women in a campaign for equal treatment. The Martínez Sierras utilize a male speaker in *Cartas a las mujeres de España* to address middle-class female consumers of clothing and encourage them to become more cognizant of the workings of the market and the unfair profits earned by middle men to the detriment of lower-class female producers. It also urges wealthy, educated women to inculcate a sense of self-worth in working women and help them demand their rights rather than acquiesce to their employers. The text speaker calls for women's labor unions and on some occasions, directly addresses working-class women to foster increased activism.

Nelken's *La condición social de la mujer en España,* published in the early 1920s, offers a longer and considerably more complex effort to forge new alliances between women of all classes as well as between working-class men and women. Written by a woman for a readership of men and women of the middle and lower classes, Nelken's study adopts a complex discursive organization that continually moves from one perspective to another. The female text speaker exemplifies the easy adoption of multiple subject positions characteristic of modernist female subjectivity as she moves from advocacy of worker's rights to a defense of women of all classes and seeks to forge connections between these various, sometimes competing groups. Writing in the aftermath of World War I, Nelken's speaker calls on Spanish women to enter an international women's community in order to resist nationalist divisions and fratricidal conflicts. Like other writers on feminist subjects and advocates of a new national consciousness, Nelken suggests that the appropriate models for Spanish women must be sought outside of Spain or in the Spanish lower class, where independence and self-sufficiency represent the norm.[20] Spanish rural or urban women workers traditionally enjoyed greater freedoms than their middle-class counterparts. As Nelken points out, their labor and earnings were always crucial to the family's survival and consequently welcomed, or at least accepted, by the male members of the family and class.

Emilia Pardo Bazán, often classified along with Espina and Blanca de los Ríos as a conservative Catholic writer, examines current Spanish social structures and the possibilities for their transformation with a much more radical vision than critics have recognized. Often the target of incredible hostility from such powerful writers as Valera, Menéndez y Pelayo, and Clarín, she interweaves her social criticism in a polyphonic textuality that both reflects the multi-voiced reality of modern culture and seeks to deflect criticism of her unorthodox positions. Pardo Bazán concurs with Nelken in contrasting lower-class female productivity with a poorly educated, ineffectual female middle class. In "La mujer española," she defines the middle-class Spanish woman as lacking independence and education and consequently unprepared for self-sufficiency, child rearing, or even the marriage she so single mindedly pursues. Lower-class women, on the other hand, have a distinctive personality and best exemplify Spanish womanhood (1976, 59–60).

Lower-class women characters assume many different identities in Pardo Bazán's fiction, with considerable emphasis on cross-class relations between servants and masters. "Sangre del brazo" (1896) reflects the cross-class ties that link female servants and the employers with whom they share intimate domestic spaces. When the wealthy María de las Azucenas needs a transfusion after giving birth, her Galician maid offers her blood when the husband refuses. The transfusion saves María's life, but the discovery of her husband's cowardice and selfishness precipitates a marital separation and María's decision to spend the rest of her life in the company of her servant, now converted to friend and sister. The short novel *Clavileño* presents a similar case of cross-class loyalty in a servant who reveals her love for the son of the household at the moment of his death. In contrast to the young man's wealthy fiancée, who cannot bring herself to touch her would-be husband, the maid passionately covers his face with kisses, proclaiming to her upper-class rival that only those who truly love are capable of such behavior.

Morriña (1889) depicts the much more passive Esclavitud and traces her instrumentality in the coming of age of the middle-class Rogelio. Rogelio's first awareness of his physical desire for the shy maid accompanies temptations of rape, evincing with absolute clarity the uneven distribution of power in their relationship. In the intimate quarters of a small Madrid apartment and facilitated by the temporary immobility of his injured mother, Rogelio's physical relations with Esclavitud develop along less violent, but still exploitative lines. Esclavitud suffers from low self-esteem in a culture that doubly censures her as illegitimate and the daughter of a priest. Naturally submissive and hungry for affection, Esclavitud easily falls prey to Rogelio's seemingly childish requests for caresses. Inevitably, Rogelio's mother grows suspicious, Rogelio lacks the will to stand up to her, and Esclavitud finds herself reassigned to an old man with a predilection for pretty young servants. In her only act of self-affirmation, Esclavitud commits suicide and the novel ends with a comment on the frequency of such cases in Spain.

Morriña examines lower-class female subjectivity from the perspective of a woman writer and although filtered through an ungendered heterodiegetic narrator, the focus on the routine of household management and other details reveal a woman's hand. The novelty of these domestic spaces and the sympathetic representation of a lower-class female protagonist produces a strong negative reaction in contemporary readers. Clarín censures the emphasis on the minutiae of domestic life and house-cleaning. He deems the ending arbitrary and asserts that Esclavitud's passivity mars her characterization. Clarín squirms at the attribution of culpability for Esclavitud's suicide to a general cultural condition, and although he argues that *Morriña* is not an effective novel, the high-pitched tone of his review—published first in *Folletos Literarios* (1888a) and then revised in *Madrid Cómico* (1889)—suggests a barely controlled fear of the impact of its message of social and sexual injustice. Valera criticizes the novel for its lack of humor, stating that the theme of a young man's sexual initiation with a maid has the makings of great comedy. He clearly envisions the lower class as the appropriate butt of middle-class humor and moves to erase Esclavitud's identity by suggesting a happy ending as more fitting to the materials (1941, 1:789). In the existing class structure, such an ending would imply Rogelio's departure for continued masculine adventures and Esclavitud's cheerful acceptance of her status as servant and sexual facilitator.

Pardo Bazán attacks middle-class blindness to lower-class realities in a number of stories. "Sobremesa" (1893) describes the conversation of a group of men enjoying after-dinner drinks around a fireplace. In comfortable surroundings, they discuss the case of a poor mother of five, abandoned by her husband and unable to survive as a rag picker, who spent her last monies on a hearty holiday meal and a carved set of the three kings and then proceeded to kill each of the children and turn on the oven to kill herself. With their feet warmed by the fire, the privileged men judge the case. The economics professor remarks that the poor lack foresight and suggests that if the mother had saved the monies she spent on the figures and special meal, she could have lasted for at least another week. The marquis, for his part, defers judgement, having stated at the beginning of the story that he remains unsure whether the woman's actions constitute a horrendous crime or simply a desperate act. This difference of opinion opens a space for a critique of orthodox views that receives greater impetus in the ironic juxtaposition of the elegant ambience of the male judges and the brutal poverty of the woman and children.

"En tranvía" (1897) offers a similar contrast between the well-dressed, contented middle and upper-class passengers who ride the trolley to Madrid's elegant Salamanca district and a lone lower-class mother, whose demeanor communicates misery and desperation. The narrator adopts a distanced tone that mimics the indifference of the passengers, who step out of their cozy space only when the poor woman informs the conductor that she lacks the full 15 *céntimos* for the fare. It is a woman who first donates monies to make up the balance and it is a man who sardonically comments on the woman's ugliness and seems to justify her husband's disappearance, as had been announced by the angry woman to the full trolley. The text emphasizes the self-centered behavior of the middle and upper classes and their inability to comprehend the lower-class female other in their uncomfortable response to the woman's outcry and their resentment that their charity did not provoke expressions of gratitude. The ungendered narrator attempts to encourage the woman with allusions to the infant boy that she carries and to some future time when he will learn a trade and support her financially. In a steadfast refusal to accept patronizing offerings, the poor woman raises her baby to show that he is blind. The text conveys a persistent sense of middle and upper-class discomfort and ignorance of the realities of lower-class female conditions.

In contrast with lower-class female vulnerability and defeatism appearing in *Morriña* and the stories just considered, Pardo Bazán inscribes agency and freedom in other depictions of the rural and urban poor. She often explores issues that lie at the heart of middle-class anxieties, perversely confronting her readers and in particular, her male public, with fictional incarnations of their worst fears. "Champagne" relates the story of a bride who drank one glass of champagne too many at her wedding reception and then brutally informed the older, wealthy husband of her parents' choice that she completely detested him. Now she lives as a prostitute, preferring what most view as the most demeaning of professions to a loveless marriage, where her sexual favors would also be required and receive payment, albeit in a legally sanctioned arrangement. Female rejection of middle-class male protection and life style also provides the narrative interest in "La Camarona" (1896), in which a fisherman's daughter, born on the beach and wrapped in a sail for her first covering, refuses to marry the canning factory heir that her parents see as a ticket to middle-class comfort. In order to continue her active life at sea, La Camarona instead marries a poor fisherman for whom she feels little attraction. Marriage in both stories is a secondary consideration, with only tangential relation to the construction of female subjectivity.

Female choice increasingly moves to the foreground in Pardo Bazán's fictions and a woman's merit is shown to depend less on the qualities and status of her partner than on her own agency. *Insolación* (1889) deals with several issues that haunt the middle-class male subconscious, including fears of sexual inadequacy in comparison with a more virile lower class. The urban environment and proximity of a lower class with more relaxed views on sexuality facilitate a personal transformation in Asís Taboada that could not occur in other spaces. Felski makes reference to the bourgeois depiction of nineteenth-century crowds through "feminizing metaphors of fluidity and liquidity" and states that the "anonymity of the mass embodies a labile, chaotic, and undifferentiated force that threatened the boundaries of autonomous individuality" (1980, 73). It also threatens class distinctions put in place to contain middle-class sexuality and distance middle and upper-class women from a more libidinous lower class. Chapter 2 of *Insolación* presents this theme through Gabriel Pardo's theory that middle-class Spaniards easily appropriate lower-class behaviors when exposed to the open air, sun, and popular ambience.

The novel relates just such an occurrence in Asís's visit to the popular celebration of the festival of Saint Isidore and consistently relates her discovery and ultimate acceptance of her sexuality to the experience of urban living and contact with the lower classes. The initial step in this trajectory occurs during an early morning walk to church in which Asís makes several detours in her obvious enjoyment of the street scenes and the compliments proffered by lower-class, street-smart young men. The mention that these admirers wear tight fitting pants draws attention to a female gaze that reappears in later descriptions of her study of the dress and appearances of her male admirers. In a first-person narration, Asís reveals that her contacts with the urban ambience produce a strong desire to run, scream, and allow her body to physically express itself.

The connections between corporal needs and the lower classes continues in her street encounter with Diego Pacheco, a young Andalusian she met briefly at the home of mutual friends. Asís feels a strong physical attraction to Pacheco, a sentiment that she specifically justifies stating that women should be allowed to express the same street compliments that she received earlier from lower-class male admirers. Although clearly of the upper class, Pacheco bears unmistakable links to popular Spanish culture and a sensuality often associated with the lower class. His Andalusian accent and disdain for middle-class norms separate him from other characters and his unconstrained behavior produces strong animosities in the more intellectual, sexually repressed Gabriel Pardo. Pacheco feels at home in the popular ambience of the Saint Isidore festival and in his company, Asís confesses that her notions of social hierarchies dissolve and she begins to enjoy the atmosphere of diverse social classes that encompasses soldiers and gypsy fortunetellers.

The gypsy woman who reads her palm alludes to Asís's lack of self-knowledge, which receives textual confirmation in her rigid separation of mind and body, personal drives and social conventions. Asís has repressed her sensual/sexual identity, having married an older man who the narrator explains treated her generously but with no effort to inspire passion. The protagonist's divided self receives expression in the novel's changing focalization, moving from Asís's first-person confession and attempts to justify her somewhat loose behavior during the excursion with Pacheco to a heterodiegetic narration, as if Asís lacked the discourse and courage to continue her story. The narrative advances cautiously toward resolving the conflict, often revealing its own reticence to openly communicate events and characters' feelings. The upper-class textual world prohibits the sincere expression of feelings and develops elaborate rituals to structure human interactions within a predictable, controlled format. During the novel Asís remains largely silent in interactions with Diego and Gabriel, unable to express her desires in a culture in which words and feelings often oppose each other. Gabriel's criticism of a rigid moral code contrasts with his doubts as to Asís's conduct, based only on the discovery of a male calling card at her house. Asís, for her part, verbalizes thoughts that the reader recognizes as contrary to her feelings and actions. The narrator offers unconvincing explanations of Asís's behavior and, in a metafictional confession of self-censure, declares the need to silence and indirectly present the materials (1980, 117).

The constant repression of unspeakable desires breaks down in the final chapter when Pacheco insists that Asís communicate whether she wants him to stay for the night. The text emphasizes the rare expression of her wishes, stating that when Asís articulates her desire that Pacheco stay, she doesn't recognize her voice as her own (1980, 191). The recuperation of a sensual identity portends a richer, multifaceted subjectivity. Asís's repression of this facet of female selfhood has produced a diffident relationship with her daughter that Pacheco wishes to transform. He speaks of his wish to win the child's affection and create a family life that has been lacking in the previous narration of Asís's story. The final paragraphs again link a fluid, variable subjectivity with lower-class culture, reiterating the gypsy forecast of the early chapters and its promise of a life full of love. Asís's acceptance of her sexuality involves acknowledgment of female roles that she has previously ignored and allows for the construction of an identity that includes a maternal and spousal self. The new Asís derives value not from her choice of husband, but from a decision to actively participate in the construction of her narrative of self.[21] Gabriel's disapproval of her choice reveals his puritanical rejection of female desire. The traditional binarism of virgin and whore, lover and wife, continues in his vision, despite his liberal outlook, and he feels relief when he realizes that he came close to marrying a woman with appetites he would prefer to ignore.

Pardo Bazán's "Allende la verdad," published in *El cuento semanal* in 1908, plays with patriarchal fear of female sexuality and its relation to the dubious verifiability of paternity. The story presents a vindictive former mistress who determines to reconquer her lover. Mercedes succeeds in marrying Quintín by convincing him that the daughter of a servant is their biological child. Despite her success, Mercedes becomes increasingly embittered, too angry at Quintín's earlier abandonment to reconstruct a loving relationship and upset that the victim of her revenge is ecstatically happy with his daughter Tinita. The narrative alternates between assumptions that the child's lower-class origins remain totally imperceptible, since Quintín, the governess, and family friends accept her legitimacy without question, and allusions to certain lower-class values that mark the child, such as her gift for language and generous love for Quintín, whom she sees as sad and mistreated by Mercedes. The privileging of biological determinism alternates with a valorization of class blind affection. The servants and Quintín himself see physical resemblances between "father" and "daughter" and Quintín considers Tinita so truly his child that when Mercedes tells him the truth in a last effort to hurt him, Quintín throws her out of the house and hugs Tinita in a clear declaration that despite the absence of biological links, she is without any question his "real" child.

In other modernist texts dealing with the issue of biological paternity, biological and psychological paternity coincide, as I pointed out in Pérez de Ayala's *Luz de domingo,* or the child used to entrap the "father" disappears from the fictive landscape as an unnecessary factor in the now reconstituted amorous relationship, as in Picón's *Dulce y sabrosa.* Pardo Bazán rejects the patriarchal ideology that stands behind such solutions while simultaneously negating traditional definitions of class and gender. Quintín's paternal devotion transcends biological definitions of fatherhood, conventional expectations of social class, and inherited stereotypes of male versus female parenting. Like many modernist writers, in the consideration of cross-class relations Pardo Bazán looks to the lower class and in particular to the lower-class woman for new possibilities of subject formation in a world that creates a variety of subject positions and an increased ability to move from one to the other. In the intersection of gender and class, she and many of her contemporaries break with the rigid categories of the previous period and with the belief in a stable, unchanging subject. By way of Quintín, she presents a subject who abjures traditional definitions of gender and moves toward the creation of a transgendered subject, which stands as another major contribution of modernist writing to the reconceptualization of human identity.

Transgendered Subjectivities

The conception of the individual that dominated nineteenth-century thought presumed a reasonably stable, autonomous selfhood that for Dennis Brown receives exemplary expression in the figure of Robinson Crusoe. Defoe's character displays integral, consistent identity that operates in a self-sufficient world of his own design and feels secure in the ability to sustain and control his environment (1989, 3). The nineteenth-century vision of subjectivity as stable and non-contradictory relates to the literary practice of realism, which as Catherine Belsey observes, moves toward closure and order (1980, 73–82). Among the stable categories constitutive of the nineteenth-century subject, gender represents a fundamental marker that differentiates male and female identity. Realist and naturalist writers and cultural commentators share a conviction that male character traits inhere without alteration in healthy male subjects and female attributes equally conjoin with female subjectivity. The emergence of male qualities in women or female properties in men signifies abnormality and disease. The belief in a gendered subjectivity has important consequences not only for male-female relations, but also for attitudes toward homosexuality. The breakdown of clearly demarcated categories of masculinity and femininity threatens conventional notions of sexuality and of social roles in a larger sense. As critics of European modernism observe, the appearance of the dandy, the "New Woman," homosexuality, as well as seemingly superficial changes in clothing style and female participation in physical activity and city life, challenge inherited views of gender. Analyzing the response to transformations in public and private deportment, Gilbert and Gubar and Elaine Showalter emphasize male fear of female challenges to conventions of feminine conduct while Rita Felski focusses on a more varied reaction among both men and women. In *The Gender of Modernity,* Felski rejects the homogeneous modernism sometimes posited by theorists of postmodernism and explores a varied, discordant modern culture that proves alternately and sometimes coincidentally advantageous and disadvantageous for women (1995, 15–17).

Studies on late nineteenth and early twentieth century Spanish culture have only recently begun to foreground questions of gender in contrast with traditional emphasis on distinguishing an escapist *modernista* current from a profound, nationalist "Generation of 1898." Critics who address issues of gender emphasize a generalized fear of a breakdown of conventional categories and the mobilization of misogynistic discourse. Susan Kirkpatrick states that during the period under consideration, "gender difference and gender confusion became key tropes in discourse about society and culture" (1995, 97) and attributes the division of the literary and cultural production of these years into two distinct movements to a desire to distinguish "the virile, energetic, *castizo* Generation of 1898 from the degenerate, feminized and nonnational *modernistas*" (100). Stephanie Sieburth identifies a modernist fear of mass culture, which she points out is typically gendered feminine, and defines modernist art as the conscious exclusion of the popular and female (1994, 158). In *Voices, Silences and Echoes: A Theory of the Essay and the Critical Reception of Naturalism in Spain,* I traced the relationship of the entwined fears of female sexuality and social revolution to the literary debates of the realist and naturalist period and analyzed the hostile, misogynistic discourse that met the increasing presence of women, in particular Emilia Pardo Bazán, in public discussions of culture. Although antagonistic responses to female cultural intervention continue during modernism, they now intersect with a variety of opposing discourses that challenge their claim to hegemonic status. Spanish modernist rejection of Restoration Spain includes a rewriting of gender roles through parody, inversion, and direct refutation. In contrast with the stable gendered subject of the preceding period, modernism explores a transgendered subjectivity that introduces debates on gender and sexuality that persist today. The adoption of new attitudes appears in the writings of the understudied women writers of the early twentieth century but also in male authors, in dialogue with traditional discourse that continues in hold overs from the previous period and in certain modernists. The vision of a transgendered subjectivity not only transcends the gender divisions of the writers of late nineteenth- and early twentieth-century Spanish literature but also traditional divisions of the period into two distinct literary groups.

Restatements of the Traditional Gendered Subject in Spanish Modernism

The changing status of women takes center stage in essay writing in the later decades of the nineteenth century and continues in the twentieth. Valera's "Las mujeres y las académicas: Cuestión social inocente" belittles the issue of women's membership in the various national academies in the title and throughout the essay. The text speaker upholds the inherited view of female subjectivity as distinct and antithetical to male selfhood and even states his belief that souls have gender and that in the spiritual afterlife, men and women will continue to exhibit sexed characteristics. He expands this argument in "Meditaciones utópicas sobre la educación humana," declaring that if the transmigration of souls existed, it would be inconceivable that a woman's soul enter a man's body or vice versa, except in a "monstrous" aberration (1941, 2:2194). The insistence on fundamental gender differences interweaves with tortured efforts to explain that "different" does not imply "unequal." Arguments supporting female superiority, exemplified by the power of the Virgin Mary, intersect with admonitions that women accept their God-given role as man's helpmate. The "monstrous" aberration here becomes a "sinful" rebellion against divine design in a two-pronged attack on women who question the established order.

The Jesuit Graciano Martínez, writing three decades later, reveals the continuity of anti-feminist rhetoric and the complicity of the Church in propagating gendered subjectivities. In the early pages of his treatise *La mujer española* (1921), the text speaker remits the reader to Biblical authority to argue against the scientific education of women that the Martínez Sierras had advocated in *Cartas a las mujeres de España*.[22] He turns to the story of Eve's fall to confirm divine opposition to female access to the tree of knowledge and also to underscore the perils that befall women who aspire to equality with men (1921, 110). The text utilizes traditional patriarchal and nationalist discourse to argue that excessive intellectual development would defeminize Spanish women, as has occurred in the cerebral, mannish, infertile North American woman. Like Valera, Martínez counters feminist vindications of women's rights by simultaneously asserting an essential feminine difference and an undeniable equality before God and within patriarchy. The speaker moves uneasily from assertions of feminine superiority in the areas of purity, amorous constancy, compassion, and resignation in the face of suffering (23) to declarations that female submission does not imply inferiority, merely paralleling the subordination of the individual to the state for the greater social good. Repudiating female intellectualism as a masculine aberration, the Jesuit advocates a strong religious education and in subtextual and at times blatant statements, encourages his female readers to use their intellectual and sexual powers of persuasion to ensure the continued religious faith of their husbands and children. He also advocates that wives trade sex to motivate the efficient management of their financial property by the husbands who control them (229). Although Martínez views women's most important role as that of mother and wife, he recognizes the growing presence of women in the labor force and calls for equal salary and fair treatment with a hope of thus avoiding a radicalization of the Spanish working-class woman.

La mujer española represents an extremely conservative Catholic position that advocates a tempered defense of women as a counterweight to socialism and radical feminism. Writing with a much more intellectual and serious tone and from a liberal outlook, José Ortega y Gasset directly confronts theories of subjectivity that contribute to changing gender definitions. His 1924 "Epílogo al libro *De Francesca a Beatrice*" differs in emphasizing that women's primary function resides not in her role as mother or wife, but rather as embodiment of the male "ideal" and argues that a woman's influence in this capacity far surpasses any power she might attain through electoral votes or educational degrees (1965, 3:327). The essence of women is "to be" while that of men is "to act," in a restatement of traditional gendered subjectivities. While the history of man traces his invention of ever more advanced laws, sciences, arts, and technologies, the progress of woman consists in her perfection of self, creating an ever more delicate femininity (330). "¿Masculino o femenino?," also of 1924, develops the idea that while men are sufficient in and of themselves, without any need for women to further their essential activity in science, war, politics, or sports, it is impossible to define women without reference to men. In keeping with Valera's vision of the female auxiliary role, in this reading women cannot construct their own narrative of identity but achieve selfhood only in a dependent, reflective process. The discussion of metaphor in "Ensayo de estética a manera de prólogo" (1914) further elaborates this concept, stressing that women, like glass, serve as a passageway to other objects:

> La esencia del cristal consiste en servir de tránsito a otros objetos: su ser es precisamente no ser él, sino ser las otras cosas. ¡Extraña misión de humildad, de negación de sí mismos, adscrita a ciertos seres! La mujer que es, según Cervantes, "un cristal transparente de hermosura" parece también condenada a "ser lo otro que ella": en lo corporal, como en lo espiritual, parece destinada la mujer a ser un aromado tránsito a otros seres, a dejarse penetrar del amante, del hijo. (1967a, 159–60)
>
> [The essence of glass consists in serving as a passageway to other objects: its being is precisely to not be itself, but rather to be other things. Strange and humble mission, of self-denial, assigned to certain beings! Woman who is, according to Cervantes, "a transparent glass of beauty," seems similarly condemned to "be other than herself": in body as well as spirit, woman seems destined to be an aromatic transit to other beings, to let herself be penetrated by her lover, her son.]

While other beings, by default masculine subjects, constitute themselves in the act of knowing or seeing, since their gaze hits against the surface of the observed object and then rebounds back, creating in all cognitive acts a duality or separation between the thing known and the knowing subject (1967a, 159), women dissolve into an auxiliary self, a pathway for the construction of identity by the male viewer who absorbs her in his search for selfhood.[23]

Ortega y Gasset insists that his analysis simply reflects the natural order of things, with no subjective valorization on his part (1990, 473). His emphasis on the objectivity of his writing relates to his correlation of masculinity with reason and science. Concomitantly, his definition of essay writing as science without explicit proof (1990, 60) explains his cultivation of this textual form to the exclusion of more imaginative, emotional kinds of writing. Feminine (non)identity relates of course to emotion, sentimentality, and illogic and Ortega's writings often associate it with sickness and disease. The speaker of *Meditaciones del Quijote* refers to sick and womanish idealism (1990, 71)[24] and in "Poesía nueva, poesía vieja," he equates French, particularly Parisian, decadentism with the feminine and contrasts it with a metaphysical, national art (1965, 1:50). Women have no place in art in the Ortegan vision and he goes to considerable lengths to refute the tradition of the female muse. The speaker of "La Gioconda" reminds the reader that the original meaning of "muse" is "leisure" and argues that male achievements owe much more to male free time than to flesh and blood female muses, suggesting that the muse represents only one of many myths that women have elaborated to create the illusion of male dependence (1965, 2:556). In this reading, Leonardo painted the picture out of a need to compete with Michelangelo, with no interest in women or in the female model. The famous portrait of the enigmatic Italian woman becomes a vehicle for the expression of masculine rivalry and the female subject is a pretext for the creation of homosocial communications and more important subject formations.

Despite the insistence on reason, objectivity, science, and the stated irrelevance of women to the formation of male subjectivity, Ortega's texts occasionally concede a certain power to the feminine. At the same time, they struggle to reassert masculine authority in rather surprising confessions of instinctive impulses. The previously commented "La Gioconda" opens with a statement that God created beauty so it could be robbed and then slides into a discussion of beautiful women, asserting that God fashioned them so they might be abducted. The use of the passive voice elides textual identification of male agents but hardly camouflages subtextual connotations of conquest and rape. "El epílogo al libro *De Francesca a Beatrice*" returns to the subject in the discussion of history as alternating between masculine and feminine periods. A masculine modality initiated human history in a world in which man viewed woman as prey: "La mujer fue primero para el hombre una presa—un cuerpo que se puede arrebatar" [Women was first an object of prey for men—a body that could be seized] (1965, 3:321). Later, men became more refined and discovered a greater pleasure in women's voluntary surrender and as a result, women became arbiters of taste. Although the text states a preference for cultural periods in which a "feminine" modality predominates, the attribution of the origins of human society to the violent act of rape as well as the comment that abduction figures in God's design endows the original "masculine" culture with a legitimacy that overshadows suggestions of feminine ascendancy. As in a number of male-authored texts of the previous period to or about Emilia Pardo Bazán, women's increased presence on the national cultural scene prompts fears of a loss of male hegemony in Ortega and an effort to shore up masculine power with theorizations of human history and male-female relations that privilege violence and physical strength.

Ortega y Gasset's textual revelations of subconscious impulses constitute a minor presence in his work, which foregrounds control, logic, and science. He discloses discomfort and antagonism toward visions of subjectivity that posit other possible subject positions. His study of Freud in "Psicoanálisis, ciencia problemática" (1911) reveals his skepticism in the title itself and specific statements within the text question the scientific validity of Freudian explorations of the subconscious. The speaker criticizes the decision to seek the causes of mental illness in the body because such an approach posits two worlds that do not communicate with each other within a single subject and also expresses doubts because Freud's theories cannot explain why things occur a certain way, possessing a purely descriptive rather than explicative value (1965, 1:237). He clarifies that the explanation he seeks occurs when connections exist between one or more series of elements, when each element in a series corresponds to one and only one element in the other series, when a more or less conclusive mathematical expression accounts for these relations (237). The demand for such precision excludes the murky, disordered realm of the unconscious. Ortega's definition of subjectivity resists Freudian challenges to the nineteenth-century stable, unchanging identity.[25] He carries forward a belief in a gendered subject and combats modernism in his review of *La corte de los poetas* because it breaks with inherited definitions of gender and sexuality. His allusions to the erotic elegance and nervous squandering of the dreamy, spineless, and feminine life of Paris (1965, 1:50) as well as his calls for a nationalist, metaphysical literature reveal a gendering of aesthetics and a repudiation of the eroticism and homosexuality that for Gert Hekma characterized Parisian life at the turn of the century (1991, 60).

Other opponents to modernism also attack its endorsement of transgendered subjectivities. Max Nordau's 1892 critique of *fin-de-siècle* decadence opens with a discussion of the exaggerated hair styles and colors used by women of the day "in such a fashion as to be startling in its effect against the law of organic harmony" (1968, 8). Nordau continually stresses the loss of harmony, which he equates with abnormal sexuality and the abolition of traditional gender roles. He characterizes the period as hysterical, associating "decadent" art forms with female sickness and imbalance. *Degeneration* rejects the blurring of borders, whether in paintings that erase the clear outlines of figures and foreground and background blend together (87), or in the fusion of genres and genders in Wagner's music, with his insistence on the presence of masculine and feminine traits in the fully developed woman (177). He shares Ortega's discomfort with definitions of the human subject that include a subconscious component, stating that the "I" refers exclusively to the "pondering, remembering, observing, comparing intellect, not, however, the 'sub-Egos'—unconnected, and for the most part at strife with each other—which are included in sub-consciousness. The individual is the judging, not the instinctive human being" (411). Like Ortega he places great confidence in science and views contradiction as a form of psychosis (166).[26]

Pompeyo Gener reiterates virtually all of Nordau's positions in *Literaturas malsanas* (1894), including a profound faith in science, a vision of contemporary literature as pathologically ill (4), and a critique of the mixing of genres in symbolism (6) and in Wagnerian music (213). He equates decadentism with feminism and the break down of conventional gender and moral categories (177) in contrast with a masculine, virile aesthetic that proclaims justice and defends life (185). Gener also insinuates a link between homosexuality and the literature he disparages which other studies, such as the anonymous "Contra los modernistas" of *El Nuevo Mercurio* (1907) continue in references to the effeminate inventors of poems about drug use (354). Associations of feminism, homosexuality, and drugs bring together movements that disrupt traditional gender borders and firm divisions separating the rational and irrational, traditionally marked as masculine and feminine, respectively. The liberal Urbano González Serrano's strident attacks on women wearing pants interweave intimations of sexual abnormality and accusations of insanity for those who exhibit characteristics conventionally associated with the opposite sex: "Mujer hombruna, la que siente como carga pesada ahora las faldas y luego el pudor, es repulsiva en el mismo grado que lo es el hombre afeminado. Son detritus y residuos de las representaciones-fronteras, donde comienza el reino de la insania" [The mannish woman, she who feels as a heavy burden now her skirts and soon her modesty, is repulsive to the same degree as an effeminate man. They are the detritus and residue of cross-over figures, where the reign of insanity begins] (1896, 186).

Fictional attacks on a modern transgendered subjectivity appear first in the works of residual realists writing into the modernist period, such as José María de Pereda, or in transitional figures such as Leopoldo Alas and Armando Palacio Valdés, both of whom appropriate modernist themes and techniques to attack what they perceive as dangerous tendencies in the redefinition of gender and sexuality. Pereda's *Peñas arriba* (1895) advocates a return to rural traditions and clear divisions of gender and gendered activity. The novel describes the male activities of the hunt and mountain hiking in comparison with female enclosure in the home and village. The imposition of strict divisions of responsibilities carries over to an unscientific description of a bear hunt, in which male hunters enter a cave where a female bear is hibernating with three cubs. The text describes the slaying of the mother bear and the arrival of the father, whose valiant attempts to protect his family fail in the face of the hunters' weapons. Despite the fact that male bears play no role in raising the young and disappear shortly after mating, Pereda constructs a story in which his vision of male as provider for and protector of the family remains intact.

Palacio Valdés also attacks modernity, but does so through the appropriation of modernist themes and language. *El maestrante* specifically links perverse behaviors to inversions of "correct" gender roles, presenting the weak-willed Conde Luis as the product of an over-protective mother who exposed her son only to "feminine" culture instead of providing him with the requisite virile education. Amalia, the oversexed and cruel heroine, is compared to a bull fighter, interjecting both an "abnormal" gender and class crossover. The novel emphasizes vicious behaviors in women or feminized characters, including Amalia's mistreatment of her illegitimate daughter and the nasty gossiping of the homosexual Manuel Antonio, described as combining male intelligence and female malice. Woman's virtue in this and such Palacio Valdés novels as *La alegría del Capitán Ribot* (1899) resides primarily in her function as the guardian of male honor. Female sexuality of any kind, even in cases of rape, presumes moral depravity and requires restitution through marriage. Although *El maestrante* avoids explicit references to the rape of Fernanda, who gets drunk at a wedding and sits in the lap of a rich, old lecher, the fact that she later attempts suicide and that after confessing to a priest, this latter confronts the culprit and with the victim's father insists on marriage to remediate the situation, leaves no doubt in the reader's mind. The narrative describes Fernanda's resistance to the marriage, but assumes her moral responsibility for her loss of honor when it reports her lament that although her sin was great, the punishment is truly terrible. *El maestrante* and other Palacio Valdés texts that describe sexual abuse disclose a voyeuristic pleasure that insinuates a misogynistic focalization. The narrator of *Las majas de Cádiz* comments that a domineering man beats his lover to satisfy his pride and also because it produces sensual pleasure (1935, 466). The presence of this erotically charged, sexually aberrant gaze links Palacio Valdés's writings to decadentist texts, but whereas decadentism challenges bourgeois presumptions regarding sexuality and morality, Palacio Valdés presents unorthodox sexual behaviors in order to shore up traditional values and visions of gender, albeit deriving voyeuristic pleasure through the depiction of depravity.

Clarín more fully integrates modernist narrative techniques and produces some strangely hybrid literary works, in which he decries the collapse of stable gender categories and yearns for a return to the past, as Susan Kirkpatrick observes (1995, 96), while simultaneously constructing a text whose decoding requires a reader that both comprehends and experiences the multiple subject positions that on some level the narrative scorns. Clarín overtly rejects feminism and any dissolution of traditional gender categories in his review of *La amistad y el sexo* (1893), in which he argues that a woman who feels enslaved in the present social conditions is either physically or spiritually masculine and a man who accepts such statements by women is either physically or spiritually effeminate (1893a, 85–86). A number of Clarín's short stories of the 1890s express anxiety regarding changing gender roles, but it is his last complete novel, *Su único hijo,* that most fully manifests the related fears of increased feminine power and spreading homosexuality. The narrative consistently characterizes the protagonists through gender inversion. Bonifacio Reyes fails to live up to his kingly surname, dependent on his wife's money and subjected to her verbal and even physical abuse. Emma Valcárcel treats him as a "kept" spouse, requiring that he appear well dressed for public affairs in a reversal of traditional masculine desires for attractive, stylishly clothed female companions. At Emma's insistence, Bonifacio nurses her through imagined illnesses and the text alludes to her continued physical desire for him, in another inversion of inherited gender roles. The sterile nature of their relationship takes symbolic form in the description of Bonifacio playing Emma's father's flute, with clear phallic connotations, while Emma moans on the couch and grasps her ailing liver. The narrative avoids depicting a fully altered "masculinity" in Bonifacio's delineation, insisting that despite his gentle touch and docility, he retains a manly character. The description of his affair with the opera soprano Serafina interweaves allusions to his effeminacy and his masculine sexual appetites, first recounting the tears that come to his eyes in his initial physical contact with Serafina and his subsequent swoon

(1966, 46–47), and then relating his masculine sexual appetites in his relationship with his lover and his wife's renewed desires for physical contact.

The text displaces suggestions of homosexuality from Bonifacio to the tenor Mochi, who directs his singing to Bonifacio during rehearsals and sends him expressive glances. When Emma discovers traces of acting powder on Bonifacio, left by an earlier embrace from Mochi, Bonifacio refers to the latter as *maldita marica,* using the pejorative Spanish term for homosexual (1966, 96). The allusion to homosexuality becomes less veiled in the tenor Minghetti's confessions of his relations with priests while working in a religious school and in reference to Emma and her friendship with Marta Körner. The narrator describes Marta as devoid of ethics and especially depraved in relations with women (162). Her pleasure at having her feet tickled by Emma, an activity she shares with only a select few female friends, connotes partial, if not full participation, in a lesbian relationship. Intimations of homosexual activity aspire to confirm the degenerate character of the society in which the narrative action takes place, which is furthered by the description of Emma's "unnatural" desire to abort her child and her disinterest after the baby is born. In contrast, Bonifacio reveals a "normal" desire for a son, in a blatant reflection of patriarchal values. The latter part of *Su único hijo* deals openly with male anxieties regarding verifiable paternity, which in Bonifacio's case proves additionally problematic since Emma concurrently has relations with her husband and Minghetti. The text leaves no doubt, however, regarding the son's legitimacy, referring to Minghetti's surprised admiration for Bonifacio's studly abilities.

The insistence on Bonifacio's paternity combines with his fervent desire to educate his son and lead an ethical life, an aspiration that in this textual economy aims to ennoble the formerly undignified protagonist. In the closing pages, Bonifacio's characterization acquires a certain grandeur that intermixes with residues of his comical, pathetic behavior. This merging of two antithetical modes constitutes what David Hayman refers to as a double-distancing, whereby the reader feels simultaneously alienated from and drawn to the fictional character or world (1966, 25). Hayman associates this technique with modernism and it combines with several other modernist traits in *Su único hijo* that relate to a new vision of subjectivity. Bonifacio and Emma often see themselves as actors and they frequently adopt different roles. Emma dresses as a lower-class woman to secretly attend the theater, she has Bonifacio pretend he is Minghetti and she, Serafina, and Bonifacio regularly adopt gestures from literary texts. The move from one subject position to another and the shifting response that it demands of the reader introduce a fluid, modernist vision of identity that stands in paradoxical opposition to the critique of the breakdown of gender roles. The narrative moves away from the stable world and totalizing vision of realism and naturalism and advances toward a different understanding of society and the self, but does not dare to pursue the transformation beyond the initial stages.

Changing Norms and Gender as Cultural Construct

Early and aggressive attacks on the breakdown of gender roles by contemporaries of the modernist movement attest to the very real presence of changing views of gender and subjectivity within modernism. In conjunction with the expressed fear of female power and sexuality that continues throughout realism and naturalism and into modernism, an alternative discourse welcomes and encourages the dissolution of inherited binarisms and advances the exploration of a transgendered subjectivity. Nineteenth-century exaltation of harmony and balance as artistic and social norm gives way to a new appreciation for diversity and contradiction. Enrique Ferrí's "Los anormales" of *La Revista Nueva* argues that history only remembers abnormal individuals, who deserve credit for all human progress (1899, 50–51). Ferrí relates this vision to a changing aesthetic, in which asymmetry and imbalance replace harmony as markers of artistic beauty and further refers to a preference for women of abnormal beauty as opposed to conventionally pretty females. He aspires to become other so that society will become other, "ser otro para que la sociedad sea otra" (54–55). The allusion to unorthodox female beauty advances feminine individuality and personality, which also expresses itself in a growing recognition of women's talent and in varied portraits of female characters, ranging from the voracious vamp of decadentism or Unamuno's stridently willful women to the moderately feminist creations of the Martínez Sierras.

Modernist journals incorporate diverse representations of women and reflect the simultaneity of traditional and changing visions of gender. *El Gato Negro* exemplifies the modernist intermixing of genres and artistic forms in its 1898 issues, with cartoons succeeding serious articles, dramatic two page four-color drawings allegorizing the horrors of war, poems, short stories, musical scores, varied fonts, and decorative graphics. A satirical poem by Luis Taboada poking fun at women writers (April 30) alternates with feminist stories by Emilia Pardo Bazán ("La redada" June 18), or a cartoon entitled "Las niñas toreras," depicting the Spanish actress María Guerrero and the American Sarah Bernardh [sic] dressed in bull fighters' costume (February 26). The drawing of cross dressing actresses allows for multiple readings, including amusement, amazement, winking acceptance, or absolute derision, and the simultaneity of various responses echoes the magazine's design and forces the reader to adopt rapidly changing responses to the varied text types and artistic forms presented on a single page or in a single issue. *Helios* (1903–4) has a less varied visual design but includes similarly diverse text types and ideological stances. The Martínez Sierras contribute feminist stories, reviewers endorse works by Pardo Bazán, the column "Fémina" includes a range of opinions by women on changing gender roles and Benavente publishes short plays, such as *Por qué se ama,* in which he depicts women as born to love and suffer, in line with Echegaray or José Feliu y Codina and in contrast with other Benavente works.

La Ilustración Española y Americana publishes sexist articles by Urbano González Serrano as well as an interesting example of transgendered subjectivity in "La mujer sabia" by Luis Calvo Revilla. The short story describes the trajectory of Enriqueta, a smart young woman who believes the mind and spirit are genderless, but recognizes that her intellectual pursuits intimidate other men and women. She leaves Santander to start over in Madrid and in the capital constructs a new identity as ignorant and disinterested in intellectual pursuits. A bachelor who dislikes educated women marries her precisely because he finds her sufficiently ignorant to make him happy and their married life proves highly satisfactory to both. Enriqueta runs a perfectly organized house and leaves the husband to pursue his study of an admired German philosopher. When he discovers to his surprise that the German philosopher is an invented identity used by his wife to publish her thoughts, the husband encourages Enriqueta to continue her studies and publications but not reveal her authorship, for fear it will expose her to ridicule in a country that does not respect knowledge, much less when originating in a woman. Despite his fear of publicly acknowledging superior feminine intellect, the text traces the absolute reversal of the husband's original antagonism toward the female intellectual and also signals the fluid subjectivity of the modern woman. Enriqueta successfully and happily moves from wife to writer, housekeeper to philosopher, Spanish woman to German man, socially isolated Santander female scholar to conventional Madrid marriageable young woman in the construction of a narrative of selfhood that adequately responds to the different facets of her modern, multidimensional life.

The anonymity of women writers exemplified by the fictional character of "La mujer sabia" continues into the modernist period in the real life cases of Caterina Albert I Paradís, who published her work under the masculine pseudonym Victor Català, and María Martínez Sierra, who hid behind her husband's name. Català's *Drames rurals* provokes a hostile review in *La Lectura,* where Ramón Péres attacks an excessively virile style and crudity of language in what he suspects is a female writer. His later review of *Solitut* proves somewhat more positive, but his general derision simply confirms the reasons for her adoption of a masculine pseudonym. However, it bears noting that Péres's voice and stance represent only one of many perspectives included in *La Lectura* in the early 1900s. The magazine publishes a number of male and female authored reviews of literature written by women. Blanca de los Ríos defends Català's narrative technique and choice of language in response to the Péres review, pointing out the paradoxical situation in which women writers find themselves, criticized for imitating male writers when that is their only model and simultaneously praised and condemned with the back-handed compliment that a woman-authored text seems to be written by a man (1905, 168). Angel Guerra publishes a favorable analysis of Concha Espina's first book of poetry in another 1905 issue and Unamuno reviews Pardo Bazán's *La Quimera,* stating that the novel speaks to him and suggests topics for his own meditations on religious and philosophical subjects. This open, dialogic response from a younger male modernist to Pardo Bazán's explorations of aesthetics and religious belief contrasts remarkably with Clarín's hostile accusations of heresy and philosophical ignorance in reaction to Pardo Bazán's review of Palacio Valdés's novelization of religious doubt in *La Fe* (1893a, 136).

The simultaneous presence of works by and about women writers in modernist magazines as well as the growing acceptance and serious treatment in the reviews published signifies a tangible change in the reception of women as authors of many different kinds of texts, which in turn reveals an openness to the consideration of women according to new definitions of gender and identity. The modernist woman writer represents one form of the "New Woman,"[27] a sexually liberated, strongly independent figure who challenges traditional visions of gendered subjectivity. Although women writers achieved considerable commercial success in the nineteenth century, their audience and choice of medium largely remained within conventionally defined "feminine" categories. Many wrote for magazines designed for a female readership, such as *El Albúm del Hogar* and *El Correo de la Moda,* or authored texts aimed at socializing young women into traditional female roles, as exemplified by the works of Angela Grassi or Pilar Sinués de Marco. Those entering areas conventionally designated masculine drew their contemporaries' wrath, as Emilia Pardo Bazán quickly discovered. Although the number of women writers during the modernist period does not show a marked numerical increase and the instance of influential women writers may even be said to decline in comparison with such important nineteenth-century figures as Gertrudis Gōmez de Avellaneda, Cecilia Böhl de Faber, Rosalía de Castro, and the early Pardo Bazán, modernist writers and artists play an increasingly active role in public affairs and in cultural arenas traditionally reserved for men. Pardo Bazán continues her work throughout the modernist period, mixing literary and cultural criticism, original literary works, and public advocacy for women's inclusion in such national cultural institutions as the Royal Academy, the University, and the Ateneo. Her sexual activity with various well-known figures, including Galdós and Lázaro Galdeano, separates her from the prescribed virginal behavior of the nineteenth-century "angel of the house," advocated by the religiously and socially orthodox Fernán Caballero and Sinués de Marco. Pardo Bazán's writings seek new avenues for female emancipation and even works that advocate a return to spiritual values incorporate criticism of traditional church attitudes and repression of women.

Photographic portraits of modernist women writers reveal a considerable shift in comparison with paintings and photos of women authors of the previous periods. Carolina Coronado's sweet appearance in the traditional Spanish mantilla with a fan folded in her demurely placed hand shows a marked contrast with the position of Carmen Castellví y Gordón and Sofía Casanova, both of whom appear seated in large chairs by equally grand desks, caught in a professional posture and looking squarely at the camera eye.[28] Casanova, like Virginia Woolf, remarks on the need to create a room of her own, and sets up a

Spanish room in her home in Warsaw to keep contact with her homeland and also establish a work space for herself (1913, 8). Carmen de Burgos created her own working location within Spanish culture in her public separation from her husband and her affair with the considerably younger Ramón Gómez de la Serna. Concha Espina also separated from her husband, and although her private and public life followed a more conventional trajectory, her success in supporting herself and her children through her writing provides a model that includes her in a growing group of independent women.

Male modernists display the same varied responses to the woman writer as to other features of the changing times. Santiago Rusiñol describes female painters as neutered and critiques their appalling preference for studying nude models rather than serving as objects of the male gaze. Unamuno has a more open attitude toward women writers and artists. He and Pardo Bazán had a cordial relationship and his "A la señora Mab" encourages an aspiring Argentinean woman writer, suggesting that although for the present women inevitably will imitate male style, since it provides their only model, they should work to create their own language. A woman's style in this view would enrich literature and language and provide a welcome alternative to the unauthentic, "feminized" style adopted by men writing for a female public (1958, 4:720). Azorín initially adopts a satirical stance with respect to Pardo Bazán when he composes a mock necrology of the still very much alive novelist in "Muertos ilustres: Doña Emilia Pardo Bazán" of *Buscapiés* (1894). In later writings, he distances himself from the antifeminism of Clarín, critiquing his archaic vision of women in *Teresa* and rescuing Rosalía de Castro from the oblivion to which Valera, Menéndez y Pelayo and other realist critics had relegated her. His essay on Castro in *Clásicos y modernos* (1913) uses *poeta* and *poetisa* interchangeably, with a preference for the gender neutral *poeta.* The text speaker utilizes the first-person plural identifying Castro as "our poet" in a gesture of inclusion that breaks with traditional separations of male and female writers into two distinct categories.

The modernist rejection of rigid dichotomies and the preference for contradiction and encounters across inherited boundaries contributes to a repudiation of biological determinism and of traditional beliefs in a divinely sanctioned division of gender roles. The conflict between church adherence to an essentialist definition of femininity and a shift toward a view of gender as socially constructed surfaces in the confrontation between the

Bishop of Granada and Manuel Torres Campos, a student of Francisco Giner de los Ríos who went on to teach at the University of Granada. As reported in the *Boletín de la Institución Libre de Enseñanza,* Torres Campos argues in a speech to the Society of Friends of Granada that the presumed "nature of women" is a contrived construction, imposed and artificial. He further proposes a move toward moderate female intervention in public life (October, 1895). At this point in the speech, the Bishop of Granada refused to allow Torres Campos to continue because his opinions contradicted church teachings (November 1895). In keeping with Torres Campos's moderate calls for female intervention, modernists often mock more radical forms of feminism. Baroja, Rusiñol, Unamuno, and Benavente publish satirical or ironic treatments of feminist characters and platforms. On the other hand, they also repudiate the belief in a gendered subjectivity and increasingly emphasize the social construction of gender as they explore new possibilities for female narratives of selfhood and for male-female relations.

Benito Pérez Galdós begins his narrative career with forceful women characters, such as the domineering protagonist of *Doña Perfecta* or Pepa Fúcar of *La familia de León Roch.* In his early thesis novels, strong women often represent intolerance and religious intransigence. In his modernist writings, Galdós continues to present women who zealously defend tradition and theocracy, but he also depicts a religiously unorthodox, socially rebellious female antagonist. Cruz of the Torquemada series (1889–95) exemplifies the transition from the defender of bourgeois values to a more questioning, activist stance. After engineering the financial salvation of her family in the process chronicled in the first three volumes of the series, Cruz takes a different view of money and social responsibility in the final pages of *Torquemada y San Pedro,* where she advocates philanthropy and questions the ethics of large concentrations of wealth. Leré of *Angel Guerra* and Catalina of *Halma* continue this depiction of female exploration of changed ethical, social, and religious principles and of women's leadership in the foundation of new communities.

Galdós's plays of the 1890s and 1900s consistently portray women who possess strong leadership and organizational skills, often in contrast with men who lack these qualities. Isidora of *Voluntad* (1895) salvages the family store through her business acumen and provides her dreamer husband with the strength and support to find a will to live. Susana of *La fiera* (1896) similarly provides the clarity of mind and strength of will to resolve the conflict between absolutist and liberal fanatics. In contrast to the early depiction of women as the voice of intransigence and tradition, these modernist Galdosian women represent openness to change and a fluid subjectivity. Susana's dialogue with her lover Berenguer establishes a gender link between traditionalism and progressive thinking that inverts nineteenth-century beliefs. While Susana insists that the past can be destroyed and love can create a new future and that as a woman, she lives in the present and looks intrepidly toward the future, Berenguer responds that he cannot follow her because as a man, he is a slave of tradition (1967, 6:867). Galdós contrasts this New Woman and the traditional view of female subjectivity in *Casandra,* a 1906 dialogue novel that he reworks in 1915 to a four-act play. The eponymous protagonist combats a wealthy older puritanical woman of fanatical religious devotion. Juana's vision of life as a valley of tears harks back to traditional Catholic ideology and female subjectivity while Casandra's repudiation of conventional definitions of marriage and morality and her defense of her rights look towards a different narrative of female selfhood. In the 1915 drama, Casandra confronts Juana and kills her, declaring that she has annihilated the Hydra that devastated the earth. Casandra incarnates a Nietzschean version of the "New Woman," refusing the Christian admonition to turn the other cheek and the bourgeois tradition of the "angel of the house." She and other Galdosian female characters of his modernist works offer a new model of feminine behavior that in its arrogation of strength and agency suggests the incorporation of what traditionally had been considered "masculine" traits.

Baroja alludes to theories of female subjectivity in many novels. Ciriaco, the Basque sea captain of *Las inquietudes de Shanti Andía,* advises the first-person narrator not to assume that women are weak, timid, or unintelligent, insisting that gender is an unreliable predictor of character (1946–48, 2:1038). The narrator of *El mundo es ansí* claims the notion of female psychology lacks scientific basis and is merely a novelistic invention (1967, 373–74). The essay "La secularización de la mujer" moves from an initial critique of women's insensitivity to calls for her greater participation in social life in order to diminish her isolation and opposition to progress. In the closing paragraphs, the speaker refuses to hierarchize women over men or men over women, abjuring the negativity of the introductory sentences for a more equal treatment. The title of the text alludes to church control of women's beliefs, a position that also surfaces in *El árbol de la ciencia,* where a combination of religious and social pressures disrupt the harmonious marriage that Andrés Hurtado had constructed. As a result of her formation, Lulú cannot imagine happiness without children and she pleads with Andrés to start a family. The text indirectly refers to the use of birth control in the first year of the marriage and to the conflict between such a modern mechanism of biological and social management and traditional religious beliefs. After Lulú speaks of her desire for children, Andrés comments that religion, traditional morals, and the idea of sin weigh heavily, allowing a reading that connects his remarks to church and cultural definitions of marriage as primarily for purposes of procreation. When Andrés relents to Lulú's pleadings, it is clear that they change their sexual behavior and as a result, she becomes pregnant.

The struggle between Lulú's socially and religiously conditioned desire for children and Andrés's interest in circumventing previously accepted biological destiny carries forward the tension between the tree of life and the tree of knowledge that structures the narrative. However, in this modernist vision, traditional dichotomies disappear, whether in the form of life over knowledge or male in opposition to female subjectivity. Modernity erases clear divisions between nature and science, instinct and socialization. The novel attributes Lulú's desire for children as much to social pressures as to an instinctive drive for succession. Science and nature collide and interweave in the narration of the birth of a still-born child and of Lulú's death. Conventional lore ascribes the loss of a child through miscarriage or early death to nature's wisdom in selecting only the most fit, but Baroja's narrative states that scientific intervention, the use of forceps, and quick medical response failed to save child or mother and the attending doctor states that perhaps in nature they might have survived. The forces responsible for the fatalities change according to the perspective of the speaker. Andrés's determination to commit suicide similarly relates both to science and nature. Throughout the novel, he has attempted to control his surroundings, to impose rational order on the chaos of nature. Lulú's death and his decision to take his life in some sense confirm the triumph of vital forces over efforts at its control, but it is Andrés's knowledge of science and possession of aconite, perhaps as part of his current investigation into the synthetic study of ammonia, that enable him to voluntarily withdraw from further participation in the life cycle. Nature and science become ever more intricately interwoven and interdependent in modernity, mutually redefining and reconfiguring their respective territories.

Andrés's relationship with Lulú similarly redefines conventional gender and social relations. In contrast with Ortega's definition of man as existing independent of woman, Baroja envisions a new kind of collectivity in which women play a primary role. The construction of a living space without interior walls breaks with typical divisions of male and female, domestic and public spheres, which is advanced by the fact that Lulú goes out to work in her store while Andrés remains at home to write his scientific articles. Their married life style rejects bourgeois, patriarchal conventions and Andrés underscores the radical nature of their difference when he warns Lulú not to listen to others, because they will want to reinstate social controls. Throughout the novel, Andrés derives his greatest happiness and pleasure when he builds community with women, children, or such marginalized individuals as his sister Margarita, the servant Venancia, his young brother Luis, his land lady Dorotea, his crippled friend Lamela, and Lulú. Here and in many texts, Baroja explores new possibilities for male-female relationships and female subjectivity. Critics traditionally regard his female characters as incomplete or unconvincing,[29] perhaps because they depart from conventional characterizations of women. Baroja rejects essentialist visions of woman as mother and of female happiness as maternity, just as he repudiates traditional images of women as objects of desire. Salvadora of *Aurora roja* and Lulú offer a different kind of companionship that contrasts with inherited concepts of male-female love. They work alongside their respective husbands and their living situations include members from outside the immediate family in a new sort of community.

Other Baroja novels present different options for the female subject: Blanca of *Los últimos románticos* lives happily as a single, childless woman, the young neighbor in *Las aventuras, inventos y mixtificaciones de Silvestre Paradox* shows an early interest in and aptitude for science, and various unconventional women characters surface in *La feria de los discretos, La ciudad de la niebla,* and the Aviraneta series. Despite traditional accusations of misogyny and his antifeminist parody of Miss Pich in *Paradox, rey,* Baroja offers multiple examples that exemplify alternate routes to the construction of a female narrative of identity. In an open affirmation of transgendered subjectivity, Baroja's autobiographical collage, *Juventud, egolatría* (1917), presents a personal solution to the tensions between the need for sexual expression and aversion to social control. In the Spanish culture of the period, male sexuality found expression either in marriage or prostitution, both of which prove unpalatable to the speaker. The inferior education provided Spanish women and the superficiality of bourgeois society make marriage an unappealing alternative while the possibility of disease, well-known to Baroja through his work as a doctor certifying disease-free prostitutes, also precludes this outlet. Rejecting both male irresponsibility and an unrealistic poetization of sexuality, such as occurs in the narratives of Trigo or Picón, Baroja voluntarily accepts sexual repression and the hysteria that accompanies such a choice. The public self-diagnosis as hysteric, a condition long associated with women, and the refusal to follow traditional male solutions to the problem of sexuality present a novel case of autobiographical transgendering.

Jacinto Benavente generally presents a more conventional female figure, although he concurs with Baroja in the repudiation of a gendered subjectivity. His dramas at times depict traditional self-effacing women while other female characters display more unorthodox behaviors. Even in the cases of the self-sacrificing woman character, Benavente often underscores that such conduct is learned rather than intrinsic. *Rosas de otoño* (1905) traces the development of the forgiving, understanding wife who helps her step-daughter come to terms with her husband's infidelity. The text ends with a conventional idealization of female abnegation, but shows the difficult evolution toward such an attitude. *Los malhechores del bien* (1905) also demonstrates the social origins of much female behavior and the incredible amount of social control required to promote what in some quarters is viewed as natural feminine conduct. *La propia estimación* (1915) introduces a moderate version of the "New Woman" in the figure of Angeles, who defies her family and loses the inheritance of a rich aunt in order to marry a man who seems incapable of holding a job and generally appears inferior to his strong-willed wife. Angeles enjoys the trappings of modern life, the speed of the automobile, and advertises her acceptance of modernity by smoking and drinking coffee in contrast with other women characters, who express fear of the new rhythms and inventions. *La sonrisa de Giaconda* (1907) revises dichotomous thinking and anticipates modern theories of alterity and identity. The play describes Leonardo da Vinci's attempts to capture the enigmatic qualities of Monna Lisa, who changes each day, at times pure and at others, perverse. When the long painting sessions provoke gossip, Monna Lisa refuses to continue sitting for the painter and sends her page instead. The young boy bears a striking resemblance to Monna Lisa and is rumored to be the illegitimate son of her father and his favorite slave. Leonardo finds the switch in models extremely productive and explains that he had never before understood the enigmatic Monna Lisa so well. The male servant and son of a slave reveals the essence of the rich, upper-class Italian woman, in a clear expression of the need for the other to reveal the identity of the self, and of the presence of a transgendered identity in one of the most famous female portraits in the history of visual art. The contrast between the versions of the painting posited by Benavente and Ortega y Gasset reveal the considerable differences in their respective visions of gender and subjectivity, with Ortega erasing female presence to underscore competition between male artists and Benavente emphasizing the interdependence of model and painter, male and female, in the portrait's creation.

The Martínez Sierras join Baroja and Benavente in presenting "feminine" behavior as culturally conditioned. Their texts typically exalt motherhood, and sometimes present it as intrinsically feminine, as in *Canción de cuna,* where a young nun intuitively knows how to care for an abandoned baby. Other works present maternity as learned behavior or as only one of multiple facets of female experience. The protagonist of *Amanecer* (1915) does not find fulfilment in marriage or motherhood, but in her transformation from protected wife to equal partner on the heels of her husband's financial losses. *El ama de casa* (1910) equates competent mothering and female self-satisfaction with work outside the home. *Mamá* (1912) specifically links inadequate mothering with a lack of equality between the sexes, voicing the lament of the female protagonist and mother that her husband's habit of treating her like a child prevented her from developing a mature, maternal relationship with her children. A number of Martínez Sierra texts repudiate current male-authored versions of female subjectivity. The female letter writer of the first part of *El amor catedrático* (1910) criticizes novels for providing erroneous depictions of women (1910, 56) and specifically attacks Trigo and others who present male fantasies of female erotic desire (118). *Almas ausentes* (1900) describes the swearing and uncontrolled aggression of women mental patients, signaling their break with conventional gender definitions: "Así andan allí rotas, derrumbadas, dispersas, de un lado la gran farsa del altruismo masculino, del otro la no menos grande comedia de la dulzura y el pudor femeninas; los dos soportes mentirosos, pero imprescindibles, que sostienen el arco de triunfo de la moralidad social. . . ." [There one finds, on the one hand, the immense farce regarding masculine altruism, in a broken, destroyed, and disperse state, and on the other, the no less enormous comedy with respect to feminine sweetness and modesty; the two false but necessary pillars that sustain the arch of triumph of social morality . . .] (1900, 82).

The Martínez Sierras represent a special case of transgendered authorship, with the collaboration of Gregorio and María, of which many readers of the period were aware (O'Connor 1977, 41). In various works, they textually elaborate an aesthetic that reflects their dual authorship and repudiation of traditional categories, including male and female and extending to form and content, science and art, abstract idea and specific artifice. "Abrazo inmenso" of *El poema del trabajo* (1899) describes the blending of a masculine force, here equated with "work," and a feminine power, related to the "idea," to produce the work of art. A similar representation appears in "Obra de amor" in *Diálogos fantásticos* of the same year. The 1905 publication of a series of critical essays in *Motivos* consistently advocates an art that blends opposites and crosses borders. Their discussion of *Antonio Azorín* takes place through a conversation between a male and female speaker whose different points of view transmute each other through dialogic interchange and enter into yet another polyphonic dialogue with the author and his projection in the character Antonio Azorín. In this multi-voiced discussion, the text calls for a melding of matter and spirit, of form and content, that carries forward the general modernist practice of traversing borders.

Feminine Men, Masculine Women, and Transgendered Identities

In contrast with the view of writers of the preceding period, whose accusations of masculine traits in female authors and feminine qualities in male authors invariably invoke harsh criticism and rejection, modernists positively value such a transgendering. A Martínez Sierras' review refers favorably to feminine perversity in Juan Ramón Jiménez and Unamuno's poem "Mano en la sombra," published in 1907 in *Renacimiento,* alludes to God using the male term for redeemer and then adds the feminine option as an equally plausible alternative. Jiménez evolves from the representation of female subjectivity as alien and incomprehensible other to an internalized component of his identity. In "Nacía gris la luna y Beethoven lloraba," the poetic speaker and a female interlocutor engage in a dialogue of incomprehension in which the woman asks about the unknown and the poetic speaker responds about the impossible. The progression towards acceptance of erotic desire accompanies a growing sense of the poetic speaker's transgendered subjectivity. "Mi frente tiene luz de luna" of *La soledad sonora* (1911) openly expresses that a woman lives within the male speaker and contributes significantly to his art: "Vive una mujer dentro de mi carne de hombre; siete ríos de plata presentan ritmo a mi lira" [A woman lives within my masculine flesh; seven silver rivers lend rhythm to my lyric].

Diario de un poeta recién casado not only carries forward the construction of a sexual subject, but also strives to come to terms with the conflict between inherited visions of the female as object of desire and a more equal relationship in which male and female subjectivity actively contribute to the construction of a new identity that incorporates both without effacing the individual self. The journal entry of March 16 struggles with the poetic tradition in which a male speaker gazes on a sleeping woman and celebrates her passivity as an opportunity to more easily refashion her identity to match his idealized version.[30] The female other becomes a creation of the male speaker's self in this traditional reconstruction of her selfhood. Jiménez's speaker feels the pull of this legacy, but refuses to follow it. He will not kiss her while she sleeps, because she has given him her soul and body with her eyes open and asleep she is no longer her real self. Another poem in the collection acknowledges the lover's active role in the construction of the poetic speaker's selfhood and the uneasy balance between a fear of this dependency and a recognition of its necessity. "Desvelo" finds the speaker awake, observing his sleeping lover and imagining that he is caught in her dream. A part of him now resides within the lover's selfhood and beyond his control. Although he knows he can wake her and end her dreaming, and in this sense retains power over her, he also confesses fear of her dream and her love. In contrast to the nineteenth-century masculine subject, symbolized by Robinson Crusoe, this modernist speaker acknowledges the ethical commitment inherent in loving relationships while confessing fear at the vulnerability that ensues from such a mutual giving of self. In the final verse, the poetic speaker reveals that it is not just his lover's dream that frightens him but love itself, in open confession of the constitutive role that the female subject plays in the construction of the heterosexual male lover's identity.

A third poem in *Diario de un poeta recién casado* seemingly reiterates a more traditional stance, but in the context of the two previously analyzed poems and within the poem itself, a different vision of the male-female relationship takes form. "Serenata espiritual" presents the speaker's contemplation of the sleeping lover and as in the poetic tradition, the speaker enjoys observing the silent woman. However, rather than project a male-constructed image of the female other, the speaker acknowledges the unknowability of the world she contains in her mind and exults in the transitory experience of giving himself fully and without possibility for reciprocity. In contrast with a traditional gaze that appropriates the observed woman into the self, here the male speaker compares his lover to God and accepts his inability to possess or fully understand as an essential component of the loving relationship. Jiménez rewrites the tradition of the sleeping female object of the gaze to imagine a mutually constituted subjectivity, in which the woman becomes an intrinsic component of the male poet's subjectivity while also resisting assimilation.

Unamuno's works also theorize a male-female relationship that defies inherited visions of desire, possession, and subordination of the female subject to male-authored definitions. In *Soliloquios y conversaciones,* he argues for sexual equality while reiterating traditional beliefs in the importance of maternity in the formation of female subjectivity (1958, 4:711). In contrast to the traditional vision of a stable subjectivity and to his own statements of a simpler, more limited female selfhood as defined exclusively by maternity, in *Cartas a mujeres* the text speaker posits that the construction of the female subject is a never-ending process. Certain poems, such as "Veré por ti," present a male speaker who guides a blind female companion, suggesting a traditional hierarchical relationship, but in typical Unamunan dialectical thinking, the ordering of the categories changes in the course of the text. The blind female provides the light that allows the male speaker to guide her, and the male speaker acknowledges that one does not begin to know the self until it is illuminated by another's subjectivity (1958, 13:419). The succeeding poem "Tu mano es mi destino" provides a reverse image of "Veré por ti," with a woman's hand guiding the male speaker, but as in the earlier poem, a dialogic and mutually constitutive subjectivity continues (412). Through her presence, life arises anew in the speaker and in a transformation of the conventionally intransitive verb *renacer* to a transitive usage, the male speaker incorporates female agency and states that he "rebirths" the female subject (*yo te renazco*).

A number of short stories explore possibilities for male-female understanding and transgendered subjectivity. "Soledad" (1911) describes the loveless existence of the female protagonist whose relationships with her father, brother, and a suitor have each proven dissatisfactory, prompting her to choose a life of solitude. The male narrator admires her intelligence and decries a culture that fosters male cruelty and female suffering. At the same time, he acknowledges a permanent gulf between male and female perspectives and expresses a desire for continued dialogue with Soledad to come to a better understanding of her vision of the world (1958, 2:583). In this textualization of the gender relationship, male and female subjectivity appear as clearly differentiated, but with strong possibilities for communication. A deliberate refusal to appropriate female subjectivity accompanies a desire to retain a productive dialogue. "Don Bernardino y Doña Etelvina" (1916) utilizes a comical tone to explore gender differences and communication. The feminist Bernardino carries on a public debate with the masculinist Etelvina and over time their intellectual exchange causes major modifications in their respective positions, but rather than a synthesis, which would imply resolution of the tension, the story introduces additional complicating forces. Bernardino and Etelvina maintain an intellectual collaboration, but each seeks an amorous partner outside of their friendship and although they marry each other to satisfy the expectations of their reading public, each has a child with another. The two couples live together and raise the children as twins, in a foursome that defies simple dualities and possibilities for synthesis (1958, 5:1065). In evident contrast with Ortega y Gasset's suppositions of male self-sufficiency, this Unamuno story posits that men and women require each other's presence to fully develop intellectually, emotionally, and sexually and further emphasizes that neither gender lays claim to greater need or potentiality in any of these areas.

Despite his own and critical emphasis on the Unamunan identification of maternity and female subjectivity, his fictional representations of women include an incredibly diverse panorama in which the maternal woman figures as only one of many types:

Soledad chooses solitude and single life; Eugenia of *Niebla* demands economic self-sufficiency and control of her choice of lower-class romantic partner; Julia Yáñez needs to become more than the object of desire in *Nada menos que todo un hombre;* and Tula desires a non-biological maternity in *La tía Tula.* In all cases, these women demonstrate a drive and strength traditionally reserved for male characters. Even when Tula seeks seemingly traditional feminine goals, she redefines the conventions of women's experience and of the terms maternity and love, as I argue in an earlier study.

El cuento semanal incorporates many conventional portraits of women and culture, as observed by the University of Paris Research Group, but also moves beyond inherited models to present alternative values and life styles. The consideration of female sexuality in a publication of mass circulation addressed to middle-class readers, particularly women, speaks to the widespread interest in modern visions of gender and sexuality. Pérez de Ayala's "Artemisa" (1907) depicts a young woman who straddles the borders of traditional womanhood and a new kind of feminine behavior. Gloria's transformation has its roots in her exposure to the outside world through the return of her brother Alfredo from his four years in an English boarding school and expresses itself in her changed relationship with her longtime boyfriend Pedro, her mode of dressing, and her participation in the masculine activity of the hunt. Gloria's transition toward new subject positions receives recognition in the multiple names assigned to her—Gloria, Diana, and Artemisa.

Pedro finds Gloria's adoption of a new hunting outfit, with short skirt and tailored cut, both shocking and arousing. Although he feigns indifference at Gloria's newly expressed desire to experiment with modern clothing styles, not for public display but private occasions with him, the text reveals his sexual desire. Like Alberto Díaz de Guzmán of *Tinieblas en las cumbres* and its sequels, Pedro cannot abide any transgression of traditional categories. When Gloria retains a virginal docility, he treats her protectively and with gentle respect, but when she takes on attributes of independence and the redefined sexuality of the "New Woman," he desires to possess her, in a response that simultaneously expresses lust and a need to control. His wish to impose his will over her increasing emancipation plays out in violent aspirations when he attempts to gain forced entry into Gloria's bedroom the night before they are to leave for the wild boar hunt. Pedro's fear of and attraction for the new Gloria parallel her own vacillation between inherited and novel roles. She alternately insists on her independence and reverts to the docile young woman who craves Pedro's approval. The conflict within and between the two characters leads to a tragic confrontation, in which Pedro accosts Gloria and accuses her of being in love with her brother. Gloria shoots her accuser and would-be assailant and then throws herself into the path of a charging wild boar. The ambiguous ending allows for several interpretations regarding the validity of the charge of incest and the nature of Pedro's motives and intentions, but the inevitability of a dramatic and violent conflict as a result of changing definitions of gender stands as a clear message. The text does not advocate a return to traditional roles; rather, it signals the presence of a critical transition. The narrative avoids clear expressions of preference for the New Woman or the Traditional Man, but subtextual comparisons of Pedro with the wild boar and the spirited portrayal of Gloria suggest the desirability of a transformed female subjectivity while recognizing conscious and subconscious forces that oppose this change.

Eduardo Marquina's contribution to *El cuento semanal* focusses on the conflicts within the New Woman and similarly paints a tragic outcome. The concert pianist protagonist of "Corneja Siniestra" (1908) attempts to reconcile her desire for fame and independence with a need for emotional and financial security. When Isabela Wagner decides to marry a younger man from the provinces, it appears that his wish that she abandon her professional aspirations in return for financial security will displace her narrative of self-sufficiency. In the end, Isabela breaks off the engagement in a refusal to return to orthodox femininity. The text avoids an unambiguous endorsement of female emancipation through the description of the female protagonist's suicide and the misreading of her final action by her fiancé, his family, and other observers. Isabela owes her future husband monies she cannot repay and decides to end her life rather than surrender her freedom. Some assume the fiancé abandoned her and that as a result, she committed suicide. Her fiancé, convinced by his parents, comes to believe that she chose to die in recognition of her moral and social inferiority. The narrative of the New Woman remains so new and strange that it has not entered the common repertoire and the public continues to rely on old stories to account for behaviors that have their origins in a very different kind of subjectivity.

The Martínez Sierras' "Aventura" (1907) moves further towards the endorsement of female erotic pleasure and expression of desire in a middle-class woman character, but silences other features of the modern female model, such as intellectual curiosity and professional aspirations. The story unfolds through a tripartite narrative that imitates a symphonic composition with changing movements: the Prelude, presented by a third person narrator, fragments of letters written by the male protagonist, more letters by the main female character, an "Intermezzo" in third person, additional letter fragments by the protagonists Pedro and Marcela, and a final "Serenata." The musical format contributes to the lyrical quality of the narrative and a sense of polyphonic construction that places the male and female voices on an equal plane. The story unassertively marks a connection between Marcela and the New Woman in her pleasure at bathing outdoors, first in the river and later in her garden. The description of her river swim, after which Pedro first sees and tries to kiss her as she emerges from the water, fails to specify whether she bathes nude or clothed but in either case, her love of body contact with nature reflects an acceptance of her sensuality. Furthermore, although she rejects Pedro's physical advances with exceptional vigor, she does not fear him and rather enjoys his desire, fantasizing about further meetings. Her expression of desire transgresses inherited views of female purity and represents with Asís of *Insolación* one of very few cases of middle-class female sexuality in the literature of the period. The closing sections of "Aventura" leave the future of this relationship open, suggesting the possibility of a mutually desired marriage but allowing for various modes of narrative closure. Whatever the denouement, the final segment, entitled "Serenata," alludes to a laughing young woman and a singing cuckoo to connote a happy ending. In this version of the modern woman, the tragic endings of Pérez de Ayala and Marquina give way to possibilities for a happier kind of amorous relationship.

María Martínez Sierra's advocacy of female sexuality and women's right to desire takes place behind the safety of her husband's pseudonym, but other women openly present their advocacy of what were traditionally masculine attributes in female characters. Sofía Casanova outlines her own evolution from rejection of the body, as encouraged by her education, to healthy acceptance in her poem "El cuerpo" of *Fugaces.* The poetic speaker relates a visit to a museum, during which a northern European woman observes the speaker's embarrassment at seeing a naked statue of Venus and proceeds to educate her on the beauty and nobility of the naked female. The closing lines of the poem reveal the speaker's transformation to a more enlightened response to nudity, while simultaneously if indirectly indicting a Spanish educational system that produces regressive attitudes in women. In her campaign to delegitimize former and current beliefs in gendered subjectivities, Pardo Bazán utilizes gender inversions in her creation of characters and takes pleasure in presenting physically strong women who prove more than capable of avenging wrongs perpetrated against them by their male counterparts in stories such as "La mayorazga de Bouzas" (1892), "Geórgicas" (1893), "El molino" (1900), and "Oscuramente," also of 1900. "Feminista" (1909) relates a comical role reversal in the case of an older husband who vociferously defends traditional sex roles. To educate his wife in his philosophy, the husband wakes her on the morning after their wedding, insists she put on his clothing, and then explains that she will never again wear the pants in the family. As a result of the husband's dissolute youth, his health quickly fails, and, although his wife dutifully cares for him, the narrator discovers that every morning she makes him put on her underwear, reminding him that as long as he lives and she nurses him, he will wear the petticoats of the family.

In the construction of a transgendered subjectivity, Pardo Bazán presents many different accounts of female selfhood. "Cuento primitivo" rewrites traditional versions of history and sexuality in order to create new possibilities. In a framed narration, in which an ungendered narrator transmits a tale composed by a male storyteller, the text offers a new rendering of Genesis, in which God creates Eve, not from Adam's rib, but from the best portions of his brain, nerves, bones, and heart. This version explains that it was Adam and not Eve who ate the forbidden apple, after Eve valiantly defended it. From then on, instead of viewing Eve as a superior being worthy of respect and admiration, Adam blamed her for his tribulations. Eve and her successors assimilate the message of culpability and come to see themselves as inferior versions of their masculine counterpart. Several elements of "Cuento primitivo" resurface in Pardo Bazán's last two major novels and relate to the appearance of the New Woman and the male backlash she produces. The Eve of the modern rewriting of Genesis provokes desire and violence in Adam, with the forceful taking of the apple easily read as a metaphor for rape. This angry response to a woman who stands as equal as well as the intertwined desire and disdain for the no-longer virginal woman reappear in the exploration of changing gender relations in *La Quimera* (1905) and *La sirena negra* (1908).

La Quimera portrays the painter Silvio Lago's search for meaning to life in modern society. Three female characters exemplify different versions of the modern woman. Espina Porcel represents the sexually liberated, cosmopolitan socialite who has traveled widely and whose inability to construct a meaningful narrative of selfhood has led to morphine and sexual promiscuity. Silvio's relationship with her follows an oscillating rhythm of attraction and repulsion, and his inability to predict or control her behavior awakens his desire to physically dominate her, as when he violently rips her clothes to see the naked body that she has hidden from him and discovers the marks left by her morphine injections (1909, 400–401). His relationship with Clara de Ayamonte follows a very different trajectory. Widowed, wealthy, sexually liberated but lacking Espina's perversity, Clara generously offers to marry Silvio in order to foster his artistic career, although she knows he does not love her. Silvio's refusal exposes a conflict between his idealization of women and his disgust at their reality (160). He cannot come to terms with the distance between a traditional feminine model and the modern exemplar. Clara's search for meaning takes a peculiar turn and she determines to enter the convent. This seemingly traditional solution acquires a different significance in relation to Silvio's friendship with Minia, an older composer who lives alone with her mother in rural Galicia. Minia, like Clara, has followed an unconventional trajectory, eschewing traditional female roles and achieving success in a male-dominated world, but retreating from the social conflict that her unorthodox choices produce. Minia's amorous history remains completely silenced and it is this absence of men who might seek to control her art and her freedom that links her narrative of selfhood to Clara's. Both find satisfaction in a single-sexed community, evading the inevitable conflicts generated by the transition of the traditional male and female towards new modes of being and sexually relating.

La sirena negra traces more directly the friction arising from the development of new gender roles. Gaspar de Montenegro reveals his resentment of women in his first-person narration, angrily criticizing his domineering sister and announcing his determination to adopt an orphan boy as a means to fatherhood without having to "submit to the yoke" of a woman (1964, 2:892). After adopting Rafael, the battle for self-sufficiency continues in his relations with Miss Annie, the British governess whose love of swimming and bike riding, preRaphaelite style, and forthright manner invoke the figure of the New Woman. Gaspar spars with her verbally and psychologically, flirting but maintaining his distance. He takes pleasure in humiliating her with the offhanded announcement that he is marrying another woman and when she responds with a forceful slap to his face, he rapes her. Gaspar attempts to justify his actions, first alluding to a manly impulse to avenge her physical assault, then referring to her flirtatious behavior, and finally mentioning a divided subjectivity in which a part he does not control asserts itself and performs a heinous deed.

Through a first-person male narrator, Pardo Bazán textualizes the violent masculine response to changing female roles and a conscious and subconscious effort to reimpose traditional behaviors. Rape signifies the ultimate expression of male power and the attempt to freeze women in a subservient position. I previously mentioned veiled allusions to rape in critical discussions of Pardo Bazán's literary production and similarly noted Ortega y Gasset's theorization of rape as inherent in human relations in essays dealing with the history of gender interaction. Pardo Bazán recognizes the hostile response to female emancipation, its links to traditional misogyny, and its profound and complicated imbrication in the identity formation of modern men. Gaspar's patriarchal dreams of family run counter to anxieties regarding women's dominance. It is significant that his adoptive son Rafael is the product of an incestuous relationship, another example of masculine control of the female body and the literal imposition of patriarchal domination. Gaspar's neurotic fear of women and his obsession with death and unhealthy sexuality only end when Rafael dies. Gaspar writes of his conversion in the final paragraphs of the narrative, suggesting escape from the cycle of domination and violence without explicating the specific form his newly acquired equilibrium will take. Pardo Bazán leaves this story open to the reader's imagination, but subtly indicates the acceptance of a transgendered subjectivity in a transformed Gaspar when he states that he is now other. His tears, acquiescence to a superior power—whether life itself or God—and the confession of dependence indicate qualities traditionally associated with women and alien to his earlier aspirations for dominance and self-sufficiency. Pardo Bazán confronts the underlying fears of her male contemporaries and attempts to bring into the open such topics as sexual anxiety, conflicted liberal reactions to female and lower-class emancipation, and conscious and unconscious efforts to regain dominance in a world of changing power relations. Although she often interweaves her perceptive observations with conventional religious discourse, she courageously explores issues of rape and masculine desire and much of her writing of the 1890s and 1900s strives to unmask underlying gender hostilities that many male writers prefer to ignore or disguise.

The increased attention to human and, in particular, female sexual activity in modernism occupies an ambiguous relation with respect to the issue of gendered as opposed to transgendered subjectivity. At times decadentist and other forms of erotic discourse simply continue or increase female passivity and subservience in the narration of masculine sexual exploits or reveal voyeuristic pleasure in the depiction of female intimacy to create a homosocial bond with male readers whose shared flaunting of bourgeois values results in a strengthened patriarchal ideology.[31] In other cases, the depiction of female sexuality opens a new space for feminine desire and contributes to an enriched female subjectivity, capable of sharing in pleasures traditionally limited to the masculine subject. The differentiation of these two modalities escapes easy identification, but a distinction can be made on the basis of evidence of female pleasure and agency as well as the presence of an ironic or parodic narrative stance. The absence of these features generally signals a continuation of traditional visions of gender and of a sexualized version of the image of the sleeping, passive female lover depicted by Bécquer and rejected by Juan Ramón Jiménez. Ramón Gómez de la Serna offers a particularly egregious example of such a figure in *El doctor inverosímil* (1914), where he describes the experimental procedure performed by a doctor on his dying mistress. The operation closely parallels the physical rape of an anesthetized patient and the text invites such a reading through erotic and violent references. The doctor-lover determines that he must deeply wound the moribund woman in the leg in order to save her and after removing her clothing, he sets upon her "como quien acomete a la mujer en la pasión" [like one who sets upon a woman in a moment of passion], thrusts the lancet into her leg, and watches as she bleeds profusely (1921, 15). The narrator/witness to the procedure writes that the unconscious woman's murmur of pain sounds like a sigh of pleasure and the erotic focalization persists in his sensual description of her white body, pink nipples, and unattractive knees (15)! The almost dead object of the procedure has no opportunity for pleasure or agency. The violent, voyeuristic presentation of her dormancy clearly ignores issues of female sexual desire, pandering instead to male preferences for female passivity that begin in Aristotle and continue to the present (Bordo 1993, 11–15).

Other Spanish modernist texts present a more active female sexuality or question inherited female passivity. The 1907 modernist anthology, *La corte de los poetas,* includes many poems that continue the traditional depiction of women alongside others that offer a more innovative portrayal. Enrique de Mesa's "Erótica" describes the desire of the speaker and a female lover who willingly participates in a sexual encounter. Unlike many works of the period, the sexual partner of this poem is not identified as a prostitute and could easily be a middle or upper-class subject. Recent criticism of the early Valle-Inclán places his depiction of the female subject within conventional objectification and erasure of identity. Noël Valis comments on the narcissistic character of the *Sonatas* and although she recognizes the parody of traditional gender roles, she underscores the perpetuation of inherited stereotypes that in her view overshadow ironic revisions. I would like to consider the representation of gendered subjectivities in the *Sonatas* as a kind of performance, following Judith Butler's work on the social construction of gender through ritualistic repetition. In this sense, the *Sonatas* and works such as *Jardín Umbrío* or *Femeninas* move away from essentialist notions of masculinity and femininity and portray gendered representations as masks that require elaborate practices for their perpetuation. Constant allusions to the characters' literary antecedents accentuate their imitation of inherited roles and the already noted ekphrastic comparisons similarly freeze characters in established poses. Valle-Inclán stylizes movements and stances and the repetition of the same gesture within a text or in different texts contributes to the sensation that the reader is witnessing a theatrical performance. With frequency, characters appropriate dramatic roles. Bradomín and Concha invent a little play in *Otoño,* so that her daughters do not discover that he has been staying at the palace. On another occasion, Bradomín writes that he was the Crusader and Concha the medieval lady who lamented his departure and confesses that while he wore his hair in the Romantic style of Espronceda and Zorrilla, he adopted the Romantic kiss as part of his performance (1963a, 53). In

Primavera, Bradomín observes himself playing the role of seducer and in the midst of his performance, he states that he feels the seductive power of his own voice (1963b, 74).

In modernism, the don Juan figure is shown to be a master of masks and of roles whose efficacy has been displaced by new modes of performance and theaters of activity. *Sonata de primavera* closes with Bradomín's rejection by the crazed young princess who continues to repeat throughout her life that he was the devil. *Estío* relates his inability to retain la niña Chole and *Invierno* never proceeds beyond verbal seduction. Concha of *Otoño* represents the only sustained amorous conquest, although Valle-Inclán even undoes this narrative of triumph in the 1906 *El marqués de Bradomín* where Concha, brought back to life in modernist defiance of chronology, sends Bradomín away so that she can nurse her dying husband. In yet another blow to tradition, Valle-Inclán invests his character with feminine qualities, insinuating a transgendered subjectivity in the traditional symbol of quintessential masculinity. Bradomín's dandyism, knowledge of feminine clothing, and desire and ability to serve as Concha's maid-of-honor reflect his assimilation of attributes conventionally ascribed to women. The difference between Bradomín and the older, stereotypically masculine Juan Manuel accentuates this contrast and brings out the historicity of gender categories and their susceptibility to change over time.

The representation of transgendered subjectivity as a productive departure from traditional conceptualizations of identity contributes only modestly to reconsiderations of homosexuality in the modernist period. Clarín's hostile allusions to same-sex relations change in form but not substance in the derisive comments sprinkled through Baroja's texts.[32] The Oscar Wilde case attracts the attention of several Spanish modernists who come to his defense after his trial for sodomy. Manuel Machado condemns British persecution of Wilde in *El amor y la muerte* (1913) while Margarita Nelken demonstrates her support with her translation of his 1905 *De profundis,* written while Wilde was in prison and published in expurgated form after his death. *Revista Latina* includes a poem by Leopoldo Díaz entitled "Al espíritu de Oscar Wilde," which portrays Wilde as a persecuted innovator, castigated by a hypocritical bourgeoisie and ignorant lower class. Sympathetic representations of homosexuality surface rarely in the period and those few allow for a double reading that wavers indeterminately between acceptance and rejection. Carmen de Burgos depicts the friendship of a retired female singer and an aristocratic artist and homosexual in "El veneno del arte" (1989b, 309–63). The narrative empathetically presents the two disillusioned individuals for the better part of the work, contrasting their sensitivity and respect for talent with the superficiality and ambition of other artists with whom they interact in turn-of-the-century Madrid. However, in the closing paragraphs Luis's characterization undergoes a sudden transformation, when he announces plans to settle down, compose politically conservative works, and marry. In response to María's surprise, given his openly homosexual lifestyle as a younger man, Luis insists that he will make a model husband precisely because of his homosexuality. On the one hand, his remark reflects a cynical decision to play by the rules, willingly deceiving an unsuspecting bride to garner social acceptance. On the other, it rebukes a system in which male and female identity formation follow such different paths that understanding between the sexes as conventionally defined proves impossible. Luis's fluid gender identity may offer greater possibilities for communication than conventional heterosexual formation. The text avoids definitive closure and accountability, but raises unsettling questions.

José María Llanas Aguilaniedo displays an interest in homosexual identity in his sociological and fictional works. He depicts gay and lesbian characters as examples of a decadent modern culture in *Navegar pintoresco* (1903) and *Pitayuso* (1908) constructs a winding plot as a pretext to catalogue sexual aberration, including sadism, rape, and homosexual bondage. In his sociological study of the Madrid under classes, Llanas Aguilaniedo refers to homosexual activities as a crime against nature but at the same time, he and his co-authors include a touching description of two lesbian lovers imprisoned in a Madrid jail who serenade each other from their separate cells (1901, 185). *Del jardín del amor* (1902) continues the sympathetic portrayal of lesbianism in the first-person narration of the frustrated love of María de los Ángeles Pacheco. The novel purposely delays the revelation of the gender of the object of María's passion until the last page, perhaps to enhance its "shock" value, but also with the effect of deferring judgement until the reader has come to empathize with the character. The opening remarks by a male friend of the female diary writer further break down preconceptions of the lesbian woman as other, portraying María as a sensitive and admirable figure. The interweaving of masculine and feminine voices, with the shadow of a male author standing behind the male frame narrator who collects and publishes the diary and letters of the female writer, contributes to the construction of a transgendered textual subject. The deferral of the identification of the female love object encourages acceptance of homosexual love as essentially the same as heterosexual love, in that María's description of her feelings and her discourse in no way deviates from conventional expressions of heterosexual amorous passion.

While the narrative in some ways feeds into conventional characterizations of the suspect sexual orientation of intellectual women, the *marimacho* referred to in traditional misogynistic discourse, it also expresses a general rejection of bourgeois conventions and stultifying social regimentation. The text mocks Restoration values and writers, ironically inserting poems by the conservative Menéndez y Pelayo or Federico Balart as epigraphs to chapters in which the female narrator explains her sense of alienation from the society in which she lives and delineates her growing passion for what is later revealed to be another woman. María's description of an insipid, hypocritical society in which individuals must mask their feelings and avoid novelty in art, dress, and ideas carries forward modernist social criticism and her appreciation for new forms of painting advances modernist aesthetics. Above all, in the persistence of a double voicing and an ambivalent discourse *Del jardín del amor* advances a vision of society, art, and gender that rejects stable categories, placing the reader precariously on the borders between inherited conceptualizations that alternately receive ironic and straight treatment and present new possibilities that bear the dual imprint of deviance and banality, menace and liberation. Poised between two worlds, the text and the subject position that it produces in the reader no longer allow for a fixed stance, but require an ethical and aesthetic response that in its very mobility represents a significant break with the past.

7

Masks and Mirrors: Modernist Theories of Self and/as Other

THE MODERNIST VISION OF SELF ACCENTUATES DISCONTINUITY, multiplicity, and interdependence with a similarly discontinuous, changing world. The changing conceptualization of human identity, with increasing emphasis on a divided subjectivity in a process of continual formation, has its roots in early modernity[1] and continues to develop throughout Romanticism and the period of classic realism, in contrast with the stable subject interpellated by realist texts.[2] Brown relates the growing acceptance of a modern vision of the subject to Freud's theorization of the unconscious and the experience of World War I (1989, 3), while Davie Roberts traces it to Nietzsche, Croce, and Heidegger and Scott Lash mentions the challenge to bourgeois hegemony by a growing worker class. As in the transformation of traditional notions of nation, time, and space, multiple factors contribute to reconceptualize the subject, including advances in philosophy, psychology, and biology, modifications in social structures and living conditions, and the ability to move rapidly from rural to urban environments. New theories of the subject arise to explain the transformed self and the changing individual and social relations.

Studies of subjectivity often focus either on a dehistoricized self or a socially, historically constrained identity with little or no emphasis on the unconscious. In the present discussion of the conceptualization and representation of the subject in Spanish modernism, I will continue to emphasize historical circumstances while also underscoring the role of the unconscious, as it developed in early theorizations during the period under consideration and has continued to evolve subsequently. Spain's transformation to post-imperial status and from a nation that defined itself as racially, ethnically, and religiously homogenous to a more pluralistic self-perception unfolds simultaneously and in dynamic interaction with changing visions of the self. Modernist rejection of empire, patriarchy, Castilian hegemony, and bourgeois values influences new definitions of the subject and its formation, while shifts in the definition of the subject necessitate modifications in the perception of nation and other collectivities.

Within the Krausist belief in reason as the path to harmonic wholeness, Krausist and Institutionist writers focus on multiple features of the subject as components of equal value. Such a vision contrasts with dualistic, hierarchical Catholic thinking, which privileges the soul over the body, eternity over life, and revelation over reason. Over time, the categories and discourse developed by Krausist/Institutionist thinkers undergo transformation in contact with positivism and advances in psychoanalysis, philosophy, and sociology. Although residues of a Catholic conception of a "fallen" human nature persist, they increasingly cede to Krausist/Institutionist and succeeding visions of human nature and to an acceptance of the various elements of the self as equally valid. Francisco Giner de los Ríos discusses two different aspects of the self that resurface in subsequent texts and in such contemporary theorists as Paul Ricoeur in *Oneself as Another.* Giner posits a temporally changing, continually diverse subject that exists alongside an unchangeable identity, ever identical to itself.[3] Modernist writers increasingly emphasize the mutating self of this dual subject, both to underscore the break with the stable subjectivity of realism and to reflect the accelerated pace of modern living, where everything finds itself in motion, including the human subject. Throughout the period, explorations of subjectivity unfold in relation to both the individual and collectivity, with a growing recognition that any entity conceived as a unit carries within itself multiple forces that interact in dynamic tension. Developments in the field of group psychology inflect the understanding of the individual subject and the reverse also holds true. Changing visions of the other, whether ethnic, religious, racial, or gendered, accompany an altered conception of the self and an increased awareness and acceptance of the other as inhering within the self.

From Dualistic Conceptions of the Self to Multiple Masks for a Modern World

Initial modernist explorations of a divided subjectivity reveal a certain reticence, with a tendency to attribute multiple subject positions to a temporally altered self or to limit their scope or number. In some early ventures into the topic, the Oriental concept of the transmigration of souls allows for the introduction of multiple subjectivities. Rubén Darío cultivates the theme in "Metempsicosis" (1893), Baroja follows in "Parábola" of *Vidas sombrías* (1900) and Valera plays with the idea in *Morsamor* (1899). The modernist vision of a temporal discontinuity between periods informs subject theory and receives expression in various texts. Unamuno's "Cuando yo sea viejo" is one of several poems that project a different older self, which will disagree with the subject presently speaking (1958, 13:203). Galdós also voices time's contribution to a divided subjectivity through the self-reflexive comments of Angel Guerra, who imagines his future self as priest, dressed in a cassock and beardless in contrast to a present hirsute, worldly identity. He refers to two I's that stand face to face, one a spectator and the other a spectacle, insinuating the notion of self as other that other writers develop more fully (1967, 5:1423).

Moving beyond a temporally based conceptualization of a multiply constituted subjectivity, writers explore the notion of the simultaneity of multiple subjectivities within a single moment. In more tentative textualizations, this appears as the shifting from one subject position to another in a rapid oscillation between opposing responses to reality. Many autobiographical poems utilize this approach, beginning with Rubén Darío's "Canto de vida y esperanza" and his self-depiction as "muy siglo diez y ocho, y muy antiguo, y muy moderno" [very eighteenth century, and very old, and very modern] and continuing in Manuel Machado's "Retrato" (1909), with his claim to be half gypsy, half Parisian, aspiring poet and frustrated bandit, and Villaespesa's "Ego sum," also of 1909, where the poet exultantly proclaims his love of the Orient and Rome, Allah and Jupiter. Unamuno often confronts two seemingly contrasting subject positions that he gradually reveals as simultaneous, intertwined, and equally constitutive of a single identity. *Del sentimiento trágico de la vida* bases its argument on the equal force of rational and affective selves and defines the human subject as an ongoing tension between these two aspects. Within the essay, Unamuno already surpasses a dualistic structuring of the self to incorporate other subject positions as father, teacher, philosopher, poet, and historically changing individual, but he often returns in this and other early works to a dualistic structuring of subjectivity.

Dualistic representations of split subjectivity easily fall back into Catholic notions of certain manifestations of the self as evil. Especially in the early years of modernism, writers and texts emphasize a difficult, conflictive process of self-discovery, with residues of a Catholic binary division of sin and virtue, body and soul. Ricardo Gil intermixes elements of a new discourse of subjectivity with traditional Catholic elements in "Mi único enemigo," in which the lyrical speaker describes a false friend who leads him astray and whose powers he cannot resist without God's intervention. In the final verse the speaker inserts the belated and surprising clarification that the enemy is the speaker himself. The sense of a newly discovered recognition of divided subjectivity and the internalization of the traditional figure of the devil as part of the self relate to modern notions of the subject, but the religious overtones and vision of an evil component that works against a better self echo Catholic versions of a fallen humanity.

Angel Ganivet also moves towards modern theorizations of selfhood combined with echoes of a religious discourse of culpability and suffering. Viewed from the perspective of subjectivity, his posthumous *El escultor de su alma* presents the sculptor protagonist's tragic struggle to create himself. In the absence of a discourse adequate to communicate modern notions of the self, the text utilizes the traditional spiritual term "soul." As the protagonist adopts ever changing subject positions, he sheds previous selfhoods in a process that this textualization presents as painful and almost sinister. He abandons Cecilia, the lover with whom he had once felt as one, and then focusses his desire on Alma, alternately presented as his prized statue or daughter. The sculptor arrives at a new subject position through his assimilation of Alma, but in the process he must eliminate other selves, as symbolized in the petrified Alma that results from his kiss. Alma reflects a certain fear of this new vision of subject formation in her feelings of antipathy and dread for her father. The references to God in the closing scene as well as the emphasis on guilt and pain carry forward Catholic approaches to the subject.

Jacinto Benavente's *Los intereses creados* (1907) and *La ciudad alegre y confiada* (1916), combine the *commedia dell'arte* tradition of masks and metatheater with a study of divided subjectivity that erases overt religious references while continuing Catholic hierarchical notions of a base as opposed to heroic identity. The earlier drama constructs and then deconstructs a number of binary oppositions, including popular, open-air in contrast to bourgeois theater, the power of money in opposition to love, appearances as opposed to identity, men versus women, and upper as against lower classes. The text moves back and forth from one polarity to the other, and emphasizes the mutually constitutive identity of Leandro, the upper-class hero, and Crispín, his lower-class servant. Crispín voices a theory of divided subjectivity to describe their relationship, asserting that he and Leandro represent a unit and that each forms a part of the other (1945, 3:175). He clarifies the hierarchical nature of such a split when he attributes the noble, heroic, and virtuous domains to Leandro and the base, manipulative, calculating features to himself (175–76). In conversations with the unscrupulous, now wealthy Polichinela, Crispín states that he is what Polichinela used to be and will become what he is presently, adding the element of a temporally changing self to his theory of the subject. This insistence on a fluid, changing selfhood contrasts with the closing lines of the play, which argue for the presence of an essential core of human identity: ". . . no todo es farsa en la farsa, . . . hay algo divino en nuestra vida que es verdad y es eterno, y no puede acabar cuando la farsa acaba" [. . . not everything is a farse in the farse, . . . there is something divine in our life that is true and eternal and does not end when the farse ends] (213). These two visions of the subject intermix Giner de los Ríos's notion of a changing and permanent self with Catholic belief in a superior and base subject but in Benavente, neither triumphs definitively. Despite the trumpeting of an eternal truth in the closing scene of *Los intereses creados,* the continuation of the dramatic action in *La ciudad alegre y confiada* and the introduction of a now cynical, unfaithful Leandro and a powerful but self-doubting Crispín shows the impermanence of the victorious moment. Although the second play ends with a passionate defense of commitment to the nation and the people in opposition to mercenary interests and suggests a more authentic, admirable Crispín, it too could unravel in future sequels. Benavente's representation of a divided subjectivity reveals uncertainty and a tendency to valorize a stable authenticity in the closing scene in contrast with the theorization of a mobile subject in the text itself. This may reflect the tyranny of the dramatic ending, with public expectation for closure inherited from Echegarayan theater, which Benavente modifies but does not entirely efface. It may also indicate the author's discomfort with a modern vision of the subject, also suggested in his reluctance to repudiate hierarchical rankings of an inferior and superior self.

The growing recognition of a plurality of selves over time and increasingly in a single temporal moment relates to the widespread modernist interest in masks and other forms of disguised identity. The revival of the painted faces of *commedia dell'arte* in Benavente's *Los intereses creados* also occurs in many of his early plays and in poems by Rubén Darío ("Los regalos de Puck," "Canción de Carnaval") and Manuel Machado ("Pierrot y Arlequín," "Pantomima"). Traditional visions of the subject perceive the mask as connoting a false visage that stands between a real, authentic self and an inauthentic other. Some modern theorists of a divided subjectivity continue this negative view. Antonio Carreño asserts that the twentieth-century search for the self ends in depersonalization and radical isolation. To know oneself leads to the recognition of the other, which Carreño designates as a "mask" that annuls the old identity and imposes a new one (1981, 13–14). Carreño's use of the mildly negatively charged verbs "annul" and "impose" and the mention of "radical isolation" suggest a bleak response to new processes of identity formation. Although some modernist writings on subjectivity recognize painful encounters and loss, Spanish writers of the period also welcome changing views of subjectivity as a means to a productive transformation of self and society. Many modernists embrace the new understanding of selfhood and develop theories of alterity that open the way for an enriched experience of life. The move toward such a stance follows an uneven trajectory and develops through many different writers. Benavente's *Teatro fantástico* (1892) includes plays of varying length that introduce different versions of Pierrot, Colombina, and their entourage. Some texts utilize masked characters to exalt love and a carnivalesque ambience while others reveal tragedy and dark passions behind the frozen faces. *Cuento de primavera* plays with multiple levels of personality and transgressions of traditional categories by introducing *commedia dell'arte* characters who disguise themselves as members of the other sex or other classes. Women dress as men, the king changes roles with Harlequin, Colombina enacts a play within a play, and the drama maximizes a sense of unstable subjectivity with multiple disguises and frequent instances of mistaken identities that playfully move towards a happy ending.

Pío Baroja's *El tablado de Arlequín* (1904) and *El nuevo tablado de Arlequín* (1917) announce his intended exploration of masked, multiple identities in the titles. The varied essays in the collections reflect shifting subject positions as does his self-presentation in the 1904 preface, where the speaker self-reflexively comments on his theory of divided subjectivity. He expresses his fascination with studying the representation of reality in his mind, comparing it to a magic show to reenforce the theatrical resonances of the book's title. Even within the metaphor of the magician's performance, the speaker refuses to rest in a fixed subject position, remarking that the performance is at times happy and enjoyable and at others tediously boring. Baroja generally takes pleasure in the construction of his own narrative of selfhood and in the representation of this process in his fictional characters. *La lucha por la vida* maps the varied trajectories of the creation of a life story taken by Roberto Hastings, Manuel, his brother Juan, and many other characters. In the context of a modern conceptualization of selfhood, the title of the series takes on an additional nuance, connoting not just a Darwinist battle for survival, but also an equally important struggle for self-definition. The trilogy and other Barojan narratives present characters who resiliently recreate themselves, to the narrator's amusement and often admiration. Alonso, el *Hombre Boa* of *Mala hierba,* embellishes his story of life in America with outlandish adventures, creating a site for his own self-preservation in defense against the misery that surrounds him in Madrid. The text validates his process by ceding him ample space in a narrative that often breezes by characters with only passing attention. Bonifacio Mingote, the Baroness, and other characters who concoct an elaborate scheme involving a make-believe son and fictional relationships receive the narrator's winking acceptance and Bonifacio, in proof of his admirable talents for survival and reinvention, resurfaces in *Paradox, rey* as a participant in yet another adventure

Baroja's autobiographical *Juventud, egolatría* (1917) adopts a fragmented structure, moving from personal data to general commentary and self to society. The text speaker flaunts his instability as subject, defying the rules of conventional self-writing in pointing out that his memoirs lack unity and are probably not even sincere. He asserts that like an individual who poses for a photograph, the author who writes about the self employs a mask (1946–48, 5:156–57). To underscore the fictional aspect of his self-writing, he describes a museum visit where he signed the guest book with the self-description "hombre humilde y errante" [a humble and wandering man], but declares he could just have easily written "hombre orgulloso y sedentario" [a proud and sedentary man] and that perhaps both or neither are true (158). The speaker admits to the co-presence of Dionysian and Apollonian personality traits, then expresses a desire to change, followed almost immediately by a statement that only geniuses are capable of true transformation (159–60). The constant pirouettes serve as a cautionary note to those who seek to define Baroja, extracting statements from his texts and then attempting to build a coherent psychological, ideological, or artistic portrait. The good humor with which Barojan speakers and narrators present the alternation of multiple subject positions communicates a vision of masks and divided subjectivities that differs from traditional beliefs in an "authentic" self. While Baroja and his contemporaries recognize the negative by-products of modern society and the threats to the individual that accompany commodification and urbanization, they also perceive historically unprecedented possibilities for the individual and society.

Azorín traces the modern understanding of the subject to the French Revolution, which he believes inaugurates a new ontological conception, in which one refers not to will but to wills, not to personality but to states of consciousness that succeed each other (1947–48, 1:418). Other writers emphasize technological advances in the evolution of a different experience of self and society. Baroja's allusion to the adoption of a camera pose in his autobiographical remarks points to a new interplay between a subject as packaged for public or private presentation. Manuel Machado reflects on the impact of the camera and fame in *El amor y la muerte* (1913) as he studies pictures of the Belgian dancer and courtesan Cleo de Merode and General Kuropatkine on two sides of a match box. The wide distribution of photographs in modern advertising sensitizes consumers to the construction of a public identity and Machado's observation of the difference between the photogenic Cleo de Merode and the stiff general prompt him to meditate on the loss of self in the assumption of the photographic pose. The absence of movement in the still photograph leads to the paradoxical situation in which the camera surprises the individual in a moment that does not characterize her/him and the developed film reveals an other: "No somos nosotros, y claro está el parecido . . . no parece. La verdad es mentira" [We are not ourselves, and of course, the similarity . . . does not appear. The truth is a lie] (1913, 182). To compensate, performers like Cleo de Merode learn to adopt a pose that projects authenticity whereas the untrained general is unable to feign a look that captures who he is.

Azorín's *Doña Inés* presents multiple factors of modern society that impact the sense of the self as changing and other. In a world of choice in clothing styles, Inés opts for sensual lower-class dress in the early chapters. The narrator focuses on glimpses of her feet and leg, the movement of her breast as she walks, and on her animated, vital presence. He later describes her daguerreotype, for which she sat motionless for three minutes, but which only captures one aspect of her being and in a distorted image. Owing to the early technology of the daguerreotype and the time that has lapsed since the picture was taken, the viewer must hold the plate at a certain angle in order to make out the figure. The image escapes and requires a certain reconstruction on the observer's part. The portrait of Inés that the painter Taroncher executes later in the text proves no more exact. Taroncher simultaneously paints pictures of Inés and her ancestor Beatriz, based on a statue of the latter. In the transition from sculpture to oil, the artist creates a new image, inflected by the medium, by his vision of other women, including Inés and the many female models he has used or seen, and by the tradition of portraiture in which he works. The changing, fluid "I" eludes reproduction, and each portrait represents only one (mis)take of the subject. The image in the mirror similarly fails to duplicate the self. Like the photograph, sculpted or oil portrait, the mirror offers an incomplete picture of a mobile selfhood, requiring the viewing subject to continually adjust the self-image to the aging reflection. The narrative underscores the impossibility of exact duplication in the mirrored chapters "Obsesión (Ella)" and "Obsesión (Él)," in which the two main characters contemplate the evening sky from their respective rooms and construct similar but slightly disparate fantasies about their relationship. Inés's acceptance of a fluid subjectivity intersects with technological advances, changing ethical standards, and altered notions of gender and nation. Her personal trajectory coincides with a global cultural transformation and the two mutually inform each other with positive effects both for the construction of Inés's narrative of identity and of the Argentine-Spanish community of which she forms a part.

Pérez Galdós also utilizes the concept of a divided subjectivity and the notion of a constructed narrative of selfhood to express his belief in the need for and possibilities of social transformation. The protagonist of *Mariucha* argues that the individual carries all the elements of good and evil within him/herself and in the course of the play, both he and the female protagonist choose a new narrative of identity that rejects aristocratic privilege in favor of productive labor and renewed contacts with the lower class. Both state at different points in the drama that they are no longer who they once were but rather other, linking the change from a traditional aristocratic society of inherited wealth and identity to a modern world in which the self must be created. Although the play closes with a sense that the main characters have found a more satisfactory identity, it avoids a return to a stable, bourgeois selfhood through an ending that represents the beginning of a struggle and will require continued changes. Benavente also joins a chosen change in social class with the notion of a constructed narrative of identity in a number of works and in *La princesa Bebé* (1904), he specifically links both to modernism. The drama presents the search of an emperor's nephew and niece for a life of their own beyond constricting court etiquette. The emperor chides his nephew for his liberalism, modernism, and links to Tostoi, Ibsen, and Nietzsche, mocking his desire to "live his own life" (1945, 3:433).[4] Both royal runaways find that their lower-class lovers do not share their rejection of class and privilege. In the end, the princess and her cousin escape from their social climbing partners and immerse themselves in a popular carnivalesque celebration. The introduction of carnival, with its use of masks and abolition of class boundaries, reflects both the socially transgressive message of the text and the vision of a mobile subjectivity[5] and links the two elements with modernist visions of the individual and society.

It bears noting that female characters and women writers figure prominently in the representation of a divided subjectivity that conjoins with a changing cultural landscape. The recognition and celebration of a modern, multiple subjectivity appears most clearly in Carmen de Burgos and Margarita Nelken. Burgos clearly enjoys the rich potential available to her as a modern woman and values the various manifestations of her mobile selfhood:

> Mi vida es compleja; varío de fases muchas veces; tantas, que me parece haber vivido en muchas generaciones diferentes . . . y yo también he cambiado de ideas . . . de pensamientos . . . ¡Qué sé yo! . . . Me río de la unidad del *yo,* porque llevo dentro muchos *yoes,* hombres, mujeres, chiquillos. . . . Viejos . . . se pelearían si discutiese con alguno . . . pero les dejo que venza el que más pueda, y haga cada uno lo que le dé la gana . . . ¡todos son buenas personas! . . . A veces imprudentes, demasiado confiados. . . . Suelen obrar con ligereza y tener de qué arrepentirse. . . . Entonces intervengo. Nada de esa debilidad que nos hace estar todo el tiempo de cara al pasado lamentándolo. . . nada de lágrimas. . . . Consuelo como puedo al culpable y despierto a

todos los demás para que lo aturdan con sus cantos . . . la . . . la . . . ra . . . la, ra, la, la, la. . . . (*Mis mejores cuentos,* 23)

[My life is complex; I change phases a lot; so much that I feel like I have lived in many different generations. And I have also changed my opinion . . . my thoughts. What can I say? I laugh at the idea of the unity of the self, because I have many selves within me, men, women, little children. . . . Old people . . . they would fight if I argued with one of them . . . but I let the strongest one win, and allow them to do what they please. . . . They are all good people! Sometimes imprudent, too presumptuous. . . . They tend to act rashly and then have to repent. . . . At that point I intervene. None of that weakness that makes us look back and lament the past . . . no tears. . . . I console the guilty party as best I can and awaken the rest to drown the sorrow with their songs . . . la . . . la . . . ra . . . la . . . , ra, la, la, la.]

Margarita Nelken also validates the experience of multiple selves, which she humorously treats in her short story "Mi suicidio," a title that introduces the seemingly impossible subject position of an "I' that relates his/her own death.[6] The story opens with the male narrator's first-person description of his recovery of consciousness in a hospital room or "setting," as he designates it in the first of multiple references to theater, acting, masks, and features of a constructed subjectivity. As the narrator gradually remembers being hit by a car while crossing a busy plaza, his nurse addresses him as "poor devil" and "unfortunate soul," also making reference to a certain Duke. When the narrator finally feels strong enough, in his own words "like his old self," to inquire about the accident and the Duke's role, the nurse hands him a newspaper that describes the mishap as the attempted suicide of a despondent young writer. Using his pseudonym "Juan de la Cumbre," in yet another insinuation of multiple subjectivities, the paper now praises his talent and extols the Duke, who has generously paid all medical expenses in what the narrator quickly recognizes is an attempt to conceal legal culpability. Juan's fame brings him new literary contracts as well as the return of an ex-lover, who invents her own version of the purported suicide as a response to her termination of their relations. Unable to resist the identities that the Duke, the newspapers, and his old girl friend have constructed for him, Juan settles into a new life complete with fame, demands for his literary contributions, and a woman he would prefer to live without. The text specifically repudiates a tragic representation of the events, designating them rather as a *sainete* in a laughing embrace of modern forms of subjectivity.

The Representation of Self as Other: Changing Categories and Textual Innovation

The modernist conceptualization of selfhood in some writers emphasizes the presence of multiple I's, as expressed by Carmen de Burgos, or states of consciousness that succeed each other, as articulated by Azorín, while in others it takes the form of a subject that contains within itself one or multiple "others." These modes of envisioning the modern subject often coexist and although their difference may appear slight, the shift in emphasis from an I constituted by multiple selves to an I that contains multiple others proves immensely productive in reimagining the self and its relations with other individuals and groups. Alejandro Sawa articulates both notions in his autobiographical *Iluminaciones en la sombra,* where he speaks of his desire to create his self, in clear expression of the constructedness of identity in modern society, and also remarks that he is always other, communicating his constant changes in his opinions, values, and subject positions and the recognition that his "I" never coincides fully with the self that he textualizes. Sawa's comments echo Rimbaud's famous statement, "Je est un autre" [I is an other] and reflect Freudian and Lacanian psychoanalysis and new notions of social relations. It coincides with Galdós's description of the quintessential modernist joke on the occasion of the woman who looks in the mirror and sees the face of another person (1909, 47). If the mask symbolizes the recognition of multiple selves, the mirror represents the concept of self as other. Valle-Inclán utilizes both in *La lámpara maravillosa,* stating at one point that he wears a hundred masks (1974, 575) and advising the reader at another to evoke the child of his/her past when looking in the mirror (533). The mirror reveals a different self in Valle-Inclán's aesthetic treatise and also in his theory and practice of the *esperpento,* which he defines as reality's deformed reflection in the carnival mirror. Even the regular mirror returns a distorted, transformed image as Villaespesa elaborates in "Los espejos":

Me busca mi mirada.
Sólo encuentro
mi propio rostro reflejado

dentro
de la luna empañada.
Todo se ve lejos . . .
¿Somos nosotros
mismos, o son otros
los que nos miran desde los espejos?

(1911, 45)

[My gaze searches for me.
I only find
my own face reflected
inside
the blurred mirror.
Everything appears distant . . .
Is it us or is it
some others
who look at us from the mirrors?]

In Spanish modernism, the exploration of self and/as other develops simultaneously on the individual and collective levels, with a clear sense of the interconnectedness of changing visions of subject and nation, self and others. Baroja makes this connection in "Lejanías," where he attacks modern state manipulation of the lower classes, in which soldiers are ordered to fire on the revolutionaries that fight for the rights of both. He ends the essay projecting a future society in which an energetic love of the self will produce love of the species (1946–48, 8:861). The more tolerant, comprehending attitude toward traditionally marginalized and alienated groups that many texts advocate has its roots in the growing recognition that the other resides within the self and that traditional attempts to establish strict borders between these two entities, on the individual and collective levels, no longer obtain. The reconsideration of the relationship with former colonies, European colonizers, and other colonized peoples, as well as redefinitions of nation, ethnicity, race, and gender accompany and inform a transformed perception of the self. Peoples formerly conceived as inferior and alien come to represent a newly discovered element of the self, as in the case of "primitive" societies that serve as models for a re-encounter with repressed features of the human experience. Categories such as illness and health break down and the easy homogenization of groups under the labels "criminal" or "insane" cedes to a more nuanced definition that recognizes the presence of these states in the general population. Llanas Aguilaniedo and Bernaldo de Queirós insist that the criminal does not differ significantly from law-abiding citizens and Baroja textualizes a similar notion in *Mala hierba,* where the criminal activities of the Madrid underclass appear in duplicate among the wealthy, socially respectable denizens of the upper classes.

Benavente's famous play about incest, *La malquerida* (1913), may also be read as a study of the criminal other who resides within the self. When Acacia's fiancé is murdered, her mother Raimunda initially blames an outsider, then comes to suspect a village resident, and finally identifies her husband Esteban as the perpetrator. Acacia's process follows a similar trajectory, moving from expressed hatred of her stepfather Esteban and his incestuous affection to the recognition of her love for him and her participation in the "crime." Pardo Bazán presents a similar case in "El aljófar," where a touring circus performer is lynched by an angry mob in his children's presence for purportedly defaming a statue of the Virgin and stealing her jewels. In the end, the police discover that a local student had committed the crime. The borders between insider and outsider, criminal and accuser, dissolve with the violent lynching a clear indicator of the element of criminality within "civilized" society. Pérez de Ayala's *La caída de los Limones* introduces a complex mix of good and evil, kindness and cruelty in the figure of Arias, whose motives for the brutal murder and rape of the woman he loves remain a mystery to his sisters and the readers. Azorín propounds a dissolution of the boundaries between criminal and non-criminal in *Sociología criminal,* where the text speaker remarks that to understand the criminal mind, the reader simply has to examine her/himself (1947–48, 1:510). He subsequently links issues of changing ethics and legal accountability to a vision of the modern individual as a series of subject positions that change over time according to circumstances. Questioning the traditional notion that the execution of the act provides sufficient basis for the attribution of responsibility, he argues that senility, insanity, immaturity, alcohol, and other factors mitigate ethical responsibility. The text establishes a correlation between a reconceptualization of the subject and social policy and although it does not elaborate a new ethics, it points to the need for a major reevaluation of the presuppositions undergirding Western law.

The question of insanity and its relation to the constitution of the subject surfaces frequently in modernism. Jacinto Grau's *El conde Alarcos* (1907) examines the internal conflict of a count ordered to kill his wife by the king. The count responds to the dilemma with frantic shifts from virtue to evil, rationality to irrationality, loyal husband to murderer. The radical changes in his mode of acting and being break longstanding conventions of character portrayal and probably contributed to the unsuccessful reception of the text, which Grau addresses in notes appended to the published version. The Martínez Sierras more successfully depict the interweaving of sanity and insanity, virtue and vice in *Almas ausentes* (1900), whose title illustrates once again the use of traditional religious terminology to designate modern psychological states for which a commonly accepted discourse has still not evolved. The text describes a stay in a residence for the mentally disturbed and in the course of the narrative, the differentiation between attendants and patients and narrator and inmates becomes increasingly tenuous. The first-person narrator's analysis of his feelings unfold in a chaotic, repetitive discourse that conflicts with the very ordered explanations of the "insane" resident who had murdered his wife. The patient who appears to have most completely lost contact with reality, waiting each night for some undefined event that he is sure will occur, becomes the hero of the action when he murders the attendant who intends to seduce a young woman. The murder raises obvious questions about (in)sanity and legal responsibility, with links to Azorín's considerations of the same topic, but also insinuates the validity of the inmate's intuitive knowledge and his sense of good and evil. The reactions of a second worker also challenge established definitions of lunacy and sanity, generosity and egotism. Lorenzo has determined to devote his life to the care of the mentally ill, and although he loves the young woman who almost fell prey to his co-worker and recognizes that she has limited possibilities for building a life for herself, he chooses to abandon her in order to pursue his goal. The narrator questions the wisdom of his decision, ironically accusing the caretaker of the mentally ill of being crazy, to which Lorenzo responds that human reason is just another form of madness (1900, 115).

The aspiration to reconceptualize categories of sanity and insanity or rationality and irrationality affects a wide range of writers and relates to redefinitions of gender, class, and race. Galdós inverts traditional visions of the hysterical woman in *La loca de la casa,* where the female protagonist reveals remarkable negotiating and business skills that she combines with philanthropic activities and religious faith. Many studies of *Don Quijote* that appear during the celebration of the third centennial of its publication valorize the melding of sanity and insanity, of the lord and his lower-class squire, of the local and universal in the novel. Gabriel Alomar sees a marvelous conjoining of native Castilian and transnational humanitarian faith in the novel (1907b, 183). Rusiñol ironically plays with prevailing definitions of madness in "El loco" of *El pueblo gris,* republished in *Pájaros de barro,* signaling the arbitrary classification of "insane" for those who refuse to enter the army, prefer to cultivate music over commerce, and choose to remain rootless and free rather that settle into bourgeois married life. The changing vision of sanity reflected in the writers of the period and the growing recognition that the madman who had traditionally represented a feared or ridiculed other resides within the self reveals itself in the open references to Juan Ramón Jiménez's struggles with mental illness and his candid remarks on his suicidal temptations and stay in a sanatorium in "Habla el poeta," published in *Renacimiento.*

The theme of the double provides another mechanism for the exploration of self and/as other. I pointed to numerous examples of this literary phenomenon in the discussion of eternal return and will here focus on its relationship to questions of subjectivity. Concha Espina's interest in the topic reflects her transition away from the Catholic vision of selfhood to a richer consideration of self and/as other. The confusion of Mariflor and Marinela in *La esfinge maragata* allows the reader to see both the commonality and difference between the young woman raised in a coastal city with the experience of education and freedom and her cousin of the inland, economically depressed and psychologically repressed region of Maragatería. While Mariflor increasingly moves toward the realization that she will have to marry Antonio and give up her dreams of a chosen marriage partner and life outside of Maragatería, Marinela persists in her fantasies to elude the grim reality that surrounds her, suggesting the coincidence of these two opposing subject positions, here personified in two distinct individuals but residing within each in varying degrees. *La rosa de los vientos* represents the self as other through a series of doubles. Soledad's tense relationship with her mother stems from her close identification with her biological father, who raised her as he would have raised the son he desired. Soledad's feelings for her stepfather, Germán Ercilla, alternate between a desire to accept him as the heir to her father's role and a rejection of him as usurper. They also oscillate based on her view of herself as her mother's rival or supportive daughter. The conflict between these various subject positions reveals itself in Soledad's identification with Amalia, Germán's deceased daughter by a previous relationship, and with Carmen, Amalia's mother. Soledad bears a remarkable resemblance to Amalia and when she sees her portrait, she feels as if she sees herself. She similarly identifies with Carmen when she reads a series of love letters addressed to her and presumably written by Germán. The confusion of roles receives additional expression when Soledad mistakes Félix Iturbe, an older and disreputable don Juan, with his noble and gentle son Agustín.

The novel's conclusion suggests a resolution of the various conflicts. Soledad comes to accept Germán's paternal affection when he rescues her from the jail in which Félix has placed her under pretext that she caused Agustín's death. The liberation by one father figure from the dark, subterranean jail cell in which another father figure had enclosed her invites Freudian readings and insinuates the resolution of the Oedipal complex in the final acceptance of a non-sexual relationship with Germán. In consonance with this development, Soledad also establishes a healthy relationship with her mother and appears to open herself to the possibility of an amorous relationship with the young Adolfo Velasco. As in other writers, the apparent stability of the characters at the end of the text unravels in future sequels. Soledad reappears in *El caliz rojo* (1923) as the disillusioned wife who has separated from Adolfo Velasco and a painfully unhappy marriage. Access to the self remains forever incomplete and the other, whether a separate individual or a part of the self, persists as both an impediment and an aid to self-knowledge.

Espina's short story of the foundling, "El jayón," revised to dramatic form with the same title, more succinctly and forcefully argues the necessity of the other for the constitution of the self. Andrés loves Irene, who is from his same lowland village and like him in character, but marries the temperamentally distinct Marcela, from a mountain town. Marcela gives birth to a son the same night that a foundling is left at their doorstep. Andrés persuades his wife to raise the abandoned infant, who looks identical to their son and is generally assumed to be Irene's illegitimate child, fathered by Andrés. Marcela continually refers to Irene as *la otra* [the other (woman)] and the villagers similarly call the foundling *el otro* [the other (man)], but the differences quickly dissipate. When Marcela discovers that her own child is a sickly hunchback, she switches the infants and *el otro* becomes the legitimate son for all but his mother. Irene continues to love the hunchback, thinking it is her child, while Andrés loves both. When he and the boys get lost in a snowstorm, Irene and Marcela seek each other out, each needing the other, and when Marcela learns that the sickly boy has died, she cedes the other son and her husband to Irene and commits suicide. The rotating of self and other does not end with her death, as the text communicates in the laments of the remaining son, who still considers himself Marcela's child, continues to call out to her as mother, and cannot bring himself to see her as other.

Modernist writers explore new forms of literary expression to better communicate the experience of self and/as other. A predilection for dialogue reflects one of many shared strategies. The narrator of the Martínez Sierras' *Almas ausentes* remarks that the insane rarely dialogue, preferring a monologic monopolization of discourse. The inability to open to the other also appears as a form of illness in Baroja's works. The advice to Fernando of *Camino de perfección* that he listens to himself too much and should take a long trip signifies a rejection of self-analysis and a call for dialogue with the other. Silvestre Paradox needs an other with whom to converse and when his sidekick Avelino Diz is not present, he argues with himself, remarking that his own ideas expressed out loud seem like they belong to another and make him want to debate (1946–48, 1:54). In a rudimentary attempt to systematize his philosophy, he declares that the self proceeds from the non-self ["El yo procede del yo no"] (69), once again linking self and other.

The critical tradition that emphasizes will and an idiosyncratic exaltation of the self in Baroja[7] overlooks the other side of the revolving coin that also has a strong presence in his work. Often when he argues for strong individualism, he uses the first person plural to make his case, fusing the I and the other in a collective identity. In "El culto del yo" he talks of the discovery of the self as a new birth, likening it to the Renaissance, and then moves on to argue that *we* must shed our morality and never sacrifice *our* personality to anyone or anything (1946–48, 5:27). "Indiferencia" includes the paradoxical statements, "Somos individualistas" [We are individualists], and "Somos así, no tenemos el sentimiento social que tienen otras razas" [We are just this way. We don't have the social sense that other races have], conjoining the collective "we" with references to a single, impenetrable self. The essay's text structure simulates a conversation, with colloquial language, ellipsis, and rhetorical questions that bring the reader into dialogic exchange to further undermine the sense of isolated, antisocial individualists. Manuel Machado utilizes a similar strategy in his poem, "Vraiment." The text assumes a dialogic structure, with the poetic speaker addressing a French woman and half-agreeing, half-disagreeing with the French generalization that Spaniards are a sad people. In a telling example of the desire to reach out to the other, the poem is written entirely in French and the final stanza starts with the words "Et nous . . ." [And we . . .] and then moves on after the ellipsis to describe the Spanish self in the language of the other (1988, 160).

Spanish modernist novelists explore new forms of narrativity to communicate the experience of the self as other to their readers. Gabriel Miró's innovative literary style and narrative strategies reflect his commitment to the abolition of the borders separating self and other and his understanding of self as other on the individual level. Many stories of *Del huerto provinciano* deconstruct the traditional opposition of good and evil, self and other. "El señor maestro" describes the frustrated attempts of a small town school teacher to instil respect for animal life in the villagers. His opposition to hunting prompts him to rescue a badly wounded crow that he names Arturo and trains to speak. Inverting self and other, the story ends when the teacher's son, a priest and avid hunter, returns to the village and shoots his father's pet. The ambiguous referent of the teacher's cries of "Arturo, hijo mío" [Arturo, my son] enhances the already evident crisscrossing of borders, insinuating the displacement of paternal feelings from the biological son to the animal and the coalescing of the son and the cruel villagers, all of whom remain estranged from the school teacher's values and sentiments. Miró exploits the possibilities of ambiguity to deconstruct established polarities and disallow the construction of new divisions.

"El sepultero" refutes human efforts to separate life and death with its continual movement back and forth between a depiction of the grave digger as inalterably alien and identical to other workers. On the one hand, the narrative argues that with a clean shirt and different hat the grave digger would be indistinguishable from a bricklayer or library worker while on the other, he suggests an inherited predisposition that explains the grave digger's chilling gaze and the projection of death in his eyes (1988, 108–9). The description of tomb decorating on All Soul's Day and of the black-robed older women whose friendship has its origins in shared cemetery visits suggests an easy familiarity with death in the general population that conflicts with the representation of the grave digger and his family as unique in their lack of fear. The closing scene carries forward the ambiguous message, introducing the thin figure of the grave digger's daughter, who had been ill with fever and who only recovers her appetite during visits to the cemetery. The image of the young girl snacking calmly on a sandwich of bread and sausage in the presence of a cadaver brought to the surface by recent rains conjoins life and death in opposition to cultural desires to maintain their separation. It also humanizes the figure of the grave digger in the depiction of his concern for his daughter's health, even while estranging both father and daughter from the reader in their possibly inherited indifference to death. Miró's language mirrors the ambiguity of his message, with affirmations leading to negations and one sentence undermining the preceding. The fourth paragraph of "El sepultero" opens with the declaration that gods, heroes, and mystics have a premonition of immortality while grave diggers never feel it. A later sentence states that the grave digger stays alone with the dead and comes to believe they belong to him and need him and that he himself will never die. The seeming contradiction between this last assertion and the earlier description of his inability to feel immortality takes on additional complexity in the subsequent reference to grave diggers as immortal, followed by a final two sentences that equate divinity with life and heaven and the grave digger with death and earth. The oscillation from one judgement to the other erases the borders separating self and other.

The syntactic inversions and reversals of "El sepultero" combine with Miró's narrative shifts in *Del vivir* (1904) to dislodge traditional prejudices regarding leprosy. The novel describes a visit to an area of the Valencian region known for its leper population and initially focalizes the narrative through the eyes of Sigüenza, sometimes described as the author's *alter ego* and more correctly as a recurring character that stands in a complex, changing relationship with the author and his narrators.[8] Sigüenza expects to find suffering in the region, but encounters pleasant villages where life appears to transpire as elsewhere. His mixed feelings for the community, based on stereotypes and alternately generous and selfish behavior, reveal themselves in his desire to comprehend and become one with the lepers and in his fear of contact and of the deformation caused by the disease. Although the text seeks to break down inherited categories and erase established borders between leper and non-leper, it continually underscores the inability to fully do so and the danger of failing to respect the alterity of the other in the process of rapprochement. Sigüenza's conflicted relationship with local lepers and healthy residents is mirrored by the narrator's oscillating judgements of the protagonist. At times the narrator fuses with Sigüenza, disappearing as a separate entity and merely voicing the character's experiences and feelings. However, on other occasions, a clearly extradiegetic narrator exposes his difference, intruding in a first person that actively differentiates itself from the protagonist or voicing harsh criticism of his shallow character. The narrator expresses disdain for Sigüenza when he visits a badly disfigured young woman and desires to see her deformity despite her wish to hide it. The narrative's defense of the dignity of the other and her right to remain free from Sigüenza's gaze conflicts with its the invasion of the leper terrain and the opening of leper suffering to the reader's scrutiny.

Miró's texts struggle to find a middle ground between the imposition of the self, with the resultant annihilation of the other, and the unproductive separation of self and other. His stylistic and structural innovations work toward a melding of difference in conjunction with a respect for the integrity of the self. Miró's frequent use of synaesthesia brings together normally distinct entities in a new relationship. He writes of "lluvia de sol" [sun rain] in *Del vivir* and in *La novela de mi amigo* a character describes how he smells the smoke from the kitchen and remembers the odors of the bedrooms and closets (1949, 145). In both cases, the solidity of one article dissolves into another less material entity, but each persists as an independent if transmuted object. Miró's metaphors have the same effect. *Del vivir* transforms inherited visions of flies as bothersome and disease-ridden by fusing them with jewels and light: "Brillaban las moscas imitando chispas de gasa y argentería" [The flies glittered imitating sparks of gauze and silver] (1949, 25). Narrative shifts in many texts signal the instability of identity and frequent melding of self and other. The first-person narrator of *La novela de mi amigo* undergoes frequent transformations in the course of the novel. In the opening chapter, the unidentified speaking I carries on a one-sided monologue that reveals the presence of a narratee in his comments that he does not smoke, but will, if his interlocutor wishes. Several pages later the focalization changes and the unnamed narratee takes over the narration and the first-person narrator of the opening paragraphs briefly becomes a character presented by an intradiegetic narration and then almost immediately, the original speaker resumes his story in first person singular. The second chapter also unfolds in first person, but here the speaking I gradually identifies himself as the narratee of the previous chapter. At times the narrative proceeds in dialogue form with almost no indication of a difference between the two friends while on other occasions, the narrator distances himself, designating his friend by his name Federico in an effort to mark their separation. At the novel's end, a heterodiegetic narrator appears for the first time to relate Federico's suicide and his final escape from an oppressive marriage and failed artistic career. In the course of the novel, as in *Las cerezas del cementerio* and other Miró texts, characters become confused with each other in the mind of the reader or other characters. Federico's daughter Lucía becomes linked in his mind with his sister-in-law and after Lucía's death, the (con)fusion becomes even stronger. The borders between self and other continually shift on a number of textual levels, ranging from lexical choice to narrative stance, characterization to effect on the reader.

Pérez de Ayala shares with Miró and other modernists the exploration of novel forms of narrativity to reflect the dynamic interplay of self and other in the formation of the subject and to force the reader to experience such a division in her/his reception of the text. His short novel *Sonreía* opens with a prologue that immediately foregrounds the text's undecidability, declaring the imperceptible difference between tragedy and the grotesque. The first-person speaker of the introductory remarks appears to differ from the first-person narrator of chapter 1, who identifies himself as Fernández and proceeds to transmit the memoirs of his friend Rodríguez that another friend López has surreptitiously obtained. Several details suggest that this threesome represents a fictional doubling or tripling of the narrative I and that the three are different elements of a single self. The narrator mentions in the initial sentences that his rhetoric teacher's prediction that he will become a great novelist seems unlikely, since he neither understands himself nor feels capable of understanding others, a comment that foregrounds the theme of identity and its slippery nature. The ordinary ring of the three names (Fernández, Rodríguez, López), and the fact that the trio meets in a small village when each is in mourning and takes a walk at the same time in exactly the same place day after day insinuates their common identity. All three are artists: López, a painter; Rodríguez, a prose writer; and Fernández, a bit of a poet. The insistence in naming himself Fernández rather than the unnamed "I" of typical narrative custom further underscores a focus on the problematics of identity, which continues in the framed narrative.

Chapter 2 relates the return to Asturias of a young man after an absence of six years. The first-person narrative presumably describes Rodríguez's life, but it never mentions his name in the ensuing ten chapters and no other character uses a specific given or surname in direct address to resolve the character's identity. Upon arriving at Pilares, the young man undertakes an ongoing dialogue with himself, in which he comments on the various changes in the town. He discovers remnants of the former city in the park and when he reads the newspaper, it takes him back to another place and time. Although born and raised in Pilares, he now uses English words and French expressions to communicate his thoughts and does not understand certain slang words used by his erstwhile friends. Feeling estranged from his native land, he suddenly remembers his fiancée, whom he had abandoned years earlier. He remarks that he feels like ancestors are living in him, compelling him to visit her in the village where she lives. In another instance of multiple selves that stand in a relationship of otherness, he inquires about his ex-fiancée and learns that she was cruelly deceived by a boyfriend, a tale that pains him until he realizes that the story he now hears as if about another simply relates his own desertion of the pitiable Esperanza.

The narrator and Esperanza resume their love, marry, and depart on their honeymoon and he appears to have resumed the original narrative of identity until Esperanza becomes ill and he has to leave her with relatives in Santander while he attends to business in San Sebastián. There he runs into a former lover from New York and completely forgetting his bride, resumes their torrid love affair for several days before returning to Santander to discover that Esperanza has died in his absence. When he views her corpse, he observes that she is smiling. The long suffering Esperanza dies with a smile on her face, in yet another manifestation of self as other, while her new husband renews a narrative of identity that excludes her and moves in an entirely different direction. The various selves that coexist in Rodríguez (or is it López or Fernández?) remain incomprehensible to the reader, who stands in a relationship of otherness to the narrator while also reading the text with a fascination that manifests a certain identification with him and his story/ies. The narrator's experience of self as other continues to the present if the three men of the prologue in fact represent different elements of his identity. All three wear mourning and temporarily reside in a village where they attempt to recover from a recent loss and their alternating friendship, hatred, and indifference suggests a vision of subjectivity as constituted by a series of selves in a relation of alterity.

A later work by Pérez de Ayala adopts a more optimistic response to the exploration of self as other. *Belarmino y Apolonio* (1921) contains multiple examples of pairings that represent two facets of a unit constituted by tensions between the components. The prologue introduces Amaranto de Fraile, who coincides with the first-person narrator in a boarding house and whose advice has now become part of the narrator's vision of the world. Chapter 1 presents another narrative level, in which the first-person narrator of the prologue describes his encounter in the rooming house with a jovial priest, whose multiple names of Pedro, Lope, Francisco, Guillén, and Eurípedes suggest a self constituted by varied subject positions, a definition which the narrative confirms. Cordial and tolerant, clearly committed to his religious vocation, Pedro Lope Guillén has no qualms in breaking the prescribed Lenten fast, but avoids public declarations of his unorthodox behavior by having his meals served to him in his room. The narrator joins him there and begins to reconstruct the story of his life, but rather than move forward with this narrative, Chapter 2 circles back to the prologue to revise the image of Amaranto and his relationship with the narrative in an ever-changing play of reproduction and distortion. Here Amaranto appears as a ghost that arises in the narrator's memory when he determines to open his story with a description of the Rúa Ruera.

The remembered/recreated figure of Amaranto advises the narrator, in a textualization of self as other, that to capture reality in its multiple variants he should adopt a dual vision and have two characters describe the scene from different perspectives. The narrator follows this counsel and introduces the painter Juan Lirio and the philosopher Pedro Lario, who offer their opposing descriptions of the street according to their preference for order or disorder, art or logic, Romanticism or Classicism. The cascading levels of narration mirror the succession of multiple narrative perspectives that unfold as the text shifts focalization from the point of view of an omniscient narrator to segments that adopt the perspective of Belarmino, the philosopher shoe maker, or his rival Apolonio, the dramatist cobbler. Certain fragments reflect the presence of the priest Guillén and reveal his own divided subjectivity as priest and former lover of his childhood sweetheart Angustias. The priest carries within him the person of Guillén the lover just as Angustias, the pure and loving young girl, continues to reside in Angustias the prostitute.

The reader's relationship with the text and the characters continually changes, at times a distanced, detached response in keeping with the grotesque nature of the characters and at times a warm attachment in consonance with the tender portrayal of the story and its actors. The narrator often comes across as arrogant, impatient, and self-serving, as when he forces Angustias to follow him to a meeting with Guillén with a brusqueness that makes her fear he plans to injure her (1989, 278) or when he makes impertinent commentaries at inappropriate moments during Guillén's narration in chapter 4. The narrator at times disappears to become one with the other tellers of the story, but on other occasions stands out as distinct and separate. The entire text insists on a rhythm of repetition and difference, duplication and change, that surfaces in the twice-told story of the attempted elopement of Guillén and Angustias and in the narrator's explicit conflation of the celebrations of the Resurrection and Pentecost in the presentation of the reencounter between Guillén and Angustias. The displacement of the resurrected figure of Christ by a former prostitute and the commemoration of the descent of the Holy Spirit and the miracle of communication across different languages through Guillén's Latin prayer of pardon and his redesignation of Angustias as his sister and ward revisits and revises Catholic liturgy.

The changing roles and appropriation of new relationships of identity and alterity receive full endorsement in the closing chapters, where the antagonistic Belarmino and Apolonio find themselves confined in a home for the aged. Apolonio's resentment of Belarmino and Belarmino's cultivated indifference to the outside world and his rival give way to a final embrace and to Apolonio's confession that he considers Belarmino his other half. Belarmino responds in kind, but in the ultimate representation that self always remains other, he communicates the same, but slightly different idea, telling Apolonio in his idiosyncratic language that he is his other hemisphere ["y tú mi otro testaferro"] (1989, 300). Pérez de Ayala has often been linked with Ortega y Gasset in his use of perspectivism, but his vision of the subject and of self as other differs considerably from that espoused by the philosopher. Ortega privileges suture over alienation, conscious rationality over the unconscious. His fear of the other precludes a consideration of self as other and of the implications of such a discovery for the individual and society. By contrast, Pérez de Ayala and other modernists internalize the concept of self as other and continually explore the consequences of this new understanding of identity for their lives as well as their art.

Theories of Intersubjectivity and Interculturality

The cultural production of Juan Ramón Jiménez, Antonio Machado, and Miguel de Unamuno reveals their shared interest in the relationship of self to other, self as other, and self and society. Each addresses these issues from a different perspective and with varying emphasis on the individual and the social, but all three underscore the significance of intersubjectivity for the formation of the self in a conceptualization that anticipates the work of Emmanuel Levinas, Paul Ricoeur, Paul Smith and other later theorists. Traditional Hispanic criticism places Juan Ramón Jiménez within the *modernista* current and Machado and Unamuno within *noventayochismo.* In tracing their respective textualizations of a theory of subjectivity, I intend to point out once more the insufficiency of these categories. Jiménez and Machado share a similar evolution as they move from the experience of divided subjectivity as a crisis of being to an understanding of intersubjectivity as a dialogue that encompasses both self and other and self as other in a dynamic, caring encounter. Machado and Unamuno more fully and specifically relate their vision of subjectivity and intersubjectivity to an analysis of social, collective relations, but all three share with Pérez de Ayala and other modernists an acceptance of the multiplicity of the self and of the always desired but ever incomplete communion with the other.

I have mentioned Juan Ramón Jiménez's transition from fear of the body to a more healthy acceptance in discussions of time and a transgendered subjectivity and this change clearly relates to his theory of the subject. His early poetic representations of a crisis of identity characterize certain components of the self as alien forces that he struggles to overcome. "Mis demonios" speaks of his tormented spirit and his desire to dissolve himself in the splendor of the white sky. Death and sex are frequent themes and the poetic speaker often fears solitude, afraid of his self-destructive impulses and the darker side of his sexuality, as in "Nocturno" of *Rimas.* The sense of crisis and self-alienation manifests itself in a fear of mirrors and sight. In the untitled poem numbered 51 in *Rimas,* the speaker feels terror when viewing his image in the mirror and senses that the shadow of another follows him. "Roja" of *Almas de violeta* presents a self that closes its eyes when seeking pleasure from foul bodies, afraid to look at the other and the self in the other. "Soy yo quien anda esta noche," of *Jardines lejanos* (1903), depicts a subject that questions whether it is he that walks in his room or the beggar who circled his garden. He feels distanced from himself, in an anguished, repetitive questioning that finds no answer. The separation of a carnal and spiritual self continues in *Las hojas verdes* (1906). "Tengo un libro de Francis Jammes" places the lyric speaker inside on a rainy winter afternoon reading about a nature he cannot access. This split of inside and outside mirrors the speaker's self-description as divided between an open spirit ("Mi alma estará de par en par" [My soul will be wide open]) and a sad, carnal self ("todo será triste y carnal" [all will be sad and carnal]) (1954, 722). A highly unusual end of verse and end of stanza division, with the splitting of the word *tarde* into two syllables between the first and second stanzas and then again in the final two verses graphically represents the internal division.

Laberinto and *Melancolía,* both of 1911, show a marked interest in the use of windows and mirrors, both of which J. M. Aguirre has identified as symbols for the relationship of self to other. Aguirre relates the window to melancholy hopelessness or hope and the mirror to despair (1979, 105), and although this correlation of images and sentiments is plentiful in the early Jiménez, in later publications he moves toward a richer, more affirmative exploration of intersubjectivity. In the 1911 publications, the feelings of sadness and disorientation suggested by the titles of the two collections alternate with a sense of connection through and with the other. Many poems in *Melancolía* describe the landscape as viewed through a train window and the mobility of the speaking I/eye creates a succession of images and emotional responses that liberate the subject from an obsessive preoccupation with the self. The train window overlays a series of changing external images on the barely visible reflection of the self in the glass. The relationship between a growing acceptance of self as carnal and spiritual and the intersubjective relationship as access to a wider experience of the external world receives expression in several poems. "Mientras ella, divina de rubor . . ." superimposes the description of the passionate kisses of the speaker and a woman aboard a train and of the villages and countryside visible through the window. In contrast to the melancholy vision of nature often present in the Jiménez of this and previous collections, the text describes tranquil brooks and laughing women intermixed with more woeful sounds and the final stanza breaks with the intruding note of sadness precisely because the speaker discovers access to the world outside through the gaze of his lover:

> Luego, la suave brisa de la tarde de agosto
> refrescó alegremente sus mejillas besadas,
> y, mientras me miraba, cogiéndose el cabello,
> en sus ojos floridos las praderas pasaban . . .
>
> (1912, 44)

> [Then, the soft breeze of the August afternoon
> happily refreshed her kissed cheeks,
> and, while she looked at me, putting up her hair,
> the meadows passed in her flowering eyes . . .]

The speaker's growing acceptance of his divided subjectivity parallels acceptance of the other and the world beyond. This same understanding resurfaces in a poem in which the lyrical speaker describes the setting sun light that he receives in his room through its reflection in the windows of a facing balcony. The sun comes to him from the East although it is positioned in the West, bringing him morning sentiments in the afternoon. This light filtered through the other brings calm to the speaker and transforms his flesh to spirit ("Un sol débil, reflejado en otro balcón").

The constitutive power of the other for the formation of the self becomes a constant theme in poems that analyze the uniqueness of his and her selfhoods in their amorous relation and their displacement by other selves in their changing relationship and as they change partners. She may love another, but will never again be what she is now for him when she engages in a different relationship. Although the poet at times emphasizes the changing selves of the female object of his love and his own constitutive power in the creation of her subjectivity, he also reveals his awareness of the same process in his own subject formation. "Soledad" of *Diario de un poeta recién casado* presents the sea as a metaphor for the unending transformations of the self from plenitude to insufficiency, self-knowledge to ignorance. "¡En ti estás todo, mar, y sin embargo, / qué sin ti estás, qué solo, / qué lejos, siempre de ti mismo!" [You are full of yourself, sea, and yet, / you are so empty of yourself, so alone, / so far away, always from yourself] (1917, 44). In this (re)vision, self and other intertwine, stars take on the form of the earth ("Las estrellas parecen en el mar, tierra, tierra divina" [Stars seem like earth, divine earth, in the sea], 260) and the sky and the sea frequently blend and then separate to blend anew. The sea struggles, alone but giving birth to itself in a continual process of self-creation ("Mar," 271). Some poetic texts scream out an exultant sense of fullness and plenitude, as in Poem 183, "Nocturno," while others describe a sea that remains blind to the observer and thus incapable of entering into the loving relationship required for self-realization, as in Poem 189, "Ciego." "Todo" reveals the succession of these two moments and their necessary coincidence in the search for the self through the other and for the other through the self. The poem's subtitle, "Al mar y al amor" clarifies that it addresses both the sea and love, linking once more communication with the world and intersubjective caring. The speaker's eyes now penetrate the mysteries that previously perplexed him and he feels in full possession of the sea and his love. All belongs to him. The final verses suddenly shift from the affirmative "all" to the negative "nothing" and the plenitude of possession cedes to emptiness. The poem does not bemoan this transformation, maintaining an exclamatory tone and punctuation to the end, in an expression of a sense of wonder at the continual succession of suture and alienation, seeming fullness of self/other and discovery of the inaccessibility of the self/other.

The poems "Yo y yo" and "Cristales" of *Piedra y cielo* depict various selves in dialogue, either in a relation of opposition or solicitous concern. Several poetic texts from *Eternidades* reflect the voyage from the terror of the other within the self, expressed in the early poetry, to a productive acceptance in the later collections and also reveal the connection between the mature understanding of the relationship of self as other and self to other. In increasingly brief poems, Jiménez condenses his thought in a language almost devoid of adjectives and alien to the sensual, sentimentally saturated creations of his early writing. In two three-line poems, he expresses his keen sense of his multiple subjectivity and of the multiple subjectivity that results in both self and other in intersubjective relations. Poem 39 consists of two verbless exclamations in which the speaker remarks on the many former selves that he has abandoned, even forgotten, but that live on within him: "Olvidos de esos yos / que, un punto, creí eternos! ¡Qué tesoro infinito de yos vivos!" [Forgetting those I's / that at one point I believed eternal! What an infinite treasure of living I's!] (1919, 58). Poem 21 recognizes a similar multiplicity of subject positions in the loving relationship: "¡Cuán extraños / los dos con nuestro instinto! / . . . De pronto, somos cuatro" [How strange / Both of us with our instinct! / Suddenly, we are four] (38). The doubling of the twosome allows for multiple readings, including but not limited to a representation of a carnal relationship that simultaneously involves a deeper emotional commitment (two carnal lovers who suddenly discover a different relation to each other) or the depiction of the dual presence of the self as seen by the respective selves and others (my vision of you in contrast to your vision of self, your vision of me in contrast with my vision of self). In both poems, the speaker recognizes his and his companion's multiple relations of identity and alterity, with each other and their respective selves, and this cognizance relates directly to the metapoetical expression of his aesthetic that also appears in *Eternidades.*

"¡Intelijencia, dame el nombre exacto de las cosas!" has received formalist readings that foreground the speaker's desire for artistic precision and suggest a belief in the authority and self-sufficiency of the artist's word.[9] This reading elides the importance of alterity in Jiménez's thinking during this period and its expression within the text:

¡Intelijencia, dame
el nombre exacto de las cosas!
. . . Que mi palabra sea
la cosa misma,
creada por mi alma nuevamente.
Que por mí vayan todos
los que no las conocen, a las cosas;
que por mí vayan todos
los que ya las olvidan, a las cosas;
que por mí vayan todos
los mismos que las aman a las cosas . . .
¡Intelijencia, dame
el nombre exacto, y tuyo,
y suyo, y mío, de las cosas.

(1918, 19)

[Intelligence, give me
the exact name of things!
. . . Let my word be
the thing itself,
created anew by my soul.
Let those who do not know things
reach them through me;
Let those who have forgotten things

reach them through me;
Let those same ones who love things
reach them through me . . .
Intelligence, give me
the exact name, and yours,
and his, and mine, of things.]

The poem posits both the relationship between what Levinas, commenting on Martin Buber, refers to as the I-It of knowledge and the I-thou of dialogue (1993, 35). The exact name of things for which the poetic speaker struggles corresponds to the knowledge of an object, but although the text suggests the possibilities of the possession of the object, it immediately clarifies that it is transitory and incomplete. The text clearly reflects the modernist belief that all reality is mediated by language in verses three to five, suggesting that the word creates the object anew. A certain ambiguity in these same verses and the remainder of the poem also insinuates that the word through which the speaker and his audience access reality changes according to the affective and temporal relationship between the I and the It. There is not one, but rather many different words and even when using the same lexical sign, it carries different meanings according to the shifting subject positions of speaker and addressees. The insertion of a redundant first-person possessive pronoun (*mío*) in the final verse illustrates the non-coincidence of the speaking I with itself, in that it calls for a word spoken by the speaker that also speaks to him and his struggle to access the object. The subject of *mío* stands in the same relationship to the speaking I as the subjects of *tuyo* and *suyo,* all of whom enter into the I-Thou of dialogue. Levinas argues that dialogue does not imply possession, but rather encounter and it "functions not as a synthesis of the Relation, but as its very unfolding" (25). Jiménez's poem represents a process of continual revision, rewriting again and again to try to discover the exact name that will inevitably change as he undergoes temporal and affective transformations in his relationship with himself and the multiple others with whom he dialogues.

The poetics of dialogue observed in Jiménez recurs in Antonio Machado and follows a similar trajectory from a sense of anguish and crisis over a divided selfhood to a productive exploration of the potential for self and society in the understanding of the ineluctable separation of self and other.[10] From his early poems he manifests a predilection for an overtly dialogic form that appears much more insistently than in Jiménez. Machado intercalates conversations, apostrophe, and other forms of direct address that engage with people, things, and places. In "Fue una clara tarde, triste y soñolienta" he speaks to a fountain, addressing it as "sister," resisting the norm of possession posited by Levinas in the I-It relation. The dialogic relationship in much of *Soledades, galerías y otros poemas* accompanies a fear of the other and a distaste for carnality that coincides in certain respects with Juan Ramón's crisis of identity. "Siempre fugitiva y siempre cerca de mí . . ." depicts a pale, enticing woman who brings both pleasure and sorrow and whose portrait invokes images of sexuality and death. "Crear fiestas de amor" also interweaves death and corporality, with a morbid pall largely displacing sexual pleasure. In some early texts, the speaking I views an other through a window and responds with the anguish to which Aguirre refers in his study[11] while others explore the notion of multiple selves with a profound despair at the impossibilities for reconciliation or productive interaction. "¡Oh, dime, noche amiga, amada vieja" presents a dialogue in which the speaker asks the night to confirm the sincerity of his tears and she responds that she cannot authenticate where his true self resides. She tried to find it in his dreams, but found him there wandering in a clouded labyrinth of mirrors.

The vision of the mirror as preventing access to the self alternates and ultimately gives way to a rich understanding of self as other and the productive interrelationship of such a concept with a new notion of intersubjectivity. The growing appreciation of the need for I-Thou dialogue within the self surfaces in "Desde el umbral de un sueño me llamaron," in which the poetic speaker answers a beloved voice that invites him to see the soul and happily accompanies the friendly guide through the long, narrow gallery. The poem allows for a reading in which the "you" stands for another facet of the self or a woman, and this ambiguity between the other as self or as a separate subject reflects their coalescence in Machado's vision. At times his poetry emphasizes an I-Thou dialogue with a collective or individual other, as in *Campos de Castilla* with its focus on the national question and on his love for his deceased wife, while in other works it privileges the self, particularly in his *Cancionero apócrifo* and *Juan de Mairena*. However, it is in the opening autobiographical poem of *Campos de Castilla* that he first enunciates a theory of subjectivity that he subsequently elaborates in prolonged and rich meditations:

Converso con el hombre que siempre va conmigo
—quien habla solo espera hablar a Dios un día—;
mi soliloquio es plática con este buen amigo
que me enseñó el secreto de la filantropía.

(1951, 732)

[I talk always to the man who walks along with me;
—men who talk to themselves hope to talk to God someday—
My soliloquies amount to discussions with this friend,
who taught me the secret of loving human beings.[12]]

Machado's conjoining of the dialogue with the self and philanthropy and his allusion to a hope to someday continue this conversation with God advances an ethical commitment that both carries forward and transcends traditional religious and social doctrines. In keeping with modernist rejection of grand narratives and in recognition of the forever deferred access to the other, Machado develops his notion of subjective/intersubjective ethics in a fragmented format that refuses claims of wholeness or completion. In a series of aphorisms and proverbs that purposely interweave philosophic and popular tradition, he encourages his reader to consider a dialogic relationship with the other while constructing a dialogue with the reader that allows for the experience of the desired behavior.

In relation to subjectivity, Machado's aphorisms focus on four related aspects of self and/as other (1951, 883–904). Many present the relation of self as other both as one of harmony and dissidence, suture and alienation. "Mas busca en tu espejo al otro, / al otro que va contigo" [But seek out the other in your mirror, / the other who keeps you company[13]] reflects suture while "Busca a tu complementario, / que marcha siempre contigo, / y suele ser tu contrario" [Look at your counterpart, / who always walks with you, / and is generally your opposite] communicates alienation. A second strain focusses on the necessity of dialogue and commitment to the other(s) and simultaneously emphasizes the need to seek approximation while cautioning against appropriation. The alterity of the other requires recognition and respect in this ethics. "Para dialogar, / preguntad primero; / después . . . escuchad" [To dialogue, / first ask; / then . . . listen] fosters a caring openness to the other as does aphorism XIV, which cautions against drawing a border or cultivating a profile. "Enseña el Cristo: a tu prójimo / amarás como a ti mismo, / mas nunca olvides que es otro" [Christ teaches: Love your neighbor /

as you love yourself / but never forget that he is other] admonishes against xenophilia while simultaneously suggesting the inaccessibility of the other, which also serves as the focus of the following text: "Dijo otra verdad; / busca el tú que nunca es tuyo / ni puede serlo jamás" [He spoke another truth: Look for the you that is never yours / nor can ever be]. A third feature establishes the link between Machado's poetics and his theory of self and/as other, stressing in aphorism XXXVI that the poet does not seek the self, but rather the other in his work and in L where he clarifies that the "you" of his poetry does not invoke the reader but refers to his own self. A final thread that appears in "Proverbios y cantares" and receives considerable emphasis in his subsequent *Cancionero apócrifo* censures a narcissistic stance. Aphorism III introduces this idea and VI further embellishes it: "Ese tu Narciso / ya no se ve en el espejo / porque es el espejo mismo" [That Narcissus of yours / can no longer see himself in the mirror / because he is the mirror itself]. The Narcissist relates to the odious bourgeois ne'er-do-well of "Del pasado efímero" who cannot look into the mirror of memory nor get outside himself to imagine a different future. He relates neither to the self nor the other, neither able to look into the mirror nor back out of it, because he is all surface. Machado's opening text to this series of aphorisms enunciates this same concept in a form that he reiterates several times in later works: "El ojo que ves no es / ojo porque tú lo veas; / es ojo porque te ve" [The eye you see is an eye / not because you see it; / it's an eye because it sees you].[14]

The vision of self and/as other enunciated in the aphorisms calls for a new relationship between author and reader and author and self that Machado constructs through his complex play of various apocryphal philosopher-poet-commentators through whom he presents his dialogue with the Spanish reader and with whom he enters into dialogue in a relationship of agreement and opposition, ironic distance and sympathetic communion, that reenacts a continual slide from suture to alienation. These heteronymous creations first appear in the 1920s with the publication of *De un cancionero apócrifo* and continue in *Juan de Mairena* and newspapers collaborations of the 1930s. The creation of Abel Martín and his disciple Juan de Mairena allows for extended dialogue between the two thinkers and writers and other figures such as Jorge Meneses, a process in which the various individuals often overlap and notions of clear authorship disappear. In a period where vanguardist art and Ortegan theories espoused in *La deshumanización del arte* posit an "artistic art" that is pure play and exalt the figure of the poet as separate from the ordinary person, Machado prefers a dialogic relation with the reader and resists the shift towards an autonomous, authoritative artist. The adoption of heteronymous counterparts and the ironic perspective under which they unfold participates in a certain playfulness, but the dialogic quality of the texts, the consistent erasure of a single authorial presence, and the interweaving of erudite philosophy and popular expressions and beliefs retain the multi-voiced, multi-perspectivist posture that characterizes Spanish modernism throughout its long duration.

Beyond this effort to sustain multiple discourses that address a variety of audiences within his hybrid philosophic-poetic production, during this period Antonio Machado enters into a collaborative authorial relationship with his brother Manuel, with whom he composes a number of plays. This late foray into theater speaks to a desire to examine questions of identity before a wider audience and to analyze the implications of new theories of intersubjectivity for the project of national reconstruction. The Machado brothers' plays cover a range of topics, but in all cases present a conflict between a fear of and desire for change which relates to questions of narcissism in opposition to caring for the other. *La Lola se va a los puertos* and *Las adelfas* explore these issues in relation to middle-class values and popular culture, while *La prima Fernanda* confronts middle-class ambitions for power and money at the expense of a caring commitment to the other, both as embodied in the individual and the nation. The concern with narcissism and its negative impact on a productive intersubjectivity leads the Machados to a reexamination of the character of don Juan in *Juan de Mañara,* a figure to which they and other modernists repeatedly turn in the reconsideration of nation and self. The shedding of identities in the don Juan of José Zorrilla's romantic drama shares certain similarities with modernist conceptualizations of the subject, but differs considerably in the narcissistic character of Zorrilla's hero. Don Juan Tenorio illustrates the motility of desire, rapidly sliding from one woman to another, from carnality to spirituality, in a relation of possession rather than dialogue or encounter. Don Juan receives Inés's love, which saves him from hell, but is unable to give or care for the other. His status as national hero not only impedes a restructuring of sexual relations, but of all forms of interpersonal communications. As Antonio Machado establishes in his aphorisms, a narcissist is incapable of change, frozen in a false but believable coincidence with his own image. He lives in a perpetual present, unable to see himself as other and incapable of finding the other through the self, a process that Galdós, Valle-Inclán, and other writers of the period deem essential to the modernist experience.

In contrast to this national hero, the Machados construct a figure who continually sees himself reflected in the eyes and lives of his victims or through his own self-reflexive meditation. The play establishes a relationship of similarity and difference between this don Juan and his predecessors, repeating the famous first name for obvious reasons of audience identification, adding the surname Mañara—with links to the historical Miguel de Mañara who purportedly served as Tirso de Molina's model for the original dramatization—and establishing loose intertextual links with Zorrilla's play in the encounter between don Juan and a young woman who is about to enter the convent. However, Zorrilla's Inés becomes Beatriz in the modernist play and receives a much more forceful characterization, while Elvira, a former conquest, breaks completely with antecedent models. Her confession that she has just murdered her abusive husband prompts Juan to offer her assistance and accept blame for her crime. He comes to this position after looking into her eyes and seeing his own crime reflected there and throughout the play, he refers to seeing himself in the mirror of her eyes in a graphic expression of the dynamic interaction between self and other and self as other (1951, 361; 362; 385). Juan acquires access to himself through Elvira and decides to flee with her and abandon Beatriz, even though Elvira expresses her hatred for him. The uneasy triangle in which Elvira needs but rejects Juan, Beatriz loves but cannot possess him, and Juan loves both but possesses neither reflects the essential heterogeneity of being, as expressed by the apocryphal Abel Martín (1951, 946), and at the same time advocates a relation of caring even in the face of a permanently deferred reciprocity.

Juan himself contrasts this vision of intersubjectivity with traditional definitions when he states that Elvira killed his Narcissism and likens Narcissus to Cain, another figure that preoccupies modernists (1951, 365). The association of self-absorbed Narcissus and fratricidal Cain links excessive self-love with a lack of caring for the other and looks toward a redefinition of the relation of self and/as other. The Juan of *Juan de Mañara* distances himself from previous textualizations of a narcissistic don Juan in the nature and form of his conversion. Esteban, a portrait painter who displaces Zorrilla's sculptor in a revealing preference for a less stable, less permanent medium, emphasizes that no skeleton or fear of death transformed Juan, but rather a glimpse into another's soul prompted him to save the other rather than himself. Juan devotes his life to giving, loving, and working with the poor in illustration of the I-Thou relationship described by Levinas. The tension between commitment to the other and recognition of the other's inalterable alterity continues to the end in the irresolvable triangle of Juan, Beatriz, and Elvira. Only at his death does Juan see the two as one, with a coincidence of his desire and being desired, but the illusion of fullness does not extend to Elvira and Beatriz, whose survival presupposes a continual slide from communication to alienation as a fundamental law of life.

Miguel de Unamuno's crisis of identity predates virtually all his published work and according to biographies and textual resonances, it lacked the obsession with sexuality that appears in Jiménez and Machado, although sharing with them an insistent preoccupation with death. This concern continues throughout Unamuno's work and intersects with his theorization of subjectivity in several different forms. Unamuno identifies the self as consisting of multiple subject positions in a number of his works. His well-known re-elaboration of Oliver Wendel Holmes's theory of the three Johns and three Thomases in the prologue of *Tres novelas ejemplares y un prólogo* (1920) reiterates Holmes's notion of the real self, the ideal self of one's own self-image, the ideal self as others imagine it, and adds a fourth dimension in the self one aspires to become (1958, 2: 982). "Ideocracia" proclaims his right to contradict himself, to become a new person every day, without every ceasing to be himself (3:431). The glib professions of a divided selfhood coincide in Unamuno with a recognition of the responsibilities and threats that accompany such a notion of subjectivity.

Unamuno often advocates the need to know the self, but simultaneously recognizes the impossibility of the task in the face of the multiplication of subject positions in the modern experience of selfhood and the consequent lack of coincidence between the knowing subject and the subject as object. "El que se enterró" describes the anguished experience of the protagonist Emilio who one day finds himself seated across a table in his home, face to face with a man who looks just like him, who mimics his gestures, but with a slight temporal disjunction. Emilio relates that at one moment he felt he was dying and when he awoke, he found himself on the other side of the table looking at his own corpse. From that moment, everything felt and looked different to him and although his friends continued to know him as Emilio, they also noticed a change (1958, 5:1026). Emilio's narration reveals the painful shedding of past subject positions and somber discovery of self as other that recurs in many Unamunan texts.

Amor y pedagogía (1902) presents early treatment of the problem in Apolodoro's tragic inability to know himself and in the disjunction between his father's image of him, his own self-image, and his lived experience. A later elaboration of the lack of coincidence between the speaking I and the self about which she/he speaks appears in *La novela de don Sandalio, jugador de ajedrez* (1933). The text parallels in narrative technique the cascading levels, changing perspectives, and collapsing of identities that characterize Pérez de Ayala's *Sonreía* and *Belarmino y Apolonio.* It opens with a prologue in which a reader provides the prologuist with a series of letters written by a friend who describes his association with don Sandalio. The prologuist defers identifying the recipient of the letters as Felipe until the first chapter, where his name appears in the epistolary salutation (1958, 2:1233). Twenty-three letters written over some three months relate the story of the letter-writer's stay in a coastal village, where he comes to know and play chess with Sandalio. The letter-writer refuses to provide details of his chess partner's life, even when Felipe pleads to learn more about Sandalio, his family, the death of his son, and the reasons for his jail stay or his death while incarcerated. The letter-writer insists on inventing his own image of Sandalio and refuses to hear Sandalio's son-in-law when he tries to provide additional information. The writer's relationship with Sandalio oscillates between concern and indifference, approximation and differentiation, a desire for distance and a need for companionship. The novel's epilogue reintroduces the voice of the prologuist, who suggests that don Sandalio, the letter-writer, and Felipe are in fact the same person, and further complicates the relation of self and/as other by insinuating the identification of characters and author in the assertion that all biographies are autobiographies (1266).

A reading of the novel as a study of the relationship between self and other within a single subject suggests the impossibility of total self-knowledge interwoven with moments of partial to almost complete understanding. The game of chess, which has often stood as a metaphor for life, includes multiple pieces that alternately stand in opposition to each other, as a bishop to an opposing or same color king, or almost completely correspond to each other, as two pawns of the same color. However, even in this last instance, the varied points of origin interject a slight difference in perspective and possibilities of movement. The view of the self as comprised by the multiple subject positions exemplified by the thirty-two chess pieces contrasts with the Robinson Crusoe image of self-identity and sufficiency and *La novela de don Sandalio* specifically mentions the Defoe text as a lost ideal that the letter-writer nostalgically invokes in initial correspondence (1958, 2:1235), but later rejects in confession of his need for Sandalio (1240).

The narrative consistently emphasizes the connection between the conception of subjectivity advanced by the narrator(s) and modern society. The letter-writer expresses a need to escape, to be alone, but finds it impossible to elude reminders of modern social organization and the dependence of the modern subject on the other(s). In the solitude of the mountain, the narrator describes his hike on paths built by paid labor and in the forest he comes upon trees hung with advertisements that sell farm machinery, alcohol, and tires. Commodification invades spaces where the individual could previously find solitude and feel at one with self and nature. The old oak tree, symbol of strength and integrity, now has a large hole in the trunk's base, but the sap continues to flow through the cambium layer and send nutrients to the leaves. When Sandalio dies, the letter writer takes refuge inside the trunk, where he cries in sorrow at the loss of Sandalio, which he describes as a loss of self. The oak no longer stands independent and opens its heart to the divided subject, who finds solace amidst his pain in this new refuge within nature. The impugned commodification of nature by the advertisements hung from the branches accompanies a more hopeful cohabitation of the modern individual and nature and the simultaneity of opposing views once again demonstrates modernism's refusal to adopt a single, permanent stance. Resistance to a stable position expresses itself in the narrator's changing preference for the modern café over the traditional casino, in the late introduction of Sandalio's surnames as Cuadrado y Redondo, literally Squared and Rounded, and in the final recommendation of the letter-writer to his friend Felipe to find a city café with lots of mirrors if he wants to know more about don Sandalio, since there, in the presence of smudged glass, he may invent his own character (1958, 2:1264).

The final suggestion that the city café allows for the discovery of the self as other stands in opposition to the letter-writer's initial desire to flee from society and in particular, urban society, in search of the self. These two positions succeed each other in a constantly rotating order in various Unamunan texts. "Las peregrinaciones de Turismundo" (1921) straddles traditional allegory and modern science-fiction. The protagonist Turismundo, with resonances of the medieval "Everyman" or Calderonian *autos sacramentales* (1958, 5:1108), finds himself in a futuristic city called Espeja, a name that clearly invokes its masculine counterpart *espejo* and the concept of mirror. In Espeja, bells ring, hot breakfasts appear, all moves in perfect order but without a sign of living human beings. Turismundo feels surrounded by eyes that observe him and voices that he dimly perceives and wants desperately to find himself truly alone. He now realizes that real solitude only occurs in the midst of crowds and discovers to his horror that he is locked in the city by invisible walls and cannot hear his own voice, even when he screams in desperation. Turismundo only recovers the ability to hear himself after he encounters Quindofa, who emerges from a tomb. Quindofa's connection with death echoes the notion of a painful shedding of previous selves expressed in "El que se enterró," but here the tone has a bemused quality. Quindofa clearly represents a new subject position within Turismundo, a new other that enriches the self and allows Turismundo to dialogue with himself, to hear his voice, to see himself in the reflection of the other rather than feel totally alone in the mirrored city, and finally to break through the invisible walls that imprison him. A continuation of the adventures appears in a third part of "Las peregrinaciones de Turismundo" that further examines the relation of self and other. Here the text describes the shifting relationship between Quindofa and Turismundo, who at times coincide entirely in gesture and at others find themselves in childish arguments, one screaming "yes" while the other yells "no." The comical expression of the coincidence/non-coincidence of the self as other also receives expression in the description of Quindofa as Turismundo's shadow, which sometimes precedes and guides him, but in the heat of midday, disappears completely.

The allusion to Espeja and the image of the mirror links with several other Unamunan texts and the theme of self and other as developed in other modernist writers, in particular Juan Ramón Jiménez and Antonio Machado. Unamuno argues consistently that knowledge of the self only ensues from knowledge of the other and that the two exist in a mutual, dynamic interaction. "¡El español . . . conquistador!" defends this position on individual and collective levels, asserting that the concept of introspection is a fantasy. One comes to know the self only in the same manner as he/she arrives at knowledge of the other: ". . . no llega a conocerse uno a sí mismo sin algo medianero. Un espejo no puede verse a sí mismo. Ni un espejo puede verse en otro espejo, sino algo que haya entre ambos [One does not come to know oneself without some intermediary. A mirror cannot see itself. Nor can a mirror see itself in another mirror, rather something that stands between both] (1958, 4:1121). Subsequently, the text speaker repeats that a mirror cannot see itself in another mirror, adding that a pure I cannot see itself in another pure I (1123). Without the other, whether an other within the self or an individual or collective other outside the speaking/viewing subject, no self-knowledge is possible. We cannot define ourselves without reference to what stands outside of and in difference to us. The correlation with Machado's aphorisms and his repudiation of narcissism needs no further comment but in Unamuno, the connection between subject and nation receives more specific and continued emphasis. In numerous essays, he insists that the Delphic precept "Know thyself" applies equally to the individual and the national collectivity,[15] placing the search for the self within the desire for encounter with the other. "¡Adentro!," with its admonishment to look inward in order to radiate out to the nation and universe (3:427) and "Soliloquios y conversaciones," which textualizes in the title and within various essays the dynamic interrelation between solitude and community, monologue and dialogue, exemplify this notion. *En torno al casticismo* argues that to love others is to love the self (1971, 214), in terms reminiscent of Baroja's "Lejanías."

Unamuno's concept of love, like his notion of dialogue, recognizes the dangers of appropriation by or of the other. The text speaker of *Del sentimiento trágico de la vida* asserts that love awakens compassion for the other, but also the desire for possession. In order to preclude assimilation and consequent dissolution by/of the other, Unamuno advocates an aggressive relationship that demands a response, a forceful dialogue that prefers conflict over agreement. The speaker of *Del sentimiento trágico* rejects the hermit's ethic and calls instead for an active, bellicose stance that compels the other to abandon complaisant self-absorption and engage in a mutually constitutive communication (1966, 238–42). "Sobre la literatura hispanoamericana" welcomes disagreement in his dialogue with his Spanish American interlocutor and declares that each new encounter and difference of opinion awakens in him a dormant part of his selfhood. He further insists on his right to contradict himself, and in his use of paradox, self-refutation, dialogue between multiple and opposing spokespersons, and cascading levels of narration and narrative perspectives, he continually strives to project an unstable, unpredictable subjectivity.[16] As in the Machado brothers' theater, the tension between the need for dialogue, desire for possession, and recognition and respect for the inalterable alterity of the other structures Unamuno's novels, short stories, and plays that deal with intersubjectivity. "Robleda, el actor" depicts the fear of possession and the endeavor to avoid the imposition of a definition of self by the other in the figure of an actor who chooses to appear on stage in a curious effort to better hide his true self from the scrutinizing eyes of the audience (1958, 5:1104). Robleda's attempt to remain untouched by the other in his continual exhibition of masks stands in a tense relation with the persistent efforts of the public to identify the face behind the disguise. "Nada menos que todo un hombre" similarly textualizes the male protagonist's effort to cling to a nineteenth-century definition of the self-sufficient subject and the ultimate failure of such a project. Alejandro Gómez, a wealthy *indiano* whose economic success in America reflects the Restoration ideal of the self-made man imported in part from Victorian England and North America, admits in his final dialogue with his dying wife that he is her creation, nothing more than the man she has made him (2:1070).

Abel Sánchez, La tía Tula, "Tulio Montalbán y Julio Macedo," and "Dos madres" all examine the constitution of the self through conflictive relationships that oscillate between love and hate, possession and loss, identity and difference, and unfold within a social context that further complicates the intersubjective dialogue with issues of gender and national identity. As early as *En torno al casticismo,* Unamuno links Spanish unsociability and the inability of the nation to develop a vital program of reconstruction to masculine brutality and posturing (1971, 232). Male competition for women fragments masculine society and male brutality in the treatment of women similarly splinters any possibility for a collectivity across gender borders. Women characters from Soledad of the story of the same title to Tula of *La tía Tula* voice their harsh judgement of masculine insensitivity, which Tula even extends to the figure of Christ and his treatment of his mother at Cana. As she remembers that Christ answered Mary's observation that the wine had run out with a brusque "Woman, what is that to me and to thee? My hour is not yet come" (John 2:4), Tula rankles at the treatment and the address of "woman" rather than "mother." In ironic criticism of the male author, Tula explains Christ's conduct by reminding herself that he was, after all, a man (1958, 2:1148).

Unamuno's essay "Sobre don Juan Tenorio" (1908) invokes the figure of don Juan as the incarnation of Spanish masculine behavior and laments its persistence and devastating effects on male-female relations and national identity (1958, 4:482). In consonance with the Machado brothers, Pérez de Ayala, Azorín, and many modernist writers, Unamuno returns to the theme and character of don Juan out of a need to reconsider the role of tradition in the formation of modern subjectivities on individual and collective levels. His dramas *El otro* (1926) and *El hermano Juan* (1929) bring together many of the considerations on subject formation that appear dispersed across his works and when considered in conjunction with each other, address the interplay of individual and society within the context of tradition and a changing conceptualization of subjectivity, gender, nation, and empire. *El otro* represents male resistance to the modern experience of subjectivity on the part of the protagonist, who recognizes his own divided subjectivity in his self-designation as *El Otro* [The other], but struggles against it and the twin who continuously reminds him of it. He insists on covering the mirrors in his house to avoid other human beings that he sees as reflecting surfaces. The painful shedding of past identities appears in Cosme's (or is it Damián's?) murder of his twin brother Damián (or is it Cosme?).

The representation of the shift from one self to another echoes that presented in the story "El que se enterró," with the protagonist's description of the arrival of an identical other who mirrored his demeanor and gestures and a gradual sensation of moving backward in time to the womb and then to rebirth, after which he found himself facing his own cadaver. The play underscores the connections between the changing identities and the story of Cain and Abel, conjoining the problem of self as other with that of self and other. As in *Abel Sánchez* and other Unamunan works, the text argues that responsibility for the murder lies with both brothers, for as El Otro contends, if Cain hadn't killed Abel, Abel would have killed Cain and if Abel had not played the role of victim, Cain would not become the victimizer. The Ama, who raised and nursed the twins, explains that Cain internalizes Abel and Abel carries Cain within him. Their hatred originates in always seeing their selves in the other, in the twin who serves as a mirror and alienates each from the other and the self. The inability of Cosme/Damián to exist as one, to create a stable identity without the presence of the other within, causes an internal divide and a gnawing sense of the lack of coincidence of the viewing, self-analyzing subject with the self that it observes. This disjunction multiplies in the amorous relationship, in which the image(s) of the self enter(s) into a complex interaction with the image(s) that the love partner holds of the object(s) of desire.

El otro represents this proliferation of subject positions in the depiction of Laura and Damiana, the twins' wives, who fight over the surviving husband in their desire to possess and continually redefine him. Both insist that they have left a physical mark on his flesh, symbolizing the aggressively dialogic nature of the Unamunan I-Thou relationship. El Otro resents their efforts and in frustration at the inability to achieve a stable subjectivity, commits suicide. The puzzle presented in the drama defies traditional and modern attempts to explicate and resolve it. Ernesto represents the rationalist, empiricist tradition and tries to decipher the enigma but, although El Otro hands him a key, he simultaneously states that the key and the mirror cannot co-exist. The key opens doors, unlocks interior spaces, moves in a linear fashion from one space to another and works at cross-purposes with the mirror, which reflects the image back to the viewer in a circular dynamic. Just before he confesses his murderous encounter with his twin, El Otro takes the key and bites it (1958, 12:809), expressing his hostility toward this ancient symbol of access and decoding. In Ernesto's possession, the key insinuates a connection to a European patriarchal tradition and its correlative colonialist aspiration. Ernesto is Laura's brother and addresses her with the diminutive “Laurita” (805) in an expression of masculine, paternalistic protection. Furthermore, he has just returned from America and his links to the colonialist Spanish past introduce a traditional discourse that ultimately proves useless to decipher the enigma of modern subjectivity. Juan, the family doctor and a dabbler in psychiatry, also fails to explain the mystery.

In contrast, both Damiana and the Ama understand El Otro and his actions. Whereas Laura represents the traditional woman who inspires desire, Damiana desires and actively seeks to impose her will on both Cosme and Damián. Damiana is pregnant, understands that life is conflict, and welcomes the birth of the twins she feels fighting within her. She has no fear of producing her own other, whether in the lover(s) that she struggled to possess or the children to whom she will give birth. The Ama similarly accepts the modern subject. She loves Cosme and Damián, sees each in the other, and forgives them for the suffering they have caused in their struggle. She rejects the insistence on truth, arguing in the final scene that there is no universal truth and no possibility for absolute knowledge of the self or the other. No one knows who she/he is; all must construct their identity in a continual process of dialogue with the self and with others.

The destabilization of the subject correlates to a destabilization of language in *El otro*. The text continually signals the ambiguity of pronominal referents and their dependence on the presence of the interlocutor for clarification. The "I" exists only in relation to the "you" and in rapid Unamunan dialogic exchange, one pronoun slides into the other in a linguistic representation of self as other. Laura responds to a question from El Otro in typical fashion:

> Otro. Eres tú quien no debe saberlo. Aunque . . . ¿lo sabes?
> Laura. ¿Yo? Tu Laura . . .
>
> (1958, 12:809)

> [Other. You are the one who should not know it. However . . . do you know it?
> Laura. Me? Your Laura . . .]

Laura cannot clarify the referent of her "I" without placing it in a relation with the Other, whereby it slides from a first to a second-person pronoun. The text takes everyday expressions and stretches their meaning, reconfiguring traditional modes of expressing and perceiving. The standard Spanish reflexive construction to denote accidental, unplanned occurrences, for which the speaker absolves her/himself of responsibility, takes on new meaning in the context of a divided subjectivity. El Otro insists that Ernesto visit the basement where the cadaver of his twin other lies and refers to the dead brother as "el que se me murió" [the one who died on me] (812), with entirely new connotations now applied to the traditional grammatical combination of first and third-person pronouns. The third person *se* and first person *me* now join in more than a syntactical form to express the imbrication of the other within the self and the question of responsibility of the self and for the other that pertains in this new relationship. The representation of the female figures of Damiana and the Ama in *El otro* both continue and break with conventional feminine roles. Damiana's strength of character departs from traditional depictions of the "angel of the house," although her self-definition through maternity carries forward inherited visions of female subjectivity. The Ama's loyalty to her charges furthers established notions of women, particularly lower class women, but her parity with Juan and Ernesto in the discussion of the nature of the subject departs from customary depictions.

El hermano Juan continues to explore these questions, with greater emphasis on ethical responsibility, its relation to Spanish cultural legacies, and the need for new social configurations. Whereas *El otro* treats self as other in the context of the Cain and Abel story, *El hermano Juan* focusses on the ethical commitment of the self to the other within the framework of the Spanish don Juan tradition. Both traditions intertwine in the national psyche and Unamuno challenges them through a radical re-vision. The presence of the don Juan figure in *El hermano Juan* carries forward the analysis of male-female roles and relations present in *El otro,* but in the second play, a transgendered subjectivity displaces traditional gendered roles. As in the Machados' depiction of Juan de Mañara, Unamuno places his don Juan within the long tradition of literary antecedents while also signaling major differences. Like his forebears, Unamuno's Juan is a theatrical personage, always on stage and in public places. His first appearance with Inés invokes Zorrilla's drama and multiple intertextual allusions reiterate this connection. However, the other female figures appearing in the play have no definite literary antecedents. Elvira, his childhood friend, introduces an unprecedented figure in the don Juan repertoire and foregrounds his new role as brother, first in his childhood relation, and subsequently, in his decision to become a monk.

This Juan differs from his predecessors in his self-reflexivity, acknowledgment of the specter of death, rejection of the notion of an authentic self, and departure from traditional discursive models. Having arrived late to a world populated with literary and historical models and prescribed behaviors, he struggles to define himself but realizes he must play multiple roles in the encounter with the other. As mentioned in the opening chapter, Bernard Waldenfels suggests that in order to avoid the danger of appropriation of the other or dissolution of the self in a process of appropriation by the other, it proves useful to abandon traditional attempts at resolving the problem through ever more exact definitions of self and other. He proposes a "theory of responsiveness" in which the other necessitates a response from us that does not pre-exist in our intentions, but comes into being in the very act of address (1995, 43). The response alters with each change of participant and as the various parties enter into relations with others who reorient the answer in complex directions. It is noteworthy that *El hermano Juan* opens with Inés's reply to a statement previously made by Juan, whose contents remain only vaguely delineated, and the drama continues in a successive interplay of address and response. Juan has no stable identity, revealing his selves in his answers to Inés, Elvira, their respective suitors, Benito and Antonio, and the remaining characters. He slides from one subject position to the other according to the presence or absence of other characters. Raised in the same home and sharing the cradle with Elvira, their relationship includes multiple components, from her desire to be desired by him and bear his child to her maternal protectiveness and their fraternal memories. With Benito, Juan assumes physical dominance, almost strangling his rival, but with Elvira he becomes childlike and weak, while he demonstrates control of his emotions and verbal facility with Father Teófilo.

Juan recognizes the origins of his identity formation in external forces that impose certain values and subject positions and that inevitably mark him. Anthony Giddens refers to the different forms of expertise that exert authority in modern society (1991, 18–19) and *El hermano Juan* incorporates multiple examples. Father Teófilo introduces church discourse, admonishing Juan and Elvira to take life seriously and prepare for the next world while Antonio, the psychiatrist, exemplifies scientific expertise. Commodification, another modern form of expertise that also impinges on the formation of the self (Giddens 1991, 196–201), appears in the final scene of act 2, where Juan quotes an advertisement for an indeterminate product that advises the user to shake well before using. Juan applies this counsel to the dilemma of life and subject formation, shifting from the traditional metaphor of life as a stage to a more modern image of life as a shaving cream container out of which varied formations, from liquid to aerated foam, ensue according to specific conditions. Elvira represents a final expertise, with her reminders regarding his childhood and a selfhood that predates his discovery of the existence of multiple roles and inherited scripts. Children, like ancient peoples, are pre-modern; they do not feel the weight of tradition, the force of their own past experiences, the inability to act spontaneously. Juan, having lived before in multiple incarnations, feels that he was born old, with preestablished roles from which he can extricate himself only with difficulty.

Although *El hermano Juan* recognizes the force of history and the considerable influence exerted by modern institutions and experts in the formation of the subject, it also underscores the possibilities for change embedded in modernity. The multiplicity of inherited roles that constitute the modern subject and in particular, don Juan, in conjunction with the definition of the self as a response to the other and to the historical context in which the response unfolds, allow for and privilege change. The modern world, with its rejection of traditional discourses, undermines the forces that sustained don Juan and a destructive legacy of male-female relations. Elvira jeers at Biblical discourse as manifested in Father Teófilo's sermons and the out-dated refrain "Vanity of vanities" (1958, 12:909). The old language of honor also gives way to a modern reformulation by Antonio, who signals its discursive origins. When Inés reproaches Juan for playing with her honor, Antonio responds that while honor figured prominently in Golden Age theater, it is hopelessly out of fashion in a world of short skirts and cropped hair. A shocked Inés asks if honor is a style, like a dress, to which Antonio replies laconically in the affirmative, asking if she thought it was part of the skin and suggesting she stop putting on Romantic airs. Discursive changes require the death of the traditional don Juan and the creation of a new model for intersubjectivity across and within genders. The seducer of virgins cannot survive without his masculine and feminine others, the father and husband who valorize virginity above all else and the helpless virgin herself.

In a world that rejects such outmoded roles, Don Juan becomes Brother Juan, here raised by women and openly flaunting a transgendered subjectivity. Whereas the traditional seducer remained locked in a narcissistic search for pleasure, Brother Juan comes to believe in the need to create, to comprehend that creating is giving oneself, and that to give oneself is to die (1958, 12:980–81). The giving of the self, the response to the other, transforms the self, creating a new "in-between" in Waldenfels's terms. This post-don Juan literally kills his self-absorbed predecessors, but in his death, he gives birth to a new model and to transformed possibilities for the relations between Inés and Benito, Elvira and Antonio, and other Spanish and non-Spanish men and women. Juan refers to his impending death as a marriage, welcoming it as a requisite step towards the creation of a new self and necessary to facilitate a new partnership between the couples he brings together. He states that to live enamored of the self, unable to become other, is much worse than death (961–62). Juan's self-definition now crosses traditional gender borders, appropriating the role of the go-between or the transgendered self-designation of *nodrizo,* appropriating the Spanish word for wet-nurse in a previously inconceivable masculine form (978). The female acceptance of the death of a self and the construction of another in the process pregnancy and birth here becomes a model for the Spanish masculine ideal. Biological roles provide the prototype, but do not impose limitations according to gender.

The modern subject, male and female, exists as the product of multiple and changing subject positions that continually change in response to the self as/and other(s). The "death" of the subject also implies its "rebirth" in a process of transformation that relates to the past as both continuity and change. Elvira twice states in the closing scene of *El hermano Juan* that everything returns, to which Antonio responds first with a dubious "¡Quién sabe!" [Who knows!] and subsequently, with a gleeful cry in praise of change: "¡Ande el movimiento!" [On with movement!] (1958, 12:998). The turning coin that characterizes the Spanish modernist conceptualization of empire, nation, time, and space, similarly marks the theorization of subjectivity, with significant implications for redefinitions of social class and gender. The recognition of the discursive basis of notions of selfhood and alterity necessitates a new relation with language and textuality, which prompts a radical reworking of inherited literary forms. Unamuno's stark theater, denuded of all but the most minimal props, foregrounds anguished, brutally frank characters who confront the audience with painful questions of identity, ethics, and social interaction. In conjunction with other modernist writers, Unamuno invites the Spanish reading and theater-going public of the period to imagine and experience new forms of encounter between self and other.

8

Author, Text, and Reader: An End to Borders

CHANGING VIEWS OF SUBJECTIVITY DURING THE MODERNIST period influence a revision of the definition of author, which in turn intersects with the conceptualization of textuality and the nature of the relationship between author, text, and reader. As traditional hegemonic centers cede to a more diffusely structured authority, the nature of the power relation and the discourse that shapes it undergo a shift from strongly marked hierarchical models to more disperse, dialogic forms. Mikhail Bakhtin comments that authoritative discourse "permits no play with the context framing it, no play with its borders, no gradual and flexible transitions" and "cannot enter into hybrid constructions" (1981, 343–44). The dissolution of former concentrations of power in the church, military, patriarchy, and aristocracy accompanies the rise of polyphonic genres such as the novel and essay, in which multiple discourses enter into play to mutually inform and influence each other. Traditional literary genres, inherited from periods with clearly defined class and gender divisions, appear increasingly limiting in thematic range and audience and undergo transformations that widen their scope and allow for broader dissemination. Writers resist the limitations of a single mode of expression, preferring to cultivate multiple genres, often incorporating music, art, and the new worlds of photography and film into their repertoire. New narrative strategies and representations of the textual speaker surface in a never-ending search for means of communication that foster a non-hierarchical relationship between author, text, and reader. The commodification of art and literature significantly impacts perceptions of the role of art and artist in modern society. The perception of the role of the reader undergoes dramatic transformation, with a new emphasis on active consumption and the adoption of multiple, often conflicting subject positions. The development of novel discursive modes relates to the aspiration for national and individual redefinition in post-imperial Spain and Spanish modernism actively seeks to move the Spanish reading public forward to previously unimagined ways of relating to the self and the community, both national and international, through new artistic experiences.

Authority and the Modernist Author

The rising power of the lower classes and women causes some writers of the period to cling to elitist definitions of art, a gendered vision of literary creativity, and a correlation of artistic value with unity and harmony. The view of the work as a symmetrical balancing of forces reflects the image of the (male) artist as a stable subject in control of his surroundings and standing above and outside artistic creation. Romantic aesthetics and Schlegel's theory of romantic irony begin to undermine this perception of the author in Spain, as elsewhere, but post-Romantic literary debates and aesthetic treatises return to an exaltation of the artist that does not always coincide with realist practices, but continues in abstract theory. Both conservatives and liberals espouse a view of author that coincides with hierarchical definitions of authority. The Krausist/Institutionist view appears in works by Francisco Giner de los Ríos and his brother Hermenegildo, who describes the noble role of the artist as both synthesizer and creator of the collective ideal of his day (1908?, 67–68), which he[1] should then make accessible to a broad readership.

Juan Valera represents a more conservative political position and, while he also extols the importance of the artist's position, he espouses an even more elitist view with respect to the dissemination of literary works. Valera's essays on literature persistently seek to reeducate writers who incorporate a social message that could foment increased demands for change and power redistribution by the lower classes.[2] His well-known insistence on idealism in art connects with his fear of a politically motivated realism and an elitist view that privileges the male artist as the purveyor of access to another, better world. Federico Balart echoes these ideas in *Impresiones: Literatura y arte* (1894), where he also remarks that a synthetic, harmonious art proves difficult in a modern world characterized by ideological conflicts (1894, 13). While recognizing the changes that impinge on traditional conceptions of art and the artist, he adheres to a more comfortable, authoritarian aesthetic. Balart openly encourages the continuation of nineteenth-century literary models, with his participation in the homage to the dramatist José Echegaray in 1905, which prompted the public opposition of modernist writers (Unamuno, Azorín, Maeztu, Darío, Villaespesa, Valle-Inclán, etc.).[3] Pompeyo Gener reveals a more sophisticated understanding of a changing aesthetics, but continues to reflect the fear of social revolution and the possible contributory role of literature, in particular the novel, to class unrest (1894, 165). He advances the view of the artist as a superior being who produces a refined sensibility in the less advanced public (6, 121) and also a gendered vision of art that marks the feminine as degenerate and ill (195). Gener, and Valera before him, oppose modernism and their vision of the artist as masculine and defense of an elitist relationship with the reading public stand in marked contrast with modernist redefinitions of art, the artist, and the reader.

The halting transition from nineteenth-century aesthetics to a modernist definition of art and the artist is observable in Joaquín Dicenta and Leopoldo Alas. Dicenta more actively encourages a social role for art in his increasingly radical plays. His advocacy of lower-class and female agency in *Daniel* (1906) and his representation of the artist as worker rather than high priest in *El crimen de ayer* (1908) connect with other modernist writers and texts, but his vision of art in many respects remains firmly tied to realist presuppositions. Concomitant with the representation of the artist as worker, *El crimen de ayer* mocks modernist interest in sound, color, smell, and a transgendered subjectivity. Manuel, the representative of realism, accuses Ruderico, a parody of modernist artists, of belonging to an androgynous generation (1915a, 32) and in both *Luciano* (1894) and *Mi Venus* (1915), bourgeois wives fail to understand the exalted mission of art and encourage their sculptor husbands to mass produce their works and sell them commercially. The sculptor of *Mi Venus* repudiates classical and religious models and calls for an original creation based on the living model that nature provides, echoing realist precepts and blindness to the mediated nature of experience.

Alas also reveals conflicted relations with modernist aesthetics and visions of the artist, which he textualizes in his essays and fictional creations. Both his denunciation of women writers' invasion of traditional male territory and his attacks on the commodification of art and lamentable democratization of literary consumption reveal discomfort with a perceived loss of the male artist's authority over a mass public that no longer heeds the advice of critical authorities (1893a, 54–55). Clarín displays these anxieties in *Su único hijo,* which confronts the diminished place of art within the modern world and relates it to changing gender and class relations and the loss of power by traditional authorities. The narrative underscores the disappearance of the Romantic ideal in an increasingly commercialized society where a few aging, residual Romantics meet in a clothing store to recite poems by Zorrilla and read historical plays and where no alternative aesthetic has yet appeared. Bonifacio Reyes admires art, finds solace in his flute playing, and reveres the opera singers who dare to live the unsettled life of the traveling artist, but he admits that he could never relinquish his own comfortable surroundings, as symbolized by his attachment to his bedroom slippers (1966, 146). The representatives of art in the text are motivated solely by money and sexual desire, and the materialism that permeates society has corrupted art as well as moral and spiritual values. The narrator continually mocks Bonifacio's expressed belief in the artistic ideal by contrasting his prosaic, vulgar, and anti-heroic figure to the exalted literary models that he imitates.

The disappearance of the artistic ideal and the authority of art correlates with the appearance of an increasingly powerful female sector. Emma Valcárcel holds the economic power in the marriage and physically and psychologically abuses Bonifacio. The reminiscences of enclosure and punishment connoted by the embedded *cárcel* of her surname reflect the inverted power relations in the marriage relationship. Bonifacio seeks refuge in his affair with the singer Serafina, whose presence reveals the growing incidence of women performers and their increased access to economic power. In Clarín's narrative, the figure of female success quickly falls, revealing a failed professional who initially satisfies her frustrated desire for domesticity in her affair with Bonifacio and then turns bitter and aggressive when he terminates their relations. In his association with both women, Bonifacio's economic dependency on his wife's money undermines his authority, leading to the curious situation in which he plays the role of lover on command in his encounters with his wife and fraternal companion in his dealings with Serafina. The narrative underscores his subordinate position as nurse to his wife during her imagined illnesses and also to Serafina, when she suffers from fever and a toothache.

Both scenes connect the loss of male authority with a diminution of the value of art and interweave the two levels through the use of phallic symbolism. While attending Emma, Bonifacio plays the flute and while keeping vigil as Serafina sleeps, he draws with a quill pen, tracing figures on a page with a motion that the text likens to the copulation of white and black (1966, 143). The drawing gradually becomes an allegory of his life, with a stormy scene representing his relations with Emma and a placid, moonlit night depicting his association with Serafina. Both the flute and the pen and ink drawing here take place in the privacy of inner spaces and the absence of an audience as well as the minor size and value given to the flute, in comparison with the full orchestra or other more prominent instruments, and to the black and white drawing, in comparison with an oil painting, communicate the art world's loss of authority in a modern, materialistic society. Bonifacio's frustrated desire to create and recuperate the former authority reveals itself both in the fortuitous spelling out of the name "Serafina" in his unplanned pen strokes and in his obsessive need for a male heir. In the end, the new-born son displaces his interest in art and in Serafina, as the representative of this world, and in his wife Emma, representative of sexuality and commercialism. Bonifacio's anxiety with respect to his paternity reflects the textualization of a blatant fear of female power and creativity, clearly enunciated in terms of biology and economic restructuring, but also strongly insinuated with respect to artistic production. *Su único hijo* recognizes and fears changes in the power structure and traditional authority, including the role of the artist as the creator of his destiny and representative of a self-sufficient, authoritative subjectivity.

Modernist writers challenge Restoration hierarchical authority and the modernist definition of art and the artist actively works to break down a one-dimensional vision of author as above and outside his work and his public. While remnants of traditional visions of a sublime art and exalted artist persist, they enter into dialogic play with self-disparaging representations and persistent efforts to undermine the figure of the artist as superior, stable, and in control. Modernist artists flaunt their use of masks and this continual reinvention of self challenges traditional notions of authorship. While pen names exist throughout the nineteenth century, they enjoy a noticeable increase in modernism and combine with other public demonstrations of multiple authorial subjectivity. Restoration writers, such as Fernán Caballero (Cecilia Böhl de Faber) or Clarín (Leopoldo Alas), who adopted pseudonyms did not also elaborate one or several poses to mediate their relation with the reading public. In contrast, modernists cultivate multiple disguises and poses. In consecutive or closely numbered issues of *Revista Nueva,* Pío Baroja signs as S. Paradox, Doctor Baroja, and P. Baroja. Luis Urrutia Salaverri notes that he also used Tirteafuera and perhaps Pío Quinto (1973, 23–24). Many other modernist writers make use of pseudonyms: José Martínez Ruiz signed as Cándido and Ahrimán before settling permanently on Azorín (Glenn, 1981, 19); Ramón del Valle-Inclán has almost completely obliterated the memory of the real Ramón Valle y Peña, which it displaced after passing experimentation with the pseudonyms Ramón del Valle de la Peña and Ramón del Valle (Lima, 1988, 22); Ramón Pérez de Ayala occasionally signed as Plotino Cuevas and José Ortega y Gasset briefly used Rubín de Cendaya.

Unamuno preferred a different type of identity transformation. In the same *Revista Nueva* where Baroja slides from one signature to another, Unamuno refers to his friend "Unamuno" and includes a long quotation by this invented other (1899c, 59). Unamuno's adoption of the uniform of the Protestant minister, with black jacket and collarless white shirt, represents the creation of another self and coincides with Baroja's habitual beret, Valle-Inclán's wire-rims and waist-long beard, Azorín's red umbrella, Villaespesa's Moorish robes, and Gómez de la Serna's conferences given from a trapeze or mounted on an elephant. These poses not only seek to attract attention, but also state publicly the modern concept of multiple subject positions as constitutive of selfhood, here transferred to the representation of author and artist. As Giddens among others has observed, the modern subject is a self-reflexive project (1991, 32) and the modernist invention of an authorial self continues as an on-going process throughout their texts and in the adoption of multiple public names and personae. The eccentric character of many of these masks mocks inherited visions of the bourgeois subject and of the author as revered guide, substituting a self-disparaging, comical presentation that redefines authorial authority.

Interest in the differentiation between a public and private self has its roots in Krausist thought, receives study in Julián Sanz del Río's *El derecho como ideal fundamental en la vida* (1882), and is later reformulated in the *Boletín de la Institución Libre de Enseñanza* by writers like Manuel Sales y Ferré. This serious consideration of the phenomenon gives way to a comical, self-mocking treatment in modernist texts. Baroja plays with the concept in his open discussion of the invention of self in his autobiographical writings, and often toys with his reading public regarding the discovery of a real self behind the speaking I. The speaker of the first chapter of *Las inquietudes de Shanti Andía* (1911) writes that reading his own experiences on paper made him feel that they had been written by someone else, and he became transformed from narrator to reader (1946–48, 2:997). "Confidencias de un hombre de pluma" of the 1904 *El tablado de Arlequín* takes this notion one step further, opening with a first person speaker-writer that, in combination with the title, leads the reader to conflate author and text speaker and assume an autobiographical discourse. A footnote in the second paragraph discloses that the speaking subject is the son of Silvestre Paradox, Baroja's doubly invented character with distinct traits and presentation in two different works, *Aventuras, inventos y mixtificaciones de Silvestre Paradox* (1901) and *Paradox, rey* (1906), who here takes on yet a third persona, in that he is now revealed to have a son and presumably, a wife. Baroja's previous use of S. Paradox as pseudonym further confuses the relationship between author, text speaker, and literary character, as does the interweaving in the hybrid essay-story of autobiographical information—in accusations of poor syntax such as Ortega y Gasset had criticized in "Ideas sobre Pío Baroja"—and fictional details in the references to an uncle and senator named Carlos Eduardo Pérez de los Pasados, conde de la Fumarada del Campo. Toward the end of the text, the speaker reveals that he totally invented the historical data he has presented, with a final destabilizing sweep that erases the borders between a real and invented self.

A similar erasure of borders that signals a destabilized, comically presented authorial subject occurs in *Las aventuras, inventos y mixtificaciones de Silvestre Paradox,* where Baroja makes a cameo appearance as Doctor Labarta, owner of a bakery and aspiring writer who reads his work to Silvestre and others during a Christmas Eve dinner. Author becomes character and writer becomes text in a dizzying *mise en abîme.* To further complicate and diminish the figure of the artist, the narrator pokes fun at the gloomy vision conveyed in Labarta's writing and its evident contrast with the doctor's healthy, happy demeanor. Julio Camba inverts conventional visions of authorial subjectivity in "El destierro," published in *El cuento semanal* in 1907, when the first person narrator interrupts the apparently fictional materials with the announcement that he is not only the author of the text but more importantly, its protagonist. Furthermore, he asserts that he already appeared as a character in a Baroja novel on which he later wrote a critical review, thus establishing his triple role as author, character, and critic and converting Baroja from author to character in the text presently in the reader's hands. A similar play of identities occurs with Baroja's appearance as a character in Azorín's *Las confesiones de un pequeño filósofo* and Martínez Ruiz's shedding of his given name for that of one of his characters. Throughout modernist texts, these and related strategies continue a generalized questioning of traditional authorial subjectivity and of the authority of the writer over and independent from his text.

Modernist writers frequently flaunt their lack of authority with self-disparaging comments and representations that alternate with self-aggrandizing poses. Picasso's self-portraits in two drawings incorporate this stance and reveal its links to the modernist frustration with having arrived late to a rich cultural heritage in which any aspiration to originality seems doomed to failure. Picasso expresses his desire for and confidence in his artistic powers and innovative creativity as well as his sense of belatedness and imitative repetition through intertextual allusion to well-known predecessors. His several reworkings of Velázquez's *Las meninas* show the artist in various sizes, enormously overshadowing the other figures in his August 17, 1957 oil painting, but smaller than his easel and similar in size to the other figures and to his predecessor in his September 18, 1957 painting. The Cubist remake of the Velázquez painting exposes the incredible difference between the two works, with the resulting revelation of Picasso's originality while also underscoring his debt to the past in selection of topic and configuration of the subjects. Picasso's 1901 reworking of Manet's *Olympia* both parodies the model, as Sander Gilman points out in "Black Bodies, White Bodies," and the artist himself, who appears naked and humbled in a self-portrait that communicates his enslavement to his desire for the black prostitute and to his artistic predecessor, whose painting continues to impose itself despite Picasso's alterations.

The Barojan narrator continually signals his lack of control by calling attention to his incomplete knowledge of his characters and narrative, and making fun of his artistic pretensions, as in *La busca* (1946–48, 1:257, 277), or calling attention to the ephemeral quality of his work, as in *La dama errante* (2:232).

Numerous Baroja characters disparage art, negating its value in the modern world. José Ignacio Arcelu of *El mundo es ansí* (1912) holds this view (1967, 426–27), as does César Moncada of the 1910 *César o nada* (1967, 115–18). Benavente mocks traditional definitions of art in his designation of the circus as a modern artistic form in *La noche del sábado* (1903) and oscillates between exaltation of art and a recognition of its diminished role in the modern era in *Amor de artista* (1892). Ricardo Gil's reference to his collection of poems as a humble music box, which he explicitly contrasts with traditional metaphorical representations of poetry as arrogant lyre, communicates his acceptance of a diminished role for art and the artist, as does Pérez de Ayala's more shocking comparison of art and prostitution in *Troteras y danzaderas* (1913). In conversation with the prostitute Verónica, Alberto Díaz de Guzmán completely destroys any notion of the exalted artist: "Tú *haces hombres,* como se dice; yo hago literatura, artículos, libros. Si la gente no nos paga o no nos acepta, nos quedamos sin comer. Tu vendes placer a tu modo; yo, al mío; los dos, a costa de la vida. En muy pocos años serás una vieja asquerosa, si antes no te mueres podrida; yo me habré vuelto idiota, si antes no muero agotado" [You do men, as they say; I do literature, articles, books. If people don't pay us or don't accept us, we are left to go hungry. You sell pleasure in your way; I in mine, both at the cost of our lives. In a few years you will be a disgusting old hag, if you don't die diseased before then; I will have become an idiot, if I don't die sooner of exhaustion] (1964–66, 1:556). The comments evidently reflect a bitterness at the modern disregard for art, but they also signal the aspiration for tolerance noted by José Ramón González García as a central concern of Pérez de Ayala's aesthetic (1992, 52). The incorporation of the perspective of the lower-class woman considerably enhances the range of vision available to the novelist and as the fictional Amaranto argues in *Belarmino y Apolonio,* the novelist must abandon the one-eyed vision of the cyclops, with its obvious association with the nineteenth-century definition of self and artist, for a multiperspectival approach (1989, 91–93), including women and lower-class experiences and views.

The contradictory combination of an aspiration for a democratization of art and a fear of the effects of commodification marks many modernist works. Valle-Inclán's exaltation of the artist in his 1916 *La lámpara maravillosa* (1974, 575) accompanies his self-description as a face with one hundred masks. These various masks succeed each other in his works, moving from the stylization of the popular and aristocratic in the *Sonatas* (1901–5) to his exaltation of popular art forms and discourse in *Los cuernos de don Friolera* (1921). The two discourses interweave in his 1914 *Farsa infantil de la cabeza del dragón,* where the intersection of the modern world with traditional literary forms such as the fairy tale produces a hybrid form that alternately mocks and approves new and inherited linguistic and generic patterns. The Martínez Sierras alternate between a vision of an exalted art that stands above science and other forms of modern knowledge and a definition of creativity as work, a dual stance reflected in the title *El poema del trabajo* (1899). Emilia Pardo Bazán presents a similarly contradictory view of art and artist in *La Quimera* (1905), which confronts the young painter Silvio Lago and the older female composer Minia. While Silvio exalts art above all things and disparages wealth in favor of fame, in a view he explicitly links to anarchism, Minia praises the medieval aesthetic of collective composition and a more socialist, egalitarian aesthetic (1909, 50–54).

Santiago Rusiñol consistently assails the commodification of art in *Desde el molino* (1894) and nostalgically evokes a classical Greek civilization that he defines as made by and for art in "La oración del domingo." Among the most bitterly anti-feminist of modernists, he derides women painters with a language and hostility reminiscent of Clarín and other Restoration writers. By contrast, his depiction of the rural and urban lower classes reveals a faith in the spontaneity and talent of these previously marginalized individuals, who often prove successful in resisting modern efforts at social control and conformity. The titles of the undated *Pájaros de barro* and *El pueblo gris* reflect his melding of commonplace themes, places, and characters with a rejection of commodification in an aesthetic that conjoins a democratizing impulse with a vision of art and the artist as privileged sites of resistance and transgression.

Galdós's increased interest and faith in the lower classes as the source of national and individual reconstruction accompanies his abandonment of a never rigidly enforced omniscient narration and a move towards dialogue and the acknowledgment of incomplete authorial control. The prologue to *El abuelo* (1897) explicitly states that the author's word has less efficacy than the direct expression of the characters (8). In *Misericordia* (1897), he openly relinquishes his control of the narrative, adopting a neutral stance with respect to the benefit or disadvantage of Antoñito's drawing of a high lottery number and avoidance of military service (1967, 5:1898) and also with regard to the truth of accusations that Benina had an illegitimate child that she placed in an orphanage (1946). The metafictional structure of the novel, in which Benina's invented employer Romualdo turns out to exist and ultimately solves the family's financial problems, furthers the sense of authorial loss of power. Creations take on a life of their own and escape authorial design. Despite an evident commitment to a democratization of art, which characterizes Galdosian narrative from the earliest novels and continues to his later dramatic and narrative production, his later works also give evidence of a countervailing tendency toward artistic experimentation and a more reduced public. *La incógnita* (1888–89) and *Realidad* (1889) demand a sophisticated reader to tease out the differences and meaning of their contrasting version of the same events and *Misericordia* similarly challenges accepted reading habits, with its play of reality and fiction. Galdós specifically voices his intention to address a select audience in the prologue to *Alma y vida* (1902) and favors the approval of this group over popular applause.

Unamuno's public representation of self also brings into paradoxical union the stern, thundering, and seemingly self-assured philosopher and a self-effacing, self-mocking figure that gives the lie to the portrait of authorial control and stable subjectivity. His well-known appearance as character in *Niebla* (1914) includes a comical parody of authorial mastery when his character Augusto confronts him and remarks that if it is difficult for an individual to know her/himself, it is all the more difficult for a novelist to truly know his/her characters (1958, 2:849). Augusto mocks Unamuno's discourse, both in his sarcastic reference to the Unamunan invention of the term *nivola* to designate his idiosyncratic narratives and in his recommendation that his author stop using such typical Spanish expressions as "no me da la real gana" [I damned well refuse] (849). The figure of the author presented in this dialogue takes on multiple facets, as the writer behind the text and the character in the text struggle to maintain control over his creation. Unamuno replays this self-mockery in *El otro* (1926), where he places his own name in the list of those who do not have full knowledge of themselves (12:862) and in *El hermano Juan* (1929), when the protagonist pokes fun at the idea of a dog mouthing funeral elegies and then committing suicide (12: 929), with obvious intertextual reference to the "Oración fúnebre por modo de epílogo" that appears at the end of *Niebla* and less noticeable connection to Unamuno's poem "Al perro 'Remo'," in which he envisions a shared anguish in dogs and human beings with regard to the question of life after death. Ortega had alluded somewhat disdainfully to evidences of Unamuno's materialism in this concern for canine afterlife (1:200), and Unamuno's self-mockery on the same subject represents a modernist ability to stand outside of the self and assimilate, with a twist, the voice of the other.

The desire to dialogue with and incorporate the other's voice relates to Unamuno's disdain for elitist aesthetics, which appears in his earliest writings and continues throughout his literary career. The text speaker of "El literatismo," published in *La Revista Blanca,* equates the "art for art's sake" school with an aristocratic conception of art and argues that in the modern consumerist world, art's salvation lies in extending its range, popularizing its forms, and encouraging appreciation among new social groups (1898, 14). "Una visita al viejo poeta," which appears in *La Ilustración Española y Americana* in 1899, expresses two different views of artists and their relation to their work in a dialogue between two speakers that echoes other Unamunan texts in which a bifurcated speaker converses with the self. The older poet, who has retired to his country home, disdains fame and cares little if his name becomes known, preferring that his voice become one with his readers and disappear in a collective chorus. The text also presents the opposing view in the speaker who fears that the self he transmits to others and that forms in response to the world will efface the self that exists in solitude. The textual focus moves back and forth from one subject position to the other, placing the artist in a place of authority and then shifting to a relationship of equality or even assimilation. A more complete fusion of these two stances occurs in "Los cerebrales," published later the same year in the same journal, in which the text speaker in typical Unamunan paradox declares that the greater the genius, the more accessible he/she is to the world, because genius is simply the individualized soul of the people (1899a, 228). A very similar vision of the artist appears in Urbano González Serrano as he moves from a nineteenth-century view of art towards an assimilation of the modernist aesthetic. In *La literatura del día* (1903), he describes the writer as half ventriloquist, half apostle to communicate his sense that art must both reflect the culture in which it appears and lead the reader toward new goals.

The idea of ownership also undergoes transformation during this period, and Marxist and socialist arguments of collective, communitarian possession of natural resources and economic production parallel a rejection of private property and ownership in the realm of artistic creation. Ricardo Velázquez Bosco denies the existence of originality in art and ridicules critics who judge artists on this basis ("La originalidad en el arte" 305). Unamuno refutes the ownership of words and ideas in his 1910 *Soliloquios y conversaciones,* (1958, 4:551), and he and other modernists revise inherited notions of plagiarism and individual creation. The borders between texts and authorial property become increasingly vague as writers simultaneously publish their textualizations of shared experiences and make no pretense to a single, stable authorized view of the events. Ciro Bayo, Pío Baroja, and his brother Ricardo travel together through the Castilian countryside in a trip that appears in narrative form in Bayo's *El peregrino entretenido* (1910) and Baroja's *La dama errante* (1908), with striking similarities amid many differences. The fragmented nature of both texts, the somber descriptions of the countryside, the backdrop of the panic after the anarchist Morral's attempt to assassinate the king and his new bride, and the introduction of adventures that never materialize join the two texts in a sort of dialogic authorship.

Llanas Aguilaniedo and José María and Bernaldo de Queirós cite Baroja's "La patología del golfo" (1899), as well as Galdós's *Misericordia* (1897), as sources in *La mala vida de Madrid* (1901), and Baroja evidently draws from the Llanas Aguilaniedo and Queirós sociological study in *La busca* (1904). The borrowings across textual lines here erase the borders between literary and sociological study, placing Baroja, Galdós, and Llanas Aguilaniedo in a relation of collaboration in the analysis of the Madrid poor. The famous description of the funeral of the young girl from Toledo in Baroja's *Camino de perfección* (1902), and Azorín's *Diario de un enfermo* (1901) and *La voluntad* (1902) calls attention to the duplication and openly defies traditional notions of textual property. The same effect occurs in the fictional retelling of the death of Alejandro Sawa, which appears in Baroja's *El árbol de la ciencia* (1911), and later in Valle-Inclán's *Luces de Bohemia* (1920). It is also worth pointing out that Valle-Inclán's famous phrase "Viva la bagatela" [Long live triviality!], inserted in *Sonata de invierno* (1905), had previously appeared in Baroja's *El mayorazgo de Labraz* (1903) as the synthesis of the philosophy of the eccentric Englishman Bothwell, who in turn cites Swiff (sic) as his source. The presumed misspelling of Jonathan Swift could easily represent a typographical error or a Barojan erasure of originary authority, underscoring the absence of ownership of ideas.

Azorín and Valle-Inclán often recycle their own work, leaving the reader with the sensation of having read the same material before and openly challenging textual and authorial borders. Revised episodes and characters from the *Sonatas* reappear in *El marqués de Bradomín,* and a similar process occurs in the remaking of the 1899 *Cenizas* in the 1908 *El yermo de las almas.* Azorín's recycling of the Toledo funeral scene in two different narratives and his reworking of the story of the knight from *El Lazarillo de Tormes* first in "Un hidalgo" in the 1905 *Los pueblos* and then in "Lo fatal" in *Castilla* (1912) reflect the wide-spread practice of erasing authorial and textual property lines. Azorín's constant reinterpretation of classical Spanish texts has a similar motivation and effect. The same abolition of borders characterizes Valle-Inclán's echo of Darío's "Año lírico" in the *Sonatas.* Antonio Machado openly acknowledges his debt to Unamuno in his "Poema de un día," but even this recognition of Unamuno's originality admixes respect and humor to diminish the exalted figure of the teacher to a more equal partner in dialogue. The rhyming of Unamuno's name with *tuno,* the Spanish word for "rogue" or "scamp," significantly levels the power relations between master and disciple: "Este Bergson es un tuno; ¿verdad, maestro Unamuno?" [This Bergson is a rascal, / wouldn't you say, Master Unamuno?][4] (1917, 202).

Antonio's collaborative work with Manuel in the production of theater further challenges notions of individual authorship and continues a tradition of co-authoring in popular theatrical production. The playwright Carlos Arniches (1866–1943) wrote seventy-seven works with co-authors in comparison with only twenty-two original works, of which fifteen were one-act plays (Berenguer 1988, 220). I have insisted throughout this study that Gregorio Martínez Sierra was in fact María and Gregorio and their collaborative efforts often extended to include Santiago Rusiñol, as in the jointly authored *Vida y dulzura* (1907). The Alvarez Quintero brothers together author some two hundred plays in the early decades of the twentieth century. Stephen Kern mentions the 1911 exercise in which Picasso and Georges Braque work side by side to produce *Ma Jolie* and *Le Portugais,* two individually titled but almost identical works (1983, 196).

In the light of this flagrant display of collaborative artistic production, the intertextual references to Antonio Machado's poetry in Manuel Machado's "La guerra literaria" take on additional significance, as do the recognizably similar autobiographical poems of Antonio and Manuel Machado and Francisco Villaespesa. All apparently written for inclusion in the Madrid newspaper *El Liberal* in a special publication of poetic self-portraits, Villaespesa's "Ego sum," Manuel's "Retrato," and Antonio's identically titled "Retrato" follow a rhythm of echo and difference that establishes their collective endeavor in the very act of producing their individual self-portraits.[5] Manuel's denial of links to don Juan Tenorio while simultaneously declaring his amorous success and particularly pointing to one who loves him and another whom he loves resurfaces in Antonio's self-description as faithful lover without being a Mañara or a Bradomín and in Villaespesa's statement that he has loved and been loved. Villaespesa's allusion to a virile aristocracy inherited from Christian princes in his delicate hands resonates in Antonio Machado's references to the virile hand of the sword-wielding Captain, whom he takes as a model for his poetry. Similarly, Antonio's insistence that he travels light, has no debts, and remains true to his poetic voice coincides with Villaespesa's claim that he seeks neither gold nor applause, but writes from the depth of his soul. The use of fourteen syllable quartets in Villaespesa's "Ego sum" and Antonio's "Retrato" further joins the two poems, while consonantal rhyme connects the three texts. All the self-portraits underscore a hybrid cultural heritage, with Antonio focussing on Seville and Castile and classicism and romanticism, while Manuel emphasizes Seville and Paris, gypsy and bohemian, classicism and lower class. Villaespesa intermingles an Arab and Christian past, Western classicism and Oriental traditions.

The similarities between the three texts belie traditional attempts to divide the Machado brothers into distinct literary schools or place Villaespesa with Manuel in opposition to Antonio in poetic outlook and literary expression but more importantly, they communicate an understanding of art as a play of tradition and innovation, individual creation and collective cultural product. This attitude carries over to the assimilation of popular literary forms within modernist literature in the work of the Machado brothers, Villaespesa and other modernists. Antonio's long poem "La Tierra de Alvargonzález" follows the *romance* form of popular Spanish poetry and identifies as its source a local peasant in the prose version originally appearing in the Parisian magazine *Mundial* in 1912, and then republished in *Campos de Castilla.* A similar melding of collective and individual authorship appears in Carmen de Burgos's "El tesoro del castillo" (1907), in which the protagonist's father, famous for his story-telling abilities, narrates a traditional tale within the frame narrative of the modern love story. The borders between the two levels do not hold fast, however, and the reader is left with the sensation that the entire story could just as easily be categorized as a popular folk-tale or the creation of the modern artist.

The conjoining of popular and cultured artistic creation, the dissolution of the individual author, as well as the self-disparaging portraits of artists that characterize modernist texts communicates a changed perception regarding the exalted artist figure of previous times, who now takes on a more complex character in which the authorial self dialogues with other authors, both contemporary and antecedent, and with a wide readership, drawn from lower and upper classes. The modernist text both challenges and welcomes the new public, forcing it to adapt to new authorial modes of self-presentation and respecting the popular classes for their contributions to a collective Spanish literary heritage. The critical tendency to focus exclusively on an elitist authorial stance overlooks this rewriting of authorship that occurs during the period and that predates in textual practice the death of the author later theorized in Foucault's "What is an Author?" and other poststructuralist writing. The challenge to authorial authority in Spanish modernism carries forward the generalized questioning of traditional hierarchies of power and in particular, of patriarchal notions of authenticity and paternal ownership which Jonathan Culler has identified as characteristic of the literary criticism that develops within patriarchal culture (1982, 60). Spanish modernists invite a different conceptualization of authority and author and their considerable efforts in this process have important consequences for the representation of authority within the text and for revisions of inherited genres and artistic forms.

Decentering and Unbinding the Text

Multiple Textual and Narrative Authorities

The dissolution of authority evident in Spanish modernist representations of the writer/artist continues in the treatment of authority within the text. Throughout *Encounters across Borders,* I have signaled the frequency of framed narratives and the cascading levels of narration that characterize a wide number of modernist novels and stories and that introduce multiple textual authorities that sometimes contradict each other, and in all cases present multiple perspectives and authorities. Constant narrative shifts in Baroja's *Camino de perfección* (1902) leave the reader puzzled as to the sources of the story. The first-person speaker and friend of the protagonist opens the novel abruptly and then disappears in the third chapter, displaced by a third-person narrator who takes control until a sudden interruption in the opening paragraph of chapter 46, where an intrusive authorial figure questions whether the preceding narrative was a manuscript or a collection of letters (1969, 176) and then clarifies that in the remaining chapters, the narrator seems to be Fernando himself. A similar erasure of narrative authority occurs in *El mayorazgo de Labraz* (1903) in the discussion of the dubious origins of the textual materials. *Aurora roja* (1905) and *El mundo es ansí* (1912) exemplify the constantly changing Barojan narrative perspective, alternately mocking and admiring of his literary characters, tender and distant in their treatment. The anarchists of both works one moment appear filtered through the perspective of a cynical unbeliever and in the next acquire heroic stature. The description of the anarchist meeting in *Aurora roja* moves through multiple viewing lenses, from grotesque to idealized distortion, suggesting various narrators with varied perspectives, and climaxing with the ambivalent "Long live literature!" cry of one character, which leaves Manuel, and by extension the reader, puzzled as to the meeting, the enthusiastic cheer, and anarchism in general (1946–48, 1:614).

A seemingly more stable narrative authority in *El árbol de la ciencia* (1911) is weakened through the contrast between chapter titles and their subject matter. In the first part of the novel, chapter titles correspond entirely with the textual information presented within. "Los estudiantes" or "Andrés Hurtado y su familia" clearly announce what will follow. In the later sections, this coincidence becomes more and more arbitrary, with enigmatic titles that are never fully clarified. The second part of the book is entitled "Las carnarias," a name that doesn't coincide with any of the characters and perhaps relates to the root "carne" [flesh] and the sexual nature of the episodes and individuals presented. The chapter heading "Las moscas" similarly remains at a distance from the chapter's content and the use of "En paz" for the chapter that describes the complete breakdown of Andrés's carefully constructed marital refuge suggests the presence of two conflicting narrative perspectives that stand in opposition to each other. The volumes of the Aviraneta series flaunt the use of multiple narrators and the dissolution of a central narrative authority, with materials drawn from many different sources that at times complement each other, but more frequently lead to contradictory representations and appraisals.

I have commented extensively on Azorín's use of changing narrative stances within and across texts that treat the same characters and of framed narratives and unreliable narrators in Miró and Pardo Bazán, all of which serve to decenter narrative authority. Galdós textualizes the loss of the author and narrator's control in *Misericordia* (1897) and also in *Nazarín* (1895), where the narrator intermixes his own observations of the unusual protagonist with information he has gathered from a journalist friend. These two sources disagree fundamentally in their judgement of Nazarín, with the reporter convinced he is lazy, dangerous, and corrupt while the friend remains more ambivalent, reasonably sure that Nazarín is a saint, but dubious as to the value of saints in the modern age. At the end of the novel's first part, the text openly foregrounds the problem of narrative authority when the narrator ponders whether he has invented the character or related the true story of a living person. He then speculates that in the light of his doubts, his readers may well wonder if he or his journalist friend wrote the text or perhaps even Chanfaina, Nazarín's landlady in Madrid (1967, 5:1691).

The abolition of the writer's authority often intersects with or is duplicated in the dissolution of the narrator's control of the materials. Ramón Gómez de la Serna works to decenter authorial and narrative authority in many publications. His book *El libro mudo* (1910) communicates in the title an ambivalent relationship between writing and silence, speaker and word, narrator and text, that continues in the play of speaking subjects presented in the work. An authorial I states in the preface that the prologuist Tristán is an alter ego and throughout the brief book, Tristán addresses Ramón in a continual reminder of the presence of the authorial position behind this play of levels and also of the loss of a stable, centered self in the modernist artistic creation. Gómez de la Serna's *Mis siete palabras* (1910) continues to communicate a humbled vision of art and artist, whose power now appears constrained to just a few words that others have already spoken. The first-person narrator confesses his desire to be a Robinson Crusoe, lamenting the fact that the stories he tells are merely toned-down repetitions of previously told narratives. Interweaving allusions to imminent death and suggestions that he is presently imprisoned in a jail cell with other comments that allow for a more metaphorical reading of his enclosure, the speaker struggles to discover new modes of expression and to throw off the tyranny of inherited discourse. The mixture of two different text forms, an aesthetic treatise and the last words of a condemned man, bring together art and politics, aesthetic theory and social protest.

In this textual representation, change requires sacrifice and death in both narratives. The execution of the political prisoner stands as a protest against the system and his right to final words, even if only seven in number, allows his voice to carry over beyond the execution to others who might continue his denunciation of current social and political structures. The death of the artist and in this textual instance, the narrator, occurs through the destabilizing doubling of the voice and the inability to establish the identity of the speaking subject, whether prisoner or artist or perhaps neither. This decentered narrative authority dissolves even more through the use of a fragmented writing style, with parenthetical remarks that bear only a tangential relation to the preceding and following comments, abundant ellipses, and closing statements that promise a future, continuing conversation with the interlocutor and end without concluding. The new artistic expression to which the speaker aspires calls for a significantly reduced dictionary, the abolition of abstractions and rhetoric of the traditional narrative center in favor of more disperse, inconclusive speaking subjects, who literally disappear from the reader's view in a persistent doubling or tripling of narrative identity that is continually constructed and deconstructed.

The play of different narrative stances or contradictory narrative authorities originates in the earliest days of the modern novel with Cervantes's *Don Quijote* and continues even during the realist period in Juan Valera's *Pepita Jiménez* (1874) and his later *Juanita la Larga* (1896). However, it is not until the modernist period that it appears with such frequency and complexity or that it combines so insistently with other forms of textual redefinition. The radical change in narrative structures and in the constitution of the narrator that occurs in modernism becomes strikingly evident in the contrast between modernist texts and novels and stories published by residual realists during the late nineteenth and early twentieth centuries. Pereda constructs a moderately divided narrative authority in *Peñas arriba* (1895), in which the citified first-person speaker assumes a position of alterity with respect to the rural habits and values of his uncle Celso and the other residents of the remote villages of northern Spain that the text holds up as exemplary of a glorious if disappearing Spain. However, this separation between narrator and textual values completely disappears over the course of the novel and in the closing chapters, the speaker has fully assimilated the discourse of the other characters and that espoused by the narrative.

Ricardo León's novels similarly emphasize a single narrative center and a harmonious perspective within the unity of the novel's textual borders. In the prologue to *El amor de los amores* (1910), a first-person authorial I addresses the reader and explains the origins of the novel in a visit he made to a Castilian village. The speaker introduces the characters about whom he is going to write and then invites the reader to enter the story. Once the narrative proper commences, the I of the prologue recedes entirely and the novelistic cosmos appears before the reader as a seamless world without any further distractions or reminders of the textual, constructed nature of the materials. A single narrative stance creates a semblance of a free-standing world and even the long, descriptive chapter titles that remind the reader of the divisions of the materials into relatively uniform chunks, and are obviously constructed by someone, so perfectly meld with the materials in tone and correct description of the narrative action that the intrusion passes largely unnoticed. In contrast with Baroja's misleading or ironic titles or Pérez de Ayala's footnotes or marginal notes that call attention to the constructed nature of the text, León dutifully follows several centuries of narrative convention and consequently, the text avoids any overt metafictional commentary and the reader, long accustomed to this novelistic code, passes over it with no break in her/his immersion in the fictive world. In contrast, the modernist text continually unbinds this neat textual unit, opening up connections between narrator and characters, readers and narrator, readers and characters, and one text and another.

In early discussions of modernism, its opponents express their strong defense of the maintenance of traditional borders. The belief in harmony and unity as essential qualities of the prized artistic work correlate with unwavering support for textual borders, clear definitions of generic differences, uniformity of discourse and language, and the avoidance of ambiguity.

Federico Balart's defense of unity in art accompanies his preference for the subordination of the detail to a unified synthesis and for the use of the strong line in pictorial art (1894, 15, 72). Emilio Ferrari's attack on modernism in his 1905 acceptance speech to the Royal Academy links his vision of beauty as harmony with a socio-political view of culture as a unified whole, clearly voicing the fear of social revolution that undergirds opposition to the new aesthetic and the dissolution of a central authority. He decries what he sees as the insubordination of individual organs with respect to the whole and the disintegration of what God created as one, organic unit (1905, 20). The Jesuit Eguía Ruiz expresses the same idea over a decade later, calling for a return to the classics and defending traditional Castilian language against foreign influence in order to maintain the unity of the artistic product (1917, 11, 22).

Nordau's efforts to undermine modernism associate the lack of harmony in art, music, and literature of the period with sexual aberrations and criminality (1968, 18). He attacks impressionist art as the result of a visual hysteria that deforms the retina and produces a vision of zigzags rather than clear lines (29). In this same vein, he defends the sense of proportion evident in Turgenev's work in contrast with the excessive detail that he observes in Tolstoi (145). The satirist Pablo Parellada, writing under the pseudonym Melitón González, publishes his parody of modernist drama in 1906 and focusses on the introduction of foreign words, new verse forms, and a general lack of classical coherence in textual construction. His play *Tenorio modernista* also mocks the conjoining of modern and classical art forms, referring to the drama in the subtitle as a film and three lapses. In Spanish as in English, the word *lapso* connotes both error and a temporal gap, in both cases signaling the lack of coherence and harmony in the modernist work. Valera echoes the belief in a universal, unchanging artistic standard that is shared by many of those who oppose modernism (1941, 2:920, 927). In defense of the purity of art and opposition to border crossings, he rejects novels that communicate a social message and generalizes that like all hybrid products, they are infertile (1140). Pompeyo Gener's previously mentioned opposition to mixing music with painting and literature and his condemnation of emphasis on detail over the whole similarly support a vision of art as a harmonious unit within traditionally delimited generic borders (1894, 211).

Ortega y Gasset essentially concurs with the vision of art and textuality as harmonic, masculine, and hierarchically ordered, although he repudiates realist aesthetics. His theorization of these positions in *La deshumanización del arte* (1925) builds on previous articles and specifically traces the beginnings of a new perception of art to approximately 1905 (1967a, 25), attempting to bring all of modernist literature within the field of vision. The text speaker coincides with other modernists in his insistence on the creation of new habits of reading and perception, but differs in his exclusive emphasis on art and abstraction over reality and human emotions. His desire to distance his aesthetics from realism and romanticism leads him to denounce any sentimental attachment to the text on the part of the reader and to oppose mimesis in favor of emotional detachment and an art that openly flaunts its condition as artefact. In contrast with the modernist turning of the coin, in the aesthetic arena he once again migrates toward a single, stable position, insisting on the impossibility of simultaneously perceiving artistic form and lived reality and classifying an art that proposes such a double vision as cross-eyed and anomalous (38).

Ortega y Gasset's inability to imagine the simultaneity of opposites or the alternation between different subject positions correlates with his distaste for mixtures and defense of borders in art as well as culture, politics, and science: "Ya veremos cómo todo el arte nuevo, coincidiendo en esto con la nueva ciencia, con la nueva política, con la nueva vida, en fin, repugna ante todo la confusión de fronteras. Es un síntoma de pulcritud mental querer que las fronteras entre las cosas estén bien demarcadas" [We shall see how all new art, coinciding in this respect with the new science, the new politics, in short, the new life, loathes above all the muddling of borders. It is a symptom of mental pulchritude to want to retain well demarcated borders between objects] (1967a, 44). Although the speaker of *La deshumanización del arte* insists on various occasions that he does not foster this new art but merely wishes to define it, the presence of numerous evaluative statements and positively charged adjectives applied to a dehumanized art reveal an evident preference for abstract art, uncluttered with human emotions and a complex reality. His desire for clearly defined borders echoes the statement of a decade earlier in *Meditaciones del Quijote* that he must hierarchize the Iberian and Germanic souls within him in order to achieve clarity (1990, 159). The need for hierarchies and the belief in authority in Ortegan aesthetic theory correlates with a similar vision with respect to European imperial expansion, Spanish national history, gender and class relations, and the definition of human subjectivity.

In contrast, the vast majority of modernists privilege a nonhierarchical, non-unitarian, non-harmonious aesthetic and continually experiment with the erasure of borders between and within texts and between and within artistic genres. In addition to the dissolution of textual boundaries between authors, with the appearance of one writer as a character in the work of another or the cameo appearance of an author within his own work, the predilection for serial narratives or the publication of several interrelated novels signals a desire for intertextual dialogue. Baroja's grouping of his novels in trilogies has raised questions among critics as to the relations between the various texts within a given trilogy that sometimes shares a common narrative ambience and characters, but in other instances seems to have little in common. Emilio González López authored a long critical study addressed to this issue and his interest and that of other critics in identifying connections across textual borders responds to a conscious effort on Baroja's part to present textuality in a more fluid, dynamic light. In placing *La dama errante, La ciudad de la niebla,* and *El árbol de la ciencia* in the trilogy entitled *La raza,* Baroja invites the reader to forge links between these three texts and to read the trajectory of María Aracil and Andrés Hurtado in a dialogic fashion that valorizes female and male experience as equally valid and places the search for individual selfhood within the national and international context, joining Madrid and London, city and country, self and community. Barojan texts also forge connections across trilogies, with references to Iturrioz, who is present in all three volumes of *La raza,* as the author of several publications read by Arcelu in *El mundo es ansí* of the trilogy *Las ciudades.* Similarly, the center of narrative action in *El mayorazgo de Labraz* of the trilogy *Tierra vasca* resurfaces in *Mala hierba* of *La lucha por la vida,* where Roberto Hastings refers to Labraz as the site of his ancestral roots.

Realist and naturalist writers like Honoré de Balzac and Emile Zolá also cultivate the serial novel in an effort to capture a whole social unit, but in modernist hands, characters from one novel reappear as transformed or totally contrary to their previous depiction, reflecting a vision of subjectivity and textuality as unstable and always amenable to change. The different versions of Antonio Azorín presented in *La voluntad* (1902) and *Antonio*

Azorín (1903) and the chronological inversions and lapses that occur in Pérez de Ayala's series on the intellectual and artistic development of Alberto Díaz de Guzmán reflect a similar interest in undoing previously established characterizations and obliging readers to revise assumptions adopted at the end of one text when they arrive at another. The retreat back in time at the beginning of the last novel in Pérez de Ayala's series, *Troteras y danzaderas* (1913), intercalates a whole narrative between parts two and three of the preceding *La pata de la raposa* (1912) and rewrites the ending of the previous novel by introducing new information on Alberto's life in Madrid during the intervening years. Pérez de Ayala utilizes the novelistic series as a means of promoting his advocacy of perspectivism, forcing the reader of *Luna de miel, Luna de hiel* and *Los trabajos de Urbano y Simona* (1923) and of *Tigre Juan* and *El curandero de su honra* (1926) to adjust to a smaller or greater degree to a new narrative stance in the passage from one novel of the cycle to the other.

Pardo Bazán also experiments with serial or two part novels, at times vastly altering the narrative stance, as when she shifts from the naturalistic discourse of *Los pazos de Ulloa* (1886) to the more lyrical representation of nature and love in *La madre naturaleza* (1887) or moves from a tragic narration of female sexuality in *Morriña* (1889) to its celebration in *Insolación* (1889), both grouped under the overarching title of *Historias amorosas.* She also shifts from one narrator to another in the two volumes included in *Adán y Eva,* moving from the ineffectual Benicio Neira of *Doña Milagros* (1894) who, as the father of the family he describes, is deeply implicated in the narrative action but comes to view it more objectively over the course of the novel, to the initially detached but ultimately emotionally committed Mauro Pareja of *Memorias de un solterón* (1896). Other novelistic cycles show less change, as in the transition from *Una cristiana* to *La prueba* (1890–91). The different treatments place the reader in an unstable position, never sure when opening the second novel whether it represents a continuation, revision, or erasure of its antecedent.

The barriers separating textuality and reality also disappear in the modernist period. The increasingly rapid dissemination of news in the urban setting quickly converts ordinary citizens into public figures who take on a certain textual reality above and beyond their biographical identity. Baroja alludes to this phenomenon in *La dama errante* (1908), in which María and her father quickly become known to a reading public that follows their adventures in the newspaper and projects an identity onto them that stands in an ambivalent relation to their self-image and their subjectivity as perceived by other characters and the reader. Galdós plays with this same idea in *Misericordia* (1897), where the residents of a poor neighborhood confuse Benina with the legendary charity worker doña Guillermina, who had previously appeared in his *Fortunata y Jacinta* (1886–87). The narrative invention of the earlier novel resurfaces in the memory of the characters of the later volume, crossing textual borders and acquiring a historical reality in the minds of the desperate lower-class characters who accost Benina in the hope of generous hand-outs and stone her in their anger at her extremely modest gifts. In the context of this metafictional novel, the confusion suggests the very porous nature of the borders that separate life and text, fiction and reality. Inventions become reality and text becomes history just as history and reality become text. Ciro Bayo points to fluid divisions between textuality and life in *El peregrino entretenido* (1910), in which he reveals that individuals he meets in his wanderings through Spain know they may emerge in his publications and act in accordance with how they want to appear in textual form. The narrator of *Las Aventuras, inventos y mixtificaciones de Silvestre Paradox* (1901) suggests that characters act in order to provide the narrator/author with material worthy of transmittal to the reader (1946–48, 1:35), in another expression of the notion that life is a text waiting to be transcribed. Unamuno's insistence that all biography is a novel and that there is no real separation between his prologue to *Tres novelas ejemplares y un prólogo* (1920) and the three narratives that follow also relates to the abolition of the borders separating fiction and reality, life and textuality.

Modernist writers similarly dissolve traditional intratextual borders and unifying strategies. In both theory and practice, they show a preference for unfinished, fragmented art forms, in which the strongly bordered text becomes unbound both at its boundaries and within. Nuances and instability displace strong paint strokes and definitive forms in the presentation of the materials. Baroja's Fernando Ossorio disdains rules in painting and detests Yécora because it lacks shading and the patina of age that softens colors and outlines (1969, 139). Salvador Rusiñol dreams of the abolition of the line and complete fusion of background and foreground, subject and landscape. The protagonist of Llanas Aguilaniedo's *El jardín del amor* expresses her preference for muted colors, subtle nuances, and only vaguely delineated figures (1902, 91–92), and like many modernists, among the classic painters she vastly prefers El Greco (95). Modernist aesthetics privileges change over permanence and seeks to capture the variability of human experience in all art forms. Even in the realm of sculpture, Baroja advocates the incorporation of mutability in his description of Juan's bust of la Salvadora, in which she appears laughing when viewed from one angle and sad from the other (1946–48, 1:535). The statue of Imperia in *La noche del sábado* (1903) also has an undecidable expression, either of triumph and life or death and descent. With reference to verbal arts, Urbano González Serrano recommends the use of silences as an antidote to rhetoric and oratory (1903, 4) and insists that words, thoughts, and living things are unstable entities that degenerate and die when fixed in an unchanging state (7).

Modernist art insistently cultivates fragments and instability over large, coherent works. Baroja's novels have long attracted critical attention and often rejection because of their use of intercalated stories, episodes that lead nowhere and have only a superficial relation to the main story, and a plot development that depends more on casual encounter than causal relations. The definition of life that results from such a textualization privileges chance over plan and change over continuity. Major events in the characters' lives result from haphazard meetings: Andrés Hurtado runs into Lulú on the street (n. d., 335) and this unplanned encounter sets in motion the renewal of their friendship and ultimately, their marriage. In Unamuno's *Niebla* a similarly random street meeting between Augusto Pérez and Eugenia initiates Augusto's existential journey, which takes many twists and turns depending on the unexpected associations of his intellectual ramblings and the casual events that cause a shift in his trajectory. Miró's texts seam together individual scenes and apparently unrelated individuals in a kaleidoscope of visual images from which the reader must attempt to create a never fully unified whole.

Azorín's work largely consists of small fragments that he publishes in collections of dubious unity. He is the master of the silences advocated by González Serrano, typically eliding critical information that the reader must interpellate while at the same time providing an overabundance of details that he alternately lists without providing the connecting frame or joins in an unusual coupling of disparate elements. I have commented on his penchant for forging connections between seemingly unrelated parts, such as the sea and Castile in *Castilla* or the Italian epigraph and epilogue inspired by and composed in France that frame and help to define *España.* Azorín continually questions limits, borders, and conventional divisions to create new relations across traditional boundaries. His 1915 *Tomás Rueda* textualizes his aesthetic rejection of limits and borders in reworking Cervantes's *El licenciado vidriera* in a modernist vein. The narrative defies efforts to affix a stable meaning, opening with the ambivalent "En Zamora o en Medina," placing the action in either of two Castilian cities in a definition of setting that then becomes even more vague in the chapter itself with the introduction of Valladolid as a third possibility (1947, 15–18).

The initial lines of *Tomás Rueda* begin with the familiar and stable "once upon a time" fairy tale opener that introduces the character as a king, but quickly gives way to a series of clarifications that explain that it was not really a king but rather a knight, and not really a knight but a brave captain, and finally that it was really just a child. The narrator breaks traditional textual limits that seal the work off from the outside world by continually shifting narrative perspective, from heterodiegetic to homodiegetic, with ample use of narrative intrusions and comments addressed directly to the reader, asking help in reminding the narrator where he left the story in the previous chapter. The narrative often continues across subchapter divisions, ending with ellipses in one segment and resuming the text with the repetition of the final words of the preceding section in the next chapter or segment (1947, 54, 62). An unstable, fragmentary text continues to the end, where the never clearly characterized protagonist, who has chosen to leave Spain and live in the Netherlands, receives a letter from Spain, yells happily for a female companion whose relationship to the main character is never defined, and gives her the letter. The narrative ends with the elliptical expression, "La carta decía así. . . ." [The letter said. . . .], in a final unfinished, unstable affirmation of a fragmented vision of reality and textuality. The text continues across the borders of the volume in yet another instance of unbinding of textual unity.

Ramón Gómez de la Serna begins with short, fragmented works and gradually constructs an entire new genre out of random associations between seemingly unrelated objects or concepts. He continually defined and redefined his *greguerías* as a metaphor plus humor, a casualty of thought, a nuance among other nuances (1955, xlviii–xli), and often relies on a paradoxical conjunction of seemingly dissimilar elements, such as the spatial configuration of a letter, its sound, and its semantic connotations ("La T es el martillo del abecedario" [T is the hammer of the alphabet], 92) or the randomly associated shapes of two different objects ("El corazón es un puño cerrado que boxea dentro del pecho" [The heart is the closed fist that boxes inside the chest], 47). The insistence on paradox in Gómez de la Serna appears in other writers of the period and relates to the rejection of coherence and fixed meaning. Baroja's choice of "Paradox" as one of his early pseudonyms and the recurring character Silvestre Paradox in novels and essays speaks to his commitment to this rhetorical and (il)logical device. Unamuno's defense and practice of paradox recurs throughout his work. In "Soliloquios y conversaciones" he attacks those who dismiss paradoxical thinking as invalid and asserts that the word "paradox" was invented by close-minded people to identify concepts they hear for the first time (1958, 4:592).

Breaking Genre Borders

Modernist defiance of inherited definitions and modes of classifying the world translates to a radical redefinition of literary genre. I have pointed to the constant mixing of "high" and "low" art forms in Ramón Pérez de Ayala, whose comparison of art and prostitution reflects his refusal to separate these two realms of human experience. His 1907–13 series of novels on the artistic and personal trajectory of Alberto Díaz de Guzmán as well as his later *Prometeo* (1916) or *Belarmino y Apolonio* (1921) intermix epic and grotesque discourse and introduce poetry or dramatic dialogue within narrative. The poems that initiate each of the chapters of the 1916 *Prometeo, Luz de domingo,* and *La caída de los Limones* introduce a different language and generic tradition that alternately opposes and echoes the prose sections of the texts. *Troteras y danzaderas* (1913) intercalates poems, the reading of the drama *Othello,* long dialogues that simulate dramatic form within the narrative structure, verses of Greek, English, Italian, and early Spanish literature in a continual recognition of multiple literary traditions and forms. Baroja also mixes cultured and popular, domestic and foreign literary forms in *El mayozago de Labraz* (1903), where Samuel Bothwell as one of several possible narrators joins his voice with traditional national discourses in a continual play of similarity and difference. Textual allusions to El Greco, the British preRaphaelites, and medieval Spanish texts as artistic models underscore the co-presence of multiple aesthetic traditions that combine the popular world of the Celestina, the aristocratic plaint of Jorge Manrique, the stylized world of the preRaphaelites, and the distorted representation of El Greco.

Baroja's *Zalacaín el aventurero* (1909) coincides with Pérez de Ayala's conjoining of epic and popular discourses, intermixing events drawn from the classic adventure story in the protagonist's escape from the Carlist forces in chapter 5 of part 2, epic elements in the sounding of the trumpet in the valley of Roncesvalles when Martín dies, with clear references to the French epic *La Chanson de Roland,* and popular Basque and Castilian songs and tales that appear throughout the novel.[6] Benavente and the Martínez Sierras often cultivate a poetic theater, with intertextual links to the classical *commedia dell'arte* or traditional drama in verse form. The Martínez Sierras's narrative works may include varied short fragments, as in the early *El poema del trabajo* (1898) or *Diálogos fantásticos* (1899). The later *El amor catedrático* (1910) consists of several different segments, including letters between two women, the first-person diary of a young male suitor, the first-person notes of an older male professor, and finally a return to the epistolary format of the opening section. Both the epistolary and diary segments have a disjointed quality that adds to the overall rejection of a uniform whole.

The insistent utilization of multiple discursive traditions within modernism and the refusal to remain within conventional generic borders correlates with the modernist tendency to cultivate a variety of literary and artistic forms. Artists of the period resist definitions that freeze them into a specific movement and energetically cultivate a variety of genres in order to establish a polymorphic identity. Galdós, who had devoted his career exclusively to the novel, moves toward a hybrid dialogue novel and then to theater in the 1890s and 1900s. Clarín had always cultivated the essay, short story, and novel, and he too moves toward theater in his final years. Pardo Bazán commenced her literary career with a volume of poetry and then quickly abandoned this genre for various prose forms, including the essay, novel, and short story. Like Galdós and Clarín, in the latter part of the nineteenth and early years of the twentieth centuries, she also turns to the theater. Her monumental *Nuevo teatro crítico,* authored, edited, and published solely by Pardo Bazán, appears monthly from 1891 to 1893 and includes short stories, literary criticism, book and dramatic reviews, feminist essays, and other social commentary. The controversial short story "No lo invento" that appears in the publication in 1891 reflects the commitment to multiple generic traditions, opening under the guise of an idyllic romance before moving through the tragic tale of premature death and lost love to the format of the ghost story and ultimately the naturalist narrative of a necrophilic grave digger. The text includes a section that imitates theatrical dialogue to represent the judge's questioning of the grave digger in another example of writing across generic boundaries.

Younger writers continue the cultivation of multiple genres. Unamuno publishes in virtually every known art form as poet, essayist, novelist, short story writer, and dramatist. In yet another instance of polymorphic artistry, he also practices origami, expertly fashioning paper birds and even writing a treatise on the subject in "Tratado de cocotología." Pérez de Ayala published essays throughout his novelistic career while Gabriel Miró cultivated the short story, the novel, as well as the essay. Valle-Inclán writes poetry, short stories, novels, and plays, as well as his extended aesthetic treatise while Azorín produces hybrid works that straddle fiction and essay. Baroja's narrative production is punctuated by short stories, essays, and dialogue novels that straddle narrative and drama in the cases of *La casa de Aizgorri* and *Paradox, rey.* I have referred several times to Antonio Machado's sorties into the world of theater and philosophy and even the quintessential poet, Juan Ramón Jiménez, produces the hybrid prose/poetry *Diario de un poeta recien casado* and the prose work *Platero y yo* (1914).

The turn toward the essay during this period merits commentary and relates to the vision of subjectivity, outlined in the previous chapter, and of textuality, as defined in the present. The essay, like the novel, arises during the modern period at a time when the dissolution of traditional centers of authority cleared a space for competing perspectives. In a world increasingly devoid of master narratives, individual voices or representatives of varied social groups seek to persuade the reader to adopt alternative visions. The essay is an essentially dialogic form that reaches back to antecedent speakers and texts and out to current readers in an effort to bring them to accept the views posited within the text. The power relationship between reader and essayistic text speaker is much more tenuous than in narrative texts. Whereas the reader of fiction enters an invented world with a willing suspension of disbelief, temporarily adopting the norms and values of the fictive world, the essay reader remains in his/her world, which she/he shares with the essayist and text speaker and which is invoked throughout the text by references to contemporary events, living figures, and other shared cultural information. In that the essay seeks to transform the reader's relation with this shared world within the context of decentered authority, essayistic discourse oscillates continuously between validation of the reader and imposition of the text speaker.

The uneven power relationship between essayistic text speaker and reader mirrors the dissolution of traditional centers of authority in modern culture and is further complicated by the appearance of new groups, such as women and the lower-class reader, who bring new values and demands. The text speaker of the modernist essay addresses an increasingly heterogeneous public and must continuously adopt new subject positions as the addressee(s) and textual topics change. Essayistic discourse and the modern perception of subjectivity develop hand in hand and this conjunction contributes to the increased prevalence of the essay among modernist writers. Subject theory has pointed to the importance of narrative in the construction of subjectivity, but has overlooked the equally significant role of the essay. Anthony Giddens postulates the need for the construction of a narrative of self-identity to meet the challenge of living in modernity. In answer to the fragmenting tendencies of modern life and institutions, the individual must continually create and recreate a selfhood (1991, 186). Paul Smith in *Discerning the Subject* suggests that every narrative type reflects and creates a different vision of the subject. In classic realism, the text seeks to construct a sense of control, cohesion, and stability in terms of the producing, fictional, and reading subjects (1988, 92). Smith and Paul Ricoeur both argue that contemporary narrative constructs a fragmented subject and Ricoeur goes on to note the similarities between contemporary narrative, autobiography, and the essay. Ricoeur posits that the modern view of the subject and character produces narrative and autobiographical texts that break with temporal continuity and the construction of a coherent character that typify traditional narrative, moving deliberately towards the more disjointed, seemingly unstructured quality of the essay (1992, 149).

If, as Paul Smith argues, the choice of discourse reflects a specific historical moment and ideological purpose that in turn is intimately related to a particular configuration of the subject (1988, 105), then the emergence of the essay in the modern period represents a significant (re)vision of the self that predates contemporary narrative's experimentation and provides a model for the modern textualization of a decentered subject. Thus, the essay writer not only addresses a collectivity composed of different and typically discordant subjects, but also configures these and the subject that is constituted in the text as an interplay of different and often discordant subject positions.[7] An incredibly large number of modernist writers cultivate the essay in one of its multiple variants and essayistic discourse appears intermixed in their publications with narrative, drama, and even poetic forms. Antonio Machado's *De un cancionero apócrifo* combines biography, philosophy, essay, and poetry and some of the poems of Enrique de Mesa and Vicente Medina have a distinctly essayistic quality. Baroja, Rusiñol, Unamuno, and Azorín author hybrid texts that straddle the borders of short story and essay and Eugenio d'Ors also tends toward works that break with traditional generic boundaries and includes essayistic components in his *La ben plantada* and *Cartas a Tina.* Pardo Bazán plays with the dissolution of genre borders in "Con una alemana" (1891), where she introduces the reader to a German woman with whom she proceeds to engage in an extended dialogue on Spanish culture, only to reveal at the end of the text that the dialogue and the German interlocutor are imaginary constructs and pretexts for her essay (1976, 213). Ganivet, Miró, Unamuno, and Baroja, among others, adopt a purposefully non-linear essayistic structure, underscoring the role of the unconscious and irrational in the construction of ideology and identity. For these writers, writing across generic borders relates to other border crossings, from redefinitions of empire and nation to reconfigurations of subjectivity.

The unbinding of the text also leads to a break down of traditional separations of the literary, visual, and musical arts. In the world of visual creation, artists replicate their literary colleagues' refusal to remain firmly fixed within a single medium. Picasso works in varied media, including oil, charcoal, sculpture, and ceramics. Dalí similarly traverses multiple artistic modalities. A number of visual artists simultaneously produce written texts, either working alone or in collaboration. The landscape artist Aureliano de Beruete also authors the seminal study *Velázquez* (1898). The painter Darío de Regoyos collaborates with the Belgian poet Émile Verhaeren to produce the book *La España negra* and Santiago Rusiñol cultivates painting, theater, poetry, and narrative. The worlds of visual and literary arts enter into increasingly intimate contact during modernism. Writers and painters coincide in the experience of bohemian Paris, where the

Baroja brothers, Picasso, Rusiñol, the Machado brothers, Alejandro Sawa and many others spent months and in some cases years in a sometimes fruitful, sometimes unproductive apprenticeship.

Increased production of paper and rapid dissemination through train transport enables publishers to meet the demands of a growing readership. Greater facility to handle graphics and photographic duplication, among other factors, transforms the numbers and kinds of publications in the modernist period.[8] Magazines such as *El Cuento Semanal* incorporate numerous drawings that accompany the texts and provide a reading experience that includes the visual alongside the verbal in a venue now open to a massive readership. *El Gato Negro,* published in Barcelona at the turn of the century, incorporates drawing and graphics on virtually every page, including sketches by the well-known Ramón Casas. *La Ilustración Española y Americana* offers engravings, drawings, and lithographs of peoples and activities occurring in remote cultures as well as Spanish urban and rural scenes. The June 8, 1893 issue includes on the same page an engraving of an Asturian farm woman with a sickle in her hand and a bare-breasted odalisque, doubly traversing the visual-verbal textual border and the national cultural boundary. Editions of 1898 include photographs from Cuba and maps of military positions, bringing the war home to the Spanish reader. The editors of *Helios* lament that costs preclude the inclusion of the visual arts and promise to revise their format as profits allow (1903, 1:99).

Illustrations and graphics accompany the early editions of Gabriel Miró's novels and under the aegis of the Caro Raggio publishing house, Ricardo Baroja's drawings accompany the republication of many of his brother Pío's earlier novels. Santiago Rusiñol publishes his own tribute to interartistic collaboration in *Oracions* (1897), in which he incorporates prose descriptions of nature, intercalated segments of musical scores, softly colored drawings and engravings, as well as black and white art. In the midst of strongly expressed opposition to a modern technology that destroys the old order, the text exploits new print technologies to create a modernist conjoining of traditionally separate art forms and to invoke primitive collective artistry, as found in the pyramids, the Parthenon, the Alhambra, and Gothic cathedrals, as models for the modern artists. The pluralist artistic tradition invoked in the text, with references to Egyptians, Greeks, Arabs, and Christians, coexists with enunciations of elitist aesthetics in a co-presence of difference that mirrors the simultaneity of diverse art forms within a single volume.

Modernist artists persistently invoke music and visual art, reflecting both their desire to break down traditional generic and artistic borders and their growing recognition of the insufficiency of the word or any single mode of expression. Ekphrastic techniques appear with great frequency in the period. Leopoldo Alas holds up the painter as the guide to a superior understanding of reality in *Doña Berta* (1892), at about the same time that he mocks verbal art in *Su único hijo* (1891). The painter of *Doña Berta* in some ways advances the exalted vision of the artist as the purveyor of a superior vision of reality to a less illustrious public. However, he also supports the modernist abolition of artistic borders in his use of both the paint brush and his evident story telling talents. His presence induces Berta to relate the story of her illegitimate child and in response, the painter invents another narrative that explains the disappearance of the lover-father and creates a biography for the lost son. This new artist, who straddles the borders of visual and verbal art, creates fictions that give meaning to life and both capture and transcend reality. The text insists on the cross-eyed vision that Ortega disdains, voicing through the painter the belief that neither painting nor poetry can capture certain realities, contrasting the portrait of the young Berta and the figure of the aged woman with the "real" Berta and underscoring Berta's arrival at a new level of understanding of self and life through the painter's visual/verbal art. Both the word and the image are necessary to this process of transformation, but neither fully apprehends reality.

Clarín's text also explores an understanding of art as convention while revealing the influential role of artistic convention for an understanding of culture. When Berta moves to Madrid in an effort to buy the painting of the dying captain that she believes is her son, she finds that the picture has been removed from the wall and is lying on the floor, ready to be packaged and shipped to the new owner's home in America. She can only view the painting by climbing a wooden ladder that a sympathetic young worker holds in place, thus allowing her to examine the work from above. As she ascends, Berta at first only perceives a series of smudges, but gradually is able to connect the random brush strokes to discern the figure of the captain. Visual art, like textual creation, consists of a series of unrelated marks on a surface that the viewer must connect in order to construct meaning. This view seemingly places visual art on the same level as verbal art, but the description of Berta's fainting and fall from the ladder emphasizes painting as more powerful than words for the apprehension of reality and underscores the memory of visual images that serves as a fundamental feature of the reader's map of reality. The narrator compares Berta's fall to another kind of painting, a Descent from the Cross. The allusion to the ladder and the evident comparison of Berta's suffering with that of Christ on the Cross invoke memories of many different pictorial versions of the removal of Christ's body by his disciples, but in particular suggest Roger Van der Weyden's *The Descent from the Cross,* which is housed in the Prado Museum, not far from the city bustle where *Doña Berta* takes place.

Van der Weyden's painting shows a wooden stepladder leaning against the cross, duplicating the ladder that Berta climbed to see her "son" and it also depicts the Virgin Mary in a faint, held up by a young apostle, visually replicating the textual description of Berta as supported by the young worker who had compassionately helped her to ascend the ladder. In the painting, Mary's position mirrors that of Christ, both figures horizontally extended with arms curved slightly outward, just as the fallen doña Berta duplicates the bodily composition of Mary, Christ, and perhaps the dying captain of the verbally described painting she has just viewed. In the context of the constant backdrop of painting in the text, the graphic description of Berta's death under the wheels of the trolley encourages the reader to visualize the accident, picturing the ivory color of skin, the ashen hue of her hair, the tobacco shades of her clothing and boots, and finally the small red trickle of blood that flows from her mouth. Throughout the text, verbal and visual images succeed each other, in a double vision that enriches the reading experience with a mutual reenforcement of visual and verbal perception. Pictorial image and text work together to reproduce and refashion reality, calling on the reader's knowledge of literary, artistic, and cultural codes to produce new aesthetic experiences and new, more productive subject positions.

The literary production of Azorín and Miró depends heavily on the reader's visual memory and her/his ability to build a mental picture from words. Azorín theorizes in *La voluntad* on the need for the artist to capture color, noise, movement, and plasticity in the description of landscape (1919, 1:862). Many of his works duplicate Clarín's study of the mutually enhancing presence of the visual and the verbal and the deficiency of each when used alone. *Los pueblos* (1905) includes references to Zuloaga, Velázquez, El Greco, in combination with recreations of classical literary texts, the narration of personal adventures, and descriptions of place in the convention of travel writing in order to recreate the ambience of Spanish villages. *Castilla* (1912) alerts the reader to the presence of ekphrastic techniques in the dedication to the landscape painter Aureliano de Beruete and continues to interweave visual and verbal art throughout. In the introduction to the volume, the speaker refers to the individual texts as *cuadros,* a term that reappears in the quotation of Modesto Lafuente's description of the poetic beauty of trains (1958, 85). The first real introduction of trains in Spain, as described in "El primer ferrocarril castellano," took place in 1830 in the form of a drawing, which is described at length. The text explains that a second drawing appeared in 1845. The speaker emphasizes the defective nature of both sketches, in particular the second, which depicted six train cars traveling across the plain with no tracks in sight. Visual art here proves incomplete while on other occasions, it is invoked to enrich verbal descriptions. Azorín frequently uses terms borrowed from painting to describe texts, as when he states that the poet Arriaza "ha pintado las capeas en los pueblos" [has painted the amateur bullfights in the villages] (105) or later refers to the canvas on which the poet painted the bull fight (105). The reader could easily perceive Arriaza's text as a painting until specific quotations from the poem reveal that it is verbal art.

The persistent conflation of the verbal and visual in *Castilla* signals that neither words nor visual images suffice. Rather, the artist must cross boundaries that have been artificially created between these two artistic forms and combine them. In "Lo fatal," the text can only capture the totality of the Spanish gentleman it seeks to describe through a combination of narrative—the retelling of the *Lazarillo*—of poetry—the prose description of a Góngora sonnet and the reproduction of two of its verses, and of painting—the reference to an El Greco portrait, most probably his *Portrait of a Gentleman.* The final text in the collection, "La casa cerrada," reiterates the mutual dependence of multiple forms of artistic expression. The text alludes constantly to visual art, with descriptions of male and female portraits on the library walls, engravings in books, a portrait of the protagonist when he was a child of eight, and a photograph of Velázquez's *Las meninas* that hangs on the wall. The use of ekphrasis takes on particular significance due to the protagonist's blindness. His only access to the paintings is through his sense of touch, which allows him to feel the oil portraits, but proves inadequate to "see" the engravings and photographs. Continuous references to the visual communicate the insufficiency of words to capture reality but at the same time, the character's lack of sight points to the inherent dependency of visual arts on a single sense. Verbal art is inadequate but visual art is also incomplete. The two must combine, crossing arbitrary borders and margins to jointly work towards a full representation.

Azorín and other modernists explore interartistic connections between verbal texts and the burgeoning world of film and cinematography. I previously mentioned the use of the film cut in Villaespesa's poetry and Pérez de Ayala's narrative as well as Azorín's verbal reproduction of the long shot and close up in *Doña Inés*. In his earlier *Antonio Azorín* (1903), he condenses multiple forms of ekphrasis in a single opening paragraph. The text commences with a dedication to the painter Ricardo Baroja and the initial chapter begins with a description that echoes the painter's preference for Castilian landscapes, with ample play of light and shadow. It then quickly moves beyond static landscape painting toward the new art of film. The emphasis on the dynamic character of light introduces movement and mention of the noise of insects and the sound of a train, followed by the appearance of the train in the distance, suggests cinematography and the presence of sound long before it actually appeared in the movie theater.

Antonio and Manuel Machado also move from traditional forms of interartistic reference to the incorporation of cinematography. Antonio's descriptive poems at times invoke impressionistic paintings while other texts rely on starker, more definitive lines and images. He compares memory to a canvas on which different images come into vision in "Algunos lienzos del recuerdo tienen. . . ." and the title "Ante el pálido lienzo de la tarde" clearly invokes the pictorial model for his description of the late afternoon scene. The Machado brothers' collaborative theater works of the 1920s draw on the experience of cinema to explore new subject positions. The stage directions of *Las adelfas* instruct the actress to use facial expressions to show happiness and surprise simultaneously, specifically referring to the rich development of facial gesture in silent movies as a model (1951, 415). Characters in *Juan de Mañara* refer to life as a movie script, in which it is always possible to add or revise a segment to construct a different ending (1951, 364). The world of cinema adds to the artistic repertoire and promotes a vision of human experience as fluid and multifaceted in consonance with the modernist outlook.

Manuel Machado's ekphrastic poetry approximates poetry, music, dance, and sculpture, in an exploration of interartistic expression that other poets also pursue. The extended "La fiesta nacional" describes the bull fight and utilizes varied metrical forms to replicate the movement of the bull, the bullfighter, picadors, banderilleros, and the public (1951, 59–64). The opening segment describes the sound of the bugle and the bull's entry into the arena and utilizes varying verses of eight and four syllables to capture the indecisive movements of the bull, which typically enters running, stops, takes stock of the situation, charges, stops again, in alternating rhythms reflected in the poetic meter. The second section describes the bull fighter's cape movements and utilizes a six line stanza of octosyllabic verses and a second stanza of four syllable verses that flow into eight syllable couplets, creating a sense of evenness, of a smooth flowing cape and rhythm uniformity. The third segment describes the violent encounters between the bull and the picador, utilizing uneven verses, ellipsis, and enjambment to capture the uneven combat, the horse's fall, the bull's attack and retreat. The description of the banderilleros predominantly utilizes six syllable lines, with a few shorter and one longer verse to capture the generally smooth movement of these members of the bullfighter's team that is punctuated with some quick footwork to place themselves properly and some long pauses, as they wait for the opportunity to insert the banderillas in the bull's shoulders. The outline of the verses on the page at times takes a physical shape that mimics the movements of the subjects of the poem, as if the verses represented movements in a ballet, and at other times signals a rhythm that evokes memories of the accompanying music.

The use of shape, outline, and contour to communicate meaning also approximates sculpture, an art form that Salvador Rueda similarly emulates in a melding of verbal and visual art that anticipates the concrete or pattern poetry of Guillaume Apollinaire's 1918 *Calligrames*. Rueda's poem "Lo que dice la guitarra" from *En tropel* (1893) utilizes a combination of six and twelve syllable lines in the opening stanza, with the hexasyllabic verses duplicating the six strings of the guitar and the ordering of the verses roughly delineating the outline of the musical instrument. More common than the intermixing of poetry and sculpture is the much commented blending of music and verbal text that Pompeyo Gener so violently opposes. Rueda utilizes many musical terms as titles of poems or sections of his poetic collections, such as "Escalas," "Cantos del mediodía," "Sinfonía callejera" and in a prose selection appended to *En tropel,* he argues for the incorporation of color and music in poetry, comparing the pen to an orchestra and an artist's palette (1893, 183). Juan Ramón Jiménez similarly draws from music for titles such as "Arias tristes," "Nocturnos" as does Ricardo Gil in his previously commented *La caja de música.* Pardo Bazán constructs her late novel *La Quimera* around the artistic discussions of a painter and a composer, and the text continually interweaves verbal, visual, and auditory art forms in content, intertextual references, and stylistic expression. Even such an unlikely candidate as Pío Baroja, rarely linked with Jiménez, Gil, or Villaespesa, exalts music as the most promising of the arts because it has the ability to express both universal and local, popular elements (1946–48, 5:163).

Speaking and Writing a Renewed Spanish

Baroja's intercalation of popular songs throughout his works reflects his conviction that popular music expresses the character of the people in ways that words alone can never convey and also his belief, shared by his contemporaries, that the Spanish language needs an infusion of new energy in terms of lexicon, syntax, and discursive variation. Modernist rejection of Restoration rhetoric takes different forms in the writers of the period, but virtually all share a desire to move away from what they see as an excessively verbose, artificial discourse toward other modes of expression. Francisco Giner de los Ríos had early argued this position and he promotes the abandonment of the more tortured style of early Krausists to a clearer expression with shorter sentences.[9] Baroja expresses this stance in *Juventud, egolatría* (1917) and both in this autobiographical text and in the prologue to *La dama errante* (1908), he advocates a rhetoric in minor key and argues that as a Basque he has the right to introduce his own idiomatic turns of phrase to Castilian (1946–48, 5:173). Like Baroja, many modernists see the way to new, more authentic and spontaneous expression in Castilian through contact with other languages, dialects, and speech registers. In contrast with Raymond Williams's description of modernism as privileging poetic over ordinary language (1989, 69–75), Spanish modernists interweave the poetic and popular, the local and foreign. The Martínez Sierras state that the Catalan language helps enrich Castilian and their long and continuous collaboration with Santiago Rusiñol manifests their commitment to the language and culture of Catalonia.

Unamuno, Baroja, the Machado brothers and their father before them, Costa, Azorín, Valle-Inclán and others foster knowledge of popular language and many interweave it in their works with more cultured forms of speech. Unamuno defends the study of popular, living language in the educational system and calls for inclusion of dialectal variations in the construction of a new, non-purist Spanish language: "Hay que hacer . . . con el castellano y sobre él, la lengua española, sin que ninguna región de la península pretenda el monopolio del casticismo de la lengua común" [It is necessary . . . with and over Castilian, to create the Spanish language, without any region of the peninsula claiming a purist monopoly of the common language] (1906, 358). His essay "Contra el purismo," initially published in *Revista Nueva* in 1899, advances the same idea and argues that traditional Castilian cannot express modern ideas. The development of new thought requires the evolution of the language, integrating the various regional and national varieties of Spanish. The text speaker aspires to move the language and culture towards *hispanismo* as opposed to *españolismo,* through free exchange of ideas, words, and discourse (1899b, 350). Unamuno writes extensively on questions of language and although he does not believe in a renovation of the Basque language, which he judges incapable of adjusting to the flexibility required of modern thought,[10] he much more positively appraises other languages spoken in the Iberian peninsula. In "Sobre el uso de la lengua catalana," he encourages Catalan writers to write in their native language rather than Spanish, in the belief that the reader will understand what they communicate better if they express their thoughts in their native language. In "Español-portugués" (1914), he expresses a similar view with respect to Portuguese and urges Spaniards to learn and read Portuguese. He believes that the two languages will eventually grow closer through a natural process of mutual assimilation and encourages this rapprochement.

It is the desire for interchange and mutual enrichment that leads him to reject what he perceives as an exclusionary spirit in Catalan nationalism and to defend Spanish as the national language against growing calls for Catalan political autonomy. The text speaker of "Por la cultura: Las campañas catalanistas" (1907) clearly fears that the Catalan language will completely displace Castilian if local Catalan authorities gain the power to determine such issues. The expressions of this anxiety during the same period that Unamuno calls for a Catalanization of Spain in his textual dialogue with Maragall reflects once again the tension between calls for pluralism and fears of dismemberment that I noted in the discussion of nation. In this particular case, Unamuno comes down on the side of a tradition of centralized political power in opposition to local political and linguistic autonomy, but his comments represent just one statement in an ongoing dialogue with Maragall and others and do not constitute a definitive, closed opinion.

Levinas's distinction between the saying and the said and the nature of the modernist essay both disallow the selection of individual texts or statements as representative of Unamunan thought. The words expressed have a meaning that transcends their content and that derives from their desire to remain in ethical relation with the other (Levinas, 1993, 142). In addressing Catalan nationalism, Unamuno insists on a continued dialogue with its representatives and on adjusting his own subject position as essayistic text speaker according to the changing nature of his readership and the subject matter. His commitment to the continuation of "saying" in the context of the Catalan-Castilian-Portuguese (and by analogy, Galician) multi-lingual presence on the cultural landscape reveals itself in his 1915 essay "Iberia," which describes his plans to publish a tri-lingual journal of the same title in collaboration with Maragall. The text speaker expresses the desire to bring the three major linguistic groups in the Iberian peninsula to a better understanding of their similarities and differences, to know each other better even if that only leads to increased dissension. Writing in the shadow of World War I, the text argues for spiritual approximation and even hopes for the amalgamation of the three languages and cultures into a single unit at some future date, while specifically abjuring any forced imposition of unification (1958, 6:774).

The same philosophy governs Unamunan consideration of Spanish American Spanish. He often refers to the vigor of the language that has developed and continues to evolve in Spanish America and welcomes its influence on a fossilized Castilian expression in order to create a new language capable of communicating new thoughts ("El pueblo que habla español," 1958, 6:826). His life-long campaign against *casticismo* and linguistic standardization by the Royal Academy reflects his belief in language as a living entity, that continually grows through integration and differentiation ("Comunidad de la lengua hispánica," 6:95) and also his belief in the enriching force of the various dialects that constitute the Spanish language, including popular speech and geographic variation throughout the Americas. The defense of virile, unadulterated Castilian by the conservative Father Juan Mir y Noguera and the satirical publication *Gedeón* directly oppose the Unamunan definition of language. Numerous articles in the latter publication specifically target Unamuno and his style along with other modernist innovations in the campaign against what conservative forces see as an adulteration of language and culture.

The purist view of language coincides with what Bakhtin designates a unitary, centripetal language that "develops in vital connection with the processes of sociopolitical and cultural centralization" (1981, 271) and that Ashcroft associates with nationalist/imperialist governments that emphasize uniformity and a centrally imposed standard (1989, 42–43). Unamuno's definition of language coincides with Bakhtinian *heteroglossia* and centrifugal linguistic dynamics, which for both Bakhtin and Ashcroft represent a resistance to standardized language and speech. Latin Americans writing on Spanish modernism in the early years of the twentieth century express a clear understanding of the connection between a changed vision of language in modernism and a transformed relation with the former colonies and the Spanish past. Rufino Blanco Fombona, in his prologue to *Letras y Letrados de Hispanoamérica,* distinguishes between Restoration writers like Clarín and Navarro Ledesmo, who rejected Spanish America, and modernist writers like Martínez Sierra, Sawa, Juan Ramón Jiménez, who with only slight differences write and think like their Spanish American colleagues (1908?, 132–33). He defends the mixing of artistic genres, in direct opposition to Menéndez y Pelayo, and contrasts closed, severe Castilian thinking with a new spirit of fraternity in the post-colonial period with the Basque Unamuno and Catalan writers (221). Enrique Gómez Carrillo and Manuel Ugarte praise the new "modernist" language, a term which the latter prefers to the discarded "decadentist" precisely because it connotes renovation, progress, and an embrace of the future in opposition to a stultifying past (1908, 43).

Unamuno, Ugarte, and Blanco Fombona all equate a change in language with a change in thought and Unamuno specifically states in "Contra el purismo" that language conditions thought: "El verbo hace la idea. Y he aquí como el trabajar sobre la lengua, trabajo de libertad, puede ser obra de emancipación intelectual" [The word produces the idea. And in this way, work on language, a labor of liberty, can be a work of intellectual emancipation] (1899b, 349). This vision of language contrasts with nineteenth-century liberal and conservative perceptions of the word as subordinate to the spirit. The krausist Sanz del Río specifically expresses this view in his study "El lenguaje," published posthumously in 1891, and Pompeyo Gener's repudiation of symbolism to a large degree stems from his discomfort at a devalorization of reason as the origin of meaning and of the word as a product of thought (1894, 213). In contrast, modernist writers place language in a dialectical relationship with human thought, both conditioned by and conditioning the society in which it develops. They anticipate the views of Hans Robert Jauss that the work both reflects and shapes the reality in which it appears (1982, 14), or as Azorín traces back to the aesthetic doctrine of the neo-classical Andrés Piquer, art rejuvenates the past and transforms while renewing ideas as it acquires new, ever-changing forms (1947–48, 683).

Modernist writers choose many different paths to the construction of a new language capable of producing new thought. Traditional criticism of the period typically focussed on stylistic, discursive changes among *modernista* writers while the discussion of the "Generation of 1898" emphasized content over form. In general, critics noted the shift from the long sentence with multiple dependent clauses of the Restoration writers to a simpler, shorter sentence in the modernist period and a change in poetry from classical meter and prosaic expression to a more exotic, personal, sensual expression.[11] In the present study, I have underscored an aspiration to both simplify and complicate expression in the modernist period. Syntactically, the sentences undergo observable simplification, the length of chapters and titles decrease, long poems give way to shorter texts, and detailed description of setting cedes to an impressionistic, incomplete depiction. The apparent simplification produces discomfort because of its sheer novelty and resists rapid assimilation through the simultaneous cultivation of other defamiliarizing techniques. The play of similarity and difference that appears in the representation of national and personal identity continues on the level of lexicon and discourse, with the introduction of foreign words, the resurrection of traditional Spanish terms, the invention of modern expressions, and the interjection of popular dialect. Clarín harshly rebukes Pardo Bazán for her introduction of

French words and expressions and also for her use of such popular clichés as *tomar el pelo* [to pull one's leg], which he rejects in conjunction with the exploration of female domesticity in *Morriña.*[12] Galdós receives less criticism from those opposed to modernism and his use of language does not generally call attention to itself in terms of innovation and linguistic creativity. On the contrary, as Stephen Gilman points out, Valle-Inclán's allusion to him as "don Benito el Garbancero" attacks him precisely because of a perceived vulgarity in his literary expression (1961, 542). Despite this often repeated criticism, Galdós frequently plays with language and as discussed in the analysis of *Tristana,* he equates the development of a new mode of expression with the appropriation of new subject positions. Tristana's amalgamation of Italian and popular Spanish language reflects her creation of a new selfhood. Galdós also signals the instability of language and underscores the presence of multiple meanings in a single lexical item in his use of name symbolism and in comical turn abouts, such as the closing words of *Torquemada y San Pedro,* where the deathbed articulation of the word "conversion" by the usurer Torquemada leaves the reader and characters in doubt as to whether it communicates acceptance of religion or continued preoccupation with debt and economic matters. Language often appears in Galdós as unstable, transforming itself in the very act of communication. Valle-Inclán, Baroja, Unamuno, the Machado brothers, Pérez de Ayala, Miró, Concha Espina, and other modernists interweave multiple dialects, languages, and discourses in a persistent effort to create new subject positions for the reading public.

The vision of language as an entity in continual formation and amenable to change from many different quarters is consonant with the unprecedented modernist emphasis on dialogue in all genres. Baroja and Unamuno privilege dialogue over description in narrative texts and both engage in on-going conversations with the imbedded readers of their novels and essays. Many Barojan novels place a key philosophical discussion in the center of the narrative, as occurs in the long conversations between Iturrioz and Andrés Hurtado in *El árbol de la ciencia* and between Arcelu and Sacha in *El mundo es ansí.* Galdós emphasizes dialogue in his long realist and naturalist narratives and then moves toward an exclusively dialogic form in *Realidad, El abuelo,* and his dramatic works. Valle-Inclán similarly evolves toward a dialogic form in his later works, which have often challenged traditional notions of generic classification. The use of ellipsis in the poetry of Manuel Machado, the invention of apocryphal figures who enter into their own internal textual dialogue in Antonio Machado, and the intercalation of sections of dialogue in texts by Azorín, Pérez de Ayala, and Pardo Bazán as well as the on-going dialogue between Unamuno and Maragall, Unamuno and Antonio Machado, or Ortega y Gasset and many of the writers of the period speak to the vision of language as living communication. "Saying" in the modernist period acquires a value that alternates with the traditional valorization of the "said," and this shift in emphasis moves the focus of attention away from finished product and toward continual process. Purist centripetal conceptions of Spanish that accentuate the speaker give way to centrifugal notions that highlight the encounter with the other and the rich diversity of linguistic variants.

The Formation of the Modernist Reader

The Reader Then

The reader of realist texts confronts a new textual experience with the advent of modernism. Gonzalo Guasp and Pompeyo Gener, among early theorists of modernism at the turn of the century, speak of the need to perturb inveterate reading habits and expose the reader to broader horizons. The artistic text replicates an increasingly destabilized world through persistent use of irony and ambiguity, which oblige the reader to adopt ever-changing responses to the work and the world. Ganivet and other opponents of an imperial, colonizing past move the reader to repudiate traditional values by putting into play competing authoritative discourses that reveal the failure of a once glorified national program. The mixing of generic forms brings the reader to experience hybridity and the frequent utilization of dialogue forces the public to take an active role in weighing evidence that has no clear authoritative source. Azorín, the Machado brothers, Pérez de Ayala, Miró, Carmen de Burgos, among many others, explore new modes of viewing reality that capitalize on advances in lens and camera production and reeducate the reader in the possibilities of simultaneous and contradictory viewing perspectives. The breakdown of narrative authority correlates with the breakdown of a centralized political, religious, social power center and the experience of reading texts in which multiple interpretations are not only possible but necessary habituates the reader to question inherited narratives and create meaning according to different and more personal standards.

Modernist works train the reader of the period to adjust to rapid changes in focus and to the speed that characterizes the modern world. Novels, poems, stories, and plays introduce multiple and changing settings, transporting the reader across boundaries that traditionally separated urban and rural society, domestic and foreign culture, the minute realm of subcellular life and the enormity of the galaxy. The unbinding of the text described earlier requires the adoption of new reading habits capable of processing a constantly changing relationship between text and narrator, narrator and reader, reader and world. Open-ended narratives, double-voicing, ironic destabilization, constant shifts in the mode of representing the textual world, and the dissolution of traditional boundaries between literary genres and different art forms place the reader in relation with an unfamiliar world, a text that is other and requires the formation of new interpretive patterns and an active reader response that enters into dialogue with the work. Lower-class protagonists in Baroja, Galdós, Pardo Bazán, or Dicenta, feminist characters who challenge the bourgeois world of the reader in Pardo Bazán, Unamuno, Azorín, or the Martínez Sierras, *indianos* who invert traditional notions of the successful economic colonizer, and revisions of history that rewrite conventional narratives of national formation place the modernist reader in a position of alterity with national cultural traditions and move him/her toward new ways of thinking and being. The introduction of novel temporalities, altered spatial configurations, unconventional visions of human subjectivity, and unusual linguistic and textual forms has the same goals and effects.

Texts with ties to decadentism, such as Bargielo's *Luciérnagas,* Valle-Inclán's *Femeninas* or *Sonatas,* introduce first-person narrators who represent values and relate actions repugnant to the middle-class reader and require a continual adjustment of emotional relation to the fictive world and the self. Leopoldo Alas, Baroja, Pérez de Ayala, Miró, Pardo Bazán, Galdós, Valle-Inclán, and many others at times bring the reader into a relation of empathy or equality with the materials presented and at times establish distance and emotional detachment. For some critics, the shift from what Barthes has called the readable, *lisible* text and the writerly, *scriptible* text coincides with the arrival of postmodernism,[13] but as Culler, Waugh, and others point out,[14] all texts contain a balance of conformity with inherited literary conventions that enables the reader to comprehend the work and of rupture that forces the reader to question received codes and create a new response. Spanish modernist texts break the illusion of the seamless world of fiction and directly confront the reader with the need to adopt new interpretive perspectives and subject positions while carrying forward certain traditional relations between reader and text, self and other. Eysteinsson has pointed out the presence in modernist texts of a realist subtext that enables the reader to make sense of the non-mimetic presentation of materials (1990, 218). In Spanish modernism, authors link back to classical Spanish literature and popular culture as well as to realist codes in a continual play of repetition and difference that forces the reader to build on and break with inherited habits of reception.

The active role of the reader receives textual expression in works that directly incorporate the reader within the text, which occurs in works by Azorín, Miró, Unamuno, as well as plays by Benavente. His prologue to *Cuento de primavera* (1892) places Ganimedes on stage addressing the theatrical audience in a metatheatrical doubling of audience as character and virtual public. Ganimedes warns the spectators to abandon traditional receptive codes, telling those who want pure entertainment to leave before the play starts and similarly dismissing those who would adopt a purely analytical relationship with the material. Instead he advocates a collaborative role between audience and author: "En suma: que colaboréis con él tanto, que al fin del espectáculo las ideas que de él esparcidas queden en vuestra idea os parezcan allí mismo nacidas, y más vuestras que suyas; de este modo la obra ha de pareceros excelente, como obra, al fin, más vuestra que suya" [In summary, may you collaborate with him so much that at the end of the performance the ideas that he disseminates and that remain in you seem to have arisen naturally and to be more yours than his. In this way the work will strike you as excellent, like a work, in the final analysis, that is more yours than his] (1945, 1:365). The textual emphasis on the active role of the reader as creator of meaning through engagement with the text also surfaces in *La noche del sábado,* where the reader appears as one among the list of characters on the opening page of the text.

Numerous modernists explicitly theorize on the need to form a new readership through the utilization of changing stylistic and textual methods. Darío's "A un poeta" (1890) calls on the writer of poetry to create a language that sounds strange to the reader and creates a struggle between text and receiver. Unamuno works continuously to defamiliarize standard language, pointing out the gaps in Spanish that reveal the ideological biases propagated in daily communication. The absence of a female equivalent of "fraternal" in Spanish forms the basis of a significant segment of his prologue to *La tía Tula* (1921) and his continual play with words, such as *recrear* in the sense of to remake and to entertain in the prologue to *Tres novelas ejemplares y un prólogo* (1920) responds to a similar desire to force the reader to question fundamental presuppositions about language and reality. Unamuno and Baroja purposefully adopt a belligerent attitude toward the reader to force a response from their public. Baroja's use of what Ortega called the *improperio* seeks to provoke an answer and Unamuno similarly launches assaults designed to produce a reaction. Other writers prefer more cordial communication, inviting the reader to join in the experience of the text or interrupting the story to direct a question to her/him.

Baroja and Unamuno specifically refer to future readers, and imagine a continually changing relationship with a public that will enter into a different dialogic communication with them in a transformed cultural context. Baroja states in *Juventud, egolatría* that he hopes the reader in another 30 years will be more in tune with his message and style and Unamuno imagines a different conversation with future readers in several poems. In "Cuando yo sea viejo" of his 1907 *Poesías,* the poetic speaker projects that when he is older he will return to the poems he presently composes and will not recognize the self he finds there. Moreover, he imagines that future readers will argue with his readings of his compositions and will discover meanings in his texts that he never considered. In a clear understanding of the continual revising of the canon and of antecedent texts, he writes that poems only live on if they say something other than what the poet wrote.

The Reader Now: Critic as Other

As I detailed in the initial chapter, subsequent readings of the poetry of Unamuno and the artistic production of his modernist contemporaries have passed through various stages. The early emphasis on a pluralistic reading of modernist art and late nineteenth, early twentieth-century culture continued through the early decades of this century with some opposition from residual nineteenth-century writers and thinkers and from the powerful Ortega y Gasset, who at times coincides with but more frequently contests modernist views of nation, gender, subject, and language. Ortega y Gasset's voice grows in authority during the 1920s, as formalist theories of art gain ascendancy in a period of anxiety over growing division between a fascist right and socialist/communist left. In Spain, this crisis plays out in the Spanish Civil War and the Franco victory accompanies a rewriting of Spanish modernism that erases the aspiration to dialogue, diversity, reconnection with a multicultural past to produce a reading that highlights centralism, opposition to modernity, and stasis.

Criticism in the post-Franco period almost invariably stands in opposition to Francoist values and ideology, but often reiterates the same judgements of the modernist period propounded by supporters of Franco. Rafael Gutiérrez-Girardot and Jo Labanyi condemn the "Generation of 1898" for the same reasons that Laín Entralgo and Díaz-Plaja exalted them. In a contemporary extension of the globalizing forces that contributed to the origins and development of Spanish modernism, the debate over its characteristics and significance continue to play out on the international cultural stage. In the reevaluation of the Spanish-American War and its aftermath, citizens of different cultures have a stake in the discussion. Latin Americans who continue to work towards full cultural, economic, and political independence bring one perspective to the debate while North Americans have their own pressing need to reexamine the United States's complicity in the changing empires that have continued to evolve over the last century. Europe, with which Spain shares a complex relation of identity and difference, continues to exclude Spain in its discussions of early twentieth-century culture and Spain sits uneasily in her position as member of the European Community while still cultivating an evolving relation with her former colonies in Spanish America.

The conflicted relations between the various constituencies involved in the reconsideration of cultural changes occurring in the critical period of late nineteenth and early twentieth-century culture need to be brought to the surface and addressed directly. The erasure of history and of personal perspective presumes an unmediated access to "truth" that disregards current understanding of language, subjectivity, and their interrelations with the external world. Students of global modernism working within an

Anglo-European tradition bring certain inherited visions of the place of Spain in their shared heritage, just as Spanish critics writing within Spain enter the dialogue at an assigned moment in Spanish national development. Native-born Spaniards who reside in the United States for political or economic reasons have their own contentious relation with the culture of their birth and that of their residence, which impacts the tone and focus of their scholarship and teaching. As an Anglo-Saxon North American woman who has devoted her life to the study of Spanish culture and derived tremendous personal and professional pleasure from Spain, its people, and its culture, my approach to Spanish modernism necessarily reflects a complex personal and culturally specific relation. In working out my own position with respect to Spain and Spanish modernism, I have been heavily influenced by the theorization of alterity developed by Spanish modernist writers and subsequent criticism and theory.

The insistence on dialogue and the adoption of multiple subject positions advocated by Spanish modernists resurfaces in Levinas's ethics of heteronomy and Bammer's cautionary remarks about the equal dangers of a phobic and philic relation to the other. The relationship between critic and text, whether individual or collective cultural product, replicates that of self and other and carries the same ethical responsibility. The phobic rejection of individual writers or an entire group of writers and works in one homogenizing sweep fails to recognize the tensions and heterogeneous forces that constitute culture at any given moment. Similarly, philic assimilation of the other, by the imposition of the identity of the observer or the erasure of difference through the observer's absorption into the other, effaces diversity and disallows dialogue. I have tried in this study to avoid both phobic rejection and philic assimilation of individual writers and of the period in its totality. The organization of the study into different thematic subjects allows for the reintroduction of writers and texts from various perspectives and the consideration of the same work or writer as both a proponent and opponent of modernist visions of reality. Within the discussion of empire, nation, time, space, subjectivity, and language, I have sought to tease out the conflicting responses of individual writers and of the collective modernist voice in their response to changing global, national, and individual conditions. While contemporary studies of culture, power, nation, time, space, class, gender, and language have provided me with invaluable conceptual and discursive tools for working out a different vision of Spanish modernism, it is in the Spanish modernist texts themselves that I have found the richest expression of innovative and transformative thinking on topics that continue to concern us as we move into the next century. Spanish modernism continues to offer models for transcultural interaction, intersubjective relation, and artistic exploration that speak to us today if we allow ourselves to enter into the dialogue to which it invites us.

Notes

Chapter 1. Modernism and Its Borders

1. The reference to Murcia invokes the long occupation of parts of Spain by Moors and peoples of African origin.

2. I use the terms global or international modernism in keeping with studies that trace artistic reflections of social, economic, and scientific transformations occurring throughout the world during this period.

3. Germán Gullón (1992) argues this position with respect to Galdós, Clarín, Unamuno, Ganivet, Baroja, Valle-Inclán, and Azorín in *La novela moderna en España,* and C. Christopher Soufas, Jr. calls for an overall identification of the literature of the early twentieth century in Spain with modernism as a general period concept (1998, 465).

4. Studies that privilege this vision of modernism include Bradbury and McFarlane (1978, 1991), Brooker (1992), Chefdor (1986), DeKoven (1991), Eysteinsson (1990), and Fokkema (1986).

5. Eysteinsson (1990) bases his decision on Ned Davison's *The Concept of Modernism in Hispanic Criticism* (1966), which presents a now surpassed vision of Hispanic modernism. Even within his synthesis of critical definitions of Spanish American modernism, Davison emphasizes a great diversity of opinion and devotes considerable time and space to considerations of the recent "epochal" conception of modernism, which bears important similarities to Eysteinsson's vision. Eysteinsson ignores this link, excluding Hispanic modernism as separate and distinct.

6. The elision of Picasso's Spanish roots surfaces consistently in studies of contemporary art and culture. Chefdor (1986) states that he could only have created "Les demoiselles d'Avignon" in France, although he had been there for only a few years when he painted it and its subject matter is Spanish. I will discuss the painting and its connections with Spanish modernism in chapter 2.

7. I am guided by Rita Felski (1995) and her definitions of modernization, modernity, and modernism (12–13). Modernization refers to the confluence of socioeconomic features (such as scientific and technological advancement, industrialization, urbanization, capitalism, and nationalism) that spread from the West to the rest of the world. Modernity designates the historical period that introduces secularism and individualism in opposition to traditional culture. Modernism represents the artistic response to late modernity that arose at the end of the nineteenth century.

8. The references are not immediately apparent, since they are indexed under Gasset, José Ortega y. Such errors make somewhat more forgivable the

comical mistake of a third year university student who on a final exam identified Ortega y Gasset as two famous philosophers.

9. A recent article by Nelson Orringer (1998), while presenting a very different classification and nomenclature for the period, also includes the early Ortega y Gasset among writers often designated as belonging to the preceding "generation."

10. This reading appears in the critical edition of Machado's text by Celma Valero and Blasco Pascual (1981) and in studies of Azorín by José-Carlos Mainer (1988) and Priscilla Pearsall (1986), among many others.

11. For definitions of Catalan modernism, see studies by Arthur Terry (1972, 1995), Oriol Bohigas in *Actas del Congreso Internacional sobre Modernismo* (1987), Cacho Viu (1988), or Valenti (1973). As I make clear in my discussion of Catalan modernism, I see the cultural movements of late nineteenth- and early twentieth-century Spain as related components of a national and international search for new modes of thinking about and representing the world.

12. I include Rubén Darío, Gómez Carrillo, and other Spanish American writers and critics who visited and published in Spain and Europe, not in an effort to subsume them within Spanish modernism, but as participants in the dialogue that occurred at this time regarding Spanish national reconstruction in relation with Europe and the Americas.

13. Sources for information on Castilian and Catalan modernist collaborations include Celma Valero (1989), Salaün and Robin (1991), and Ribbans (1993).

14. Díaz-Plaja includes this quotation in his study of Catalan modernism, which he appends to *Modernismo frente a Noventa y ocho* (1966, 337). In a revealing case of critical blindness, Díaz-Plaja ignores the presence of the adjective "virility," which flies in the face of his insistent description of Catalan and Castilian modernism as feminine in contrast to the masculine Generation of 1898.

15. See *Voices, Silences and Echoes: A Theory of the Essay and the Critical Reception of Naturalism in Spain* (1992) for further information on this subject.

16. Jiménez's description of Darío replicates Darío's self-portrait and in both cases, the emphasis on indigenous heritage signals the acceptance of a pluralist cultural formation.

17. Bernardo Gicovate makes such a statement in "Antes del modernismo" (1974, 90–91).

18. Even writers presumably sympathetic to a global vision of Hispanic modernism fall into a more restricted rhetorical tradition. Donald Fogelquist provides a sympathetic study of modernism, but also includes disparaging comments regarding its superficial beginnings and posits its evolution toward the expression of what is profoundly Spanish and universal (1986, 331). The echoes of Salinas's categorization of a superficial modernism and authentic generation of 1898 are evident.

19. Bakhtin's theory of the dialogic character of language informs this approach to the critical reception of modernism. In *Voices, Silences and Echoes,* I developed a theory of the essay based on such a view of language and textuality and this definition of essayistic discourse forms the basis for the discussion of the essays dealt with in *Encounters across Borders.* In the earlier study, I argued for the use of the term "text speaker" in order to break with a tendency to interpret statements made in essayistic discourse as unequivocal, univocal expressions of authorial opinion. I will also use "text speaker" in the present study, but at times I will introduce the author's name to help the reader keep

track of the writer under discussion. This does not imply a change in my vision of the essay and its dialogic nature; rather, I hope to facilitate the task of reading in a work that covers many authors and texts.

20. See Valle-Inclán (1987), Azorín (1904b), and González Blanco (1907c).

21. See Baroja (1946–48, 2:203–4) and Valle-Inclán (1987).

22. Litvak incorporates Deleito y Piñuelo's article in *El Modernismo* (1986) as an example of anti-modernism. Although it offers strong criticism of certain aspects of modernism, it does so in the context of attempting to channel other aspects for a socially progressive movement.

23. Many studies show how global modernism eschews past master narratives that offer totalizing explanations for life and the human experience. Marshall Berman's suggestive title, *All that is Solid Melts into Air* (1982), communicates the impossibility of stable, enduring definitions within the modernist experience. Spanish modernism openly expresses this same repudiation of overarching systems and attempts at homogeneity, but critics have typically interpreted such statements as examples of confusion or weakness rather than a defining characteristic of the period.

24. Translation by Alan S Trueblood (1982, 101).

25. Critics who have taken these statements as evidence of a rejection of modernism by Machado and Darío include Leopoldo de Luis (1988) and Fiodor Kelin (1968).

26. Carl Cobb (1971), among others, interprets Unamuno's words as a clear rejection of "art for art's sake." This reading does not take into account the dialogism that characterizes modernist writing and its openness to the other.

27. Nordau defines abulia, or lack of will, as characteristic of the decadent personality that he studies in *Degeneration* (1968). Spanish modernists, both those traditionally associated with decadentism and those aligned with regenerationism, work to promote an energetic, active reader.

28. Peter Bly interprets the allusions to dream and beauty as utopian statements that hide a profound disbelief in the possibilities for change (1998, 133). Such a reading disregards the modernist belief in the power of art and the word to transform society, here combined with concrete regenerationist recommendations.

29. Celma Valero and Blasco Pascual continue this tradition in their critical edition of the text.

30. Mainer (1988), Pearsall (1986), and Iglesias Feijoo (1999) are only three of many critics who repeat this view.

31. Translation by Alan S Trueblood (1982, 105).

32. Fuentes (1995) lists 1934 as the date for "El concepto de generación literaria" and does not mention the second article at all in his study. Salinas left Spain in 1936 for a teaching position at Wellesley and remained in the United States until his death in Boston in 1951.

33. Significantly, the internal division of Spain into *noventayochista* and modernist geographic areas largely coincides with regions that supported Franco during the Spanish Civil War (*noventayochista*) and those that supported the Republic (modernist), with the exception of the Republican capital Madrid and the more ambivalent Basque countries, whose relations with the Republican government were strained.

34. Labanyi is one of the most interesting and intelligent scholars working in contemporary Spanish literature and culture and while I disagree with her conclusions in the article under discussion, I generally admire her work and her contribution to Hispanic scholarship, She herself has publicly spoken of a revi-

sion in her view of Spanish writers and their representation of the past at a lecture delivered at Rutgers University, March 31, 2000.

Chapter 2. Changing Empires

1. Spanish control of various enclaves in Northern Africa continues into the twentieth century. Although these territories do not participate in the same level of mutual cultural and economic exchange of other former colonies, they influence national and foreign policy in important ways over the next decades.

2. Information on trade relations between Spain and Cuba comes from Ubieto, et al. (1971) and Carr (1970).

3. See, for example, R. Becerro de Bengoa (1892, 22) or G. Reparaz (1893).

4. The spate of publications that appeared during the centennial continue this same rhetoric. See Cacho Viu (1997), Romero Tobar (1998), and Mainer and Gracia (1998).

5. A more complete discussion of Cuban slavery and the Spanish response to it can be found in Raymond Carr (1970) and Ubieto, et al. (1971).

6. Noel Valis (1993) has pointed out the conjoining of negative and positive attributes in the protagonist's name, including peace/war and life/death. I would add that it signals his mercurial nature as well as the paradoxical melding of church and state, slavery and Christianity, brutality and protection, that constitutes the Conquest.

7. This reading differs considerably from that offered by Catherine Jagoe (1995), who sees the novel as fearful of progress and hybrid gender forms. Like other modernist novels, *Angel Guerra* does not articulate a full program of social reform, but it explores possibilities for change that implicitly and explicitly repudiate traditional social, economic, and cultural values and institutions.

8. See Antonio Llopis y Pérez's study and edition of Salmerón's political speeches (1915, 346–50) and Altamira's *Manual de Historia de España* (1946).

9. José-Carlos Mainer's 1988 study of the period also cites writers and texts that advocate active military, economic, or a more genteel cultural imperialism. Many of his examples are political figures, but others are writers or intellectuals. While it is important to recognize that the weight of past military and colonial glory and the habits of speech and thought that accompany it often intrude even in writers and thinkers who combat colonial and militarist aspirations, there exists a considerable current of modernist writing that struggles against the national tradition in search of both a new discourse and a new way of relating with former colonies.

10. Subirats reiterates these ideas in *Después de la lluvia: Sobre la ambigua modernidad española.*

11. Domingo Ynduráin characterizes Ganivet's *La conquista del reino de maya* as a Nietzschean justification of conquest and hence colonialism (1988), but that text also includes overt anti-colonialist statements as well as multiple subtextual challenges to the European justification of empire. I do not view it as a contradiction of *Idearium español,* but rather a correlative text.

12. Pérez Triana in *Helios* exemplifies progressive opposition to United States racism in contrast to other more nationalist statements (1903).

13. John Butt (1993, 41) excludes both Blasco Ibáñez and Pío Baroja from his expanded definition of modernism and although I concur with his view of

Blasco, I very much disagree regarding Baroja, as I make clear in subsequent chapters.

14. Mainer (1997) notes the importance of illegitimacy in Galdós's theater and alludes to changing relations of class and gender, but does not relate them to the revision of history and of relations with the colonies that I am tracing here.

15. In yet another destabilizing move that welcomes alternative traditions, the text adopts the Jewish concept of matrilineal inheritance to deconstruct European patriarchal norms.

16. I am indebted to Hoon Kim, who first called my attention to the problem of the gaze in this novel in a graduate paper that he wrote in a course on Spanish modernism.

17. Gilbert and Gubar trace this process in nineteenth-century English-speaking women writers.

18. The *huipil* was apparently imposed by Spanish missionaries and then remarked as native by the elaborate weaving of patterns and colors. For the reader of the novel, it represents a mark of difference that Valle-Inclán deconstructs through comparison to Andalusian clothing.

19. Litvak (1985) points to comparisons between Chole and the exotic East as reflecting the belief that indigenous Americans and Asians share a common ancestry. I would emphasize that the comparison between Lilí, Bradomín's European love interest, and Chole, the indigenous American, breaks down racial borders in the present, and not just in a remote past.

20. Pieropán (1989) also recognizes the differences between these two versions of the story, without suggesting their importance for a rewriting of Spanish imperialist traditions.

21. This reading of a revised male gaze differs considerably from Luis Fernández Cifuentes's study of the Latin American and Spanish vision of Paris (1998), which I review more fully in chapter 5.

22. Levinas builds on Buber's work to theorize intersubjectivity as a reciprocal ethical responsibility between the I and the Thou in the first three essays of *Outside the Subject* (1993).

23. Roberta Johnson expresses this view in *Crossfire* (1993) with specific reference to *Doña Inés* and Ortega y Gasset characterizes Azorín's work as the immobilization of nature and life in his "Azorín: Los primores de lo vulgar" (1965).

24. I concur with Gonzalo Navajas (1998, 284) on this point, but wish to emphasize the staking out of new ground that neither adopts a philic appropriation of the other nor glorifies European imperialistic identity.

25. Scott Lash (1991) defines foundationalism as "the opposite of self or autonomous legislation." Its authority comes from another, universal source, such as reason or God (9). Modernism is antifoundationalist, rejecting theological, scientific, philosophical, or other totalizing visions.

26. Sipsom's statement both represents and parodies the modernist tenet of relative aesthetic values, in yet another example of the constantly revolving coin.

27. It is interesting to note the cultural accuracy of Benavente's depiction of African custom. Those who view his work as escapist and bourgeois have not paid adequate attention to this and other texts that reveal a changing view of the other and a concern with faithful depiction of others' culture. Marcelino Peñuelas (1968) represents this tendency when he classifies the work as a fantasy play, stripping it of its political and social implications.

28. See for example Luis Fernández Cifuentes (1982, 111–12).
29. Fusi and Palafox (1997, 185) attribute Spanish neutrality in World War I to impotence and indifference, but many of the writers and intellectuals invoke an impassioned anti-imperialism as good reason for remaining outside the conflict.
30. This same vision of the writers of the period continues in *Después de la lluvia* by Eduardo Subirats (1993) and " Cartografías del 98" by Luis Fernández Cifuentes (1998).
31. The changing Andalusian stereotype from the happy, exotic land of nineteenth-century texts to the tragic, gloomy land of twentieth-century works reflects the historicized nature of the other.
32. As in the case of Maeztu, I would like to stress the importance of distinguishing between the fascist posture of the later d'Ors and these earlier acclamations of modernist outlook.
33. Ortega y Gasset states this view in "Arte de este mundo y del otro" and also in *Meditaciones* (1990, 132).
34. Even in *La ben plantada,* in which d'Ors argues for a classical, harmonious form to represent the ideal Catalan woman, the text introduces multiple features that undermine the supposed balance, not the least of which are the use of the Castilian name Theresa for the exemplary Catalan woman and the designation of Uruguay as her birthplace.
35. Translation taken from Evelyn Rugg and Diego Marín's *Meditations on the Quijote* 98.
36. These ideas appear both in "Las Atlántidas" and "El sentido histórico."
37. Sofía Casanova also rejects the exaltation of Greek culture of some of her contemporaries, pointing out in her poem "El Gineceo" that the culture of Beauty and Art had its basis in slavery and exploitation (*Fugaces* 95–97).
38. Max Nordau, an important influence on Baroja, publishes an article in *El Nuevo Mercurio* in which he debunks racial theories of Gobineu, Richard Wagner, Houston Stewart Chamberlain.
39. Unamuno states this opinion in "La otra España" and also in *En torno al casticismo.*
40. See, for example, "Los pueblos civilizados" and "Indiferencia."

Chapter 3. Nation, History, and the Past as Other

1. A number of contemporary writers on literature and philosophy have dealt with the changing perception of time during the period under consideration. Those that most directly inform these introductory comments include Art Berman, Stephen Kern, Scott Lash, and Richard Sheppard.
2. As E. Inman Fox and others have demonstrated, *intrahistoria* has its roots in Krausist and Institutionist visions of history. Often presented as Unamuno's invention, it develops over the last decades of the nineteenth century in the work of many different writers. It rejects traditional emphasis on military battles, political systems, and rulers (the surface or conscious level of history) to focus on the substrate or unconscious, the everyday lives of the common people.
3. A quotation from Menéndez y Pelayo included in *La invención de España* reveals the passion underlying these beliefs and the staunch rejection of a pre-Catholic Spain, as in the Roman or Arab periods. The style of expression, with echoes of a litany in the repetition of attributes, reenforces a Catholic outlook: "España, evangelizadora de la mitad del orbe, España martillo de herejes, luz

de Trento, espada de Roma, cuna de San Ignacio . . . ; ésa es nuestra grandeza y nuestra unidad; no tenemos otra. El día en que acabe de perderse, España volverá al cantonalismo de los arévacos y de los vetones o de los reyes de Taifas . . . " [Spain, evangelizer of half the globe, Spain, scourge of heretics, light of Trent, sword of Rome, cradle of St. Ignatius . . . ; this is our greatness and our unity; we have no other. The day that we lose it, Spain will return to the cantonalism of pre-Roman tribes or of the Moorish kings . . .] (188).

4. The term appears in italics in the original Italian in the Aguilar *Obras completas,* while it is given a hispanized spelling in the Caro Raggio and Espasa-Calpe editions. In either case, the word retains its foreign origin and membership in a cultured, specialized lexicon.

5. Lissorgues and Salaün refer to the modernist disruption of established modes of reception through the use of enjambment and unusual distribution of pauses and syntagmatic sequences (1991, 189). They do not mention the relationship between these innovations and new perceptions of time, an important element in the creation and reception of the modernist lyric.

6. "La enseñanza de la historia" begins in the March 31 issue and continues into April of 1891.

7. Studies of Unamuno's definition of *intrahistoria* typically emphasize the metaphor of the sea, with the surface waves as representing history and the ocean depths *intrahistoria,* generally glossing over the first-mentioned metaphor of the rushing river. See, for example, Peggy Watson's *Intra-historia in Miguel de Unamuno's Novels.* The rushing river and rich sediment that it carries with it suggest movement and change and a much more rapid temporal succession than the metaphor of the sea.

8. In contrast with other texts, *En torno al casticismo* places greater emphasis on the role of the *pueblo* in this bidirectional process. The ambiguous meaning of the term, denoting either "people," "nation," or "lower classes," suits Unamuno's purposes and helps to break down the barriers that normally separate social classes and urban and rural populations. Many critics assume that *pueblo* in Unamuno refers exclusively to the rural lower classes, but the bulk of his narrative work deals with the "people" of urban and small town settings, either middle or lower class, and a broader definition of the term allows for a more complete connection between his theoretical writings in essayistic discourse and his creative production.

9. Inman Fox emphasizes the Castile-centered nature of Unamunan reconstructions of nation. I find the insistence on medieval culture to reflect a vision of nation as rooted in a more dynamic interplay of races, religions, and regional authorities. Later in the chapter, I will deal more fully with Unamuno's rejection of Castilian hegemony over regional identity.

10. In their study *Ideología y texto en El cuento semanal,* the research group of the University of Paris identifies the publication with mainstream values. Although most of the stories published do not overtly challenge bourgeois ideology, many include a transgressive tendency that either interweaves with or openly defies more orthodox thinking.

11. See, for example, Seone and Manuel Gil, among others.

12. Lima emphasizes the movement's aesthetic appeal in his biography of Valle-Inclán (1988, 86).

13. This same expression appears in an early essay and novel by Baroja, an intertextual link I discuss further in the final chapter of this study.

14. Tension between advocates of regional autonomy and defenders of strong central power dates from the early days of the Hapsburg dynasty and continues

through the present, flaring with considerable force in the early 1870s with the Carlist upheaval in the north, cantonalism in the south, and a central government that foundered in large part on this very question.

15. Critics who accuse modernists of opposing regional autonomy fail to recognize the complex overlay of traditional and progressive discourses in discussions of the topic. Co-optation of calls for change remains an ever-present danger in late nineteenth and early twentieth century Spain, where multiple voices compete for the attention and loyalty of the reading public.

16. Iris Zavala observes similarities with Bakhtin's thought in her study of Unamunan dialogism.

17. See, for example, the studies by Cardwell (1984) and Gutiérrez Girardot (1983), among many others.

18. Rand (1956) began this emphasis, which continues in the recent work of Inman Fox.

19. Andreas Huyssen equates the culture of enlightened modernity with imperialism and identifies some forms of modernism with enlightened modernity (in Natali, 1993, 148) and Natali and Hutcheon reenforce this reading in the preface to part 3 of their anthology when they quote Stephen Slemon's equation of Eurocentrism, colonialism, empire, and the modern.

20. See Pratt (1992) or Corbey and Leerssen (1991a).

21. I trace the subtleties of this challenge in *Voices, Silences and Echoes* .

22. See "Berenice," "La sed de Cristo," and "El martirio de Sor Bibiana."

23. The information provided is historically accurate and reveals the modernist interest in foreign affairs and the availability of news about distant and lesser known areas of the world. The Bhãbist movement in Persia did attempt to assassinate Shah Naser od-Din. In this context, it is ironic that the text should present Avila as unreal, but not insinuate the same with regard to Persia.

24. See Clemessy (1981, 366), Hemingway (1983, 65), and Charnon-Deutch (1994, 65–67).

25. For further information, see Brody's *The Disease of the Soul* (1974). Sander Gilman points out that Karl Marx associates Jews, blacks and leprosy in describing his rival Ferdinand Lassale (1992, 181).

26. María del Carmen Simón Palmer (1990) writes that Acuña's father dies in 1883, some 10 years prior to the performance and publication of the play, in which case the sorrowful expression of what appears to be a recent loss appears even more clearly as a cover for another message.

27. Current studies of Calderonian drama underscore the complexities of his discourse and covert critique of the honor code contained in his texts. Valle-Inclán uses a more traditional reading of Calderón and Golden Age honor plays as a foil in order to underscore the need for a radical rethinking of the national past.

28. Tortella Casares et al. observe that after the Franco-Moroccan Treaty of 1912, Spain controlled five percent of Moroccan territory with approximately one million inhabitants while France counted five million Moroccans and the remaining land among its colonial possessions (1981, 494).

29. The insistence on a shared identity between Spain and North Africa also characterizes imperialist, militarist discourse during this period. The common tradition justifies Spanish claims to historical rights over North African lands and peoples. The discourse itself is neither intrinsically progressive nor regressive. As Felski observes, specific features in modernism are both repressive and liberating, dissident, and conformist. In the particular case of similarity be-

tween Spanish and North African lands, cultures, and peoples, the context in which the argument is put forth must be considered in determining the ideological implications.

30. Spanish modernism largely overlooks the gypsy in the reconsideration of marginalized or forgotten subcultures. The Martínez Sierras criticize Spanish mistreatment of the gypsy in "Por el sendero florido" in *Teatro de ensueño* and Gabriel Miró sensitively describes the issue in *Los pies y los zapatos de Enriqueta.* Dicenta's "Del Camino," published in *El cuento semanal,* communicates this message to a wider audience.

31. Unamuno extends a warm embrace to Machado and once more illustrates the shared purpose of these writers who felt linked in a common cause and welcomed a diversity of strategies in the effort to transform Spanish literature and culture: "¿Por qué los que sentimos sobre nuestras diferencias—mi manera de poetizar es muy otra que la de Machado, y si yo intentara lo de él, lo haría tan mal como si el intentase lo mío,—por qué los que sentimos sobre nuestras diferencias unos inmensos brazos impalpables que nos ciñen en uno, por qué no hemos de apretarnos en haz de hermandad contra la tropa de los bárbaros a los que une su barbarie?" [Why should we who feel above and beyond our differences—my manner of writing poetry is very different than that of Machado, and if I tried his way, I would do it as badly as if he tried my way,—why should we who feel above and beyond our differences some immense, impalpable arms that encircle us as one, why should we not close ranks in brotherly unity against the troop of barbarians that are joined in their barbarity?] (quoted in "Variedades y revista de revistas" 7:826).

32. Schyfter (1978, 78) assumes he is a Sephardic Jew, while Casalduero calls him an Arab follower of Judaism (1974, 228).

33. Peter Bly refers to sexual desire on the part of Almudena, which he judges impedes a spiritual relationship with Benina (1998, 128). While Almudena expresses a desire to enter into a marital, sexual relationship, he abandons such thoughts when Benina informs him that she is too old for such an arrangement. The ease with which he assumes a more fraternal role and his blindness work against the tradition of the male gaze.

Chapter 4. Modern Times

1. See, for example, Lily Litvak (1980, 11ff) and Graham and Labanyi (1995, 12–13).

2. Aureliano Beruete's study arguing the dual Velázquez-del Mazo authorship of the Prado painting predates Machado's poem by several years.

3. Although the validity of scientific theories espoused in Baroja's novels matters less than the impact of conflicting theories on his thinking, it is worth noting that recent studies of the Galapagos finch by Peter and Rosemary Grant, reported in Jonathan Weiner's *The Beak of the Finch,* confirm the existence of sudden evolutionary changes. Stephen Jay Gould defends this view in a number of works and in particular, in his 1972 co-authored article with N. Eldredge.

4. In contrast with Michael Ugarte's insistence on a negative, pessimistic message in the trilogy (1996), I find a constant oscillation between criticism and hope, failure and new possibilities.

5. Excellent studies on the use of time, memory, and their relation to Machado's theory of poetry and communication can be found in the work of Cobb (1971), Guillén (1971), Ricardo Gullón (1958), and Havard (1988). Building on

the findings of these and other critics, I will link Machado's vision of temporality and his poetic practice to a general modernist definition of time and its connection with individual and social change.

6. Havard, among others, emphasizes the connection between Bergson's notion of duration and Machado's rejection of linear time (1988, 78). In the present discussion, I wish to underscore the dual motion across temporality within the individual and between the individual and the collectivity. Machado recuperates his own past self and the reader's and nation's discarded selves and weaves them together in a poetics that is both personal and social, individual and collective.

7. Michael Predmore signals the danger of separating these periods and modalities into distinct, separate entities in "Un nuevo enfoque sobre la evolución de la poesía de Antonio Machado" (1981b).

8. Laín Entralgo begins this emphasis on a pessimistic reading of Machado in general and "A Orillas del Duero," in particular (1967, 25, 98–100, 129–30), which continues in Dolores Franco (418) and more recently in David Darst's introduction to the poem in *Sendas literarias: España* (1988).

9. Cobb (81) interprets the Duero as symbol of the outflow of people and the loss of the best Castilians to the new world. Alongside this signification, there also exists an emphasis on the river as connecting to the outside as a constructive feature in contrast to an inward-looking myopia.

10. In their study of Azorín, Carmen Hernández Valcárcel and Carmen Escudero Martínez view the idea of time as flow and time as eternal return as contradictory. The surface differences between the two temporalities disappear when seen as dual challenges to traditional religious time.

11. Translation from Betty Jean Craige.

12. Although the text leaves the entry into the convent unresolved, Curra's conversion and the daughter's repeated desire to expiate her family's sins point to such an outcome.

13. See Rafael María de Hornedos's publication of Menéndez y Pelayo's letters in *Razón y Fe* (1956).

14. Translation from Alan Trueblood.

15. Specific theorization and practice of this vision can be found in the "Los naturales y los espirituales" (1958, vol. 3), in the angry protestations of Augusto Pérez at Unamuno's unilateral decision to kill him off, and in the creation of characters who converse for the sake of conversing.

16. Glenn holds this view (1981, 19) as does E. Inman Fox in his introduction to *Antonio Azorín* (1970).

17. Glenn (1981) disagrees with E. Inman Fox's introduction to the 1970 Labor edition of *Antonio Azorín* and with José María Valverde (1971), who minimize the differences between the Azorín of the two texts. Building on Glenn's observations, I wish to point out the importance of the concept of eternal return to a reading of the character and the novels.

18. A complex example appears in the embedded story related by Azorín when a group of anarchists asks him to address them. Other cases occur in Azorín's description of his trip through the Castilian countryside as a reliving of classical texts or the dual depiction of the scandal ensuing from the noisy embrace of Azorín and Sarrió in a Madrid theater after an extended separation, first narrated as an episode in the novel and then repeated as related in a newspaper report.

19. In later works, the decadentist impulse cedes to the grotesque as the preferred mode to transcend the omnipotence of death. *Romance de lobos* con-

trasts the traditional superstition of the Galician peasantry who fear death and see it in the shadows of the night with a modern desire to look death in the face. Juan Manuel Montenegro insists on lifting the stone lid from his wife's crypt and leaving it off until he can join her in the tomb. *Las galas del difunto* represents a complete rejection of traditional respect for and fear of death. Juanito Ventolera, unlike his ancestor Juan Tenorio, refuses to bow to church messages of hell and damnation and coolly steals the medals and uniform of the dead pharmacist in order to score with a waiting date.

20. Lacan takes the concept of *glissement* from Saussure to denote the sliding of the signifier over the signified or more generally, of one system over another. See "L'Instance de la lettre dans l'inconscient ou la Raison depuis Freud" (1957) for a full discussion.

21. Landeira emphasizes these differences (1985, 62ff) as does Rosa Rossi (1967).

22. Johnson joins other critics in dismissing the concept of eternal return as having limited possibilities for change and renewal (1993, 72) and as I have argued throughout this section, in this respect I hold a different view.

Chapter 5. From the Subatomic to the Galactic: Modernist Spaces

1. See Kern (1983, 152) and Sheppard (1993, 14).

2. The mention of Espina in the same category as Baroja, the early Maeztu, and Azorín will undoubtedly provoke nervous denials or perhaps derisive laughter among quarters that continue to devalue women writers, to classify authors according to expressed religious conviction, and to presume that the political stance adopted by an individual during the Spanish Civil War marks all previous and subsequent writing. This critical tradition and its residue enforces a separation of late nineteenth- and early twentieth-century literature into distinct and separate movements and prefers to emphasize rivalry and petty jealousy over epochal similarity and common purpose. Feminist and postructuralist criticism have provided us with the tools to tease out the tensions within texts and to identify transgressive impulses among writers too easily discarded by previous criticism as marginal and unworthy of study. Cultural studies abjures evaluative judgements of texts and writers, recognizing the ideological biases that inform such judgements, and looks to literary and non-literary texts as a source of the stresses that define a given period and culture.

3. In my 1980 book on Concha Espina, I failed to see the full impact of this interaction with natural forces that Felski and recent psychoanalytical and feminist theories help to elucidate.

4. It is for this reason that I prefer to translate *trabajo* as "work" over Patricia O'Connor's use of "labor," using "work" as in physics to denote a measure of energy transfer when an object is moved by an external force. The Spanish term *trabajo* allows for both meanings, but the scientific focus of the text and the emphasis on energy and change support the use of the term as used both in physics and human endeavor.

5. See Ricardo Gullón's "Simbolismo y modernismo" in José Olivio Jiménez's *El simbolismo* (1979).

6. See John Wilcox's study (1987) for a discussion of the various periods in Jiménez's poetry.

7. Translation by Trueblood (1982).

8. Gayana Jurkevich has published excellent studies on the use of ekphrasis in Azorín and its relation to his use of time and space. See her article "A Poetics of Time and Space": Ekphrasis and the Modern Vision in Azorín and Velázquez."

9. For a discussion of *mise en abîme* see Gerhard Joseph (1985), Sylvia Tomasch (1985), and Jean Ricardou (1981).

10. The ideas expressed by Ortega recur throughout Azorinian criticism and most recently appear in the book by Carmen Hernández Valcárcel and Carmen Escudero Martínez (1986).

11. Tuberculosis appears with some frequency in texts of the period, at times associated with an urban environment, but on other occasions with a more rural setting. Andrés Hurtado's younger brother contracts the disease in Madrid, improves considerably under a strict regime of diet and sunshine in the country, and then relapses and dies in Valencia. Antonio Machado's young wife contracted the disease in the small town of Soria, fell ill in Paris, and died in Soria.

12. Fernandez Cifuentes's 1997 study of Spanish rejection of Paris makes no mention of Sawa, Picasso, or Rusiñol, all of whom represent, among other varied responses, an enthusiastic endorsement of Parisian life. I also find problematic his reconstruction of a vision of turn-of-the-century Paris in texts written by Spanish writers in the 1930s and 1940s and then compared to texts from the 1890s to early 1900s by Spanish American authors. The temporal jump and age difference between the authors at the time of writing their impressions is too great to authorize a comparison.

13. For more detail, see "Voices of Authority and Linguistic Autonomy in *Niebla.*"

14. Bakhtin studies the idyllic chronotope in *The Dialogic Imagination* (1981, 224ff).

15. Stephanie Sieburth's assumption that "Unamuno's intrahistorical women would be long-suffering women" (1994, 213) certainly does not describe the women of this text nor of many of his stories of rural or small-town society.

16. My 1993 study of *La tía Tula* analyzes the complex antipatriarchal arguments of the novel.

Chapter 6. Class and Gender in the Construction of Modernist Subjectivity

1. See my study *Voices, Silences and Echoes* for further information on the topic.

2. Laín Entralgo (1967) begins this trend, which is continued by Francisco José Martínez Martínez in his study of Machado (1989) and Jo Labanyi (1994).

3. The Spain of 1900 had a population of 18.5 million with 70% engaged in agriculture (Ubieto, 1971, 700–705) and through the first third of the twentieth century, the rural sector represents the critical element with respect to social policy (Ubieto, 1971, 813).

4. Eysteinsson (1990) has studied the persistence of realism as the prevailing cultural form against which modernism struggles but remains in a permanently oppositional relation.

5. Bammer's analysis of phobic and philic responses to the other (1995) accurately depicts the first two responses of Spanish writers to the lower classes outlined here.

6. See Graham and Labanyi (1995, 14) and also my own comments in *Voices, Silences and Echoes,* chapter 3.

7. Gagen (1999) views the novel as a sophisticated study of the complex relations between various sectors of the proletariat. While the novel may succeed in avoiding simplistic portrayals of cross-class animosities, the segregation of the rural lower-class world from the outside and from other classes allows only for self-destructive behaviors directed against those who share the same economic exploitation and lower-class conditions. The dispassionate tone of Blasco's narratives further distance the reader from a world that appears remote and impenetrable.

8. See Giddens (1991, 14–23) and Ortega y Gasset (1993, 68–76) for their discussions of a globalized modernity.

9. See Giddens (1991), Chapter 4 and Ortega y Gasset (1993, 76–81) for their discussion of risk and choice.

10. Giddens (1991) discusses the possibilities for individual and social emancipation in his closing chapter and Smith's entire study seeks to provide for agency and political resistance in a theory that recognizes the fluid character of modern subjectivity.

11. See Sawa's *Iluminaciones en la sombra* (1910, 23) and Roberto Hasting's comments in Baroja's *La busca* (1946–48, 1:291–92).

12. The theme reappears in Pardo Bazán's "La redada," published in 1900 in *Historias y cuentos de Galicia* but probably written earlier, as were other texts in the collection. "La redada" makes explicit the subtextual anxieties of *Memorias de un solterón,* with a first-person male narrator relating how he ended his engagement upon discovering his physical inferiority in comparison with a lower-class fisherman whose body his fiancée vocally admired (1990, 2:92–94).

13. Most critics judge this a pre-*esperpento,* with characteristics that grow more pronounced in later texts.

14. Leonardo Romero discusses this critical response in his introduction to the Castalia edition (1975).

15. Azorín's review of the play reveals the modernist rejection of Clarín's attitudes. He rebukes what he terms an archaic thesis and specifically links the vindication of the rights of workers and women, refusing to subordinate one to the other. Echoing Nietzschean repudiation of Christian resignation, he argues that turning the other cheek simply strengthens the oppressor (1947–48, 1:232).

16. For a more detailed study of Feíta's invention of a new language see my study "Text and Intertext in Emilia Pardo Bazán's *Memorias de un solterón.*"

17. Susan Kirkpatrick (1995, 96) and Paulette Wilson (1996, 85–87) have argued this point in their studies.

18. Male characters prove resistant to an altered view of honor. When Verónica rejects Travesedo's offer of marriage, he asks if it is because she has scruples about her past and does not really understand the significance of the look of surprise that accompanies her strong denial that such a motive has anything to do with her rejection of his proposal (1964–66, 1:812).

19. In "Espíritu recio," Pérez de Ayala offers one of the few cases where a middle-class woman and lower-class man enter into mutually desired sexual relations. However, the text mainly utilizes the lower-class male character as a counterpoint to middle class and church repudiation of sexuality. None of the

characters show evidence of intersubjective influence. To the contrary, they remain locked in opposing stances with regard to life, death, sexuality, and religion.

20. For a longer discussion of the interweaving of discourses and subjectivities in Nelken's study, see my essay in *Spanish Women Writers and the Essay: Gender, Politics and the Self.*

21. Critics, beginning with Clarín in *Folletos Literarios* (1888a) and continuing to some degree even in sympathetic readers like Lou Charnon-Deutsch (1994, 167–68), have questioned Asís's choice of Pacheco as a mate. Such a reading reflects in part a refusal of Pardo Bazán's underlying contention that a woman's value rests not in her selection of partner, but in her decision to take charge of the construction of her selfhood. On Clarín's part, it may also manifest an underlying discomfort with Pacheco's association with lower-class sexuality and values.

22. Graciano Martínez erroneously cites *Feminismo, feminidad, españolismo* as his source, confusing it with *Cartas a las mujeres de España* in an interesting case of homogenization of the other. One feminist text is the same as the next, irrespective of differences of format or title.

23. In yet another difference between Ortega y Gasset and other writers of the period, his vision of glass as having a single dimension stands in stark contrast with Machado's view of it as reflecting in and out, allowing passage through but resistant to absolute assimilation.

24. Later editions change feminine to puerile, revealing once again the links between woman, child, and primitive peoples already analyzed in other Ortegan texts.

25. I use the exclusive male possessive here for reasons that should be clear from the discussion.

26. Nordau's rejection of doubt and deviation from established definitions of gender relates to Echegaray's theater and explains his popularity among a public that shared such anxieties. Echegaray's theater presents women in traditional terms as the repository of male honor and destined to suffer. The plays typically end in melodramatic confrontations that produce an emotional and complete resolution to the limit situations that constitute the dramatic tension. *La duda* (1898) synthesizes rejection of contradiction, presenting doubt as literally driving the protagonist crazy and then incarnating it in her aunt, whom the main character kills at the end of the play. There is literally and figuratively no room for doubt on this stage.

27. Elaine Showalter's study of the New Woman appears in chapter 3 of *Sexual Anarchy.*

28. Portraits of many Spanish women writers of the nineteenth and early twentieth centuries are included in María del Carmen Simón Palmer's biobibliographic study.

29. See for example D. L. Shaw, who finds the absence of love scenes and the presence of friends on Sacha Savarof's honeymoons totally unconvincing (1975, 105).

30. Two famous examples of the tradition can be found in Bécquer's Rima XXVII, "Despierta, tiemblo al mirarte" and Neruda's sonnet "Me gustas cuando callas."

31. Eve Sedgewick's 1985 study of the homosocial bond, often constructed over the exchange of the female body, proves useful in the consideration of erotic writing, but does not fully explain the transgressive power of this literature.

32. Baroja's homophobic stance remains constant throughout his work, sur-

facing in his portrait of the sadistic lesbian Laura in *Camino de perfección* and continuing in mocking references to gay and lesbian characters in later novels.

Chapter 7. Masks and Mirrors: Modernist Theories of Self and/as Other

1. Belsey analyzes the appearance of the split subject in Renaissance literature (1980, 86–90).

2. Some theorists associate a divided, fluid subjectivity with postmodernism, in an effort to distinguish it from early periods. Zygmunt Bauman contrasts postmodern ambivalence, doubt, and plurality, both in the world and the self, with a modern obsession with sameness (1991, 98). Although Bauman does not specifically link modern(ity) with modernism, his placement of postmodernism in opposition to an overarching modern period that precedes it subsumes the period under study here within the general designation of modern(ity). Spanish modernism clearly embraces the view of the subject that Bauman identifies with postmodernism, and the same can be argued for other national literatures and international modernism in general.

3. Giner's theorization appears in Fernando de los Ríos Urruti's *La filosofía del derecho en don Francisco Giner* (1916, 17) and coincides with Ricoeur's discussion of sameness and selfhood or *idem* and *ipse,* which he develops in *Oneself as Another* (1992, 2–3 and 116ff).

4. The emperor's words at one point reflect an interesting hybrid discourse that contains both a rejection of traditional culture and a defense of inherited visions of subjectivity. He mocks his nephew's desire to be himself (conventional bourgeois view of the subject) rather than submit to the demands of society (rejection of bourgeois society). This inherited conceptualization of identity could reflect the emperor's own mentality or the continued power of inherited discourse and modes of thinking in a text that seeks to break with the past. Benavente's presentation of subjectivity in this and other texts suggests a theory of the self that abjures one, stable identity

5. Bakhtin's study of Dostoievsky (1984a) and Stallybrass and White's work on transgression (1986) both examine the significance of carnival and its relation to the themes presented here.

6. This unusual narrative stance evidently perplexed the editors of *La novela corta,* who gave the text the more conventional title "Un suicidio" on the magazine cover when it appeared in 1924.

7. Among others who emphasize this aspect of Baroja's work, Leo Barrow has an entire chapter on "Yoismo, Ego-identification, and Poetic Moments."

8. José Domingo continues the critical tradition that sees Sigüenza as Miró's alter ego in Díez Borque's *Historia de la literatura española* (1988, 103) while G. G. Brown underscores the frequency with which the novelist mocks his character (1972, 47).

9. Mervyn Coke-Enguídanos presents such a reading (1982, 47) and John Wilcox (1987) privileges this aspect in his definition of Jiménez's modern period, in which this poem appears.

10. I agree with Marco (1989) regarding an evolving vision of self as other in Machado.

11. See for example XV. "La calle in sombra . . . " of *Soledades* or LVI. "Sonaba el reloj la una" of *Humorismos, Fantasías, Apuntes.*

12. This translation comes from Robert Bly's *Times Alone.*
13. This translation comes from Alan Trueblood.
14. This translation also comes from Alan Trueblood.
15. "Renovación" and "Civilización y cultura" both express this concept.
16. Resistance to modern conceptualizations of the subject as multiple and self-contradictory continues in many critics, who insist on locating a stable, coherent Unamuno. Manuel Alvar describes such a subject in his prologue to Unamuno's *Poesías,* when he refers to his "armónica y ciclópea unidad" [harmonic and cyclopic unity] and his "exacta coherencia" [exact coherence] (1997, 21).

Chapter 8. Author, Text, and Reader: An End to Borders

1. I have purposely left the masculine pronoun used by Giner de los Ríos, who does not address the issue of women writers, but who very clearly identifies women readers as conservative, intransigent, and in need of male-directed reorientation (1908, 67).
2. See "Disonancias y armonías de la moral y de la estética: Al Señor don Salvador Rueda" (1891).
3. See Díaz-Plaja's *Modernismo frente a noventa y ocho* for a description of the protest and his tortured attempt to explain away the participation of members of what he sees as two discrete groups in a common enterprise (1966, 195–96).
4. Translation taken from Alan S Trueblood.
5. Villaespesa's poem is included in his 1909 *El libro de Job,* Manuel's "Retrato" opens his 1909 *El mal poema* and Antonio's appears as the lead poem in his 1912 *Campos de Castilla.*
6. For a full study of the interweaving of these different discourses see my study "Zalacaín el aventurero como aventura textual" in *Explicación de textos literarios.*
7. In my article on the essayistic production of Margarita Nelken, I trace the changing vision of the subject and its relation to essayistic discourse in greater detail. See "Margarita Nelken's *La condición social de la mujer en España:* Between the Pedagogic and the Performative."
8. See Salaün and Serrano (1991) for more detailed studies on these topics.
9. According to the 1878 prologue to the second edition of *Lecciones sumarias de psicología,* Giner undertook revisions motivated primarily by a desire for simpler, clearer expression (xiii).
10. See his early essays on the Basque language published in *Revista de Vizcaya* in 1886, later collected in his *Obras completas* or his later "Más sobre la lengua vasca" in *La Nación* (1907).
11. See among others the early work of Díaz Plaja (1966) and Laín Entralgo (1967) as well as the more recent studies of Celma Valero (1989) and Giovanni Allegra (1985).
12. See his article on "Morriña" in *Madrid Cómico* and on "Emilia Pardo Bazán y sus últimas obras" in *Folletos literarios.*
13. Mary Bittner Wiseman establishes such a taxonomy in her study of Barthes (1989, 86).
14. See Culler's *Structuralist Poetics* (1975, 190–91) and Waugh's *Metafiction* (1984, 6).

Works Consulted

Actas del Congreso Internacional sobre el modernismo español e hispanoamericano, Córdoba, October, 1985. 1987. Córdoba: Imprenta San Pablo.

Acuña, Rosario de. 1893. *La voz de la patria.* Madrid: R. Velasco.

Adam, Paul. 1907. Mis sensaciones de España. *Nuevo Mercurio.* (April): 363–79.

Aguirre, J. M. 1979. The Window as Symbol in Spanish Modernista Poetry: Outline of a Model. In *Waiting for Pegasus: Studies of the Presence of Symbolism and Decadence in Hispanic Letters,* edited by Roland Grass and William R. Risley, 103–24. Macomb: Western Illinois UP.

Alas, Leopoldo (Clarín) 1887. *Nueva campaña (1885–1886).* Madrid: Fernando Fe.

———.1888a. Emilia Pardo Bazán y sus últimas obras. *Folletos literarios.* Vol 7. Madrid: Fernando Fe.

———. 1888b. *Folletos literarios.* Vols. 4–5. Madrid: Fernando Fe.

———. 1889. Morriña. *Madrid Cómico* (November 23, 1889): 3, 6.

———. 1892. *Ensayos y revistas.* Madrid: Manuel Fernández y Lasanta.

———. 1893a. *Paliques.* Madrid: Librería de Victoriano Suárez.

———. 1893b. *El señor y los demás son cuentos.* Madrid: Manuel Fernández y Lasanta.

———. 1896. *Cuentos morales.* Madrid: La España Editorial.

———. 1966. *Su único hijo.* Madrid: Alianza.

———. 1975a. *Adiós, cordera y otros cuentos.* Madrid: Espasa Calpe.

———. 1975b *Teresa.* Edited by Leonardo Romero. Madrid: Castalia.

———. 1980a. *La Regenta.* Madrid: Alianza.

———. 1980b. *Superchería. Cuervo. Doña Berta.* Madrid: Taurus.

Albert I Paradis, Catalina. 1982. *Drames rurales.* Barcelona: Ediciones 62.

———. 1983. *Solitud.* Barcelona: Selecta.

———. 1984. *La infanticida I altres textos.* Barcelona: La Sal.

Al lector. 1907. *Renacimiento* 1:5–6.

Allegra, Giovanni.1985. *El reino interior: Premisas y semblanzas del modernismo en España.* Translated by Vicente Martín Pindado. Madrid: Ediciones Encuentro.

Alomar, Gabriel. 1907a. Futurismo. *Renacimiento* 5 (July): 257–76.

———. 1907b. Sobre el Quijote. *Renacimiento* 1:169–203; 265–84.

Alonso, Martín. 1968. *Diccionario del idioma.* 3 Vols. Madrid: Aguilar.

Altamira, Rafael. 1891. La enseñanza de la historia. *Boletín de la Institución Libre de Enseñanza* (March 31, 1890 to Sept. 15, 1891).

———. 1898. El patriotismo y la universidad. *Boletín de la Institución Libre de Enseñanza.* (Sept. 30, 1898): 257–70; (Oct. 15, 1898): 291–96; (Oct. 30, 1898): 323–27.

———. 1917? *La guerra actual y la opinión española.* Barcelona: Araluce.

———. 1946. *Manual de Historia de España.* Buenos Aires

———. 1976. *Psicología del pueblo español.* Madrid: Doncel.

Alvar, Manuel. 1997. Prologue. *Poesías* by Miguel de Unamuno. Madrid: Cátedra.

Anderson, Benedict. 1991. *Imagined Communities.* London: Verso.

Anderson, Perry. 1984. Modernity and Revolution. *New Left Review* 144: 96–113.

Arniches, Carlos. n. d. *Las estrellas. Teatro escogido.* Madrid: Editorial Estampa.

Ashcroft, Bill. 1989. *The Empire Writes Back: Theory and Practice in Post-Colonial Literatures.* London: Routledge.

Azcárate, Gumersindo. 1910. Carácter científico de la historia. *Boletín de la Institución Libre de Enseñanza* (April-May): 601–2.

———. 1967. *Minuta de un testamento.* Barcelona: Cultura Popular.

Bakhtin, Mikhail. 1981. *The Dialogic Imagination.* Translated by Caryl Emerson and Michael Holquist. Austin: University of Texas Press.

———. 1984a. *Problems of Dostoevsky's Poetics.* Translated by Caryl Emerson. Minneapolis, Minn.: University of Minnesota Press.

———. 1984b. *Rabelais and His World.* Translated by Helene Iswolsky. Bloomington: University of Illinois Press.

———. 1986. *Speech Genres and Other Late Essays.* Translated by Vern W. McGee. Austin: University of Texas Press.

———. 1993. *Toward a Philosophy of the Act.* Translated by Vadim Liapunov. Austin: University of Texas.

Balart, Federico. 1894. *Impresiones: Literatura y arte.* Madrid: Fernández Fe.

———. 1929. Salutación. *Poesía completa.* Vol. 2. Barcelona: Gustavo Gili.

Balbín de Unquera, Antonio. 1901. El discurso del Sr. Unamuno. *Gente Vieja* (Oct. 10): 8.

Bammer, Angelika. 1995. Xenophobia, Xenophilia, and No Place to Rest. In *Encountering the Other(s): Studies in Literature, History, and Culture,* edited by Gisela Brinker-Gabler. Albany: State University of New York Press.

Bargielo, Camilo. 1900. *Luciérnagas.* Madrid: J. Poveda.

Bark, Ernesto. 1901. *Modernismo.* Madrid: Biblioteca Germinal.

———. 1904. *Estadística social.* Barcelona: Lezcano y Compañía.

Baroja, Pío. 1901. Elizabelde el vagabundo. *La Lectura* 1:24.

———. 1946–1948. *Obras completas.* 8 vols. Madrid: Biblioteca Nueva.

———. 1967 *Las ciudades: César o nada. El mundo es ansí. La sensualidad pervertida.* Madrid: Alianza.

———. 1968? *El árbol de la ciencia.* New York: Las Américas.

———. 1969. *Camino de perfección.* New York: Las Américas Publishing House.

Barrow, Leo. 1971. *Negation in Baroja.* Tucson: University of Arizona Press.

Barthes, Roland. 1974. *S/Z.* New York: Hill and Wang.

Bauman, Zygmunt. 1991. *Modernity and Ambivalence.* Ithaca: Cornell University Press.

Bayo, Ciro. 1910. *El peregrino entretenido.* Madrid: Bailly-Baillere.

———. 1927. *Por la América desconocida.* Madrid: Caro Raggio.

———. 1965. *El lazarillo español.* Madrid: Espasa-Calpe.

Becerro de Bengoa, R. 1892. Por ambos mundos. *La Ilustración Española y Americana* 1 (January 8): 19, 22.

———. 1896. Por ambos mundos. *La Ilustración Española y Americana.* 46:350.

Behler, Ernst. 1990. *Irony and the Discourse of Modernity.* Seattle: University of Washington Press.

Belsey, Catherine. 1980. *Critical Pactice.* London: Routledge.

Benavente, Jacinto. 1893. La tienda de flores. In *Versos.* Madrid: Tipografía Franco-Española.

———. 1945. *Obras completas.* 6 vols. Madrid: Aguilar.

Benítez, Rubén. 1975. Introducción. In *Pequeñeces* by Luis Coloma, 9–43. Madrid: Cátedra.

Benjamin, Walter. 1968. *Illuminations.* Translated by Harry Zohn. New York: Harcourt, Brace and World.

Berenguer, Angel. 1988. El teatro hasta 1936. *Historia de la literatura española.* Vol 5. Edited by José María Díez Borque. Madrid: Taurus.

Bergson, Henri. 1911a. *Creative Evolution.* Translated by A. Mitchell. London: Macmillan.

———. 1911b. *Matter and Memory.* Translated by N.M. Paul and W. S. Palmer. London: Allen & Unwin.

———. 1972. *Mélanges.* Paris: Presses Universitaires de Frances.

Berman, Art. 1994. *Preface to Modernism.* Urbana: University of Illinois Press.

Berman, Marshall. 1982. *All that is Solid Melts into Air: The Experience of Modernity.* New York: Simon & Schuster.

Beruete, Aureliano de. 1898. *Velázquez.* Paris: Libraire Renouad.

Bhabha, Homi. 1990. DissemiNation: Time, Narrative, and the Margins of the Modern Nation. In *Nation and Narration,* edited by Homi Bhabha. London: Routledge.

Blanco Fombona, Rufino. 1908? *Letras y letrados de Hispanoamérica.* Paris: Ollendorf.

Blasco, Eusebio. 1895. *Juan León.* Madrid: Florencio Fiscowich.

Blasco Ibáñez, Vicente. 1961. *Obras completas.* 3 vols. Madrid: Aguilar.

Bloom, Harold. 1979. *The Anxiety of Influence.* London: Oxford University Press.

Bly, Peter. 1998. Benito Pérez Galdós: Noventayochista desencantado antes del 98. In *El camino hacia el 98.* Edited by Leonardo Romero Tobar, 117–38. Madrid: Visor.

Bly, Robert. 1973. *Times Alone.* Translation of *Soledades* by Antonio Machado. Port Townsend, Washington: Gray Wolf Press.

Bobadilla, Emilio. (Fray Candil). 1903. Desde mi celda: G. Nuñez de Arce. *Alma Española* (Nov. 8): 10.

Bohigas, Oriol. 1987. La arquitectura modernista: Renovación estilística y raíces ideológicas. In *Actas del Congreso Internacional sobre el modernismo espanol e hispanoamericano. Córdoba, October, 1985,* 143–68. Córdoba: Imprenta San Pablo.

Bordo, Susan. 1993. *Unbearable Weight.* Berkeley: University of California Press.

Bordonado, Angela Ena, ed. 1989. *Novelas breves de escritoras españolas (1900–1936).* Madrid: Castalia.

Bouchard, Andrée. 1988. *Los españoles ante las campañas de Marruecos.* Madrid: Espasa Calpe.

Bradbury, Malcolm and James McFarlane. 1978. *Modernism: A Guide to European Literature 1890–1930.* Sussex: Harvester Press.

———. 1991. 2d ed. London: Penguin Books.

Bretz, Mary Lee. 1987. Voices of Authority and Linguistic Autonomy in *Niebla. Studies in Twentieth-Century Literature* 2 (Spring): 229–38.

———. 1989. Text and Intertext in Emilia Pardo Bazán's *Memorias de un solterón. Symposium* 13 (Summer): 83–93.

———. 1990–1991. Zalacaín el aventurero como aventura textual. *Explicación de textos literarios* 19:48–58.

———. 1992. *Voices, Silences and Echoes: A Theory of the Essay and the Critical Reception of Naturalism in Spain.* London: Tamesis.

———. 1993. The Role of Negativity in Unamuno's *La tía Tula. Revista Canadiense de Estudios Hispánicos* (Fall): 17–30.

———. 1998. Margarita Nelken's *La condición social de la mujer en España:* Between the Pedagogic and the Performative. In *Spanish Women Writers and the Essay,* edited by Kathleen Glenn and Mercedes Mazquiarán de Rodríguez. Columbia, Missouri: University of Missouri Press.

Brinker-Gabler, Griselda, ed. 1995. *Encountering the Other(s): Studies in Literature, History and Culture.* Albany: State University of New York Press.

Brody, Saul Nathaniel. 1974. *The Disease of the Soul: Leprosy in Medieval Literature.* Ithaca: Cornell University Press.

Brooker, Peter, ed. 1992. *Modernism / Postmodernism.* London and New York: Longman.

Brooks, Linda Marie, ed. 1995. *Alternative Identities.* New York: Garland Publishing.

Brooks, Peter.1993. *Body Works: Objects of Desire in Modern Narrative.* Cambridge: Harvard University Press.

Brotherston, Gordon. 1976. *Manuel Machado.* Taurus: Madrid.

Brown, Dennis. 1989. *The Modernist Self in Twentieth-Century English Literature.* Hampshire: MacMillan.

Brown, G. G. 1972. *A Literary History of Spain: The Twentieth Century.* London: Ernest Benn.

Bueno, Manuel. 1899. La Eva futura. *Revista Nueva* (August-December): 193–97.

Burgos, Carmen de. 1907. El tesoro del Castillo. *El cuento semanal* VI.

———. 1909? *Por Europa.* Barcelona: Casa Editorial Maucci.

———. 1919. Los negociantes de la Puerta del Sol. *La novela corta.* (September 27).

———. 1980. *El hombre negro* Madrid: Emiliano Escolar.

———. 1986. *Mis mejores cuentos.* Barcelona: Editoriales Andaluzas Unidas.

———. 1989a. En la Guerra (Episodios de Melilla). In *La flor de la playa y otras novelas cortas* 163–218. Madrid: Castalia.

———. 1989b. *La flor de la playa y otras novelas cortas.* Madrid: Castalia.

Butt, John. 1980. The "Generation of 98": A Critical Fallacy? *Forum for Modern Language Studies* 16: 136–53.

———. 1993. Modernismo y *Modernism.* In *¿Qué es el Modernismo?: Nueva Encuesta, Nuevas lecturas,* edited by Richard A. Cardwell and Bernard McGuirk, 39–58. Boulder, Co.: Society of Spanish and Spanish American Studies.

Cacho Viu, Vicente. 1988. Catalonian Modernism and Cultural Nationalism. In *The Crisis of Institutionalized Literature,* edited by Wlad Godzich and Nicholas Spadaccini, 229–50. Minneapolis, Minn.: Prisma Institute.

———. 1997. *Repensar el noventa y ocho.* Madrid: Biblioteca Nueva.

Calvo Revilla, Luis. 1894. La mujer sabia. *La Ilustración Española y Americana.* 1:318–19.

Camba, Julio.1907. El destierro. *El cuento semanal* 25.

———. 1934. *Playas, ciudades y montañas.* Madrid: Espasa-Calpe.

Cardwell, Richard A. 1981. Modernismo frente a noventa y ocho: The case of Juan Ramón Jiménez (1890–1900). In *Estudios sobre Juan Ramón Jiménez,* 119–41. University of Mayagüez, Puerto Rico.

———. 1984. Myths Ancient and Modern: Modernismo frente a Noventayocho and the Search for Spain. In *Essays in Honor of Robert Brian Tate,* edited by Richard A. Cardwell, 9–21. Nottingham: University of Nottingham Press.

———. 1998a. Antonio Machado and the Search for the Soul of Spain: A Genealogy. *Anales de la literatura española contemporánea* 23:51–79.

———. 1998b. Los componentes del fin de siglo. In *En el 98 (Los nuevos escritores),* edited by José-Carlos Mainer y Jordi Gracia, 173–75. Madrid: Visor.

———. 1998c. Los Machado y Juan Ramón Jiménez en el 98: buscando nuevas trazas por las ciudades muertas y las sendas abandonadas. In *En el 98 (Los nuevos escritores),* edited by José-Carlos Mainer y Jordi Gracia, 137–57. Madrid: Visor.

Cardwell, Richard A. and Bernard McGuirk, editors. 1993. *¿Qué es el modernismo?: Encuesta, Nuevas lecturas.* Boulder, Colo.: Society of Spanish and Spanish American Studies.

Carnavaggio, Jean, ed. 1995. *Historia de la literatura española. El siglo XX.* Vol. 5. Translated by Clara Urbaldina Lorda. Barcelona: Ariel.

Carr, Raymond. 1970. *Spain: 1808–1939.* Oxford: Oxford University Press.

Carreño, Antonio. 1981. *La dialéctica de la identidad en la poesía contemporánea.* Madrid: Gredos.

Casalduero, Joaquin. 1974. *Vida y obra de Galdós.* Madrid: Gredos.

Casanova, Sofía. 1898. *Fugaces.* La Coruña: Andrés Martínez.

———. 1910. La mujer española en el extranjero. Conference read in Ateneo of Madrid, April 9, 1910. Madrid: R. Velasco.

———. 1913. *La madeja.* Madrid: R. Velasco.

———. 1916. *De la guerra: Crónicas de Polonia y Rusia.* Madrid. R. Velasco.

———. 1919. *Triunfo de amor. La novela corta.* (July).

Castillo, Homero, ed. 1974. *Estudios críticos sobre el modernismo.* Madrid: Gredos.

Castoriadis, Cornelius. 1991. Time and Creation. In *Chronotopes: The Construction of Time,* edited by John Bender and David Wellbery, 38–64. Stanford: Stanford University Press.

Castro, Américo. 1925. El verdadero hispanoamericanismo. *Boletín de la Institución Libre de Enseñanza:* 43–46.

———. 1971. *La realidad histórica de España.* Mexico: Porrúa.

Catena, Elena. 1990. Introducción. *Doña Inés* by José Martínez Ruiz (*Azorín*). Madrid: Castalia.

Cejador y Frauca, Julio. 1915–1922. *Historia de la lengua y literatura castellana.* Madrid: Revista de Archivos, Bibliotecas y Museos.

Cela, Camilo José. 1975. *Diccionario secreto.* 3 vols. Madrid: Alianza.

Celma Valero, María Pilar. 1989. *La pluma ante el espejo.* Salamanca: University of Salamanca.

———. 1991. *Literatura y periodismo en las revistas del fin de siglo: Estudio e indices (1888–1907).* Madrid: Jucar.

Celma Valero, María Pilar and Francisco Blasco Pascual, eds. 1981. *Manuel Machado. La guerra literaria.* Madrid: Narcea.

Certeau, Michel de. 1988. *The Practice of Everyday Life.* Translated by Steven Rendall. Berkeley: University of California Press.

———. 1989. *Heterologies: Discourse on the Other.* Translated by Brian Massumi. Minneapolis: University of Minnesota Press.

Chapelle, Daniel. 1993? *Nietzsche and Psychoanalysis.* Albany: State University of New York Press.

Charnon Deutsch, Lou. 1994. *Narratives of Desire.* University Park: Pennsylvania State University Press.

Charnon Deutsch, Lou and Jo Labanyi, eds. 1995. *Culture and Gender in Nineteenth-Century Spain.* Oxford: Clarendon Press.

Chavarri, Eduardo L.1902. ¿Qué es el modernismo? *Gente Vieja* (April 10): 1–2.

Chefdor, Monique, Ricardo Quinones and Albert Wachtel, eds. 1986. *Modernism: Challenges and Perspectives.* Urbana and Chicago: University of Illinois Press.

Cidrón, Manuel 1902. ¿Qué es el modernismo? *Gente Vieja* (November 30): 5–6.

Ciges Aparicio, M. 1914. *Villavieja.* Madrid: Jaime Ratés Martín.

Cirici Pellicer, A. 1972. *1900 in Barcelona.* Barcelona: Polígrafo.

Clemessy, Nelly. 1981. *Emilia Pardo Bazán como novelista.* 2 vols. Translated by Irene Gambra. Madrid: Fundación Universitaria Española.

Cobb, Carl W. 1971. *Antonio Machado.* Boston: Twayne.

Coke-Enguídanos, Mervyn. 1982. *Word and Work in the Poetry of Juan Ramón Jiménez.* London: Tamesis Books.

Colmeiro, José and Christina Dupláa, Patricia Green, Juana Sabadell, eds. 1995. *Spain Today: Essays on Literature, Culture, Society.* Hanover, N.H.: Dartmouth College.

Coloma, Luis. 1975 . *Pequeñeces.* Madrid: Cátedra.

Colorado, Vicente. 1903. Modernismo. *Gente Vieja* (April 20): 8.

¿Conoce Ud. España? 1907. *El Nuevo Mercurio* (August): 843–52.

Contra los modernistas. 1907. *El Nuevo Mercurio* (March): 354–55.

Corbey, R. and J. Th. Leerssen, eds. 1991a. *Alterity, Identity, Image: Selves and Others in Society and Scholarship.* Amsterdam: Rodopi.

———. 1991b. Freud's Phylogenetic Narrative. In *Alterity, Identiy, Image: Selves and Others in Society and Scholarship,* edited by R.Corbey and J.Th. Leerssen. 37–56. Amsterdam: Rodopi.

Cortázar, Julio. 1994. *Cuentos completos.* Madrid: Alfaguara.

Corte de los poetas, La. 1907. Edited by Emilio Carrere. Madrid: Pueyo.

Cosas que fueron: Un episodio de la guerra de Africa. 1904. *Gente Vieja.* (May 15): 1–2.

Costa, Joaquín. 1967. *Oligarquía y caciquismo, colectivismo agrario y otros escritos.* Madrid: Alianza.

Craige, Betty Jean, Translated by. 1978. *Selected Poems of Antonio Machado.* Baton Rouge: Louisiana State University Press.

Culler, Jonathan. 1975. *Structuralist Poetics.* Ithaca, Cornell University Press.

———. 1982. *On Deconstruction.* Ithaca, Cornell University Press.

Darío, Rubén. 1901? *España contemporánea.* Paris: Casa Editorial Garnier Hermanos.

———. 1917. *Tierras solares. Obras completas.* Vol III. Madrid: Mundo Latino.

———. 1952. *Poesía.* Mexico: Fondo de cultura económica.

———. 1971. *Cantos de vida y esperanza.* Salamanca: Anaya.

Darst, David. 1988. *Sendas literarias. España.* New York: Random House.

Davison, Ned J. 1966. *The Concept of Modernism in Hispanic Criticism.* Boulder, Colo.: Pruett Press.

De Arte. 1903. *Helios* 1:99.

DeKoven, Marianne. 1991. *Rich and Strange: Gender, History, Modernism.* Princeton: Princeton University Press.

Deleito y Piñuela, José. 1902. ¿Qué es el modernismo? *Gente Vieja* (April 10): 1–2.

Del Río, Angel. 1963. *Historia de la literatura española.* Vol 2. New York: Holt, Rinehart and Winston.

De Ojeo. 1897. *Gedeón.* (February 18).

Un desengaño. 1896. *La Voz de Galicia.* (February 15): 1.

Díaz, Leopoldo. 1907. Al espiritu de Oscar Wilde. *Revista Latina* 1:3.

Díaz-Fernández, José. 1928. *El blocao: Novela de la guerra marroquí.* Madrid: Historia nueva.

Díaz-Plaja, Guillermo. 1966. *Modernismo frente a noventa y ocho.* Madrid: Espasa-Calpe.

———. 1976. *1898.* Madrid: Editora Nacional.

Dicenta, Joaquin. 1894. *Luciano.* Madrid: Florencio Fiscowich.

———. 1907. *Lorenza.* Madrid: Teatro español.

———. 1908. Del camino. *El Cuento semanal:* 3.

———. 1912. *Los bárbaros.* Madrid: Renacimiento.

———. 1913a. *Aurora.* Barcelona: Teatro de Cataluña.

———. 1913b. *Los de abajo.* Madrid: Antonio Marzo.

———. 1915a. *El crimen de ayer.* Barcelona: Teatro mundial.

———. 1915b. *Mi Venus.* Madrid: Biblioteca Hispania

———. 1930. *El señor feudal.* Madrid: Prensa moderna.

———. 1931. *Daniel.* Madrid: Prensa moderna.

———. 1965. *Juan José.* Madrid: Taurus.

Díez Borque, José, ed. 1988. *Historia de la literatura española. Siglo XX.* Madrid: Taurus.

Domingo, José. 1988. La prosa narrativa hasta 1936. In *Historia de la literatura española: Siglo XX,* edited by J. María Díez Borque, 71–121. Madrid: Taurus.

D'Ors, Eugenio. 1920. *Glosas.* Translated by Alfonso Maseras. Madrid: Saturniño Calleja.

———. 1967. *Cartas a Tina.* Barcelona: Plaza y Janes.

———. 1969. *La bien plantada.* Barcelona: Montaner y Simón.

Dos palabras al lector. 1907. *El Nuevo Mercurio* (January): 3–4.

Dust, Patrick ed. 1989. *Ortega y Gasset and the Question of Modernity.* Minneapolis, Minn.: The Prisma Institute.

Echegaray, José. 1898. *La duda.* Madrid: Teatro español.

Eguía Ruiz, Constancia. 1917. *Literaturas y literatos: Estudios contemporáneos.* Barcelona: Librería Religiosa.

Eldredge, N. and Stephen Jay Gould. 1972. Punctuated Equilibria: An Alternative to Phyletic Gradualism. In *Models in Paleobiology,* edited by T. J. M. Schopf. 82–115. San Francisco: Freeman, Cooper and Co.

El modernismo. 1907. *El Nuevo Mercurio.* 2–12.

Espina, Concha. 1972. *Obras completas.* 2 vols. Madrid: Fax.

Espinosa y González Pérez, Francisco. 1910. La cuestión del Rif. *La España Moderna* 253:155-64.

Eysteinsson, Astradur. 1990. *The Concept of Modernism.* Ithaca: Cornell University Press.

Fabra, Nilo María. 1896. Los Estados Unidos en Cuba. *La Ilustración Española y Americana.* (March 22): 171, 174.

Feliu y Codina, José. 1895. *Miel de la Alcarría.* Madrid. R Velasco.

Felski, Rita. 1995. *The Gender of Modernity.* Cambridge: Harvard University Press.

Fernández Almagro, Melchor. 1943. *Vida y literatura de Valle Inclán.* Madrid: Editora Nacional.

Fernández Cifuentes, Luis. 1982. *Teoría y mercado de la novela en España: Del 98 a la república.* Madrid: Gredos.

———. 1997. Apasionadas simetrias: Sobre la identidad del 98. *Anales de la Literatura Española Contemporánea.* 22: 103–30.

———. 1998. Cartografías del 98: fin de siglo, identidad nacional y diálogo con América. *Anales de la Literatura Española Contemporánea* 23: 117–45.

Fernández Flórez, Wenceslau. 1980. *Volvoreta.* Madrid: Cátedra.

Ferrari, Emilio. 1905. *Discursos leídos ante la Real Academia Española en la recepción pública de Emilio Ferrari.* Madrid: Ambrosio Pérez y Cía.

Ferreres, Rafael. 1955. Los límites del modernismo y la Generación del noventa y ocho. *Cuadernos Hispanoamericanos.* 73:66–84.

Ferrí, Enrique. 1899. Los anormales. *Revista Nueva* 1:49–57.

Fiddian, R. W. 1976. Cyclical Time and the Structure of Azorín's *La voluntad. Forum for Modern Language Studies.* 12:163–75.

Fogelquist, Donald F. 1986. Helios, voz de un renacimiento hispánico. In *El modernismo,* ed. Lily Litvak, 327–35. Madrid: Taurus.

Fokkema, Douwe and Hans Bertens. 1986. *Approaching Postmodernism.* Amsterdam/Philadelphia: John Benjamins Publishing Co.

Foucault, Michel. 1977. What is an Author? *Language, Countermemory, Practice.* Ithaca: Cornell University Press.

———. 1972. *The Archeology of Knowledge.* Translated by A. M. Sheridan Smith. New York: Harper Colophon.

Franco, Dolores. 1959. *España como preocupación.* Madrid: Guadarrama.

Fuentes, Victor. 1995. More than Three Forms of Distortion in 20th Century Spanish Literary Historiography: Counterpoint Alternatives. In *Spain Today: Essays on Literature, Culture and Society,* edited by José Colmeiro, Christina Dupláa, Patricia Greene, Juana Sabadell, 21–33. Hanover, N.H.: Dartmouth College.

Fusi, Juan Pablo and Jordi Palafox. 1997. *España: 1808–1996. El desafío de la modernidad.* Madrid: Espasa-Calpe.

Fusi, Juan Pablo and Antonio Niño, eds. 1997. *Vísperas del 98: Orígenes y antecedentes de la crisis del 98.* Madrid: Biblioteca Nueva.

Gabriele, John P., ed. 1992. *Suma Valleinclaniana.* Barcelona: Anthropos.

Gagen, Derek. 1999. ¿El santo o la esfinge? El teatro ante la crisis de 1898. *Rilce* 15: 253–66.

Ganivet, Angel. 1903. Epistolario. *Helios* 1:257–70.

———. 1943. *Obras completas.* 2 vols. Madrid: Aguilar.

———. 1962. *Idearium español.* Madrid: Austral.

Gato Negro, El. 1898. (January-December).

García Goyena, Juan. 1901. La muerte del modernismo. *Revista Contemporánea.*(March): 641–48.

Gener, Pompeyo. 1894. *Literaturas malsanas: Estudios de patología literaria contemporánea.* Barcelona-Madrid: Fernando Fe, 1894.

———. 1902a. *Historia de la literatura.* Barcelona: Montaner y Simón.

———. 1902b. *Leyendas de amor.* Tarragona: Francisco Sugrañes.

———. 1907. Ultimos días de Miguel Servet. *El cuento semanal.* Vol. 27.

———. 1911. *Servet: Reforma contra renacimiento. Calvino contra humanismo.* Barcelona: Maucci.

Génesis. 1903. *Helios.* 1:3–4.

Gicovate, Bernardo. 1974. Antes del modernismo. In *Estudios críticos sobre el modernismo,* edited by Homero Castillo, 190–202. Madrid: Gredos.

Giddens, Anthony. 1991. *Modernity and Self-Identity.* Stanford, Calif.: Stanford University Press.

Gil, Ricardo. 1972. *La caja de música.* Edited by Richard Cardwell. Exeter: University of Exeter.

Gil Cremades, Juan José. 1981. *Krausistas y liberales.* Madrid: Dossat.

Gilbert, Sandra and Susan Gubar. 1979. *The Madwoman in the Attic.* New Haven: Yale University Press.

Giles, Steve, ed. 1993. *Theorizing Modernism: Essays in Critical Theory.* London: Routledge.

Gilman, Sander. 1992. Plague in Germany 1939/1989. In *Nationalisms and Sexualities,* edited by Andrew Parker, Mary Russo, Doris Sommer and Patricia Yaeger. 175–200. New York: Routledge.

———. 1995. Black Bodies, White Bodies. In *Feminist Cultural Studies.* Vol. 2, edited by Terry Lovell. Cambridge: Cambridge University Press.

Gilman, Stephen. 1961. La palabra hablada y *Fortunata y Jacinto. Nueva Revista de Filología Hispánica.* 15:542–60.

Giner de los Ríos, Francisco. 1920. *Lecciones sumarias de psicología. Obras completas.* Vol. 4. Madrid: La Lectura.

———. 1925. El problema de la educación nacional y las clases productoras. *Educación y enseñanza. Obras completas.* Vol. 12. Madrid: La lectura.

———. 1965. Paisaje. *Ensayos y cartas.* Mexico: Fondo de Cultura Económica.

Giner de los Ríos, Hermenegildo. 1908? *Teoría de la literatura y de las artes.* Madrid: Manuales Soler.

Glenn, Kathleen. 1981. *Azorín.* Boston: Twayne Publishers.

Godzich, Wlad and Nicholas Spadaccini, eds. 1988. *The Crisis of Institutionalized Literature in Spain.* Minneapolis, Minn.: The Prisma Institute.

Gómez Aparicio, Pedro. 1971. *Historia del periodismo español: De la revolución de septiembre al desastre colonial.* Madrid: Editora Nacional.

Gómez Carrillo, E. 1905? *El modernismo.* Madrid: Fernando Fe.

———. 1907. Mis orientales. *El Nuevo Mercurio* 9:1044–69.

Gómez-Lobo, Arturo. 1908. *La literatura modernista y el idioma de Cervantes.* Ciudad Real: Impresión del "Diario".

Gómez de la Serna, Ramón. 1910. *Mis siete palabras.* n.p.: Pastoral.

———. 1921. *El doctor inverosímil.* Madrid: Alrededor del Mundo.

———. 1955. *Total de greguerías.* Madrid: Aguilar.

———. 1987. *El libro mudo.* Mexico: Fondo de Cultura Económica.

González Blanco, Andrés. 1907a. *Los contemporáneos.* Paris: Garnier Brothers.

———. 1907b. El modernismo. *El Nuevo Mercurio.* 7:797–805.

———. 1907c. Movimiento literario reciente. *Nuestro Tiempo.* 108:322.

———. 1908. Un amor de provincia. *El cuento semanal.* Vol. 27.

González García, José Ramón. 1992. *Etica y estética: Las novelas poemáticas de la vida española de Ramón Pérez de Ayala.* Valladolid: University of Valladolid.

González López, Emilio. 1971. *El arte narrativo de Pío Baroja.* New York: Las Américas.

González Serrano, Urbano. 1892. *Estudios psicológicos.* Madrid: n.p.

———. 1896. Los derechos de la mujer. *La Ilustración Española y Americana.* 2:183.

———. 1898. Novedades Añejas. *La Revista Blanca.* 1:2:52–55.

———. 1899. El arte contemporáneo. *Revista Nueva.* 2:193–98.

———. 1903. Silencio. *Helios.* 5:3–7.

Graham, Helen and Jo Labanyi. 1995. *Spanish Cultural Studies: An Introduction* Oxford: Oxford University Press.

Gramsci, Antonio. 1992. *Prison Notebooks.* New York: Columbia University Press.

Grass, Roland and William R. Risley. 1979. *Waiting for Pegasus: Studies of the Presence of Symbolism and Decadence in Hispanic Letters.* Macomb: Western Illinois University Press.

Grau, Jacinto. 1917. *El Conde Alarcos.* Madrid: Minerva.

Grupo de Investigación de la Universidad de Paris VIII-Vincennes. 1986. *Ideología y texto en El cuento semanal (1907–1912).* Madrid: Ediciones de la Torre.

Guasp, Gonzalo. 1902. ¿Qué es el modernismo? *Gente Vieja* 56:2–3.

Guerra, Angel. 1903. Fuera de Espana: Retazos. *Helios* 2:291–300.

———. 1910. Cuestiones contemporáneas. *La Espana Moderna.* 361:n.p.

———. 1905. Mis flores, Concha Espina. *La Lectura.* 2:75.

Guixé, Juan. 1904. La "idea" de Espana. *La España Moderna.* 303–4:53–63.

Guillén, Claudio. 1971. *Literature as System: Essays Towards the Theory of Literary History.* Princeton: Princeton University Press.

Guimerà, Angel. 1912. *Mar y cielo.* Translated by Enrique Gaspar. Madrid.

———. 1914. *Terra baixa.* Barcelona: La Renaixensa.

Guindos, Manuel de. 1902. ¿Qué es el modernismo? *Gente Vieja.* 52:3–4.

Gullón, Germán. 1992. *La novela moderna en España (1885–1902).* Madrid: Taurus.

Gullón, Ricardo. 1958. *Las secretas galerías de Antonio Machado.* Madrid: Taurus.

———. 1969. *La invención del 98 y otros ensayos.* Madrid: Gredos.

Gutiérrez Girardot, Rafael. 1983. *Modernismo.* Barcelona: Montesinos

Havard, Robert G. 1988. *From Romanticism to Surrealism: Seven Spanish Poets.* Totowa, N.J.: Barnes and Noble.

Hayman, David. 1987. *Reforming the Narrative: Towards a Mechanics of Modernist Fiction.* Ithaca: Cornell University Press.

Hekma, Gert. 1991. From Sade to Fassbinder: Aesthetics of Cruelty and Male Love in Homosexual Artists. In *Alterity, Identity, Image: Selves and Others in Society and Scholarship,* edited by R. Corbey and Th. Leerssen. Amsterdam: Rodopi.

Hemmingway, Maurice. 1983. *Emilia Pardo Bazán: The Making of a Novelist.* Cambridge: Cambridge University Press.

Hernández Valcárcel, Carmen and Carmen Escudero Martínez. 1986. *La narrativa lírica de Azorín y Miró.* Alicante: Cajas de Ahorros de Alicante y Murcia.

Herzberger, David. 1995. Introduction: Reading Beyond Location. *Siglo XX/20th Century.* 3:5–12.

Hornedo, Rafael María de. 1956. Menéndez y Pelayo y el P. Coloma. *Razón y Fe.* 701:759–72.

Hughes, Robert. 1981. *The Shock of the New.* New York: Alfred Knopf.

Huyssen, Andreas. 1986a. *After the Great Divide: Modernism, Mass Culture and Postmodernism.* Bloomington: Indiana University Press.

———. 1986b. Mass Culture as Woman. In *Studies in Entertainment: Critical Approaches to Mass Culture,* edited by Tania Modleski. 188–207. Bloomington: Indiana University Press.

Iglesias Feijoo, Luis. 1999. Sobre la invención del 98. *Del 98 al 98:Literatura e historia literaria en el siglo XX hispánico. Rilce, Revista de Filología Hispánica.* 15:3–12.

In fragranti. 1900. *Blanco y Negro.* (January 13): Cover drawing.

Inman Fox, E. 1970. Introducción. In *Antonio Azorín,* by José Martínez Ruiz (Azorín). Barcelona: Labor.

———. 1991. Hacia una nueva historia literaria para España. *Dai modernismi alle avanguardie. Atti del Convegno dell'Associazione degli Ispanista Italiani. Palermo, Italy, 1990,* 7–17. Palermo: Flaccovio Editore.

———. 1997. *La invención de España: Nacionalismo liberal e identidad nacional.* Madrid: Cátedra.

La Institución Libre de Enseñanza. 1980. *Historia.* 5:4:67–93.

Insúa, Alberto. 1907. Las señoritas. *El cuento semanal.* Vol. 28.

Jackson-Veyán, José. 1900. El modernismo. *Blanco y Negro* (April 7): 10–11.

Jagoe, Catherine. 1995. Monstrous Inversions: Decadence and Degeneration in Galdós's *Angel Guerra.* In *Culture and Gender in Nineteenth-Century Spain,* edited by Lou Charnon Deutsch and Jo Labanyi, 161–81. Oxford: Clarendon Press.

James, William. 1977. The Stream of Thought. In *Writings of William James,* edited by John J. McDermott. 21–74. Chicago: University of Chicago Press.

Jauss, Hans Robert. 1982. *Toward an Aesthetic of Reception.* Translated by Timothy Bahti. Minneapolis: University of Minnesota Press.

Jeschke, Hans. 1954. *La generación de 1898.* Translated by Y. Pino Saavedra. Madrid: Editora Nacional,

Jiménez Landi, Antonio. 1973. *La Institución Libre de Enseñanza.* Madrid: Taurus.

Jiménez, Juan Ramón. 1907. Habla el poeta. *Renacimiento* 8:422–25.

———. 1912. *Melancolía.* Madrid: Revista de Archivos.

———. 1917. *Diario de un poeta recién casado.* Madrid: Calleja.

———. 1918. *Eternidades.* Madrid: Angel Alcoy.

———. 1919. *Piedra y cielo.* Madrid: Fortanet.

———. 1954. *Primeros libros de poesía.* Madrid: Aguilar.

———. 1957. *Libros de poesía.* Madrid: Aguilar.

———. 1962. *El modernismo: Notas de un curso (1953).* México: Aguilar.

Jiménez, José Olivio, ed. 1979. *El simbolismo.* Madrid: Taurus.

Johnson, Roberta. 1993. *Crossfire: Philosophy and the Novel in Span (1900–1934).* Lexington: University of Kentucky Press.

Joseph, Gerhard. 1985. The Echo and the Mirror en abîme in Victorian Poetry. *Victorian Poetry,* 23:403–12.

Jrade, Cathy L. 1988. Modernism on Both Sides of the Atlantic. *Anales de la literatura española contemporánea* 23:181–96.

Jurkevich, Gayana. 1995. A Poetics of Time and Space: Ekphrasis and the Modern Vision in Azorín and Velázquez. *Modern Language Notes* 110:284–301.

Kelin, Fiodor. 1968. Rubén Darío. *Estudios sobre Rubén Darío.* Edited by Ernesto Sánchez Mejía. México: Fondo de Cultura Económica.

Kern, Stephen. 1983. *The Culture of Time and Space: 1880–1918*. Cambridge: Harvard University Press.

Kiely, Robert, ed. 1983. *Modernism Reconsidered*. Cambridge: Harvard University Press.

Kirkpatrick, Susan. 1995. Gender and Difference in *Fin de siglo* Literary Discourse. In *Spain Today: Essays on Literature, Culture, Society,* edited by José Colmeiro, Christina Duplaá, Patricia Greene, Juana Sabadell. 95–101. Hanover, N.H.: Dartmouth College.

Kristeva, Julia. 1980. *Desire in Language*. Translated by Thomas Gora, Alice Jardine, Leon S. Roudiez. New York: Columbia University Press.

Labanyi, Jo. 1993, ed. *Galdós*. London: Longman.

———. 1994. Nation, Narration, Naturalization: A Barthesian Critique of the 1898 Generation. In *New Hispanisms: Literature, Culture, Theory,* edited by Mark I. Millington and Paul Julian Smith, 127–49. Ottowa: Dovehouse Editions.

Lacan, Jacques. 1957. L'Instance de la lettre dans l'inconscient ou la raison depuis Freud. *La Psychanalyse* 3:47–81. [English translation by Jan Miel. *Yale French Studies*. 36–37 (1966): 112–47.]

Laín Entralgo. Pedro. 1967. *La generación del noventa y ocho*. Madrid: Espasa-Calpe.

Landeira, Ricardo. 1985. *The Modern Spanish Novel: 1898–1936*. Boston: Twayne.

Lash, Scott. 1991. *Sociology of Postmodernism*. London: Routledge.

Lanza, Silverio (Juan Bautista Amorós). 1899. Barcelona. *Revista Nueva* 2: 28:199–200.

León, Ricardo. 1908. *Casta de Hidalgos*. Madrid: n.p.

———. 1959. *El amor de los amores. Las mejores novelas contemporáneas*. Vol. 4. Barcelona: Planeta.

Levinas, Emmanuel. 1993. *Outside the Subject,* Translated by Michael B. Smith. Stanford: Stanford University Press.

———. 1994. *The Levinas Reader*. Edited by Seán Hand. Oxford: Blackwell Press.

Lima, Robert. 1988. *Valle-Inclán: The Theater of His Life*. Columbus: University of Missouri Press.

———. 1989. Crisis and Response: The Dynamics of Spain's "Generation of 1898". In *Los hallazgos de la lectura: Estudio dedicado a Miguel Enguídanos*. Madrid: Porrúa Turanzas.

Lissorgues, Yvan and Serge Salaün. 1991. Crisis del realismo. In *1900 en España,* edited by Serge Salaün and Carlos Serrano. Madrid: Espasa-Calpe.

Litvak, Lily. 1980. *Transformación industrial y literatura en España (1895–1905)*. Madrid: Taurus.

———. 1985. *El jardin de Alah*. Granada: Don Quijote.

———. 1986. Editor. *El modernismo*. Madrid: Taurus.

———. 1990. *España 1900: Modernismo, Anarquismo y Fin de Siglo*. Barcelona: Anthropos.

Llanas Aguilaniedo, José María. 1902. *Del jardín del amor* Madrid: Fernando Fe.

———. 1903. *Navegar pintoresco*. Madrid: Fernando Fe.

———. 1991. *Alma contemporánea: Estudio de estética.* Huesca: Instituto de Estudios Altoaragoneses.

———. n. d. *Pitayuso.* Madrid: Fernando Fe.

Llanas Aguilaniedo, José María and Bernaldo de Queirós. 1901. *La mala vida en Madrid.* Madrid: B. Rodriguez Serra.

Llanos, Adolfo. 1893. España en el Rif. *La Ilustración Española y Americana.* 38:233–34.

Llopis y Pérez, Antonio. 1915. *Historia política y parlamentaria de D. Nicolás Salmerón y Alonso.* Madrid: Imprenta de Ediciones España.

López Martínez, Adelaida. 1988. Significación del *esperpento* en el contexto del pensamiento europeo del siglo XX. In *Valle-Inclán: Nueva valoración de su obra,* edited by Clara Luisa Barbeito. Barcelona: PPU.

López Pinillos, J. 1908. Los enemigos. *El cuento semanal.* Vol. 4.

Lorrain, Jean. 1905? *Las Españas.* In *El modernismo,* E. Gómez Carrillo, 125. Madrid: Fernando Fe.

Loureiro, Angel G. 1988. *Estelas, laberinto, nuevas sendas: Unamuno, Valle-Inclán, García Lorca, La Guerra Civil.* Barcelona: Anthropos.

Lovell, Terry. 1995. *Feminist Cultural Studies.* Vol. 2. Cambridge: Cambridge University Press.

Luis, Leopoldo de. 1988. *Antonio Machado: Ejemplo y lección.* Madrid: Fundación Banco Exterior.

Lyotard, Jean-Francois. 1989. *The Postmodern Condition: A Report on Knowledge.* Translated by Geoff Bennington and Brian Masumi. Minneapolis: University of Minnesota Press.

MacDonald, Ian R. 1975. *Gabriel Miró: His Private Library and his Literary Background.* London: Tamesis.

Macklin, John. 1993. Las cumbres del modernismo: Aproximación a la novela finisecular española. *¿Qué es el modernismo?: Nueva Encuesta, Nuevas lecturas,* edited by Richard Cardwell and Bernard McGuirk. 199–215. Boulder, Colo.: Society of Spanish and Spanish American Studies.

Machado, Antonio. 1917. *Poesías completas.* Madrid: Residencia de Estudiantes.

Machado, Antonio and Manuel. 1951. *Obras completas.* Madrid: Plenitud.

Machado, Manuel. 1904. Nuestro Paris. *Helios* 3:32–35.

———. 1913. *El amor y la muerte.* Madrid: Imprenta Helénica.

———. 1922–1924. *Obras completas.* Vols 1–5. Madrid: Mundo Latino.

———. 1981. *La guerra literaria.* Edited by María Pilar Celma Valero and Francisco J. Blasco Pascual. Madrid: Narcea.

———. 1988. *Alma. Ars moriendo.* Edited by Pablo del Barco. Madrid: Cátedra.

Maeztu, Ramiro. 1903. Plumas hidalgas. *Alma Española* 5:3.

———. 1919? *La crisis del humanismo.* Barcelona: Minerva.

———. 1967. *Hacia otra España.* Madrid: Rialp.

Maier, Carol. 1988. ¿Palabras de armonía?: Reflexiones sobre la lectura, los límites y la estética de Valle-Inclán. In *Estelas, laberintos, nuevas sendas: Unamuno, Valle-Inclán, García Lorca, La Guerra Civil,* edited by Angel Loureiro. Barcelona: Anthropos.

Maier, Carol and Roberta L. Salper, eds. 1994. *Ramón María del Valle-Inclán: Questions of Gender.* Lewisburg, Pa.: Bucknell University Press.

Mainer, José-Carlos. 1988. *La doma de la Quimera.* Barcelona: Gellaterra.

———. 1997. Galdós a escena: una campaña teatral (1892–1896). *Vísperas del 98: Orígenes y antecedentes de la crisis del 98,* edited by Juan Pablo Fusi y Antonio Niño, 257–68. Madrid: Biblioteca Nueva.

Mainer, José-Carlos and Jordi Gracia, eds. 1998. *En el 98 (Los nuevos escritores).* Madrid: Visor.

Maragall, Juan. n. d. *Artículos.* 5 vols. Barcelona: Gustavo Gili.

Marco, Joaquín. 1989. Las máscaras en la obra machadiana. In *Antonio Machado: El poeta y su doble,* 9–36. Barcelona: Departamento de Filología Española.

Marquina, Eduardo. 1900. *Odas.* Barcelona: La Academia de Serra Hermes y Russell.

———. 1908a. Corneja siniestra. *El cuento semanal.* Vol. 14.

———. 1908b. *Las hijas del Cid.* Madrid: R. Velasco.

———. 1914. *En Flandes se ha puesto el sol.* Madrid: Renacimiento.

Martínez, Graciano. 1915. *La Institución Libre de Enseñanza y la gestión de los dos primeros Directores Generales de Instrucción pública.* Madrid: Asilo de Huérfanos.

———. 1921. *La mujer española: Hacia un feminismo cuasi dogmático.* Madrid: Asilo de Huérfanos.

Martínez Marín, Ana. 1986. Carmen de Burgos: Defensora de la mujer. In *Mis mejores cuentos,* by Carmen de Burgos. Seville: Biblioteca de la Cultura Andaluza.

Martínez Martínez, José Francisco. 1989. Antonio Machado ante la modernidad. In *Antonio Machado y la filosofía,* edited by José Luis de la Iglesia, Ana Lucas, Juan Manuel Martínez, Franciso José Martínez, Luis Martínez de Velasco. Madrid: Orígenes.

Martínez Ruiz, José. (Azorín). 1900. *Los hidalgos.* Madrid: Fernando Fe.

———. 1904a. Arte y utilidad. *Alma Espanola* 3:4.

———. 1904b. Somos iconoclastas. *Alma Espanola* 10:15–16.

———. 1919. *La voluntad. Obras completas.* Vol 2. Madrid: Caro Raggio.

———. 1921. *Al margen de los clásicos.* Madrid: Caro Raggio.

———. 1947. *Tomás Rueda.* Madrid: Espasa-Calpe.

———. 1947–1948. *Obras completas.* 3 vols. Madrid: Aguilar.

———. 1953a. *Antonio Azorín.* Madrid: Biblioteca Nueva.

———. 1953b. *Los pueblos. Obras selectas:* Madrid: Biblioteca Nueva.

———. 1954. *España.* Madrid: Espasa-Calpe.

———. 1958. *Castilla.* Buenos Aires: Losada.

———. 1969. *La generacion del 98.* Edited by Angel Cruz Rueda. Salamanca: Anaya.

———. 1976. *Las confesiones de un pequeño filósofo.* Madrid: Espasa-Calpe.

———. 1990. *Doña Inés.* Madrid: Castalia.

Martínez Sierra, Gregorio and María. 1900. *Almas ausentes.* Madrid: B. Rodríguez Serra.

———. 1903a. De como el arte en esta tierra no acierta a reír. *Helios* 2:308–12.

———. 1903b. La monja maestra. *Helios* 1:153–64.

———. 1903c. El poble gris. *Helios* 8:385.

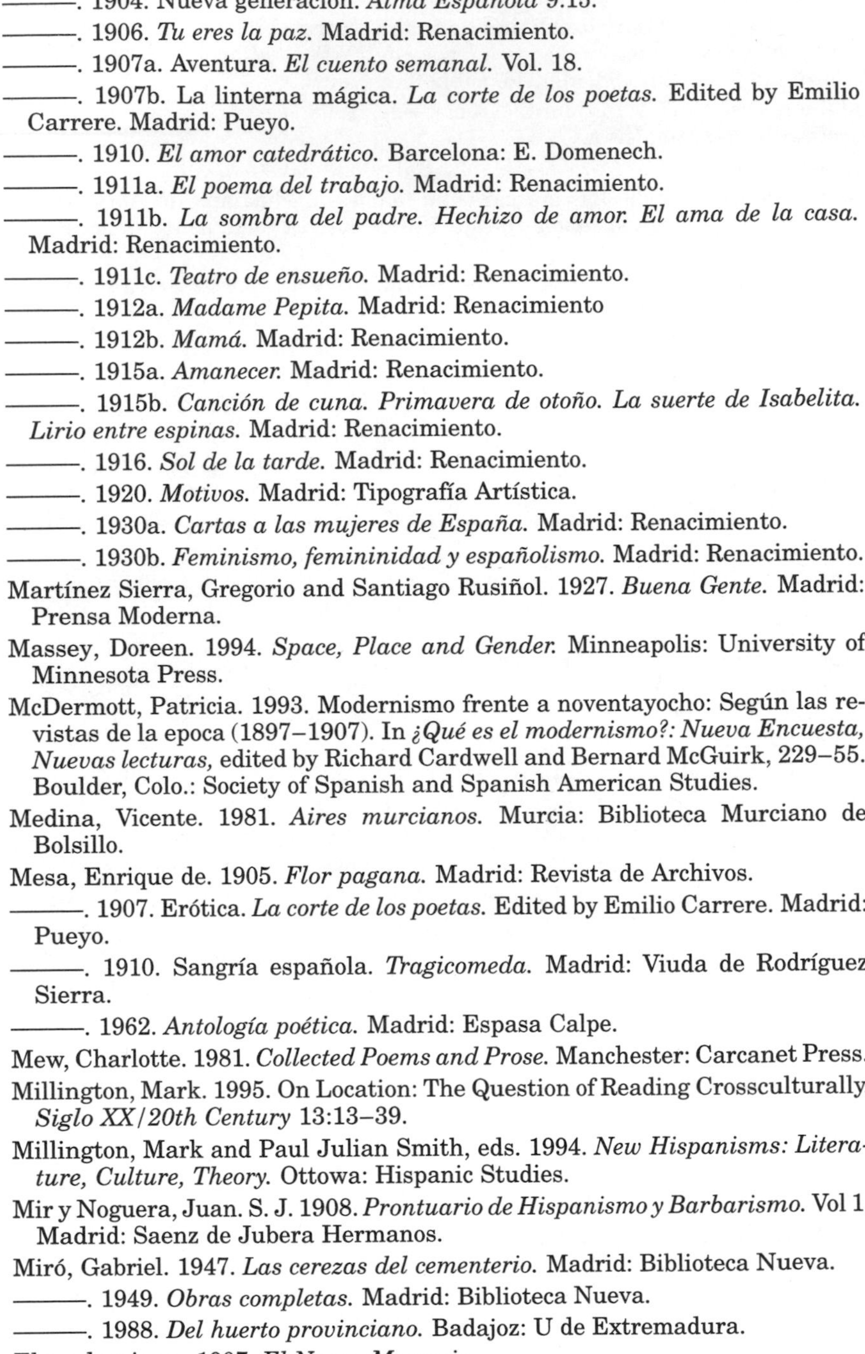

———. 1904. Nueva generacion. *Alma Española* 9:15.

———. 1906. *Tu eres la paz.* Madrid: Renacimiento.

———. 1907a. Aventura. *El cuento semanal.* Vol. 18.

———. 1907b. La linterna mágica. *La corte de los poetas.* Edited by Emilio Carrere. Madrid: Pueyo.

———. 1910. *El amor catedrático.* Barcelona: E. Domenech.

———. 1911a. *El poema del trabajo.* Madrid: Renacimiento.

———. 1911b. *La sombra del padre. Hechizo de amor. El ama de la casa.* Madrid: Renacimiento.

———. 1911c. *Teatro de ensueño.* Madrid: Renacimiento.

———. 1912a. *Madame Pepita.* Madrid: Renacimiento

———. 1912b. *Mamá.* Madrid: Renacimiento.

———. 1915a. *Amanecer.* Madrid: Renacimiento.

———. 1915b. *Canción de cuna. Primavera de otoño. La suerte de Isabelita. Lirio entre espinas.* Madrid: Renacimiento.

———. 1916. *Sol de la tarde.* Madrid: Renacimiento.

———. 1920. *Motivos.* Madrid: Tipografía Artística.

———. 1930a. *Cartas a las mujeres de España.* Madrid: Renacimiento.

———. 1930b. *Feminismo, femininidad y españolismo.* Madrid: Renacimiento.

Martínez Sierra, Gregorio and Santiago Rusiñol. 1927. *Buena Gente.* Madrid: Prensa Moderna.

Massey, Doreen. 1994. *Space, Place and Gender.* Minneapolis: University of Minnesota Press.

McDermott, Patricia. 1993. Modernismo frente a noventayocho: Según las revistas de la epoca (1897–1907). In *¿Qué es el modernismo?: Nueva Encuesta, Nuevas lecturas,* edited by Richard Cardwell and Bernard McGuirk, 229–55. Boulder, Colo.: Society of Spanish and Spanish American Studies.

Medina, Vicente. 1981. *Aires murcianos.* Murcia: Biblioteca Murciano de Bolsillo.

Mesa, Enrique de. 1905. *Flor pagana.* Madrid: Revista de Archivos.

———. 1907. Erótica. *La corte de los poetas.* Edited by Emilio Carrere. Madrid: Pueyo.

———. 1910. Sangría española. *Tragicomeda.* Madrid: Viuda de Rodríguez Sierra.

———. 1962. *Antología poética.* Madrid: Espasa Calpe.

Mew, Charlotte. 1981. *Collected Poems and Prose.* Manchester: Carcanet Press.

Millington, Mark. 1995. On Location: The Question of Reading Crossculturally. *Siglo XX/20th Century* 13:13–39.

Millington, Mark and Paul Julian Smith, eds. 1994. *New Hispanisms: Literature, Culture, Theory.* Ottowa: Hispanic Studies.

Mir y Noguera, Juan. S. J. 1908. *Prontuario de Hispanismo y Barbarismo.* Vol 1. Madrid: Saenz de Jubera Hermanos.

Miró, Gabriel. 1947. *Las cerezas del cementerio.* Madrid: Biblioteca Nueva.

———. 1949. *Obras completas.* Madrid: Biblioteca Nueva.

———. 1988. *Del huerto provinciano.* Badajoz: U de Extremadura.

El modernismo. 1907. *El Nuevo Mercurio.*

Monasterio, Antonio de. 1903. ¿Qué es el modernismo? *Gente Vieja* 82:5–7.

Monleón, José. 1975. *El teatro del 98 frente a la sociedad española.* Madrid: Cátedra.

Montilla. R. 1903. América. *Gente Vieja.* 90:3.

Mukarovsky, Jan. 1977. *The Word and Verbal Art.* Translated by John Burbank and Peter Steiner. New Haven: Yale University Press.

La mulata. 1896. *La Voz de Galicia* (March 8): 1.

Mulvey, Laura. 1989. *Visual and Other Pleasures.* London: Macmillan.

Natali, Joseph and Linda Hutcheon. 1993. *A Postmodern Reader.* Albany: State University of New York Press.

Navajas, Gonzalo. 1998. La modernidad como crisis. El modelo español del declive. *Anales de la literatura española contemporánea* 23:277–94.

Nelken, Margarita. 1924. Mi suicidio. *La novela corta.* 9:474.

———. 1975a. *La condición social de la mujer española.* Madrid: CVS Ediciones.

———, trans. 1975b. *Oscar Wilde. De profundis.* Madrid: Felmar.

Niemeyer, Katharina. 1992. *La poesía del premodernismo español.* Madrid: CSIC.

Nogales y Nogales, José. 1901. *El último patriota.* Barcelona: Maucci.

Nordau, Max. 1907. Las razas humanas. *El Nuevo Mercurio* 1:5.

———. 1968. *Degeneration.* Translated by George L. Mosse. New York: Howard Fertig.

Nuestras impresiones. 1896. *La Voz de Galicia* (January 17):1.

O'Connor, Patricia W. 1977. *Gregorio and María Martínez Sierra.* Boston: Twayne.

Onís, Federico de. 1961. *Antología de la poesía española e hispanoamericana.* New York: Las Américas Publishing Co.

O'Riordan, Patricia. 1973. Helios, revista del modernismo. *Abaco: Estudios sobre literatura española.* 1:57–150.

Orringer, Nelson R. 1998. Redefining the Spanish Silver Age and '98 within It. *Anales de la literatura española contemporánea* 23:315–26.

Ortega y Gasset, José. 1965. *Obras completas.* Vols. 1–3. Madrid: Revista de Occidente.

———. 1967a. *La deshumanización del arte.* Madrid: Revista de Occidente.

———. 1967b. *La España invertebrada.* Madrid: Espasa Calpe.

———. 1990. *Meditaciones del Quijote.* Madrid: Cátedra.

———. 1993. *La rebelión de las masas.* Madrid: Alianza.

Palacio Valdes, Armando. 1892. *La fe.* Madrid: M. G. Hernández.

———. 1893. *El maestrante.* Madrid: Hijos de M. G. Hernández.

———. 1917. *La espuma.* Madrid: Victoriano Suárez.

———. 1920. *Años de juventud del Doctor Angélico.* Madrid: Victoriano Suárez.

———. 1921. *Papeles del Doctor Angélico.* Madrid: Victoriano Suárez.

———. 1923. *La alegría del Capitán Ribot.* Madrid: Victoriana Suárez.

———. 1935. *Las majas de Cadiz. Revista literaria: Novelas y cuentos* 331.

———. 1945. *La aldea perdida.* Madrid: Espasa-Calpe.

Pardo Bazán, Emilia. 1891–1893. *Nuevo teatro crítico,* 1–30.

———. 1908. Allende la verdad. *El cuento semanal.* Vol. 23.

———. 1909. *La Quimera. Obras completas.* Vol. 29. Madrid: Renacimiento.

———. 1910? *Una cristiana—La prueba. Obras completas* Vol 22. Madrid: Renacimiento.

———. 1911? *De siglo a siglo. 1896–1901. Obras completas.* Vol. 24. Madrid: Renacimiento.

———. 1964. *Obras completas.* 3 vols. Madrid: Aguilar.

———. 1976. *La mujer española y otros artículos feministas.* Edited by Leda Schiavo. Madrid: Editora Nacional.

———. 1980. *Insolación.* Madrid: Taurus.

———. 1990. *Cuentos completos.* 4 vols. La Coruña: Galicia Editorial.

———. n. d. *Por la Europa católica. Obras completas.* Vol. 26. Madrid: Renacimiento.

Parellada, Pablo. (Melitón González). 1906. *Tenorio modernista.* Madrid: Editorial Siglo XX.

Parker, Andrew and Mary Russo, Doris Sommer, Patricia Yaeger, eds. 1992. *Nationalisms and Sexualities.* New York: Routledge.

Parlow, Hans. 1899. Estudio de la literatura española. *Revista Nueva* 3:145–63.

Patt, Beatrice. 1971. *Pío Baroja.* Boston: Twayne.

Pearsall, Priscilla. 1986. Azorín's Myth of the Generation of 1898: Toward an Aesthetic of Modernism. *Revista canadiense de estudios hispánicos* 11:179–85.

Peñuelas, Marcelino. 1966. Benavente, autor satírico. *Papeles de Son Armadans.* (July-September): 283–93.

———. 1968. *Jacinto Benavente.* Boston: Twayne.

Pereda, José María. 1897. *Discursos leídos ante la Real Academia Española en la recepción pública del Sr. D. José María de Pereda.* Madrid: Viuda e hijos de Tello.

———. 1959. *Pachín González. Obras completas.* Vol. 3. Madrid: Aguilar.

———. 1963. *Peñas arriba.* Madrid: Aguilar.

Peres, Ramon D. 1903. Otros libros. *La Lectura.* May: 293–94.

———. 1905. Victor Catalá. *La Lectura.* September: 562–66.

Pérez, Janet. 1988. *Contemporary Women Writers of Spain.* Boston: Twayne.

Pérez de Ayala, Ramón. 1903a. La aldea lejana. *Helios.* 1:5–14.

———. 1903b. Liras o lanzas. *Helios* 2:513–21.

———. 1907. Artemisa. *El cuento semanal.* 12.

———. 1923. *A. M. D. G.* Madrid: Mundo latino.

———. 1957. *Obras selectas.* Barcelona: AHR.

———. 1964–1966. *Obras completas.* 3 vols. Madrid: Aguilar.

———. 1989. *Belarmino y Apolonio.* Madrid: Cátedra.

Pérez Galdós, Benito. 1903. Soñemos, alma, soñemos. *Alma Española.* 1:1–2.

———. 1909. *El caballero encantado.* Madrid: Viuda e hijos de Tello.

———. 1967. *Obras completas.* Vols. 4–6. Madrid: Aguilar.

———. 1979. *El abuelo.* Madrid: Hernando. Pérez Triana, Santiago. 1903. Apuntes internacionales: El porvenir de Paco Tudela. *Helios* 2:342–54.

Pérez y González, Felipe. 1893. Los muertos en Melilla. *La Ilustración Española y Americana.* 41:287.

Said, Edward W. 1979. *Orientalism.* New York: Vintage Books.

———. 1994. *Culture and Imperialism.* New York: Vintage Books.

Salaün, Carlos and Carlos Serrano, eds. 1991. *1900 en España.* Madrid: Espasa-Calpe.

Salaün, Carlos and Claire-Nicole Robin. 1991. Artes y espectáculos: tradición y renovación. In *1900 en España,* edited by Carlos Salaün and Carlos Serrano, 131–59. Madrid: Espasa-Calpe.

Sales y Ferré, Manuel. 1905. La conciencia social espontánea. *Boletín de la Institución Libre de Enseñanza.* 543:176–80.

Salinas, Pedro. 1949. *Literatura española: Siglo XX.* Mexico: Librería Robredo.

Sanz del Río, Julián. 1891. El lenguaje. *Boletín de la Institución Libre de Enseñanza.* 354.

Sanz y Escartín, Eduardo. 1902. La filosofía del anarquismo. *La Lectura.* (August): 161–73.

Sauvage, L. F. 1907. España en Francia: El amor español. *El Nuevo Mercurio.* 5:552–56.

Sawa, Alejandro. 1903. Dietario de un alma. *Helios.* 2:284–90; 436–48; 560–76.

———. 1904. Juventud trinfante. *Alma Española.* 9:10–11.

———. 1910. *Iluminaciones en la sombra.* Madrid: Renacimiento.

———. n. d. *Micromegas: Historia filosófica.* Madrid: Imprenta Popular.

Schwarz, S. 1912. La emigración judía de España y Portugal. *La España Moderna.* June: 103–8.

Schyfter, Sara E. 1978. *The Jew in the Novels of Benito Pérez Galdós.* London: Tamesis.

Scott-James, R. A. 1908. *Modernism and Romance.* New York: John Lane.

Sedgewick, Eve Kosofsky. 1985. *Between Men.* New York: Columbia University Press.

Senabre, Ricardo. 1992. Algunas claves de Antonio Machado. In *Estudios sobre Antonio Machado,* edited by Theodor Berchem and Hugo Laitenberger. Münster: Aschendorrff Münster.

Seone, María José Alonso. 1979. Introducción. *Ramón del Valle-Inclán. La guerra carlista.* Madrid: Espasa-Calpe.

Shaw, D. L. 1975. *The Generation of 1898 in Spain.* London: Ernest Benn Limited.

Sheppard, Richard. 1993. The Problematics of European Modernism. In *Theorizing Modernism: Essays in Critical Theory,* edited by Steve Giles. London: Routledge.

Showalter, Elaine.1990. *Sexual Anarchy. Gender and Culture at the Fin de Siècle.* New York: Viking.

Sieburth, Stephanie.1994. *Inventing High and Low: Literature, Mass Culture, and Uneven Modernity in Spain.* Durham, N.C.: Duke University Press.

Simón Pilar, María del Carmen, ed. 1990. *Rosario de Acuña: Rienzi el Tribuno / El padre Juan.* Madrid: Castalia.

———. 1991. *Escritoras espanolas del siglo XIX.* Madrid: Castalia.

Smith, Paul. 1988. *Discerning the Subject.* Minneapolis: University of Minnesota.

Smith, Verity. 1973. *Ramón del Valle-Inclán.* Boston: Twayne.

Soufas, C. Christopher Jr. 1998. Tradition as an Ideological Weapon: The Critical Redefinition of Modernity and Modernism in Early Twentieth-Century Spanish Literature. *Anales de la literatura española contemporánea* 23:465–77.

Spires, Robert. 1988. *Transparent Simulacra: Spanish Fiction (1902–1926)*. Columbia: University of Missouri Press.

Spivak, Gayatri.1998. Can the Subaltern Speak? In *Marxism and the Interpretation of Culture,* edited by Cary Nelson and Lawrence Grossberg, 271–313. London: MacMillan.

Stallybrass, Peter and Allon White. 1986. *The Politics and Poetics of Transgression.* Ithaca: Cornell University Press.

Subirats, Eduardo. 1993. *Después de la lluvia: Sobre la ambigua modernidad española.* Madrid: Temas de Hoy.

———. 1995. Ambigua modernidad. Distinguished Graduate Lecture Series. Rutgers-The State University of New Jersey. New Brunswick, 24 March.

Terry, Arthur. 1972. *A Literary History of Spain: Catalan Literature.* London: Ernest Benn.

———. 1995. Catalan Literary Modernism and Noucentisme: From Dissidence to Order. In *Spanish Cultural Studies: An Introduction,* edited by Helen Graham and Jo Labanyi, 55–57. Oxford: Oxford University Press.

Tiffin, Chris and Alan Lawson, eds. 1994. *De-Scribing Empire: Post-Colonialism and Textuality.* London: Routledge.

Todorov, Tzvetan. 1993. *On Human Diversity.* Translated by Catherine Porter. Cambridge: Harvard University Press.

Tomasch, Sylvia. 1985. Breaking the Frame: Medieval Art and Drama. *Early Drama to 1600,* edited by Albert H. Tricorni. 13: 81–93.

Torrente Ballester, Gonzalo. 1968. *Panorama de la literatura española contemporánea.* Madrid: Guadarrama.

Torres Campos, Rafael. 1895. El movimiento a favor de los derechos de la mujer. *Boletín de la Institución Libre de Enseñanza.* 427–28.

Torres Nebrera, Gabriel. 1988. Introducción. *Del huerto provinciano* by Gabriel Miró. Badajoz: Universidad de Extremadura.

Tortella Casares, Gabriel and Casimiro Martí, José María Jover Zamora, José Luis García Delgado, David Ruiz. 1981. *Revolución burguesa, oligarquía y constitucionalismo (1834–1923). Historia de España.* Dir. Manuel Tuñón de Lara. Vol 8. Barcelona: Labor.

Trigo, Felipe. 1914. *Jarapellejos.* Madrid: Renacimiento.

———. 1974. *El médico rural.* Madrid: Turner.

Trueblood, Alan. 1982. *Selected Poems.* Translations of Antonio Machado. Cambridge: Harvard University Press.

Ubieto, Antonio and Juan Reglá, José María Jover, Carlos Seco. 1971. *Introducción a la historia de España.* Barcelona: Teide.

Ugarte, Manuel. 1908. *Las nuevas tendencias literarias.* Valencia: F. Sempere y Compañía.

Ugarte, Michael. 1996. *Madrid 1900: The Capital as Cradle of Literature and Culture.* University Park, Penn.: Pennsylvania State University Press.

Unamuno, Miguel de. 1898. El literatismo. *Revista Blanca.* 1:11–15

———. 1899a. Los cerebrales. *La Ilustración Española y Americana.* 3:227.

———. 1899b. Contra el purismo. *Revista Nueva.* 1.8:348–61.

———. 1899c. De la enseñanza superior en España. *Revista Nueva.* 1.18:830–37; 2.19:1–9; 2.20:51–60; 2.21:108–11; 2.22:165–71; 2.23:201–08; 2.24:40–44; 2. 25:59–65.

———. 1899d. Una visita al viejo poeta. *La Ilustración Española y Americana.* 33:135.

———. 1903. Vida y arte. *Helios.* 5:46–50.

———. 1905. La Quimera, de Emilia Pardo Bazán. *La Lectura.* (August): 424–32.

———. 1906. La enseñanza de la gramática. *Boletín de la Institución Libre de Enseñanza.* 561.

———. 1907. Razon y vida. *Renacimiento.* 5 (July): 1–12.

———. 1911. *Rosario de sonetos líricos.* Madrid: Imprenta española.

———. 1953. Nuestra egolatría de los del 98. *De esto y de aquello.* Buenos Aires: Sudamericana.

———. 1958. *Obras completas.* 15 vols. Barcelona: Afrodisio Aguado.

———. 1966. *Del sentimiento trágico de la vida.* New York: Las Américas.

———. 1971. *En torno al casticismo.* Madrid: Alcalá.

Urrutia Salaverri. Luis. 1973. Prólogo. *Hojas sueltas,* by Pío Baroja. Madrid: Caro Raggio.

Valenti Fiol, Eduardo. 1973. *El primer modernismo literario catalán y sus fundamentos ideológicos.* Barcelona: Ariel.

Valera, Juan. 1888. *Cartas americanas* Madrid: Fuentes y Capdeville.

———. 1941. *Obras completas.* 2 vols. Madrid: Aguilar.

———. 1982. *Juanita la Larga.* Madrid: Alianza.

Valis, Noel M. 1994. The Novel as Feminine Entrapment: Valle-Inclán's *Sonata de otoño.* In *Ramón María del Valle-Inclán,* edited by Carol Maier and Roberta L. Salper, 56–76. Lewisburg, Penn.: Bucknell University Press.

———. 1993. *Angel Guerra,* or the Monster Novel. In *Galdós.* Edited by Jo Labanyi. London and New York: Longman.

Valle-Inclán, Ramón del. 1899. *Cenizas.* Madrid: Administración.

———. 1917. *La media noche: Visión estelar de un momento de guerra.* Madrid: Imprenta Clásica Española.

———. 1919. *La pipa de kif.* Madrid: Sociedad General de Librería.

———. 1920a. *Flor de santidad.* Madrid: Helénica.

———. 1920b. *Jardín umbrío. Opera omnia.*Vol. 12. Madrid: Topografía Europa.

———. 1922a. *Aguila de blasón.* Madrid: Saez Hermanos.

———. 1922b. *Romance de lobos. Opera omnia.* Vol 15. Madrid: Saez Hermanos.

———. 1954. *Obras completas.* Madrid: Plenitud.

———. 1963a. *Sonata de otoño y Sonata de invierno.* Madrid: Espasa-Calpe.

———. 1963b. *Sonata de primavera y Sonata de estío.* Madrid: Espasa-Calpe.

———. 1968. *Luces de bohemia.* Madrid: Espasa-Calpe.

———. 1974. *Obras escogidas.* (*Epitalamio. Femeninas. La lámpara maravillosa*). 2 vols. Madrid: Aguilar.

———. 1979. *La guerra carlista. Los cruzados de la causa. El resplandor de la hoguera. Gerifaltes de antaño.* Madrid: Espasa-Calpe.

———. 1987. Breve noticia acerca de mi estética cuando escribí este libro. In *Artículos completos y otras páginas olvidadas,* edited by J. Serrano Alonso, 204–8. Madrid: Istmo.

———. 1990. *Martes de carnaval: Las galas del difunto, Los cuernos de don Friolera, La hija del capitán.* Madrid: Espasa-Calpe.

Valmala, Antonio de. 1906. *Ripios colombianos.* Bogotá: Librería Nueva.

———. 1908. *Los voceros del modernismo.* Barcelona: Luis Gili.

Valverde, José María. 1971. *Azorín.* Barcelona: Planeta.

Variedades y revista de revistas y periódicos. El cerebro espanol. 1907. *El Nuevo Mercurio.* 4:468–69.

Variedades y revista de revistas y periódicos. Las poesías de Manuel Machado. 1907. *El Nuevo Mercurio.*7:815–28.

Vega, Ricardo de la. 1899. *Amor engendra desdichas o el guapo y el feo y verduleras honradas.* Madrid: n.p.

Velázquez Bosco, Ricardo. 1905. La originalidad en el arte. *Boletín de la Institución Libre de Enseñanza.* 544.

Vicenti, Alfredo. 1896. Los judíos. *La Ilustración Española y Americana.* 23:367–70.

Vidal y Careta, Franciso. 1902. ¿Qué es el modernismo? *Gente Vieja.* 57:4; 63:7–8.

Vilanova, Mercedes. 1971. *La conformidad con el destino en Azorín.* Barcelona: Ariel.

Villaespesa, Francisco. 1911. *Torre de marfil.* Paris: Ediciones literarias.

———. 1915? *La leona de Castilla.* Madrid: Hispania.

———. 1930. *Aben Humeya.* Madrid: Prensa Moderna.

———. 1954. *Poesías completas.* 2 vols. Madrid: Aguilar.

Waldenfels, Bernhard. 1995. Response to the Other. In *Encountering the Other(s): Studies in Literature, History, and Culture,* edited by Gisela Brinker-Gabler. Albany: State University of New York Press.

Watson, Peggy W. 1993. *Intrahistoria in Miguel de Unamuno's Novels: A Continual Presence.* Potomac, Maryland: Scripta Humanistica.

Waugh, Patricia. 1984. *Metafiction.* London: Methuen.

Weiner, Jonathan. 1995. *The Beak of the Finch.* New York: Vintage Books.

White, Hayden. 1978. *Tropics of Discourse: Essays in Cultural Criticism.* Baltimore: Johns Hopkins University Press.

Wilcox, John. 1987. *Self and Image in Juan Ramón Jiménez.* Urbana: University of Illinois Press.

Williams, Raymond. 1989. *The Politics of Modernism.* London: Verso.

Williamson, Judith. 1986. "Woman is an Island: Femininity and Colonization. In *Studies in Entertainment,* edited by Tania Modleski. 99–118. Bloomington: Indiana University Press.

Wilson, Elizabeth. 1995. The Invisible Flâneur. *Feminist Cultural Studies.* Vol. 2. Edited by Terry Lovell. Cambridge: Cambridge University Press.

Wilson, Paulette. 1996. Culpability and Gender in the Novels of Emilia Pardo Bazán and Benito Pérez Galdós. Ph. D. diss. Rutgers University.

Wiseman, Mary Bittner. 1989. *The Ecstasies of Roland Barthes.* London: Routledge.

Ynduráin, Domingo.1988. Galdós and the Generation of 1898. In *The Crisis of Institutionalized Literature,* edited by Wlad Godzich and Nicholas Spadaccini, 149–66. Minneapolis, Minn.: Prisma Institute.

Zahareas, Anthony. 1968. *Ramón del Valle-Inclán: An Appraisal of his Life and Works.* New York: Las Américas Publishing Co.

Zamacois, Eduardo. 1899. Lo inconfesable. *La Vida Galante.* 36:506.

Zavala, Iris. 1991. *Unamuno y el pensamiento dialógico.* Barcelona: Anthropos.

———. 1992. *Colonialism and Culture: Hispanic Modernisms and the Social Imaginary.* Bloomington, Indiana: Indiana University Press.

Zayas, Antonio. 1907. El Escorial. In *La corte de los poetas,* edited by Emilio Carrere. Madrid: Pueyo.

Zulueta, Luis de. 1920. Soliloquios de un español: La última esperanza. *La libertad.* (Feb. 19). Rprt. *Boletín de la Institución Libre de Enseñanza.* 719: 158–60.

Index